PANDEMICS, PUBLIC HEALTH, AND THE REGULATION OF BORDERS

This book examines how the COVID-19 pandemic has engendered a new and challenging environment in which borders drawn around people, places, and social structures have hardened and new ones have emerged.

Over the course of the COVID-19 pandemic, borders closed or became unwelcoming at the international, national, sub-national, and local levels. Debate persists as to whether those countries and territories that tightly managed their borders, like New Zealand, Australia, or Hong Kong, got it 'right' compared to those that did not. Without doubt, a majority of those who suffered and died throughout the pandemic have been those from vulnerable populations. Yet on the other hand, efforts taken to manage the spread of the disease, such as through border management, have also disproportionately affected those who are most vulnerable. How then is the right balance to be struck, acknowledging, too, the economic and other imperatives that may dissuade governments from taking public health steps? This book considers how international organizations, countries, and institutions within those countries should conceive of, and manage, borders as the world continues to struggle with COVID-19 and prepares for the next pandemic. Engaging a range of international, and sub-national, examples, the book thematizes the main issues at stake in the control and management of borders in the interests of public health.

This book will be of considerable interest to academics in the fields of health law, anthropology, economics, history, medicine, public health, and political science, as well as policymakers and public health planners at national and sub-national levels.

Colleen M. Flood is Dean of the Faculty of Law at Queen's University, Canada.

Y.Y. Brandon Chen is Associate Professor at the University of Ottawa's Faculty of Law (Common Law Section), Canada.

Raywat Deonandan is Epidemiologist and Associate Professor with the Interdisciplinary School of Health Sciences at the University of Ottawa, Canada.

Sam Halabi is Professor at the Georgetown University School of Health and Co-Director of the Center for Transformational Health Law at the O'Neill Institute for National and Global Health Law.

Sophie Thériault is Full Professor in the Faculty of Law (Civil Law Section) at the University of Ottawa, Canada.

PANDEMICS, PUBLIC HEALTH, AND THE REGULATION OF BORDERS

Lessons from COVID-19

Edited by Colleen M. Flood, Y.Y. Brandon Chen, Raywat Deonandan, Sam Halabi and Sophie Thériault

Routledge
Taylor & Francis Group
a GlassHouse Book

Designed cover image: Vitezslav Vylicil/Getty Images

First published 2024
by Routledge
4 Park Square, Milton Park, Abingdon, Oxon OX14 4RN

and by Routledge
605 Third Avenue, New York, NY 10158

Routledge is an imprint of the Taylor & Francis Group, an informa business

A GlassHouse book

British Library Cataloguing-in-Publication Data
A catalogue record for this book is available from the British Library

Library of Congress Cataloging-in-Publication Data
Names: Flood, Colleen M., editor.
Title: Pandemics, public health, and the regulation of borders : lessons from Covid-19 / edited by Colleen M. Flood, Y.Y. Brandon Chen, Raywat Deonandan, Sam Halabi, and Sophie The´riault.
Description: Abingdon, Oxon [UK] ; New York, NY : Routledge, 2024. Includes bibliographical references and index.
Identifiers: LCCN 2023047570 (print) | LCCN 2023047571 (ebook) | ISBN 9781032494746 (hardback) | ISBN 9781032494784 (paperback) | ISBN 9781003394006 (ebook)
Subjects: LCSH: COVID-19 (Disease)—Law and legislation. | COVID-19 Pandemic, 2020– | Public health laws. | Border crossing.
Classification: LCC K3575.C68 P33 2024 (print) | LCC K3575.C68 (ebook) | DDC 342.08/2—dc23/eng/20231013
LC record available at https://lccn.loc.gov/2023047570
LC ebook record available at https://lccn.loc.gov/2023047571

ISBN: 978-1-032-49474-6 (hbk)
ISBN: 978-1-032-49478-4 (pbk)
ISBN: 978-1-003-39400-6 (ebk)

DOI: 10.4324/9781003394006

Typeset in Sabon
by Apex CoVantage, LLC

University of Ottawa and Colorado State University

CONTENTS

ABOUT THE CONTRIBUTORS

Fernando Aith is Director of the University of São Paulo's Health Law Research Center and Full Professor in the Department of Policy, Governance and Health at the University of São Paulo Public Health School. He graduated in law, earned a master's degree in philosophy and general theory of law, and a doctorate in public health from University of São Paulo. He specialized in medical and health law at Université de Paris – Saint-Denis (France), and did post-doctoral work in the area of public law at Université de Paris – Panthéon-Assas (France). At the University of São Paulo, he is also a member of the UNESCO Chair on Education for Peace, Human Rights, Democracy, and Tolerance.

Joseph Belliveau is Executive Director of Doctors Without Borders/Médecins Sans Frontières (MSF) Canada. He began supporting MSF humanitarian medical teams in a refugee camp in eastern Zambia in 2000 and subsequently worked in Democratic Republic of the Congo, Liberia, Cote d'Ivoire, Sierra Leone, Pakistan, and Zimbabwe before overseeing operations at MSF's HQ in Amsterdam. Belliveau has expertise in humanitarian negotiations, political and context analysis, and organizational change. He has also been at the forefront of MSF's efforts to integrate climate awareness into its programs and ways of working. Belliveau has been a consistent champion of MSF's advocacy work, speaking out against the policies and actions that cause human suffering and the restrictions that prevent an adequate humanitarian response. Belliveau has a master's degree in international relations from the University of Toronto and currently lives in Toronto with his family.

Céline Bellot is Professor at the School of Social Work of the Université de Montréal. She obtained her PhD in criminology from the Université de Montréal in 2001 and completed a post-doctoral fellowship at the Université du Québec à Montréal. She directs the Observatoire des profilages (ODP) and is a member of the Centre international de criminologie comparée (CICC). Currently, she is researching the judicialization of homeless populations and populations living in poverty in Canada (homeless people, drug users, Indigenous populations, and youth living on the margins). She also conducts evaluations of innovative interventions with marginalized populations, either in terms of their social participation or their social and professional integration.

Caroline D. Bergeron is a healthy aging advocate and researcher. She has a doctorate in public health from the University of South Carolina, a master's in communications from the University of Montreal, as well as a bachelor's in communications and a bachelor's in Spanish from the University of Ottawa. To date, Caroline has studied falls, ageism, social participation, sexual health, health communication, organ donation, chronic disease management, pain, age-friendly cities, dementia, resilience, alcohol consumption, and suicide among older adults. She has worked in healthy aging at the World Health Organization, the Public Health Agency of Canada, the Quebec National Public Health Institute, and the Mayo Clinic. She is presently Senior Research Advisor at the Employment and Social Development Canada.

Emmanuelle Bernheim has a dual background in social sciences (PhD—École normale supérieure de Cachan) and law (LLD—UMontréal). She is currently Professor at the Civil Law Section of University of Ottawa Faculty of Law and holds the Canada Research Chair in Mental Health and Access to Justice. Her research focuses on the role of law and courts in the production and reproduction of social inequalities, more specifically, through the study of judicial practices and the experience of litigants in the justice system. Her current projects focus on mental health, youth protection, and self-representation. As an extension of her work, Emmanuelle is part of the founding team of the Outaouais Social Rights Interdisciplinary Clinic, a legal clinic serving marginalized groups in Outaouais region.

Y.Y. Brandon Chen (SJD, MSW, JD, University of Toronto) is Associate Professor at the University of Ottawa's Faculty of Law, Common Law Section. A lawyer and social worker by training, his research program examines legal, policy, and ethical questions at the intersection of international migration and health. His published work has touched on such topics as migrants' health and rights, social determinants of health, philosophy of healthcare, and medical tourism. He has served on the board of directors of such organizations as the HIV Legal Network, Community Alliance for Accessible Treatment, and Canadian Centre on Statelessness.

Pascale Dangoisse is a PhD candidate and research assistant at the Humanities Data Lab of the University of Ottawa. Dangoisse has developed an expertise in revealing where systemic discrimination lies through the critical analysis of political and media discourses.

Vincent Delhomme is Lecturer in EU Law at Leiden University, Netherlands, and Guest Lecturer at Université Saint-Louis—Bruxelles, Belgium. His research covers various constitutional and substantive aspects of EU health law, including the prevention and control of noncommunicable diseases and the COVID-19 pandemic and its consequences.

Raywat Deonandan is Epidemiologist and Associate Professor with the Interdisciplinary School of Health Sciences at the University of Ottawa, and holder of the Research Chair in University Teaching. He is a researcher with the Centre for Health Law, Policy and Ethics and the Life Research Institute, as well as Senior Fellow with Massey College at the University of Toronto. During the pandemic, he has been an active consultant to pharmaceutical companies, law firms, labour unions, the media, and government on epidemiological aspects of the disease.

Amélie Doucet is a doctoral candidate in Work and Organizational Psychology at the Université du Québec à Montréal (UQAM). She is a junior researcher at the Canada Border Services Agency and vice-president of the Communications Committee of the Société Québécoise de Psychologie du Travail et des Organisations. Amélie specializes in research related to equity, diversity and inclusion issues in the workplace (particularly ageism). She is also interested in issues relating to mental health in the workplace and the continuous improvement of workplace practices.

Stephen Duckett is Honorary Enterprise Professor in the School of Population and Global Health at the University of Melbourne. He has held top operational and policy leadership positions in healthcare in Australia and Canada, including as Secretary of what is now the Commonwealth Department of Health. He has a reputation for creativity, evidence-based innovation, and reform in areas ranging from the introduction of activity-based funding for hospitals to new systems of accountability for the safety of hospital care. An economist, he is Fellow of the Academy of the Social Sciences in Australia and of the Australian Academy of Health and Medical Sciences.

Krystyna Dzwonkowska-Godula is Sociologist and Assistant Professor in the Department of Sociology of Social Structure and Social Change at the

University of Łódź in Poland. Her research interests include gender roles and stereotypes, gender inequality, and feminist activism. She is co-author of the book *Gender, Age, and Gendered Age in Relation to Attitudes to One's Own Appearance and Health (Chosen Aspects)* (2017) and a book (in Polish) based on her doctoral thesis: *Traditional or modern? Patterns of motherhood and fatherhood in Poland* (2015). She conducts comparative research on reproductive politics and reproductive justice in Poland and Canada. In 2021–2022, she was a visiting researcher at the Institute of Feminist and Gender Studies at the University of Ottawa, with a scholarship in the Bekker Programme of the Polish National Agency for Academic Exchange. Her more recent publications deal with social inequalities in regard to reproductive rights in Poland, activism for reproductive justice in Poland, and self-managed abortions.

Tim G. Evans is Inaugural Director and Associate Dean of the School of Population and Global Health (SPGH) in the Faculty of Medicine and Associate Vice Principal (Global Policy and Innovation) at McGill University. He joined McGill after a six-year tenure as Senior Director of the Health, Nutrition and Population Global Practice at the World Bank Group. From 2003 to 2010, he was Assistant Director-General at the World Health Organization (WHO). Prior to this, he served as Director of the Health Equity Theme at the Rockefeller Foundation. Earlier in his career, he was an attending physician of internal medicine at Brigham and Women's Hospital in Boston and was Assistant Professor in International Health Economics at the Harvard School of Public Health. Tim has been at the forefront of advancing global health equity and strengthening health systems delivery for more than 20 years. At WHO, he led the Commission on Social Determinants of Health and oversaw the production of the annual World Health Report. He has been a co-founder of many partnerships, including the Global Alliance on Vaccines and Immunization (GAVI) as well as efforts to increase access to HIV treatment for mothers and innovative approaches to training community-based midwives in Bangladesh.

Jennifer Fang is Project Manager and Research Fellow with the Pacific Institute on Pathogens, Pandemics and Society (PIPPS) and the Pandemics and Borders Project based at Simon Fraser University. Her research interests include the commercial determinants of health, global health, and development. Ms. Fang holds a master of public health degree from the University of Liverpool and a bachelor of science in nutritional sciences from UBC. Previously, she conducted research on the global activities of the Chinese tobacco industry. Before joining Simon Fraser University, she worked in Beijing on building China-Africa health collaboration.

David Fisman is a physician-epidemiologist with research interests that fall at the intersection of applied epidemiology, mathematical modelling, and applied health economics. Dr. Fisman completed a residency in Internal Medicine at McGill and Brown Universities before completing a fellowship at the Beth Israel Deaconess Medical Centre in Boston and an MPH at Harvard School of Public Health. He was also an AHRQ fellow in Health Policy (1998–2001) at Harvard Centre for Risk Analysis and has held faculty appointments at McMaster, Princeton, and Drexel Universities. He is currently Professor of Epidemiology at the University of Toronto and Fellow of the Canadian Academy of Health Sciences and coleads the Pandemic Readiness Stream at the University of Toronto's new Institute for Pandemics.

Colleen M. Flood (FRSC, FCAHS) is Dean of the Faculty of Law, Queen's University. Prior to this, she was the University of Ottawa Research Chair in Health Law and Policy and Inaugural Director of the Ottawa Centre for Health Law, Policy and Ethics. Her research interests are focused on the role of law in shaping health and healthcare systems and the appropriate roles for the public and private sectors. She is the editor of *Halsbury's Laws of Canada—Public Health* (2019 reissue), co-editor of *Vulnerable: The Law Policy & Ethics of COVID-19* (2020), and teaches a course called the Law of Modern-Day Plagues.

Lisa Forman is an international human rights law scholar whose research explores the contribution of the right to health in international law to remediating global health inequities. She holds a Canada Research Chair Tier 2 in Human Rights and Global Health Equity. From 1996 to 1999, Forman worked as a human rights lawyer on HIV/AIDS at the Centre for Applied Legal Studies at the University of the Witwatersrand and then as a consultant on HIV/AIDS and human rights at the South African National Commission on Gender Equality. From 2009 to 2017, she was Lupina Assistant Professor in Global Health and Human Rights at the Dalla Lana School of Public Health and Director of the Comparative Program on Health and Society (CPHS) at the Munk School of Global Affairs. She is now tenured Associate Professor at the Dalla Lana School of Public Health.

Véronique Fortin is Professor in the Faculty of Law at Université de Sherbrooke. She is interested in the different modes of control of marginalized populations, such as people experiencing homelessness, people with mental health problems, and social assistance recipients. Her research focuses on the judicialization of homelessness, penal governance, the control of public space, the concept of decriminalization, and punitive measures in social assistance. She favours an empirical approach, most often ethnographic, for her research. Professor Fortin holds a double degree in civil law and common law from McGill University, as well as a master's degree in sociology of law from Oñati International Institute for the Sociology of Law (Basque Country, Spain). In 2015, she completed a PhD in criminology, law, and society at the University of California, Irvine. During her doctoral research, her ethnographic approach led her to work closely with people experiencing homelessness and protesters who had received tickets for their occupation of public space in Montreal.

Alexandra Fyfe is a student at the City Law School (City, University of London). Alongside her studies, she is a research and administrative assistant to Professor Tamara Hervey, supporting her projects on transnational, global, and comparative health law. Alexandra is an aspiring English solicitor. Her recent extracurricular achievements include running the British Inter-University Commercial Awareness Competition and helping host the final at Fieldfisher LLP's London office in December 2022. She is also passionate about access to justice and has been Vice President of City University's Pro Bono Society since September 2021.

Katherine Ginsbach is a senior associate with the Center for Transformational Health Initiative at the O'Neill Institute. Her primary research areas include pandemic preparedness and response legislation, global health governance, and disease surveillance. Her other areas of interest include Indigenous health law and One Health with a specific focus on the Arctic Region. Prior to joining the O'Neill Institute, she worked as a medical-legal partnership attorney at the Alaska Native Medical Center. Ginsbach holds a JD and an MS in global health from University of Notre Dame.

Roojin Habibi is Assistant Professor in the Faculty of Law, University of Ottawa and Senior Visiting Fellow at the United Nations University's International Institute for Global Health. As a law academic who bridges disciplines of international law, health law, and human rights, her research examines the impact of transnational institutions, actors, and norms on global health equity and the realization of health as a human right. In 2022, Roojin was appointed to the WHO expert committee mandated to advise countries on proposed amendments to the 2005 International Health Regulations. She was the only Canadian representative appointed to the Committee. She is a Pierre Elliott Trudeau Foundation Scholar and holds a Joseph-Armand Bombardier Doctoral Award for her doctoral research at Osgoode Hall Law School, York University, and has a law degree (JD) from the University of Ottawa's French Common Law program, a specialization in transnational law from the University of Geneva Faculty of Law, and a master's of science in global health from McMaster University. She is Barrister and Solicitor in Good Standing with the Law Society of Ontario and is fluent in English, French, and Farsi.

Sam Halabi (JD, MPhil) is Co-Director of the Center for Transformational Health Law at the O'Neill Institute for National and Global Health Law and Professor at the Georgetown University School of Health. His research career has focused on the ethical, legal, and regulatory dimensions of biomedical innovation and collaboration, especially in the context of epidemic and pandemic preparedness and response. He has published four books and more than 70 manuscripts in areas including data sharing during infectious disease emergencies, the development and deployment of vaccines in routine and emergency circumstances, the philosophy of medicine, international technology transfer, public health ethics, and vector-borne disease surveillance.

Tamara Hervey is Jean Monnet Professor of EU Law ad personam at the City Law School (London, UK). Tamara is currently working in three broad areas: transnational, global, and comparative health law; equality and diversity; and legal education. She is Editor of the Health Law section for the *OUP Encyclopaedia of EU Law*. She was Principal Investigator of Health Governance after Brexit, an ERSC-funded project that investigated the effects of Brexit on health and the NHS. She is currently working with the Nuffield Trust to track the ongoing effects, especially in Northern Ireland. Tamara is also working on the EU's COVID-19 law. She contributed to *COVID Lex-Atlas*, a major comparative study of legal responses to the COVID-19 pandemic.

Adam R. Houston (BSc, JD, MA, LLM, PhD) works at the intersection of health, human rights, and globalization with a particular focus on access to medicines and the role of law in the response to infectious disease. He has worked with organizations across Canada and around the world on a wide range of issues, from reconciling disparate human rights/policy approaches towards HIV and tuberculosis to United Nations accountability for the Haitian cholera epidemic. He is currently Medical Policy and Advocacy Officer for Médecins Sans Frontières/Doctors Without Borders Canada (MSF). He has also taught courses on topics relating to health, human rights, and international law at multiple Canadian universities.

Adelina Iftene is Associate Professor in the Schulich School of Law at Dalhousie University. She teaches criminal law, evidence, sentencing, and imprisonment and prison policy. Her past, current, and upcoming major research projects investigate issues surrounding aging in Canadian penitentiaries; the regulation of healthcare provision in prisons; the regulation of end-of-life and medical assistance in dying in prisons; prison release mechanisms, in particular, compassionate release; access to justice behind bars; and sentencing of older and sick individuals.

Esyllt W. Jones is Professor at the Department of History/Community Health Sciences in University of Manitoba. She teaches and conducts research into the history of health and disease in Canada and elsewhere. She also specializes in 20th-century health and social activism, working-class history, and the history of Winnipeg. Her publications include *Influenza 1918: Disease,*

Death and Struggle in Winnipeg (2007). Her work also encompasses a collection of essays entitled *Epidemic Encounters: Influenza, Society, and Culture in Canada, 1919–1920*, co-edited with Magda Fahrni (2012).

Jeff King joined the University College London Laws as Senior Lecturer in 2011 and has been Professor of Law since 2016. He is currently Visiting Professor at the Faculty of Law, University of Oxford, and was Legal Adviser to the House of Lords Select Committee on the Constitution between 2019–2021. His research interests include UK and comparative public law (including international law), constitutional theory, and socio-legal studies. Within these, he is particularly interested in the relationship between public law, democracy, and social policy. He is currently working on the use and abuse of delegated powers and comparative legal responses to COVID-19 and is writing a book on the social dimension of the rule of law.

Myka Kollmann is currently completing her articling at the Public Interest Advocacy Centre in consumer protection. She completed a Bachelor of Arts degree at The University of British Columbia in Gender and Environmental studies and graduated with her Juris Doctor from the University of Ottawa where she worked as Research Assistant for Professor Vivek Krishnamurthy. Her interests include international human rights law, competition law, and AI. She is particularly focused on exploring the intersection of human rights and the regulation of emerging technologies.

Vivek Krishnamurthy is Associate Professor and Director of the Samuelson-Glushko Technology Law and Policy Clinic at the University of Colorado Law School. Vivek's teaching, scholarship, and clinical legal practice focus on the complex regulatory and human rights–related challenges that arise in cyberspace. He advises governments, activists, and companies on the human rights impacts of new technologies and is a frequent public commentator on emerging technology and public policy issues. Vivek is Faculty Associate of the Berkman Klein Center for Internet & Society at Harvard University, Senior Associate of the Human Rights Initiative at the Center for Strategic and International Studies, and an alternate member of the Global Network Initiative's board of directors.

Martine Lagacé was appointed Associate Vice President for research, promotion, and development at the University of Ottawa in August 2018 for a five-year term. She is Professor in the Department of Communication and is affiliated with the school of psychology. Professor Lagacé was Vice Dean of the Governance of the Faculty of Arts from 2014 to 2018 and Director of the Department of Communication from 2011 to 2012. In addition to her administrative experience, she has extensive expertise in journalism, having worked at Radio-Canada for more than en years. Professor Lagacé has contributed greatly to the advancement of knowledge on the psychosocial aspects of aging, particularly as they relate to discrimination based on age. She has led several field surveys in Canada and abroad, with workers as well as elderly patients to better understand the impact of age-based discrimination.

Sarah J. Lazin is an LLM Candidate at the University of Ottawa. She completed her juris doctor at the University of Alberta and her bachelor of arts at the University of Victoria, graduating with distinction from both programs. Her primary areas of interest include reproductive rights and autonomy, global and public health, organ donation and transplantation, and similar intersections between law, medicine, and ethics. Her thesis, supervised by Professor Jennifer Chandler, will look at legal and ethical questions surrounding autonomy and consent in the organ donation context.

Kelley Lee is Professor and Tier 1 Canada Research Chair in Global Health Governance in the Faculty of Health Sciences, Simon Fraser University. She was previously Professor of Global Health Policy at the London School of Hygiene and Tropical Medicine, where she co-directed the WHO Collaborating Centre on Global Change and Health. Trained in International Political Economy and Public Administration, her research focuses on collective action to address transboundary health risks, including major infectious disease outbreaks. She currently heads the Pandemics and Borders Project which analyses the use of travel measures during the COVID-19 pandemic and supports efforts to strengthen decision-making in their future use. She has published 15 books, 200-plus papers, and 60-plus book chapters, including the *Oxford Handbook of Global Health Politics* (edited with Colin McInnes and Jeremy Youde, 2020).

Audrey Macklin is Professor and Chair in Human Rights Law at the University of Toronto's Faculty of Law. She holds law degrees from Yale and Toronto and a bachelor of science degree from Alberta. After graduating from Toronto, she served as law clerk to Mme. Justice Bertha Wilson at the Supreme Court of Canada. Professor Macklin's teaching areas include criminal law, administrative law, and immigration and refugee law. Her research and writing interests include transnational migration, citizenship, forced migration, feminist and cultural analysis, and human rights.

Carissima Mathen, LSM (BA McGill, LLB Osgoode, LLM Columbia), is Professor of Law at the University of Ottawa. A noted constitutional scholar, she is the award-winning author of *Courts Without Cases: The Law and Politics of Advisory Opinions* (2019) and *The Tenth Justice: Judicial Appointments, Marc Nadon and the Supreme Court Act Reference* (2020). As former Director of Litigation for the Women's Legal Education and Action Fund (LEAF), she was involved in path-breaking *Charter of Rights* cases. Professor Mathen is committed to public education and legal literacy. She is a Law Society

Medalist (Law Society of Ontario) and the recipient of the 2022 David W. Mundell Medal (Government of Ontario). In addition to her numerous books, Professor Mathen has published widely on all aspects of constitutional law, as well as criminal law, legal theory, and law and technology.

Jason W. Nickerson is Humanitarian Representative to Canada for Doctors Without Borders/Médecins Sans Frontières (MSF), based in Ottawa. Dr. Nickerson is also appointed as Clinical Scientist at the Bruyère Research Institute in Ottawa and as Adjunct Professor of Common Law at the University of Ottawa's Centre for Health Law, Policy and Ethics. He leads MSF's humanitarian diplomacy in Canada and provides advice on humanitarian operations, medical advocacy and policy, and access to medicines to MSF's operations in more than 70 countries affected by crises. He has over ten years' clinical experience as a respiratory therapist working in adult critical care and anesthesia and has worked extensively in global public health response in Canada and internationally during armed conflicts, disease epidemics, and sudden onset disasters.

Chidi Oguamanam is Professor in the Faculty of Law (Common Law Section), University of Ottawa. He holds the research chair in sustainable bio-innovation, indigenous knowledge systems, and global knowledge governance. He is affiliated with the Centres for Law, Technology and Society, the Environment and Global Sustainability as well as Health Law, Policy and Ethics. Dr. Oguamanam has diverse interdisciplinary research interests in the areas of global knowledge governance in general, especially as manifested in the dynamics of intellectual property and technology law with emphasis on biodiversity; biotechnology, including agricultural biotechnology; as well as global public health. He identifies the policy and practical contexts for the exploration of the intersections of knowledge systems, particularly Western science and the traditional knowledge of Indigenous peoples and local communities within the development discourse and knowledge governance paradigms. Dr. Oguamanam is associated with several research consortia, including the Open African Innovation Research (Open AIR) Partnership and the Access and Benefit Sharing Canada (ABS-CANADA).

Samantha Oostlander is a fourth-year PhD candidate supervised by Dr. Tracey O'Sullivan in the population health program at the University of Ottawa. She is a recipient of the EntourAGE scholarship from the LIFE Research Institute which supports her dissertation research exploring the adaptive capacity of older adults during the COVID-19 pandemic. Samantha has experience in a research assistant capacity on many projects exploring the far-reaching impacts of the pandemic; she recently joined Public Health Ontario in a research coordinator role on a public health emergency preparedness project. Samantha also holds a master's of science in occupational therapy and has experience practicing clinically in an acute care setting.

Tracey O'Sullivan is Full Professor in the Faculty of Health Sciences at the University of Ottawa. Her research program focuses on community resilience and public health emergency preparedness, with specific emphasis on strategies to support high-risk populations in health-related disasters, such as pandemics. Dr. O'Sullivan's work underscores the importance of social participation in an all-of-society approach and how discourse in disaster media (e.g., ageism, ableism in media coverage) can support or undermine inclusive engagement of high-risk populations in social policy development.

Eva Ottawa is Atikamekw Nehirowisiw Researcher from Manawan, Quebec, and Assistant Professor at the Faculty of Law, University of Ottawa. She holds a bachelor of laws degree from Laval University and a master's degree from the University of Ottawa. She decided to pursue graduate studies following an exceptional career path. She has been very involved for over 20 years in the political life of her nation and has served as Grand Chief of the Atikamekw Nation for two terms, from 2006 to 2013. In this capacity, she assumed, among other things, major responsibilities in connection with the negotiation of the Atikamekw's land claims and self-government and the implementation of innovative governance approaches within the nation. More recently, she served as a commissioner with the Quebec Human Rights and Youth Commission.

Julianne Piper is Project Manager for the Pandemics and Borders project and Research Fellow with the Pacific Institute on Pathogens, Pandemics and Society (PIPPS) under the supervision of Dr. Kelley Lee in the Faculty of Health Sciences at Simon Fraser University (SFU). Julianne holds a master in international affairs from the Graduate Institute of International and Development Studies, Geneva, and a bachelor of arts in international relations from the University of British Columbia. She is currently pursuing a PhD in health sciences at SFU. Her research interests include global health governance, health security, and development. Prior to joining SFU, Julianne worked in administration at UBC's School of Public Policy and Global Affairs and as Research Officer for the Global Health Centre at the Graduate Institute in Geneva.

Florence Robert is a Part-time Professor at the University of Ottawa and a member of the Barreau du Québec since 2023. She holds a Bachelor of Civil Law (LL.L.) degree from the University of Ottawa and is currently completing her Master of Laws (LLM) at the University of Toronto. Her research focus on Indigenous legal orders and legal pedagogies.

Philippe Rodrigue-Rouleau (PhD) is a post-doctoral fellow at the Faculty of Arts, University of Ottawa. In his post-doctoral position, he studies the effects of ageism perceptions on older workers' and employers' attitudes and behaviors in Canada. Prior to this, he completed a PhD at the University of Ottawa, during which he examined journalists' discourses about their own industry. His research interests cover ageism and intergenerational contacts at work, as well as journalism and media representations.

Priyanka Saksena is a consultant working for the School of Population and Global Health at McGill University. Previously, she was Health Systems Adviser with the World Health Organization's Country Office for Tunisia, where she was responsible for supporting overall health policies in the country. Before Tunisia, she worked for WHO in Geneva and New Delhi. Earlier in her career, she worked for the London School of Hygiene and Tropical Medicine and the International Labour Organization. Priyanka has degrees in economics from McGill University, in public health from the London School of Hygiene and Tropical Medicine, and in law from the University of London.

Christabelle Sethna is Historian and Full Professor in the Institute of Feminist and Gender Studies, University of Ottawa. She has published widely on sex education, contraception, and abortion histories, focusing on Canada. She is the co-author or co-editor of the following books: *Animal Metropolis* (2017), *Just Watch Us* (2018), *Abortion Across Borders* (2019), and *No Place for the State* (2020). She is currently Principal Investigator on a SSHRC-funded project about women's transnational travel for abortion services from 1960s to 1990s.

Wei William ("Will") Tao is Canadian Immigration and Refugee Lawyer. He co-founded Heron Law Offices in 2021 and provides legal services in all areas of Canadian immigration and refugee law with a particular focus on complex refusals, appeals, and judicial reviews of international student, family class, and foreign worker-related applications. He won the Canadian Bar Association (CBA) Immigration Section Founders' Award for his accomplishments in his first five-years of practice (2020) and won the CBA Immigration's Volunteer Recognition Award (cowinner) for his work with the Section's Anti-Racism Committee (2021). Will also provides strategic advice and consultation to government, media, educational institutions, and businesses on immigration-refugee, decolonization, and race/inclusion-related issues. Will previously taught immigration law through the UBC Certificate in Immigration: Laws, Policies and Procedures (CILPP) program. He is currently studying the impact of Canadian immigration's use of automated decision-making systems and artificial intelligence on applicants from the Global South.

Sophie Thériault is Professor in the Civil Law Section at the University of Ottawa. She is also a member of the Barreau du Québec (2003) and of the

Global Young Academy (2020–2025). Professor Thériault's research focuses on Indigenous peoples' rights in the context of natural resources extraction, Indigenous environmental governance, environmental justice and environmental rights, and food security and sovereignty for Indigenous peoples. She is a co-editor of *Vulnerable: The Law Policy & Ethics of COVID-19* (2020).

Bryan Thomas is Senior Research Fellow with Faculty of Law, Queen's University. His research spans a wide range of topics, including Canadian and comparative health law and policy, health rights litigation, long-term care, global health law, and the role of religious argument in legal and political discourse. Dr. Thomas holds an SJD from University of Toronto and a master's degree in philosophy from Dalhousie University.

Michael Veale is Associate Professor at the University College London's Faculty of Laws. His research sits at the intersections of emerging digital technologies, Internet and data law, technology policy, and human-computer interaction. His work has previously examined areas such as how the law applies to machine learning techniques in practice, how civil servants grapple with issues of algorithmic discrimination, how data protection law copes with new data processing practices, and the use and limitations of data rights. He is currently working on areas including the compliance of online tracking and advertising systems, such as 'real-time bidding' with data protection law, the legal tensions caused by encrypted data analysis and business-side privacy-enhancing technologies (PETs), and the implications of synthetic content (such as so-called 'deepfakes').

Pedro A. Villarreal is Senior Research Fellow at the Max Planck Institute for Comparative Public Law and International Law, and the German Institute for International and Security Affairs. His research focuses on international and comparative law on human health issues, as well as its intersections with international economic law. He received his PhD in law from the National Autonomous University of Mexico (UNAM). His book *Pandemics and Law: A Global Governance Perspective* (published in 2019 in Spanish) was awarded the Prize for the Best Doctoral Dissertation in Law and Social Sciences at said university. He is a member, among other associations, of the Global Health Law Consortium, the Global Health Law Committee of the International Law Association, and the German Alliance for Global Health Research. He is currently a member of the editorial board of *Lex-Atlas: COVID-19*.

Siouxsie Wiles is Associate Professor in the Faculty of Medical and Health Sciences, Molecular Medicine, and Pathology at the University of Auckland. She studied medical microbiology at the University of Edinburgh, followed by a

PhD in microbiology at the Centre for Ecology and Hydrology in Oxford. Siouxsie heads up the Bioluminescent Superbugs Lab, which searches for new antibiotics as well as tries to understand how bacteria evolve to become more infectious. Siouxsie also has a keen interest in demystifying science. She has won numerous awards for her research and science communication efforts. When the pandemic arrived, Siouxsie joined forces with *The Spinoff* cartoonist Toby Morris to make the science of the pandemic clear and understandable. Their award-winning graphics have been translated into multiple languages and adapted by governments and organizations around the world. Siouxsie was named as one of the BBC's 100 influential women of 2020 and Kiwibank New Zealander of the Year for 2021.

Brenda J. Wilson is Professor in the Division of Community Health and Humanities at Memorial University of Newfoundland. As a public health physician and health services researcher, she has research interests in two related areas: the population and health system aspects of developments in genetics, genomics, and precision health; and promoting evidence-based approaches to shared decision-making about prevention and screening in primary care. Her research work is usually interdisciplinary and spans many questions about how we judge the usefulness of a test or technology (to people, the health system, or society), how we promote the appropriate use of those that do seem to be useful, and how we build a system that supports people and professionals in making good decisions about health interventions.

Kumanan Wilson is interim CEO/Chief Scientific Officer at the Bruyère Research Institute and VP Research and Academic at the Bruyère Continuing Care. Dr. Wilson is also a Specialist in General Internal Medicine and Senior Scientist at the Ottawa Hospital and Full Professor and Faculty of Medicine Clinical Research Chair in Digital Health Innovation at the University of Ottawa. He is a scholar at the O'Neill Institute for National and Global Health Law at Georgetown University and is Co-Founder and Chief Scientific Officer of CANImmunize, a science-based technology company specializing in immunization software. Dr. Wilson's research focuses on digital health, health data, immunization, pandemic preparedness, and public health policy and innovation. He has received support from multiple organizations, including the Canadian Institutes of Health Research (CIHR), the World Health Organization (WHO), The Bill & Melinda Gates Foundation, and Canada's Immunity Task Force.

ACKNOWLEDGEMENTS

It is no small feat to put together an edited volume, let alone doing so during the third year of a global pandemic. We, therefore, owe a debt of gratitude to everyone who generously supported and assisted us on this journey.

In particular, we owe thanks to the University of Ottawa's Centre for Health Law, Policy and Ethics for logistical and financial support. Special thanks go to Giles Holland, the centre's operations officer, and Bryan Thomas, former Adjunct Professor and Senior Research Fellow with the centre. Giles played a crucial role in the planning and organization of a two-day conference held in Ottawa in October 2022, where many of the papers contained in this collection were workshopped. Bryan provided us with tremendous help in relation to research and editing for this volume. Without their superb work, this book project would not have been possible.

We would also like to thank the University of Ottawa's Faculty of Law, including its Research Office, and the University's Office of the Vice President Research. They were strong supporters of our conference and made valuable financial contributions that allowed this volume to be published open access.

Acknowledgements are likewise due to the Social Science and Humanities Research Council of Canada, as well as the Institute of Population and Public Health of the Canadian Institutes of Health Research. Funding from the former was critical to supporting both the conference and this open-access publication, whereas the latter partially covered the cost of a dinner event associated with the conference.

We are also grateful to our team of exceptional research assistants made up of juris doctor and master of laws students at the University of Ottawa's Faculty of Law. They include Nicole Davidson, Sarah J. Lazin, Caroline Mercer, Michael Piaseczny, and Saly Sadek. Their skills and attention to detail are invaluable to us throughout this project.

We further express our deepest gratitude to all the colleagues who reviewed the papers contained in this volume, including Isabel Barbosa, Marie Bismark, Zack Buck, Céline Castets-Renard, Kalowatie Deonandan, Nathalie Des Rosiers, Eric Friedman, Martin Gaal, Vanessa Gruben, Lorian Hardcastle, Anne Lévesque, Peter Oliver, Tim Sly, Elizabeth Steyn, and Barbara von Tigerstrom. They were incredibly generous with their time and care, and the quality of this book is enhanced because of them.

Finally, we dedicate our book to those whose lives have been lost, fractured, or harmed by COVID-19. At the time of writing, the disease has wrought nearly 7 million confirmed deaths globally, with millions more disabled or economically hobbled. Pandemics have a way of breaking the world. We hope our efforts here can in some way contribute towards healing and preparing us for the next public health crisis.

BORDERS, BOUNDARIES, AND PANDEMICS

Preface

The COVID-19 pandemic ushered in a new and challenging environment in which existing borders drawn around people, places, and social structures have hardened and new ones have emerged. Countries placed restrictions on movement at the international, domestic, and individual levels meant to contain the spread of COVID-19, often squarely pitting public health against human rights and equity concerns, particularly among the most marginalized populations.

Although a vast literature has already emerged analyzing the various aspects of the world's failure to prepare for and respond to the magnitude of the threat posed by COVID-19, this is the first volume to analyze this literature through the lens of borders, boundaries, circumscriptions, and their accompanying meaning for future pandemic preparedness and response. This book brings together global and country-specific experts from multiple disciplines to examine how countries, international organizations, and institutions manage borders during the COVID-19 pandemic, with the goal of developing sustainable and equitable border interventions for future pandemics. Throughout this volume, the authors address the unique border challenges presented by COVID-19 pandemic, with a focus on applicable lessons that can inform future responses.

Structurally, the book moves through history, background, and conception through concentric topical approaches that emphasize the local, the regional, the national, and the international. The opening chapters examine current and historical border controls during pandemics, highlighting the regional, national, and sub-national border measures taken during the

COVID-19 pandemic. Threaded through these chapters is the historical, continuing, and persistent gap between what borders mean as symbolic targets for measures taken by governments and the actual public health benefit border measures impart.

In one of the most important comparative analyses available to date, scholars from Australia, Brazil, New Zealand, and the United States synthesize the internal and external effects of border measures in their respective countries. Placed against the broader theme in the book covering Canadian policy and practice during the pandemic, this section will make for one of the most useful resources for local, national, and international decision-makers.

Following this background, context, and comparison, the volume moves through the impact of border controls on migrants, refugees, and asylum seekers. These constituencies, vulnerable under almost all circumstances in any case, find their paths to liberation, protection, and security even more obstructed by scapegoating, political expediency, and the vicissitudes of diplomatic relations between countries. What emerges from these examinations is special pressures the pandemic applied to families, disfavoured ethnicities, and those at greatest risk of persecution during perilous flight.

The following sections highlight the controversial implementation of vaccine passports, noting allegations of interference with fundamental rights and potential technological implications. These chapters, which represent a special strength and pronounced contribution of the volume, thoroughly examine the inevitable balancing legislators, regulators, and judges in liberal constitutional systems must undertake as between the fundamental rights and freedoms enjoyed by individuals and the public health demands that social distancing, regulation of gathering places, and especially, evidence of prophylaxis impose for the community's welfare.

These rights and freedoms are analyzed in special detail, where they face the greatest pressure—social institutions constructed around the most vulnerable. Restrictions drawn and enforced around elder care facilities, prisons, and psychiatric care institutions posed special problems in the balance between individuals already in confined circumstances and how the pandemic led to special measures, often imposing a disparate impact on these vulnerable populations.

The volume concludes with the future of global health law and how borders will be internalized as places for pandemic preparedness and response under a new international pandemic instrument and amendments to the primary agreement that already exists—the International Heath Regulations. Focusing on the free movement of healthcare workers, the need for countries to better cooperate and communicate with one another, and the role of the World Health Organization, this final section draws the curtain on what the future of borders and pandemics hold.

The volume makes for a crucial convening of some of the world's leading scholars, activists, and policymakers on a conceptual core of the world's future health security: borders, boundaries, and the force with which they may guide policy, cooperation, and response when the next pandemic emerges.

Lawrence O. Gostin

Preface

For legal geographers, borders and boundaries are fruitful and productive tools and constructs. They allow us to differentiate between things, people, and practices. As David Delaney once wrote:

> we draw a line, we establish an inside, and an outside, a this side and a that side, we assign a set of if . . . thens, to precise locations with respect to the line or to the act of crossing the line.

In defining borders and setting boundaries, we use space as a powerful tool to protect and save but also to exclude and push away, to confine, sometimes for our own sake but also to expel and to refuse to share.

The pandemic has reminded us of that power and of such consequences. As we created borders and boundaries, sometimes fixed, often fluid, pushing the others away and staying in closely knitted bubbles, we aimed at protecting the most vulnerable, protecting those inside from the outside, away from the virus and imminent death. In doing so, we have saved many lives and gained some precious time in our race for the vaccine.

Those staying inside, however, have in some cases suffered the consequences of confinement, from the isolation of our youth and the violence of an abusive spouse to our children's hunger. In some cases, confinement meant heightened danger and contagion, such as in prisons, shelters, and long-term care facilities, creating further vulnerabilities and inequalities.

On the outside, many were exposed to even greater risks, as they did not have the privilege of staying inside—like essential workers, operating the front line in places of care, in schools, in grocery stores or food-processing facilities. Others, including the homeless and the poor, who live and survive in public spaces, faced repression and banishment, as they were excluded from the outside, traced and ticketed for being in public parks or in the streets, punished for not having the luxury of a backyard or a property line in times of curfew.

The pandemic has blurred the lines between protection and exclusion, between in place and out of place, challenging our understanding of borders and boundaries. In many ways, and with the use of technologies, we have removed boundaries and ignored borders, creating virtual spaces of communication and meeting, reducing physical constraints, and shortening distances. Yet we have also reinforced borders between the countries who could pay for the precious masks and protective gear and then the vaccines and those who had to wait and die, and we have created new boundaries, as some of us have developed long-term disabilities. The pandemic has revealed pre-existing vulnerabilities and injustices but also, hopefully, our common humanity.

In this book, contributors from different disciplines and different jurisdictions wrestle with the conceptual and practical implementation of COVID-19 border restrictions between countries, provinces, regions, and limits on entry to different institutions and dependent on one's vaccine status. There is on occasion sharp disagreement as to the approaches to be taken and how the weight of potential benefit of border closure should be calibrated against the impact on people, particularly those that society marginalizes. Together, this collection of essays shed critical light on our pathways forward so we can make transparent the bases for differences in views and how to navigate these to make better decisions in the future.

Marie-Eve Sylvestre

PART I

Introduction

1

INTRODUCTION

Borders, Boundaries, and Pandemics

Colleen M. Flood, Y.Y. Brandon Chen, Raywat Deonandan, Sam Halabi and Sophie Thériault

1.1 Introduction

Around the world, as the COVID-19 pandemic emerged, many countries placed restrictions on entry at their borders. Whereas some countries did so to buy time to respond to the COVID-19 pandemic, others had hoped that such restrictions would slow or even stop transmission. In addition to restrictions on international travel, borders *within* countries were drawn (e.g., between states/provinces/regions/territories) as well as around high-risk sites, such as long-term care homes, psychiatric institutions, and prisons. With the arrival of vaccines, border drawing was individualized, as some jurisdictions required proof of vaccination when crossing borders for entry into non-essential settings like restaurants and movie theatres and for certain categories of employment. Worldwide, layers of bordering were imposed not only by governments and other public institutions but also by private actors and businesses.

This book is about how international organizations, countries, and sub-national governments and institutions conceived of, and managed, borders throughout the COVID-19 pandemic, both to understand what happened and to prepare for the next pandemic or public health challenge. How can we best protect those who are at high risk on both sides of borders? How can we manage borders as a public health response to best account for the vulnerability of those impacted—vulnerability which may stem either from *the specific public health precautions taken* or from a *failure to act*? How can we ensure the decision to close borders avoid xenophobic, racist, and otherwise oppressive calculations and/or effects? How should public health actors respond to and *communicate* the rapidly evolving scientific evidence

DOI: 10.4324/9781003394006-2

relating to pandemics, vaccination, medication and precautions, and the need for border measures? At the same time, how should they combat the inevitable spread of misinformation? How can public officials communicate that if the disease is uncontrolled, borders may effectively shut on their own accord, as people fall to disease and death? And what role does law play in all of this, in framing and mediating debates about international law and human rights, including the right to health, mobility rights, and more?

In what follows, we explore these questions. This introduction encompasses Part I, and in Part II, we explore some of the histories of pandemics and international border restrictions, with a particular focus on how border restrictions were communicated. In Part III, our contributors explore regional border restrictions, for example, within the European Union, and restrictions imposed within nations, for example, between provinces or borders established by Indigenous groups. Analyzing the disparate effect of border restrictions is the theme of Part IV, as contributors from New Zealand, Australia, United States, and Brazil offer insights into their experiences. Migrants and refugees are made even more vulnerable if border restrictions are not implemented with their needs in view. Contributors in Part V explore how, on the one hand, essential workers were frequently composed of migrant labour and yet, on the other hand, how little effort was made to attenuate the impact of border restrictions on these groups and their families. One of the most controversial measures of the pandemic was the implementation of vaccine mandates and passports. Contributors in Parts VI and VII explore restricting individuals' movements depending on their vaccine status and the balancing of civil liberties, like privacy, against public health goals of pandemic containment. Borders were also drawn around high-risks sites, and in Part VIII, contributors explore the harsh effects of borders drawn around sites like long-term care homes, prisons, and institutions for those living with mental illness. As borders closed around the world, concerns were raised about supply lines and access to critical services and care—and our contributors explore these issues in Part IX. Finally, in Part X, our contributors return to the global level to contemplate what kind of rules should be implemented in the future to guide border restrictions as a response to global health threats.

1.2 Layers of Bordering

Throughout this book and, indeed, embedded in this book's very structure is the idea of how border restraints, in response to COVID-19, have been layered, from the international to the national, to the sub-national, and right down to restrictions impacting an individual depending on their vaccine status.

At the *international* level, the first layer of bordering came in the global response in the first few critical months of the pandemic. The response was heterogeneous, with a group of countries moving swiftly to impose strong border restrictions, in defiance of the World Health Organization recommendations at the time, and other countries moving more slowly, if at all.

Singapore, for example, moved quickly—first closing to individuals with a recent travel history to Hubei province, and, soon after, to travelers through all of mainland China on 31 January 2020.[1] New Zealand closed its border to non-citizens from mainland China and non-citizens who had traveled through mainland China on 3 February 2020, four days after the WHO's declaration of a global health emergency.[2] Israel suspended all flights from China on 30 January 2020, extending the ban to Thailand, Hong Kong, Macau, and Singapore on 17 February.[3] A mandatory 14-day quarantine for all travelers was imposed on 9 March 2020.[4] In contrast, Canada was much slower to implement border closures and resisted a border closure targeting travelers from China for the first two months of the pandemic and then, finally, implemented a partial closure (non-US travelers) on non-essential travel on 16 March 2020; non-essential travel from the US was barred 5 days later.[5] Germany closed its borders with select neighbouring countries (Austria, Switzerland, France, Luxembourg, and Denmark) on 16 March 2020 and imposed a 14-day quarantine requirement on all visitors on 9 April 2020.[6] The UK did not impose border closures at all, instead requiring that all passengers entering the country complete a locator form and self-isolate for 14 days.[7] Sweden did not close its border; its leading state epidemiologist at the time, Anders Tegnell, dismissed the idea as "ridiculous" in an interview with *Nature*.[8]

Border restrictions have been one of the most highly contested aspects of the COVID-19 pandemic management, and debate persists as to whether those countries that moved quickly at the beginning of the pandemic and tightly managed their borders got it "right". We address this question in Part IV of this book, exploring and contrasting different border management approaches in Canada with those of New Zealand, Australia, Brazil, and the US. As we see, the answer to this question is a relative and contextual one; the benefit of a border closure depends, for instance, on the risk gradient between it and other countries. Canada, with its deeply integrated supply lines with the US, would have found any hard border closure extremely difficult to sustain, even though the risk of contagion from the US, where fewer precautionary measures were implemented, was significant. New Zealand, by comparison, with most travelers arriving by air, was able to maintain tight control until vaccines were available, saving many lives as a result. Relatedly, debate is ongoing as to the extent to which the World Health Organization's International Health Regulations (IHR) (2005) should be revised, given how many countries acted unilaterally and, at times, arbitrarily to restrict their borders to stop the spread of COVID-19.

An important question here is whether there should be one rule for all or whether there should be an opportunity for countries, taking the measures of their own capacities and relative risks, to close borders in response to a public health threat. And if countries are permitted to take individualized assessment and actions, how can we ensure international human rights and humanitarian norms are consistently interpreted and sufficiently taken into account in each country's border management? If border controls are used as a political tool to keep out "foreign viruses" and systematically discriminate against those from racialized countries, then they cannot be tolerated. Throughout this book we wrestle with these questions. Part II sets the context for our discussions by examining the history of border management and communication thereof.

Moving from the international level to borders *within* regions and states, there were contests and challenges as to whether economic regions or subnational units could close their borders to others. As we explore in greater detail in Part III, Canada's smaller eastern provinces restricted travel across their borders, which, combined with other measures, appeared a significant factor in reducing their death rates from COVID-19. For limited periods of time, there were even travel restrictions between two of Canada's largest provinces, Ontario and Quebec. Some questioned not only the practical realities but also the very constitutional permissibility of these kinds of provincial border restrictions. Nonetheless, as Professor Wilson explores in her chapter, a constitutional challenge arguing infringement of mobility rights in response to Newfoundland and Labrador's border restrictions was unsuccessful, with the ruling emphasizing the importance of the precautionary principle, where the evidence is not complete but the risk to population health is very significant if action is not taken.[9] Both within federations such as Canada and regional organizations such as the European Union as discussed by Professor Hervey and her colleagues, concerns about public health are juxtaposed against individual claims to "freedom" and mobility—whether for work or personal reasons. Within countries, Indigenous groups took actions to restrict mobility to and from their lands. These measures are analyzed by Professors Thériault, Ottawa, and Robert, reflecting on how colonization has rendered Indigenous peoples more vulnerable both to the ravages of coronavirus itself as well as to the harms flowing from border controls.

At the local level, we saw hard borderlines drawn around sites of extreme risk. For example, Canadian provinces and many other jurisdictions put in place tight entry requirements around long-term care homes, prisons, and mental health institutions. We discuss the impacts of these border measures in Part VIII, with expert contributors from different disciplines underscoring the extraordinary suffering inflicted upon the residents of long-term care homes, prisons, and psychiatric institutions, as well as on homeless people. What can we learn from these experiences so that, going forward, public health restrictions do not cause unnecessary harms? How can we ascertain that such restrictions are truly motivated by public health imperatives rather than based on stereotypes and prejudices against marginalized groups and individuals? And how can we ensure that these measures are calibrated to respect the dignity and needs of those most impacted? And yet, at the same time, how can we ensure that individuals residing in these congregate institutions are protected from the virus itself? What seems needed is both an assessment of the relative effectiveness of the proposed measures in combating the virus and careful calibration of these measures' implementation so that as much as possible, the dignity and autonomy of residents are respected. However, we must also be clearheaded that should a novel airborne asymptomatic transmission (as in the case of COVID-19) were to go unchecked within congregate facilities, then much greater harms to human rights can occur through suffering and death.

Finally, we have also seen borders (in a sense) drawn around individual people. Once COVID-19 vaccines became available, many governments implemented border restrictions requiring proof of vaccination. This was done primarily to prevent transmission but also more indirectly to promote vaccine uptake so as to prevent healthcare system overload. Canada's federal government put in place requirements of proof of vaccination when flying (whether internationally or domestically) or traveling by train, as well as at all federal workplaces.[10] Canadian provincial governments, and other jurisdictions worldwide, imposed vaccination requirements on people working in long-term care settings and demanded proof of vaccination for entering into non-essential settings (e.g., restaurants, bars, etc.).[11] Many private and non-governmental sectors too—large banks, universities, and so on—required proof of vaccination from employees and visitors.[12] Although implemented to protect those who could not be vaccinated and to spur the hesitant to vaccinate, vaccine mandates and passports in a sense were viewed by some to draw borders around an individual depending on their vaccination status and, as a result, were deeply controversial. In Parts VI and VII of this book, our expert contributors explore the human rights claims made in the context of vaccine passports and mandates, including those relating to freedom of religion and conscience and privacy rights. In doing so, they unpeel layers of issues relating to the changing evidence (precipitated by vaccine evolution and efficacy, as well as the changing nature of the virus), the spread of misinformation, and changing trust levels in governments and public health actors.

1.3 Vulnerabilities on All Sides

As we debate issues of how to manage borders throughout a pandemic (between countries, within regions or countries, around specific institutions, and around individuals), it behooves us to acknowledge the extreme vulnerability on both sides of the trade-offs to be made. Without a doubt, a majority of those who have suffered and died throughout the pandemic have been those from vulnerable populations. Yet on the other hand, efforts to manage the spread of the disease, such as through border management, can disproportionately burden those who have been made vulnerable through structural inequities resulting from racial and other forms of discrimination. How is the right balance to be struck, acknowledging, too, the economic and other imperatives that may dissuade governments from implementing public health measures? To underscore the latter point, some governments may be reluctant to take protective measures such as border closures not because they are concerned about the impact of precautions on marginalized communities but rather for fear of the short-term economic impact of those measures.

Border decision-making is frequently politicized, and politics can trump public health. Border management to protect against public health harms may be eschewed by governments who want to keep open important supply lines and travel routes and may be relatively unconcerned about the resulting death/morbidity, particularly if borne by marginalized groups and individuals. In other words, some governments may not want to take measures to protect public health such as border management because they are prioritizing economic and trade issues over public health. For example, Canada delayed implementing measures to manage its border with the US, a choice that would not seem supported by the relative risk profiles of the US compared to some other countries subjected to the restrictions, which had very low rates of COVID-19.

An unwanted flavour of politicization is when border measures are implemented in racist or xenophobic ways. One manifestation of this sort sees border restrictions used to penalize lesser-resourced countries, causing them to be isolated from the medicines, personnel, and supply lines they depend on. Upon detection of the Omicron variant in South Africa, the country moved rapidly to inform the World Health Organization and the global community of this latest threat. In response, several countries, including the US, Canada, the UK, and the EU—who had all been slow to initiate travel restrictions at the onset of the pandemic—immediately announced travel bans from South Africa and other southern African nations.[13] Clearly, any new attempt at revising the IHR must insist that states are evenhanded in their responses, applying the same severity of measures based on risk and not based on geopolitical importance or racism.

Likewise, any guidelines on the use of border management as a public health measure must recognize the disproportionate impact of these measures on migrants, refugees, and medical travelers, so as to better reconcile public health objectives with the interests of people whose security and well-being depend on international mobility. Canada, notwithstanding its initial stance to the contrary, closed its borders to virtually all asylum seekers for over 18 months in response to the COVID-19 pandemic. All the while, other migrants, including seasonal agricultural workers from Mexico and the

Caribbean, were permitted to enter the country. No reasons were ever given for why asylum seekers warranted a more stringent treatment.[14] Arguably, asylum seekers' need to find safety in another country should have supported their exemption from border restrictions. At the same time, COVID-19 outbreaks were frequently reported from Canadian farms and factories that employed a large number of migrant workers and warehoused them in often overcrowded quarters.[15] This raises concerns about whether enough has been done by the government to protect the health of those migrants whom it has chosen to admit despite public health-motivated border closures.

How can we develop global rules to ensure that *public health* drives decision-making, as opposed to racism and xenophobia, and how can we ensure that countries and people adversely impacted by travel restrictions, including migrants and refugees, are protected from harsh consequences? In Part V of this book, immigration experts grapple with this question and, using Canada as a case study, consider the possible tension between pandemic-related border measures and international migration. In Part IX, leading scholars and practitioners debate a range of access to care issues that result from border restrictions, including cross-border access to reproductive and maternal health services, humanitarian assistance, and access to vaccines. Meanwhile, in Part X, leading global health experts attempt to map a way forward by discussing potential reforms in global health law, including reforms to the IHR, and strategies for shoring up much needed human resource capacity in the global health law sector. Professor Fisman, a well-known Canadian infectious disease specialist, discusses the kind of evidence that decision-makers should weigh in, considering when and how to manage borders, focusing on risk gradients which must factor in not only the impact of controls on the introduction of pathogens but also the in-country measures taken to reduce spread. This is a critical point and yet may be difficult to assess at the outset of a pandemic when the mode(s) of transmission may not be fully understood still. This raises the question of whether countries should be entitled to rely on the precautionary principle, which animates much of public health, in making border closure decisions. The precautionary principle stands for the principle that where the risks to the population are potentially high, protective actions can be taken even in the absence of scientific certainty. The IHR presently requires nation states to provide evidence justifying the need for border closure, arguably negating the possibility of relying on the precautionary principle to justify a border closure.

1.4 Evidence

A theme that our contributors will wrestle with throughout the volume is the question of evidence: what evidence counts and what quality of evidence should be relied upon when placing restrictions on borders.

The precautionary principle, so critical to public health, highlights that in the early days of a public health threat, decision-makers are called upon to make decisions with often scant scientific evidence. Early in the pandemic, there was some disagreement about the seriousness of the disease, with some scientists predicting a much lower global infection fatality rate (IFR, the fraction of cases who will die of the disease) than was being observed and, therefore, arguing for a slowing of mitigation efforts, travel restrictions prime among them. Should countries, regions, or areas that are able to implement effective border controls as a mitigation measure be prevented by international law from protecting their population because the science supporting border closures is not definitive?

Fueling this tension was disagreement on the quality of evidence needed to trigger these decisions. The tenets of evidence-based medicine demanded that only the highest quality of clinical evidence, randomized controlled trials, should dictate decision-making, and yet it is not clear that this kind of evidence is ever feasible when considering issues like vaccine mandates, social restrictions, institutional closures, and mandatory masking. Many leaned on the precautionary principle to allow a lower standard of evidence, such as that gleaned from laboratory studies, mathematical models, and ecological studies, to trigger public health action and avoid possible mass suffering and deaths. Going forward, how should decision-makers (and the jurists reviewing their decisions) approach questions of the evidence required to trigger border restrictions and reopenings? What role should predictive modelling play in informing decision-makers regarding borders restrictions?

1.5 Our Goal

In what follows, we explore how the COVID-19 pandemic has ushered in a new and challenging environment in which existing borders drawn around people, places, and social structures have hardened and new ones have emerged. Whilst effective border management has in some circumstances saved many lives and reduced morbidity, it has also too frequently resulted in rigid, arbitrary, and inequitable distinctions between "ingroups" and "outgroups". In other words, the brunt of the impact of border drawing too frequently seems to have been borne by the most marginalized, reinforcing structural inequities and discrimination grounded in age, gender, disability, race, and immigration status.

Reflecting the need for nuanced and thoughtful analysis of the complex issues involved in border management, the contributors to this volume span multiple disciplines (e.g., constitutional law, ethics, history, human rights, public health, global health, immigration, and refugee law). Our contributors represent both country-specific and global experts on the changing ways that national, sub-national, and even figurative interpersonal borders have been managed in response to the pandemic threat. Going forward, our collective aim is to determine how public and private actors should best respond to pandemic outbreaks with border management responses. Our goal, with legal and policy reform, is to save lives, avoid harms, and specifically, reduce wherever possible the harmful impacts on those made vulnerable in society.

Notes

1 "Precautionary Measures in Response to Severe Pneumonia Cases in Wuhan, China" (2 January 2020), online: *Ministry of Health Singapore*. www.moh.gov.sg/news-highlights/details/precautionary-measures-in-response-to-severe-pneumonia-cases-in-wuhan-china.
2 "Timeline—Coronavirus—COVID-19", online: *New Zealand Doctor*. www.nzdoctor.co.nz/timeline-coronavirus
3 Rina Rozenburg Kandel & Ido Efrati, "Israel suspends all flights from China, Isolates arrivals over coronavirus outbreak" (30 January 2020), online: *Haaretz*. www.haaretz.com/israel-news/2020-01-30/ty-article/.premium/israel-suspends-all-flights-from-china-isolates-arrivals-over-coronavirus-outbreak/0000017f-e1c2-d804-ad7f-f1fa42640000.
4 "Israel bans foreigners coming from East Asian countries over virus fears" (17 February 2020), online: *The Times of Israel*. www.timesofisrael.com/israel-bans-foreigners-coming-from-east-asian-countries-over-virus-fears/.
5 Lauren Vogel & Laura Eggertson, "COVID-19: A timeline of Canada's first-wave response" (12 June 2020), online: *CMAJ News*. cmajnews.com/2020/06/12/coronavirus-1095847/.
6 "The federal and state governments have agreed on uniform quarantine rules for people entering the country" (9 April 2020), online: *Federal Ministry of the Interior and Homeland (Germany)*. www.bmi.bund.de/SharedDocs/pressemitteilungen/DE/2020/04/muster-verordnung.html.
7 Jeff King & Natalie Byrom, "United Kingdom: Legal response to Covid-19" in Jeff King & Octávio LM Ferraz, eds, *The Oxford Compendium of National Legal Responses to Covid-19* (Oxford University Press, 2021), at para 81. Doi: 10.1093/law-occ19/e17.013.17.
8 Marta Paterlini, "'Closing borders is ridiculous': The epidemiologist behind Sweden's controversial coronavirus strategy" (21 April 2020), online: *Nature*. www.nature.com/articles/d41586-020-01098-x.
9 Taylor v Newfoundland and Labrador, 2020 NLSC 125.
10 "Government of Canada to require vaccination of federal workforce and federally regulated transportation sector" (13 August 2021), online: *Government of Canada*. www.canada.ca/en/treasury-board-secretariat/news/2021/08/government-of-canada-to-require-vaccination-of-federal-workforce-and-federally-regulated-transportation-sector.html.
11 Debra Parkes & Carissima Mathen, "Canadian universities must act now to protect their communities" (2 August 2021), online: *The Vancouver Sun*. vancouversun.com/opinion/debra-parkes-and-carissima-mathen-canadian-universities-must-act-now-to-protect-their-communities.
12 Bryan Thomas et al, "Vaccine ins and outs: An exploration of the legal issues raised by vaccine passports" (13 July 2021), online: *C.D. Howe Institute*. www.cdhowe.org/public-policy-research/vaccine-ins-and-outs-exploration-legal-issues-raised-vaccine-passports; Bryan Thomas et al, "Privacy rights and private sector vaccination requirements" (28 January 2022), online: *C.D. Howe Institute*. www.

cdhowe.org/sites/default/files/2022-01/IM_Tho-Flo-Kri-Tan-Wil_2022_0128. pdf.; "Proof of COVID-19 vaccination", online: *Government of Ontario*. www. ontario.ca/page/proof-covid-19-vaccination#medical-exemptions.

13 Deepa Shivaram et al, "As omicron spreads, studies suggest that travel bans alone don't do much good" (29 November 2021), online: *NPR*. www.npr.org/sections/ coronavirus-live-updates/2021/11/28/1059619823/omicron-travel-bans-covid.

14 Audrey Macklin, "(In)Essential bordering: Canada, COVID, and mobility" in Anna Triandafyllidou, ed, *Migration and Pandemics: Spaces of Solidarity and Spaces of Exception* (Cham: Springer, 2021) 23.

15 Y.Y. Brandon Chen, "Beyond the rhetoric of essentiality: Canada's neoliberal migrant worker policy during the COVID-19 pandemic" in Sabrina Germain & Adrienne Yong, eds, *Beyond the Virus: Multidisciplinary and International Perspectives on Inequalities Raised by COVID-19* (Bristol: Bristol University Press, 2023) 164.

PART II

Histories, Contests, and Communication of Borders as Public Health Tools

2

THE ESSENTIAL ART OF COMMUNICATION ABOUT BALANCE IN BORDER CLOSURES

Raywat Deonandan

2.1 The Role of Public Health Communication

When considering the SARS epidemic of 2003, Suok Kai Chew identified transparency in communication as the first best lesson to be applied to future pandemics.[1] The agents of communication include state actors, individual researchers, and international bodies like the World Health Organization, with an audience that would include all such agents, policymakers, media, and the general public. Chew noted that "Infectious diseases such as SARS do not respect international borders." If prompt and accurate cross-border sharing of information had been achieved, "history may have taken a different course."[2] With the arrival of the COVID-19 pandemic, it behooved us to take this lesson to heart, to strengthen our public health communication wherewithal as we sought to curtail both the leaking of infection through porous international borders and the explosive spread of cases within our borders.

Public health communication, loosely defined, has a history going back thousands of years, as individuals have always sought to alert their communities to impending threats.[3] Its contemporary manifestation, though, has struggled to find formalized structure. There is no official consensus on the specific roles of public health communication during a crisis. But they are arguably to alert the public to the nature of the emergency, enumerate steps that authorities are taking and that the public should be taking, inform the public of key developments during the evolution of the crisis, explain some technical points, and lastly, assuage panic. Encouraging behavior change can be considered a longer-term goal of public health communication, as evidenced by the decades-long antismoking or safe sex campaigns. The

DOI: 10.4324/9781003394006-4

effectiveness of such campaigns depends not only on the clarity and accuracy of their content but also on the extent to which missives are well received and deemed acceptable and convincing by the intended audience. Culture, science literacy, numeracy, and ideology are, therefore, necessarily factors gating the impact of any information campaign.

Formal guides or frameworks for proper communication are few. The US Centers for Disease Control (CDC) maintains the Crisis and Emergency Risk Communication (CERC) manual as a guide for public health professionals to reach and engage with stakeholders across society.[4] The manual suggests a six-point framework for this work, including the important qualities of accuracy, honesty, and promptness.[5] While these are indeed crucial virtues, they have proven to be insufficient in a new age in which information and misinformation can spread faster than the disease itself.[6] There is an unspoken assumption in the application of this framework: that the communicator is reaching out from a position of trust and authority. That advantage can no longer be assumed, as cultural and ideological shifts have eroded public confidence in the trustworthiness of state-centred public messaging,[7] at least for a vocal segment of the population.

The trust issue is not specific to messaging from state actors. The ability of independent voices of authority, such as research scientists, to offer guidance has also been compromised by the new realities of public life.[8] Public health communication in many jurisdictions is not centralized. Local health authorities vie with national messaging centres, mass broadcast media, and now independent social media voices. With such a diversity of voices, confusion can reign. Confusion is further sown by the addition of false voices, such as "bots" on social media, which serve to amplify fringe narratives to give the appearance of greater support.

But such diversity is unavoidable and sometimes even desirable. Evidence has long pointed to the tendency of differing communities to seek emergency guidance from different authoritative sources. Rural populations turn to local authorities first, whereas urban residents turn to broadcast media first.[9] Some ethnic communities respond differentially to information that is tailored to their cultural realities or from a known personal source, like a family doctor, rather than a governmental figure.[10]

Trust is unfortunately further challenged by uncertainty, though uncertainty is a pillar of proper science. Early in the pandemic, there was considerable variability in opinion around the nature of the threat and how to assuage it. The method of transmission was not clear nor was the quality of the actual societal challenge. Was COVID a mortal threat to people or mostly an existential challenge to healthcare systems? Later, changing guidance around mask wearing further fueled public confusion.[11] Uncertainty bred inconsistency in message content and that in turn fomented distrust and created opportunities for counternarratives, such as those of the COVID minimizers, who argued that the disease was no worse than the flu, in terms of its lethality and overall threat to society.[12]

Yet regardless of controversy around its scale and trajectory, disease transmission was undeniably happening, people were getting sick, and many were dying. Action had to be taken. In the initial pre-vaccine phase of the pandemic, nations who fared best, in terms of limited transmission, morbidity, and mortality, had three things in common: their COVID testing infrastructure was extensive, their response was fast and decisive, and their national borders were closed or monitored to control importation of new cases. The ability to manage borders and act decisively was gated by two further phenomena: a clear understanding of the science of infectious disease dynamics and the ability to resist the nefarious spread of misinformation and disinformation serving to slow any needed response.

Those two factors have proven to be drivers of greater distrust and division and continue to hobble public health leaders' ability to communicate to the public information essential for community and self-protection and for and understanding and acceptance of why policy decisions were taken. For the essential art of public health communication to best inform and guide in times of difficult policy choices, such as the decision to restrict border crossings, the communication hinderances of innumeracy and disinformation must be addressed.

2.2 Did Border Closures Work?

A common objective of science communication is to find and distill the appropriate evidence around the issue at hand. But evidence concerning the effectiveness of closures to slow the spread of COVID-19 is variable. Among 24 countries notable for having delayed the introduction of the disease within their populations, having had border closures and travel restrictions are a common factor,[13] suggesting that it was an important policy choice in the early phase of the pandemic. Examined African countries, though, showed minimal impact of borders closures on COVID incidence.[14] Similarly, analyses of countries already seeded with disease found no statistical difference in growth rate between those with strong closure policies and those with weaker ones.[15] And a more rigorous analysis of time-series data found "no evidence in favor of international border closures."[16]

However, a meta-analysis of border closures within China early in the pandemic found that travel restrictions slowed the spread of the disease considerably but only in its initial phase. Similarly, the ban on travel out of Wuhan prevented nearly 80% infections from spreading to countries outside China in the weeks after it was imposed.[17] Further complicating this seemingly simple question is a modelling study showing that restrictions on international movement reduced exportation of cases globally by

10% within the first month, though the effect diminished in subsequent months.[18]

Depending on how the studies are parsed and used, border closures could be expressed to the public and decision-makers as justified or not. An important nuance to these data is that any advantage in closures is thought to be temporary and, in the case of the Chinese studies, might be more in line with the prevention of outward exportation of infection rather than of importation of foreign infection. The challenge in communicating the rationale of border management then becomes twofold: the public's ability to accept and digest nuanced scientific uncertainty, including whether a 10% reduction in case exportation is significant; and the possibility that a policy that some controversially expected to be hurtful[19] might have limited utility domestically but still reduce caseload globally. As noted earlier, it seems the first barrier to effective public communication in the COVID-19 pandemic is simple innumeracy.

2.3 The Innumeracy Pandemic

2.3.1 The Lesson of Exponential Growth

Innumeracy, a discomfort or unfamiliarity with mathematics among the base population, is a persistent challenge to medical communication[20] and continues to be unaddressed as a public policy priority in the long term. And in the near term, communication strategies fail to account for its insidious effects. The result is a population unable to emotionally or intellectually grasp the urgency of action or the scale of the threat. In the context of a pandemic, expressing the magnitude and speed of case growth is a communication priority, as well as the distinction and relationship between small and large numbers.

Physicist Albert Allen Bartlett once wrote that "the greatest shortcoming of the human race is our inability to understand the exponential function." In April of 2021, when asked on a CBC radio show[21] why the province had waited so long before enacting the COVID-19 restrictions for which medical experts had been pleading, Ontario Solicitor General Sylvia Jones replied, "We wanted to make sure that the modelling was actually showing up in our hospitals." This was a curious answer that possibly explained the slow government responses to the pandemic to that point. Ms. Jones's inability to understand the explosive nature of exponential growth prevented her from realizing that action must be taken *before* the modelling numbers manifest as measurable cases.

German statisticians suggested that "people mistakenly perceive the coronavirus to grow in a linear manner, underestimating its actual potential for exponential growth." The authors go on to say that this cognitive failure "influences political opinions about matters of life and death."[22] Indeed, exponential growth comes in two phases. As labelled by author Richard Baldwin, the first is the "imperceptible progress" phase and the second is "explosive progress." In the first phase, growth is acknowledged but easily dismissed. But in the second phase, we are overwhelmed by growth and act surprised that it is happening at all.[23] Failure to consider the implications of exponential growth leads to failure in prompt response and an inability to mitigate the importation of infection from outside national borders.

The lesson of exponential growth as it pertains to public health is this: When we know it is happening, when we are still in the "imperceptible progress" phase, we must act decisively. If we wait until the "explosive progress" phase, we risk not having the resources to mount a sufficient response. As noted, evidence suggests that border closures are most effective early in the outbreak and lose their utility later, likely due in large part to this essential property of exponential growth, the need to enact the policy in this early "imperceptible progress" phase of incidence growth.

2.3.2 Individual versus Population Risk

Similar to the cognitive misfiring that prevents deep appreciation for exponential growth, a failure to distinguish between individual risk and population risk is a recurring frustration in pandemic communication, often underlining a key difference between public health and clinical medicine. The latter is focused on the treatment of individual patients, while the former manages impacts upon communities and populations. Not understanding this difference, news media continuously asked professionals from one group to offer public pandemic guidance on the matters of the other group, further adding to the disarray and confusing nature of public messaging.

Overlain atop this disarray is the improper application of the tenets of evidence-based medicine (EBM), which is a set of practices and philosophies for guiding clinical medicine. EBM has been transformative in ensuring that the highest quality of evidence is used to inform clinical care of a patient. It holds the randomized clinical trial (RCT) and systematic reviews of RCTs as the highest forms of evidence. Often, the absence of RCT evidence is used by EBM adherents to discount therapies and interventions that show promise in the laboratory. The adoption of mask wearing as a pandemic mitigating strategy, for example, continues to be challenged by those demanding the high bar of RCT evidence of its effectiveness.

But EBM is not the appropriate paradigm for decision-making in the context of either public health or a public health emergency. There are no RCTs to determine whether seatbelts are efficacious, for example, or indeed to determine whether cigarette smoking causes lung cancer. Yet effective public health policy was enacted with respect to those issues without the need for the highest pinnacle of EBM evidence. Laboratory and observational evidence have proven more than sufficient to inform those policies.

Similarly, there have been no RCTs to prove the effectiveness of soldiers' gas masks in battle conditions or that of parachutes for those plummeting from airplanes. Laboratory studies of each have repeatedly been deemed to offer adequate evidence of high utility. Endless further examples abound of population-level policies and procedures having been enacted without the need for RCTs, yet calls for the application of EBM-style evidence seems disproportionately loud in the context of the COVID-19 pandemic.

Even if one wished to apply EBM standards to a public health emergency like a pandemic, the demands for action and policy decision-making are too urgent to wait for the slow and deliberate process of EBM evidence collection. As one group of authors observed, "While RCTs are important, exclusion of other study designs and evidence sources has been particularly problematic in a context where rapid decision making is needed in order to save lives and protect health."[24] While EBM remains the appropriate evidence paradigm for individual care and risk, a different evidence hierarchy is relevant for population-based risks and health challenges characteristic of a public health emergency.

Technically, risk assessors use the term "population risk" to mean the number of deaths caused by some hazard. But "individual risk" is the incremental probability of death that the hazard imposes on a given person.[25] The ideal of personalized risk assessment is the ultimate goal of much of clinical medicine. But the computation of risk is itself by definition a population-based measure. The extrapolation of individual risk from measures in a population is inherently flawed and indeed oxymoronic.[26]

A glaring example of this disconnect is a misunderstanding of the scale of the infection fatality ratio (IFR) of COVID-19. The IFR is that fraction of all COVID cases who will die from the disease. It is impossible to compute IFR directly since it is impossible to know of all cases, as many people never get tested and thus never know of their infection status. But most modelling studies place the COVID IFR, before the advent of vaccines, at around 1%.[27] This led to a rallying cry among COVID-minimizers, "Why be afraid of a disease with a 99% survival rate?" At the individual level, a 99% survival rate seems comfortable. But if millions become infected, then tens of thousands die. Tens of thousands more become hospitalized or disabled. The population level impact of this seemingly benign number is substantial.

The individual/population disconnect is evident in the ongoing efforts to encourage vaccination. For most healthy people with low probability of a bad COVID outcome, the best rationale for seeking vaccination is to add to overall population immunity and slow the penetration of the disease into the population—in other words, to protect others.

However, the messaging has instead focused on individual protection and vaccine efficacy against symptomatic disease and worse outcomes. For example, the CDC website offers the following rationale for getting vaccinated against COVID-19: "Getting a COVID-19 vaccine is a safer, more reliable way to build protection than getting sick with COVID-19. COVID-19 vaccination helps protect you by creating an antibody response without you having to experience potentially severe illness or post-COVID conditions."[28] Similarly, the government of Canada's social media campaign to encourage booster doses states, "By triggering more antibodies and other parts of the immune system, a booster dose can improve the immune response and help increase protection against infection and sever illness from COVID-19."[29] Messaging around the positive community impacts of vaccination is comparatively very rare.

Similarly, the risk of infected persons crossing managed borders has been consistently presented as a matter of individual impact and consequence. Concern for the inconvenience of individual travelers was paramount. The justification of border closures as being for the global good rather than the national or personal good requires an acceptance of global population risk as being as worthy of mitigation as is individual or national risk. This tension can be described as antagonism between individual liberty and community responsibility, which unavoidably aligns with political ideologies.

2.4 Fighting the Infodemic

2.4.1 Merchants of Misinformation

Ideological divide has proven to be a potent accelerant for many kinds of societal distrust, with opinions on the rationality of COVID restrictions falling neatly along ideological lines. This in turn allowed malignant actors to prise social divisions further apart through the introduction of seductive scientific untruths.

In April of 2021, the Canadian Security Intelligence Service (CSIS) tweeted that "Disinformation about COVID19 is being spread by threat actors to discredit government efforts and diminish confidence in vaccine rollout efforts."[30] The suggestion was that organized entities, perhaps foreign powers, were working specifically to disrupt Canadian public health communication with counternarratives and outright lies. Combined with unorganized falsehoods shared by simply misinformed individuals, some have taken to calling this phenomenon an "infodemic."[31] The synergy between the directed disinformation efforts and the aforementioned barriers to proper communication is particularly concerning. For instance, it has been shown that those with the least scientific literacy are most susceptible to mis- and disinformation, particularly when it comes to vaccine issues.[32]

The specific false claims within the infodemic are too many to list. But they include false (and sometimes dangerous) cures and treatments; erroneous origins of the virus; erroneous routes of transmission; incorrect levels of risk posed by the disease (almost always underestimating its seriousness); nefarious motivations of scientists and public health leaders; and a host of false claims about the effectiveness, source, and safety of COVID vaccines.

It is unclear how the infodemic helped shape border closure policies. Suggestions that the virus was a Chinese bioweapon might have increased acceptance of closed borders. But more common erroneous insistences on low IFR[33] (meaning that the disease was less lethal than experts claimed), oversensitive PCR testing (suggesting that there is no real pandemic but a "casedemic" caused by the testing apparatus),[34] and bad pandemic math (suggesting that the pandemic was already over, just weeks after it was declared)[35] served to hinder acceptance of all COVID mitigation measures, border closures among them.

In the wake of such forces, public health communicators are compelled to become soldiers in an information war. It is no longer sufficient to follow the various frameworks that call simply and naively for accuracy and promptness. Active combatting of falsehoods is required, given the speed at which social media spreads easily digested and seductive lies. Strategies for waging this battle are still emerging. But they include regular fact-checking of all public claims;[36] heightening the credibility of communicators by amplifying those with recognizable credentials;[37] disseminating more factual information at scale;[38] and as earlier, continuously reinvesting in both health and media literacy.[39]

2.4.2 The Flow of Information across Borders

A largely unexamined communications phenomenon arising from the closing of borders is the extent to which information, not just people, was constrained from flowing freely between jurisdictions. The Suok Kai Chew paper originally cited at the beginning of this paper[40] stressed that transparency in communication is most essential between disparate agents scattered across the globe, each seeking to combat a pandemic with the limited tools at hand; information is one of those critical tools. In the words of Plasek *et al*, "Global data on disease trajectories and the effectiveness and economic impact of different social distancing measures are essential to facilitate effective local responses to pandemics."[41]

Information sharing can be either formal or informal. Some refer to the latter as "social remittances," which are essentially the transfer of ideas, practices, and behaviors, a phenomenon well established in migration studies. Pandemic restrictions enacted in several countries, such as mask wearing, social distancing, and eschewing in-person meetings, lead to changes in everyday activity that have been referred to as a "new normal" for citizen behavior. But the effect of border closures has been to compel transnational families and organizations to reconcile "new normality" in a heterogenous and multinational way.[42] For such groups to best navigate their new reality, it's important to have access to the legal and behavioral expectations of their members in foreign domains, as well as to the public health data expressing the status of the epidemic locally. The role of public communications is important in this context, packaged in a way that is digestible to an international audience, and without overreliance on the jargon or the societal or governmental nuances specific to a given jurisdiction.

More critical to the scientific management of the pandemic is the rapid global sharing of surveillance data, laboratory findings, clinical observations, and the local vicissitudes of incidence patterns. These types of information permit public health leaders, among other things, to brace for the arrival of new viral variants, to calibrate performance expectations of diagnostic tests and therapeutics, to characterize disease presentation to help with the treatment of infected patients, and to project the likely course of the local epidemic. The free flow of data is an essential good in times of global emergency to enable quicker validation of biotechnological innovations and refinement of mitigation strategies.

Much of this task has been automated, with heavy reliance on open data for disease surveillance and aggregator feeds for news reports that can be accessed online from anywhere with an Internet connection. But open data, while crucial, is insufficient to the task. An actual flesh-and-blood human communicator lends context and interpretation to numbers, transforming data into information and information into narrative. The roles of a public health communicator in times of global emergency and border restriction, then, is not only to interpret, assuage, clarify, inform, and reassure but also to do so in a manner that allows wide geographical exportation and comprehension.

2.5 Conclusion

The old frameworks for public health communication are no longer sufficient. The pandemic has offered new challenges, both external and baked into our society. A rehabilitated approach is now needed, one that not only meets the traditional public health goals of disease control but also that is both hardened against targeted disinformation and catalysed by a renewed commitment to addressing public innumeracy and scientific illiteracy and that appreciates the global and diverse nature of the audience.

Notes

1 S. K. Chew, "SARS: How a global epidemic was stopped" (2007), *The Bulletin of the World Health Organization* 324.
2 *Ibid* at 1.

3 C. T. Salmon & T. Poorisat, "The rise and development of public health communication" (2020) 35:13 *Health Communication* 1666.
4 Centers for Disease Control and Prevention, *Crisis and Emergency Risk Communication (CERC) (Manual)* (US Department of Health & Human Services, 2018).
5 M. A. Sauer et al, "A failure to communicate? how public messaging has strained the COVID-19 response in the United States" (2021) 19:1 *Health Secure* 65.
6 C. H. Basch et al, "A global pandemic in the time of viral memes: COVID-19 vaccine misinformation and disinformation on TikTok" (2021) 17:8 *Human Vaccines & Immunotherapeutics* 2373.
7 H. J. Larson, E. Gakidou & C. J. L. Murray, "The vaccine-hesitant moment" (2022) 387:1 *New England Journal of Medicine* 58.
8 L. Steffen, "Are we there yet? Reflections on life during a pandemic" (2021) 27:3 *Create Nursing* 153.
9 R. J. Wray et al, "Communicating with the public about emerging health threats: Lessons from the pre-event message development project" (2008) 98:12 *The American Journal of Public Health* 2214.
10 M. Alsan et al, "Comparison of knowledge and information-seeking behavior after general COVID-19 public health messages and messages tailored for black and latinx communities: A randomized controlled trial" (2021) 174:4 *Annals of Internal Medicine* 484–492.
11 K. Koehler & A. Rule, "Understanding changing guidance on mask use" (24 April 2020), online: *HUB*. https://hub.jhu.edu/2020/04/24/covid-19-mask-glove-use/.
12 J. P. A. Ioannidis, "Reconciling estimates of global spread and infection fatality rates of COVID-19: An overview of systematic evaluations" (2021) 51:5 *The European Journal of Clinical Investigation* e13554.
13 Z. Li et al, "Countries with delayed COVID-19 introduction—Characteristics, drivers, gaps, and opportunities" (2021) 17:1 *Global Health* 28.
14 T. I. Emeto, F. O. Alele & O. S. Ilesanmi, "Evaluation of the effect of border closure on COVID-19 incidence rates across nine African countries: an interrupted time series study" (2021) 115:10 *Transactions of the Royal Society of Tropical Medicine and Hygiene* 1174.
15 L. Timur & Y. Xie, "Is border closure effective in containing COVID-19?" (2021) 44 *Travel Medicine and Infectious Disease* 102137.
16 M. A. Shiraef et al, "Did border closures slow SARS-CoV-2?" (2022) 12:1 *Scientific Reports* 1709.
17 M. Chinazzi et al, "The effect of travel restrictions on the spread of the 2019 novel coronavirus (COVID-19) outbreak" (2020) 368:6489 *Science* 395.
18 T. W. Russell et al, "Effect of internationally imported cases on internal spread of COVID-19: A mathematical modelling study" (2021) 6:1 *Lancet Public Health* e12.
19 L. Lin & S. Y. Xie, "Economic costs accumulate as countries worried by delta variant extend border closures" (11 September 2021), online: *Wall Street Journal*. www.wsj.com/articles/economic-costs-accumulate-as-countries-worried-by-delta-variant-extend-border-closures-11631387873.
20 G. Gigerenzer & A. Edwards, "Simple tools for understanding risks: From innumeracy to insight" (2003) 327:7417 *BMJ* 741.
21 R. Bresnahan, "Ottawa morning" (2021), online: *CBC*. www.cbc.ca/listen/live-radio/1-100-ottawa-morning?cmp=DM_SEM_Listen_Titles.
22 J. Lammers, J. Crusius & A. Gast, "Correcting misperceptions of exponential coronavirus growth increases support for social distancing" (2020) 117:28 *Proceedings of the National Academy of Sciences of the United States of America* 16264 at 16266.
23 R. E. Baldwin, The Globotics Upheaval: Globalization, Robotics, and the Future of Work (Oxford University Press, 2019).

24 T. Greenhalgh et al, "Adapt or die: How the pandemic made the shift from EBM to EBM+ more urgent" (2022) 27:5 *BMJ Evidence-Based Medicine* 253.
25 M. D. Adler, "Against 'Individual risk': A sympathetic critique of risk assessment" (2005) 153:4 *The University of Pennsylvania Law Review*.
26 J. W. McEvoy et al, "Risk and the physics of clinical prediction" (2014) 113:8 *The American Journal of Cardiology* 1429.
27 G. Meyerowitz-Katz & L. Merone, "A systematic review and meta-analysis of published research data on COVID-19 infection fatality rates" (2020) 101 *International Journal of Infectious Diseases* 138.
28 "Benefits of getting A COVID-19 vaccine" (22 December 2022), online: *CDC*. www.cdc.gov/coronavirus/2019-ncov/vaccines/vaccine-benefits.html.
29 "COVID-19: Social media and promotional resources for health Canada and public health agency of Canada" (2022), online: *Government of Canada*. www.canada.ca/en/public-health/services/diseases/2019-novel-coronavirus-infection/digital-resources.html.
30 CSIS Canada, "Disinformation about #COVID19 is being spread by threat actors to discredit government efforts and diminish confidence in vaccine rollout efforts. Be sure to verify information before you share it. Follow @CPHO_Canada & @GovCanHealth for accurate info on the pandemic in Canada" (29 April 2021), online: *Twitter*. https://twitter.com/csiscanada/status/1387799417676238853.
31 D. Banerjee & K. S. Meena, "COVID-19 as an 'infodemic' in public health: Critical role of the social media" (2021) 9 *Front Public Health* 610623.
32 S. K. Lee et al, "Misinformation of COVID-19 vaccines and vaccine hesitancy" (2022) 12:1 *Scientific Reports* 13681.
33 Ioannidis, *supra* note 12.
34 D. Gorski, "There is no COVID-19 'casedemic.' The pandemic is real and deadly" (23 November 2020), online: *Science Based Medicine*. https://sciencebasedmedicine.org/no-covid-19-casedemic/.
35 B. F. Ostrov, "Cue the debunking: Two Bakersfield doctors go viral with dubious COVID test conclusions" (28 April 2020), online: *Cal Matters*. https://calmatters.org/health/2020/04/debunking-bakersfield-doctors-covid-spread-conclusions/.
36 P. Lurie et al, "COVID-19 vaccine misinformation in English-language news media: retrospective cohort study" (2022) 12:6 *BMJ Open* e058956.
37 B. Swire-Thompson & D. Lazer, "Public health and online misinformation: Challenges and recommendations" (2020) 41 *Annual Review of Public Health* 433.
38 J. L. Pomeranz & A. R. Schwid, "Governmental actions to address COVID-19 misinformation" (2021) 42:2 *Journal of Public Health Policy* 201.
39 S. Ratzan, S. Sommariva & L. Rauh, "Enhancing global health communication during a crisis: lessons from the COVID-19 pandemic" (2020) 30:2 *Public Health Research & Practice* e3022010.
40 Chew, *supra* note 1.
41 J. M.Plasek et al, "Following data as it crosses borders during the COVID-19 pandemic" (2020) 27:7 *Journal of the American Medical Informatics Association* 1139.
42 N. Galstyan & M. Galstyan, "Social remittances during COVID-19: on the 'new normality' negotiated by transnational families" (2021) 9:1 *Comparative Migration Studies* 51.

3

THE WOLF AND THE SHEEPFOLD

Borders, Containment, and Contested Discourses of Public Health in the Great Influenza Pandemic Era

Esyllt W. Jones

The 1918–1919 influenza pandemic in Canada generated heterogeneous state and public responses, even as a catastrophic death toll (over 50,000 Canadians lost) challenged faith in the efficacy of public health measures. The influenza pandemic was not the only, nor necessarily, the most impactful infectious disease crisis, short- or long-term, in the early history of Canadian public health. However, it provides an interesting encapsulation of themes that resonate especially clearly in the light of COVID-19, as the public response to containment measures has become fractured and politicized. In the influenza pandemic's aftermath, public health critically examined its own shortcomings, and diverse state approaches to disease control confronted equally diverse popular responses. This paper re-evaluates trust, authority, and legitimacy in public health debates and discourses and highlights the value for us today of examining discord, resistance, and multiple sites and spaces of governance in shaping reactions to disease outbreaks.

In Canada, as in other constitutionally federal systems, the response to pandemic influenza was decentralized and variable. In the fight against a highly communicable virus, and in the context of war, containment at the borders of the nation was never seriously attempted. Regional- and local-level tensions emerged over governance, the exercise of legitimate authority, and public trust in other forms of containment. In the post-pandemic era, public health searched for a new paradigm. Institutional frameworks for international health cooperation were bolstered. Canada created its first national department of public health. The pandemic strengthened a shift in disease containment from compulsion to cooperation (at least, in the Western metropole). Given the failures of medicine and public health in 1918–1920, however, many questioned the assumption that expertise

DOI: 10.4324/9781003394006-5

and science alone could provide solutions to infectious disease and health inequality.

3.1 Borders, Compulsion, and Containment: Brief Histories

Robert Koch's discovery of the cholera bacillus in 1884 bolstered the contagionist view of disease over earlier environmental and sanitationist traditions and encouraged individual vector containment rather than social solutions to disease prevalence. Public health placed a growing emphasis upon quarantine, isolation, and disinfection.[1] Compulsory measures were enacted, especially in colonial settings, where racialized bodies were perceived as incapable of self-governance and subordinated to colonial rule.[2] In the North American context, critical analyses of containment through immigrant medical screening have demonstrated how public health discourse and practice at the turn of the 20th century were socially and politically contingent, were interwoven with histories of capitalism and colonialism, and theories of racial difference. For example, Amy Fairchild's *Science at the Borders* explores the relationship between the labour needs of capitalism, racism, and nativism and attempts to define the most dangerous infectious diseases entering the US as brought by "dirty" and "ignorant" newcomers.[3] Prevailing public health discourses depicted health threats as external, not internal, despite evidence that internal social and economic inequality were wreaking havoc on the health and wellness of millions. In Canada, Isabelle Wallace's work on the public health debate about involuntary screening of South Asian migrants for hookworm (not a deadly disease or at all common in Canada) has clarified the role of public health in the infamous case of the Komagata Maru and Canada's attempts to keep South Asian migrants from entering the country.[4] Until the First World War (after which immigration policies explicitly lowered the overall numbers of newcomers admitted to Canada and the US), health inspection at the borders was designed to prevent those perceived as diseased and physically or mentally disabled migrants from compromising the vitality of the nation—even while inspection legitimized the mass migration necessary to fuel the demand for cheap labour and white settlement. Public health was less focused on surveilling or controlling the movement of specific infectious diseases.

Thus, historians of disease and global public health for the past two decades have been fruitfully engaged in exploring the intersection between public health policies and practices, borders and migrant inclusion/exclusion, racialized and class-based disease containment regimes, and how each of these acted in service of "the nation." Indeed, we now understand that the history of the modern nation state and the history of public health regimes are inseparable, in a variety of contexts. For example, in works like *Imperial Hygiene: A Critical History of Colonialism, Nationalism and Public Health*, published almost two decades ago, historian Alison Bashford asserted that "lines of hygiene were boundaries of rule . . . the whole mission of public health was that it formed an important part of the larger modern projects of nation, of race, and of colonization."[5] A critical perspective on the integral relationship between nation-building, territoriality, racial and ethnic inequality, and public health has shaped a generation of innovative scholarship in the history of disease outbreaks.

At the same time, the strength of modern state *apparati*, "at home" and in the colonies, made preventive campaigns of quarantine, isolation, and disinfection increasingly practicable at the local level. In the context of imperial rivalries deploying health and bodily politics in the struggle for territory and legitimacy, compulsion was frequent, as a number of scholars have noted.[6] Compulsory measures did frequently encounter resistance and criticism. Over time, popular opposition was a central factor in a shift towards a more voluntary approach, along with the general ineffectiveness of mandatory measures such as mandatory isolation and segregation of the exposed and infected. Approaches to smallpox prevention is one example. Within liberal democratic states, notions of bodily autonomy and the primacy of parental authority informed well-organized opposition to compulsory smallpox vaccination across class lines.[7]

By the time of the influenza pandemic, compulsory measures were viewed by many health officials as double-edged swords, and public health officials were aware that containment policies might become fraught. In countries with decentralized health systems like Canada, the work of resolving these tensions and gaining public support during the pandemic was done almost exclusively at the provincial and municipal government levels.

3.2 The Influenza Pandemic in Canada

As Mark Humphries has demonstrated, the failure of Canada's national border and quarantine system to contain the influenza pandemic was inseparable from the war effort.[8] Local health officers were frequently highly critical of military decision-making and failure to adequately quarantine those exposed to influenza.[9] Both the spring and fall 1918 waves of influenza moved from the US into Canada via soldiers' movements. Soldiers were not the only vectors—civilian travel also played a role—but military mobilization was key to the virus's spread within Canada's borders as well. In fall of 1918, influenza was spread across the country, not by soldiers "coming home" from the European theatre but by troops moving from east to west across Canada as members of the Canadian Siberian Expeditionary Force (CSEF). During the pandemic, the CSEF was deployed to Vladivostok to reinforce the Allied presence in Russia and strengthen forces opposed to the Bolshevik Revolution. Infected soldiers who were part of this mobilization were left at military bases across the country and became key vectors for the spread of the disease.

With a permeable border and a lethal variant of the influenza virus spreading across the country in fall 1918, provincial public health legislation enabled local health boards to take interventionist disease control measures that restricted human interaction, such as placarding, quarantine, and isolation measures and the closure of public spaces and schools. However, critical decisions about which measures to deploy and when, and how to enforce them, while facilitated by provincial law, were made at the municipal level. Unsurprisingly, local responses were varied and lacking in consensus.

In Winnipeg health officials initially opted against compulsory isolation in hospital or placarding infected homes—measures that were within their provincial mandate and had been used in past outbreaks. During the first month of the pandemic, the mandatory reporting of cases formed the backbone of their response to the disease. Winnipeg's chief medical officer, Alexander Douglas, had little faith in placarding infected households (that is, placing signs on the doors of infected households and requiring all the inhabitants to isolate by law). Instead, those infected and their contacts were asked to respect a voluntary period of isolation. City officials sought to foster cooperation and encouraged the public to seek treatment.[10]

They were cautious about public health measures that might discourage the infected from notifying health authorities or seeking treatment. W.J.T. Watt, Chief Inspector of Communicable Diseases, argued that the placarding of houses, which was unpopular with the public, would tend to make people less willing to report their illnesses to authorities.[11] This might mean public health would lack accurate information about the location and numbers of cases and ultimately further spread the disease rather than contain it. Public trust was seen as a priority. The health department employed education, rather than compulsion. On 19 October, they announced measures focused upon the working-class newcomer residents of the north end. Douglas announced:

> Means [are being] taken to educate the foreign residents of that district as to the grave danger of delay in combating the disease. Literature, printed in Yiddish and Ruthenian, giving warning and advise [sic] will be distributed North of the CPR tracks today.[12]

The health department also worked with immigrant organizations to establish volunteer nursing and relief organizations specific to their communities.

Soon, however, conflict emerged between Winnipeg and the province over more stringent measures to limit public interaction. The provincial medical officer, Dr. M. Stuart Fraser, preferred more restrictive measures and punishment for those failing to follow public health orders. In opposition to Winnipeg's health officers, on 30 October 1918, Fraser called for strict mandatory quarantine of everyone infected with influenza. Health authorities saw the placarding of all infected houses as impracticable, but on 1 November, a full placarding initiative was announced by city health authorities.[13]

Douglas's moderate stance on mandatory containment measures was overcome at the pandemic's peak. Despite public proclamations, however, strict quarantine was never effectively enforced. The health department was short-staffed, as health inspectors and police officers were themselves severely affected by influenza. Health department data suggest that approximately 4,000 homes were officially quarantined and placarded in 1918; far fewer were inspected to ensure compliance. There were 13,059 cases of influenza reported to the health department; the total number of cases was far in excess of that figure and dwarfed the number of quarantines issued or enforced.[14]

In Ontario, the local-provincial dynamic was reversed. The chief provincial health officer, John W.S. McCullough, focused on educating local public health officers, physicians, and the public. He advised against measures such as closures of schools, churches, and meeting places. But the provincial board of health had no legal right to determine local municipal public health measures, only to advise. Public health officials in some Ontario cities (including London and Windsor) enacted public closures despite the province's recommendations.[15]

In British Columbia, the closure of schools and meeting places was referred to as "town closure." As with quarantine measures in Winnipeg and Ontario, provincial and local authorities in BC were not always in agreement and vied for authority and public support. Vancouver's health officer, Frederick Underhill, viewed public closures as ineffective and hoped to avoid mandatory measures in favour of sanitary preventive measures and public education. By contrast, 16 surrounding municipalities applied to the province for town closures. Some of these municipal leaders viewed Vancouver as a disease reservoir and its health officer as too lax and requested that the province impose a town closure on Vancouver. Victoria also requested that it be quarantined from the mainland if the outbreak in Vancouver was not controlled. As the pandemic intensified, public and political opinion shifted in favour of greater intervention. Ultimately, like Douglas on the issue of quarantine in Winnipeg, Underhill was forced to compromise and close schools and places of public assembly in Vancouver, for a time.[16]

Events in Saskatchewan illustrate another layer of response—locally-initiated cordons sanitaires. Forty-five towns informed the Canadian Pacific Railway that they would not be allowed to drop off goods or people. According to Maureen Lux, in railway line communities, residents congregated on station platforms to stop anyone from disembarking. At Lloydminster and North Battleford, armed guards patrolled roads in and out of the community. To assert its decision-making authority, the province argued that these local measures were illegal and not in keeping with public health expertise.[17] Humphries has referred to these efforts as "vigilante."[18]

In the pandemic context, however, individual and community assertions of authority, sometimes outside of health policy and law, were not infrequent.

At times, more intervention was demanded of public health, involving additional limits on human interaction and movement, whether in the form of quarantining the exposed, isolating the sick, closing all but essential public spaces, or closing off entire towns from "outsiders." By the pandemic's worst weeks in late fall 1918, calls for stringent measures became more dominant. At the same time, some members of the public ignored education and advice to limit contacts and avoid crowds. And not all mandatory measures were supported. In Alberta, where the wearing of masks was compulsory, masking was ridiculed and resisted. Public health decision-makers had to balance these competing viewpoints and interests and challenges to their judgment and authority.

3.3 Reckoning, Reform

These examples illustrate the extent to which spatial boundaries and compulsory containment measures were contested concepts during the pandemic—although not necessarily in the ways we might expect in light of the COVID-19 experience. Influenza's aftermath contributed to changes in public health but not necessarily to unified opinion. The most obvious impact the influenza pandemic had on federal policy was the creation in 1919 of the country's first national Department of Health. The federal government had faced public criticism over its failure to contain influenza at the border or to coordinate preventive efforts across the country; even under wartime censorship, leading newspapers held the government to account. Reformers had called for a greater national role and coordination for years, but the pandemic proved the catalyst to its creation. Some spoke of the new department as essential for national security or, as did Peter Bryce, as a reflection of a trade-off between individual freedoms surrendered and "sanctions" in order to protect "community and nation, and for mankind."[19]

By contrast, for some the pandemic illustrated deeper flaws in notions of health, nation, and borders. Social gospeller Newton Rowell, addressing a gathering to celebrate the centenary of the Methodist Church in Canada, argued:

> we may think in lines of nationality; we may try to build up walls between one nation or people and another; but . . . humanity is essentially one and [that] which affects any for weal or woe, affects all.[20]

This social reformist perspective was echoed by voices beyond Canada, in multiple nations. At the first postwar meeting of the permanent committee of the Office international d'hygiene publique in June 1919, its president, Santoliquido, referred to the five years since the last session as having seemed more like five centuries. Norman Howard-Jones, an early historian of the organization, noted that Santoliquido called for "a complete change of orientation in international health affairs . . . the idea of erecting barriers against contagion was invalid, and the 'quarantine concept' was an obsolete scientific superstition."[21] As the British Ministry of Health commented in 1921 regarding influenza, "there is no question of shutting the wolf out of the sheepfold."[22]

Public health and medicine in Canada did its own soul-searching, in which a sense of failure was palpable. In his article specifically addressing the role of quarantine, Edmonton's medical officer of health, Dr. T.H. Whitelaw, spoke of "the apparent futility of practically all measures of prevention, some of which were, at the outset, acclaimed with great assurance by members of our profession."[23] Alberta's compulsory mask order, which lasted almost a month, had no apparent impact upon the increasing number of flu cases: as Whitelaw noted, "public confidence in it as a prevention soon gave place to ridicule."[24] Similarly, the citizens of Edmonton viewed quarantine and the placard with suspicion and scepticism or as "an injustice," in part because there was no laboratory diagnosis of influenza. Some suspected their neighbours of concealing cases from the authorities and "charges of discrimination were frequently made against the officials of the health department."[25] John McCullough, Chief Officer of the Ontario Provincial Board of Health, voiced similar concerns.

> The matter of placarding, and quarantining for this effection [sic] is regarded . . . as being impracticable . . . Many people with colds would be improperly quarantined, and in short the operation of the law would, as it has been in many of the States to the south of us, be a dead letter.[26]

3.4 Conclusion

Whether and in what ways the 1918–1919 influenza pandemic shaped public health and disease containment approaches is an underdeveloped theme in regional, national, and global studies of public health in the 20th century. In some ways, this is hardly surprising since the pandemic was largely absent from 20th-century histories until studies slowly began to emerge in the 1970s. The question of remembrance and forgetting is now integral to influenza history.[27] While it is difficult to imagine why a pandemic with massive mortality virtually worldwide seemed to leave so few concrete traces, we know that lost histories are possible. In part, gaps and silences are the product of historians' own preoccupations, as much as broader social and cultural amnesia. Nonetheless, the influenza pandemic should be better integrated into 20th-century public health history.

At the same time, any examination of public health's engagement with issues of trust and legitimacy today would benefit from closer attention to historical experience, especially local community responses to past disease outbreaks. In a COVID-era discussion of the influenza pandemic, Barratt and Bashford have called for a fine-grained local approach to Australia's influenza history in order to do the following:

> analyse the exercise of authority, as much as law, including the micro-authorities claimed by local residents' groups . . . authority . . . —lawful and sometimes lawless—was both devolved and assumed at a finer scale than historical scholarship has recognized.[28]

The influenza pandemic illustrates the possibility that popular resistance to public health might mean a call for more—not less—intervention. Local communities in Canada sometimes implemented their own intra-provincial and even extra-state control measures, asserting and policing spatial boundaries, in an effort to keep the pandemic out of local communities. In other contexts, the public resisted compulsory measures, such as mask wearing or quarantine. When we look beyond elite voices within public health and government, multi-valent views and actions emerge, however competing and contradictory. During and after the influenza pandemic, questions about boundaries and containment gave rise to diverse perceptions of what a functioning public health system should accomplish and how; and, they revealed those struggles over legitimacy and decision-making that characterize all major disease outbreaks historically, including COVID-19. Tracing how these views coalesced (or failed to do so) into wider shifts in policy and discourse remains an unfinished task.

Notes

1 Richard Evans, "Epidemics and Revolutions: Cholera in Nineteenth-Century Europe," in Terence Ranger and Paul Slack, eds, *Epidemics and Ideas: Essays on the Historical Perception of Pestilence* (Cambridge: Cambridge University Press, 1992) at 171.

2 See, for example, David Arnold, "Cholera and Colonialism in British India," (1986) 113 Past and Present or Deborah Neill, *Networks in Tropical Medicine: Internationalism, Colonialism, and the Rise of a Medical Specialty, 1890–1930* (Stanford, CA: Stanford University Press, 2012).

3 Amy Fairchild, *Science at the Borders: Immigrant Medical Inspection and the Shaping of the Modern Industrial Labor Force* (Baltimore: Johns Hopkins University Press, 2003). See also Natalia Molina, *Fit to Be Citizens? Public Health and Race in Los Angeles, 1879–1939* (Berkeley: University of California Press, 2006); Nayan Shah, *Contagious Divides: Epidemics and Race in San Francisco's Chinatown* (Berkeley: University of California Press, 2001); Renisa Mawani, "Island of the Unclean: Race, Colonialism, and 'Chinese Leprosy' in British Columbia, 1891–1924," (2003) 1:1 *Journal of Law, Social Justice, and Global Development.*

4 Isabelle Wallace, "Komagata Maru Revisited: Hindus, Hookworm, and the Guise of Public Health Protection," (2013) *BC Studies* 178.

5 Alison Bashford, *Imperial Hygiene: A Critical History of Colonialism, Nationalism and Public Health* (Basingstoke: Palgrave Macmillan, 2004) at 1.
6 See for example Warwick Anderson, *Colonial Pathologies: American Tropical Medicine, Race and Hygiene in the Philippines* (Durham, NC: Duke University Press, 2006); David Arnold, *Colonizing the Body: State Medicine and Epidemic Disease in 19th Century India* (Oakland: University of California Press, 1993); Neill, supra note 2; Randall Packard, *A History of Global Health: Interventions into the Lives of Other Peoples* (Baltimore: Johns Hopkins University Press, 2016).
7 Katherine Arnup, "'Victims of Vaccination?': Opposition to Compulsory Immunization in Ontario, 1900–1990," (1992) 9 *Canadian Bulletin of Medical History*; Paul Adolphus Bator, "The Health Reformers Versus the Common Canadian: The Controversy over Compulsory Vaccination against Smallpox in Toronto and Ontario, 1900–1920," (1983) 75:4 *Ontario History*; Nadja Durbach, "Class, Gender, and the Conscientious Objector to Vaccination," (2002) 41 *Journal of British Studies*; and Nadja Durbach,"'They Might As Well Brand Us': Working-Class Resistance to Compulsory Vaccination in Victorian England," (2000) 13:1 *Social History of Medicine*.
8 Mark Humphries, "The Horror at Home: The Canadian Military and the 'Great' Influenza Pandemic of 1918," (2005) 16:1 *Journal of the Canadian Historical Association* 235.
9 For the US, see Carol R. Byerly, *Fever of War: the Influenza Epidemic in the U.S. Army During World War I* (New York, NY: New York University Press, 2005).
10 Esyllt W. Jones, "'Co-Operation in All Human Endeavour': Quarantine and Immigrant Disease Vectors in the 1918–1919 Influenza Pandemic in Winnipeg," (2005) 22:1 *Canadian Bulletin of Medical History* at 71. See also: Esyllt W. Jones, *Influenza 1918: Disease, Death and Struggle in Winnipeg* (Toronto: University of Toronto Press, 2007).
11 Winnipeg Tribune(29 October 1918) at 1.
12 Manitoba Free Press (19 October 1918) at 5.
13 Jones, *supra* note 10 at 72.
14 City of Winnipeg Archives, Annual Report of the City Health Department for the Year Ending December 31 (1918), at. 111, 99.
15 Mark Osborne Humphries, *The Last Plague: Spanish Influenza and the Politics of Public Health in Canada* (Toronto: University of Toronto Press, 2013) at 118.
16 Margaret W. Andrews, "Epidemic and Public Health: Influenza in Vancouver, 1918–1919," (1977) 34 *BC Studies* at 30–33.
17 Maureen Lux, "'The Bitter Flats': The 1918 Influenza Epidemic in Saskatchewan," (1977) 49:1 *Saskatchewan History* at 9.
18 Humphries, *supra* note 15 at 113.
19 *Ibid* at 175.
20 Quoted in Mark Osborne Humphries, *ibid* at 117.
21 Norman Howard-Jones, *The Scientific Background of the International Sanitary Conferences, 1851–1938* (Geneva: World Health Organization, 1975) at 93.
22 Quoted in J. Andrew Mendelsohn, "From Eradication to Equilibrium: How Epidemics Became Complex After World War I," in Christopher Lawrence and George Weisz, eds, *Greater Than the Parts: Holism in Biomedicine, 1920–1950* (Oxford: Oxford University Press, 1998) at 310.
23 T. H. Whitelaw, "The Practical Aspects of Quarantine for Influenza," (1919) 9 *Canadian Medical Association Journal* at 1070.
24 *Ibid* at 1071.
25 *Ibid.*
26 John W.S. McCullough, "The Control of Influenza in Ontario," (1919) 9 *Canadian Medical Association Journal* 1084.

27 Guy Beiner, ed., *Pandemic Re-Awakenings: The Forgotten and Unforgotten 'Spanish' Flu of 1918–1919* (Oxford: Oxford University Press, 2022); Esyllt W. Jones, "Open Secrets: Silence, Suppression and Memory in the History of Canada's 1918–1920 Influenza Pandemic," (2022) 39:1 *Canadian Journal of Health History* 99.

28 Tiarne Barratt and Alison Bashford, "Lines of Hygiene: Pandemic Border Control in Australia, 1919," (2022) 53:2 *Australian Historical Studies* 284.

4

BORDERING AND THE FALLACY OF DISEASE DIRECTIONALITY

Ebola, SARS-CoV-2 and Africa's Confidence Deficit with Global Public Health

Chidi Oguamanam

4.1 Introduction

Global public health (GPH) evolved along colonial trajectories. And it continues to perpetuate a universe of yet-to-be-weaned colonial biases. Those range from various forms of discriminations thematized along racialization of diseases and poverty, isolation and othering of non-Western peoples,[1] most notably Africans. These trends manifest through kneejerk border measures and skewed migration policies, bifurcation of the targets of protection against the burdens of infectious disease down the hardlines of power and privilege that expose Africa's vulnerability on each turn. Mindful of its fraught nature, the management of Ebola and COVID-19 pandemic has refocused attention on the historic fault lines of GPH. The Ebola and COVID-19 experiences magnified the primacy of infectious diseases control unevenly in GPH pendulum against other considerations such as equitable public health services delivery and capacitation. The latter is outside the focus of this chapter.

Ebola and COVID-19 experiences demonstrate that bordering, control or regulation of movements in their various details are cardinal tools of GPH for disease control. The two pandemic events have also shown that GPH, especially in a time of crisis, is a theatre for regulatory free-for-all that victimizes the most vulnerable. This is evident in the discriminatory and reactionary response to border control, based on often patentably false or contested ideas about disease directionality that isolates Africa more than any other region. Disease directionality, in this context, refers to the false assumption that infectious diseases travel unidirectionally mainly from non-Western countries and old colonial outposts to the West, for which the latter is justified to isolate the former. This tendency poses a conflict between powerful

DOI: 10.4324/9781003394006-6

states bent on fencing off the subaltern othered in cases of infectious disease emergencies and global health authorities' inclination for objective and scientific approach to disease control. It also casts serious doubt over the supposed panoptical reach of GPH.

This chapter sketches the continuing historic fault lines of GPH at the intersection of skewed use of migration policy as a strategy of disease control for the protection of imperial and colonial interests. It maps the transition from the Eurocentric or colonial phase of GPH to the modern era, which is marked by the entry of the WHO. It highlights principles-based constitutional approach of GPH through the WHO constitution and IHR. Focusing on Africa's experience with Ebola and COVID-19, it examines how the handling of these two experiences resulted in no improvement from the colonial legacies of GPH. Rather, despite the new principles-based constitutional approach, Africa's isolation in the extant GPH order lays bare the unequivocal vulnerability of the continent. The chapter concludes on the need to give effect to the principles-based constitutional framework of both the WHO constitution and IHRs for a truly inclusive GPH that moderates the role of politics and truly leverages science and the imperative for international solidarity.[2]

4.2 Global Public Health, Migration and Disease Control: A Historical Sketch

Arguably dating back to 16th and 17th centuries of European imperialist expeditions that resulted in founding of colonial outposts in the 18th and 19th centuries, GPH is rooted in migration.[3] Europe, literally, is the major catalyst for the escalation of diseases across borders. Even regarding Eurasia—a combination of Europe and Asia—that sits on same tectonic plate with no seas demarcating them,[4] Africa is an uneven recipient of global disease transfers. Africa's complicity in the origin of diseases is mainly a factor of its tropical credential as well as its status as part of the Old World. Both features are implicated in the Eurasia region. While pathogen exchange between Old and New Worlds is uneven,[5] Africa is only a fraction of the Old World. The continent was and remains a victim of European adventurism that resulted in the global spread of diseases. European encounter with the New World and with colonial Africa, as part of the Old World, was pivotal in the escalation of global infections disease transfers.[6] Yet in the GPH dynamic, Africa remains isolated as a continent of affliction and the major source of contagion from which the whole world needs to be saved. The European imperialist encounter with Indigenous inhabitants of remote colonial outposts, including those in Africa, Asia, the Middle East and elsewhere, resulted in radical disruption of populations and demographics not only of Indigenous peoples[7] but also of the ecological order. Colonial settlers were infected by new diseases from their subjects and from the new environment. Perhaps on a disproportionate scale, they also exposed the native inhabitants of their new destinations to strange afflictions. In some instances, European encounter led to the decimation of entire native tribes.[8] For their part, European colonizers and, by extension, Europe, also bore the brunt of infectious tropical diseases such as malaria. This experience is best captured in the metaphoric designation of the Western African region, for example, as the "Whiteman's grave"[9] due to malaria.

The colonial experience with infectious diseases encountered in the so-called harsh tropical regions of the colonial outposts provided impetus for the rise of tropical medicine and the development of germ theory for the understanding and prevention of diseases.[10] It also spurred attention to specific diseases and epidemics, notably cholera, and a population approach to epidemiology and public health. These strategies prepared Europe for better engagement and mitigation of human casualty in its colonial quests.[11] They were also to safeguard European personnel and agents operating through institutional tools of conquest such as its military[12] and bureaucratic accoutrement entrenched in strange lands in pursuit of trade, proselytizing and other spheres of influence. The resulting colonial medical services and research were designed as segregationist policies that essentially catered to the health of European settlers to shield it from disease-prone others with a baseless notion of disease directionality. According to Palilonis, "[t]his was at a time of great violence towards native populations and colonial medical officials implemented sometimes draconian public health measures, such as forced quarantines, as a means to 'civilize' native populations".[13]

Before WWI, the international health framework was deeply entrenched in its colonial emphasis on the control of infectious disease. The post-WWII order, under the auspices of the United Nations (UN), was saddled with consolidating and centralizing the disparate colonial trajectories driven mainly via international sanitary conferencing models in the evolution of GPH. This new development positioned the emergent global health regime for a more plural outlook coinciding with the equally emergent new independent and 'postcolonial' states. This was the circumstance under which the WHO was formed in 1948.

4.3 WHO, IHR and Principles-Based Constitutional Approach to Global Public Health

At the core of WHO is a principles-based constitutional approach frontally enunciated in its constitution. Those principles are linked to the organization's primary objectives of attainment "by all peoples", not colonial powers only, "of the highest possible level of health".[14] Pursuant to principles-based orientation, the WHO objective is linked to "fundamental rights of every human being without distinctions of race, religion, political beliefs, economic or social conditions".[15] The WHO constitutional framework supports equity in health promotion and in infectious disease control among nations.[16] It links public health to the attainment of peace and security by all,[17] not only powerful states. The WHO constitutional principles approach identifies the imperative of harmonious living amidst environmental changes[18] as integral to public health. It also identifies access to medical, relevant psychological knowledge alongside informed opinion and active cooperation of the public within a range of unspecified social measures relevant to the improvement of public health.[19]

A complement of the WHO's principles-based constitutional approach is the 2005 International Health Regulations (IHR).[20] The WHO constitution vests the World Health Assembly (WHA) with the power to make regulations to prevent international spread of disease through the 2005 IHR.[21] The IHR provide elaborate protocols for preventative, containment and other measures of public health response to international spread of disease. It mandates WHO Member States, pursuant to detailed yardsticks, to notify WHO of events in their jurisdictions that may constitute a public health emergency of international concern (PHEIC).[22] It, in turn, empowers the Director-General of WHO—pursuant to detailed criteria, including expert committee processes, consultations and engagements with concerned Member States—to make declaration of specific PHEIC with consequential recommendations. Article 3 of the IHR, titled 'Principles', outlines three principles for its implementation: a) "full respect for the human dignity, human rights and fundamental freedoms of persons",[23] b) "the Charter of the United Nations and the Constitution of the World Health Organization"[24] and c) "international law and sovereign rights [of states] to legislate and implement legislation in pursuance of their health policy" while upholding the IHR.[25] Those were supposed to contrast with prior global health order of unfettered European discretion and arbitrariness. The question is whether WHO-IHR approach has influenced a culture shift in infectious disease control, away from the unscientific and colonially-biased sense of disease directionality. That question is perhaps best addressed in reference to how the WHO has implemented the IHR since 2007 regarding two recent pandemics, Ebola and COVID-19, in the context of Africa's experience of isolations, vulnerability and discrimination.

4.3.1 Africa and the Ebola Outbreak

Ebola haemorrhagic fever, or the Ebola virus disease (EDV), is a fatal viral affliction. It is extremely transmissible through secretions of fluids from a range of mammals, notably porcupines, fruits bats[26] and other primates to humans. It was first discovered in 1976, before the IHR, in the rural tropical rainforests of Central and West African countries (Guinea, Congo, Sierra

Leonne, Liberia, etc.). Since its discovery, there have been sporadic episodes of Ebola spreading to other West African countries and parts of East Africa.[27] Despite its high mortality rate (estimated at 66%) the disease did not attract serious and concerted international emergency response for mitigation and containment pursuant to PHEIC and other interventions.

The period 2014–2016 was the peak of Ebola outbreak to date. At that time, IHR was seven years in operation. While Ebola was spreading across mainly security-challenged, impoverished and least-developed African countries, with little economic significance to Western capitals, it was not considered a PHEIC. WHO's belated attempt to deploy the IHR and to implement PHEIC over Ebola happened in a dramatic circumstance. In July 2014, a high-profile, Ebola-positive patient flew from Liberia to Nigeria. The patient landed in Lagos, the commercial capital of Nigeria, the continent's largest economy by GDP.

The presence of Ebola in one of Africa's international air travel hubs attracted the attention of Western media which highlighted the imminent danger of the disease to the Western world. Before then, the spread of Ebola across African countries was of no consequence. Had the Liberian poster case of Ebola spread traveled low profile across African land borders into Nigeria, as did cases of Ebola's spread across Guinea, Congo,[28] Liberia, Sierra Leonne, Senegal, etc., conceivably, the Western media would likely not have given significant attention to Ebola let alone created awareness towards making it PHEIC, which the WHO did less than one month after the Nigeria index case.[29]

Ebola has been an off-and-on epidemic. Despite its spread to some Western countries, including the United States, the virus remains largely within Central and West African countries. In March 2016, the WHO lifted Ebola's PHEIC status in West Africa, but Congo recorded major outbreak in August 2018. Similarly, the WHO was tardy in declaring Ebola a PHEIC in the subsequent outbreak in DRC: another year passed before the WHO declared an Ebola PHEIC in DRC, on 17 July 2019.

Like the Nigerian experience, the WHO's decision was linked to the presence of Ebola in an economically significant location—Goma, a city of 2 million people in Eastern DRC serviced by an international airport bordering Rwanda. Since its emergence from the genocide, Rwanda has transitioned to a significant African country with impressive development credentials, strong Western patronage and growing tourist and business significance. Meanwhile, DRC remains the source of the spread of Ebola into Uganda. With paucity of local spread of Ebola within Uganda,[30] the WHO could not declare Ebola PHEIC in that country.

The WHO's laxity in the management of Ebola and dubious application of IHR was subtly attested to through the United Nations' direct intervention. While diplomatically acknowledging the role of WHO, the UN General

Assembly passed Res 69/1 on 19 September 2014, setting up the UN Mission for Ebola Emergency Response (UNMEER).[31] UNMEER went on record as the "first-ever UN emergency health mission".[32] It was also backed by an earlier United Nations Security Council Resolution[33] which addressed "the unprecedented extent of the Ebola outbreak in Africa" as constituting "a threat to international peace and security".[34] Both the GA and UNSC resolutions on Ebola characterized it as a matter of grave and deep concern that was getting out of hand beyond Africa and was fast constituting a ravaging threat to the West. Beyond direct UN involvement, Ebola was fought through grave sacrifices of global public health humanitarian interventions of non-state actors.[35] Ironically, associated humanitarian health workers suffered some backlash of social discrimination because of their exposure to Ebola and association with Ebola hotspots. Returning to their bases in the West, they were targets of random border or isolation measures.[36]

4.3.2 Africa and COVID-19 Omicron Variant

SARS CoV-2 is the latest in the family of coronaviruses. Unlike Ebola, on 30 January 2020, it was declared a PHEIC by the WHO a month after outbreak in China.[37] Before and following the declaration, many countries did not await recommendations and protocols from the WHO before embarking on ad hoc measures focusing on travel restrictions, quarantine protocols and, later, vaccine passports across states and sub-national units.[38]

The politicization of travel restrictions and the attitude of developed countries regarding WHO's leadership and recommendations pursuant to PHEIC pitted countries of the Global North against themselves. Even EU members and the US could not maintain a harmonized implementation of travel restrictions in the early stages. COVID-19 rattled Western countries out of their peerage and solidarities of power and privilege. Most resorted to defining thresholds of statistical prevalence of cases in individual countries as triggers to impose travel restrictions.

Africa's experience of travel restrictions with COVID-19 in general, especially the Omicron variant, clearly reflected a pattern of continuing racialization of disease along biased colonial patterns of 'othering' Africa in skewed assumption of disease directionality.[39] The experience is not saved by WHO's recommendation for limited travel restrictions as opposed to a carpet ban on international travels.[40] Neither was it mitigated by WHO's insistence on scientific principles as the basis for implementation of measures including travel restrictions. Despite Africa being spared a major outbreak of COVID-19 cases, the continent was lumped together with other high prevalence regions as targets of travel bans by Western countries. COVID-19 provided a pretence for implementing stricter and discriminatory immigrations policies against Africa. Traditionally, the continent is a major source of migrants to the West in a manner that is grossly lopsided in relation to Western migration to Africa.[41] That reality makes Africa worse off as the most bordered and most othered or restricted in the chase game of infectious disease control in a GPH that is dubiously global and patently selective.

In relation to African or non-European countries, there is little regard for implementing IHRs in manners consistent with the WHO-IHR principles-based approach. Rather, there were clear camaraderie of privilege, power and economic considerations resulting in discretionary softening or outright exemption from restrictions among Western countries. For example, against overwhelming statistical evidence, the US exempted the UK from its European travel ban.[42] African countries suffered travel bans when the region had comparatively low prevalence of COVID-19 cases. These practices of discriminatory application of international travel restrictions by developed countries has dehumanizing and unjustifiable impacts on African and other non-Western countries. Emphasis on arbitrary and external travel restrictions and punitive border measures targeting Africa and travelers from the Global South resulted in lack of adequate attention towards curbing domestic spread of COVID-19 among populations within developed countries, notably US, Canada and Europe.[43]

Unlike Ebola, COVID-19 is characterized by its global spread and rapid mutations into variants and subvariants. Among the prominent variants and associated countries/region of initial identification are Alpha (United Kingdom), Beta, Omicron (South Africa), Delta (India) and Gamma (Brazil). Because of the characteristics of these variants, declaration of PHEIC involves sustained surveillance and exchange of information to pre-empt the capacity of these variants to undermine existing public health measures, including ongoing research into their effects or lack thereof on existing vaccines.

Despite Africa's low rates of COVID-19 infection, developed countries' attitude to the continent, as evident in the travel bans and other public health measures, are reminiscent of pre-WHO colonial attitude and dubious assumptions about disease directionality. The inclusion of South Africa and other African countries in travel bans by Europe, United Kingdom, United States, Canada, Australia, Japan, Israel, etc., in the wake of the Omicron variant of COVID-19 affirms that claim. To the credit of South African scientists and of that country's surveillance capacity, South Africa was the first country to report the discovery of Omicron variant even when there was evidence of the variant's probable presence earlier in the Global North.[44] At the time of the kneejerk reaction through which the whole world slammed its doors on African countries, starting with Southern Africa, the Omicron variant was only confirmed in Botswana and South Africa. Other countries where the variants were detected, such as UK, Canada, Germany, the Netherlands, etc., did not face these swift travel bans.

The decision to arbitrarily impose travel bans on African countries owing to South Africa's role in the discovery of the Omicron variant of COVID-19 was not consistent with WHO-IHR principles-based constitutional approach. The WHO insists that such bans must be premised on a risk-based and scientific approach.[45] Amidst the outrage, the WHO noted that "with the Omicron variant now detected in several regions of the world, putting in place travel bans that target Africa attacks global solidarity".[46] The Omicron Africa travel bans were later lifted in the light of their outright hypocrisy. However, the symbolism of the ban is indicative of the fragility of the WHO, the IHRs and their subservience to the old order. It is also indicative of historical and unsubstantiated tarring of Africa as the default source of the afflictions that threaten global health.

4.4 Conclusions

Africa's experiences with Ebola and the COVID-19 Omicron variant offer some lessons for GPH. The mismanagement of Ebola from the GPH perspective could partly be blamed on domestic capacity deficit of Central and Western African countries. Most of them had no focal point, not to mention critical public health crisis management infrastructure. Also, the 2014–2016 Ebola outbreak happened within the fledgling phase of the IHR, warranting WHO to commission a critical introspective and retrospective review of its Ebola experience.[47] In the case of Omicron, as a counterintuitive matter, an Africa country stepped up with capacity and competence, while Western countries, where the variant could possibly have been spotted earlier, dropped the ball. Yet despite a decade and half of implementation of IHR, South Africa and the rest of African countries were carpeted with international travel bans and restrictions without regard to principles-based constitutional approach and WHO's insistence on scientific parameters.

Despite the emergency and expedient nature of GPH, even within the WHO constitutional system, preference is given of sovereign rights of nations regarding the making of public health decisions.[48] Unfortunately, the Zero Draft of the WHO Convention, Agreement or other International Instrument on Pandemic Prevention, Preparedness and Response (WHO CA+)[49] starts off with a reinforcement of the sovereignty principles. Paragraph 1 of the preamble to the Zero Draft reaffirms, "the principle of sovereignty of States Parties in addressing public health matters, notably pandemic prevention, preparedness, response and health systems recovery".[50] Like the IHRs, the anticipated WHO C+ will be consequently susceptible to political considerations incidental to the exercise of sovereign rights. This approach threatens to make politics rather than science and international solidarity[51] to trump such decisions. And so long as there is no sanction or accountability required of countries who deviate from scientific parameters of GPH response in times of crisis, the world will be plunged into a counterproductive regulatory free-for-all, with the most vulnerable regions such as Africa as major victims. The lesson of these recent global health emergencies of both epidemic and pandemic proportions is that prioritizing science and international solidarity are important to moderate politically driven relapse to sovereignty and nationalism that leaves a suboptimal and inequitable outcome in global health crisis management.

The fallacy of disease directionality has historically burdened African countries from colonial times. With anticipated pandemic incidences linked to intensification of climate change-induced zoonoses,[52] that fallacy will be more pronounced. In this renewed crisis lies a new opportunity for creating a 21st-century GPH architecture based on science, international solidarity as opposed to national indiscretion, which is the bases for nonapplication and abuse, at worst, or selective application, at best, of principles-based constitutionalism. For Africa, the experience with Ebola and COVID-19 reinforces the urgency of premising a reimagined GPH on inclusive and non-discriminatory protection of everyone, above systemic biases. Such systemic biases and fallacy of disease directionality have continued to burden Africa, Africans and many marginal communities negatively portrayed as sources and reservoirs of diseases that afflict all humankind.[53] In the era of an unregulated social media, this systemic misinformation is now ubiquitous across multiple planforms and unregulated fields. In many cases, they are stuff of grotesque imageries requiring a deliberate consciousness over the ethics of speaking disease and of naming disease. It is along these sentiments that the WHO announced the renaming of monkeypox to mpox in exercise of its power of international disease classification. The change in name is aimed to address "racist and stigmatizing language online, in other settings and in some communities" associated with the name 'monkeypox'.[54] Through continuing reforms, the WHA can recalibrate the IHR with some biting teeth. It can also rejig GPH on the path of inclusivity as opposed to entrenchment of its colonial origins that confines Africa and non-Western peoples as the diseased other. There is a breath of fresh air in the Zero Draft's elaboration of One Health[55]—a signification of the prominence of zoonotic and vector-borne pathogens, interconnectedness of humans, animals and other life forces and ecological order with ramification of shared health and vulnerabilities.[56] Logically, that same principle implicates One Health in which diseases respect no boundaries across geographical and geopolitical regions and in which no one region should be continuously treated disdainfully as being the source of diseases that threaten the whole world.

Notes

1 Matiangai Sirleaf, "Entry Denied: COVID-19, Race, Migration and Global Health" (2020) 2:599157 *Frontiers in Human Dynamics*.
2 See Allyn Taylor et al, "Solidarity in the Wake of COVID-19: Reimagining the International Health Regulations" (2021) 396:10244 *The Lancet* 82.
3 M. A. Polilonis, "An Introduction to Global Health and Global Health Ethics: A Brief History" (2015) at 2, online (pdf): https://bit.ly/3CWz7Xi.

4 For example, diseases like smallpox, influenzas and measles are associated with Eurasia farming culture. In addition, despite contested histories, diseases such as bubonic plague, dysentery, smallpox, chickenpox, cholera, mumps, diphtheria, typhus, etc., were little known in Africa and the New World before European contact. Even in situations where a disease, such as leprosy, was endemic to a region of Africa, the arrival of Europeans was instrumental in some cases to its spread in other parts of Africa and the world.
5 See Nathan D. Wolfe, Claire Panosian Dunavan & Jared Diamond, "Origins of Major Human Infectious Diseases" in *Improving Food Security Through a One Health Approach* (Washington: Institute of Medicine, National Academy Press, 2012) A16.
6 *Ibid.*
7 Sirleaf, *supra* note 1.
8 Polilonis, *supra* note 3 at 2.
9 P. D. Curtin, "The Whitman's Grave: Image and Reality 1780–1850" (1961) 1:1 *Journal of British studies* 94.
10 Polilonis, *supra* note 3 at 2.
11 *Ibid.*
12 *Ibid* at 3.
13 *Ibid* at 3.
14 See WHO Constitution, art. 1, July 22, 1946, 14 UNTS 185 (entered into force April 7, 1958).
15 *Ibid*, para 2 of the preamble.
16 *Ibid*, para 5.
17 *Ibid*, para 3.
18 *Ibid*, para 6.
19 *Ibid*, paras 7–9.
20 WHO, International Health Regulations 2005 (3rd ed., 2016) [IHR].
21 *Ibid*, in effect 2007.
22 *Ibid*, art 1.
23 *Ibid*, art 3(1).
24 *Ibid*, art 3(2).
25 *Ibid*, art 3(3).
26 Fruit bats of the Pteropodidae family are associated as the natural host of the Ebola virus.
27 At the time of writing (September–October 2022), a new Ebola outbreak is reported in Uganda and elsewhere.
28 Also, the Democratic Republic of the Congo (DRC).
29 WHO declared Ebola in the West African region a PHEIC on August 8, 2014.
30 During the 2018–2019 period.
31 "UN Mission for Ebola Emergency Response (UNMEER)", online: *Global Ebola Response*. https://ebolaresponse.un.org/un-mission-ebola-emergency-response-unmeer.
32 *Ibid.*
33 Resolution 2177/2014 (adopted 18 September 2014).
34 *Ibid.*
35 Linda M. Mobola et al, "A Humanitarian Response to the West African Ebola Virus Disease Outbreak" (2018) 3:10 *Journal of International Humanitarian Action*.
36 Michelle Nicholas, "Ebola Health Worker Restriction Could Deter Others" (29 October 2014), online: *Reuters*. https://reut.rs/3g8WCU4.
37 Declared a pandemic 11 March 2020.
38 Our World in Data maintains real live and historic statistics of the trend, see online: https://bit.ly/3g2Elb9.

39 Sirleaf, *supra* note 1.
40 For the chronology and evolution of WHO COVID-19 travel advisories, see WHO, "Coronavirus Disease (COVID-19) Travel Advice", online: www.who.int/emergencies/diseases/novel-coronavirus-2019/travel-advice.
41 However, African nations are on record to have imposed travel restrictions against the US, Europe and China in 2020. See: Joe Penney, "African Nations Turn the Tables, Imposing Travel Restrictions against U.S., Europe, and China to Stave Off Coronavirus" (15 March 2020), online: *The Intercept*. https://bit.ly/3CeHwnL.
42 Donald Trump's exclusion of the UK from his coronavirus travel ban was a brazen demonstration of political—as opposed to scientific—influence on travel bans. See Patrick Wintour, "Why did Donald Trump Exclude UK from his Corona Virus Travel Ban?" (12 March 2020), online: *The Guardian*. https://bit.ly/3CBDwyI.
43 At its early stage, researchers found that imported cases of COVID-19 did account for an insignificant percentage of domestic spread. See Timothy W. Russell et al, "Effect of Internationally Imported Cases on Internal Spread of COVID-19: A Mathematical Modelling Study" (7 December 2020), *The Lancet*.
44 In its December 3, 2021, brief, the Advisory Board offered three plausible explanations on the origin of Omicron. See Advisory Board, online: https://bit.ly/3M7qg8c.
45 WHO, "Advice for International Traffic in Relation to Omicron Variant", online: https://bit.ly/3MtuAPq.
46 "South Africa Presidents Calls for Lifting Omicron Travel Bans" (29 November 2021), online: *BBC News*. https://bbc.in/3S6Zdvq.
47 WHO, "Report of Ebola Interim Assessment Panel", online (pdf): https://bit.ly/3VpCqxr.
48 See also IHR, *supra* note 20, art 3(4).
49 See WHO, *Zero draft of the WHO CA+ for the consideration of the Intergovernmental Negotiating Body at its fourth meeting*, A/INB/4/3, February 2023. In December 2021, the WHA established the International Negotiating Body for WHO CA+.
50 *Ibid*. See also IHR, *supra* note 20, art 3(4).
51 See Taylor et al, *supra* note 2.
52 See Collin J. Carlson et al, "Climate Change Increases Cross-Species Viral Transmission Risk (2022) 607 *Nature* 555.
53 See "African Journalists Decry Racist Monkeypox Reporting" (22 May 2022), online: *TRT World*. https://bit.ly/3FdDGOh.
54 See "WHO Recommends New Name for Monkeypox Disease" (28 November 2022), online: *WHO*. https://bit.ly/3gMCFDq.
55 Zero Draft of WHO CA+, *supra* note 49, art 18.
56 See Wolfe, Dunavan & Diamond, *supra* note 5, associating "One Health" to food security and the agriculture value chain.

5

TOWARDS REIMAGINING THE IHR ARTICLE 43 ON TRAVEL RESTRICTIONS[1]

Lisa Forman and Roojin Habibi

5.1 Introduction

In international law as in many other disciplines, the role of borders as public health tools has been strongly contested. The International Health Regulations (IHR)—the world's primary international law instrument to address public health emergencies of international concern (PHEIC)—were adopted precisely to ensure that States respond to infectious diseases threats in ways commensurate with public health risks and which avoided unnecessary interferences with international traffic.[2] As regulations adopted pursuant to Article 21(a) of the Constitution of the World Health Organization (WHO), they bind all 194 WHO Member States.

The control of disease and the limitation of needless restrictions of international traffic are mutually dependent, as excessive restrictions of international traffic threaten to 'disincentivize countries from reporting new risks to international public health authorities.'[3] The IHR outline legal requirements for adopting travel restrictions in Article 43, a provision which requires that health measures adopted by States in response to public health risks or PHEICs 'not be more restrictive of international traffic and not more invasive or intrusive to persons than reasonably available alternatives that would achieve the appropriate level of health protection.'[4] In addition, States must base their policy choices on scientific principles, available scientific evidence of health risks, and advice from the WHO.[5] States implementing such measures must provide the WHO with the public health rationale and scientific information that such decisions are based on.[6] Where such measures significantly interfere with international traffic,[7] States must inform the WHO within 48 hours of implementation

DOI: 10.4324/9781003394006-7

unless these measures are covered by a temporary or standing WHO recommendation.[8]

COVID related travel restrictions have interfered with international traffic in extraordinary ways, and the question of whether these restrictions have been commensurate with risk and strictly necessary continues to divide legal and public health scholars. When news of the spread of a novel coronavirus emerged in late 2019, the WHO discouraged international travel and trade restrictions, even as the WHO Director-General determined that the outbreak constituted a PHEIC. The WHO Director-General instead called for the global community 'to demonstrate solidarity and cooperation, in compliance with Article 44 of the IHR (2005).'[9]

However we may understand the legitimacy of these restrictions within the International Health Regulations and international law more broadly, the most challenging part of COVID-related restrictions is what appears to be an almost total failure of States to consider IHR Article 43's requirements to base decisions on scientific principles, available scientific evidence of health risks, and advice from the WHO,[10] and to notify the WHO if they took measures beyond those recommended by a temporary or standing WHO recommendation.[11] Indeed, these restrictions have persisted in spite of the fact that WHO discouraged international travel and trade restrictions from the start of the pandemic and in spite of the extraordinary social, economic, and human rights impacts of these restrictions.

The worst instance of these restrictions came when travel bans were imposed on South Africa after it complied in good faith with duties to notify Omicron, followed by bans on African States where Omicron had not been detected but not on European countries where Omicron was already present. These measures were not just grossly discriminatory but deeply threatening to continued compliance with the IHR's aims of assuring prompt notification of future disease outbreaks or COVID-19 variants. Such discriminatory, ongoing, and disproportionate restrictions are totally at odds with the objectives of the IHR and undermine the legitimacy not simply of Article 43 but of the IHR more broadly. They underscore the need for reforms to make this instrument 'fit for purpose',[12] whether through amendments to the IHR, monitoring mechanisms within other governance bodies of the WHO,[13] or the forthcoming pandemic treaty that will supplement and perhaps supplant the IHR in key dimensions of pandemic prevention, preparedness, and response.

In this chapter, we consider whether, and in what circumstances, travel restrictions are legally permissible under IHR Article 43. We survey scholarly debates over the legality of travel restrictions under Article 43, emerging evidence of the efficacy of travel restrictions during COVID-19, and evolving WHO recommendations and guidance and what these suggest about the necessity and proportionality of travel restrictions. We conclude by noting that these considerations should inform the kinds of reforms necessary to bolster the utility of this provision in future infectious disease outbreaks.

5.1.1 Contextualizing the Debates in Relation to IHR Article 43

To understand Article 43, it needs to be located in the context of the IHR more broadly, particularly the central twofold purpose of the regulations to prevent, protect against, control, and provide a public health response to the international spread of disease commensurate with and restricted to public health risks and to do so in ways which avoid unnecessary interference with international traffic and trade.[14] We argue that this latter focus on necessity is the crux of both the IHR and Article 43. When the IHR were last revised in 2005, it was precisely to prevent States from implementing overly harsh and costly travel restrictions in response to disease threats that disincentivized transparent notification.[15] Article 2 also emphasizes that interferences with international traffic should not be unnecessary if they are to comply with the general objective of the regulations. Necessity is thus central to whether additional cross-border health measures, such as travel restrictions, can be passed under this instrument, and limiting interferences with international traffic is a core plank of the IHR.

Article 43 itself outlines the criteria and process for determining what a necessary interference with international traffic might entail. The article allows States to implement health measures beyond WHO recommendations so long as (1) the measures accord with relevant national law and international law obligations; (2) are not more restrictive of international traffic or "invasive to people than reasonably available alternatives that would achieve the appropriate level of health protection";[16] and (3) are based on assessments of (a) scientific principles, (b) available scientific evidence of a risk to human health, or where such evidence is insufficient, available information from WHO or other relevant intergovernmental organizations, and (c) any available specific guidance or advice from WHO.[17] States that implement measures not covered by WHO recommendations must inform WHO within 48 hours of the measures implemented and their public health rationale. They must within three months review such measures, taking into account WHO advice and available science.

Even a cursory read shows how challenging it is to interpret key elements of this provision: What are reasonably available alternatives? What is the appropriate level of health protection? How do we define scientific principles or scientific evidence? Moreover, when evidence of risk is lacking as it may be with a novel pathogen, what should risk assessments be based on given that there is no recourse under Article 43 to a precautionary approach?

5.1.2 Debates Over the Legal Interpretation of Travel Restrictions under IHR Article 43

These questions have fueled legal debate over the appropriate interpretation of Article 43. Prior to COVID-19, general legal opinion was that immediate resort to travel restrictions to control the international spread of disease was unlawful under the IHR given the inconclusive nature of scientific evidence on the public health benefits of travel restrictions and the historically chilling impact of travel restrictions on good faith reporting of subsequent disease outbreaks of international concern.[18]

In early 2020, we joined more than a dozen other global health law scholars to argue that many COVID-related travel restrictions violated international law because they lacked the support of scientific evidence or WHO advice as required by the IHR. We argued that travel restrictions flouted widely accepted international human rights norms and principles, including the *Siracusa Principles on the Limitation and Derogations Provisions in the International Covenant on Civil and Political Rights* (Siracusa Principles) which require that restrictions of human rights be strictly limited to measures that are necessary (as determined by their legitimacy, non-arbitrary and non-discriminatory nature), legal, and proportional.[19] We argued that in this context, travel restrictions should be weighed against less restrictive alternatives with high public health efficacy, including social distancing and robust contact-tracing measures.[20] This proved to be a highly contentious and contested proposition.

In the early days of the pandemic, Foster argued that Article 43 afforded States a margin of appreciation in taking actions (including travel restrictions) beyond those recommended by WHO, consistent with their sovereign rights articulated elsewhere in the IHR.[21] Villareal argued that Article 43's obligations were '"contingent" in nature . . . [and] highly dependent on the circumstances' given the abstract formulation of the provision.[22] Tigerstrom and Wilson argued that the unprecedented situation of COVID-19 meant that 'we should not assume that all travel restrictions violated international law,' and that 'some travel restrictions were more likely to be justified than others . . . depending on . . . how they [were] designed and local capacity to implement less restrictive measures.'[23] Tigerstrom, Halabi, and Wilson argued that under the IHR, the WHO has a key role in identifying justifiable travel restrictions and that it should be combining its 'formal recommendations, informal guidance and the text of the IHR [to] provide guidance to Member States on how to continue or modify travel restrictions in compliance with their international obligations.'[24] These legal debates are far from resolved.

How then should Article 43 be interpreted from an international law perspective? The *Vienna Convention on the Law of Treaties* guides treaty interpretation, indicating that the ordinary meaning of treaty terms should be interpreted in their textual context and in light of a treaty's object and purpose and subsequent State practice. This ordinary meaning is apparent from the text of Article 43, which allows additional health measures in response to a specific public health risk or to a PHEIC but only if these achieve the same or greater levels of health protection than recommendations issued by the WHO,[25] or health measures otherwise prohibited by specific articles of the IHR,[26] and only provided certain preconditions are met. These preconditions include that (1) health measures accord with relevant national law and international law obligations and (2) are not more restrictive of international traffic and 'not more invasive or intrusive to persons than reasonably available alternatives that would achieve the *appropriate* level of health protection.'[27]

Article 43(1) thus embeds a proportionality clause rooted in State obligations under international law. The whole text of the IHR is indeed guided by international human rights law. According to Article 3 of the IHR, implementation of the regulations must be with full respect for the dignity, human rights, and fundamental freedoms of persons and guided by the United Nations Charter and WHO Constitution, both of which include human rights provisions. In addition, Article 57 requires States to interpret the IHR to be compatible with other relevant international agreements which in this case includes international human rights treaties which govern a range of human rights implicated in travel restrictions for travelers, for people unable to travel because of restrictions, and for the populations of countries impacted by restrictions. It is important to note that the drafting history of Article 43 indicates that earlier drafts far more explicitly constrained governments from imposing 'measures exceeding those recommended by WHO,'[28] with one draft only allowing States to exceed WHO recommended measures if such measures did not conflict with international human rights law entitlements.[29] While this explicit reference to international human rights law was removed from the final version of Article 43, the references to less 'invasive' and 'intrusive' measures, focus on necessity and on least restrictive alternatives arguably reflect the continuing imprint of these criteria, as do these other explicit indications that human rights are guiding principles for the IHR. An assessment of whether travel restrictions are a necessary response to a public health threat requires, therefore, not just that States assess the evidence for public health risks but also consider evidence for the efficacy and by extension, both the necessity and proportionality of these measures themselves, including by reference to their impact on human rights.

5.1.3 Risk Assessment Given Evolving Science and WHO Guidance

5.1.3.1 Scientific Evidence of the Effectiveness of Travel Restrictions during COVID-19

The IHR emphasizes that decision-making on travel restrictions must be guided by scientific evidence and principles, rather than public perceptions, media characterizations of risk, religious or cultural tenets, or sociopolitical considerations. Risk in science is understood in terms of probability and severity of harmful events.[30] Studies of past travel restrictions have indicated that travel restrictions delay disease spread by a few days to a few weeks, at most.[31] They also suggest that travel restrictions may divert resources and public attention from other necessary interventions and disrupt aid and technical support to other countries.[32] Studies of COVID-19 restrictions suggest that they delayed but did not curtail the international spread of the disease. Wells et al's study of China's cordon sanitaire on Wuhan and other cities in Hubei province found that it had averted the export of 71% cases out of China and bought world crucial time but that COVID-19 had already spread to several continents.[33] Grepin et al did a systematic review of 29 studies of early phase travel measures (including advice, entry and exit screening, medical examination or vaccination requirements, isolation or quarantine, refusal of entry, and entry restrictions).[34] They found a high level of agreement that measures led to important changes in dynamics of early phases of the pandemic albeit that most studies investigated initial export from Wuhan. They suggest that early implementation was an important determinant of effectiveness and that any such effectiveness was short-lived.[35] They found that 'travel measures alone are unlikely to significantly change the trajectory of the outbreak unless commensurate domestic measures [like testing, contact tracing and physical distancing] are also implemented.'[36] Russell et al's modelling study found that in May 2020, imported cases accounted for more than 10% total incidence and that by September 2020, imported cases accounted for far less total incidence. Their findings suggest strict untargeted travel restrictions were probably unjustified in many countries other than those with good international travel connections and very low local COVID-19 incidence, or "where epidemics are close to tipping points for exponential growth."[37] They argue that, before implementing, countries should consider local COVID-19 incidence, local epidemic growth, and travel volumes.[38] Burns et al's systematic review of 62 studies found varied beneficial effects and delays in outbreak spread for up to 85 days and that effectiveness depended on levels of community transmission, travel volumes and duration, public health measures in place, and specification and timing of the measure.[39] In a recent quasi-experimental study, Poirier et al examined real-world data from 166 countries to examine the impact of travel restrictions on the spread of COVID-19. They found that while targeted border closures banning non-essential travel from some countries had some effect in slowing the spread of COVID-19 at country level, total border closures banning non-essential travel from all countries had the effect of drastically reducing global transmission.[40] In sum, these studies suggest some efficacy for short-term early restrictions as well restrictions applied without discrimination to all non-essential travel. However, any such efficacy considerably wanes over time, and a one-size-fits-all approach that does not take account of context is not appropriate or effective.

5.1.3.2 WHO Guidance on Travel Restrictions

In tandem with accumulating scientific evidence, travel advice issued by the WHO also evolved through the course of the COVID-19 pandemic as evidenced in its recommendations issued through both the IHR Emergency Committee (EC) and the Secretariat. The EC's initial recommendations even as COVID-19 was determined a PHEIC on 30 January 2020 were that travel restrictions not be implemented.[41] In its May 2020 statement, the EC continued to advise against trade restrictions[42] and further advised States to 'review travel and trade measures based on regular risk assessments, transmission patterns at origin and destination, cost-benefit analysis, evolution of the pandemic and new knowledge of COVID-19.'[43] These latter recommendations arguably were efforts to assure greater proportionality in the impact of these restrictions insofar as they impacted on individual human rights and public health responses to COVID-19 and insofar as less restrictive public health measures like screening, contact tracing, and quarantine could be used instead.

In July 2020, the WHO recommendations clarified that the risk of case importation from international travel depends on, *inter alia*, the intensity of SARS-CoV-2 virus transmission between the country of arrival and the country of departure. Where two countries share a similar profile of SARS-CoV-2 virus transmission, for instance, the WHO indicated that there is 'no substantial risk of potential impact' on the country of arrival's epidemiological situation.[44] This WHO advice marked a break from advice issued in past PHEICs—changing the narrative of the Organization from one of recommending *against* travel restrictions to one of advising States to exercise caution in *lifting* travel restrictions. The advice notably omitted mention of IHR Article 43. In December 2020, the WHO offered further detail on the criteria and steps necessary to assess a risk-based approach to international travel in relation to COVID-19, recommending that such risk assessments be conducted 'systematically and regularly (ideally every two weeks).'[45] The WHO further recommended making such assessments on the basis of detailed information regarding the following:

> the local epidemiology . . . in departure and destination countries; travel volumes between countries; the public health and health services capacity and performance to detect and care for cases and their contacts, including among travellers, in the destination country; public health and social measures implemented to control the spread of COVID-19 in departure and destination countries and available evidence on adherence and effectiveness of such measures in reducing transmission; [and] contextual factors, including economic impact, human rights and feasibility of applying measures, among others.[46]

Here, the WHO specifically indicated the permissibility of implementing travel restrictions:

> in accordance with their national legislation, and as per relevant provisions of the IHR . . . as long as such measures are risk-based, evidence-based, coherent, proportionate to the public health risk, and, therefore, do not constitute an unnecessary interference with international traffic and trade.[47]

In its January 2021 statement, as evidence of SARS-CoV-2 variants emerged, the EC recommended to the States:

> Implement coordinated, time-limited, risk-based, and evidence-based approaches for health measures in relation to international traffic in line with WHO guidance and IHR provisions. Careful consideration should be given to when and if travel bans should or should not be used as tools to reduce spread. Such decisions should be based on the best available evidence.[48]

On 2 July 2021, the WHO issued further guidance to address the dramatic emergence of virus variants of concern and the spectre of new forms of discrimination against travelers from countries with few or no vaccines or travelers from countries that have rolled out unfavoured (per the destination country) vaccines. The WHO recommended that countries without adequate capacities to respond to emerging variants of concern 'adopt a precautionary approach and implement time-limited, more stringent travel restrictions . . . subject to the *principle of proportionality* [citing the IHR; emphasis added].'[49] Despite tacitly approving travel restrictions in limited circumstances in mid-2021, by January 2022, the flurry of Omicron-related travel restrictions targeting travelers from South Africa and other African States (including several with limited access to vaccines) prompted the EC and the Secretariat to urge lifting travel restrictions, as these 'contribute to the economic and social stress'[50] experienced by States. The Secretariat instead urged States to implement measures commensurate with 'travellers' dignity, human rights and fundamental freedom, as outlined in the IHR' and to show 'global solidarity in rapid and transparent information sharing.'[51]

This overview illustrates how the WHO's travel guidance has evolved from strictly endorsing the futility of travel restrictions to gradually promoting a 'risk-based approach to international travel,' while still denouncing discriminatory manifestations of travel restrictions insufficiently rooted in public health evidence. Importantly, such guidance has evolved under the shadow of the pandemic to emphasize the correlative contribution of global solidarity. This progression in WHO's COVID-19–related guidance on international traffic illustrates the dynamic, high-stakes, and fast-changing nature of scientific evidence during an evolving global public health emergency and, therefore, of the measures that may be justified as necessary on public health grounds under international law.

5.2 Proportionality Analysis

Feared losses in trade, tourism, and reputation disincentivized governments from reporting under the previous IHR (1969). A 1991 cholera outbreak in Peru resulted in USD 700 million loss given trade restrictions on Peruvian imports.[52] A 1994 plague outbreak in Surat, India, met with flight cancellations, border closures, and restrictions on Indians living abroad.[53] India incurred nearly USD 2 billion losses.[54] China delayed disclosing information about SARS in 2003 and delayed notification of COVID-19 outbreaks in the city of Wuhan, Hubei province, in late 2019.[55]

Even where travel restrictions may be scientifically supported, their use is only justified under Article 43(1) in a manner that helps achieve 'an appropriate level of health protection.' Several studies show travel restrictions are only useful when combined with non-pharmaceutical interventions[56] like contact tracing, physical distancing, and diagnostics[57] and government assistance to enable citizens to follow public health guidelines. How travel restrictions are implemented matters. Sudden border closure announcements may induce a rapid inflow of travelers, inadvertently becoming super spreader events.[58] They can also disproportionately harm tenuously employed migrant workers who are left stranded without employment or assistance.[59] While the IHR leave it largely up to individual States to determine what constitutes an *appropriate* level of health protection, it is certain that a measure that offers no health protection, or worse, aggravates the public health crisis, would be in non-compliance with Article 43(1).

In considering reasonably available alternatives to travel restrictions that would achieve the *appropriate* level of health protection, international human rights law principles of legitimacy, necessity, and proportionality can guide States in assessing less restrictive measures.[60] In past outbreaks, experts have recommended exit screening at departure as the least restrictive mechanism that would achieve the level of health protection sought by travel restrictions,[61] but as WHO noted, screening would only partially assist in COVID-19, where pre-symptomatic and asymptomatic individuals are as likely to transmit the virus as individuals with symptoms.[62] Mandatory quarantine hotels have also been resorted to in several jurisdictions, including Canada, Australia, and Hong Kong, but their safety has been called into question through growing scientific consensus around the airborne nature of the SARS-CoV-2 virus.[63]

With few alternatives to controlling the international spread of the virus beyond travel restrictions, solidarity, collaboration, and assistance are key to achieving the purpose of the IHR and giving effect to proportionality analysis under Article 43(1). Article 43 must, therefore, be read alongside the duty to collaborate under Article 44 and imperatives for collaboration in World Health Assembly (WHA) Resolution 58.3. Article 44 of the IHR indicates that States must collaborate in detection, assessment, response to PHEICs, technical cooperation and logistical support, particularly in relation to public health capacities, and financial resources. WHA Resolution 58.3 calls on States to provide assistance to developing countries and countries with economies in transition in the building, strengthening, and maintenance of required public health capacities. These provisions place the onus on States to ensure that travel restrictions do not jeopardize the efficacy and implementation of the IHR. To minimize the risk that prolonged travel restrictions will disincentivize States from reporting future disease outbreaks arguably requires States to support the economies and public health response of countries disadvantaged by such restrictions (e.g., if such an economy relies on tourism). It also requires the support of equitable manufacturing and distribution of effective vaccines, particularly as vaccination became a prerequisite for international travel with dramatic equity and human rights implications for people from low and middle-income countries.

As this chapter has shown, assessments of proportionality and risk in determining travel restrictions under the existing IHR are perennially hampered by the ease with which Article 43 lends itself to highly subjective interpretation. Since 2022, a new avenue has opened to amend the IHR to reflect lessons learned from the COVID-19 pandemic. At the 75th WHA, States agreed to embark on potential amendments to the IHR through a Working Group on Amendments to the IHR (WGIHR).[64] The Assembly tasked the WGIHR with proposing 'a package of potential amendments,' taking into account the report of the Review Committee regarding amendments to the IHR by the 77th WHA in 2024. The Review Committee submitted its technical report on over 300 proposed amendments to the IHR in January 2023, and the WGIHR has since been leading negotiations to bring together a package of final amendments.[65]

Ultimately, there is no single amendment but rather a combination of them—that can help States achieve better outcomes in response to future public health threats under the IHR. **First**, Article 43 should be revised to offer a clearer and better-defined process to determine when restrictions may be justified for a novel pathogen and what processes could assure measures rooted in necessity, proportionality, non-discrimination, equity, and solidarity. Proportionality would require that travel restrictions not include blanket provisions, must be clear, and can only be used for a legitimate aim to ensure that the individual is protected from arbitrary interference and must be time-bound.[66] To a large extent, ensuring that WHO's recommendations take account of human rights criteria could offer a feasible model for how to conceptualize travel restrictions going forward. **Second**, if restrictions are imposed, there must be solidarity in mitigating their impacts by supporting the economies and public health response of countries disadvantaged by such restrictions (including, for example, States whose economies rely heavily on tourism). **Third**, there must be accountability for non-compliance. Currently, State reporting to the WHO under Article 43 is not made public. Some of the only information we have on this is in the DG's annual reports on the functioning of the IHR, where they indicate what percentage of countries in the preceding year notified the WHO of measures exceeding their recommendations—and occasionally, reports produced by DG-appointed IHR Review Committees. We have no real-time data on who has notified or not, and there are no consequences of any kind for non-compliance with the IHR, dramatically undercutting its efficacy. Transparency in reporting alone could go a long way towards increasing at least reputational costs for non-compliance. Yet equally important is creating enforcement and monitoring mechanisms that could bolster compliance with this instrument. **Fourth**, this accountability could be bolstered through greater linkages between the WHO and UN human rights bodies[67] to allow WHO authority to address human rights compliance through new and existing IHR-related monitoring and evaluation tools, such as the Universal Health Preparedness Review, a Member State driven intergovernmental process, or the Joint External Evaluation tool, a voluntary evaluation process initiated at the request of the country. These linkages could help identify the most urgent needs within national health systems, prioritize efforts and enhanced preparedness, response, and action, and engage current and prospective donors and partners in targeting resources in the most effective way.[68] Alternatively, existing UN mechanisms could be used to push for human rights compliance around IHR-related functions, including the Universal Periodic Review (UPR), where UN Member States' human rights records are reviewed.[69] In the absence of greater accountability, the effectiveness of the IHR as the world's primary tool to address public health emergencies of international concern will continue to be hampered. Moreover, unmitigated, needless, and disproportionate bans and restrictions will continue to dissuade States from promptly reporting novel diseases or variants in ways that will continue to undermine global health security for all.

5.3 Conclusion

Article 43, read in the context of the IHR as a whole and in relation to States' duties under international human rights law, require States to implement less restrictive measures than travel restrictions, where these would achieve the same level of health protection. In all cases, such restrictions should be legitimate, necessary, and proportional as directed by the Siracusa Principles. WHO advice coheres with international human rights law in indicating that if States implement travel restrictions, they should be risk-based, evidence-based, coherent, proportionate, and time-limited. If WHO advice has shifted at all to accommodate the imposition of travel restrictions, it is primarily to acknowledge the limited evidence of their utility in the earliest phase of a novel disease outbreak. Moreover, where travel restrictions are imposed, both the IHR and international human rights law require that their negative impacts be mitigated by cooperative actions. As international travel increasingly becomes dependent on proof of COVID-19 vaccination, the imperative to advance equitable access in low- and middle-income countries will become an increasingly critical aspect of the global cooperation and solidarity inherent to the IHR. These are elements of the IHR needing explicit reform, alongside strengthened mechanisms for accountability in the case of non-compliance.

Notes

1 This chapter is based on L. Forman and R. Habibi, "Revisiting the legality of travel restrictions under international law during COVID-19," (2022) 71:3 *International and Comparative Law Quarterly* 743–760. www.cambridge.org/core/journals/international-and-comparative-law-quarterly/article/revisiting-the-legality-of-travel-restrictions-under-international-law-during-covid19/78D8D2DF06E659D2BC3C529954DB7E59. This article is available Open Access: https://creativecommons.org/licenses/by/4.0/.
2 International Health Regulations (adopted 23 May 2005, entered into force 15 June 2007) 2509 UNTS 79 [IHR], art 2.
3 R. Habibi et al, "Do not violate the International Health Regulations during the COVID-19 outbreak" (2020) 395 Lancet 664.
4 See IHR, *supra* note 2, art 43(1).
5 *Ibid*, art 43(2).
6 *Ibid*, art 43(3).
7 "Significant interference" is generally taken to mean under article 43(3) as "refusal of entry or departure of international travellers, baggage, cargo, containers, conveyances, goods, and the like, or their delay, for more than 24 hours."
8 IHR, *supra* note 2, art 43(5).
9 "Statement on the second meeting of the International Health Regulations (2005) Emergency Committee regarding the outbreak of novel coronavirus (2019-nCoV)," (30 January 2020), *WHO*. www.who.int/news/item/30-01-2020-statement-on-the-second-meeting-of-the-international-health-regulations-(2005)-emergency-committee-regarding-the-outbreak-of-novel-coronavirus-(2019-ncov).
10 IHR, *supra* note 2, art 43(2).
11 *Ibid*, art 43(5).
12 World Health Organization, "WHO's work in health emergencies: Strengthening preparedness for health emergencies: Implementation of the International Health Regulations (2005)," A74/9. Add.1, 5 May 2021, para.6.
13 See, for example, World Health Organization, "Standing committee on health emergency prevention, preparedness and response," (30 May 2022), EB151(2),

1151st session, online (pdf): https://apps.who.int/gb/ebwha/pdf_files/EB151/B151(2)-en.pdf.
14 IHR, *supra* note 2, art 2.
15 Catherine Z. Worsnop et al, "The unintended consequences of information provision: The World Health Organization and border restrictions during COVID-19," (2022) *International Studies Perspectives* 1.
16 IHR, *supra* note 2, art 43(1). Note: "intrusive" is defined under article 1 of the IHR as "possibly provoking discomfort through close or intimate contact or questioning," while "invasive" is defined as "the puncture or incision of the skin or insertion of an instrument or foreign material into the body or the examination of a body cavity."
17 *Ibid*, art 43(2). Note: under IHR article 1, "scientific principles" are "the accepted fundamental laws and facts of nature known through the methods of science." "Scientific evidence," on the other hand, is defined as "information furnishing *a level of proof* based on the *established* and *accepted* methods of science."
18 A. Tejpar and S. J. Hoffman, "Canada's Violation of International Law during the 2014–16 Ebola Outbreak," (2017) 54 *CanYIL* 366; Habibi et al, *supra* note 8.
19 Habibi et al, *supra* note 3; American Association for the International Commission of Jurists, "The Siracusa Principles on the limitation and derogation provisions in the international covenant on civil and political rights," (1985) 7 *HRQ* 3.
20 B. M. Meier, R. Habibi and Y. T. Yang, "Travel restrictions violate international law," (2020) 367 *Science* 1436.
21 C. Foster, "Justified border closures do not violate the international health regulations 2005," (11 June 2020), *EJIL: Talk!*. www.ejiltalk.org/justified-border-closures-do-not-violate-the-international-health-regulations-2005/.
22 P. A. Villarreal, "COVID-19 symposium: 'Can they really do that?' States' obligations under the international health regulations in light of COVID-19 (Part I)," (31 March 2020), *Opinio Juris*. http://opiniojuris.org/2020/03/31/covid-19-symposium-can-they-really-do-that-states-obligations-under-the-international-health-regulations-in-light-of-covid-19-part-i/.
23 B. J. V. Tigerstrom and K. Wilson, "COVID-19 travel restrictions and the international health regulations (2005)," (2020) 5 *BMJ* Global Health e002629.
24 B. J. V. Tigerstrom, S. F. Halabi and K. R. Wilson, "The international health regulations (2005) and the re-establishment of international travel amidst the COVID-19 pandemic," (2020) 27:1 *Journal of Travel Medicine* 127.
25 IHR, *supra* note 2, art 43(1)(a).
26 *Ibid* art 43(1)(b).
27 *Ibid* art 43(1). Note: "intrusive" is defined under article 1 of the IHR as "possibly provoking discomfort through close or intimate contact or questioning," while "invasive" is defined as "the puncture or incision of the skin or insertion of an instrument or foreign material into the body or the examination of a body cavity."
28 Lisa Forman, Benjamin Meier and Sharifah Sekalala, "The world health organization, international health regulations & human rights law," (2022) 19 *International Organizations Law Review* 37.
29 World Health Organization, Review and Approval of Proposed Amendments to the International Health Regulations: Draft Revision, A/IHR/IGWG/3 (September 30, 2004).
30 L. Gostin and E. Wiley, *Public Health Law: Power, Duty & Restraint* (University of California Press, 2016) at 56.
31 An integrative review of the limited evidence on international travel bans as an emerging infectious disease disaster control measure. See Nicole A. Errett, Lauren M. Sauer and Lainie Rutkow, "An integrative review of the limited evidence on international travel bans as an emerging infectious disease disaster control

measure," (2020) 18:1 *Journal of Emergency Management* 7; Ana L. P. Mateus et al, "Effectiveness of travel restrictions in the rapid containment of human influenza: A systematic review," (2014) 92:12 *Bulletin of the World Health Organization* 868; P. Bajardi et al, "Human mobility networks, travel restrictions, and the global spread of 2009 H1N1 pandemic," (2011) 6 *PLoS One* e16591; S. Ryu et al, "Nonpharmaceutical measures for pandemic influenza in nonhealthcare settings—International travel-related measures," (2020) 26:5 *Emerging Infectious Diseases Journal*; T. C. Germann et al, "Mitigation strategies for pandemic influenza in the United States," (2006) 103 *Proceedings of the National Academy of Sciences* 5935; J. S. Brownstein, C. J. Wolfe and K. D. Mandl, "Empirical evidence for the effect of airline travel on inter-regional influenza spread in the United States," (2006) 3 *PLoS Medicine* e401.

32 See: "Updated WHO recommendations for international traffic in relation to COVID-19 outbreak," (29 February 2020), *WHO*. www.who.int/news-room/articles-detail/updated-who-recommendations-for-international-traffic-in-relation-to-covid-19-outbreak.

33 C. R. Wells et al, "Impact of international travel and border control measures on the global spread of the novel 2019 coronavirus outbreak," (2020) 117 *Proceedings of the National Academy of Sciences of the United States of America* 7504.

34 K. A. Grepin et al, "Evidence of the effectiveness of travel-related measures during the early phase of the COVID-19 pandemic: A rapid systematic review," (2021) 6:3 *BMJ Global Health*.

35 *Ibid* at 1.

36 *Ibid* at 19–20.

37 T. W. Russell et al, "Effect of internationally imported cases on internal spread of COVID-19: A mathematical modelling study," (2021) 6 *Lancet Public Health* e12 at e12.

38 *Ibid.*

39 J. Burns et al, "International travel-related control measures to contain the COVID-19 pandemic: a rapid review," (2021) 3 *Cochrane Database of Systematic Reviews* 1.

40 M. J. P. Poirier et al, "Quasi-experimental evaluation of national border closures on COVID-19 transmission," (2023) 3:2 *PLoS Global Public Health* e0000980.

41 World Health Organization, *supra* note 32.

42 "Statement on the third meeting of the IHR (2005) Emergency Committee regarding the outbreak of coronavirus disease (COVID-19), World Health Organization," (1 May 2020), *WHO*. www.who.int/news/item/01-05-2020-statement-on-the-third-meeting-of-the-international-health-regulations-(2005)-emergency-committee-regarding-the-outbreak-of-coronavirus-disease-(covid-19).

43 *Ibid.*

44 "Public health considerations while resuming international travel," (30 July 2020), *WHO*. www.who.int/news-room/articles-detail/public-health-considerations-while-resuming-international-travel.

45 "Considerations for implementing a risk-based approach to international travel in the context of COVID-19," (16 December 2020), *WHO* https://apps.who.int/iris/bitstream/handle/10665/337858/WHO-2019-nCoV-Risk-based_international_travel-2020.1-eng.pdf?sequence=1&isAllowed=y.

46 *Ibid.*

47 *Ibid.*

48 "Statement on the sixth meeting of the International Health Regulations (2005) Emergency Committee regarding the coronavirus disease (COVID-19) pandemic," (15 January 2021), *WHO*. www.who.int/news/item/15-01-2021-statement-on-the-sixth-meeting-of-the-international-health-regulations-(2005)-emergency-committee-regarding-the-coronavirus-disease-(covid-19)-pandemic.

49 "Policy considerations for implementing a risk-based approach to international travel in the context of COVID-19," (15 January 2021) at 3, *WHO*. www.who.int/publications/i/item/WHO-2019-nCoV-Policy-Brief-Risk-based-international-travel-2021.1.

50 "Statement on the tenth meeting of the International Health Regulations (2005) Emergency Committee regarding the coronavirus disease (COVID-19) pandemic," (15 January 2021), *WHO*. www.who.int/news/item/19-01-2022-statement-on-the-tenth-meeting-of-the-international-health-regulations-(2005)-emergency-committee-regarding-the-coronavirus-disease-(covid-19)-pandemic.

51 "WHO advice for international traffic in relation to the SARS-CoV-2 Omicron variant (B.1.1.529)," (30 November 2021), *WHO*. www.who.int/news-room/articles-detail/who-advice-for-international-traffic-in-relation-to-the-sars-cov-2-omicron-variant.

52 D. P. Fidler, "Return of the Fourth Horseman: Emerging infectious diseases and international law," (1997) 81:4 *Minnesota Law Review* 771 at 815–816.

53 R. A. Cash and V. Narasimhan, "Impediments to global surveillance of infectious diseases: Consequences of open reporting in a global economy," (2000) 78:11 *Bulletin of the World Health Organization* 1358.

54 *Ibid* at 1362.

55 T.-Y. Lin, "The forgotten role of WHO/IHR in trade responses to 2009 A/H1N1 influenza outbreak," (2010) 44:3 *Journal of World Trade* 515; Gostin & Katz, *supra* note 3 at 267; M. M. Kavanagh, "Authoritarianism, outbreaks, and information politics," (2020) 5:3 *The Lancet Public Health* e135.

56 G. Kessler, "Trump's claim that he imposed the first 'China ban,' " (7 April 2020), *The Washington Post*. www.washingtonpost.com/politics/2020/04/07/trumps-claim-that-he-imposed-first-china-ban/; A. Nowrasteh & A. C. Forrester, "How US travel restrictions on China affected the spread of COVID-19 in the United States," (2020), *Cato Institute HWCO*. https://search.bvsalud.org/global-literature-on-novel-coronavirus-2019-ncov/resource/en/grc-740552.

57 Y. Liu et al, "The impact of non-pharmaceutical interventions on SARS-CoV-2 transmission across 130 countries and territories," (2021) 19 *BMC Medicine* 40; S. Flaxman et al, "Estimating the effects of non-pharmaceutical interventions on COVID-19 in Europe," (2020) 584 *Nature* 257.

58 D. Saunders, "Why travel bans fail to stop pandemics," (15 May 2020), *Foreign Affairs*. www.foreignaffairs.com/articles/canada/2020-05-15/why-travel-bans-fail-stop-pandemics.

59 "Migrants left stranded and without assistance by COVID-19 lockdowns," (8 April 2021), *UN News*. https://news.un.org/en/story/2021/04/1089302; Omar Sachedina and Ryan Flanagan, "Hundreds of migrant workers expect to be stranded in Canada over Christmas," (22 December 2020), *CTV News*. www.ctvnews.ca/canada/hundreds-of-migrant-workers-expect-to-be-stranded-in-canada-over-christmas-1.5242287?autoPlay=true.

60 R. Habibi et al, "Stellenbosch consensus on legal national responses to public health risks: Clarifying article 43 of the international health regulations," (2020) *International Organizations Law Review* 1 at 60.

61 I. Bogoch et al, "Assessment of the potential for international dissemination of Ebola virus via commercial air travel during the 2014 west African outbreak," (2015) 385 *Lancet* 29.

62 M. A. Johansson et al, "SARS-CoV-2 transmission from people without COVID-19 symptoms," (2021) 4 *JAMA Network Open* e2035057; "Updated WHO recommendations for international traffic in relation to COVID-19 outbreak," (29 February 2020), *WHO*. www.who.int/news-room/articles-detail/updated-who-recommendations-for-international-traffic-in-relation-to-covid-19-outbreak.

63 T. Greenhalgh et al, "Ten scientific reasons in support of airborne transmission of SARS-CoV-2," (2021) 387:10285 *The Lancet*.
64 Earliest traces of an impetus to amend the IHR can be found in the WHO Executive Board's decision EB150(3). At the 75th WHA, Member States agreed to revise the mandate of the Working Group on Strengthening WHO Preparedness and Response to Health Emergencies, now renamed to WGIHR, to focus exclusively on potential amendments of the IHR. See WHA75(9).
65 Report of the Review Committee regarding amendments to the International Health Regulations (2005), A/WGIHR/2/5.
66 Forman et al, *supra* note 28.
67 B. Toebes, L. Forman and G. Bartolini, "Towards human rights consistent responses to health emergencies: What is the overlap between core right to health obligations and core International Health Regulation capacities?" (2020) *Harvard Health and Human Rights Journal* 1.
68 "Joint External Evaluation (JEE)," *JEE Alliance*. alliancehsc.org.
69 Forman et al, *supra* note 28.

PART III

Border and Mobility Restrictions as Public Health Tools within Regional and National Boundaries

6

MANAGEMENT OF THE EUROPEAN UNION'S (INTERNAL AND EXTERNAL) BORDERS DURING THE COVID-19 PANDEMIC

Tamara Hervey, Alexandra Fyfe and Vincent Delhomme

6.1 Introduction

The European Union (EU) is a deeply integrated regional trade bloc. Most commentators agree that it is (now) more: the depth and breadth of EU integration suggest that the EU is a 'quasi-constitutionalised' entity. Some key characteristics of that entity include a profound reliance on law and rule-based modes of operation; a commitment to economic openness, free and fair trade, including all factors of production (capital, goods, services and persons); and a significantly greater attention than in other trade blocs to the position of human beings (especially EU citizens[1]) as individuals with innate dignity, not merely as economic actors.

The EU's 'quasi-constitutional' powers flow from the treaties which create the EU and establish its legislative, executive and judicial institutions. These institutions are empowered to make law and policy decisions in a range of delineated 'competences'. Competences not formally granted to the EU remain with the Member States. In practice, and according to EU law, many EU powers are exercised in collaboration with national institutions. The EU is thus in a heterarchical relationship with its Member States when it comes to law and policymaking/governance.

The EU's governance of borders during the COVID-19 pandemic was (and continues to be) supported by the European Centre for Disease Control (ECDC). Established in 2004, the ECDC supports EU public health governance, through information gathering, analysis and dissemination. Formally independent from the EU legislature and executive, the ECDC is the hub in a heterarchical network of national agencies concerned with communicable disease.[2] The ECDC's accounts of 'scientific evidence' are presented as

DOI: 10.4324/9781003394006-9

neutral, pertaining to the EU level, and non-partisan in the sense of not following any one particular Member State. But in practice, the ECDC works closely with the World Health Organization, as well as with national public health agencies. The COVID-19 pandemic involved such scientific uncertainty that the EU institutions also respected national scientific assessments.[3]

6.2 European Union Border Laws

In principle, EU law aims to secure open borders within the EU, and a single border at its edge. This 'in-principle' statement hides a massively complex set of border rules and practices. EU border law continues to change significantly over time and differs depending on what 'factor of production' is crossing a border. This chapter focuses only on EU law concerning movement of people across borders.

In understanding EU border law, we need to distinguish between the EU's *internal* borders (between EU Member States) and the EU's *external* borders.

Internal EU borders include land borders between any two EU Member States, sea borders and the border involved when someone travels by air from any EU Member State to any other. EU internal border law as it applies to *people* (as opposed to products, services or capital) flows from three main sources: the rules in the EU's founding treaties,[4] rules adopted by the EU's legislature[5] and court rulings interpreting these sources.[6] The main principles behind this internal border law are to give rights to cross internal EU borders to a wide group of human beings, including EU citizens, long-term residents and their family members, irrespective of nationality. The EU shares competence with its Member States to make law on the 'internal market', within which internal EU border control law falls.[7] Public health protection formally falls within both EU and Member State competence[8] and is embedded in many ways by EU internal market law.[9] Member States may restrict free movement on the basis of a narrowly defined list of exceptions, including public health, which apply through a relatively strict version of the principle of proportionality.[10]

EU *external* border law, as it applies to people, consists of an overlapping set of legal rules, reflecting the EU's complex and evolving competences over human migration into the EU from the rest of the world. The key legal instrument here is the Schengen Borders Code, which governs the Schengen Area[11] and progressively abolishes border controls on *inter alia* people moving within the Schengen Area. Although the Schengen Borders Code is thus a measure of *internal* EU border law, it also reflects the EU's attempt to agree a common set of rules for migration into the Schengen Area from countries outside the EU. However, the detail of external migration policy fundamentally remains a national competence.

Under the Schengen Borders Code, Schengen countries may reintroduce border controls or restrict movement of people who would otherwise be entitled to cross the EU's external border, in response to a serious threat to public policy and internal security,[12] including the 'risk posed by a contagious disease'.[13] If border controls are reintroduced, a notification requirement applies.[14] Border checks are permitted to ensure that someone crossing an external EU border is not 'likely to jeopardise the . . . public health . . . of any of the Member States'.[15] The EU's external border law is significantly less comprehensive, or stable, than its internal border law. For example, in response to the 'migration crisis', and the significant numbers of people from Syria seeking safety in the EU arriving through Greece, the EU had already allowed Austria, Denmark, Germany, Norway and Sweden to reintroduce temporary internal border controls on people.[16]

The EU thus has partial competence to regulate the migration of people over its external borders, while having greater competence over internal border control. The EU's legislature has adopted key legislation, much of which is enforceable by an individual, against a violating Member State government. EU law makes provision for a 'preliminary reference', from a national court seized of a question of EU law, to the EU's Court of Justice, to determine the correct interpretation of EU law. The main aim of the legislation is to secure freedom of movement for people (and especially EU citizens and their families) within the EU.

6.3 European Union Border Laws under COVID-19

Given the centrality of free movement of people to the EU, and the depth of legal and policy integration in this field, the events of spring 2020 were perhaps a surprise.[17] The EU's Member States, acting individually and in an uncoordinated way, adopted an array of border controls on people moving within and into the EU.[18] Other parts of the world were also closing their borders to people moving from the EU, not always in very logical ways.

Starting from the back foot, the EU institutions began to act from quite early on. The European Commission did so drawing on data and advice provided by the ECDC. ECDC scientific guidance formed the basis of EU assessments of the travel-related risks of COVID-19 transmission and when, and to whom, borders should be closed.[19] The ECDC advised on quarantine and testing requirements, also in the context of the arising COVID-19 variants.[20] The ECDC worked with the EU Aviation Safety Agency to adopt an Aviation Health Safety Protocol which also contains guidance on testing and quarantine.[21] The ECDC also advised on travel by ship and rail.[22]

Many aspects of EU COVID-19 border governance were consistent with previous EU law and policy in crisis contexts and with the EU's general law and policy on its borders. But some aspects of EU COVID-19 border governance were rather more unexpected, given the EU's legal competences. We outline later the key EU COVID-19 border laws, first on the EU's *internal* borders and then on its *external* borders. The following analytical part of the chapter considers how we might assess the EU's contribution from a public health perspective.

6.3.1 EU Internal Borders

The Union's overall approach is illustrated well by the *Joint European Roadmap*[23] and *Council Recommendation 2020/1475*.[24] Both are soft law measures. Both focus on removing travel restrictions and are imbued with narratives of 'opening up' and 'freedom'. Both purport to be based on 'science'.[25] Both seek to establish common criteria for adoption of travel restrictions. Under the *Recommendation*, travel restrictions are to be based on the density of positive COVID-19 cases in any particular area. The EU's Member States provided weekly data, and the EU portrayed that data in a map, broken down by region, using a 'traffic light' system.[26] The EU Council recommended no restrictions on movement of people coming to or from 'green' areas on the map. Quarantine or compulsory testing could be adopted for non-essential travelers to and from 'orange' and 'red' areas. The *Recommendation* was amended in early February 2021, as new, more infectious variants of COVID-19 proliferated,[27] to add a new category ('dark red') for areas with very high infection rates. In June 2021, vaccine rollout was factored into the *Recommendation* and maps.[28]

As 'soft' law, Member States were able to ignore the EU's recommendations, and as far as we are aware, virtually every Member State did so at one point or another.[29]

From the beginning, the Commission made recommendations for 'effective border management',[30] creating a model of 'restrictive selection' or 'selective mobility'.[31] The focus was on encouraging Member States to permit people who are mobile 'by definition' (frontier, posted and seasonal workers) and 'essential workers' in sectors such as health, food, essential infrastructures or transportation[32] to cross internal borders. EU action thus focused on preserving the EU's internal market while recognizing that a response to a global pandemic needed to restrict human movement. A similar logic applied to extra-Union travels but, as explained later, was more restrictive of cross-border movement.[33]

Consistent with a focus on the internal market, the EU moved as quickly as it could towards coordinating progressive *lifting* of internal border restrictions. This approach was central to *Recommendation 2020/1475*.[34] The logic of COVID-19 border controls, in the context of a 'single' EU market, including people as a 'factor of production', is suspect. As one academic commentator puts it: 'Why should a journey from Berlin to Frankfurt be permitted, while travelling from Luxembourg to Frankfurt is not, even though both destinations currently constitute high-risk areas?'[35] And if movement is unfettered within a Member State, but national borders are controlled, even where neighbouring countries face a similar health situation, the restrictions on cross-border movement would normally be a disproportionate limitation in EU law.[36]

But the EU did not use its hard law powers to underpin the desire to secure free movement within the EU's internal market. The European Commission did not take any formal legal action against Member States. Instead, the Commissioners for Justice and Home Affairs wrote informally to all Member States in February 2021, urging them to adhere to the recommendations on travel restrictions.[37] It was also reported that letters were sent to six individual Member States, calling on them to bring their travel restrictions in line with EU law.[38]

The EU took its next significant step towards lifting border controls in June 2021 for the summer season.[39] This step did involve 'hard' law but law that seeks to *coordinate* Member State action, rather than to adopt a binding harmonized regional approach to COVID-19 border control. The EU adopted legislation to ensure that the certificates recognized by its Member States, as evidencing COVID-19 vaccination, recovery or negative test, would be mutually recognized in all the EU Member States. These digital certificates are used in various contexts, including border control. Mutual recognition of a single 'EU Digital Certificate' aims to secure ease of cross-border movement both within and into the EU.[40] Initially planned to expire on 30 June 2022, the regulations were extended until June 2023.[41]

The EU Digital Certificate is controversial. The EU's concerns, alongside mutual recognition and interoperability, focused on removing border restrictions, also included protection of privacy and data protection.[42] The EU has strong data protection laws, and the technical design of the EU Digital Certificate was intended to ensure compliance with those.[43] Although legally speaking, the EU Digital Certificate is not *required* for exercise of EU free movement rights, *in practice,* movement within the EU is significantly impeded for people who do not have the certificate. This has raised concerns about inequalities across the EU, as the issuing of the certificates is a national, not EU, competence.[44] Regulation 2021/953 has been legally challenged, but the relevant claims were held to be inadmissible.[45] Perhaps surprisingly, there seems to be less concern about fraud, than about privacy, even though the system meant that the whole EU was as vulnerable as the weakest link in vaccination certification.[46]

6.3.2 EU External Borders

One of the earliest measures of EU COVID-related border control concerned travel into the EU from outside its external borders. The Commission recommended a temporary restriction on non-essential travel on 16 March 2020.[47] The recommendation did not apply to EU citizens or long-term and other legal EU residents. Nor did it define 'non-essential travel', but instead, it provided a non-exhaustive list of essential functions and needs, including health- and elder-care professionals and health researchers; frontier workers; transport and haulage workers; diplomats and other international workers, including those providing humanitarian aid; imperative family reasons; humanitarian protection; and passengers in transit. The next day, the Heads of State and Government of the EU Member States and the four Schengen Associated States agreed to implement the temporary restriction.[48] As with measures on internal borders, the relevant measure took the form of soft law. These initial restrictions were repeatedly extended.[49]

By summer 2020, the EU focus had changed to progressive lifting of the restrictions on non-essential travel into the EU.[50] A June 2020 *Council Recommendation* requested that Member States lift travel bans from certain countries.[51] The recommendation listed non-EU countries in a regularly-updated annex, for which travel into the EU for their residents should be facilitated. Inclusion on the list was supposed to be based on epidemiological criteria, including the number of COVID-19 cases, decreasing case numbers, testing and containment. This recommendation was amended in May 2021 to take into account vaccine rollout.[52]

In its original form, in June 2020, the list of 'third countries whose residents should not be affected by temporary external borders restriction on non-essential travel into the EU' included Australia, Canada, Japan, New Zealand, South Korea and Thailand. China was included on a reciprocal basis only. The only African countries were Algeria, Morocco, Rwanda and Tunisia. By early June 2021, after the vaccine rollout, the list was shorter, no longer included Canada, included Israel and the only country in Africa that was included was Rwanda. By 18 June 2021, the list had been amended again, to include the USA, but no other country in Africa had been added. By early July 2021, Canada was back on the list but still no other country in Africa. By mid-July 2021, no country in Africa was on the list. Rwanda returned to the list in late September 2021 to be joined by Namibia from late October to early December 2021.[53]

Because of possible changing global virus mutations, the May 2021 recommendation includes an 'emergency brake', allowing Member States to rapidly adopt new restrictions on an individual basis, subject to subsequent coordination at EU level. The EU's provisions thus not only took the form of soft law but also permitted uncoordinated Member State action, on the proviso only that coordination took place later.

6.4 Analysis and Conclusions

The political dynamics of the (perhaps ill-founded) reassurance that comes from border closure were at play in the EU's unfolding COVID border (soft) law and policy.[54] The EU Member States' governments shared a view that both internal[55] and external borders should be closed. The EU institutions played into this consensus by articulating an idea of the EU as 'protective' of its citizens and residents.

The key features of EU COVID border law and policy can be summarized as follows. The EU relied on 'soft' law, based on technocratic/'science-based' decision-making. The EU's initial activities only much later led to measures of 'hard' law. EU law and policy is imbued with a focus on 'freedom' and 'opening' up. EU law and policy makes a distinction between the EU's internal borders and its external borders. All of these features of EU COVID law on borders have important implications for public health. Each is discussed in turn.

First, the EU's initial responses, and the vast majority of its ongoing governance of the pandemic, took the legal form of soft law. The EU's institutions relied on Commission communications and guidelines, Council recommendations and technical/scientific guidance of EU agencies, in particular, the ECDC. The ECDC played a crucial role, as a body in charge of collecting, evaluating and disseminating relevant scientific data, providing scientific opinions and assistance and exchanging information and best practices.[56] The European Commission also sought to coordinate scientific guidance through a 'scientific advice platform', bringing together advisors from national governments of the Member States, which met once or twice a month from November 2020 until June 2023.[57] This approach is very much 'classical' international law: using statements of good practice and sharing recommendations based on comparative data in order to steer Member States towards particular behaviors. It is quite different from the 'ordinary' EU law of border control and human migration, as outlined briefly earlier.

The public health implications of a soft-law approach are difficult to measure. On the one hand, the EU's approach meant significant and irrational variance in border control within and into the EU. On the other hand, soft law leaves significant discretion at national, or even sub-national, levels for Member States to determine their own border control laws and policies. The EU's approach meant that the irrationality and disproportionality of EU Member States' border control laws were not tackled with the EU's legal powers. There were no legal/constitutional challenges to EU border controls, equivalent to those seen in Canada or Australia.[58] But given that border control is an effective proportionate response to a global pandemic only in certain circumstances,[59] and given that the EU has very limited competence to adopt necessary other measures, perhaps we should 'forgive' the EU for the effects on public health of its soft-law approach.

Second, the EU's approach was portrayed as based on 'technocratic' or 'scientific' decision-making: the EU 'regulatory state' in its normal mode of governance.[60] The EU produced its own interpretations of 'the science' and disseminated those among its Member States. It took the view that both EU and national law and policymaking should be based on 'sound science'. Of course, in the context of the COVID-19 pandemic, 'the science' was highly contested. Furthermore, the EU did not operate in a vacuum but worked with the World Health Organization and with its Member States, in both gathering and analysing data and in developing its policy recommendations.[61] The EU allowed more latitude than usual to the risk assessments of its Member States. In this way, the EU was able to portray its COVID-19 border governance as legitimate, and even 'depoliticised', by decision-making residing with technocratic agencies.[62] However, the EU actually took many 'political' decisions in its response to the pandemic, including collective vaccine procurement, the COVID-19 Digital Certificate or the Next Generation EU recovery and resilience plan.[63]

This aspect of the EU's approach is consistent with the EU's tendency to articulate certainty where it is not present and raises questions about how responsive the EU is to political or ethical concerns.[64] Public health governance, as understood broadly across this book, *includes* its ethical and political dimensions: it is not a purely technocratic undertaking (even if that were possible). In its depoliticized portrayal of its COVID-19 border control, the EU obfuscated its political choices. The EU's approach also left almost no space for discussion of ethical dimensions, especially not through legal processes, which allow for holding executives to account.

Third, the narratives of the EU's COVID-19 border governance are striking in their focus on 'freedom'. While the Member States were closing borders, even from the very beginning of the pandemic's hold in Europe, the EU was articulating recommendations that focused on *opening* borders. These began as articulations of shared EU concepts of essential migration, be that key workers, or repatriation of residents or humanitarian protection for vulnerable or displaced people. They developed into 'science-led' recommendations to open the EU's internal borders and, eventually, the EU's external borders. They 'hardened' into mutual recognition of the 'EU Digital COVID Certificate'.

The implications for public health on 'opening' and 'freedom' are difficult to assess. In the earlier phases of the pandemic, before effective vaccines were available, they were obviously at odds with most other global legal and policy responses. To protect populations, health systems and individuals, major restrictions on freedom were justified. But especially as vaccines were rolled out, it became necessary to consider also the other health (especially mental health) and wider effects of the initial lockdowns. Perhaps the EU's articulations of 'freedom' and 'opening up' felt rather inappropriate in summer 2020, when so many people across the world were still to be fully vaccinated. They certainly sit at odds with any values of global health equity, given the lack of global approach to vaccine rollout and the consequent lack of access to essential medicines across many least-developed countries.[65]

A fourth key feature of the EU's response is a focus on opening internal borders, at the expense, if necessary, of closing or keeping closed external borders. As Commissioners Johansson and Reynders put it in February 2021, the EU supported the Member States' choice 'to be strict when it comes to travel to the Union, while maintaining the necessary mobility within the Union'.[66] The characterization of internal mobility as 'necessary' is revealing and, as we have seen in other chapters in this book, bears little resemblance to public health indicators. The differential treatment in EU law of internal and external borders was already well-established in EU law and policy, for example, in response to the so-called 'migration crisis'.[67] It resonates with notions of 'citizenship' and 'nationhood', for instance, as at issue in the Canadian *Taylor* case.[68] While the focus of the EU was on 'opening' and 'lifting' border controls, when it came to borders external to the EU, these were to be lifted only 'in a second stage'.[69] The EU's COVID-19 border laws perpetuated the existing differential treatment of different types of human migration in EU law, rather than considering the inherent dignity of all migrant human beings present within the EU or seeking to come to the EU. Further, they embed global structural inequalities that flow from (post)colonial relations.[70] In this regard, we can consider the EU's response as deficient.

Overall, despite significant EU competence over internal borders and some over external borders, the EU COVID-19 border laws respected a very wide range of divergence between the Member States in how the risks associated with the pandemic were managed.[71] Despite the *narratives* of 'science-based' decision-making, in practice, both internal and external EU borders were closed for longer than necessary from a public health point of view, for reasons which can be understood as political. Advice from both the WHO and the EU's own ECDC[72] to the effect that undifferentiated border closures are overall ineffective[73] was not heeded by the Member States. The European Commission did nothing to challenge these national politically-based decisions. Roles for law and legal accountability were diminished, meaning that scrutiny of executive power deployed to control borders within and at the edges of the EU was also diminished. Effective public health governance should be subject to the rule of law: in this regard, the EU's COVID-19 border law and policy may be found lacking.

Notes

1 An EU citizen is a citizen of one or more EU Member States, see *Consolidated version of the Treaty on the Functioning of the European Union*, [2016] OJ, C 202 Art 20 [TFEU]. The EU does not have power to grant freestanding citizenship, see *EP v Préfet du Gers*, C-673/20, OJ 2021/C 98/06.

2 See Scott L Greer, ed, "The politics of communicable disease control in Europe," (2012) 37:6 *Journal of Health Politics, Policy and Law*.

3 See Iris Goldner Lang, "'Laws of fear" in the EU: The precautionary principle and public health restrictions to free movement of persons in the time of Covid-19,"

(2021) *The European Journal of Risk Regulation* 1; Gareth Davies, "Does evidence-based EU law survive the Covid-19 Pandemic? Considering the status in EU law of lockdown measures which affect free movement," (2020) 2 *Frontiers in Hum Dynamics*. www.frontiersin.org/articles/10.3389/fhumd.2020.584486/full.

4 *TFEU, supra* note 1 at arts *20,21* (free movement of EU citizens); *TFEU, supra* note 1 at art 45 (free movement of workers); *TFEU, supra* note 1 at art 49 (freedom of establishment); *TFEU, supra* note 1 at art 56 (freedom to provide and receive services); EC, *Charter of Fundamental Rights of the European Union,* [2000] OJ, 2000/C 364/01 at art 45 (freedom of movement and residence).

5 See Directive 2004/38/EC on the right of citizens of the Union and their family members to move and reside freely within the territory of the Member States, [2004] OJ L158/77 [Directive 2004/38/EC]; EC, Directive 2003/109/EC concerning the status of third-country nationals who are long-term residents, [2004] OJ L 16/44 [Directive 2003/109/EC].

6 There are literally thousands of these, both interpretations by national courts in the EU Member States and interpretations by the EU's Court of Justice.

7 *TFEU, supra* note 1 at art 4.

8 *Ibid* at arts 6, 168.

9 For details, see Tamara Hervey & Jean McHale, *European Union Health Law: Themes and Implications* (Cambridge: Cambridge University Press, 2015).

10 *TFEU, supra* note 1 at arts 21(1), 36, 52, 62,45(3); *Directive 2004/38/EC, supra* note 5 at arts 27, 29; *Directive 2003/109/EC, supra* note 5 at arts 6, 9(3), 17, 18.

11 *Regulation (EU) 2016/399 on a Union Code on the rules governing the movement of persons across borders (Schengen Borders Code)*, [2016] OJ, L77/1. (Currently, 22 of the 27 EU Member States, as well as Iceland, Norway, Switzerland and Lichtenstein are part of the Schengen Area. EU Member States that are not part of the Schengen Area are Bulgaria, Croatia, Cyprus, Ireland and Romania).

12 *Schengen Borders Code, supra* note 11 at arts 6(1)(d), 8(3)(vi), see also *Schengen Borders Code, ibid* at art 25(1) about internal borders, and arts 25, 28 and 29 on procedural safeguards and temporal limitations.

13 EC, European Commission COVID-19 Guidelines for border management measures to protect health and ensure the availability of goods and essential services [2020] OJ C 86 I/01 at para 18. Notably, the Schengen Borders Code itself does not expressly mention public health as a reason for the reintroduction of border controls.

14 *Schengen Borders* Code, *supra* note 11 at art 27.

15 *Ibid* at art 8 (3)(vi).

16 See, e.g., Council Implementing Decision (EU) 2017/818 setting out a recommendation for prolonging temporary internal border control in exceptional circumstances putting the overall functioning of the Schengen area at risk [2017] OJ L 122/73.

17 See also Vincent Delhomme & Tamara Hervey, "The European Union's response to the Covid-19 crisis and (the legitimacy of) the Union's legal order" (2022) 41 YB Eur L 48.

18 For an overview of the measures adopted, see Alberto Alemanno, "The European response to COVID-19: From regulatory emulation to regulatory coordination?" (2020) 11 *European Journal of Risk Regulation* 307; Carrera & Chun Luk, supra; Stefano Montaldo, "The COVID-19 emergency and the reintroduction of internal border controls in the schengen area: Never let a serious crisis go to waste" (2020) 5 European Papers 521.

19 EC, *European Centre for Disease Prevention and Control* "Considerations for travel-related measures to reduce spread of COVID-19 in the EU/EEA" (26 May 2020).

20 EC, *European Centre for Disease Prevention and Control* "Technical Report—Guidance for COVID-19 quarantine and testing of travellers" (2021).

21 EC, *European Centre for Disease Prevention and Control & European Union Aviation Safety Agency*, "COVID-19 Aviation Health Safety Protocol—Guidance for the management of airline passengers in relation to the COVID-19 pandemic" (2020); EC, *European Centre for Disease Prevention and Control & European Union Aviation Safety Agency* "Guidelines for COVID-19 testing and quarantine of air travellers—Addendum to the Aviation Health Safety Protocol" (2 December 2020).

22 EC, *European Centre for Disease Prevention and Control,* "Considerations for travel-related measures to reduce spread of COVID-19 in the EU/EEA," (26 May 2020); EC, *European Centre for Disease Prevention and Control* "COVID-19 Rail Protocol: Recommendations for safe resumption of railway services in Europe" (21 July 2020).

23 European Commission and European Council, *Joint European Roadmap towards lifting COVID-19 containment measures* [2020] OJ C 126/1 [Joint Roadmap].

24 EC, Council Recommendation (EU) 2020/1475 on a coordinated approach to the restriction of free movement in response to the COVID-19 pandemic [2020] OJ L337/3 at para 8. Recommendation 2020/1475 was later replaced by EC, Council Recommendation (EU) 2022/107 on a coordinated approach to facilitate safe free movement during the COVID-19 pandemic and replacing Recommendation (EU) 2020/1475 [2022] OJ L18/110. Both recommendations have also been applicable to the Schengen Area: see EC, Council Recommendation (EU) 2020/1632 of 30 October 2020 on a coordinated approach to the restriction of free movement in response to the COVID-19 pandemic in the Schengen Area [2020] OJ L366/25.

25 Joint Roadmap, *supra* note 23.

26 Archives of data and maps may be accessed at "Maps in support of the Council Recommendation on a coordinated approach to travel measures in the EU" (last modified 21 July 2022), *European Centre for Disease Prevention and Control.* www.ecdc.europa.eu/en/covid-19/situation-updates/weekly-maps-coordinated-restriction-free-movement.

27 EC, Council Recommendation (EU) 2021/119 amending Recommendation (EU) 2020/1475 on a coordinated approach to the restriction of free movement in response to the COVID-19 pandemic, [2021] OJ L 36I/1.

28 EC, Council Recommendation (EU) 2021/961 amending Recommendation (EU) 2020/1475 on a coordinated approach to the restriction of free movement in response to the COVID-19 pandemic, [2021] OJ L 213I/1.

29 For details on individual EU Member States' border controls, see the country entries in "Lex-Atlas: Covid-19," https://lexatlas-c19.org/.

30 EC, Covid-19 Guidelines for border management measures to protect health and ensure the availability of goods and essential services [2020] OJ C 861; EC, Communication from the Commission Guidelines concerning the exercise of the free movement of workers during COVID-19 outbreak [2020] OJ C/102I/12.

31 Sophie Robin-Olivier, "Free Movement of Workers in the Light of the COVID-19 Sanitary Crisis: From Restrictive Selection to Selective Mobility," (2020) 5 *European Papers* 613.

32 *Ibid* at 616–617. See EC, COVID-19 Guidelines for border management measures to protect health and ensure the availability of goods and essential services [2020] OJ C 861, para 23; EC, Communication from the Commission Guidelines concerning the exercise of the free movement of workers during COVID-19 outbreak [2020] OJ C/102I/12.

33 EC, Communication to the European Parliament, the European Council and the Council, COVID-19: Temporary Restriction on Non-Essential Travel to the EU in view of COVID-19 COM/2020/115; see also EC, Council Recommendation (EU) 2020/912 of 30 June 2020 on the temporary restriction on non-essential travel into the EU and the possible lifting of such restriction, [2020] OJ L208I/1 at annex II.

34 Joint Roadmap, *supra* note 23.
35 Daniel Thym & Jonas Bornemann, "Schengen and Free Movement Law During the First Phase of the Covid-19 Pandemic: Of Symbolism, Law and Politics" (2021) 2020 5 *Eur Papers* 1143 at 1168; for other critiques in this vein, see, e.g., European Parliament, *In the name of COVID: An Assessment of the Schengen Internal Border Controls and Travel Restrictions in the EU*, by Sergio Carrera and Ngo Chun Luk (Brussels: Study requested by the LIBE committee, 2020); Davies, *supra* note 3; Goldner Lang, *supra* note 3.
36 Cf *R v Henn and Darby*, C-34/79, [1979] ECR 1979–03795 (by analogy).
37 EC, Letter from Commissioners Johansson and Reynders Addressed to the EU Ministers for Home Affairs and Justice on Travel Restrictions in the Context of the Covid 19 Pandemic (17 February 2021) Brussels, Ares (2021) 1401977.
38 "EU commission urges six member states to remove some of their COVID-19 border restrictions," (24 February 2021) *Schengen Visa Info News*.
39 EC, "Communication from the Commission to the European Parliament, the European Council and the Council—A common path to safe and sustained re-opening COM" (2021) 129.
40 The certificate consists of two separate regulations, one for Union citizens and their families and one for third-country nationals who are legally staying or residing in the Union. See EC, *Regulation (EU) 2021/953 on a framework for the issuance, verification and acceptance of interoperable COVID-19 vaccination, test and recovery certificates (EU Digital COVID Certificate) to facilitate free movement during the COVID-19 pandemic*, [2021] OJ L211/1; EC, *Regulation (EU) 2021/954 on a framework for the issuance, verification and acceptance of interoperable COVID-19 vaccination, test and recovery certificates (EU Digital COVID Certificate) with regard to third-country nationals legally staying or residing in the territories of Member States during the COVID-19 pandemic*, [2021] OJ L211/24.
41 EC, *Regulation (EU) 2022/1034 amending Regulation (EU) 2021/953 on a framework for the issuance, verification and acceptance of interoperable COVID-19 vaccination, test and recovery certificates (EU Digital COVID Certificate) to facilitate free movement during the COVID-19 pandemic*, [2022] OJ L173/37; EC, *Regulation (EU) 2022/1035 amending Regulation (EU) 2021/954 on a framework for the issuance, verification and acceptance of interoperable COVID-19 vaccination, test and recovery certificates (EU Digital COVID Certificate) with regard to third-country nationals legally staying or residing in the territories of Member States during the COVID-19 pandemic*, [2022] OJ L173/46.
42 See also EC, Commission Implementing Decision (EU) 2021/1073 laying down technical specifications and rules for the implementation of the trust framework for the EU Digital COVID Certificate established by Regulation (EU) 2021/953, [2021] OJ L230/32.
43 *Ibid* (In this context, the e-Health network adopted guidelines on interoperability, and the Health Security Committee adopted a common dataset to be included in the COVID-19 test certificates: EC, "eHealth and COVID-19," https://health.ec.europa.eu/ehealth-digital-health-and-care/ehealth-and-covid-19_en).
44 See, e.g., Henry T. Greely, "COVID-19 immunity certificates: science, ethics, policy, and law," (2020) 7 *JL & Bioscience* lsaa035; Alberto Alemanno and Luiza Bialasiewicz, "Certifying health: The unequal legal geographies of COVID-19 certificates," (2021) 12 *The European Journal of Risk Regulation* 273; Sarah Ganty, "The veil of the COVID-19 vaccination certificates: Ignorance of poverty, injustice towards the poor," (2021) 12 *European Journal of Risk Regulation* 343; Mark A. Hall and David M. Studdert, "'Vaccine passport' certification—Policy and ethical considerations," (2021) 385 *The New England Journal of Medicine* e32; Iris Goldner Lang, "EU COVID-19 certificates: A critical analysis," (2021) 12 *European Journal of Risk Regulation* 298.

45 *Lagardère, unité médico-sociale v Commission*, T-503/21, [2022] ECLI:EU:T:2022:78; *Abenante and Others v Parliament and Council*, T-527/21.
46 See Michael Veale, in this volume.
47 EC, Communication to the European Parliament, the European Council and the Council, COVID-19: Temporary Restriction on Non-Essential Travel to the EU in view of COVID-19, COM(2020)115. (The Commission gave further guidance on the implementation of the travel restrictions: see EC, Communication from the Commission COVID-19 Guidance on the implementation of the temporary restriction on non-essential travel to the EU, on the facilitation of transit arrangements for the repatriation of EU citizens, and on the effects on visa policy, [2020] OJ C102I/3).
48 European Council, News Release, "Conclusions by the president of the European council following the video conference with members of the European Council on COVID-19," (17 March 2020).
49 The 30-day limitation placed on travel into the EU via EC, Communication from the Commission: COVID-19: Temporary Restriction on Non-Essential Travel to the EU, COM(2020)115 was prolonged by further EC, Commission Communications on a Temporary restriction on Non-Essential Travel to the EU in view of COVID-19, COM(2020)148; EC, Communication on the second assessment of the application of the temporary restriction on non-essential travel to the EU, COM(2020)222; EC, Communication on the third assessment of the application of the temporary restriction on non-essential travel to the EU, COM (2020)399.
50 EC, Council Recommendation (EU) 2020/912 on the temporary restriction on non-essential travel into the EU and the possible lifting of such restriction, [2020] OJ L 208I/1.
51 EC, Communication from the Commission, Guidelines concerning the exercise of the free movement of workers during COVID-19 outbreak, [2020] OJ C 102I/12.
52 EC, Council Recommendation (EU) 2021/816 amending Recommendation (EU) 2020/912 on the temporary restriction on non-essential travel into the EU and the possible lifting of such restriction, [2021] OJ, L 182/1.
53 This list echoes the message of Chidi Oguamanam, in this volume, about the colonial patterns of othering Africa in border control and also the relative lack of access to COVID-19 vaccines in countries in Africa.
54 Thym & Bornemann, *supra* note 35; Sarah Wolff, Ariadna Ripoll Servent and Agathe Piquet, "Framing immobility: Schengen governance in times of pandemics" (2020) 42 *Journal of European Integration* 1127.
55 Stefan Salomon and Jorrit Rijpma, "A Europe without internal frontiers: Challenging the reintroduction of border controls in the Schengen area in the light of Union citizenship," (2021) *German Law Journal* 1.
56 *Regulation (EC) No 851/2004 establishing a European Centre for disease prevention and control*, [2004] OJ L 142 at art 3; See Tamara Hervey, "The role of the European court of justice in the Europeanization of communicable disease control: Driver or irrelevance?" (2012) 37 *Journal of Health Politics, Policy and Law* 975.
57 EC, *EU Scientific Advice platform on COVID-19*. https://health.ec.europa.eu/health-security-and-infectious-diseases/preparedness-and-response/eu-scientific-advice-platform-covid-19_en.
58 See Brenda Wilson, in this volume (Canada), and Stephen Duckett, in this volume (Australia).
59 See, e.g., Lisa Forman, in this volume; David Fisman, in this volume; Raywat Deonandan, in this volume; see also Julia Belluz, "Vietnam defied the experts and sealed its border to keep Covid-19 out. It worked," (23 April 2021), *Vox*. www.vox.com/22346085/covid-19-vietnam-response-travel-restrictions.

60 Giandomenico Majone, "The regulatory state and its legitimacy problems," (1999) 22 *West European Politics* 1.
61 See, e.g., EC, European Centre for Disease Prevention and Control, *Introducing a Coherent European Framework for Tuning COVID-19 Response Measures* (17 March 2021).
62 Maria Weimer and Anniek de Ruijter, "Regulating risks in the European Union : The co-production of expert and executive power," in Maria Weimer and Anniek De Ruijter, eds, *Regulating Risks in the European Union : The Co-Production of Expert and Executive Power* (Hart Publishing, 2017) at 3; see also Damian Chalmers, "Food for thought: Reconciling European risks and traditional ways of life," (2003) 66:4 *The Modern Law Review* 532; Damian Chalmers, "Risk, Anxiety and the European mediation of the politics of life," (2005) 30:5 *The European Law Review* 649.
63 Delhomme & Hervey, *supra* note 17; Vivien A. Schmidt, "Theorizing institutional change and governance in European responses to the Covid-19 pandemic," (2020) 42 *Journal of European Integration* 1177; Sarah Wolff and Stella Ladi, "European Union responses to the Covid-19 pandemic: Adaptability in times of permanent emergency," (2020) 42 *Journal of European Integration* 1025.
64 Sheila Jasanoff, *Designs on Nature: Science and Democracy in Europe and the United States* (Princeton University Press, 2007); Maria Weimer, *Risk Regulation in the Internal Market: Lessons from Agricultural Biotechnology* (Oxford University Press, 2019); Ellen Vos and Michelle Everson, eds, *Uncertain Risks Regulated* (Routledge-Cavendish, 2009); Marjolein BA van Asselt and Ellen Vos, "The precautionary principle and the uncertainty paradox," (2006) 9 *Journal of Risk Research* 313; Ellen Vos, "EU food safety regulation in the aftermath of the BSE crisis," (2000) 23 *Journal of Consumer Policy* 227; regarding the Court of Justice's case law on free movement provisions, see Gareth Davies, "Internal market adjudication and the quality of life in Europe," (2015) 21 *The Columbia Journal of European Law* 289–298.
65 See Sam Halabi, in this volume, and Adam Houston, in this volume.
66 EC, Letter from Commissioners Johansson and Reynders Addressed to the EU Ministers for Home Affairs and Justice on Travel Restrictions in the Context of the Covid 19 Pandemic, Ares (2021) 1401977.
67 Thym & Bornemann, *supra* note 35 at 1555–1557.
68 *Taylor v Newfoundland and Labrador*, 2020 NLSC 125, discussed in Brenda Wilson, in this volume.
69 European Commission and European Council, Joint European Roadmap towards lifting COVID-19 containment measures, [2020] OJ C 126/1.
70 See Chidi Oguamanam, in this volume.
71 Davies, *supra* note 3; Peter Van Elsuwege, "Lifting travel restrictions in the Era of COVID-19: In search of a European approach," (2 June 2020), online (blog): *Verfassungsblog*. https://verfassungsblog.de/lifting-travel-restrictions-in-the-era-of-covid-19-in-search-of-a-european-approach; Alessio M Pacces & Maria Weimer, "From diversity to coordination: A European approach to COVID-19," (2020) 11 *The European Journal of Risk Regulation* 283.
72 EC, Communication to the European Parliament, the European Council and the Council, "COVID-19: Temporary Restriction on Non-Essential Travel to the EU in view of COVID-19" COM (2020)115.
73 WHO, News Release, "Policy and technical considerations for implementing a risk-based approach to international travel in the context of COVID-19" (2 July 2021); EC, *European Centre for Disease Prevention and Control*, "Considerations for travel-related measures to reduce spread of COVID-19 in the EU/EEA," (26 May 2020).

7

PUBLIC HEALTH EVIDENCE FOR PROVINCIAL BORDER MANAGEMENT

Brenda J. Wilson

7.1 Background

Newfoundland and Labrador (NL) is one of Canada's ten provinces, with nearly 526,000 residents[1] and a land mass exceeding 405,000 square kilometres. 40% of the population lives in the St. John's metropolitan area; the rest—including distinct Indigenous groups—reside in small communities, many very remote.

7.1.1 Public Health Legislation

In 2019, NL's Legislative Assembly passed the *Public Health Protection and Promotion Act (PHPPA)*,[2] with the purpose of promoting and protecting the health of the population and promoting health equity. In introducing the legislation,[3] the health minister's comments appeared prescient:

> during the commemoration and honouring of those who served in the First World War, what gets forgotten is in the immediate aftermath of all those soldiers coming home, the Spanish Flu of 1918 and '19 infected half a billion people worldwide: 500 million people. At the time, the population of the planet was maybe a fifth of what it is today. It had an appalling effect on our population, and it wiped out Indigenous communities in Okak and Hebron, up in the Big Land [a commonly used provincial nickname for Labrador].[4]
>
> We are living in a world with SARS and Ebola and you are one plane flight away from a significant health problem and we need legislation that can adapt and deal with that.

DOI: 10.4324/9781003394006-10

Section 28(1) of the *PHPPA* specifies the special measures available to the province's Chief Medical Officer of Health (CMOH) in the situation of a declared public health emergency.[5]

7.1.2 The Pandemic in NL

The first presumptive case of COVID-19 in NL was recorded on 14 March 2020.[6] The minister of health declared a public health emergency on March 18, and the CMOH, Dr. Janice Fitzgerald, issued a number of special orders, closing many businesses and facilities, limiting gathering size, prohibiting visitation to personal care homes, and requiring people entering the province to self-isolate for 14 days.

On March 16, a cluster of cases was linked to a funeral home in St. John's, the so-called "Caul's outbreak".[7] This generated 178 cases, all of which could be ultimately tracked back to incoming travelers. Five people were admitted to ICU and two died.

As concerns grew, amended special measures were implemented on May 4,[8] restricting entry to the province to NL residents, certain groups of (asymptomatic) workers, and those in a number of defined exemption categories, with additional exemptions added May 5[9] (box). The province effectively entered near total isolation from the rest of Canada and the world. As of July 2020, almost no COVID-19 cases came from an unknown source, indicating highly effective case identification and control of virus spread.[10]

7.2 The Challenge

Kimberley Taylor lived in Nova Scotia but was born and raised in NL. On 5 May 2020, her mother passed away unexpectedly in her NL home. Ms. Taylor was denied an exemption to enter NL on May 8; the decision reversed a few days later on appeal. She challenged section 28(1)(h) of the *PHPPA*, which provides that the CMOH may "make orders restricting travel to or from the province or an areas within the province",[11] as being outside the province's jurisdiction and the decision to refuse her entry as contrary to her sections 6 and 7 *Charter* rights to mobility and liberty. She did not challenge the CMOH's authority or procedural or fairness aspects of the decision. The Canadian Civil Liberties Association (CCLA) joined her in the challenge. The case was heard in the period before vaccines became widely available.

7.3 The Decision

Arguments were heard by Justice Donald Burrage, who considered four questions:[12,13]

1 Were the special measures a valid law?
2 Did they violate the *Charter* right to mobility (section 6)?

3 Did they violate the *Charter* right to liberty (section 7)?
4 If the *Charter* mobility right was violated, was it justifiable under section 1?

7.3.1 The Validity of the Special Measures

Justice Burrage ruled that the special measures were valid and that Ms. Taylor's *Charter* right to mobility was violated but not her right to liberty. He ruled that the infringement of her *Charter* rights was justified under s. 1 of the *Charter*, in response to the COVID-19 pandemic.

In his determination, Justice Burrage distinguished the *purpose* of the legislation (to protect the health of NL residents—the desired effect) from the *means* to achieve this (denying entry to a non-resident). He concluded that neither federal powers over interprovincial works and undertakings[14] nor federal emergency powers to make laws for the peace, order, and good government of Canada[15] applied in this case and that section 28(1)(h) of the *PHPPA*, as a public health measure, fell under the province's authority over matters of a local or private nature[16] or over property and civil rights.[17]

7.3.2 Rights to Mobility and Liberty (Sections 6, 7)

Noting that no previous decision had addressed the simple right to mobility (right simpliciter)—not linked to earning a living or taking up residence[18]—Justice Burrage indicated that no precedent "squarely addresses" this and that "Mobility Rights has a common meaning until one attempts to seek its outer limits".[19] In his reasoning, he considered the purpose and nature of mobility rights, precedent, and consistency with international obligations. He articulated three distinct mobility rights: to enter Canada, to remain in Canada, and to leave Canada,[20] framing these as "positive" rights, i.e., "rights of action"—to choose, to travel for livelihood or residence, to come and go as one pleases.[21]

He reasoned that the right extends to all of Canada, and exercising it means being able to traverse provincial and territorial boundaries.[22] Provinces could not render this right "practically ineffective" by closing their borders, drawing a domestic analogy:

> we would regard the right to come and go from one's home, and to remain in it, as surely including the right to wander from room to room.[23]

Absent case law, Justice Burrage noted that a pre-*Charter* commentary by Justice Rand found favour with the Supreme Court of Canada[24] in its discussion of mobility rights:

> Canada is a unified federation, not a series of republics. We are one people with one common country. The right to traverse Canada thus gives Canadian citizenship its true meaning and prevents artificial barriers from being

erected between the provinces. . . . In this manner the country may not be "converted into a number of enclaves and the 'union' which the original provinces sought and obtained disrupted."[25]

He essentially stated that personal mobility is fundamental to nationhood and one of the "most cherished rights of citizenship".[26]

Finally, reiterating the presumption that the *Charter* should provide at least as much protection as any international human rights treaties ratified by Canada, he referred to Article 12 of the International Covenant on Civil and Political Rights (ICCPR)[27] and Article 13 of the Universal Declaration of Human Rights.[28] His final interpretation was framed as a "purposive and generous approach to mobility",[29] concluding that the right to travel includes the right to cross provincial boundaries, not limited to residence or livelihood—a right simpliciter.[30]

Justice Burrage noted that including mobility rights under s. 7 would create parallel rights with different tests and standards, risking incoherence in the *Charter*.[31] But ultimately, considering all the circumstances, he ruled that Ms. Taylor's "decision [to attend her mother's funeral] did not rise to the level of a 'fundamental personal choice', as defined in case law, so as to attract constitutional protection".[32]

7.3.3 Section 1 Analysis: Intersection with Public Health Perspectives

"[If] government . . . is going to tell a citizen . . . that she cannot travel to Newfoundland and Labrador, it had better have a very good reason".[33] Justice Burrage applied the *Oakes* test,[34] analyzing the effects (or potential effects) of the pandemic on the health of the NL population and comparing the means (travel restrictions) to prevent or mitigate these effects against those less drastic. He concluded that the circumstances of the pandemic meant that the goal of section 28(1)(h) met the requirements for being both "pressing and substantial". In his proportionality analysis, he considered two lines of quantitative evidence: epidemiological data on COVID-19 impact and severity and predictive modelling estimates of the likely effect of the travel restriction. He also considered how far the Court should defer to the CMOH's expertise in making critical decisions during a pandemic emergency.

7.3.3.1 Epidemiological Evidence

The epidemiological evidence addressed the seriousness of *SARS CoV-2* virus infection and the particular vulnerability of the NL population to serious outcomes. Data were drawn from Canadian reports, indicating a high mortality rate (proportion of total population dying from COVID-19) and high case fatality rate (death rate in people known to be infected with COVID-19).[35]

Additional data on severity were based on reports from China, the United Kingdom, and the United States;[36] taken together, these described a disease roughly "ten times more lethal than influenza".[37] Data from China, the United States, and Ontario indicated higher risks of death or serious illness in people who were older, obese, or with pre-existing chronic health conditions like heart or lung disease or diabetes.[38] Data from Statistics Canada and the Canadian Institute for Health Information suggested that NL would fare worse than the rest of Canada because the population was older and had a higher prevalence of these risk factors.[39] After the early "Caul's cluster" episode,[40] public health efforts had apparently been extremely effective in controlling viral transmission through testing, contact tracing, isolation, and physical distancing interventions: healthcare capacity had not been exceeded. The applicants argued the province "had already been successful at flattening the curve"[41] and the travel restrictions were unnecessary. Rejecting this, Justice Burrage accepted the epidemiological analysis that these efforts meant the population had extremely low immunity; therefore, *preventing* new chains of transmission before they started was critical. Of central importance was the significant pre-existing strain on NL's health system capacity, with average pre-pandemic ICU occupancy rates of 50–60%.[42] How much would it take for COVID-19 cases to overwhelm critical care capacity, especially if exacerbated by non-residents and tourists falling ill?

7.3.3.2 Predictive Modelling

To what extent was the low viral transmission in NL due to the travel restrictions and not the assiduous application of the other public health interventions? The situation was not conducive to experimentation, and it is impossible to prove a counterfactual. Justice Burrage placed considerable weight on the modelling carried out by the province's Predictive Analytics Technical Team. Citing Justice Bastarache, Justice Burrage stated that "in the absence of determinative evidence, the Court is entitled to rely on logic, reason and the application of common sense to what is known."[43]

The province's team used two very different predictive modelling methodologies,[44] allowing them to examine the robustness of their findings. "What would have happened" was *estimated* by the number of cases (predicted by modelling) that would have been *expected* without the travel restrictions. The models embedded varying assumptions about volume of inward travel, proportion of incomers infected, compliance of incomers with self-isolation rules, number of exemptions granted, and so forth. The two sets of results largely agreed with each other: over a nine-week time frame, the case count would have been five to 20 times higher, depending on the model and the assumptions.[45] Reducing entry by 90% would still equate to around 1,000 arrivals weekly—so three infected people failing to self-isolate in a single week is a conservative assumption. These were not empirical observations, they were predictions, but Justice Burrage considered the modelling results to be "convincing evidence".[46]

7.3.3.3 *Deference to Public Health Expertise*

In considering whether the travel restrictions were the least drastic means available, Justice Burrage reflected on the extent to which the CMOH should be afforded flexibility in developing measures against COVID-19, quoting Justice LaForest:[47]

> Given that the objective is of pressing and substantial concern, the Legislature must be allowed adequate scope to achieve that objective. It must be remembered that the business of government is a practical one. The Constitution must be applied on a realistic basis having regard to the nature of the particular area sought to be regulated and not on an abstract theoretical plane.

He equated the travel restrictions to "a medical decision directed towards protecting the health of those in this province",[48] concluding that the CMOH had the qualifications to make such a decision while the courts did not. He noted that while the travel restrictions had not been debated or approved by the legislative assembly, the latter had bestowed the powers on the CMOH in the first place and that it was the minister of health's declaration of the public health emergency that had activated the conditions for their exercise.

Justice Burrage did, however, agree that "the pandemic is not a magic wand which can be waved to make constitutional rights disappear" and that "the decision of the CMOH is not immunized from review".[49] He explored and dismissed other measures, e.g., tailoring restrictions more closely to incoming travelers likely to be at higher risk or relying on (or trying to enforce) self-isolation requirements. In doing this, he reflected on the situation as it existed in April 2020, noting the importance of the precautionary principle in public health decision-making: the margin for error is small when handling a severe and ever-evolving emergency.[50] He also accepted that public health interventions were often multifaceted and had to be so, especially when handling a complex emergency.

7.4 Discussion and Conclusions

This may be the first case to test the simple right to mobility under Canada's *Charter of Rights and Freedoms*. The analysis extended to the historical aspirations of confederation, considering how the right to mobility "defines the relationship of citizens to their country",[51] so is fundamentally linked with nationhood. But it also spoke to Canada's international human rights obligations and "concern for the dignity of the individual".[52]

The Court's decision rested on accepting extrapolations of epidemiological observations from other settings and estimates from mathematical models, assembled at a time when data and experience were inevitably limited. Saltelli and colleagues raise concerns that the results of mathematical modelling are inherently uncertain; while "a great way to explore questions", they are "a dangerous way to assert answers."[53] It is not within this chapter's scope (nor its intention) to examine the validity of the modelling results or their interpretation by the Court; inescapably, the models were the only available substitute for actual measurements of the travel restrictions' effects in this situation. The *Taylor* case has provided insight into the challenge of navigating a path between protecting collective interests and individual rights when the evidence is technical, complex, and necessarily incomplete.

The Court also explicitly considered the actions taken by the CMOH as equivalent to medical treatment of individual patients. The professional competencies required for medical practice in the discipline of public health are encompassed in the general CanMEDS framework.[54] The specific objectives of training in the specialty of Public Health and Preventive Medicine emphasize not only sufficient expertise to interpret relevant scientific data but also skills for "diagnosis and intervention" at the population level.[55] Public health physicians are also expected to "responsibly use their expertise and influence to advance the health and well-being of individuals, families, groups, organizations, communities, and populations" and "use judgement in balancing efforts to achieve health for all."[56] In many jurisdictions, clarity is lacking about the power and authority of the CMOH role.[57] Although the "population-as-patient" concept is common in public health—and inherent in the CanMEDs competencies—there is an inevitable tension between these expectations of a medical professional and the practical ability to exercise them if a physician is in a public servant role.

BOX EXTRACT FROM SPECIAL MEASURES ORDER (AMENDMENT NO. 11)[58] AND EXEMPTION CATEGORIES[59]

1 For the purpose of this order, "resident" means an individual who is the following:

  a is lawfully entitled to be or to remain in Canada;
  b makes his or her home in the province; and
  c is ordinarily present in the province but does not include a tourist, transient, or visitor to the province.

2 All individuals are prohibited from entering Newfoundland and Labrador, except for the following:

- a residents of Newfoundland and Labrador;
- b asymptomatic workers and individuals who are subject to the Updated Exemption Order effective April 22, 2020; and
- c individuals who have been permitted entry to the province in extenuating circumstances, as approved in advance by the Chief Medical Officer of Health.

[Exemption categories added.]

1 Individuals who enter the province:

- a who have a significant injury, condition, or illness and require the support of family members resident in Newfoundland and Labrador;
- b who are visiting a family member in Newfoundland and Labrador who is critically or terminally ill;
- c to provide care for a family member who is elderly or has a disability;
- d to permanently relocate to the province;
- e who are recently unemployed and who will be living with family members;
- f to fulfil a short-term contract, education internship, or placement;
- g who are returning to the province after completion of a school term out of province; and
- h to comply with a custody, access, or adoption order or agreement. (This includes a child/children arriving in the province, as well as individuals who are accompanying the child/children.)

are exempted from the prohibition of entering Newfoundland and Labrador, provided they make a formal request to the Chief Medical Officer of Health in accordance with the direction provided at *gov.nol.ca/covid-19* and provided they comply with all other Special Measures and Exemption Orders.

Notes

1 "Newfoundland and Labrador Statistics Agency (NLSA)" (July 2022), online: *Government of Newfoundland and Labrador*. www.stats.gov.nl.ca/.
2 Public Health Protection and Promotion Act, SNL 2018, c P-37.3 [PHPPA].
3 Newfoundland, House of Assembly, *Proceedings*, vol XLVII No 44 (20 November 2018) at p 2620.
4 *Ibid*.
5 *PHPPA, supra* note 2, s 28(1)(h).
6 *Taylor v Newfoundland and Labrador*, 2020 NLSC 125 (Affidavit, Janice Fitzgerald at para 19) [*Taylor*].
7 *Ibid* at paras 63–67.

8 *PHPPA*, Special Measures Order (Amendment No. 11) SNL 2020 [*PHPPA* Amendment].
9 *PHPPA*, Special Measures Order (Travel Exemption Order) SNL 2020 [*PHPPA* Order].
10 *Taylor, supra* note 6 at para 62.
11 PHPPA, *supra* note 2.
12 *Taylor, supra* note 6 at para 8.
13 Other questions considered relating to Canadian Civil Liberties Association standing and temporary suspension of declaration of invalidity in the case of a violation of *Charter* rights not saved by section 1 are not considered here.
14 *Constitution Act, 1867* (UK), 30 & 31 Vict, c 3, s 92(10), reprinted in RSC 1985, Appendix II, No 5.
15 *Ibid*, s 91.
16 *Ibid*, s 92(16).
17 *Ibid*, s 92(1).
18 *Taylor*, *supra* note 6 at para 303.
19 Skapinker v Law Society of Upper Canada, [1984] 1 SCR at 13.
20 *Taylor*, *supra* note 6 at para 343.
21 *Ibid* at para 345.
22 *Ibid* at para 348.
23 *Ibid* at para 353.
24 *Ontario (Attorney General) v Winner* 1951 Carswell NB 31, [1951] SCR 887 at paras 118–119.
25 *Taylor*, *supra* note 6 at para 356.
26 *Ibid* at para 357.
27 *International Covenant on Civil and Political Rights,* 19 December 1966, 999 UNTS 171 art 12 (entered into force 23 March 1976, accession by Canada 19 May 1976).
28 *Universal Declaration of Human Rights*, GA Res 217A (III), UNGAOR, 3rd Sess, Supp No 13, UN Doc A/810 (1948) 71.
29 *Taylor*, *supra* note 6 at para 364.
30 *Ibid* at para 365.
31 *Ibid* at para 380.
32 *Ibid* at para 384.
33 *Ibid* at para 397.
34 *R v Oakes*, [1986] 1 SCR 103, 1986 CanLII 46.
35 *Taylor*, *supra* note 6 (Affidavit, Janice Fitzgerald) at para 48.
36 *Ibid* at tabs 7–11.
37 *Taylor*, *supra* note 6 (Affidavit, Brenda Wilson) at tab 2.
38 *Taylor*, *supra* note 6 (Affidavit, Janice Fitzgerald) at tabs 12–15.
39 *Taylor*, *supra* note 6 (Affidavit, Patrick Parfrey) at tab 3.
40 *Taylor*, *supra* note 6 (Affidavit, Janice Fitzgerald) at paras 63–67.
41 *Taylor*, *supra* note 6 at para 125.
42 *Taylor*, *supra* note 6 (Affidavit, Janice Fitzgerald) at para 43.
43 *Harper v Canada (Attorney General)*, 2004 SCC 33 at para 78.
44 *Taylor*, *supra* note 6 (Affidavit, Proton Rahman) at tab 2.
45 *Taylor*, *supra* note 6 at paras 443–449.
46 *Ibid* at para 441.
47 *R v Videoflicks Ltd* et al [1986] 71 NR 161 at para 214.
48 *Taylor*, *supra* note 6 at para 457.
49 *Ibid* at para 463.
50 Quebec, National Collaborating Centre for Healthy Public Policy/Institut national de santé publique du Québec, *Public policies guided by the precautionary principle*, by Valérie Beloin (Montreal: National Collaborating Centre for Healthy

Public Policy/Institut national de santé publique du Québec, 2009), online: www.ncchpp.ca/docs/VBeloinAnC_MEP.pdf.

51 *Black v Law Society (Alberta)*, [1989] 1 SCR 591.

52 *Taylor*, *supra* note 6 at para 358.

53 Andrea Saltellie et al, "Five ways to ensure that models serve society: a manifesto" (2020) 582 Nature at 482.

54 Royal College of Physicians and Surgeons of Canada, *CanMEDS 2015 Physician Competency Framework*, Ottawa: Royal College of Physicians and Surgeons of Canada, 2015.

55 Royal College of Physicians and Surgeons of Canada. *Objectives of Training in the Specialty of Public Health and Preventive Medicine.* 2014, Editorial Revision—March 2018, version 1.1.

56 *Ibid.*

57 Patrick Fafard et al, "Contested roles of Canada's Chief Medical Officers of Health" (2018) 109 Can J Pub Health 585.

58 *PHPPA* Amendment, *supra* note 8.

59 *PHPPA* Order, *supra* note 9.

8

FIRST NATIONS JURISDICTION, COVID-19, AND THE IMPLICATIONS OF SPATIAL RESTRICTIONS IN A SETTLER COLONIAL CONTEXT

Sophie Thériault, Eva Ottawa, and Florence Robert

8.1 Introduction

Throughout the COVID-19 pandemic, First Nations communities[1] in Canada have asserted their authority to protect their members from the disease, for example by restricting mobility to and from their lands, refusing entry to all visitors and non-residents (except for essential workers), and implementing travel bans, curfews, and quarantine protocols.[2] These community-led actions were effective in decreasing the transmission of the virus within First Nations communities.[3]

However, the capacity of First Nations communities to develop and enforce efficient COVID-19 measures adapted to their specific needs and circumstances has been hindered by institutional and material constraints directly resulting from the legacies of settler colonialism. In particular, the historical and ongoing dispossession of First Nations' lands and sovereignty has impeded their ability to implement and enforce their COVID-19 protocols, especially where their protective measures were contested either by their own members or by outsiders.[4] Moreover, in the context of the systemic discrimination experienced by First Nations in accessing essential services and goods on reserve, mobility restriction measures to contain the spread of the virus adopted by First Nations communities, as well as by the federal and provincial governments, have exacerbated pre-existing structural inequalities and amplified harms experienced by community members, such as gender-based violence, mental illness and addiction.[5]

This chapter reflects on the unique implications for First Nation people of the spatial restriction measures adopted by First Nations, provincial, and federal authorities in response to the COVID-19 pandemic. It also assesses

DOI: 10.4324/9781003394006-11

how to protect vulnerable community members against the virus, while mitigating the cultural, emotional, and economic impacts of barriers to mobility. We argue that the recognition of Indigenous peoples' inherent jurisdiction to protect their communities, lands, and territories according to their own laws, along with the immediate implementation of the measures needed to address longstanding social inequalities in First Nations' access to services and infrastructures on reserves, are both necessary parts of the equation. Beyond enabling First Nations to adequately respond to current and future pandemics, such transformative changes are imperative for Canada to honour its commitment to implement the *United Nations Declaration on the Rights of Indigenous peoples* (*UNDRIP*).[6]

8.1.1 Keeping the Virus at Bay: First Nations Jurisdiction and Mobility Restriction Measures

First Nations communities across the country adopted various measures tailored to their unique needs and circumstances to contain the spread of COVID-19. These measures largely mirrored those implemented by the federal and provincial governments, though often in stricter forms. For instance, many First Nations declared a state of emergency and adopted stringent COVID-19 protocols and by-laws, including lockdowns, quarantine, curfews, and travel restrictions in and out of the reserve.[7] Like other infranational jurisdictions,[8] several First Nations erected checkpoints to control access to their communities by non-residents, including shoppers, tourists, recreational hunters, and cottage owners, among others.[9] Many First Nations communities adopted such measures through the *Indian Act*, which empowers Band Councils to enact by-laws "to provide for the health of residents on the reserve and to prevent the spreading of contagious and infectious diseases"[10] or via treaty or land claims agreement provisions. First Nations also anchored their responses in their inherent jurisdiction and legal orders, often in conjunction with Section 35 of the *Constitution Act, 1982*,[11] and their right to self-determination recognized by the *UNDRIP*.[12]

Indigenous-led responses to the pandemic are critical to preserving ancestral cultures, knowledge, and practices,[13] whereas the imposition of measures by governments that do not recognize the specific role and jurisdiction of Indigenous peoples can undermine these practices and knowledge.[14] Respecting the autonomy of First Nations to manage the pandemic locally is essential to adequately protect the health of First Nations in a culturally acceptable manner. As the United Nations Special Rapporteur on the Rights of Indigenous Peoples stated, "Indigenous peoples enjoying their collective right to autonomy as part of their right to self-determination are best placed to control the virus and to cope with months of isolation".[15] This observation is echoed by authors who have argued that "First Nations, as the most proximate government, are best positioned to make policy and law in response to COVID-19 and that they should be supported financially in that endeavour by the federal government".[16] However, First Nations' responses to the COVID-19 pandemic, especially measures aiming to control access to their territory, have been hampered and undermined by government actions and inaction.[17]

Keeping with usual colonial practices, federal and provincial pandemic measures were applied to First Nations communities often without meaningful consultation or consent. The dynamics resulting from the provincial and federal governments' lack of communication and coordination with First Nations became particularly visible when state authorities unilaterally decided to reopen the economy without taking into account the needs of First Nations communities and the COVID-19 measures they already had in place. For example, in British Columbia, while First Nations were erecting checkpoints to prevent outsiders—and the virus—from entering their communities, the provincial government declared fishing and hunting "essential services", thus opening the door to travel within First Nations' traditional territories without any prior consultation and coordination with potentially impacted communities.[18] Similarly, governments have deemed mining an essential activity, allowing large-scale mining operations to continue thereby increasing the risk of COVID-19 spreading to First Nations communities living near mining sites.[19] For its part, following the reopening of Quebec's economy in the aftermath of the pandemic's first wave, the Mohawk community of Kanesatake saw its efforts to keep visitors at bay through checkpoints thwarted by complaints from the neighbouring town's officials. The mayor of Oka served the Mohawk Council and the provincial police force with legal notices alleging the checkpoints were "illegal" and urging them to be dismantled immediately, invoking the impact on the town's economy as justification.[20] As these examples show, "First Nations communities will continue to face challenges from those who do not respect their inherent jurisdiction, particularly if their pandemic and recovery plans are not coordinated across jurisdictions".[21]

The effectiveness of the mobility restriction measures adopted by First Nations in response to the COVID-19 pandemic—including checkpoints, lockdowns, quarantine protocols, and curfews—was also constrained by insufficient or otherwise defective institutional and material support from federal and provincial authorities.[22] For instance, while the federal government provided significant financial support for First Nations' pandemic response, First Nations communities reported that the funding opportunities did not adequately meet their needs.[23] Rather, the support often came with a heavy administrative burden, especially for small communities with limited capacity (what some researchers have aptly termed "colonialism by paper cuts").[24] Furthermore, state authorities failed to meaningfully support the implementation of First Nations jurisdiction and, in some cases, to recognize their authority altogether.[25] Due to the lack of enforcement capacity within communities,[26] many First Nations sought to collaborate with provincial and federal partners during the COVID-19 pandemic with respect to law enforcement.[27] However, First Nations were often ignored by state authorities or refused assistance and were instead instructed that the enforcement of First Nations by-law on reserve is the primary responsibility of Band Councils (while these same authorities readily enforced federal and provincial COVID-19 measures against First Nations people).[28] Some First Nations checkpoints even encountered strong opposition from state law enforcement, particularly when located on public roads.[29]

Finally, First Nations decried the insufficient and fragmented COVID-19 information and data sharing practices, which impeded the ability of First Nations communities to adequately respond to the pandemic. As observed in a study conducted with the Tsilhqot'in Nation in British Columbia, while the Tsilhqot'in Nation "exercised its jurisdiction over public health and safety by implementing [. . .] pandemic response measures", they did so "in the absence of specific data about positive cases and potential exposures within and near Tsilhqot'in communities".[30] Similar issues were experienced by First Nations communities across the country.[31] In the words of then Regional Chief Marlene Poitras, "[t]oo often [F]irst [N]ations were the last to receive information and were left out of the decision-making process at the federal, provincial and territorial tables".[32] The reluctance of governmental authorities to share COVID-19 data with First Nations authorities "*as governments*"[33] undermined their ability to plan for appropriate and timely pandemic measures adapted to the changing levels of infection within and outside their communities.

In sum, instead of providing First Nations communities with the tools and resources to support the implementation and enforcement of their inherent jurisdiction and right to self-determination over the pandemic response, the federal and provincial governments unilaterally imposed their own pandemic management approaches on these communities and their citizens without considering their unique needs and realities. As discussed in the next section, these measures disproportionately impacted First Nations, whose mobility is already considerably constrained by various settler colonial policies and practices.

8.1.2 Colonialism, Systemic Discrimination, and the Unique Implications of Mobility Restriction Measures for First Nations

Although recognized as effective tools to control the circulation of the virus, mobility restriction measures have unique implications for First Nations, who are already facing a health crisis resulting from historical and ongoing colonial and discriminatory laws, policies, and practices.[34] These pre-existing conditions exacerbated First Nations' vulnerability to both the virus and the containment measures implemented either by federal, provincial, or First Nations authorities.[35]

The severity of these impacts varied according to the geographical location and colonial trajectories of the different Nations and communities. For example, the Cree Nation of Eeyou Istchee, which is party to a land claims agreement (the 1975 *James Bay and Northern Quebec Agreement*[36]) and the 2002 *Paix des Braves*[37], could rely on extensive local services and infrastructure—including hospital services in their territory—during the "travel ban" orders enacted by their government.[38] By contrast, First Nations living on reserve lands where basic services and infrastructures are lacking were heavily impacted by the virus and related containment measures.[39]

In particular, pre-existing issues with housing shortages exacerbated the inequities experienced by First Nations. The imposition of containment measures such as mandatory quarantine, lockdowns, and curfews disproportionately impacted First Nations' citizens living in overcrowded, often multi-generational households, which made maintaining physical distancing nearly impossible.[40] Deficient infrastructure on reserve inhibited many communities from providing adequate self-isolation facilities to prevent the transmission of the virus within households.[41] Consequently, some communities had to send infected citizens to quarantine in nearby urban centres, outside the community, separating sick individuals from their support network.[42] Ironically, government-funded plans to alleviate the housing and infrastructure crisis on reserve were considerably delayed by the pandemic as a result of shortages in construction material and the public health restrictions that prevented non-resident workers from accessing construction sites on reserve.[43] Delays caused by the COVID-19 pandemic have also been used by the federal government to explain its failure to meet its pledge to end boil-water advisories on reserve by 2021. This claim has been contested by communities and commentators.[44]

Mobility restriction measures also heavily impacted First Nations living in communities where access to essential goods is limited, including food and other necessities. For example, in northern Manitoba, eight mothers from a First Nation community were heavily fined for defying their community's stay-at-home orders as they drove to the nearby town to buy milk, diapers, and other essential goods for their children, which were not readily accessible on the reserve.[45] Notwithstanding the critiques that could be directed to the First Nation authorities for the enforcement of their by-laws in these circumstances, the incident illustrates the dilemma faced by First Nations who aim to protect their most vulnerable members against a deadly virus in the context of the dire lack of services and goods on reserve.

On a different note, restrictions on mobility and gatherings significantly impacted First Nations' access to land—especially outside of reserves—for traditional harvesting activities, ceremonies, and other Indigenous healing practices.[46] In some communities, these barriers exacerbated existing food insecurity issues, in addition to disrupting culture, knowledge, and language transmission practices (although some communities have reported an increased in land-based activities during the pandemic).[47] For Indigenous peoples, connection to the land, the harvesting and sharing of traditional foods and medicines, as well as ceremonies are central to community and individual health and well-being. These practices, as well as the laws and relationships in which they are grounded, are also integral to some First Nations' pandemic plans.[48] However, some First Nations' traditional activities and ceremonies on and off reserve have been disrupted during the pandemic by state-authored public health measures—such as gathering restrictions and travel bans—ill-adapted to Indigenous laws, traditions, and cultures.[49]

Pandemic measures have also exerted pressure on community and kinship networks within and across reserves' boundaries, for instance, by preventing individuals living on reserve to visit and provide support to family members who, for reasons not always under their control, live off reserve. Moreover, the increased social tensions induced by ill-conceived COVID-19 measures took place in the context of traumatic events that have impacted Indigenous peoples during the pandemic. For example, in the Atikamekw Nehirowisiw community of Manawan, as community members were coping with the virus and confinement measures, they were confronted with the trauma left by residential schools as more than 100 unmarked graves were discovered in Kamloops and other sites, as well as by the tragic death of Joyce Echaquan amidst the racist insults of a nurse at the Joliette hospital.[50] These cumulative traumatic experiences have led to an aggravation of mental health issues within the community and an overuse by public health authorities of coercive measures against individuals in crisis, including involuntary admissions in psychiatric hospitals located outside the community.[51]

8.2 Looking Forward: *UNDRIP* and the Future of First Nations' Pandemic Preparedness

First Nations in Canada responded quickly to the COVID-19 pandemic to protect their citizens. Their actions were prompted by the knowledge accumulated through past pandemics, including SARS and the H1N1 flu virus, by the increased vulnerability of their citizens resulting from the prevalence of underlying health conditions in many communities (including diabetes and chronic respiratory diseases) and by the lack of access to adequate healthcare and other essential services, especially on reserve.[52] Commentators throughout the pandemic emphasized that First Nations' authority to make policies and laws in response to COVID-19 according to their own laws, needs, and priorities must be respected.[53] Yet the exercise by First Nations of their jurisdiction to protect their citizens from the virus has been significantly constrained both by the colonial jurisdictional framework and by the material conditions in which First Nations are bound to operate. The capacity of First Nations to respond efficiently and adequately to public health crises requires deep structural changes to decolonize the relationships between the Canadian state and Indigenous peoples and to "[comprehensively address] the systemic inequities in government services for First Nations peoples".[54]

In June 2021, as First Nations were battling to keep the virus out of their communities, Canada enacted the *UNDRIP Act*, which affirms that "[t]he Government of Canada must, in consultation and cooperation with Indigenous peoples, take all measures necessary to ensure that the laws of Canada are consistent with the Declaration".[55] We argue that the *UNDRIP* contains all the tools necessary to enable First Nations to protect their communities and citizens in times of crisis, such as during a global pandemic. The implementation of *UNDRIP* in the Canadian legal system should form an essential component of Canada's future pandemic preparedness plans.

The capacity of First Nations to respond to health crises hinges on the recognition and respect for their inherent jurisdiction to protect their communities and their traditional lands, territories, and resources, in light of the rights to self-determination and to free, prior, and informed consent affirmed in the *UNDRIP*.[56] In the words of the Truth and Reconciliation Commission of Canada:

> Self-determination holds the key to better Aboriginal health by allowing communities to develop programs that are suited to their own needs, and to do so in a holistic way, avoiding the jurisdictional disputes that have plagued progress in health and so many other areas where the residential schools still cast a large shadow.[57]

While the Supreme Court of Canada has yet to confirm the existence of an inherent right to self-government protected under Section 35 of the *Constitution Act, 1982*, it may do so in a near future when deciding the case *Reference to the Court of Appeal of Québec in relation with the Act respecting First Nations, Inuit and Métis children, youth and families*.[58] In this case, the Quebec Court of Appeal, referring considerably to the *UNDRIP*, recognized that a generic right to self-government over child and family services for Aboriginal peoples is protected under Section 35. We propose that this right, if upheld by the Supreme Court of Canada, could lead to a recognition of a similar right in other sectors including public health for Indigenous peoples.

Ultimately, however, for First Nations to respond efficiently to public health crises, it is urgent for the state to remedy, without any further delay, the systemic discrimination experienced by Indigenous peoples in the healthcare system, as well as in the access to essential services, infrastructure, and goods, especially on reserve. In that regard, the *UNDRIP* affirms that "Indigenous peoples have the right, without discrimination, to the improvement of their economic and social conditions, including, inter alia, in the areas of education, employment, vocational training and retraining, housing, sanitation, health and social security".[59] At the individual level, "Indigenous people have an equal right to the enjoyment of the highest attainable standard of physical and mental health".[60] To this end, as argued by researchers, the Canadian Human Rights Tribunal decision in *Caring Society v Canada*,[61] which found inequitable funding of children's services for First Nations families was discriminatory and issued a number of remedial orders, may "provide a comprehensive roadmap of the federal government's legal obligations for the funding and provision of measures designed to prevent and respond to health crises".[62]

The recognition of Indigenous peoples' jurisdiction and the meaningful application of their legal orders are imperative for First Nations to respond to the COVID-19 pandemic and future ones efficiently, equitably, and in a culturally appropriate manner. The implementation of the *UNDRIP* in the Canadian legal system offers a pathway towards the realization of this urgent objective.

Notes

1 This chapter focuses exclusively on First Nations. We do not address the situation of Métis and Inuit communities, which may have specificities of their own.

2 Assemblée des Premières Nations Québec-Labrador (APNQL), "Bilan et perspectives. Première vague de la pandémie de COVID-19 chez les Premières Nations au Québec" (2020) at 15, online (pdf): https://files.cssspnql.com/index.php/s/wP64MQx9UQT5WLo. [APNQL]; Emma Feltes, Jocelyn Stacey and Crystal Verhaeghe, "Dada Nentsen Gha Yatastig: Tsilhqot'in in the Time of COVID: Strengthening Tsilhqot'in Ways to Protect Our People" (2021) at 17–27, online (pdf): *Tsilhqot'in Nation*. tsilhqotin.ca/wp-content/uploads/2021/03/TNG-COVID-REPORT-FINAL.pdf; Erik White, "At least 18 first nations in Northeastern Ontario close borders to keep outsiders and COVID-19 away" (8 May 2020), online: *CBC News*. www.cbc.ca/news/canada/sudbury/first-nations-borders-checkpoints-law-1.5557691; Yellowhead Institute, "COVID-19 in community: How are first nations responding?" (April 2020), online: *Yellowhead Institute*. https://yellowheadinstitute.org/2020/04/07/corona-in-community-the-first-nation-response/ [Yellowhead Institute].

3 APNQL, *supra* note 2 at 7; Feltes, Stacey & Verhaeghe, *supra* note 2 at 17–27.

4 Aimée Craft, Deborah McGregor & Jeffery G Hewitt, "COVID-19 and first nations' Responses" in Colleen M. Flood et al, ed, *Vulnerable: the Law, Policy and Ethics of COVID-19* (Ottawa: University of Ottawa Press, 2020) at 49–67; Anne Lévesque & Sophie Thériault, "Systemic discrimination in government services and programs and its impacts on First Nations peoples during the COVID-19 pandemic" in Flood et al (*ibid* at 381–392); UNGA, Report of the Special Rapporteur on the Rights of Indigenous Peoples, José Francisco Cali Tzai, "Rights of Indigenous Peoples", A/75/185, 20 July 2020 at para 48 [UNGA]; Shiri Pasternak & Robert Houle, "No such thing as natural disasters: infrastructure and the First Nation fight against COVID-19" (9 April 2020), online: *Yellowhead Institute* https://yellowheadinstitute.org/2020/04/09/no-such-thing-as-natural-disasters-infrastructure-and-the-first-nation-fight-against-covid-19/.

5 APNQL, *supra* note 2 at 15; Feltes, Stacey & Verhaeghe, *supra* note 2 at 67.
6 United Nations Declaration on the Rights of Indigenous Peoples Act, SC 2021, c 14 [UNDRIP Act].
7 APNQL, *supra* note 2 at 10; Feltes, Stacey & Verhaeghe, *supra* note 2 at 21; Craft, McGregor & Hewitt, *supra* note 4 at 59; Yellowhead Institute, *supra* note 2.
8 See Part III and IV in this volume.
9 Craft, McGregor & Hewitt, *supra* note 4 at 60–62; White, *supra* note 2.
10 *Indian Act*, RSC 1985, c I-5, s 81(1)(a).
11 *Constitution Act, 1982*, s 35, being Schedule B to the Canada Act 1982 (UK), 1982, c 11.
12 UNGA, *United Nations Declaration on the Rights of Indigenous Peoples* (*UNDRIP*), A/RES/61/295, 2 October 2007, art 3–5 [UNDRIP]. See Craft, McGregor & Hewitt, *supra* note 4 at 59; Feltes, Stacey & Verhaeghe, *supra* note 2 at 57.
13 UNGA, *supra* note 4 at para 48.
14 *Ibid.*
15 *Ibid* at para 12.
16 Craft, McGregor & Hewitt, *supra* note 4 at 52.
17 Jade Dumoulin, "The 'new normal': Defending first nations jurisdiction during COVID-19" (8 April 2021) at 1, online: *Yellowhead Institute.* yellowheadinstitute.org/2021/04/08/the-new-normal-defending-first-nations-jurisdiction-during-covid-19/.
18 Hamdi Issawi, "How first nations are finding ways to keep COVID-19—and outsiders—at bay" (9 June 2020), online: *Macleans.* www.macleans.ca/news/canada/how-first-nations-are-finding-ways-to-keep-covid-19-and-outsiders-at-bay/.
19 Julien Gignac, "Shut it down: Yukon first nations call for halt to mining operations in light of coronavirus" (3 April 2020), online: *The Narwhal.* thenarwhal.ca/shut-down-yukon-first-nations-call-halt-mining-operations-light-coronavirus/; Brandi Morin, "Pipeline, mine work sites deemed essential services worry some canadians" (21 April 2020), online: *Huffpost.* huffpost.com/archive/ca/entry/pipelines-essential-services-coronavirus-mines-pipelines-indigenous_ca_5e9668b8c5b6ead1400463a0; Natalia Balcerzak, "How the tahltan nation is weighing coronavirus concerns against Red Chris mine operations in northern B.C" (7 April 2020), online: *The Narwhal.* thenarwhal.ca/how-the-tahltan-nation-is-weighing-coronavirus-concerns-against-red-chris-mine-operations-in-northern-b-c/; Sarah Cox, " 'Send everybody home': Potential coronavirus outbreak at Site C dam a threat to Fort St. John, local officials say" (26 March 2020), online: *The Narwhal.* thenarwhal.ca/send-everybody-home-potential-coronavirus-outbreak-at-site-c-dam-a-threat-to-fort-st-john-local-officials-say/.
20 Jaela Bernstien, "Kanesatake Mohawks block entrance to Oka provincial park" (20 May 2020), online: *CBC News*www.cbc.ca/news/canada/montreal/visitors-barred-entry-at-oka-provincial-park-1.5577093; Lindsay Richardson, "Town of Oka and Kanesatake territory at odds over COVID-19 check points" (13 May 2020), online: *APTN News.* www.aptnnews.ca/national-news/town-of-oka-and-kanesatake-territory-at-odds-over-covid-19-check-points/.
21 Craft, McGregor & Hewitt, *supra* note 4 at 62.
22 Feltes, Stacey & Verhaeghe, *supra* note 2 at 56–62; House of Commons, COVID-19 and Indigenous Peoples: From Crisis Towards Meaningful Change: Report of the Standing Committee on Indigenous and Northern Affairs (March 2021) (Chair: Bob Bratina) at 68–72, online: www.ourcommons.ca/Content/Committee/432/INAN/Reports/RP11143866/inanrp06/inanrp06-e.pdf. [House of Commons]; Issawi, *supra* note 18.
23 House of Commons, *supra* note 22 at 68–72.
24 Jocelyn Stacey, Crystal Verhaeghe, Emma Feltes, "How 'colonialism by paper cuts' has undermined Indigenous pandemic leadership" (22 June 2021), online:

The Conversation. https://theconversation.com/how-colonialism-by-paper-cuts-has-undermined-indigenous-pandemic-leadership-161542; see also House of Commons, *supra* note 22 at 68–72.
25 Feltes, Stacey & Verhaeghe, *supra* note 2 at 53–64. See also Emma Feltes, Jocelyn Stacey & the Tŝilhqot'in National Government, "Crisis, colonialism and constitutional habits: Indigenous jurisdiction in times of emergency" (2023), *Canadian Journal of Law and Society*. https://doi.org/10.1017/cls.2023.2.
26 On issues pertaining to the enforcement of Indian Act by-law, see, e.g., Nick Sowsun, "Solving the Indian Act by-law enforcement issue: Prosecution of Indian Act by-laws", online: *Olthuis Kleer Townshend LLP*. oktlaw.com/solving-the-indian-act-by-law-enforcement-issue-prosecution-of-indian-act-by-laws/#citation1.
27 Feltes, Stacey & Verhaeghe, *supra* note 2 at 62–64.
28 *Ibid* at 63–64. See, for example, David Shield & Creeden Martell, "RCMP 'had no understanding' of sun dance ceremony that was interrupted, dancer says" (12 May 2020), online: *CBC News*. www.cbc.ca/news/canada/saskatoon/beardys-okemasis-sun-dance-1.5566551. Provincial laws of general application—such as public health laws—apply to First Nation people both on and off reserve, either of their own force (*ex proprio vigore*) or by way of section 88 of the *Indian Act*, *supra* note 10.
29 Feltes, Stacey & Verhaeghe, *supra* note 2 at 57–61.
30 *Ibid* at 43. See also Feltes, Stacey & the Tŝilhqot'in National Government, *supra* note 25 at 17.
31 APNQL, *supra* note 2 at 16; House of Commons, *supra* note 22 at 29–31.
32 House of Commons, *supra* note 22 at 46.
33 Feltes, Stacey & Verhaeghe, *supra* note 2 at 45.
34 Craft, McGregor & Hewitt, *supra* note 4 at 53–55; Lévesque & Thériault, *supra* note 4 at 384–387; Pasternak & Houle, *supra* note 4.
35 UNGA, *supra* note 4 at paras 5, 12.
36 *James Bay and Northern Quebec Agreement and Complementary Agreements*, Publications du Québec, Québec 1998, online: http://www3.publicationsduquebec.gouv.qc.ca/produits/conventions/lois/loi2/pages/page4.en.html.
37 *Agreement concerning a new relationship between le gouvernement du Québec and the Crees of Québec*, Publicatiobns du Québec, Québec 2002, online: 02_-agreement_concerning_a_new_relationship_between_le_gouvernement_du_q.pdf.
38 Cree Nation Government, *COVID-19 Information for the Public*, online: www.cngov.ca/covid-19/ (see the *Law Respecting Measures to Contain the Spread of COVID-19 through Mandatory Self-Isolation* and the other measures adopted by the Cree Nation Government in response to the pandemic).
39 See, e.g., Olivia Levesque, "Strict protocols to stay in effect in many First Nations even as Ontario eases them, NAN Grand Chief says" (18 February 2022), online: *CBC News*. www.cbc.ca/news/canada/thunder-bay/northern-ontario-grand-chief-covid-restriction-1.6355874.
40 House of Commons, *supra* note 22 at 17–19; Julia Christensen, "Housing is health: Coronavirus highlights the dangers of the housing crisis in Canada's North" (16 April 2020), online: *The Conversation*. https://theconversation.com/housing-is-health-coronavirus-highlights-the-dangers-of-the-housing-crisis-in-canadas-north-135594 >; Lévesque & Thériault, *supra* note 4 at 385–386.
41 Feltes, Stacey & Verhaeghe, *supra* note 2 at 38.
42 House of Commons, *supra* note 22 at 18; Marie-Laure Josselin, "COVID-19: Les communautés autochtones du Québec rattrapées par la deuxième vague" (19 November 2020), online: *Radio-Canada*. https://ici.radio-canada.ca/espaces-autochtones/1750612/covid-19-les-communautes-autochtones-du-quebec-rattrapees-par-la-deuxieme-vague.

43 Olivia Stefanovich, "COVID-19 may delay Liberal pledge to end long-term boil water advisories on First Nations" (29 October 2020), online: *CBC News*. www.cbc.ca/news/politics/stefanovich-reconciliation-throne-speech-2020-1.5738098.
44 Olivia Stefanovich & Ryan Patrick Jones, "Federal government vows again to end boil water advisories but offers no new target date" (10 March 2021), online: *CBC News*. www.cbc.ca/news/politics/ottawa-new-website-term-drinking-water-advisories-1.5943388; Nicole Thompson, "Pledge to end boil-water advisories on First Nations by 2021 delayed by COVID-19, Trudeau says" (23 October 2020), online: *National Observer*. www.nationalobserver.com/2020/10/23/news/trudeau-pledge-delayed-boil-water-advisories-first-nations.
45 Lenard Monkman, "$5K fines given to Manitoba First Nations mothers who defied COVID-19 lockdown to buy groceries" (7 February 2022), online: *CBC News*. cbc.ca/news/indigenous/5k-fines-ncn-mothers-groceries-lockdown-1.6342985.
46 House of Commons, *supra* note 22 at 48–49; Shield & Martell, *supra* note 28; Anne-Marie Yvon, "La chasse à la Bernache: une tradition touchée par le coronavirus" (9 April 2020), online: *Radio-Canada*. https://ici.radio-canada.ca/espaces-autochtones/1692211/bernache-chasse-autochtones-innus-cris-atikamekw.
47 House of Commons, *supra* note 22 at 48–49; Feltes, Stacey & Verhaeghe, *supra* note 2 at 79–80; Elisa Levi & Hayley Lapalme, "Getting back to normal? Not if 'normal' means indigenous food and health insecurity" (13 July 2021), online: *Yellowhead Institute*. https://yellowheadinstitute.org/2021/07/13/getting-back-to-normal-indigenous-food-and-health-insecurity/.
48 Craft, McGregor & Hewitt, *supra* note 4 at 63.
49 See, e.g., Shield & Martell, *supra* note 28; Yvon, *supra* note 46.
50 Antoni Nerestant, "Racism, prejudice contributed to Joyce Echaquan's death in hospital, Quebec coroner's inquiry concludes" (1 October 2021), online: *CBC News*. www.cbc.ca/news/canada/montreal/joyce-echaquan-systemic-racism-quebec-government-1.6196038.
51 Under the *Act Respecting the Protection of Persons Whose Mental State Presents a Danger to Themselves or to Others*, SQ 1997, c P-38.001. On psychiatric coercion during COVID-19, see Bernheim in this volume.
52 Craft, McGregor & Hewitt, *supra* note 4 at 51; Lévesque & Thériault, *supra* note 4 at 384–387.
53 Craft, McGregor & Hewitt, *supra* note 4 at 52.
54 Lévesque & Thériault, *supra* note 4 at 390.
55 *UNDRIP Act*, *supra* note 6 at art 5.
56 *UNDRIP*, *supra* note 12 at arts 3, 4, 19, 32(2).
57 *Canada's Residential Schools: The Legacy (The Final Report)*, vol 5 (Winnipeg: Truth and Reconciliation Commission, 2015), cited in Craft, McGregor & Hewitt, *supra* note 4 at 52.
58 Renvoi à la Cour d'appel du Québec relatif à la Loi concernant les enfants, les jeunes et les familles des Premières Nations, des Inuits et des Métis, 2022 QCCA 185 (CanLII). Appeal heard by the Supreme Court of Canada (as of right) 7–8 December 2022. At the time of writing, the Supreme Court of Canada has not yet issued its decision.
59 *UNDRIP*, *supra* note 12 at art 21.
60 *Ibid* at art 24(2).
61 First Nations Child and Family Caring Society of Canada et al v Attorney General of Canada (for the Minister of Indian and Northern Affairs Canada) 2016 CHRT 2.
62 Lévesque & Thériault, *supra* note 4, at 388.

PART IV

Border Measures in Comparative Perspective

9

BORDER CONTROLS AS PART OF AOTEAROA NEW ZEALAND'S RESPONSE TO THE COVID-19 PANDEMIC

Siouxsie Wiles[1, 2]

9.1 Introduction

Aotearoa New Zealand is an island nation of approximately five million people, located in the Pacific Ocean. The country covers a land area of almost 270,000 km^2 and consists of two large islands and hundreds of smaller islands. Aotearoa New Zealand was first settled by Polynesian voyagers in the 13th century and then colonized by the British in the 1800s. One in six people in Aotearoa New Zealand identify as having indigenous Māori ethnicity and almost 8% of the country's population identify as being of Pacific origin.[1] While English is the predominant language spoken, Aotearoa New Zealand's official languages are New Zealand sign language and te reo Māori.[2]

9.2 Border Controls in Aotearoa New Zealand's Early Pandemic Response

On the 30th of January 2020, the World Health Organization (WHO) declared Coronavirus Disease 2019 (COVID-19) a public health emergency of international concern, and COVID-19 became a notifiable disease in Aotearoa New Zealand. Despite the country's geographic isolation, we knew that the arrival of COVID-19 was imminent due to the numbers of citizens or residents who travel overseas and the large numbers of tourists and

[1] Bioluminescent Superbugs Lab, Department of Molecular Medicine and Pathology, Waipapa Taumata Rau University of Auckland, Auckland, Aotearoa New Zealand
[2] Te Pūnaha Matatini, Aotearoa New Zealand

DOI: 10.4324/9781003394006-13

students who enter the country each summer, predominantly from Europe and mainland China. Soon, border-related controls were implemented to try to control the entry of the disease into the Aotearoa New Zealand. These border-related measures and a timeline of when they were actioned are provided in Figure 9.2.

The first border-related control used by the New Zealand government was to bar entry to travelers from China, except for New Zealand citizens, permanent residents, and their families. This came into force on the 3rd of February 2020. Days later, a repatriation flight arrived from Wuhan, with passengers transferred to a military base to quarantine.

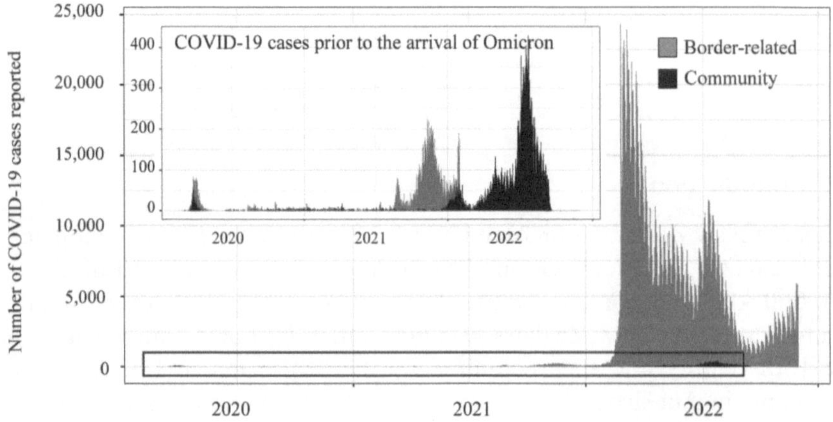

FIGURE 9.1 Cases overlaid with border closures and Alert Levels.

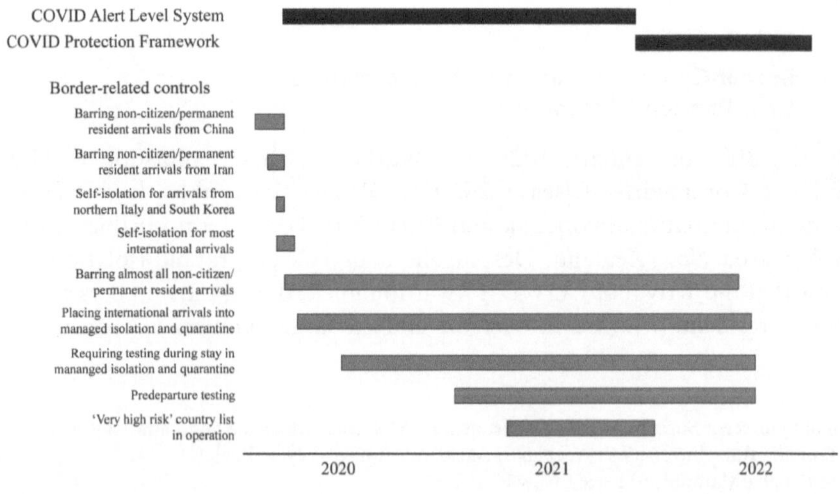

FIGURE 9.2 Border measures.

By the end of February 2020, with cases appearing around the world, health officials began screening passengers arriving on direct flights from Hong Kong, Japan, South Korea, Singapore, and Thailand. When Aotearoa New Zealand's first COVID-19 case was reported on the 28th of February, in a traveler from Iran, the government extended the bar on entry to travelers from Iran too. As with China, New Zealand citizens, permanent residents, and their families were exempt. However, they were required to self-isolate for 14 days on arrival. Days later, the government introduced self-isolation requirements for arrivals from Northern Italy and South Korea.

On the 11th of March 2020, the WHO declared COVID-19 a pandemic. Aotearoa New Zealand's second case was also reported that day, related to travel from Italy. Over the following days, several new cases were reported. On the 16th of March, the government prohibited cruise ships from docking and required all international arrivals to self-isolate for 14 days. Just a day later, it was reported that Immigration New Zealand had placed two foreign tourists into quarantine for defying the self-isolation requirement.

During February and March, there was much discussion, both within Aotearoa New Zealand and beyond, of the optimal strategy to deal with the growing pandemic.[3] Under consideration were factors such as minimizing morbidity and mortality, preventing health systems from being overwhelmed, and managing the economic impacts for a novel transmissible disease for which there were no known treatments or vaccines. By then, exponential growth of the virus had been brought under control in Wuhan, China, using non-pharmaceutical interventions including isolation, quarantine, and internal travel restrictions.[4] This showed that elimination—bringing cases to zero or near zero in a particular location—was possible, at least in the short term. To achieve this would require both controlling transmission within the location in question and preventing the seeding of new transmission chains from other locations.

This is the strategy that Aotearoa New Zealand adopted, and the country closed its borders on the 19th of March 2020. At that time, 28 cases had been reported in the country, spread over a wide geographical area from the North to the South Island. Globally, confirmed cases were approaching a quarter of a million. The border closure meant only citizens and permanent residents could enter Aotearoa New Zealand, and they had to self-isolate for 14 days. There were a small number of exceptions to the closed border. Samoan and Tongan citizens who needed to travel to Aotearoa New Zealand for essential reasons, like accessing healthcare, were still permitted entry, as were essential health workers and people seeking to enter the country for humanitarian reasons.

Just two days later, on the 21st of March, health officials announced they had identified the country's first cases of COVID-19 with no obvious links to international travel. With the prospect of undetected community transmission becoming increasingly likely, the government introduced a four-tiered Alert Level system, specifying the public health and social measures the country would take to control the spread of COVID-19.[5] By mid-March, researchers at Te Pūnaha Matatini, a Centre of Research Excellence in Complex Systems, had begun developing mathematical models to study the potential spread of COVID-19 in Aotearoa New Zealand.[6] These would prove crucial in aiding the government's decision-making on, for example, changing Alert Levels. So to was Aotearoa New Zealand's relatively low per capita allocation of emergency intensive care beds.[7]

On the 25th of March 2020, a state of national emergency was declared, and the country moved to Alert Level 4. This was effectively a nationwide stay-at-home order, which entailed a stringent lockdown of all non-essential services. Within two weeks, the measures were clearly working and daily case numbers were beginning to fall (Fig. 9.1).[8] On the 27th of April, the country began moving down the Alert Levels. The outbreak had seemingly peaked on the 2nd of April, with 89 confirmed cases reported that day (Fig. 9.1). By the 8th of June 2020, and with no active cases, Aotearoa New Zealand moved to Alert Level 1, where the only control measures that remained were those in place at the border.

9.3 Aotearoa New Zealand's First Wave of COVID-19

Analysis of Aotearoa New Zealand's first COVID-19 "wave" showed that between the 26th of February and the 1st of July 2020, there were a total of 1,178 laboratory-confirmed COVID-19 cases and a further 350 probable cases. Genomic sequencing of samples from more than half of the confirmed cases revealed 277 separate introductions of the virus into the country, though less than half of them resulted in any onward transmission.[9] The sequences represented nearly all the genomic diversity present in the global viral population at the time,[10] showing importations had come from a wide range of countries. Genomic sequencing also supported epidemiological evidence that there had been several super spreading events prior to the country's move to Alert Level 4.[11] These included a wedding (98 cases), social events associated with a school (96 cases), a hospitality venue (77 cases), aged residential care facilities (56 cases and 51 cases), a private function (40 cases), and a conference (39 cases).[12]

One of the factors in Aotearoa New Zealand's success in eliminating COVID-19 is the country's low population density of approximately 19 people per square kilometre. Yet almost 80% of Aotearoa New Zealand is uninhabited.[13] A more appropriate measure would be lived density which is the population density experienced by the average person in a region. Geospatial data analyst Adam Campbell calculated the lived density for Aotearoa New Zealand as 425.4 people per square kilometre, meaning that if the country was a US State, it would rank near the middle.[14] In other words, Aotearoa New Zealand is more urban than its low population density suggests.

Binny and colleagues used their stochastic branching process model of COVID-19 transmission to simulate Aotearoa New Zealand's first COVID-19 wave in the presence and absence of both border controls and the stay-at-home orders of Alert Levels 3 and 4.[15] While limiting the number of people arriving into a country using border controls demonstrably reduced the number of introductions of the virus in Aotearoa New Zealand and other countries,[16] Binny and colleagues' data shows that border restrictions and self-isolation alone would not have been sufficient to prevent a serious outbreak from occurring. With no other measures in place, by the 13th of May 2020—the date that Aotearoa New Zealand's stay-at-home orders were lifted—there could have already been over 60,000 reported cases and over 1,100 deaths.[17] Allowed to continue spreading unimpeded, by the end of October 2020, there could have been over 1.81 million reported COVID-19 cases and 31,905 deaths.[18] Instead, the border restrictions and stay-at-home orders allowed time for testing and contact tracing capacities to be improved.

9.4 Differential Vulnerabilities to COVID-19

It is worth reflecting here on the communities that would have been hardest hit by COVID-19 had the earlier scenario played out. Socioeconomic and demographic factors, as well as long-term health conditions, render populations vulnerable to different diseases in different ways. Indeed, previous pandemics have shown that Māori and Pacific people are at greater risk of negative outcomes.[19] For example, the Māori mortality rate during the 1918 influenza pandemic was more than seven times higher than that of New Zealand Europeans. Similarly, during the 2009 H1N1 influenza pandemic, Māori and Pacific people were infected, hospitalized, and died at higher rates than New Zealand Europeans.[20]

Beyond pandemics, there are decades of research showing that Māori and Pacific people in Aotearoa New Zealand have poorer access to healthcare services and higher unmet health needs.[21] Indeed, modelling showed that even after controlling for age and pre-existing conditions, Māori would have 2.50 times greater odds of hospitalization from COVID-19, and Pacific people have three times greater odds than non-Māori, non-Pacific people.[22] Modelling also suggested that Māori and Pacific communities were at a high risk of suffering a large outbreak, which could remain undetected for a long time.[23] Similarly, Wiki and colleagues used nationwide data on a wide range of risk factors, including age, ethnicity, population density, socioeconomic deprivation, smoking, long-term health conditions, and health service awareness to create area-level COVID-19 vulnerability maps for Aotearoa New Zealand, finding notable spatial variations.[24]

These differences in vulnerability were apparent even in Aotearoa New Zealand's first COVID-19 wave. Most of the early cases were linked to imported cases—meaning that their demographics were predominantly those of people with the means to travel internationally. They were mainly in younger adults, in people of European ethnicity, and in those of higher socioeconomic status.[25] While locally acquired cases were less common, unsurprisingly, they had more severe outcomes and were associated with more vulnerable populations, including older people, those living in aged residential care, and those of Pacific ethnicity.[26] Importantly, the cases associated with aged residential care facilities also showed that staff and visitors were a more important driver of transmission than residents.[27]

9.5 Border Controls for Maintaining the Elimination Strategy

With Aotearoa New Zealand adopting an elimination strategy for COVID-19, stopping the virus from continually reentering the country and reseeding community outbreaks was going to be crucial. But closing the border was not an easy decision to make. The country's economy heavily relies on tourism, comprising almost 10% of direct and indirect contributions.[28] For example, in 2019, there were over 3.8 million overseas visitor arrivals. Indeed, prior to the COVID-19 pandemic, international tourism expenditure reached NZ$17.5 billion per year, and almost 14% of working residents were employed by the tourism industry.[29]

Another important contribution to the economy of Aotearoa New Zealand is international education, which supported nearly 50,000 jobs in the country before the pandemic. International student fees contributed NZ$1.21 billion to the country's economy in 2019, while the total economic contribution of international education was NZ$5.23 billion. Students from China were the largest cohort in the country in 2019, followed by India.[30]

Early estimates suggested a pre-symptomatic incubation period for COVID-19 of up to two weeks, or even longer, which meant a large proportion of infected travelers would not be detected on arrival.[31] Subsequent modelling showed that the safest option was for arrivals to spend 14 days in managed isolation in a facility where opportunities for transmission between guests and from guests to staff were minimized, where guests required a negative test result for release, and where staff would also be tested regularly.[32] This regime reduced the risk of an infectious case reaching the community to less than 1% per arriving case. Modelling also showed that shorter quarantine periods, or reliance on testing only with no quarantine, would substantially increase the risk of COVID-19 entering the community.[33] Others modelling the risk of importation of COVID-19 into the United Kingdom came to similar conclusions.[34]

9.6 Dealing with International Arrivals

During April 2020, the New Zealand government established a hotel-based managed isolation and quarantine system for all international arrivals, colloquially referred to as MIQ. Those with symptoms on arrival into Auckland were immediately transferred to a hotel close to Auckland International Airport, set up to cater for those known or suspected to have COVID-19. Arrivals into all MIQ facilities were tested for COVID-19 at regular intervals by real-time reverse transcription PCR (rRT-PCR). Those who tested positive, as well as their traveling companions, were then transferred to the facility for those with COVID-19. While some countries set up purpose-built isolation and quarantine facilities—and others used technology to isolate people in their homes or other chosen location (for example, Taiwan[35])—using large hotels was a pragmatic solution that made use of and financially supported existing infrastructure that had become redundant when the borders closed to international travelers.

Over the months that followed, further hotels were converted to MIQ facilities, and further measures were introduced to reduce the likelihood of someone arriving from overseas seeding a community outbreak. In June 2020, Prime Minister Jacinda Ardern announced that the New Zealand Defence Force would oversee the country's border and MIQ facilities and that people would require a negative COVID-19 test before being able to leave a facility. In August, New Zealand Defence Force personnel replaced private security guards at MIQ facilities and border areas. In September 2020, regular COVID-19 testing was brought in for everyone working at the country's border. In response to increasing demand, an allocation system for MIQ spaces was introduced in October 2020, and in early November 2020, returnees could no longer board a flight to Aotearoa New Zealand without a prebooked voucher for MIQ.

In February 2021, the New Zealand medicines regulator Medsafe provisionally approved the Pfizer-BioNTech mRNA COVID-19 vaccine for use in Aotearoa New Zealand. With people working in MIQ having the highest risk of exposure to COVID-19, they were amongst the first to receive the new vaccine; indeed, it was made a legal requirement for anyone working in high-risk border environments to be vaccinated by the 1st of May 2021. However, modelling also showed that depending on vaccine efficacy in preventing transmission, routine testing of vaccinated border workers would be important to prevent them becoming a silent source of infection into the unvaccinated community.[36]

9.7 Border Incursions

In the first year of operation, over 135,000 people entered Aotearoa New Zealand via MIQ;[37] 1,454 of whom tested positive for COVID-19. The use of genomic sequencing established that at least some cases were a result of inflight transmission. For example, in September 2020, seven passengers started their journey to Aotearoa New Zealand from five different countries. They all took the same connecting flight from Dubai to Auckland and sat within four rows of each other. After testing positive for COVID-19 while in MIQ, sequencing revealed their viral samples were genetically identical, except for a single mutation in one sample.[38]

Also in the first year of MIQ operation, there were 13 known community outbreaks, resulting in 225 community cases and three deaths.[39] Of the 13 outbreaks, seven originated in MIQ facilities, three were from airline workers who were not required to use MIQ, and one was related to a visiting cargo ship. The sources of the remaining two outbreaks, which resulted in stay-at-home orders being issued for the country's largest city, Auckland, remain unknown.[40]

The first MIQ-related outbreak comprised two people who were granted a compassionate exemption to exit MIQ early to attend a funeral. While there were no secondary infections from these cases, it did underscore the risk of granting such exemptions. A small outbreak also occurred when a New Zealand Defence Force (NZDF) member was infected at the MIQ facility in Auckland where he worked. Contact tracing identified three additional cases in Wellington (500 kilometres from Auckland), where his close contact lived. There was one additional case linked to the outbreak, in a worker at a retail outlet approximately 50 metres from one of the locations visited by the NZDF member.[41] Another MIQ-related case occurred when a maintenance worker became infected after using an elevator within minutes of someone staying in the facility who had arrived from overseas.[42] Another elevator-related transmission event occurred at a different MIQ hotel, which also experienced transmission through the hotel's air circulation system. New arrivals to the facility were suspended and its air filtration systems improved.[43] Within MIQ-transmission late in someone's 14-day stay also triggered a small community outbreak with further spread on a domestic flight.[44]

The most serious of the post-elimination outbreaks in 2020 occurred after Aotearoa New Zealand had gone 102 days with no community cases. In August 2020, four cases of COVID-19 were found among workers at a cold storage facility in Auckland.[45] The city was immediately moved to Alert Level 3 (stay-at-home orders for most workers), while limits on gathering sizes were put in place for the rest of the country. Genomic sequencing rapidly identified that cases were the result of a single introduction of the virus, though the source was never identified, in part because of bias and gaps in global sequencing data.[46] The outbreak grew to a total of 179 cases, including three deaths.

9.8 The Emergence of More Infectious SARS-CoV-2 Variants and the End of Elimination

During 2020, variants of the SARS-CoV-2 virus began emerging that posed an increased risk due to their increased transmissibility, ability to cause more severe disease, and/or ability to escape pre-existing immunity. This prompted the WHO to begin characterizing particular variants as variants of interest (VOIs) and variants of concern (VOCs) and to assign them a letter of the Greek alphabet.[47]

In early April 2021, the WHO declared SARS-CoV-2 lineage B.1.617.2 a VOI, as it was driving a significant second wave of COVID-19 cases in India.[48] They designated the variant the letter Delta. Shortly afterwards, the New Zealand government suspended travel from India. The WHO upgraded the Delta variant to a VOC on the 11th of May 2021. In July 2021, a cluster of cases within MIQ provided further evidence of both airborne transmission of COVID-19 and the increased infectiousness of the Delta variant. Solo traveler A and travel group BCDEF arrived in Aotearoa New Zealand on different flights from different countries on different dates and were transferred to different MIQ hotels.[49] When A and E both tested positive for COVID-19, the two groups were transferred to the same isolation hotel, though on different dates. They were housed on the same floor in separate, nonadjacent rooms less than 2 metres apart. When persons C, D, and E tested positive, genome sequencing linked their infections to person A, not person E.[50] Investigation revealed transmission occurred either via the synchronous opening of the hotel room doors or via leakage of air under the doors. Protocols were immediately revised so that synchronous door opening would no longer occur and the HEPA filtration units reoriented to mitigate against movement of respiratory aerosols across the corridor.[51]

Also in 2021, Aotearoa New Zealand and Australia formed a quarantine-free travel bubble which opened on the 18th of April. On the 29th of June, the agreement was paused due to multiple COVID-19 outbreaks in Australia. On the 23rd of July, the travel bubble was suspended, and anyone returning to Aotearoa New Zealand after the 30th of July was required to stay in MIQ. Then on the 17th of August 2021, a second stay-at-home order was placed on Aotearoa New Zealand after the detection of a single community case of COVID-19 with no immediate epidemiological link to the border. Genome sequencing showed that the subsequent outbreak was linked to a single introduction of the Delta variant into the community and that the first sequenced case was genomically indistinguishable to samples from two separate travel groups who had returned from New South Wales, Australia, via MIQ in the week prior to the community outbreak being detected.[52] With Delta proving difficult to eliminate and Aotearoa New Zealand approaching high levels of vaccination in early October 2021, the country moved from elimination to suppression as a strategy.[53] MIQ remained in place, but on the 14th of November 2021, the isolation period reduced to seven days.

At 8 A.M. local time on the 25th of November 2021, researchers in South Africa met with government ministers to discuss a new COVID-19 variant, B.1.1.529, detected less than two days before.[54] On the 26th of November, the WHO declared B.1.1.529 a VOC and designated it Omicron.[55] On the 27th of November, the New Zealand government imposed travel restrictions on several African countries (designating them "Very High-Risk") with entry to Aotearoa New Zealand restricted to New Zealand citizens and their time in MIQ increased to 14 days. Days later, the Alert Level system was replaced by the COVID-19 Protection Framework, which removed stay-at-home orders as a tool for reducing controlling COVID-19.[56] The country's first confirmed case of Omicron in MIQ was reported on the 16th of December 2021, and within days, all countries had been removed from the "Very High-Risk" list and the length of stay for all arrivals into MIQ increased to 14 days.

The first community cases of Omicron were reported on the 23rd of January 2022. Over the months that followed, border restrictions began to lift and the country's MIQ system reverted to being hotels. On the 3rd of May 2022, the government announced that borders were opening and that unvaccinated visa holders, permanent residents, and Australian citizens normally residing in Aotearoa New Zealand would be able to travel without using MIQ. The government ended the COVID-19 Protection Framework on the 12th of September 2022. As of the 5th of December 2022, there have been 1,979,614 confirmed cases of COVID-19 in Aotearoa New Zealand, with 22,064 hospitalizations, 587 people requiring intensive care, and 2,235 deaths.[57]

9.9 Conclusion

Prior to the arrival of the Omicron variant, Aotearoa New Zealand's elimination and then suppression strategy produced the best mortality protection outcomes amongst countries belonging to the Organization for Economic Cooperation and Development (OECD). The country had the lowest cumulative COVID-19 death rate, at 242 times lower than average of the 38 countries in the OECD and the lowest number of "excess deaths", with approximately 2,000 fewer deaths than expected.[58] As well as saving lives, Aotearoa New Zealand's COVID-19 strategy also saved livelihoods. The country performed better than the OECD average in terms of adverse impacts on GDP and employment.[59] These findings were supported by an analysis by Oliu-Barton and colleagues, who concluded that elimination was superior to mitigation for GDP growth and preventing deaths, and that among OECD countries, liberties were most severely impacted in those countries that chose mitigation.[60]

Border controls were crucial to the success of the elimination strategy, by reducing as much as possible the continual reseeding of COVID-19 into the community. While the emergence of increasingly infectious and immune-evasive SARS-COV-2 variants made the elimination of COVID-19 increasingly difficult, following the strategy allowed for the widespread rollout of COVID-19 vaccines in Aotearoa New Zealand.

Notes

1 "New Zealand's Population Nears 5.1 Million" (23 September 2020), online: *Stats NZ*. www.stats.govt.nz/news/new-zealands-population-nears-5-1-million.
2 "Our Languages" (2022), online: *Ō Tātou Reo | Ministry for Ethnic Communities*. www.ethniccommunities.govt.nz/resources-2/our-languages-o-tatou-reo/.
3 See, for example, Roy M. Anderson et al, "How Will Country-Based Mitigation Measures Influence the Course of the COVID-19 Epidemic?" (2020) 395:10228 *The Lancet* 931. See also Michael G. Baker, Amanda Kvalsvig & Ayesha J. Verrall, "New Zealand's COVID-19 Elimination Strategy" (2020) 213:5 *The Medical Journal of Australia* 198.
4 Huaiyu Tian et al, "An Investigation of Transmission Control Measures during the First 50 Days of the COVID-19 Epidemic in China" (2020) 368:6491 *Science* 638; "Coronavirus Disease 2019 (COVID¬19) Situation Report—44" (4 March 2020), online (pdf): *World Health Organization*. www.who.int/docs/default-source/coronaviruse/situation-reports/20200304-sitrep-44-covid-19.pdf.
5 "History of the COVID-19 Alert System", online: *Unite against COVID-19*. https://covid19.govt.nz/about-our-covid-19-response/history-of-the-covid-19-alert-system.
6 Shaun Hendy et al, "Mathematical Modelling to Inform New Zealand's COVID-19 Response" (2021) 51:sup1 *Journal of the Royal Society of New Zealand* S86.
7 Nick Wilson et al, "Potential Health Impacts from the COVID-19 Pandemic for New Zealand If Eradication Fails: Report to the NZ Ministry of Health" (23 March 2020), online (pdf): www.health.govt.nz/system/files/documents/publications/report_for_moh_-_covid-19_pandemic_nz_final.pdf.
8 Sarah Jefferies et al, "COVID-19 in New Zealand and the Impact of the National Response: A Descriptive Epidemiological Study" (2020) 5:11 *The Lancet Public Health*.
9 Jemma L. Geoghegan et al, "Genomic Epidemiology Reveals Transmission Patterns and Dynamics of SARS-CoV-2 in Aotearoa New Zealand" (2020) 11:1 *Nature Communications* 6351.
10 *Ibid.*
11 *Ibid.*
12 Shaun Hendy et al, "Mathematical Modelling to Inform New Zealand's COVID-19 Response" (2021) 51:sup1 *Journal of the Royal Society of New Zealand* S86.
13 Andrew Douglas-Clifford, "Nobody Lives Here: Uninhabited Areas of New Zealand," online: *The Map Kiwi*. www.andrewdc.co.nz/project/nobody-lives-here-uninhabited-areas-of-new-zealand.
14 Adam J. Campbell, "What Is the Population Density of New Zealand?" (2020), online: *Adam J Campbell PhD*. www.adam-campbell.com/post/what-is-the-population-density-of-new-zealand/.
15 Rachelle N Binny et al, "Early Intervention Is the Key to Success in COVID-19 Control" (2021) 8:11 *Royal Society Open Science* 210488.
16 Jordan Douglas et al, "Real-Time Genomics for Tracking Severe Acute Respiratory Syndrome Coronavirus 2 Border Incursions after Virus Elimination, New Zealand" (2021) 27:9 *Emerging Infectious Diseases* 2361.
17 Binny et al, *supra* note 15.
18 *Ibid.*
19 Nick Wilson et al, "Differential Mortality Rates by Ethnicity in 3 Influenza Pandemics over a Century, New Zealand" (2012) 18:1 *Emerging Infectious Diseases* 71.
20 *Ibid.*
21 "Health Services and Outcomes Inquiry" (2019), online: *Waitangi Tribunal*. https://waitangitribunal.govt.nz/inquiries/kaupapa-inquiries/health-services-and-outcomes-inquiry.

22 Nicholas Steyn et al, "Māori and Pacific People in New Zealand Have Higher Risk of Hospitalisation for COVID-19" (2021) 134:1538 *The New Zealand Medical Journal* 28.
23 A. James et al, "A Structured Model for COVID-19 Spread: Modelling Age and Healthcare Inequities" (2021) 38:3 *Mathematical Medicine and Biology: A Journal of the IMA* 299.
24 Jesse Wiki et al, "Understanding Vulnerability to COVID-19 in New Zealand: A Nationwide Cross-Sectional Study" (2021) 51:sup1 *Journal of the Royal Society of New Zealand* S179.
25 Jefferies et al, *supra* note 8.
26 *Ibid.*
27 James et al, *supra* note 23.
28 "Tourism Satellite Account: Year Ended March 2020" (22 December 2020), online: *Stats NZ*. www.stats.govt.nz/information-releases/tourism-satellite-account-year-ended-march-2020.
29 *Ibid.*
30 Jenny Sinclair, "International Students Supported 50,000 Jobs in 2019, Figures Show" (22 February 2021), online: *Research Professional News*. www.researchprofessionalnews.com/rr-news-new-zealand-2021-2-international-students-supported-50–000-jobs-in-2019-figures-show/.
31 Jacob Burns et al, "Travel-Related Control Measures to Contain the COVID-19 Pandemic: A Rapid Review" (2020) 10:9 *Cochrane Database of Systematic Reviews*; Chad R. Wells et al, "Impact of International Travel and Border Control Measures on the Global Spread of the Novel 2019 Coronavirus Outbreak" (2020) 117:13 *Proceedings of the National Academy of Sciences of the United States of America* 7504.
32 Nicholas Steyn et al, "Managing the Risk of a COVID-19 Outbreak from Border Arrivals" (2021) 18:177 *Journal of the Royal Society Interface* 20210063.
33 *Ibid.*
34 Samuel Clifford et al, "Strategies to Reduce the Risk of SARS-CoV-2 Importation from International Travellers: Modelling Estimations for the United Kingdom, July 2020" (2021) 16:39 *Eurosurveillance* 2001440.
35 C. Wang et al, "Response to COVID-19 in Taiwan: Big Data Analytics, New Technology, and Proactive Testing" (2020) 323:14 *Journal of the American Medical Association* 1341.
36 Michael J. Plank et al, "Vaccination and Testing of the Border Workforce for COVID-19 and Risk of Community Outbreaks: A Modelling Study" (2021) 8:9 *Royal Society Open Science* 210686.
37 "Managed Isolation and Quarantine: Daily 14 Day Forecast" (2021), online: *Ministry of Business, Innovation and Employment*. www.mbie.govt.nz/dmsdocument/14219-miq-daily-update-2021-05–01.
38 Tara Swadi et al, "Genomic Evidence of In-Flight Transmission of SARS-CoV-2 Despite Predeparture Testing" (2021) 27:3 *Emerging Infectious Diseases* 687.
39 Douglas et al, *supra* note 16.
40 *Ibid.*
41 *Ibid.*
42 *Ibid.*
43 *Ibid.*
44 Nick Eichler et al, "Transmission of Severe Acute Respiratory Syndrome Coronavirus 2 during Border Quarantine and Air Travel, New Zealand (Aotearoa)" (2021) 27:5 *Emerging Infectious Diseases* 1274.
45 Douglas et al, *supra* note 16.
46 Jemma L. Geoghegan et al, "Use of Genomics to Track Coronavirus Disease Outbreaks, New Zealand" (2021) 27:5 *Emerging Infectious Diseases* 1317.

47 "Tracking SARS-CoV-2 Variants", online: *World Health Organization*. www.who.int/activities/tracking-SARS-CoV-2-variants.
48 *Ibid.*
49 Andrew Fox-Lewis et al, "Airborne Transmission of SARS-CoV-2 Delta Variant within Tightly Monitored Isolation Facility, New Zealand (Aotearoa)" (2022) 28:3 *Emerging Infectious Diseases* 501.
50 *Ibid.*
51 *Ibid.*
52 Lauren Jelley et al, "Genomic epidemiology of Delta SARS-CoV-2 during transition from elimination to suppression in Aotearoa New Zealand" (2022) 13 *Nature Communications* 4035.
53 Alicia Blair et al, "The End of the Elimination Strategy: Decisive Factors towards Sustainable Management of COVID-19 in New Zealand" (2022) 3:1 *Epidemiologia* 135.
54 Siouxsie Wiles, "Siouxsie Wiles Explains the Omicron Variant of Covid-19" (26 November 2021), online: *The Spinoff*. https://thespinoff.co.nz/science/26-11-2021/siouxsie-wiles-explains-the-nu-variant-of-covid-19.
55 "Tracking SARS-CoV-2 Variants", online: *World Health Organization*. www.who.int/activities/tracking-SARS-CoV-2-variants.
56 "History of the COVID-19 Protection Framework (Traffic Lights)", online: *Unite against COVID-19*. https://covid19.govt.nz/about-our-covid-19-response/history-of-the-covid-19-protection-framework-traffic-lights.
57 "COVID-19: Case Demographics" (2022), online: *Ministry of Health NZ*. www.health.govt.nz/covid-19-novel-coronavirus/covid-19-data-and-statistics/covid-19-case-demographics.
58 Nick Wilson et al, "Use of the Elimination Strategy in Response to the COVID-19 Pandemic: Health and Economic Impacts for New Zealand Relative to Other OECD Countries" (2021) *MedRxiv*.
59 *Ibid.*
60 Miquel Oliu-Barton et al, Miquel, "SARS-CoV-2 Elimination, Not Mitigation, Creates Best Outcomes for Health, the Economy, and Civil Liberties" (2021) 397:10291 *The Lancet* 2234.

10

BORDERS WITHIN BORDERS WITHIN BORDERS

A Legitimate Approach to Controlling the First Two Years of the SARS-CoV-2 Pandemic in Australia

Stephen Duckett

10.1 Introduction

Within a few weeks of its first COVID-19 case in January 2020, Australia closed its borders to China, slowing the arrival of the pandemic into the country and giving it a 4-to-6-week benefit in terms of reduced infections.[1] The border closure eventually extended to all countries, and returning citizens had to spend two weeks in quarantine. Stringent public health measures—including what were known in Australia as 'lockdowns'—were imposed by state authorities to manage the inevitable breaches of quarantine.[2]

Within Australia, states closed their borders against each other, and within one state, Victoria, there was an internal border separating the capital, Melbourne, from the rest of the state, with tighter restrictions in Melbourne than the rest of the state. These restrictions on freedom of movement and association saved about 18,000 lives over the two years 2020–2021.[3] Australians, especially in those states where restrictions were imposed, watched daily media conferences where state premiers, health ministers, and chief health officers reported on the number of new cases and whether there would be any change in restrictions; a New South Wales judge suspected that one New South Wales public health order 'was the mostly widely read legal instrument in the history of NSW.'[4]

The public health measures which underpinned this success in terms of deaths averted were contentious and subject to legal challenge, with courts asked to review whether the measures infringed an explicit guarantee of absolute freedom of intercourse clause of the Australian Constitution; whether they inappropriately infringed implied individual freedoms, specifically freedom of movement, freedom of association, and freedom of religion; and

DOI: 10.4324/9781003394006-14

TABLE 10.1 Key challenges to the validity of movement restrictions

Date of judgment	*Court*		
	High Court of Australia	*Federal Court of Australia*	*State Superior Court*
January–June 2020			6 June: Bassi 1 and 2[6] 11 June: Supple[7] 19 June: Kumar-NUS[8]
July–December 2020	10 December: Gerner[9]		3 July: Gray[10] 26 July: Gibson[11] 9 October: Holcombe[12] 12 October: Thomson[13] 2 November: Loielo[14]
January–June 2021	24 February 2021: Palmer[15]	10 May 2021: Newman[16] 1 June 2021: LibertyWorks[17]	
July–December 2021		6 September: Athavle[18]	17 August: Cotterill[19] 18 October: Baker[20] 8 December: Henry[21]

whether they were properly and reasonably made. This chapter reviews some of the legal issues raised in the challenges to the erection of borders to manage the pandemic (see Table 10.1). A comprehensive analysis of the Australian (national) government's response to the pandemic is available elsewhere.[5]

The public health measures were mostly imposed following declarations of states of emergency under state or Commonwealth legislation.[22,23] Every challenge based on infringement of individual rights—as opposed to collective rights of assembly—was dismissed.

In addition to challenges to restrictions on freedom of movement, there were also challenges to the validity of the freedom of the body border or 'bodily integrity,' specifically the validity of vaccine and mask mandates.[24] The anti-vaccination stance of high-profile tennis player, Novak Djokovic, was a factor in his being deported from Australia, precluding his participation in the Australian Open tennis championship in January 2022.[25] These cases are not considered here.

10.2 Closing the External Border to Citizens

Although the World Health Organization advises against border closures as an epidemic response strategy, and they were not part of Australia's pandemic preparations,[26] one of Australia's first responses to the pandemic was to close its borders to China on 1 February 2020 and then to Iran, South Korea, Italy, and subsequently, to all countries. Although exemptions were possible, citizens of other countries found it difficult to enter Australia, and Australian citizens needed to get special approval to leave. Australia, an island nation, went into isolation—an approach broadly supported by the public and upheld by the courts.

Closing the external border separated families and friends. There was a dramatic reduction in arrivals into the country with the rate-limiting factor being available space in specifically designated hotels for the required two-week quarantine period. Caps on seats meant planes were only partially full and ticket prices escalated, pricing flights to return to Australia out of reach for many. Managing consular support for 'stranded Aussies'—citizens stranded overseas—was not handled well,[27] causing distress for many.[28]

A central right of citizens is often thought to be the right to enter and leave one's own country,[29] but the pandemic showed that right might legitimately be constrained.

The Australian restrictions started early. Part of the border control regime was to introduce controls on people leaving the country, with those who expected to return in the near future finding it difficult to get exit approval, as their return would add to pressure on quarantine facilities. This was challenged by a conservative group, *LibertyWorks*, which was established to invest in 'people, projects & causes that expand liberty.'[30] An employee of *LibertyWorks* applied to travel to London to assess potential conference venues, his application was denied, and *LibertyWorks* challenged the decision in the Federal Court.[31]

In brief, the exit controls were imposed by the Minister for Health and Aged Care under Commonwealth legislation, namely, the *Biosecurity Act 2015* (Cth). This act gave the Minister very broad powers to address biosecurity emergencies, of which the SARS-CoV-2 pandemic was declared to be one under the *Biosecurity Act (Human Biosecurity Emergency) (Human Coronavirus with Pandemic Potential) Declaration 2020* (Cth). The case turned on the precise phrasing of the act, but the breadth of powers was determined by the Federal Court as legitimate in an emergency.

The parallel right of Australian citizens to return to Australia was also constrained and, for a brief period, stopped altogether for citizens seeking to return from India. In response to a worsening outbreak in that country, in May 2021, the government completely banned arrivals from India, even of Australian citizens, an ethically challenging decision of dubious legality in terms of international law.[32]

Whatever its merit in terms of international law, the arrival ban was found to be a legitimate exercise of the same powers challenged by *LibertyWorks*.[33] In *Newman*, it was held that the recognized common law rights of Gary Newman—an Australian citizen living in India—to return to Australia could legitimately be constrained under the appropriate legislation: the *Biosecurity Act 2015* (Cth).[34]

10.3 Controlling Movement between States: Closing Internal Borders

Australia is a federation, and although the Constitution grants the Commonwealth parliament power to override state laws about quarantine,[35] states can make independent decisions about public health, and they did so during the pandemic.[36] Just as external border control was quickly adopted as a strategy to stop the spread of the virus, so, too, did states quickly erect internal border controls. The first state to do so was the island state of Tasmania, which introduced entry controls on 19 March 2020, but within a week, Northern Territory, Queensland, South Australia, and Western Australia all closed their borders to the eastern states, where the virus was spreading rapidly, causing disruption to the lives of families and friends caught on opposite sides of a state border.[37]

But core to the Australian federalism project was the deceptively simple but well litigated section 92 of the Constitution: 'trade, commerce, and intercourse among the States, whether by means of internal carriage or ocean navigation, shall be absolutely free.'[38]

Australian mining oligarch Clive Palmer, who lived in Queensland but had interests in Western Australia, launched a constitutional challenge in the High Court of Australia in May 2020 to the Western Australian border closure,[39] with the facts remitted to the Federal Court for determination.[40] Rangiah J of the Federal Court found that border controls were an effective strategy in combating COVID-19:

> The border restrictions have been effective to a very substantial extent to reduce the probability of COVID-19 being imported into Western Australia from interstate. . . . If the current border restrictions were replaced by mandatory hotel quarantining for all entrants to Western Australia for 14 days, Western Australia could not safely manage the number of people in hotel quarantine. If the border restrictions were replaced by a suite of measures including exit and entry screening, mandatory wearing of face-masks on aeroplanes, PCR testing on the second and twelfth days after entry and mandatory wearing of face masks for fourteen days after entry, they would be less effective than the border restrictions in preventing the importation of COVID-19. If the border restrictions were replaced by that suite of measures plus a "hotspot" regime, involving either quarantining or banning persons entering from designated hotspots, they would be less effective than the border measures in preventing the importation of COVID-19. In view of the uncertainties involved in determining the

> probability that COVID-19 would be implied into Western Australia from elsewhere in Australia, and the potentially serious consequences if it were imported, a precautionary approach should be taken to decision-making about the measures required for the protection of the community.[41]

The High Court was unanimous in its conclusion that Western Australia's border closures were not discriminatory or protectionist, the underlying issue which led to section 92, and were appropriate as a legitimate exercise of its emergency powers.[42] The epidemiological evidence reviewed by Rangiah J formed the context which allowed Kiefel CJ and Deane J in their joint decision to conclude:

> It must be accepted that the restrictions are severe but it cannot be denied that the importance of the protection of health and life amply justifies the severity of the measures.[43]

Although its conclusions were unanimous, the reasoning was not, with, in particular, a sharp and explicit disagreement about whether 'structured proportionality'[44] provides a useful frame for assessment. Gageler J explicitly rejected its use,[45] while Gordon J thought determining the legitimacy of the Western Australian border controls 'not assisted by adopting structured proportionality as a tool of analysis.'[46]

In contrast, Edelman J explicitly used structured proportionality:

> Structured proportionality makes explicit and transparent the only three independent grounds upon which a law might be held invalid as contrary to s 92. First, a law will be invalid if its very purpose is to undermine the freedom guaranteed by s 92. Secondly, a law will be invalid if its means of achieving its legitimate purpose are not "reasonably necessary", in the sense that those means burden the freedom guaranteed by s 92 substantially more than obvious and compelling alternatives which could achieve the purpose of the law to the same extent. Thirdly, and in absolutely exceptional cases, a law will be invalid if its legitimate, but trivial, purpose is inadequate to support the extent of the burden placed upon the high constitutional purpose of s 92.[47]

Keifel CJ and Deane, in their joint judgment, also adopted structured proportionality as the frame,[48] arguing that it 'certainly seems preferable to its main competitors.'[49]

The effect of the border closures was to impose the same quarantine requirements on interstate travelers as were required of international travelers, namely, at the time, a two-week stay in hotel quarantine. In *Baker*, the Victorian Supreme Court, in a judicial review case, accepted that a decision of Victoria's Acting Chief Health Officer to require Olivia Baker to stay in hotel quarantine was reasonable and that the Acting Chief Health Officer had made a fair assessment of the risks inherent in Baker's proposed alternative, home quarantine.[50]

10.3.1 Controlling Movement within a State

Public health restrictions varied across Australia during 2020 and 2021, with Victorians enduring the longest and most severe restrictions.[51] These public health measures, especially 'lockdowns,' effectively created a personal border, requiring people to stay in their own homes with limited rights to exercise within a 5 kilometre radius. In Victoria, a night curfew was also imposed and an internal border between Melbourne and the rest of the state created for some periods of the pandemic.[52] Freedom of assembly and protest was also curtailed.

Australians generally supported state government responses to the pandemic,[53] but a minority did not and challenged the legitimacy of movement restrictions, both politically and through legal action. The legal actions were mostly unsuccessful.

Victoria's night curfew was challenged in *Loielo* on the grounds, i.a., that the restrictions on human movement imposed by the curfew unreasonably curtailed freedom of movement, contrary to Victoria's Charter of Human Rights.[54] The challenge failed, as the Court accepted the decision-maker's conclusion that the curfew—as one of a set of related restrictions—was 'reasonably necessary to protect public health.'[55]

In *Athavle*, the Federal Court of Australia declined to grant a requested interlocutory order allowing the applicants to freely practise their religion and conduct services on important religious days. This case tested whether the relevant public health measures (in both Victoria and New South Wales) unreasonably interfered with an implied freedom of religion. The Court found that if the injunctive relief was granted, "there is a risk that members of the public will become infected, some will inevitably require hospitalisation, and some might also die."[56] The Court also found that accommodations could be made that would allow some form of observance to be held which was consistent with the public health measures.

The orders restricting people's movement also restricted freedom of assembly and the right to protest. Although initially, some authorities thought the SARS-CoV-2 virus was transmitted by droplets, it is, in fact, aerosol spread.[57] This means that outdoor transmission was less likely than indoor transmission, but it still may occur, and hence, there is a public health risk from outdoor assemblies. These risks can be mitigated—but not eliminated—by good management of the assembly.

Importantly, in *Gerner*, the High Court reaffirmed that there was no implied freedom of movement in the Australian constitution which precluded legitimate movement regulation by states.[58] Again in Victoria, Kerry Cotterill, who left her home to exercise and protest movement restrictions, failed to establish a legally protected right to protest included as a permissible ground for leaving home.[59] A New South Wales case—challenging requirements to be vaccinated in certain work roles but which also touched on freedom of movement—also upheld that state's public health measures.[60]

During 2020, the New South Wales police commissioner sought orders to prevent a number of outdoor demonstrations/assemblies.[61] As Cavanagh J pointed out in one of those cases, "(e)ach case must turn on its own facts and on the evidence adduced by the parties,"[62] and so some rallies were approved and some not.

The death at police hands of George Floyd in the United States led to widespread concern and protests globally, with a 'Black Lives Matter' assembly planned in Sydney for June 2020. The public health interest and the right to assembly were considered by the New South Wales Supreme Court which prohibited the proposed assembly.[63] Fagan J noted:

> It is self-evident that the social distancing measures adopted to this point have been the key element in minimising the spread of this disease. A gathering of 5,000 people who are interested in this particular cause, at a time when the entire community is under direction not to gather in groups of more than ten, is an unreasonable proposition. The exercise of the fundamental right of assembly and of expression of political opinion by gathering in numbers is not taken away by the current Public Health Order; it is deferred.[64]

On appeal, this decision was overturned, largely on procedural grounds,[65] with the public health issues not canvassed in the judgment, and so the rally went ahead.

In the same week, a rally about the rights of refugees was prohibited[66] and just over a week after that the NSW Supreme Court again returned to the right of assembly, and again refused a Black Lives Matter rally, both decisions made on grounds similar to those articulated by Fagan J.[67] In contrast, another Black Lives Matter and related issues rally in Newcastle was allowed to proceed, with the decision taking into account the view of the Chief Health Officer that the risk was 'low' and that there had been no transmissions of unknown origin in the previous four weeks.[68] A few weeks later, in *Gibson*, the Supreme Court supported the prohibition of a Sydney rally about Aboriginal deaths in custody with Ierace J, concluding the following:

> In my view, the balancing of the competing concerns of the right to free speech and to demonstrate, as against the safety of the community at large, at this particular phase of the pandemic, necessitates the granting of the order prohibiting the holding of the public assembly. In so finding, I take

> into account the defendant's proposed safety measures, but also the absence of a mechanism to enforce them and the current rating of the risk of transmission of the COVID-19 virus at public assemblies as being 'medium'. "[69]

A few months later, the NSW Supreme Court again considered the competing interests of great importance, to use the NSW Court of Appeal phrasing.[70] In the first case, *Holcombe*, the right for a rally for transgender rights, was refused.[71] Later that same week, in *Thomson*, the Court weighed the right to protest differently against the potential threat to public health.[72] In *Thomson*, the rally was to be about proposed changes to Commonwealth government funding of universities. The rally organizers proposed a number of risk mitigation actions which, in the Court's view, meant the following:

> [T]he health risks associated with this proposed assembly are so low, having regard to the way in which it will be conducted and the expected numbers (even allowing for higher numbers) that the right to free speech and assembly outweighs whatever health risks there might be.[73]

Although Gordon fairly described the New South Wales Supreme Court's reasoning in these cases as a 'mixed bag,'[74] one can discern a thread through these freedom of assembly cases, including consideration of the assessed risk of transmission by public health officials (low versus medium), the expected size of the rallies, and the perceived efficacy of risk mitigation strategies advanced by the organizers. The higher the risk, the more the Court weighed the public health concerns over the democratic right to freedom of assembly/protest.

Movement—or lack thereof—was also the subject of a number of family court decisions about the impact of border closures and concerns about the SARS-CoV-2 virus in the context of pre-pandemic custody-sharing or child support orders.[75] Each case turned on its individual circumstances with Judge Harland in the Federal Circuit Court of Australia concluding:

> [T]hat the current state of emergency and restrictions that are put in place do not provide a general excuse for not complying with parenting orders of the Court.[76]

10.4 Conclusion

A central part of Australia's response to the SARS-CoV-2 pandemic involved an infringement of human rights—in particular, the right to freedom of movement. However, no human right is unfettered and, during the pandemic, public health authorities concluded that greater movement would lead to greater transmission of the virus.

Public health protection took priority in the public health emergency created by the pandemic and so movement restrictions were imposed. This balance—of individual freedom of movement against controlling virus spread—was challenged in several cases, but each time, the courts found that the public health measures were a legitimate exercise of emergency powers. Each of the decisions in these cases also considered whether other less stringent measures might have been equally effective, with the courts concluding, on the basis of public health evidence, that they would not have been.[77] The exception to the rule can be found in the freedom of assembly cases, where occasionally, the democratic right to protest was upheld despite a non-zero risk of transmission.

Australia, a liberal democracy, thus became a case study of imposition of stringent restrictions to prevent the spread of the SARS-CoV-2 virus which were supported by the public[78] and also found to be a legitimate exercise of state power following judicial review.

But this is not to say that there cannot be improvements in the way state power was exercised. The pandemic created a new environment for freedom of assembly cases, and more explicit codification of the matters to be taken into account by decision-makers (such as community prevalence, risk mitigation strategies) might give greater certainty to applicants seeking the right to protest.[79]

In some states, the movement restrictions were imposed by public health officials, in others, by politicians. Ginnane J in *Loielo* questioned the Victorian position at the time, which was for public health officials to make the determination:

> There is an issue of whether a health expert . . . is able to properly balance the social and economic consequences of a decision primarily based on health considerations.[80]

The public health mindset often emphasizes 'prevention is better than cure' and the 'precautionary principle', the latter positing that in the absence of definitive evidence public health policy should err on the side of caution.[81] But such an approach sits uneasily with the Victorian Charter of Human Rights, creating an 'inherent tension between that principle and the Charter's *demonstrably* justified test.'[82] Political decision-makers may well adopt the precautionary principle, too, but are probably better placed to assess where the public sits in terms of the trade-offs to be made. Different politicians may make different assessments of the trade-offs, as was seen in the divergent responses of the Commonwealth and most state governments in the Australian response to the first two years of the pandemic.[83]

But for political and public health decision-makers alike, weighing 'social and economic considerations' was difficult given the poor availability of contemporaneous information about the social and economic impacts of the pandemic, an issue common to many countries.[84] Victoria subsequently shifted decision-making power to elected officials, with a requirement for the politicians to seek advice from the Chief Health Officer, with that advice to be made public.[85]

The premise of emergency powers is that there are times when extraordinary actions are necessary to protect the public. In those circumstances, 'judicial deference'[86] may be seen: 'the judiciary has a tendency to defer to the Executive.'[87] Giving more power to the executive may thus create the risk that freedoms will be more likely to be infringed.

But if the Australian political experience is any guide, the reality is that the state governments which erred on the side of caution in managing the pandemic were convincingly reelected (South Australia being the exception) while the federal government, which adopted more of the 'freedom' discourse, was not. Although one has to be cautious in using electoral tests, this political validation suggests that a model where there is clear political accountability for public health decisions—and a politician is the decision-maker about public health restrictions—should become the common model in Australia for the exercise of public health powers in emergencies.

Notes

1 Valentina Costantino, David J. Heslop & C. Raina MacIntyre, "The effectiveness of full and partial travel bans against COVID-19 spread in Australia for travellers from China during and after the epidemic peak in China" (2020) 27:5 *Journal of Travel Medicine* taaa081; Adeshina Adekunle et al, " Delaying the COVID-19 epidemic in Australia: Evaluating the effectiveness of international travel bans" (2020) 44: 4 *Australian and New Zealand Journal of Public Health* 257.
2 Leah M. Grout et al, "Estimating the failure risk of quarantine systems for preventing COVID-19 outbreaks in Australia and New Zealand" (2021) 215: 7 *Medical Journal of Australia* 320.
3 COVID-19 Excess Mortality Collaborators, "Estimating excess mortality due to the COVID-19 pandemic: A systematic analysis of COVID-19-related mortality, 2020–21" (2022) 399:10334 *The Lancet* 1513.
4 *Kassam v Hazzard* [2021] NSWSC 1320, Beech Jones CJ in CL, para 43.
5 Stephen Duckett, "Public health management of the COVID-19 pandemic in Australia: The role of the morrison government" (2022) 19:16 *International Journal of Environmental Research and Public Health* 10400.
6 Commissioner of Police v Bassi [2020] NSWSC 710 [Bassi 1]; *Raul Bassi v Commissioner of Police (NSW)* [2020] NSWCA 109 [Bassi 2].
7 *Commissioner of Police (NSW) v Supple* [2020] NSWSC 727 [Supple].
8 *Commissioner of Police, New South Wales Police Force v Kumar (OBO National Union of Students)* [2020] NSWSC 804 [Kumar-NUS].
9 *Gerner v Victoria* [2020] HCA 48 [Gerner].
10 *Commissioner of Police v Gray* [2020] NSWSC 867 [Gray].
11 *Commissioner of Police (NSW) v Gibson* [2020] NSWSC 953 [Gibson].
12 *Commissioner of Police v Samuel Holcombe also known as April Holcombe (on behalf of Community Action for Rainbow Rights)* [2020] NSWSC 1428 [Holcombe].
13 *Commissioner of Police v Thomson* [2020] NSWSC 1424 [Thomson].
14 *Loielo v Giles* [2020] VSC 722 [*Loielo*].
15 *Palmer v Western Australia* [2021] HCA 5 [Palmer].

16 *Newman v Minister for Health and Aged Care* [2021] FCA 517 [Newman].
17 *LibertyWorks Inc v Commonwealth of Australia* [2021] FCAFC 90 [LibertyWorks].
18 *Athavle v State of New South Wales* [2021] FCA 1075 [Athavle].
19 *Cotterill v Romanes* [2021] VSC 498 [Cotterill].
20 *Baker v Department of Health and Human Service* [2021] VSC 673 [Baker].
21 *Henry v Hazzard* [2021] NSWCA 299 [*Henry*].
22 Holly Mclean & Ben Huf, "Emergency powers, public health and COVID-19 Melbourne" (August 2020), online (pdf): *Department of Parliamentary Services*. https://nla.gov.au/nla.obj-2849026124/view.
23 Paula O'Brien & Eliza Waters, "COVID-19: Public Health emergency powers and accountability mechanisms in Australia" (2021) 28: 2 *Journal Law of Medicine* 346.
24 See, for example, *Kassam v. Hazzard, supra* note 4; *Larter v Hazzard (No 2)* [2021] NSWSC 1451; *Harding v Sutton* [2021] VSC 741; *Kimber v Sapphire Coast Community Aged Care Ltd*, [2021] FWCB 6015; *Construction, Forestry, Maritime, Mining and Energy Union v British Concrete Pty Ltd T/A British Concrete* [2022] FWC 1774 (8 July 2022); *Paul Kallipolitis v Australian Postal Corporation* [2022] FWC 1739 (5 July 2022); *Boles & Walsh v Vonk & ors* [2022] QCAT 144; *Colebourne v State of Queensland (Queensland Police Service)* [2022] QIRC 40; *Clay And Dallas* [2022] FCWA 18. A scatter gun challenge to public health measures was summarily dismissed in *Knowles v Commonwealth of Australia* [2022] FCA 741.
25 *Djokovic v Minister for Immigration, Citizenship, Migrant Services and Multicultural Affairs* [2022] FCAFC 3.
26 Auditor-General, *Management of International Travel Restrictions during COVID-19* (ANAO, 2021).
27 Auditor-General, *Overseas Crisis Management and Response: The Effectiveness of the Department of Foreign Affairs and Trade's Management of the Return of Overseas Australians in Response to the COVID-19 Pandemic* (ANAO, 2022); Pippa McDermid et al, "How have governments supported citizens stranded abroad due to COVID-19 travel restrictions? A comparative analysis of the financial and health support in eleven countries" (2022) 22:161 *BMC Infectious Diseases* 1.
28 Pippa McDermid et al, "Examining the psychological and financial impact of travel restrictions on citizens and permanent residents stranded abroad during the COVID-19 pandemic: International cross-sectional study" (2022) 12:5 *BMJ Open* e059922; Olivera Simic, "Locked in and locked out: A migrant woman's reflection on life in Australia during the COVID-19 pandemic" (2021) 22:9 *Journal of International Women's Studies* 400.
29 Alberto Boretti, "Legitimacy in international law of Australian border closure to own citizens" (2022) 19:1 *Éthique & Santé* 54. See also *Potter v Minahan* (1908) 7 CLR 277.
30 LibertyWorks, online: www.libertyworks.org.au/people.
31 *LibertyWorks Inc v Commonwealth of Australia* [2021] FCAFC 90.
32 Regina Jefferies, Jane McAdam & Sangeetha Pillai, "Can we still call Australia home? The right to return and the legality of Australia's COVID-19 travel restrictions" (2021) 27:2 *Journal of Human Rights* 211; Olivera Simic, "Australia, Covid-19, and the India Travel Ban" (2022) 9:2 *The Griffith Journal of Law & Human Dignity* 35; Diego S. Silva, "The abandonment of Australians in India: An analysis of the right of entry as a security right in the age of COVID-19" (in press) Monash Bioethics Review; Olivera Simic & Kim Rubenstein, "The challenge of 'COVID-19 free' Australia: International travel restrictions and stranded citizens" (in press) *International Journal of Human Rights* 1; Elizabeth Hicks, "A right to come home? Repatriation rights & policy in Australia" (15 April 2022), online (pdf): *Melbourne School of Government*. https://papers.ssrn.com/sol3/papers.cfm?abstract_id=3829313.

33 Liz Hicks & Sangeetha Pillai, "Proportionality, rights and Australia's COVID-19 response: Insights from the India travel ban" (2021) *Australian Public Law*; Priam Rangiah, "COVID travel bans, citizenship and the constitution: Do Australian citizens have a constitutional right of Abode?" (in press) *Federal Law Review* 0067205X221107456.
34 *Newman, supra* note 16.
35 Kim Moloney & Susan Moloney, "Australian quarantine policy: From centralization to coordination with mid-pandemic COVID-19 shifts" (2020) 80: 4 *Public Administration Review* 671.
36 Issues about Australian federalism and COVID-19 have been canvassed in Scott Stephenson, "The relationship between federalism and rights during COVID-19" (2021) 32:3 *Public Law Review* 222.
37 Kate Ogg & Olivera Simić, "Becoming an internally displaced person in Australia: state border closures during the COVID-19 pandemic and the role of international law on internal displacement" (in press), *The Australian Journal of Human Rights* 1; Dirk H. R. Spennemann, " 'No entry into New South Wales': COVID-19 and the historic and contemporary trajectories of the effects of border closures on an Australian cross-border community" (2021) 10:6 *Land* 610; Lily McCann et al, "Police, permits and politics: Navigating life on Australia's state borders during the COVID-19 pandemic" (in press), *The Australian Journal of Rural Health*.
38 David Meale, "The history of the federal idea in Australian constitutional jurisprudence: A reappraisal" (1992) 8 *Australian Journal of Law & Society* 25; Gonzalo Vilalta Puig, "Intercolonial free trade: The drafting history of section 92 of the Australian constitution" (2011) 30:2 *The University of Tasmania Law Review* 1.
39 *Palmer, supra* note 15.
40 *Palmer v Western Australia* (No 4) [2020] FCA 1221 [Palmer FCA].
41 *Ibid*, para 366.
42 Samuel Whittaker & Leah Triantafyllos, "Clive Palmer, section 92, and covid-19: Where 'absolutely free' is absolutely not: 'Palmer v Western Australia' (2021) 388 ALR 180" (2021) 42:2 *Adelaide Law Review* 623; David Hume, "Palmer v Western Australia (2021) 95 ALJR 229; [2021] HCA 5: trade, commerce and intercourse shall be absolutely free (except when it need not)" (23 June 2021), online: *Australian Public Law*. www.auspublaw.org/blog/2021/06/palmer-v-western-australia-2021-95-aljr-229–2021-hca-5.
43 *Palmer, supra* note 15, para 81.
44 Evelyn Douek, "All out of proportion: The ongoing disagreement about structured proportionality in Australia" (2019) 47:4 *Federal Law Review* 551.
45 *Palmer, supra* note 15, para 94.
46 *Ibid*, para 198.
47 *Ibid*, para 265.
48 *Ibid*, para 62.
49 *Ibid*, para 56.
50 Baker, *supra* note 20.
51 Australian Bureau of Statistics, state economies, and the stringency of COVID-19 containment measures, December quarter 2020 (ABS, 2021).
52 Annie Wright, *Chronology of Victorian border closures due to COVID-19* (Parliamentary Library and Information Service, Parliament of Victoria, 2021).
53 Bruce Keith Tranter, "Your money or your life? Public support for health initiatives during the COVID-19 pandemic" (in press), *The Australian Journal of Social Issues*.
54 *Loielo, supra* note 14.
55 *Ibid,* para 256.
56 *Athavle, supra* note 18, para 111.

57 Trisha Greenhalgh, Mustafa Ozbilgin & David Tomlinson, "How covid-19 spreads: Narratives, counter narratives, and social dramas" (2022) 378 *BMJ* e069940. Interestingly, the evidence presented by a NSW health official in *Thomson* was still based on droplet transmission: see *Thomson*, *supra* note 13, para 84.
58 *Gerner*, *supra* note 17.
59 *Cotterill*, *supra* note 19.
60 *Henry*, *supra* note 21.
61 The statutory framework and pandemic cases are discussed in Jeffrey Gordon, "Protest Before and During a Pandemic" (2022) 50:4 *Federal Law Review* 421.
62 *Thomson*, *supra* note 13, para 60.
63 *Bassi 1*, *supra* note 6.
64 *Ibid*, paras 30 and 31.
65 *Bassi 2*, *supra* note 6.
66 *Supple*, supra note 7.
67 *Kumar-NUS*, *supra* note 8.
68 *Gray*, *supra* note 10, paras 32 and 33.
69 *Gibson*, *supra* note 11, para 84. The decision was upheld on appeal, with the appeal mainly dealing with procedural issues *Padraic Gibson (on behalf of the Dungay family) v Commissioner of Police (NSW Police Force)* [2020] NSWCA 160.
70 *Bassi 2*, *supra* note 6, para 7.
71 *Holcombe*, *supra* note 12.
72 *Thomson*, *supra* note 13.
73 *Ibid*, para 92.
74 Gordon, *supra* note 61 at 448.
75 See, for example, *Kardos & Harmon* [2020] FamCA 328; *Collingwood & Collingwood* [2020] FamCA 390; *Department of Child Safety, Youth and Women & Comar and Anor* [2020] FamCA 505; *Martyn v Martyn* [2020] FamCA 526; *Floros v Floros* [2021] FamCA 13; *Department of Communities and Justice v Kingsley (No 2)* [2021] FamCA 308; *Banham & Banham* [2020] FCCA 1201.
76 *Mafton & Salmet* [2020] FCCA 256, para 31.
77 For example, see Rangiah J. in *Palmer*, *supra* note 26.
78 Tranter, *supra* note 32.
79 The problematic nature of the current criteria-less decision-making is criticized by Gordon (*supra* note 61) in his comprehensive review of the NSW freedom of assembly cases.
80 *Loielo*, *supra* note 14, para 258.
81 Jeffrey K. Aronson, "When I use a word . . .. The precautionary principle: A definition" (2021) 375 *BMJ* n3111; Jeffrey K. Aronson, "When I use a word . . . The precautionary principle: A brief history" (2021) 375 *BMJ* n3059.
82 Bruce Chen, "The Victorian COVID-19 Response: Reflections on Loielo V Giles" (2021) 32:3 *Public Law Review* 8 at 12, emphasis in original.
83 Duckett, *supra* note 5.
84 Geoff Mulgan, Oliver Marsh & Anina Henggeler, "Navigating the crisis: How governments used intelligence for decision making during the COVID-19 pandemic London" (2022), online (pdf): *International Public Policy Observatory*. https://theippo.co.uk/wp-content/uploads/2022/12/Navigating-the-crisis-Intelligence-Report-12.12.pdf.
85 Stephen Duckett, "Australia's COVID-19 response" in *Democracy in Asia*, edited by Ryan Hass & Patricia M. Kim (Brookings Institution, 2022) 105–112.
86 Claudia Geiringer & Andrew Geddis, " Judicial deference and emergency power: A perspective on Borrowdale v Director-General" (2021) 31:4 *Public Law Review* 376.
87 Chen, *supra* note 82 at 13.

11

THE UNITED STATES RESPONSE TO COVID-19

A Patchwork of Border Regulations

Katherine Ginsbach

On January 30, 2020, the World Health Organization (WHO) declared SARS-CoV-2 a Public Health Emergency of International Concern (PHEIC).[1] On January 31, 2020, the Trump administration in the United States also declared it a public health emergency, with a formal declaration of a state of emergency on March 13, 2020.[2] The Trump administration acted to close both the southern and northern international borders, and American states imposed various travel restrictions. Twenty-seven states issued executive orders placing restrictions on out-of-state visitors. Further, municipal and tribal governments also adopted measures to protect the public health within their jurisdictions. These inconsistent and variable responses resulted in wide-ranging results. Although federal powers such as the commerce clause grant some level of authority to the federal government to regulate public health, most public health measures in the United States have historically been enacted by state and local governments pursuant to a broadly defined state police power.

11.1 Federal Response

On January 17, 2020, the US Centers for Disease Control and Prevention (CDC) implemented health screenings in three US airports (San Francisco, JFK in NY, and Los Angeles) for travelers coming from Wuhan, China.[3] On March 11, 2020, the same day that the WHO declared COVID-19 a global pandemic, President Trump announced new travel restrictions to and from 26 European countries. These travel restrictions did not apply to the United Kingdom and Ireland,[4] and included exemptions for Americans who had undergone appropriate screenings. On March 16, 2020, the Trump

DOI: 10.4324/9781003394006-15

administration announced that the travel ban would extend to foreign nationals who had been physically present in the United Kingdom or Ireland in the previous 14 days.[5] On May 28, 2020, a proclamation was announced imposing an entry ban on foreign nationals who had been in Brazil in the past two weeks, in addition to restrictions from China (not including Hong Kong or Macau), Iran, Ireland, the United Kingdom, and those countries in the Schengen Area. It was not until November 8, 2021, that the Biden administration issued a proclamation revoking the country-specific COVID-19 travel restrictions, allowing entrance for fully vaccinated nonimmigrant travelers.[6]

Approximately three weeks later, on November 26, 2021, and in response to the identification of the Omicron variant, the Biden administration issued a proclamation prohibiting travel into the US for travelers who were physically present in Botswana, Eswatini, Lesotho, Malawi, Mozambique, Namibia, South Africa, and Zimbabwe.[7] These restrictions were revoked on December 31, 2021, but individuals were still subject to COVID-19 vaccination and testing requirements.[8]

On March 23, 2020, to limit further spread of COVID-19, the United States reached agreements with both Canada and Mexico to limit all nonessential travel across borders.[9]

Under the Code of Federal Regulations (CFR), the Department of the Treasury announced the notification of temporary travel restrictions applicable to land ports of entry and ferry service between the United States and Canada and the United States and Mexico.[10] This document announced the decision of the Secretary of Homeland Security to continue to temporarily limit the travel of individuals from Canada and Mexico into the United States at land ports of entry along the United States–Canada border and the United States–Mexico border.[11] On March 24, 2020, DHS published notice of the Secretary's decision to temporarily limit the travel of individuals from Canada and Mexico into the United states to "essential travel."[12] Under the authority granted to the Secretary through 19 U.S.C. 1318(b)(1)(C) and (b)(2), it was determined that land ports of entry along the United States–Canada and United States–Mexico borders would suspend normal operations and would allow processing for entry into the United States only for those travelers engaged in "essential travel."[13] These restrictions were not intended to interrupt legitimate trade between the nations or disrupt critical supply chains that ensure food, fuel, medicine, and other critical materials to reach individuals on both sides of the border.[14] Essential travel was defined to include US citizens and lawful permanent residents returning to the United States, individuals traveling for medical purposes, individuals traveling to attend educational institutions, individuals traveling to work in the United States, individuals traveling for emergency response and public health purposes, individuals engaged in lawful cross-border trade, individuals engaged in official government travel or diplomatic travel, members of the US Armed Forces and the spouses and children of members of the US Armed Forces returning to the United States, and individuals engaged in military-related travel or operations.[15] Essential travel did not include individuals traveling for tourism purposes.[16] These orders did not apply to air, freight rail, or sea travel between the United States and Canada but did apply to passenger rail travel, passenger ferry travel, and pleasure boat travel between the United States and Canada.[17]

The decision was set to be in place for 30 days, at which point, each party would review it. Additionally, during this time, the US Customs and Border Protection would not detain undocumented immigrants in holding facilities and would immediately return them to the country from which they entered, either Canada or Mexico; if that was not possible, Border Protection would return these individuals to their country of origin.[18] On April 20, 2020, the US, Mexico, and Canada all agreed to extend restrictions to non-essential travel across their shared border for 30 additional days.[19] On May 19, 2020, it was announced that the restrictions were extended for yet another 30 days while also working to keep legitimate commercial trade flowing while limiting those seeking to enter the country for non-essential purposes.[20] The order, while only initially extended for 30 days, was extended 18 times, becoming the longest border restriction in the shared history of the United States and Canada and the United States and Mexico. On November 8, 2021, the United States allowed vaccinated travelers to cross the United States–Canadian land border, following a similar ease in restrictions by Canada in August 2021.[21]

Similarly, at the United States–Mexico border, non-essential travel resumed on November 8, 2021, for foreign travelers who were fully vaccinated for COVID-19, could present proof of COVID-19 vaccination status, and had appropriate documentation to enter the United States.[22] The vaccination requirements did not apply to United States citizens, lawful permanent residents, or United States nationals.[23] While land borders were closed, there was no similar restriction preventing Canadians or Mexicans from entering the United States by airplane; however, Americans were unable to fly into Canada without a special exemption.[24] The United States placed restrictions on arrivals by air travel for non-US citizens throughout COVID-19 coming from various countries, but the ban never included Canada or Mexico.[25]

Travel to the United States was limited by country-based entry bans with the travel restrictions being uncoordinated, often shortsighted, and enacted after the optimal time to slow the spread of COVID-19 and allow for resources to be put in place.

11.2 States' Responses

State governors and local officials had wide latitude to enforce directives during the COVID-19 pandemic. This has resulted in a patchwork of restrictions including travel requirements, mask mandates, public gatherings, and school closures. On April 13, 2020, President Trump said, "when someone is president of the United States, the authority is total."[26] On April 16, the president backtracked and delegated responsibility to each of the 50 governors to do what they thought was best.[27] The Supreme Court has recognized that states may act to protect their own citizens from disease outbreaks, until Congress says otherwise.[28] However, this power is not unrestricted, and in judging a governor's or local official's authority to exercise such powers under the 10th Amendment, courts require a "compelling government interest" be shown and evidence that the action has been narrowly tailored to achieve that interest.[29]

States took different approaches: no state closed their land borders, but Alaska and Hawaii were in unique positions by being disconnected from the continental United States. Alaska was impacted by the United States–Canada border closure that did not allow individuals to travel through Canada to Alaska for non-essential travel.[30] On March 21, 2020, Governor Ige of Hawaii issued a second supplemental emergency proclamation ordering all individuals, both residents and visitors arriving or returning to the State of Hawaii to a mandatory 14-day self-quarantine. The mandate was the first of its kind in the nation, applying to all arrivals at state airports from both the continental US and the international destinations and extended to other private and commercial aircrafts.[31] Mandatory quarantines required one to remain in a designated quarantine location for a period of 14 days or the duration required by the state, whichever was shorter.[32] The failure to comply with the order was a misdemeanor, punishable by a maximum fine of $5,000 USD or imprisonment of not more than one year, or both.[33] On August 1, 2020, the Governor of Hawaii announced that the state would require a valid COVID-19 test prior to arrival, and proof of a negative test result was required to be shown in order to avoid the 14-day quarantine.[34] Out-of-state travelers arriving in Hawaii were required to get a PCR test prior to arrival from any testing location approved by the Hawaii State Department of Health.[35] The State of Hawaii travel restrictions ended on March 25, 2022, with no COVID-related requirements remaining for arriving domestic or international passengers.[36]

In Alaska, more than 60,000 people live in remote communities that are off-the-road systems and only accessible by plane, boat, or snowmobile.[37] This resulted in statewide responses that were not seen in other states with restrictions imposed at the intrastate travel. On March 17, 2020, the Governor Dunleavy issued Health Mandate 4, requiring travelers returning from an area with widespread, ongoing community spread—such as the Schengen Area in Europe, China, and other countries—to stay home, avoid contact with other household members, and abstain from physically attending work or school for a 14-day period after their return.[38] In addition, Health Mandate 12 took effect March 28, 2020, prohibiting all in-state travel between communities, whether resident, worker, or visitor, unless the travel was necessary to support critical infrastructure or for critical personal needs.[39] If a business was included in "Alaska's Essential Services for Critical Infrastructure" list, individuals were required to submit a travel plan or protocol for maintaining critical infrastructure that outlined how they would avoid the spread of COVID-19 and not endanger the lives of the communities in which they operated.[40] Health Mandate 16, which came into effect April 24, 2020, sought to balance the ongoing need to maintain diligent efforts to slow and disrupt the rate of infection with the corresponding critical need to resume economic activity in a reasonable and safe manner.[41] On May 12, 2020, the Governor Dunleavy rescinded Health Mandate 12, with the newer Health Mandate 18 permitting travel between communities on the road system and in-state travel by the Alaska Marine Highway System.[42]

States in the Continental 48 showed a range of responses; none closed borders but put restrictions in place. On June 24, 2020, Governors Lamont, Murphy, and Cuomo of Connecticut, New Jersey, and New York, respectively, announced a joint incoming travel advisory whereby all individuals traveling from states with significant community spread of COVID-19 were required to self-quarantine for 14 days. This applied to any person arriving from a state with a positive test rate higher than ten per 100,000 residents or a state with a 10% or higher positivity rate over a seven-day rolling average.[43] Travel restrictions were dropped at different times, with Connecticut removing its mandatory quarantine period on March 19, 2021. On April 1, 2021, New York removed its mandatory quarantine rule for domestic travelers coming from any other US state or territory. And in April 2021, New Jersey removed its mandatory quarantine if individuals had been fully vaccinated or had recovered from COVID-19 in the past three months.[44] These restrictions came with no real enforcement mechanisms, as there were no border checkpoints. However, the Governor Murphy of New Jersey said that the Department of Health would pursue cases of non-compliance as they became aware of them.[45]

In Kentucky on March 30, 2020, Governor Beshear issued Executive Order 2020–258, which prohibited its residents from traveling to any other state except for when required by fairly narrowly-defined circumstances.[46] This travel restriction was challenged in a federal district court and the judge struck down a portion of the restrictions.[47] In the executive order, individuals were only permitted to leave the state for employment, to receive or provide healthcare, to obtain groceries or other needed supplies, and to travel outside the state to assist in caring for the elderly, a minor, dependents, or vulnerable or disabled persons. However, the provision prohibited Kentucky residents who lived near the state's border from visiting family members in another state, while it allowed them to travel much longer distances within state lines.[48] The Court ruling stated that enforcing travel restrictions near interstate bridges would result in "massive traffic jams" due to necessary checkpoints and that the state would have to set up quarantine facilities to house the numerous people who violated the interstate travel rules.[49] The travel restrictions were lifted on April 29, 2020, as part of an outline for the gradual reopening of businesses and lifting of travel restrictions.[50] An executive order was signed on May 22, 2020, that rescinded any provisions related to travel.[51] After the Court ruling, Governor Beshear and the Department of Health continued to dictate additional advisories but no further executive orders. On July 20, 2020, the Kentucky Department of Public Health issued a new travel advisory that recommended a 14-day self-quarantine for travelers who had visited the following eight states: Alabama, Arizona, Florida, Georgia, Idaho, Mississippi, Nevada, South Carolina, and Texas—any states reporting a positive testing rate equal to or greater than 15%.[52] On August 12, 2020, the Governor recommended a 14-day self-quarantine for individuals who had traveled to states that were reporting a positive coronavirus testing rate equal to or greater than 15%; the states that met the requirement at the time included Florida, Nevada, Mississippi, Idaho, South Carolina, Texas, Alabama, and Arizona.[53]

Other state travel restrictions included Ohio, Vermont, and West Virginia. In Ohio, Governor DeWine announced a travel advisory for all individuals coming into Ohio from states reporting positive COVID-19 testing rates of 15% or higher. The self-quarantine recommendation applied to those who lived in Ohio and to people who were traveling into Ohio from any of the previously listed states.[54] In Vermont on June 2020, a 14-day quarantine requirement was imposed for those traveling from counties in New England and New York with more than 400 active cases of COVID-19 per one million residents. On July 1, this policy was expanded to counties below this threshold in Delaware, Maryland, New Jersey, Ohio, Pennsylvania, Virginia, and West Virginia.[55] On March 24, 2020, Governor Justice of West Virginia issued a stay-at-home order; while the order did not address travel out of or into the state, on June 3, 2020, Governor Justice announced that private and state park campgrounds could open on June 10, 2020, but that out-of-state guests would be limited to stays of no longer than seven days.[56] A common feature of these orders was a requirement that entrants self-quarantine for 14 days; however, it should be noted that states did not seem to actively monitor compliance.[57] In the United States, COVID-19 continues to have many different trajectories of spread in 2023, and this trajectory has been matched by the various different jurisdictional boundaries and states taking different approaches to respond to surges.

11.3 Tribal Response

American Indian and Alaska Native Tribes across the country used their self-governing power to enact stricter rules than many states and county governments to prevent the spread of the virus.[58] In South Dakota, the Oglala Sioux Tribe and the Cheyenne River Sioux Tribe erected checkpoints on roads entering their reservations to protect their citizens. The Oglala Sioux Tribe adopted a COVID-19 Pine Ridge Reservation Border Monitoring Health Order and Coordinated Border Monitoring Plan and adopted Ordinance No. 29–18 ("Shelter-In-Place") to help decrease the spread of infection within the boundaries of the Pine Ridge Reservation. The order was put in place to ensure that the residents of Pine Ridge Indian Reservation were fully protected from the spread of COVID-19 and recognized that Indian Tribes and Reservations were among the most vulnerable populations and locations for the COVID-19 pandemic—especially as the number of positive COVID-19 cases continued to rise in the surrounding areas.[59] This order also included adopting a Border Monitoring Health Order and Coordinated Border Monitoring Plan that went into effect Friday April 3, 2020. The Ordinance stated:

> The Pine Ridge Indian Reservation is hereby closed to all non-residents for non-essential travel, except for all state highway entrances for pass-through vehicles. Essential travel is allowed and includes supply trucks/vehicles, workers and essential businesses as defined in the Shelter-In-Place order. Violations of this ordinance shall carry a civil fine of $1,000.[60]

The Cheyenne River Sioux Tribe enacted COVID-19 Checkpoint Policies on April 20, 2020, with residents only allowed to travel for "essential activities," including travel to a non-hotspot within South Dakota if it was for an essential activity and following the completion of a health questionnaire. Residents could only travel to a hotspot in South Dakota or out of state if it was for one of three purposes: essential work, medical appointments, or obtaining or delivering essential supplies or services that were not available within the Cheyenne River Sioux Reservation.[61] If a resident had to travel off the reservation, they were required to quarantine for 14 days when they returned, unless they first obtained a travel permit.[62]

By early May, South Dakota Governor Noem explicitly told the tribes to "remove their checkpoints or face the consequences."[63] Cheyenne River Sioux Tribal Chairman Harold Fraizer declined, saying that doing so would "seriously undermine our ability to protect everyone on the reservation."[64] The Governor pushed back, threatening a lawsuit and to pull essential COVID-19 relief aid and end law enforcement contracts—even asking President Trump for federal intervention to end "these unlawful tribal checkpoints/blockades."[65] The Trump administration did start the work to suspend the Cheyenne River Sioux Tribe's 638 contract to provide its own law enforcement services in lieu of the federal government's provision of such services.[66] Before the Bureau of Indian Affairs actually suspended the contract, Mark Meadows, then President Trump's chief of staff, was brought in to try and negotiate with the Cheyenne River Sioux Tribe to close their checkpoints. Meadows stated that without legal authority, the tribes could not "have checkpoints on a federal road" and proceeded to threaten withholding of the Tribe's COVID-19 relief money, which Congress had set aside by statute.[67] In June 2020, the Cheyenne River Sioux Tribe filed a complaint against the federal government, alleging that forcing tribes to shut down COVID-19 checkpoints would undermine tribal sovereignty and the people's health and well-being.[68] The Tribe brought a declaratory judgment action in an attempt to preclude the suspension of the law enforcement contract and to prevent other unlawful actions against the Tribe. This declaratory judgment case was stayed pending administration proceedings regarding the legality of the contract suspension.[69] In March 2021, the Cheyenne River Sioux Tribe ceased operation of its checkpoints.[70]

In Alaska, village closures were met with support from the Governor as demonstrated by the state's policy of limiting in-state travel to off-road villages. Native villages are often disconnected from the road system and may only be reachable by plane. While the isolation can make accessing medical treatments more challenging, it makes it easier to control people moving in and out and to quarantine or isolate individuals if necessary.[71] On March 23, 2020, in Fort Yukon, Alaska—a 580-person town—where the nearest big city is 150 miles away, leaders suspended all inbound passenger air travel, exempting only medical personnel, patients returning from treatment, public safety officers, and those who made it through a restrictive waiver process.[72] Anyone who arrived after March 14, 2020, was subject to a mandatory two-week quarantine, and patrolling villagers discouraged anyone from entering the settlement by snowmobile.[73] As some villagers were away from home when the orders went into effect and were thus stranded at their location, the village leaders worked to help cover their expenses incurred while waiting to return home.[74] Some stranded Fort Yukon residents rode in on snowmobiles; after refusing to leave, they agreed to isolate in their homes, resulting in the village restarting a community-wide 14-day lockdown.[75]

Other parts of Alaska required quarantine and testing upon arrival. The City of Nome reduced the number of flights per day from Anchorage from two to one, and passengers were required to complete an online health form prior to arrival.[76] It should be noted that these villages depend on air shipments and resupply by bush planes, but without many passengers to fly, Alaska's bush airlines drastically reduced their services, leading some to worry that fewer flights could result in food shortages in towns that were only accessible by air.[77] These shortages materialized in rural communities, especially with the sudden bankruptcy and closure of Ravn Airlines, an airline service that served much of rural Alaska. Communities were cut off from scheduled air service and with disruptions to freight supply for local grocery stores. For those communities connected to the road system, quarantine requirements made it difficult to drive to larger towns where groceries could be purchased more affordably.[78]

Reservations deployed state-of-emergency declarations and executive orders limiting the movements of persons in and out of reservations and native villages. In a state like Alaska where villages are located off the road system, there was less conflict with state and federal governments over border closures. In South Dakota—where porous borders and life for many reservation residents is continuous between their reservation home and neighbors—more conflict arose stemming from different approaches to suppress the spread of COVID-19.

11.4 Conclusion

The United States responded to the threat of COVID-19 in an incoherent, chaotic, and mismanaged patchwork of regulations, especially when it came to border restrictions. The federal government closed northern and southern borders while leaving it to states to determine their own interventions to slow the spread. With states having a patchwork of interventions, tribes were left to navigate their own responses that either complemented or conflicted with state responses. The COVID-19 pandemic revealed and exploited gaps in the United States response to disease outbreaks and makes a strong case for rules and norms that foster collaboration among federal, states, and tribes to coordinate preparedness and responses for disease outbreaks.

Notes

1 World Health Organization, "COVID-19 Public Health Emergency of International Concern (PHEIC) Global Research and Innovation Forum" (12 February 2020), online (pdf): www.who.int/publications/m/item/covid-19-public-health-emergency-of-international-concern-(pheic)-global-research-and-innovation-forum.

2 Administration for Strategic Preparedness & Response, "Determination That a Public Health Emergency Exists" (31 January 2020), online: aspr.hhs.gov/legal/PHE/Pages/2019-nCoV.aspx; White House Archives, "Proclamation on Declaring a National Emergency Concerning the Novel Coronavirus Disease (COVID-19) Outbreak" (13 March 2020), online: trumpwhitehouse.archives.gov/presidential-actions/proclamation-declaring-national-emergency-concerning-novel-coronavirus-disease-covid-19-outbreak/.

3 Ryan Goodman & Danielle Schulkin, "Timeline of the Coronavirus Pandemic and U.S. Response" (3 November 2020), online: *Just Security*. www.justsecurity.org/69650/timeline-of-the-coronavirus-pandemic-and-u-s-response/.

4 The exemption for the UK and Ireland was debated, as Trump said that the UK was doing "a very good job controlling the virus." The countries that were banned are located in the Schengen free travel area in Europe. Another reason is that Boris Johnson and Trump have a close relationship—both populists, nationalists, and focused on strong borders. See Frank Langfitt, "U.K. Not Included in Trump's European Travel Ban, Even as COVID-19 Spreads There" (12 March 2020), online: *NPR*. www.npr.org/2020/03/12/815097880/u-k-not-included-in-trumps-european-travel-ban-even-as-covid-19-spreads-there. It should be noted that Trump's travel ban sidestepped his own European resorts. See Ryan Heath, "Trump's travel

ban sidesteps his own European resorts" (12 March 2020), online: *Politico*. www.politico.com/news/2020/03/12/trump-coronavirus-travel-europe-resorts-126808.

5 "White House Extends COVID-19 Travel Ban to UK, Ireland" (14 March 2020), online: *BAL News*. www.bal.com/bal-news/us-covid-19-summary-of-current-travel-restrictions/.

6 Caroline Tang & Mark Wu, "White House Permits Air Travel Into the United States for Fully Vaccinated Nonimmigrant Travelers, Beginning November 8, 2021" (27 October 2021), online: *Ogletree Deakins*. ogletree.com/insights/white-house-permits-air-travel-into-the-united-states-for-fully-vaccinated-nonimmigrant-travelers-beginning-november-8–2021/.

7 Rosa M. Corriveau & Jacob A. Kanyusik, "Back to the Future: White House Restricts Travel to the United States from 8 Countries Due to New COVID-19 Variant" (1 December 2021), online: *Ogletree Deakins*. https://ogletree.com/insights/back-to-the-future-white-house-restricts-travel-to-the-united-states-from-8-countries-due-to-new-covid-19-variant/.

8 Emory University, "Omicron COVID-19 Variant Travel Restrictions Lifted" (4 January 2022), online: *International Student and Scholar Services*. https://isss.emory.edu/about/news/2021/omicron.html#:~:text=The%20US%20government%20has%20revoked,read%20the%20presidential%20proclamation%20here.

9 Homeland Security, "Fact Sheet: DHS Measures on the Border to Limit the Further Spread of Coronavirus" (23 March 2020), online: www.dhs.gov/news/2020/10/19/fact-sheet-dhs-measures-border-limit-further-spread-coronavirus.

10 "The Federal Register" (21 October 2021), online: *Federal Register*. www.federalregister.gov/documents/2021/10/21/2021-23005/notification-of-temporary-travel-restrictions-applicable-to-land-ports-of-entry-and-ferries-service.

11 Department of Homeland Security, "Notification of Temporary Travel Restrictions Applicable to Land Ports of Entry and Ferries Service Between the United States and Canada" (19 May 2020), online (pdf): www.dhs.gov/sites/default/files/publications/20_0519_as1_frn_us-canada-border.pdf; Department of Homeland Security, "Notification of Temporary Travel Restrictions Applicable to Land Ports of Entry and Ferries Service Between the United States and Mexico" (19 May 2020), online (pdf): www.dhs.gov/sites/default/files/publications/20_0519_as1_frn_us-mexico-border.pdf.

12 *Ibid.*

13 *Ibid.*

14 *Ibid.*

15 *Ibid.*

16 *Ibid.*

17 *Ibid.*

18 *Ibid.*

19 Homeland Security, "Acting Secretary Chad Wolf Statement on Non-Essential Travel" (20 April 2020), online: www.dhs.gov/news/2020/04/20/acting-secretary-chad-wolf-statement-non-essential-travel.

20 See "White House Extends COVID-19 Travel Ban," *supra* note 5.

21 Holly Honderich, "US-Canada border: After 19 months, families reunite" (9 November 2021), online: *BBC News*. www.bbc.com/news/world-us-canada-59167718.

22 San Diego Tourism Authority, "US-Mexico Border," online: www.sandiego.org/plan/visitors-information-services/border.aspx.

23 *Ibid.*

24 See Honderich, *supra* note 21.

25 "Fact Sheet: DHS Notice of Arrival Restrictions on China, Iran and Certain Countries of Europe" (17 March 2020), online: *Department of Homeland Security*. www.dhs.gov/news/2020/03/17/fact-sheet-dhs-notice-arrival-restrictions-china-iran-and-certain-countries-europe.

26 C-Span, "President Trump with Coronavirus Task Force Briefing" (13 April 2020) at 00h:59m:51s, online (video): www.c-span.org/video/?471160-1/president-trump-coronavirus-task-force-briefing.
27 Jeff Thaler, "Can Governors Close Their Borders to Pandemic Risks?" (20 April 2020), online: *Just Security*. www.justsecurity.org/69770/can-governors-close-their-borders-to-pandemic-risks/.
28 *Compagnie Francaise de Navigation a Vapeur v. Board of Health of State of Louisiana*, 186 US 380 (1902). The Supreme Court held state laws requiring the involuntary quarantine of individuals to prevent the spread of disease were constitutional. Louisiana's quarantine laws were a reasonable exercise of the state's police power that conflicted with neither the Dormant Commerce Clause nor the Due Process Clause of the 14th Amendment.
29 "How Much Authority Do State and Local Officials Have during a Health Emergency, such as the COVID-19 Pandemic" (May 2020), online: *American Bar Association*. www.americanbar.org/news/abanews/publications/youraba/2020/youraba-may-2020/state-local-authority-during-covid/.
30 Tess Williams, "Alaska Towns Near the Canadian Border Prepare for Another Summer of Restrictions" (2 May 2021), online: *Anchorage Daily News*. www.adn.com/alaska-news/2021/05/02/alaska-towns-near-the-canadian-border-prepare-for-another-summer-of-restrictions/.
31 "Governor Ige Orders Mandatory 14-Day Quarantine For All Individuals Arriving or Returning to the State of Hawai'I" (21 Mar 2020), online: *State of Hawaii Department of Transportation*. https://hidot.hawaii.gov/blog/2020/03/21/governor-ige-orders-mandatory-14-day-quarantine-for-all-individuals-arriving-or-returning-to-the-state-of-hawai%CA%BBi/.
32 Office of the Governor State of Hawaii, "Secondary Supplement Proclamation" (21 March 2020), online (pdf): https://governor.hawaii.gov/wp-content/uploads/2020/03/2003152-ATG_Second-Supplementary-Proclamation-for-COVID-19-signed.pdf.
33 *Ibid.*
34 Office of the Governor, News Release, "State to launch COVID-19 Pre-travel Testing Program for Out-of-state Travelers August 1" (24 June 2020), online: https://governor.hawaii.gov/newsroom/latest-news/office-of-the-governor-news-release-state-to-launch-covid-19-pre-travel-testing-program-for-out-of-state-travelers-august-1/.
35 *Ibid.*
36 "Pre-travel Testing Requirements for Travelers Lifted" (2022), online: *COVID-19 Updates-Hawaii Tourism*. www.hawaiitourismauthority.org/covid-19-updates/.
37 Ruby Fried et al, "COVID-19 in Remote Alaska Communities: A Longitudinal View of a Novel Pandemic" (22 May 2022), online: *Arctic Research Consortium of the United States*. www.arcus.org/witness-the-arctic/2022/3/highlight/1.
38 Governor Michael J. Dunleavy, "COVID-19 Health Mandate 4" (17 March 2020), online (pdf): https://gov.alaska.gov/wp-content/uploads/sites/2/03172020-SOA-COVID-19-Health-Mandate-004.pdf.
39 Governor Michael J. Dunleavy, "COVID-19 Health Mandate 12" (27 March 2020), online (pdf): https://gov.alaska.gov/wp-content/uploads/sites/2/03272020-SOA-COVID-19-Health-Mandate-012.pdf.
40 *Ibid.*
41 Governor Michael J. Dunleavy, "COVID-19 Health Mandate 16" (22 April 2020), online (pdf): https://content.govdelivery.com/accounts/AKDHSS/bulletins/287f1b5.
42 Office of Governor Mike Dunleavy, Press Release, "Governor Issues COVID-19 Health Mandate 18" (12 May 2020), online: https://gov.alaska.gov/newsroom/2020/05/12/governor-issues-covid-19-health-mandate-18/.

43 Office of State of Connecticut Governor Ned Lamont, Press Release, "Governor Lamont, Governor Cuomo, and Governor Murphy Announce Joint Incoming Travel Advisory That All Individuals Traveling From States with Significant Community Spread of COVID-19 Self-Quarantine for 14 Days" (24 June 2020), online: https://portal.ct.gov/Office-of-the-Governor/News/Press-Releases/2020/06-2020/Governor-Lamont-Governor-Cuomo-and-Governor-Murphy-Announce-Joint-Incoming-Travel-Advisory.
44 Laura Dannen Redman, "New York and Connecticut Drop Mandatory Quarantine; NJ Loosens Restrictions" (8 April 2021), online: *AFAR*. www.afar.com/magazine/what-to-know-about-the-ny-nj-and-ct-travel-advisory-during-covid-19.
45 *Ibid*.
46 Governor of Kentucky, "Executive Order 2020–258: State of Emergency Relating to Travel" (30 March 2020), online (pdf): https://governor.ky.gov/attachments/20200330_Executive-Order_2020-258_Out-of-State-Travel.pdf.
47 David Wells, "Kentucky's COVID-19 Travel Ban Ruled Unconstitutional" (4 May 2020), online: *Courthouse News Service*. www.courthousenews.com/federal-judge-rules-kentuckys-covid-19-travel-ban-is-unconstitutional/.
48 *Ibid*.
49 *Ibid*.
50 C. Staley & S Kitchen, "Gov. Beshear Outlines Road Ahead for Gradual Reopening of Businesses" (29 April 2020), online: *Office of the Governor, Kentucky*. www.kentucky.gov/Pages/Activity-stream.aspx?n=GovernorBeshear&prId=148.
51 Governor of Kentucky, "State of Emergency Relating to Travel" (22 May 2020), online (pdf): https://govsite-assets.s3.amazonaws.com/hCKid1hmTrmshmdgoP7A_Executive%20Order%202020-415%20Relating%20to%20Travel.pdf.
52 Governor of Kentucky, "Kentucky's Response to COVID-19" (20 October 2020), online (pdf): https://governor.ky.gov/Documents/20201020_COVID-19_page-archive.pdf.
53 *Ibid*.
54 Ohio Department of Health, Press Release, "Governor DeWine Issues Statewide Mask Order, Travel Warning" (22 July 2020), online: https://coronavirus.ohio.gov/resources/news-releases-news-you-can-use/gov-dewine-issues-statewide-mask-order-travel-warning.
55 Office of the Governor of Vermont, Press Release, "Governor Phil Scott Expands Trusted Travel Policy" (26 June 2020), online: https://governor.vermont.gov/press-release/governor-phil-scott-expands-trusted-travel-policy.
56 "State Governors' 'Stay-at Home' and Prohibition of Elective Procedures Orders" (13 October 2020), online: *McGuireWoods*. www.mcguirewoods.com/client-resources/Alerts/2020/10/state-governors-stay-at-home-prohibition-elective-procedures-orders.
57 David M. Studdert, Mark A. Hall & Michelle M. Mello, "Partitioning the Curve—Interstate Travel Restrictions During the COVID-19 Pandemic" (24 September 2020) 383 *The New England Journal of Medicine* e83.
58 Mary Auld, "COVID-19 Restrictions Put Tribal Sovereignty to the Test" (30 October 2020), online: *Montana Public Radio*. www.mtpr.org/montana-news/2020-10-30/covid-19-restrictions-put-tribal-sovereignty-to-the-test.
59 "Oglala Sioux Tribe Border Monitoring & Curfew Public Service Announcement" (3 April 2020), online (pdf): *COS-OM/COVID-19 Task Force Public Information Officer*. www.helplinecenter.org/wp-content/uploads/Oglala-Lakota-County-Curfew-Ordinance.pdf.
60 *Ibid*.
61 Bryan Bender, "Summary of CRST COVID-19 Checkpoint Policies" (20 April 2020), posted on *Cheyenne River Sioux Tribe*, online: *Facebook*. www.facebook.com/photo.php?fbid=3463114000368790&set=pcb.2774350765997474&type=1&theater.

62 *Ibid.*
63 Kalen Goodluck, "Tribes Defend Themselves against a Pandemic and South Dakota's State Government" (2 Oct 2020), online: *High Country News*. www.hcn.org/articles/indigenous-affairs-covid19-tribes-defend-themselves-against-a-pandemic-and-south-dakotas-state-government.
64 *Ibid.*
65 *Ibid.*
66 A 638 contract gives Indian tribes the authority to contract with the federal government to operate programs serving their tribal members and other eligible persons. The idea behind suspending the Tribe's law enforcement contract was apparently that the Tribe could not operate the checkpoints if it no longer had law enforcement power. Public Law 93–638, *Indian Self-Determination, and Education Assistance Act*, as amended.
67 Frank Pommersheim, "An Emeritus Prose Podcast: The Pandemic Checkpoints of the Cheyenne River Sioux Tribe: A Teaching Essay" (November 2021), online (pdf): *TurtleTalk*. https://turtletalk.files.wordpress.com/2021/11/the-pandemic-checkpoints-of-the-cheyenne-river-sioux-tribe.pdf.
68 *Ibid.*
69 Case No: 1:20-cv-01709, *In the United States District Court for the District of Columbia* (filed 23 June 2020), online (pdf): www.indianz.com/covid19/wp-content/uploads/2020/06/crstvtrump.pdf.
70 "Tribe removes disputed coronavirus reservation checkpoints" (26 March 2021), online: *AP News*. https://apnews.com/article/joe-biden-police-south-dakota-coronavirus-pandemic-kristi-noem-dd5ee196986decd0c504a21a55255bbb.
71 Nathaniel Hertz, "Most Villages Lack Road Access to Hospitals. Here's How They'll Fight the Coronavirus" (15 March 2020), online: *Alaska Public Media*. https://alaskapublic.org/2020/03/15/most-alaska-villages-lack-road-access-and-hospitals-heres-how-theyll-fight-the-coronavirus/.
72 Alejandro De La Garza, "Alaska's Remote Villages Are Cutting Themselves Off to Avoid Even 'One Single Case' of Coronavirus" (31 March 2020), online: *Time*. https://time.com/5813162/alaska-coronavirus/.
73 *Ibid.*
74 *Ibid.*
75 *Ibid.*
76 Emily Hofstaedter, "What to Expect When Traveling to Nome Based on City Requirements" (22 January 2021), online: *KNOM Radio Mission*. www.knom.org/wp/blog/2021/01/22/what-to-expect-when-traveling-to-nome-based-on-city-requirements/.
77 *Ibid.*
78 N. Johnson et al, "The Impact of COVID-19 on Food access for Alaska Natives in 2020" (7 December 2021), online: *Arctic Program*. https://arctic.noaa.gov/Report-Card/Report-Card-2021/ArtMID/8022/ArticleID/957/The-Impact-of-COVID-19-on-Food-Access-for-Alaska-Natives-in-2020.

12

BRAZILIAN DISCRIMINATORY BORDER CONTROL POLICY BASED ON "HEALTH RESTRICTIONS" DURING COVID-19 PANDEMIC

Fernando Aith

12.1 Introduction

The Brazilian Constitution of 1988 protects individual and collective rights, stating that "all are equal before the law, without distinction of any kind, guaranteeing Brazilians and foreigners residing in the country the inviolability of the right to life, liberty, equality, security and property."[1]

At the same time, while it recognizes and protects civil and political individual rights, the Brazilian Constitution also protects some social rights: "education, health, work, housing, leisure, security, social security, maternity and childhood protection."[2]

Regarding the right to health, Article 196 of the Brazilian Constitution expressly recognizes health as a "right of all and a duty of the State."[3] The same article stipulates that one of the State's duties in guaranteeing the right to health is to reduce the risk of diseases and other health problems. This is an extremely complex task since the very notion of risk—and specifically, health risk—depends on a series of variables, especially environmental, economic, cultural, social, moral, and political variables.

Since its recognition by the Brazilian Constitution, the right to health has been growing to respond to the recurrent demands of society for the reduction or elimination of risks to the health of the population, with the publication of some important laws to protect the right to health, such as the Unified Health System Organic Law (Law 8080/1990) and the law that organized the financing of the Unified Health System (Complimentary Law 141/2011). Also, the increase in epidemics related to arboviruses in the country, notably Dengue, Zika, and Chikungunya, clearly demonstrates the importance that state action has in the field of health surveillance. The arrival of the

DOI: 10.4324/9781003394006-16

coronavirus and the COVID-19 pandemic gave rise to legislative innovations on public health measures, requiring a careful look at the way in which the country has been regulating health surveillance, including with regard to the free movement of goods, services, and people. The careful look is essential to understand how these legal innovations protect effectively the right to health, especially because most of the new legislation will continue valid even after the pandemics slowed its impact in the society.

Of the legislative innovations introduced, this chapter will highlight those aimed at controlling the entry of foreign travelers into Brazilian territory during the COVID-19 pandemic. Therefore, this chapter aims to analyze the Ordinances for closing the Brazilian air and land borders published in Brazil throughout 2020, identifying the legal and sanitary aspects involved, notably with regard to the protection of the right to health and the human rights of travelers who wanted to enter Brazil during the pandemic. Special emphasis is given to the negative discrimination imposed on Venezuelan travelers compared to travelers from other bordering countries.

12.2 Legal-Normative Organization of Health Surveillance in Brazil for the Control of COVID-19

Health surveillance, in focusing on risk, requires a global view that considers the possibility of risk being anywhere and presenting itself in diverse ways. In this way, health surveillance encompasses the surveillance of diverse human activities, such as medical activities (clinical, surgical, therapeutic, etc.); population movements across borders by air, sea, and land; the production, commercialization, dispensing of, and consumption of medicines; the work environment; the use of health equipment in health facilities (including machines, surgical material, disposable materials, etc.); the use of drugs by the population; violence rates; and finally, surveillance of any and all remaining phenomena, actions, procedures, products, and substances of interest to health.

The Federal Constitution obliges the Brazilian State to provide adequate funding and institutional structure to develop sanitary surveillance (Art. 200, I and II), epidemiological surveillance (Art. 200, II), surveillance related to the environment (Art. 200, VIII), and surveillance related to workers' health (including that of the work environment) (Art. 200, II and VIII). This surveillance requirement dates back to the 1970s.[4]

Brazil is a federation, gathering the national government, 26 States, the federal district (where the capital is located), and 5,570 municipalities. The Brazilian Organic Health Law (Federal Law 8.080/90), in turn, provides that the federal government, States, federal district, and municipalities must organize their own health surveillance systems through a network of public services capable of detecting the risks of diseases and health problems, while also working to understand the sanitary measures needed, and execute the appropriate measures to eliminate or control the risks.[5]

At the same time, the BC protects the individual rights and freedoms of citizens against arbitrary measures by the State that might be adopted in the name of public health. Any State measures aimed at protecting health and limiting individual freedoms must be provided for by law, in compliance with the principles of equality and legality expressed in the BC's Article 5, caput, item II. An important decision taken from the Brazilian Supreme Court about the obligatory vaccination during the pandemic treated very well this type of conflict between liberty and public health.[6]

In seeking this balance, Federal Decree 7616 was published in 2011, regulating the Declaration of Public Emergency of National Importance and instituting the National Force of the Unified Health System (FN-SUS)—important instruments to control more serious health risks. In the wake of this decree, and with the worsening of Dengue, Zika, and Chikungunya epidemic risks in Brazil, Law 13,301 was approved in June 2016, providing rules for the application of health surveillance measures when a situation of imminent danger to public health was verified (namely, by the presence of the mosquito that transmits these diseases). This law also amended Law No. 6,437, which created sanitary infractions and its penalties in Brazil, including a new penalty for sanitary infractions related to promoting mosquito's outbreak or failure to comply with the health authority's requirements or the control of mosquito-related outbreaks.

12.3 The COVID-19 Pandemic Law

At the very beginning of the COVID-19 pandemic, Law No. 13,979 brought significant innovations to the Brazilian legal system insofar as it regulates matters including the imposition of isolation and quarantine of people and animals; the mandatory performance of laboratory tests, vaccination, examinations, and medical treatments; the temporary restriction of people and goods entering and leaving the country; the requisition of private goods and services by the State, among others; and instituting limits and safeguards in relation to the exercise of fundamental rights and freedoms captured by the Federal Constitution.[7] However, its scope was limited exclusively to "confronting the coronavirus responsible for the 2019 outbreak," valid only during the Public Health Emergency of International Concern,[8] declared by the World Health Organization (WHO) on 11 March 2020.[9,10]

The first safeguard provided for by the Pandemic Law in Brazil is that measures to combat the pandemic could "only be determined on the basis of scientific evidence and analysis of strategic health information, and must be limited in time and space when essential minimum for the promotion and preservation of public health."[11]

Public health measures can, in fact, "invade the sphere of individual freedom in a very aggressive way"—an invasion that, "in the context of a Democratic State, will always be allowed when carried out in accordance with the law and in defense of the public health interest."[12] In this case, "the protection of public health against health risks identified in the society" must be based on "a broad social debate on the rules and procedures that the State must adopt."[13] Immunization programs, increasingly attacked by anti-vaccination campaigns, are a very revealing example of the complexity of this issue.[14]

It follows that, in democratic States, measures restricting fundamental rights and freedoms must be regulated in detail in order to ensure that they are duly motivated, reasonable, and proportionate, as well as efficacious; in the field of health, in particular, it is imperative that they are based on scientific evidence.

However, the Brazilian quarantine law under consideration was made in a hasty way, at a time of notorious decline in democracy and human rights in Brazil, while trying to resolve decades of legislative lethargy in the field of health surveillance.[15]

12.4 The Ordinances for Closing Borders Published in Brazil throughout 2020

Since the declaration of Public Health Emergency of International Concern by the WHO, Brazil has adopted numerous measures to close borders within its territory, rooted in the country's COVID-19 Pandemic Law. These measures were published in successive Inter-ministerial Ordinances, periodically renewed with identical or very similar texts. Throughout 2020, several Ordinances were published on border control during the pandemic. The first comprehensive Ordinance on the matter was the Inter-ministerial Ordinance of the Civil House of the Presidency of the Republic, Justice and Public Security, Infrastructure and Health n. 157, from 27 March 2020. After this first Ordinance, the Federal Government published several modifications of this first text by publishing the following similar Ordinances (with slight changes): Ordinance 204 (29 April 2020), Ordinance 255 (22 May 2020), Ordinance 340 (30 June 2020), Ordinance 419 (26 August 2020), Ordinance 456 (24 September 2020), Ordinance 470 (2 October 2020), Ordinance 478 (14 October 2020), Ordinance 518 (12 November 2020), Ordinance 615 (11 December 2020), Ordinance 630 (17 December 2020), and Ordinance 648 (23 December 2020).

The Ordinances were based on the following:

> on the exceptional and temporary restriction of entry into the country of foreigners of any nationality, pursuant to the provisions of item VI of the caput of art. 3 of Law No. 13,979, of February 6, 2020, as a **result of a technical and reasoned recommendation from the National**

> **Health Surveillance Agency—Anvisa for health reasons related to the risks of contamination and spread of the SARS-CoV-2 coronavirus (COVID-19).**[16]

The main rule dictated by these Ordinances was that the entry into the country by foreigners of any nationality, by highways or other land means, would be restricted and pursuant to the requirements established by the Ordinances.

In general, the Ordinances also provided for some exceptions to the rule of closing land and water borders, determining that the restrictions mentioned did not apply to (1) Brazilians, born or naturalized; (2) **immigrants with permanent residence, for a fixed or indefinite period, in Brazilian territory;** (3) foreign professionals on a mission at the service of an international organization, provided they are duly identified; (4) foreign officials accredited with the Brazilian Government; (5) foreigners who are (a) **spouse, partner, child, parent, or guardian of a Brazilian;** (b) whose entry is specifically authorized by the Brazilian Government in view of the public interest or for humanitarian reasons; and (c) **holder of a National Migration Registry;** and (6) cargo transport.[17]

Each new Ordinance published replaced the previous one and presented some variation in relation to the previous Ordinance. However, there is a pattern that remains in all of them: negative border policy discrimination against Venezuelan land travelers and positive border policy discrimination in favour of Paraguayan land travelers (understanding as "positive discriminations" the ones that benefit the discriminated group and as "negative discriminations" the ones that bring some prejudice to the discriminated group).

Thus, the Ordinances were always based on identical factual and legal motivations, which may be summarized as follows:

> Considering the Public Health Emergency of International Concern by WHO on January 30th, 2020, as a result of human infection with the coronavirus SARS-CoV-2 (COVID-19);
>
> "Considering that it is a principle of the National Public Security and Social Defense Policy, provided for in item VI of the *caput* of art. 4 of Law No. 13,675, of June 11, 2018, efficiency in preventing and reducing risks in emergency situations that may affect people's lives;
>
> Considering the manifestation of the National Health Surveillance Agency—Anvisa, with a recommendation of exceptional and temporary restriction of entry into the country, as well as the need for operational alignment with other bodies or entities of the Federal Public Administration.[18]

A manifestly discriminatory article against Venezuelan immigrants has been inserted in all Ordinances, beginning with the first pandemic-related

Ordinance (Ordinance 615/2020). The exceptions regarding immigrants with permanent residence, whether for a fixed or indefinite period, as well as the exceptions regarding foreigners who are the spouse, partner, child, parent, or guardian of a Brazilian or who are holders of a National Migration Registry, would not apply to Venezuelans. In other words, with no scientific or epidemiological reason, these exceptions would not apply only to Venezuelans, revealing an evident and quite aggressive and negative discrimination against certain people based on their nationality.

The discrimination against foreigners from Venezuela was not based on public health reasons, as various other countries sharing a land border with Brazil had higher numbers of cases, as will be shown later. The Federal Government has never explained, in any of the Ordinances published, why exactly the discrimination against Venezuelans were inserted in the Ordinance's text. The motivations included in the Ordinances only referred to the ANVISA's recommendation, but this recommendation has never said anything about discriminating Venezuelans for any reason because the scientific evidences would never support such discrimination.

Another discrimination against Venezuelans arose in the rules that regulated the traffic of border residents in "twin cities," where presenting certain documents at the border guaranteed travelers with treatment equal to that received by Brazilian citizens. Without any plausible justification, successive Ordinances provided that this rule would not apply to the border with the Bolivarian Republic of Venezuela.

The Border Closure Ordinances also presented another discriminatory rule, this time in what we can call unjustified "positive discrimination." They established that restrictions on entry by land would not prevent the movement of foreigners between the Federative Republic of Brazil and the Republic of Paraguay. As we will see, Paraguay did not present at the time any epidemiological data related to COVID-19 that justified having its land border opened in total dissonance with the other neighboring countries and, even more, in absolute dissonance with the draconian measures adopted towards Venezuela and its citizens.

The closing of land borders adopted in Brazil during the pandemic was disproportionate and the regulatory options imposed did not align with the available epidemiological data, as detailed later. This fact becomes quite evident when we consider that the Ordinances for closing borders with Brazil were much more flexible for the entry of foreigners into the country by air. If foreigners can enter by air subject to certain conditions, the same treatment should be given to foreigners who are entering by land. This border policy control can be characterized as economic discrimination, once travelers coming by air are often richer than travelers coming by land.

Failure to comply with the rules established in the Ordinances could result in several penalties, such as (1) civil, administrative, and/or criminal liability; (2) immediate repatriation or deportation; and (3) disqualification from requesting refuge. These penalties reveal a punitive policy of border control that did not mirror Brazil's history of international relations since it practically criminalized foreigners who wanted to enter Brazil for the simple fact of wanting to enter Brazil.[19]

The analysis of epidemiological data from the countries clearly bordering Brazil shows us the inconsistencies of the Ordinances that restricted access to Brazil through border policy control, especially with regard to Venezuelans and also with regard to the contradiction about the privileged opening of the border with Paraguay. The ANVISA Technical Note used to justify all Ordinances is a generic and shallow document, which did not justify the closing of borders as these Ordinances advocated, much less the discrimination against Venezuelans.

12.5 Pandemic Situation in Brazil and in Neighbouring Countries

Since April/May 2020, some regions of Brazil were already clearly experiencing sustained COVID-19 transmission, especially the large metropolises in the southeast and some capitals in the north and northeast—that is, regions that had greater international exchange. However, the whole country was progressively affected by the pandemic, and since August 2020, the rates of deaths in metropolitan areas and in the interior of the country had overlapped, pointing to synchronous behaviors throughout the national territory and signaling the failure of transmission-blocking measures.[20]

Brazil is one of the countries most affected by the pandemic across the globe. In South America, a region heavily affected by COVID-19, Brazil stood out in terms of incidence and mortality rates relative to population size in their calculation, along with Argentina, Peru, Colombia (countries neighboring Brazil), as well as Chile and Ecuador (see Table 12.1). It is worth noting that French Guyana had the highest incidence of COVID-19, but this was probably due to the greater availability of tests to confirm the diagnosis, given that it is part of French territory and likely had the support of its European counterpart in facing the pandemic. This hypothesis is reinforced by the significantly lower mortality rate than its neighboring countries.

The country that has suffered the least from the impact of the pandemic in South America is Uruguay, which only began to show clear signs of sustained transmission in 2021.

Another country with an incidence below the regional average is Venezuela. Even though this information should be accepted with some caution, due to the political and economic crisis that it has been facing for some years (and that may be negatively influencing the capacity of its information system, thus making underreporting plausible), it is worth remembering that the country had a good record of quality surveillance in the pre-crisis period and

TABLE 12.1 Incidence and mortality rates by COVID-19 in South American countries (2020**)

Country	*Population*	*Cases*	*Incidence rate**	*Deaths*	*Mortality rate**
Brazil	209,500,000	6.904.618	32.958	181.485	867
Venezuela§	28,870,000	107.783	3.734	4.543	34
Suriname§	563,402	5.353	9.502	117	208
Guyana§	777,859	5.920	7.611	155	200
French Guyana §	290,691	11,855	40,783	71	245
Colombia§	49,070,000	1,425,774	29,056	39,053	796
Peru§	30,170,000	984,973	30,618	36,677	1,141
Bolivia§	11,050,000	147,150	13,317	9,018	817
Paraguay§	6,811,000	93,582	13,740	1,953	287
Argentina§	44,270,000	1,498,160	3,842	40,766	921
Uruguay§	3,457,000	9,708	2,809	92	27
Chile	18,050,000	573,830	31,792	15,931	883
Ecuador	16,620	202,180	12,165	13,875	835

Source: *Per 1,000,000 inhabitants

** Data updated until 12/14/2020

§ Countries bordering Brazil

This table was created by the author using data from The Coronavirus App, online: <https://coronavirus.app/map> (accessed 14 December 2020).

a health system with a structure at least equal to the average of the countries in the region.[21]

Therefore, it is unlikely that the magnitude of morbidity and mortality from COVID-19 will be greater than that of the neighboring countries most heavily affected by the pandemic (namely, Brazil, Peru, and Colombia) and may even be smaller since the economic restrictions that it has been suffering can considerably reduce international exchanges.

Considering that Brazil was—at the time of passing its various Ordinances—in a phase of sustained transmission throughout its territories (in metropolitan areas, medium, and small cities) and was among the most affected countries in South America, it is clear that discriminatory restrictions for entering the country from neighboring countries (and especially from Venezuela) were not justified. Added to this argument is the fact that all states in the northern region of the country (including those bordering Venezuela), with the exception of the state of Pará, had incidence rates well above the average incidence in Brazil. Considering this epidemiological reality, usual measures including tracking cases among migrants entering the country and requiring temporary isolation or quarantine would have constituted sufficient control measures.

The lack of technical and sanitary grounds to justify the discriminatory measures adopted against Venezuelans was the motivation for the publication, on 11 June 2021, of a recommendation from the National Council of Human Rights (NCHR) demanding for the Brazilian federal government to amend points of Ordinance 654/2021 in order to receive vulnerable migrants trying to cross borders from Brazil, especially the Venezuelans.

According to the recommendation, the group of people in vulnerable situations is composed of "pregnant women, children and adolescents separated or accompanied by their parents or family nucleus, elderly people, people with disabilities, indigenous population, traditional communities affected, people with serious illness, people in need of urgent healthcare and other vulnerable social groups."[22] The NCHR also stated that asylum seekers and people in a situation of vulnerability due to a migratory flow caused by a humanitarian crisis or a serious and generalized violation of human rights also fall into this group of vulnerable people.

The Recommendation 19/2021 of the NCHR also states that "since March 2020, the federal government has published 29 Ordinances imposing restrictions on entry into the country, with provisions that violate international standards and treaties and national laws on migration and refuge" and that "restrictions shall not impede the provision of health and social care services."[23] Citing WHO (World Health Organization) measures, the advisors point out that screenings, COVID-19 tests and quarantine are effective measures to contain the spread of the virus without having to harm the rights of refugees.

12.6 Final Considerations

The recognition of health as a right for all and a duty of the State imposed by the Federal Constitution generated a series of legal consequences worthy of both attention and broad public debate. By forcing the State to adopt public policies aimed at reducing the risk of diseases and other health problems, the Brazilian Constitution requires the creation of a network of public services capable of identifying problems existing in our society and adopting appropriate public health measures to combat them. This duty, inscribed within the scope of the principle of health security, can be summarized by the duty of health surveillance of the Brazilian State, to then be guaranteed through a network of public services linked to the Unified Health System. Sanitary border control is part of this range of public health protection services.

The measures to close land and water borders are extreme measures that must be adopted with caution, respecting the principles of legality, motivation, reasonableness, public interest, and efficiency. They must also respect fundamental rights, such as right to health and humanitarian and immigration human rights.

In this sense, the discrimination against Venezuelans, as codified by Brazilian law, was not based on scientific evidence or good practices for the control and mitigation of COVID-19. Even more, the degree of spread and mortality of COVID-19 in Brazil makes the closing of borders, as carried out, totally unjustified—since the country emerged as a territory with high degrees of infection and death.

Even if discriminatory measures were successful in preventing new cases from entering Brazil, they would not have been necessary. The control and containment measures recommended by the WHO in regards to air transport (and adopted by numerous Member States, including Brazil) were sufficient, thus eliminating the need to close borders entirely. Thus, measures created for foreigners entering Brazil by air—such as the requirement for PCR tests taken between 48 and 72 hours before departure, recommendations for social distancing and reducing internal movement within Brazil, and the obligation to report to the health authority if the foreigner experiences any COVID-19 symptoms—would be sufficient to control and mitigate the risks of foreigners entering Brazil by land too. The ANVISA Technical Note was thus insufficient to justify the content of the Ordinance as a whole, particularly regarding land borders and Venezuelan's discrimination.

In light of the epidemiological reality of the countries bordering Brazil, there was no public health justification available for selectively opening the land border with Paraguay. The country had increasing rates of infection that would even justify the opposite, if the measure of closing borders were, in fact, adequate for containing COVID-19 in Brazil. The justification for this exception is not of a sanitary nature but was likely motivated by political and/or economic factors.

It is worth remembering that the first safeguard provided for by the Pandemic Law in Brazil is that measures to combat the Pandemic could "only be determined on the basis of scientific evidence and analysis of strategic health information, and must be limited in time and space when essential minimum for the promotion and preservation of public health."[24]

Finally, with regard to the discrimination against Venezuelan foreigners, the measures recommended by the Ordinances studied are unconstitutional for violating the principles of isonomy (Article 5, *caput*) and the purpose of administrative acts (Article 37 of the BC), which must always be made in the public interest.

The Ordinances also violated article 32 of the International Health Regulations (IHR), which provides that States Parties have numerous obligations in minimizing "any discomfort or anguish associated with restrictive measures," including treating all travelers with courtesy and respect; taking into account travelers' gender and sociocultural, ethnic, or religious concerns; providing adequate food and water, appropriate accommodation and clothing, protection for luggage and other goods, appropriate medical treatment, and necessary means of communication, "if possible, in a language they can understand"; and other appropriate assistance to travelers who are quarantined, isolated, or subject to other procedures for public health purposes.[25] These safeguards should be expressly provided for in the Ordinances and should guide the action of governmental bodies, notably, the Federal Police and the National Health Surveillance Agency (ANVISA). The absence of such safeguards exposes travelers to potential violence, risking the violation of their fundamental human rights, as recognized by Brazil in its Constitution (Article 5) and in several human rights treaties ratified by the country, including some protections provided by the IHR itself.

Notes

1 Brazilian Constitution of 1988, art. 5, *caput*.
2 *Ibid*, art. 6.
3 *Ibid*, art. 196.
4 See, e.g., Laws 6,437/1977 (sanitary surveillance) and 6,259/1975 (epidemiological surveillance).
5 Federal Law 8.080/90.
6 Brazilian Supreme Court. Recurso Extraordinário com Agravo (ARE) 1267879, reported by Minister Ricardo Lewandowsky.
7 Law no. 13,979, of February 6, 2020. This law provides for measures to address the public health emergency of international importance arising from the coronavirus responsible for the 2019 outbreak: Official Gazette of the Federative Republic of Brazil, Brasília, DF, 7 February 2020.
8 *Ibid*, at para 3.
9 In the absence of a legal definition, the WHO generally defines a pandemic as the international spread of a new disease. In the case of the new coronavirus, however, the statement refers to the speed of spread, the number of serious cases, and the inadequacy of the response. See World Health Organization, "WHO Director-General's opening remarks at the media briefing on COVID-19–11 March 2020" (11 March 2020), online: www.who.int/director-general/speeches/detail/who-director-general-s-opening-remarks-at-the-media-briefing-on-COVID-19–11-march-2020 ["Opening Remarks"].
10 The first denomination adopted by the WHO was "2019 novel coronavirus," later changed to "SARS-CoV-2." On February 11, 2020, the WHO started to call the disease resulting from the virus "COVID-19," which is the acronym for "coronavirus disease," combined with the year related to the appearance of the outbreak (2019). See "Opening Remarks," *ibid*. This chapter adopts the title made within Brazilian law, "coronavirus responsible for the 2019 outbreak," simplified to "new coronavirus."
11 Law no. 13,979, *supra* note 7, art III, § 1.
12 Carolina Barbieri et al, "Child (non)vaccination between culture and law: the meanings attributed by middle class couples in São Paulo, Brazil" (2017) 33:2 CAD Public Health, e00173315.
13 Fernando Aith & Sueli Dallari, "Health surveillance in Brazil: the challenges of health risks in the 21st century and the need to create a national health surveillance system" (2009) 10:2 Journal of Health Law 121.
14 See Barbieri et al, *supra* note 12. ("The mandatory vaccination represents a protection to the common public good of prevention and health promotion, but it

should not be taken in an absolute way, being always subject to flexibility in cases where non-vaccination does not represent relevant risks to public health. It is a conflict between individual freedom and public health that must always be considered in the light of the legal principles of reasonableness and proportionality, balancing health protection with the protection of individual freedoms in the best possible way.")

15 Deisy de Freitas Lima Ventura, Fernando Mussa Abujamra Aith & Danielle Hanna Rached, "A emergência do novo coronavírus e a "lei de quarentena" no Brasil/The emergency of the new coronavirus and the 'quarantine law' in Brazil" (2021) 12:1 Revista Direito e Práxis.

16 Ordinance of the Civil House of the Presidency of the Republic, Justice and Public Security, Infrastructure and Health n. 157, from 27 March 2020 [Ordinance n. 157] [emphasis added].

17 These exceptions appear in all the ordinances published since the first one, with the exact same text. Emphasis added.

18 Ordinance n. 157, *supra* note 16 [emphasis added].

19 For example, forbidding requests of refuge is in total dissonance with Law 13,445/2017, which deals with immigration rules and requests for refuge in Brazil, as well as with the Refuge Law (Law 9,474/1997).

20 Oswaldo Cruz Foundation. "Technical note—The end of the cycle of internalization, the synchronization of the epidemic and the difficulties of care in hospitals." COVID-19 Observatory.

21 Pan-American Health Organization, "Health in the Americas (2017)," online (pdf): https://iris.paho.org/bitstream/handle/10665.2/34323/9789275719671por.pdf?sequence=8&isAllowed=y.

22 Brazilian National Council on Human Rights. Recommendation 19/2021.

23 *Ibid.*

24 Law no. 13,979, *supra* note 7, art III, § 1.

25 WHO, "International Health Regulations" (2005), online: www.who.int/publications/i/item/9789241580496.

PART V

Border Controls, Migrants, and Refugees

13

PANDEMIC PATHWAYS TO PERMANENT RESIDENCE

Audrey Macklin

13.1 Pandemic Pivots

The logic and discourse of deservingness in migration operates on a field already dominated by securitization, which has emerged as the dominant frame for border governance in the 21st century. Securitization portrays both terrorism and contagious disease as essentially foreign existential threats to the life and health of the body politic. This representation of risk in turn legitimates exceptional border and migration measures that would test the limits of justifiable rights violations if imposed on citizens.[1]

In 2003, the Severe Acute Respiratory System (SARS) outbreak in Ontario propelled reform of the federal *Quarantine Act*[2] to expand the legal authority to screen and detain travelers arriving by air, and to add the power to exclude classes of travelers from countries with communicable disease outbreaks.[3] From the onset of the COVID-19 pandemic in early 2020, the federal government chose to govern through the *Quarantine Act*, a federal statute centrally concerned with cross-border movement, rather than the *Emergencies Act*. Government only invoked the *Emergencies Act* only in February 2022 in response to the Freedom Convoy protest.

Governing through border control, rather than mechanisms that apply equally to citizens and non-citizens, enables the state to deploy legal instruments that maximize executive power and minimize accountability. The *Immigration and Refugee Protection Act* provides more power and fewer procedural protections than the *Anti-Terrorism Act*, and the *Quarantine Act* authorizes broad and virtually unreviewable discretion, whereas the *Emergencies Act* is subject to Parliamentary oversight and *post-facto* evaluation.

DOI: 10.4324/9781003394006-18

13.2 From Undeserving to Deserving Refugees

Canada's approach to asylum seekers before and during the pandemic reveals how the public and, eventually, government policy mobilized and recombined logics of deservingness in contingent and even contradictory ways. We begin, however, by bracketing one program that should not be linked with deservingness, namely, vaccination. Refugee claimants and migrants with temporary (or no) legal status are excluded from provincial healthcare coverage across Canada and thus do not carry provincial healthcare insurance cards that medical providers require prior to receiving publicly funded healthcare.

During the pandemic, however, everyone was eligible for provincially administered COVID-19 vaccinations, regardless of immigration status. This expansive coverage owes little to a cosmopolitan ethos that values the lives and welfare of resident citizens and non-citizens equally. Rather, it reflects the epidemiological fact that unvaccinated non-citizens pose a health risk to citizens. So a cosmopolitan-lite 'we-are-all-in-this-together' rationale for vaccinating everyone (regardless of healthcare coverage or immigration status) coincides with national self-interest. Indeed, traces of the exclusionary logic of status persisted at the operational level. Vaccine distribution to non-status or temporary migrants was hampered by an online booking system that relied on possession of government-issued health insurance cards, which non-status migrants, some international students, and some temporary workers did not hold.

Border control management tells a more complex story about the pandemic, refugees, and deservingness. Shortly after Donald Trump took office as President of the United States in 2017, increasing numbers of asylum seekers in the United States began crossing irregularly into Canada near Roxham Road, Quebec, and a handful of other Canadian locations. Their actions were neither clandestine nor illegal under Canada's *Immigration and Refugee Protection Act*[4] or the *UN Convention Relating to the Status of Refugees*.[5] The number of irregular border-crossers was small in absolute terms and compared to other states, but they were vilified in the media as illegal, dangerous and bogus and the liberal government was assailed for failing to control the border.

The Canada-US *Safe Third Country Agreement* ('STCA') in force until 2023 required asylum seekers traveling overland to lodge their refugee claim in the first country of arrival, as between Canada and the United States. Because Canada is geographically more remote than the United States, US-bound asylum seekers rarely need to pass through Canada, while the route for Canada-bound asylum seekers often passes through the US. Thus, Canada's political objective in pressing the US to enter into the STCA was to enable Canada to evade its international legal obligations towards refugees and minimize the number of asylum seekers entering Canada from the United States. By design, the STCA did not apply inside Canadian territory, at airports, or between official ports-of-entry.[6]

At the onset of the pandemic, the federal government issued travel bans preventing entry to Canada by non-citizens or permanent residents at official air, sea, or land ports-of-entry, save for limited exceptions that did not include resettled refugees or asylum seekers.[7] The government initially declared that asylum seekers entering Canada irregularly from the United States would be required to submit to screening, testing, and quarantine. This latter announcement aligned with the United Nations High Commissioner for Refugees' exhortation to states to recognize the vulnerability and peril faced by asylum seekers and use available measures to manage the public health risks.

A month into the pandemic, the federal government reversed course and invoked the *Quarantine Act* to ban asylum seekers entering irregularly across the Canada-US border.[8] Apprehended asylum seekers would be transferred back into the United States, with an unenforceable assurance that they could return to Canada to pursue their refugee claim when the ban was lifted. The government provided no explanation of why its prior arrangement for asylum seekers (similar to those for other entrants) was inadequate. Securing the health of the body politic against foreign vectors of infection did not merely outweigh refugees' deservingness (given the availability of alternatives); it negated it. In so doing, Canadian policy affirmed that state practices of refugee protection ultimately rest on a fragile benevolence that can be withdrawn without need for justification. Canada's reversal served to validate UN High Commissioner Filippo Grandi's 'worr[y] that that measures enacted on the pretext of responding to COVID-19 are being used as cover to exclude and deny asylum to people fleeing violence and persecution.'[9]

In November 2021, after individual vaccine and testing requirements replaced travel bans, Canada lifted the ban on asylum seekers crossing into Canada irregularly. It turned out, however, that the pandemic pushback supplied a precedent for Canada to seek a negotiated expansion of the Canada-US Safe *Third Country Agreement* across the entire land border. Canada and the US signed a protocol to expand the STCA in spring 2022, and it was announced and went into force in March 2023.

13.3 Essential Workers

The admission to Canada of migrant workers during the pandemic temporarily but significantly reconfigured the hierarchy of labour migrants according to ascribed skill. Apart from enjoying better wages, working conditions, and opportunities to change employers, 'high-skill' migrant workers possess viable options for transitioning to permanent residence. A 'low-wage' worker has few to no options for transitioning to permanent residence. Yet during the first months of the pandemic, when the borders slammed shut to those who were neither citizens nor permanent residents (including asylum seekers), the Canadian government facilitated the entry of thousands of 'low-skill, low-wage' temporary workers on the basis that they performed 'essential' work. Essential work was defined by degree of necessity to the Canadian economy and infrastructure, with a special focus on agriculture, food production/preparation, and health and home care. Work deemed essential according to this metric did not necessarily align with work that attracted high wages or recognition as 'high skill,' and yet it was prioritized for admission.

Importantly, migrant workers admitted during this period did not benefit from improved wages, working conditions, or health and safety provision. For some in the agricultural sector, the putative transnational mobility that brought them to Canada was belied by confinement to the workers' premises after arrival. The conditions imposed on 'essential' migrant workers exposed the gap between valuing work as essential and valuing the workers who do it.

Migrant and refugee organizations, long committed to securing status for precarious migrants, leveraged the flagrancy and incongruity of that gap by advocating for programs to regularize the status of migrants performing essential work. This included workers on temporary permits, asylum seekers,[10] and non-status migrants. The campaign traded on the outpouring of public gratitude to 'essential workers' in healthcare and low-wage service sectors. It encouraged the public to recognize non-citizen essential workers as deserving of permanent resident status because of their extraordinary service to Canada and Canadians in a time of crisis.

The federal government responded with two distinct 'pandemic pathways' to permanent residence. A range of factors determine the scope and content of any policy instrument; here, we foreground the messages communicated by the pandemic pathways about who merits permanent resident status and why. The first initiative grew out of Quebec, where media and civil society drew particular attention to asylum seekers working in healthcare, home care, and senior/nursing home sectors. The media dubbed them 'anges gardiens' (guardian angels), and the federal government opened negotiations with provincial counterparts to launch a countrywide, short-term regularization scheme.

The Guardian Angel Pathway was opened in December 2020 and expired on 31 August 2021. It offered a route to permanent residence for asylum seekers with valid work permits who had been employed for a minimum period in jobs that involved direct provision of care to patients and residents of nursing homes. The terms of the program excluded holders of temporary work permits who were not asylum seekers, non-status migrants working without a permit, workers in hospitals and nursing homes who did not provide direct care (cleaning staff, security guards, food service workers, etc.), and workers beyond health and nursing care sectors. Of course, workers in all these sectors also performed essential work, often for low wages, in poor working conditions, and at high risk to their own health and well-being. So why were only refugee claimants engaged in direct patient care deemed deserving of access to membership and belonging?

According to rumour, Quebec insisted on a narrower program than the federal government and other provinces. One reason for limiting the program to refugee claimants providing direct care was simply to minimize the number of qualified applicants. One Quebec journalist estimated the number of eligible refugee claimants at under 1,000 in that province, thereby reaping the symbolic political benefits of the program at low practical cost.[11]

Government media releases referenced the 'sacrifice' by refugee claimants 'who raised their hand to serve'[12] during the pandemic, and contained the following quote from the Minister of Immigration, Refugees and Citizenship:

> The government recognizes the extraordinary contribution of asylum claimants working in Canada's health-care sector during the COVID-19 pandemic, particularly in long-term care centres. As these individuals face an uncertain future in Canada, the current circumstances merit exceptional measures in recognition of their service during the pandemic.[13]

Confining the program to refugee claimants providing direct care to ailing or elderly Canadians also linked deservingness to the personalized, intimate nature of the care they provided. The 'guardian angel' label evokes tropes of feminized emotional and physical labour and self-sacrificing, humanitarian, and pastoral care. Apart from physicians, most front-line healthcare is feminized work that still trades on the 'labour-of-love' stereotype applied to women who perform low or unpaid care.

The federal immigration minister also praised these refugee claimants as demonstrating "a uniquely Canadian quality in that they were looking out for others.'[14] There was, of course, a certain irony to rewarding refugee claimants for their enactment of 'Canadian-ness,' which they exhibited by doing work that Canadians would not do.

So while Canada relied on COVID-19 to bar undeserving asylum seekers from reaching Canada through irregular entry, it simultaneously relied on COVID-19 to regularize an undisclosed number of deserving asylum seekers, many of whom presumptively entered irregularly. The logic remains obscure: Did this subclass of 'essential' workers deserve permanent residence *because* of their heightened vulnerability and uncertain future as asylum seekers, or did they deserve permanent residence *despite* their portrayal as illegal, bogus border crossers who would have been cast back to the United States had they arrived after March 2020? Either way, caring for vulnerable Canadians appeared to elevate asylum seekers and make their own distinctive vulnerability visible and policy-salient. The pandemic pathway for 'guardian angels' bypassed the system of refugee adjudication and conferred permanent residence on them (but not other migrants who were not asylum seekers) for performance of a restricted range of tasks (but not all 'essential' labour).

In March 2021, the federal government announced a second 'pandemic pathways' program. Pandemic border restrictions had reduced Canada's ordinary intake of permanent residents to a trickle. The second pandemic pathway program sought to partially offset the shortfall in newcomers arriving from outside Canada by enabling migrants already in Canada to transition to permanent residence.

This second program, the 'Temporary Resident to Permanent Resident Pathway Program' ('TR to PR Pathway') was launched in May 2021 with a closing date of November 2021. It comprised three streams for a total of 90,000 entrants: migrant workers employed in healthcare (20,000), migrant workers employed in 'essential' non-healthcare occupations (30,000), and recently graduated international students employed in any occupation (40,000). Asylum seekers were ineligible for the TR to PR Pathway, even though the 'guardian angel' pathway for refugee claimants was generally more restrictive in its criteria and limited to a much narrower subset of occupations.[15]

'Essential' occupations encompass jobs at all points of the skill spectrum, but the government had already facilitated access to permanent residence for high-skill or trades-related temporary workers working in any occupation in Canada by significantly easing the requirements under the regular immigration route. Under the TR to PR Pathway, Canadian-educated university graduates employed in any job could now access permanent residence. Migrant workers lacking Canadian post-secondary education only qualified for permanent resident status if they performed 'essential' work.[16]

Having delinked the performance of 'essential' work from acquisition of permanent resident by international graduates, the government announcement of the TR to PR Pathway mentions the 'contribution of newcomers,' but orients the rationale more explicitly towards the conventional economic and demographic benefits of permanent immigration:

> These special public policies will grant permanent status to temporary workers and international graduates who are already in Canada and who possess the skills and experience we need to fight the pandemic and accelerate our economic recovery.
>
> As we continue the fight against the pandemic, immigration will remain critical to our economic recovery by addressing labour shortages and adding growth to our workforce.
>
> With an accelerated pathway to permanent residency, these special public policies will encourage essential temporary workers and international graduates to put down roots in Canada and help us retain the talented workers we need, particularly in our health-care system.

> Today's announcement will help us achieve our 2021 Immigration Levels Plan, which will see Canada welcome 401,000 new permanent residents. The skilled newcomers and international graduates welcomed under our plan will help create jobs and drive long-term growth in Canada.[17]

Within weeks, the quota for international graduate applications filled up; within about three months, the quota for 'essential' non-healthcare applications was reached. Yet by the closing date of November 2021, Immigration, Refugees and Citizenship Canada applications for migrant workers employed in healthcare had scarcely reached 20% of the quota. As Naomi Alboim et al document, "a significant pool of health workers in these lower-skilled health care occupations [] include many racialized women and men who have worked tirelessly during the pandemic."[18]

The class of non-healthcare 'essential workers' is obviously much larger than the pool of healthcare workers, but the latter easily exceeds 20,000. So why was this stream so dramatically undersubscribed? Alboim et al observe that the TR to PR Pathway erected several impediments for temporary workers in lower-skilled occupations. These included the high cost of applying (without even considering the cost of legal assistance); the risk of refusal (and forfeiture of fees); the complex and technically demanding application process (requiring extensive documentation, biometrics, etc.); the exhaustion and lack of time available to health workers; and limited access by applicants to technology and digital literacy, compounded by limited language proficiency. Alboim et al persuasively argue that the financial, logistical, technical, and linguistic barriers combined to make the TR to PR Pathway practically inaccessible to a large segment of low-wage temporary workers in essential occupations, especially in healthcare. Just as restrictive eligibility criteria constricted the number of 'deserving' applicants under the Guardian Angels program, so too did the demands of the TR to PR Pathway process put it beyond the reach of many who seemed eminently 'deserving' of permanent residence.[19]

13.3.1 Conclusion: Future Directions

Overall, the government's pandemic strategy for transitioning temporary migrant workers to permanent resident status mobilized two divergent logics and routes. High-skill migrant workers could transition to permanent residence under the ordinary (*albeit* relaxed) criteria of the regular immigration system.[20] The time-limited TR to PR Pathway offered Canadian university-educated workers an opportunity to access permanent residence without working in a skilled occupation. Both classes were admitted to permanent residence on the basis of their human capital, as measured through the proxies of skill designation or post-secondary education. This is the standard logic animating economic immigration to Canada since the 1960s. It values the human capital of immigrants as predictive of anticipated future performance in the labour market.

In contrast, workers in the two 'essential occupation' categories of the TR to PR Pathway gained admission under a logic of deservingness oriented to past labour performance. These candidates deserved permanent residence because they delivered an essential service to Canada during a pandemic. Migration advocates have long campaigned in favour of permanent residence for all migrants residing in Canada on the basis of long residence, contribution to Canada through the performance of necessary labour, and/or humanitarian considerations. The TR to PR Pathway addresses only the second rationale. The Minister of Immigration, Refugees and Citizenship was mandated by the Prime Minister in December 2021 to '[b]uild on existing pilot programs to further explore ways of regularizing status for undocumented workers who are contributing to Canadian communities.'[21] The TR to PR Pathway created an exceptional, time-limited, and narrow precedent that advocates could, in principle, leverage in support of normalizing past labour contribution as a reason to enable all migrant workers (including irregular migrants) to transition to permanent residence.

Notes

1 Until the 'Freedom Convoy' protests almost two years into the pandemic, the federal government relied exclusively on the expansive powers afforded under the *Quarantine Act*, which imposed fewer legal constraints and less accountability at the border than the *Emergencies Act*.
2 *Quarantine Act*, SC 2005 c 20.
3 *Ibid*, s 58.
4 Immigration and Refugee Protection Act, SC 2001, c 27, s 27(2).
5 *The Refugee Convention*, 28 July 1951, UNHCR art 31 (entered into force 22 April 1954).
6 For greater elaboration on the STCA, see Audrey Macklin, "Citizenship, Non-Citizenship and the Rule of Law" (2018) 69 UNBLJ 19; Efrat Arbel, "Shifting Borders and the Boundaries of Rights: Examining the Safe Third County Agreement between Canada and the United States" (2013) 25 Intl J Refugee L 65.
7 One should not overstate the significance of this ban. Canada *de facto* attempts to prevent the entry of asylum seekers at all times and seeks to prevent their arrival in Canada through various extraterritorial measures.
8 Elise Mercier & Sean Rehaag, "The Right to Seek Asylum in Canada (During a Global Pandemic)" (2021) 57 Osgoode Hall Law Journal 3 705 at 706.
9 "UN high commissioner for refugees calls on states to lift remaining pandemic-related asylum restrictions" (20 May 2022), online: *The UN Refugee Agency*. www.unhcr.org/news/press/2022/5/6287a0634/un-high-commissioner-refugees-calls-states-lift-remaining-pandemic-related.html.
10 Once screened into Canada for eligibility to claim refugee protection, asylum seekers receive a temporary work permit.
11 Agnés Gruda, "Demandeurs d'asile: remercier à reculons" (18 August 2020), online: *La Presse*. www.lapresse.ca/debats/editoriaux/2020–08–18/demandeurs-d-asile-remercier-a-reculons.php. As of September 2022, the government has not released data on the number of applicants admitted under this program.

12 Immigration, Refugees and Citizenship Canada, News Release, "IRCC announces opening date of special measures for refugee claimants working in health care during the pandemic" (9 December 2020), online: *Government of Canada*. www.canada.ca/en/immigration-refugees-citizenship/news/2020/12/ircc-announces-opening-date-of-special-measures-for-refugee-claimants-working-in-health-care-during-the-pandemic.html.

13 Immigration, Refugees and Citizenship Canada, News Release, "Pathway to permanent residency recognizes exceptional service of asylum claimants on front lines of COVID-19 pandemic" (14 August 2020), online: *Government of Canada*. www.canada.ca/en/immigration-refugees-citizenship/news/2020/08/pathway-to-permanent-residency-recognizes-exceptional-service-of-asylum-claimants-on-front-lines-of-covid-19-pandemic.html.

14 The Canadian Press, "Asylum seekers working on front-lines of COVID-19 pandemic to have early chance at permanent residency" (14 August 2020), online: *The Globe and Mail*. www.theglobeandmail.com/canada/article-asylum-seekers-working-on-front-lines-of-covid-19-pandemic-to-have/.

15 Immigration, Refugees and Citizenship Canada, "Temporary public policy to facilitate the granting of permanent residence for foreign nationals in Canada, outside of Quebec, with recent Canadian work experience in essential occupations—ANNEX B—Other Eligible Essential Occupations" (14 April 2021), online: *Government of Canada*. www.canada.ca/en/immigration-refugees-citizenship/corporate/mandate/policies-operational-instructions-agreements/public-policies/trpr-canadian-work-experience.html#annex-b.

16 For an overview and critical analysis, see Naomi Alboim, Karen Cohl & Tommy Pham, "Equitable access: Implementing the temporary resident to permanent resident pathway" (June 2021) *CERC Policy Paper No. 3*.

17 Immigration, Refugees and Citizenship Canada, News Release, "New pathway to permanent residency for over 90,000 essential temporary workers and international graduates" (14 April 2021) online: *Government of Canada*. www.canada.ca/en/immigration-refugees-citizenship/news/2021/04/new-pathway-to-permanent-residency-for-over-90000-essential-temporary-workers-and-international-graduates.html.

18 Alboim, Cohl & Pham, *supra* note 16 at 4.

19 *Ibid*.

20 *Ibid* at 2.

21 Letter from Prime Minister Justin Trudeau to IRCC Minister Sean Fraser (16 December 2021), online: *Canada*. https://pm.gc.ca/en/mandate-letters/2021/12/16/minister-immigration-refugees-and-citizenship-mandate-letter.

14

SPOUSES OF THE PANDEMIC

Data, Racism, and Mental Health

Wei William ("Will") Tao[1]

14.1 Introduction

Limited academic and public attention have been paid to the plight of temporary immigration-seeking family members of Canadian work permit and study permit applicants and holders. Canada's changing COVID-19 entry policies, laws, and procedures had a major impact on these applicants, many of whom were spouses or dependents who had their family reunification plans barred or hindered. In addition to introducing new policies, Canada also pivoted towards increased reliance on data as evidence-based decision-making. Both developments suggest a need to better understand, empirically, the impact the pandemic had on these applicants.

To that end, this chapter examines whether immigration data alone adequately captures the hardships faced by these spouses and partners during the pandemic. My central research question is whether the hardships were shared equitably between applicants from the Global North (predominantly visa-exempt applicants) and the Global South (predominantly visa-requiring applicants),[2] and if not, whether the pandemic reinforced the border/overseas visa processing as a "colour line."

I argue that looking solely at statistical data and formal policy provides us with an incomplete understanding of the experiences of spouses and partners, as it leaves out evidence of such hardship as racism and mental health stress. This speaks to the need for paying greater attention to qualitative social science evidence to capture and contextualize the challenges facing migrants during the present and future pandemics.

DOI: 10.4324/9781003394006-19

14.2 Pandemic Policies/Laws that Impacted Spouses and Partners Seeking Entry to Canada

Two days following the closure of Canada's borders on 18 March 2020, an Order in Council ("OIC") setting out exceptions was introduced.[3] These exceptions notably excluded immediate family members of temporary residents, including those of international students and temporary foreign workers.[4] But the OIC did carve out border entry exceptions for immediate family members of Canadian citizens and permanent residents. Following criticism of the harsh consequences of separating loved ones,[5] Immigration, Refugees and Citizenship Canada ("IRCC") expanded the immediate family member exemption in October 2020, to include couples in a "serious committed relationship."[6] However, to qualify for this expanded exemption, immediate family members need to already hold an entry visa for Canada.

Consequently, the benefit of the expanded border entry exemption was not experienced equitably by all family members looking to reunite with their loved ones. Overseas temporary resident visa processing had grinded to a halt (and was temporarily suspended for 21 days in April 2020) as a result of the pandemic.[7] Overseas visa offices closed in droves, and processing volumes were significantly reduced.[8] This meant that many family members were having difficulty securing the necessary visa to avail themselves of Canada's newly expanded border entry rules.

Pursuant to the *Immigration and Refugee Protection Act*, an individual that seeks entry to Canada is presumed to seek immigration, unless they can demonstrate qualification for appropriate temporary resident visas.[9] While the contours of each temporary resident category (i.e., worker, student, visitor) slightly differ, an underlying similarity is the central legal test that requires a visa applicant to demonstrate they can leave Canada at the end of their authorized stay.[10] Typical grounds given by visa officers for finding applicants failing to demonstrate their ability to leave concern:

- purpose of an applicant's visit;
- an applicant's personal assets and financial status;
- limited employment prospects in an applicant's country of residence;
- an applicant's family ties in Canada and in their country of residence;
- an applicant's travel history; and/or
- an applicant's immigration status.

In contrast, visitors from countries that Canada categorizes as visa-exempt have access to an Electronic Travel Authorization (eTA), which automatically approves one's application for entry to Canada unless irregularities are flagged. This greatly facilitates visa-exempt individuals' border entry.

During the COVID-19 pandemic, significant modifications were made to the entry of the spouses of both temporary foreign workers and international students seeking to hold work permits. This chapter specifically examines C41 and C42, two exemptions from the Labour Market Impact Assessment ("LMIA") that allow spouses of certain skilled workers and those of full-time students enrolled at a designed learning institute to enter Canada with an open work permit. Without such exemptions, foreign nationals looking to work in Canada typically must seek an employment-specific work permit that requires an employer to test the labour market or prove they could not hire a Canadian citizen or permanent resident before hiring the foreign national.

Specific to C41 (spouses of skilled workers) and C42 work permits (spouses of full-time students), two changes were also made during this COVID-19 period. For both sets of spouses/partners, IRCC program delivery instructions were updated on 27 September 2021 to ask for additional "proof of relationship" as a front-end requirement.[11] This change is in line with an increased scrutiny of the genuineness and purpose of these relationships by immigration officials.[12]

Meanwhile, for accompanying spouses of students seeking entry to Canada, pandemic-era regulations permitted only the entry of spouses who could "help the principal applicant establish in Canada." This directly contradicts the requirement to show an individual would leave Canada at the end of their authorized stay, as it implicates several refusal grounds mentioned earlier that are typically seen as implying strong establishment and ties in Canada.[13] Furthermore, the OIC broadly interpreted discretionary and, therefore, restricted travel as "including tourism, recreation, and entertainment."[14] This ended up being used by IRCC and Canada Border Services Agency to deny entry to spouses seeking to come to Canada to visit and temporarily stay with their study permit-holding spouses, particularly when the study permit holder was already in Canada prior to the travel restrictions.[15]

The ability of spouses of workers and students to enter Canada was also impacted by larger blanket travel bans imposed by the government. While not directly targeting spouses, the prolonged ban of travel from India and Pakistan from April to June 2021 due to the Omicron variant[16] and from ten African countries from November 2021 to December 2021[17] had the direct impact of limiting applicants' ability to travel to Canada to reunite with their permit-holding loved ones. Spouses of Indian skilled workers, in particular, experienced further delays in processing with many applicants receiving refusal letters only once their work permit-holding spouses had less than six months remaining on their permits, rendering them no longer eligible for the C41 spousal open work permit.

14.3 Data-Driven Realities: Refusals of C41 (Spouses of Workers) and C42 Applicants (Spouses of Students) and the Current Shortcomings of Data-Based Evidence

IRCC spent much of the pandemic deepening its new digital transformation, including greater reliance on advanced analytics and data-driven decision-making to increase processing efficiency.[18] An underlying assumption of this development is that data and objective evidence should be preferred over applicants' subjective submissions, as the primary driver for consistent decision-making. However, the turn to artificial intelligence-based triaging raises concerns of historical data bias. Encapsulated in the old computer science adage of "garbage in, garbage out" (framed in the artificial intelligence world as "bias in, bias out"), this new way of decision-making could prevent some applicants from obtaining visas while creating black boxes respecting the reasons why.[19]

14.3.1 Data from the Pandemic: C41 and C42 Refusals Rose during Pandemic, but Not Equitably for All Applicants

To better understand the impact of COVID-19–related border policies on family migrants, my team wrote to IRCC's Chief Data Officer Branch ("CDO") and requested disaggregated data pertaining to C41 and C42 work permits for the five years leading up to May 2022. We specifically asked for statistics relating to the volume of these applications, as well as approval and refusal rates, broken down by country of citizenship, country of residence, and processing visa office.[20]

14.3.2 Overall C41 and C42 Refusal/Decision Volume Data

Analysis of the data received shows that overall, the COVID-19 pandemic did have an impact on refusal rates.

The refusal rate of C41 applicants increased 2.3% between 2019 and 2020 before falling to pre-pandemic levels in 2021 and 2022.

For C42 applicants, 2020 saw a more pronounced increase in the refusal rate, rising from 45.18% in 2019 to a high of 54.59% in 2020 before falling to pre-pandemic levels in 2021 and 2022.

Meanwhile, a decrease was observed in the total volume of C41 and C42 decisions made, going from 36,592 in 2019 to 21,594 in 2020, representing a decrease of 61.8%.[21]

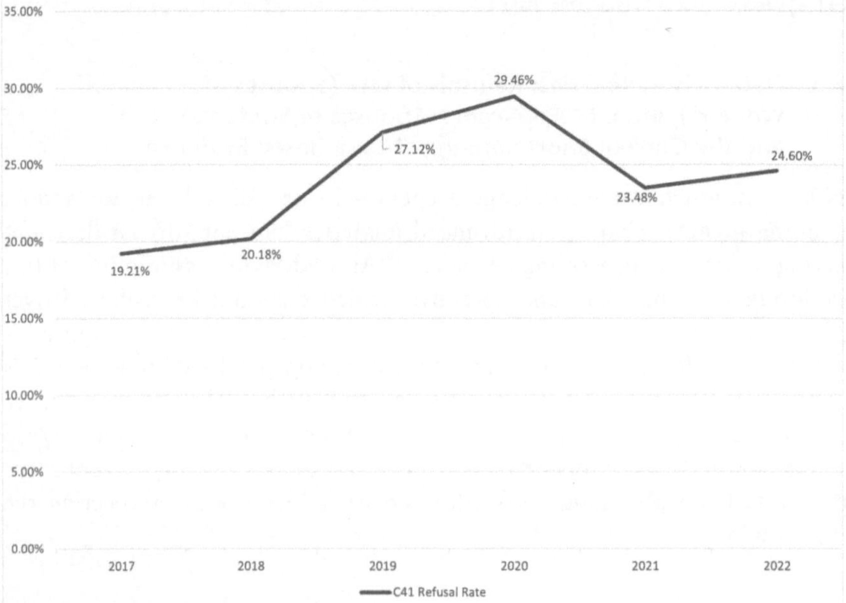

FIGURE 14.1 C41 refusal rate over years.

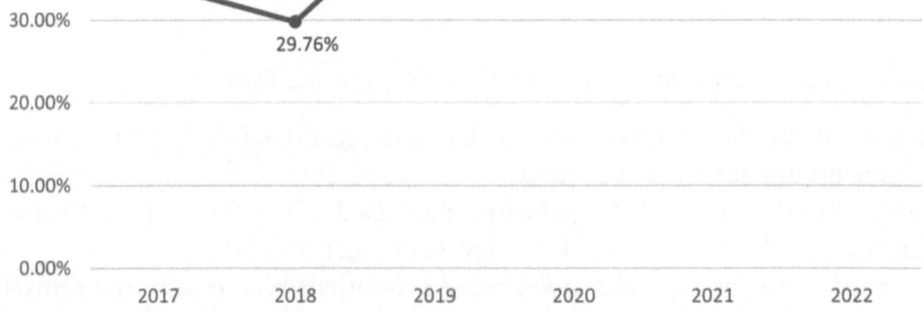

FIGURE 14.2 C42 refusal rate over years.

14.3.3 Disproportionate Impact on Global South

When the C41 data is broken down by citizenship, the highest refusal rates are found in Global South countries like Pakistan, India, and Nigeria (see Table 14.1, data ordered by 2020 refusal rate). The refusal rates for a

TABLE 14.1 C41 refusal rate over years, sorted by 2020 refusal rate

	Year					
Citizenship	*2017*	*2018*	*2019*	*2020*	*2021*	*2022*
Pakistan	56.52%	33.56%	45.89%	56.14%	45.64%	45.65%
India	16.14%	19.67%	31.60%	43.06%	29.70%	24.35%
Nigeria	65.28%	33.05%	27.18%	41.38%	38.89%	25.45%
Iran	11.94%	7.44%	17.30%	25.00%	33.69%	52.15%
Philippines	40.69%	28.64%	24.79%	24.80%	16.02%	22.26%
People's Republic of China	18.44%	15.12%	19.68%	21.82%	20.44%	24.55%
Brazil	10.58%	11.18%	8.43%	14.48%	22.07%	20.30%
Japan	13.04%	5.56%	13.33%	14.29%	4.88%	10.53%
France	14.80%	15.50%	24.23%	10.37%	22.78%	23.41%
United Kingdom and Overseas Territories	12.79%	7.55%	13.79%	8.00%	6.34%	9.52%
Turkey	6.49%	8.16%	6.78%	7.69%	9.68%	23.53%

TABLE 14.2 C42 refusal rate over years, sorted by 2020 refusal rate

	Year					
Citizenship	*2017*	*2018*	*2019*	*2020*	*2021*	*2022*
India	32.42%	27.47%	54.29%	67.72%	55.91%	34.69%
Pakistan	76.71%	56.47%	49.00%	66.32%	75.59%	68.75%
Nigeria	63.91%	27.84%	22.16%	61.67%	46.38%	35.22%
Philippines	63.23%	43.38%	36.05%	43.93%	30.04%	36.47%
Brazil	28.30%	21.17%	20.06%	39.07%	21.17%	24.45%
Iran	18.11%	10.30%	29.79%	37.98%	34.75%	32.07%
People's Republic of China	26.23%	25.60%	29.31%	26.95%	26.55%	26.87%
Turkey	22.97%	23.38%	14.39%	22.70%	46.28%	33.33%
France	17.27%	14.93%	21.26%	22.68%	26.70%	33.96%
Japan	30.77%	18.18%	17.65%	18.18%	17.39%	28.57%
United Kingdom and Overseas Territories	28.17%	14.29%	27.12%	16.83%	19.42%	29.63%

majority of these countries escalated post pandemic, and only some countries saw their refusal rates returning to pre-pandemic levels by 2022.

In contrast, Global North countries like France, the United Kingdom, and Turkey have the three lowest refusal rates for C41 in 2020. Surprisingly, for these countries, the refusal rates actually decreased or minimally increased during the pandemic.

C42, as shown in Table 14.2, shows a similar pattern in which Global South citizens tend to receive a higher refusal rate than citizens from the

Global North. Similarly, Global South countries experienced the largest percentage rise of C42 refusal during the pandemic, and in many cases (e.g., India, Pakistan, Nigeria), the refusal rate did not return to pre-pandemic levels in 2021.

14.3.4 Limitations

Our analysis uncovered several limitations in IRCC's data. First, the data itself is made publicly available by IRCC but is not publicly accessible. Requests have to be made on a case-by-case basis, at a cost of CDN $100 per request. Also, when requesting the particular data presented here, the CDO initially pushed back on the request for country of citizenship data, arguing that only country of residence data was available and that country of citizenship data could misrepresent the reality.[22] Yet looking only at country of residence data, particularly those from Global North countries, risks masking the plight and possibly higher visa refusal rates of residents who are Global South nationals.

The other challenge with government data is its incompleteness. For example, the data set obtained here does not clearly indicate whether the C41 and C42 applicants were refused alongside the principal applicants ("PAs") or separately. This renders it more difficult to ascertain whether the disparities in family migrants' visa approval rates are attributable to discrimination or other factors such as the differences in PAs' visa status.[23]

Indeed, a significant roadblock to proving the discrimination hypothesis is that IRCC still does not collect race/ethnic-based data. This makes it challenging to uncover discrepancies within a country of citizenship or residence, such as those between white and Black South Africans or Tamil and Singhalese Sri Lankans.[24]

Finally, the data is unable to speak to another anecdotal trend, namely, processing delays faced by applicants in the Global South with "complex cases." With applications now being triaged between visa offices and other cases sitting unprocessed for beyond a year, a mere look at yearly approval and refusal rates and volumes at Global South visa offices may not show the full impact of the COVID-19 pandemic on family migrants.

14.4 Three Counternarratives: Stories of Pandemic Spouses/ Common-Law Partners Not Captured in the Data

The tenet of the critical race theory to tell counternarratives or counter-stories is important as a tool to fight against dominant narratives.[25] Dominant narratives of the pandemic suggest that negative impacts were borne by all immigration sectors and applicants, regardless of race, gender, and location of application, and that Canada's policy struck an effective balance between protecting our health and security and supporting Canada's immigration objectives.[26]

The following real-life counternarratives, whose specifics have been modified to ensure anonymity, surface concerns of racism and mental health that are not fully captured by the statistical data or the dominant immigration narratives during the pandemic.

- Amit works in Ontario as a software engineer for a leading global tech company. He held an employer-specific work permit but was separated from his spouse, an Indian national, during the pandemic. He applied for a C41 work permit for his spouse, but the travel ban of applicants from India delayed the processing time. He then applied for a temporary resident visa ("TRV") for his spouse, but the application was refused on the belief that his spouse would not return to India at the end of her authorized stay. He is now experiencing mental health issues as a result of family separation.
- Ishaan is a study permit holder in Canada beginning year two of a five-year PhD program. His spouse, Swail, is a Pakistani national who takes care of Ishaan's three children and is supported by Ishaan's former employer in Dubai, who agreed to continue to renew his UAE residency permits until he returns to take a management position following studies. Ishaan has tried numerous times during the pandemic to get Swail and their children to Canada, starting with a C42 and, eventually, even trying a TRV. All applications were refused, as a lack of family ties outside Canada and concerns about the family's immigration status in the UAE led to a finding that the family would not return to UAE at the end of Ishaan's studies. Ishaan believes Canada is racially discriminating against his family because they are non-Emirates and are not legally able to obtain permanent resident status in the UAE while simultaneously punishing them for holding citizenship of Pakistan, where resident and citizen refusals are already high.
- Ola is a Nigerian work permit holder, who also has an immigration application that is nearing the end stages of processing. His recently married spouse is also a Nigerian citizen. He had submitted a TRV application in support of his spouse, but he faced a long delay due to IRCC deciding to focus on processing applications received after 7 September 2021.[27] He then applied for a C41 work permit for his wife, just days after the African travel ban was introduced. The COVID-19 vaccine was not deemed safe for pregnant women in Nigeria, and therefore, his wife was not vaccinated. Canada, at the time, required proof of vaccination for entry to Canada and did not provide exceptions for pregnant women. Over a year has passed, and neither the TRV nor the C41 application has been decided. Ola recently had to rush back to Nigeria for the birth of his first son, which meant potentially sacrificing his own immigration process.

Ola believes Canada's travel ban against Africans is racist and is suffering from sleep issues as a result of excessive worry for his spouse during the pregnancy.

These narratives highlight issues such as racism, gender discrimination, and mental health and their intersection with immigration.[28] While they have largely been overwhelmed by the prevailing public discourse during the pandemic, they have received resonance in some corners of the immigration system. Some immigration-related government institutions, for example, have recently performed internal audits and developed new frameworks/guidelines to assess and address growing concerns around racism and gender inequality.[29]

14.4.1 Legal and Policy Barriers for Applicants to Challenge Racism and Mental Health Stressors

These recent efforts notwithstanding, concerns about discrimination and/or harm to applicants' mental health have traditionally not had much influence on visa officers' decision-making.

One reason for this has to do with the difficulty of introducing social science evidence in the judicial review process. The *Immigration and Refugee Protection Act* explicitly excludes temporary residents from seeking *de novo* appeals of decisions they receive.[30] A refused applicant's only recourse, other than seeking reconsideration by the same decision-maker, is to judicially review the decision at the Federal Court in hopes of having the file sent to a new officer for reconsideration (or in rare instances, as now permitted, a directed decision). And yet the Federal Court process limits the ability of temporary resident visa applicants to introduce new social science evidence through judicial review,[31] including evidence that may shed light on the discriminatory and/or mental health impact of relevant decisions. This is so even though many IRCC decisions themselves may rely on or be informed by their own undisclosed data and social science evidence.[32]

The second reason for the inadequate consideration of racism and mental health in visa officers' decision-making has to do with policy. To date, other than its adoption of Gender-based Analysis Plus (GBA+), which focuses largely on ameliorating gender-based discrepancies created by government policy,[33] the federal government has no truly intersectional or anti-oppressive framework for how racial consequences of policy decisions should be considered. Only recently, following public scrutiny over the possible racial biases embedded in an automated immigration decision-making system (i.e., Chinook) that was largely developed during the pandemic, did the government pledge to introduce a new Racial Impact Assessment Tool.[34] At the time of writing, however, no details exist about what this assessment entails.

Consideration of mental health, on the other hand, is largely limited to determination processes involving people who apply for or have already obtained permanent status in Canada. For example, it is part of the assessment for those seeking permanent residence on humanitarian and compassionate grounds[35] and for vulnerable individuals seeking to appeal refusals rendered by the Immigration and Refugee Board.[36] For those seeking temporary residence, raising mental health concerns in their applications is often stigmatized for fear of flagging to IRCC's attention possible issues of medical inadmissibility.[37]

The concerns and experiences of temporary residents, particularly the spouses outlined in this chapter, with racism and mental health challenges suggest the need for a new approach to visa processing and border management. An intersectional/anti-oppression lens[38] must be applied to both the development of policies and guides and the provision of tools allowing visa applicants to directly challenge racist and discriminatory policies. Among others, policies during the pandemic that prioritize certain applicants of temporary resident visas, as well as such policies' racialized implication, must be examined and remedied. This should entail paying closer attention to the narratives of affected individuals and communities both now and in the future. As Canada increasingly relies on artificial intelligence to make immigration and visa decisions based on past data, careful consideration of such human narratives and social science evidence will be key to ensuring that future policy- and decision-making does not perpetuate racial inequities and silence around mental health issues facing visa applicants.

14.5 Conclusion: Need for Balanced and Wholesome Understanding of Migrants' Experiences during the Pandemic

This chapter highlights the negative impact of Canada's pandemic-era border policies on the spouses and partners of study permit and work permit holders. Drawing on limited quantitative and qualitative data that are available, I illustrate how the burden flowing from such border policies has not been borne equally among spouses of temporary residents nor has liberalization of border restrictions benefited all these spouses to the same degree. Racialized individuals from Global South face greater challenges when seeking to reunite with their spouses in Canada, and these struggles impair the mental health of all parties involved. However, the Canadian legal system does not provide effective avenues for migrants to raise these issues of discrimination and mental health through the use of social science evidence during the judicial review of visa officers' decisions. It remains to be seen whether such rejection of social science evidence by courts would persist in the wake of *Vavilov*,[39] which is currently Canada's leading decision on the standard of judicial review. In that case, the Supreme Court of Canada suggests that decision-makers have a heightened responsibility to consider the impact or harm of their administrative decisions on individuals.

Any postmortem on Canada's pandemic-era border policies will need to take into account social science evidence alongside statistical data, which may not always be complete. By applying social science tools, such as the concept of counternarratives championed by critical race theorists, one is able to uncover experiences and consequences that are overlooked by prevailing public and policy discourse. This in turn will allow us to better draw connections between immigration policy and public health outcomes, including the effects of racism on mental health.

Notes

1 The author would like to thank Stuart Wang, data scientist, for his graphs and input for part 2 of this paper. The author would also like to highlight the contributions of his Heron Law Offices team, especially Jessye Kilburn, for her careful edits and review. The author is appreciative of Y.Y. Brandon Chen for his assistance in framing the abstract, careful edits, and invitation to speak at the symposium.

2 See list of temporary resident visa (TRV)-exempt (Electronic Travel Authorization [eTA] Requiring) and TRV-requiring countries: Immigration, Refugees and Citizenship Canada, "Entry requirements by country or territory" (4 July 2022), online: *Government of Canada*. www.canada.ca/en/immigration-refugees-citizenship/services/visit-canada/entry-requirements-country.html.

3 Government of Canada, "Minimizing the risk of exposure to COVID-19 in Canada order (Prohibition of Entry into Canada from any country other than the United States)", *Order in Council*, 2020–0162 (22 March 2020) [OIC 2020–0162]. https://orders-in-council.canada.ca/attachment.php?attach=38959&lang=en.

4 *Ibid* at ss 1 and 3. https://orders-in-council.canada.ca/attachment.php?attach=38959&lang=en.

5 See, e.g., Marina von Stackelberg, "Engaged Canadian-American couples kept apart despite new exemption for cross-border families", *CBC News* (20 June 2020), online: www.cbc.ca/news/canada/manitoba/fiances-separated-canada-us-border-1.5620261.

6 Immigration, Refugees and Citizenship Canada, "Update on travel restriction exemptions for extended family members for compassionate reasons", *Government of Canada* (2 October 2020), online: www.canada.ca/en/immigration-refugees-citizenship/news/2020/10/update-on-travel-restriction-exemptions-for-extended-family-members-and-for-compassionate-reasons.html.

7 "OPP-DART-2022–18159-TRV SP Intake and Approval Rates by COC & CoR and Visa Office", received by author on 26 September 2022 from Statistical Reporting Group, Chief Data Officer Branch of Immigration, Refugees and Citizenship Canada (between 2019 and 2020, volume of TRV decisions made decreased by 81.2% and refusal rate increased by 3.8%).

8 Public Safety Canada, "Impact of COVID-19 on IRCC operations" (4 September 2020), online: *Government of Canada*. www.publicsafety.gc.ca/cnt/trnsprnc/brfng-mtrls/prlmntry-bndrs/20200724/035/index-en.aspx.

9 *Immigration and Refugee Protection Act*, S.C. 2001, C-27, ss. 11 & 20(1)(b) [*IRPA*].

10 *Immigration and Refugee Protections Regulations* (SOR/2002–227), ss.179(b), 200(1)(b), 216(1)(b).

11 Immigration, Refugees and Citizenship Canada, "Program delivery update: Public policy, competitiveness and economy [R205(c)(ii)—C41, C42, C43, C44, C45]—Canadian interest—International Mobility Program" (last modified 27 September 2021), online: *Government of Canada*. www.canada.ca/en/immigration-refugees-citizenship/corporate/publications-manuals/operational-bulletins-manuals/updates/2021-competitiveness-economy.html.
12 See, e.g., *Singh v. Canada (Citizenship and Immigration)*, 2021 FC 93; *Gill v. Canada (Citizenship and Immigration)*, 2020 FC 934; *Matharoo v. Canada (Citizenship and Immigration)*, 2020 FC 664; *Maan v. Canada (Citizenship and Immigration)*, 2020 FC 118.
13 See Will Tao, "Establishment of a contradiction—Why accompanying dependents stuck with COVID study permit instructions" (6 December 2022), online (blog): *Vancouver immigration Blog*. https://vancouverimmigrationblog.com/tag/establishment-covid/.
14 OIC 2020–0162, *supra* note 3 at s 3.
15 Immigration, Refugees and Citizenship Canada, "Students—Travel to Canada: COVID-19 program delivery", *Government of Canada* (12 October 2022), online: www.canada.ca/en/immigration-refugees-citizenship/corporate/publications-manuals/operational-bulletins-manuals/service-delivery/coronavirus/temporary-residence/study-permit/travel.html.
16 Transport Canada, "Government of Canada suspends flights from India and Pakistan" (22 April 2021), online: *Government of Canada*. www.canada.ca/en/transport-canada/news/2021/04/government-of-canada-suspends-flights-from-india-and-pakistan.html;Transport Canada, "Canada announces extension of flight ban from India as it prepares for the return of direct flights", *Government of Canada* (21 September 2021), online: www.canada.ca/en/transport-canada/news/2021/09/canada-announces-extension-of-flight-ban-from-india-as-it-prepares-for-the-return-of-direct-flights.html.
17 Public Health Agency of Canada, "Government of Canada introduces new measures to address COVID-19 Omicron variant of concern", *Government of Canada* (26 November 2021), online: www.canada.ca/en/public-health/news/2021/11/government-of-canada-introduces-new-measures-to-address-covid-19-omicron-variant-of-concern.html; Public Health Agency of Canada, "Government of Canada introduces additional measures to address COVID-19 Omicron variant of concern", *Government of Canada* (30 November 2021), online: www.canada.ca/en/public-health/news/2021/11/government-of-canada-introduces-additional-measures-to-address-covid-19-omicron-variant-of-concern.html; see also Bianca Mugyenyi, "Canada's Africa-only travel ban reveals the racism shaping Canada's international policy", *NB Media Coop* (20 December 2021), online: https://nbmediacoop.org/2021/12/20/canadas-africa-only-travel-ban-reveals-the-racism-shaping-canadas-international-policy/.
18 Immigration, Refugee and Citizenship Canada, "IRCC Minister Transition Binder 2021: Digital Platform Modernization and Transformation at IRCC", *Government of Canada* (date modified 25 January 2022), online: www.canada.ca/en/immigration-refugees-citizenship/corporate/transparency/transition-binders/minister-2021/digital-platform-modernization-transformation.html.
19 See Immigration, Refugees and Citizenship Canada, "Policy playbook on automated support for decision-making" (February 2021) (2021 Edition—Draft), obtained via Access to Information Request A-2021–28399.
20 The data utilized in this section is captured in CDO's OPP-Dart-2022–17369-C41+C42 WP Intake and Approval Rates by COC & CoR and Visa Office received on 19 July 2022.
21 *Ibid.*

22 This was cited in emails from IRCC's Statistical Reporting Group, Chief Data Officer Branch ("CDO") on 7 June and 7 October 2022, although CDO eventually provided C41 and C42 data disaggregated for country of citizenship.

23 Preliminary data that we recently received and are still processing suggests that study permit refusal rates between 2019 and 2020 (for example) dropped by 11.6% from 49.79% to 38.18% and volume of decisions-made dropped by 54.14% from 232,777 to 106,733. We do not have the same information for work permit holders, which anecdotally appeared to be where many spouses (e.g., C41 spouses of Indian applicants) were refused/delayed.

24 An applicant's digital photo is prominently attached to every application, creating the possibility for racial bias. See Project Implicit, online: https://implicit.harvard.edu/implicit/blog.html.

25 Kimberlé Williams Crenshaw, "Demarginalizing the intersection of race and sex: A black feminist critique of antidiscrimination doctrine, feminist theory and antiracist politics", (1989) *The University of Chicago Legal Forum* 139.

26 See, e.g., Royal Society of Canada, "Supporting Canada's COVID-19 resilience and recovery through robust immigration policy and programs", *An RSC Policy Briefing* (March 2021), online: https://rsc-src.ca/sites/default/files/Immigration%20PB%20ES_EN.pdf

27 See Citizenship and Immigration, "CIMM—Temporary resident visa processing strategy", *Government of Canada* (3 March 2022), online: www.canada.ca/en/immigration-refugees-citizenship/corporate/transparency/committees/cimm-mar-03-2022/temporary-resident-visa-processing-strategy.html.

28 See, e.g., "Sudbury woman says Jamaican husband may miss child's birth after Canadian residency request rejected", *CBC News* (19 July 2022), online: www.cbc.ca/news/canada/sudbury/permanent-residence-denied-canada-1.6524222); Nicholas Keung, "'It's a racist system': Some couples say Canada's visa system is cruelly extending their COVID-19 separations", *Toronto Star* (22 October 2020), online: www.thestar.com/news/canada/2020/10/22/its-a-racist-system-some-couples-say-canadas-visa-system-is-cruelly-extending-their-covid-19-separations.html.

29 See, e.g., Immigration Refugees and Citizenship Canada, "Gender-based Analysis Plus", *Government of Canada* (3 March 2022), online: www.canada.ca/en/immigration-refugees-citizenship/corporate/publications-manuals/departmental-plan-2022-2023/gender-based-analysis-plus.html; Immigration, Refugees and Citizenship Canada, "IRCC Anti-racism employee focus groups", *Final Report (Prepared for: Immigration, Refugees and Citizenship Canada)* (23 June 2021), online (pdf): https://epe.lac-bac.gc.ca/100/200/301/pwgsc-tpsgc/por-ef/immigration_refugees/2021/122-20-e/POR_122–20-Final_Report_EN.pdf [Archived]; Canada Border Services Agency, "Evaluation of travellers processing through a GBA+ lens: Appendix A: Management response and action plan", *Evaluation Report (Internal Audit and Program Evaluation Directorate)* (5 July 2022), online: www.cbsa-asfc.gc.ca/agency-agence/reports-rapports/ae-ve/2022/appa-eng.html.

30 *IRPA*, *supra* note 9, s 63.

31 *Namgis First Nation v. Canada (Fisheries and Oceans)*, 2019 FCA 149 at para 7.

32 The challenges of introducing social science evidence in Federal Court was highlighted in a pre-pandemic case *Begum v. Canada (Citizenship and Immigration)* ("*Begum*") 2018 FCA 181. The Federal Court of Appeal dismissed a constitutional challenge against the section of the IRPR that requires Canadians who wish to sponsor their overseas family members for permanent residence in Canada to possess a minimum necessary income. In rejecting the allegation that the minimum necessary income requirement is discriminatory, the Court upheld the decision of first instance that the social science evidence submitted by the constitutional claimant on this point was too generic and indirect. Specifically, the Court rejected evidence provided by three expert witnesses in this case concerning the

link between lack of family support for marginalized persons and their decreased labour market participation. It held that such evidence was not relevant, as it did not directly relate to the constitutional claimant's own situation. The Court was ultimately persuaded more by data evidence from IRCC, which appeared to show that female applicants were not disproportionately disadvantaged by the minimum necessary income requirement.

33 See IRCC, "Departmental plan 2022–2023: Gender-based Analysis plus", online: www.canada.ca/en/immigration-refugees-citizenship/corporate/publications-manuals/departmental-plan-2022-2023/gender-based-analysis-plus.html; see also: Government of Canada, "What is gender-based analysis plus", online: https://women-gender-equality.canada.ca/en/gender-based-analysis-plus/what-gender-based-analysis-plus.html.

34 "Government Response to the Eighth Report of the House of Commons Standing Committee on Citizenship and Immigration Entitled, 'Differential Treatment in Recruitment and Acceptance Rates of Foreign Students in Quebec and in the Rest of Canada' ", online: www.ourcommons.ca/content/Committee/441/CIMM/GovResponse/RP11946588/441_CIMM_Rpt08_GR/DepartmentOfCitizenshipAndImmigration-e.pdf.

35 *IRPA*, *supra* note 9, s. 25. See also: IRCC, "Humanitarian and compassionate assessment: Hardship and the H&C assessment", (2 May 2016), online: www.canada.ca/en/immigration-refugees-citizenship/corporate/publications-manuals/operational-bulletins-manuals/permanent-residence/humanitarian-compassionate-consideration/processing/assessment-hardship-assessment.html.

36 Immigration and Refugee Board, "Guideline 8: Procedures with respect to vulnerable persons appearing before the IRB", online: https://irb.gc.ca/en/legal-policy/policies/Pages/GuideDir08.aspx.

37 See, e.g., Background Declaration questions on IMM 1294 and IMM 1295 forms, which asks: "Do you have any physical or mental disorder that would require social and/or health services, other than medication, during a stay in Canada?"

38 See, e.g., Derrick A. Bell, Jr., "Brown v. Board of education and the interest-convergence Dilemma", (1080) 93 *The Harvard Law Review* 518; Mari J. Matsuda, "Looking to the bottom: Critical legal studies and reparations", (1987) 22 *The Harvard Civil Rights – Civil Liberties Law Review* 323.

39 *Canada (Minister of Citizenship and Immigration) v. Vavilov*, 2019 SCC 65.

PART VI

Vaccine Passports

Civil Liberties, Human Rights, and Public Health

15

VACCINE REFUSALS AND FREEDOM OF RELIGION

A Moving Target in a Pandemic Age

Carissima Mathen[1]

The COVID-19 pandemic upended both health security and rights protection. Across the world, governments employed tools of varying severity to battle the virus' spread. Once vaccines were developed, many nations (as well as regional governments and private enterprises) turned to proof of vaccination programs as the "passport" back to normal activity, such as restaurant dining, theatre attendance, and travel. In some cases, vaccines were required as a condition of employment or schooling.[2] Those programs collided with pre-existing anti-vax sentiment, disinformation systems, and extreme political polarization.[3]

Requiring vaccination as a precondition to full participation in society deeply implicates personal freedom and raises serious constitutional questions. One of the rights frequently raised in objection to vaccine mandates is freedom of religion. This chapter investigates the parameters for refusing a vaccine on the basis of religious conviction.

There are relatively few reported cases dealing with COVID vaccine refusals.[4] The analysis in this chapter, therefore, draws on challenges to other public health measures. The cases to date suggest that claimants may encounter difficulties establishing a sufficient "nexus" between a refusal to be vaccinated and a pre-existing religious worldview. Under the Canadian constitution, if claimants can establish that such a choice is *prima facie* protected under freedom of religion, governments likely will have strong arguments that such vaccination regimes are nonetheless justified as a "reasonable limit" and, therefore, may be sustained. Such arguments include the persistence of COVID as a threat both to individuals and to the broader healthcare system.[5]

After briefly reviewing the importance of freedom of religion, the chapter looks at a number of issues that arise in relation to its scope. It then

DOI: 10.4324/9781003394006-21

examines issues of justification and proportionality for situations where a vaccine regime might legitimately conflict with religious freedom. A number of the Canadian cases discussed arise under human rights legislation, not the constitutionally entrenched *Charter of Rights*, and some do not involve the government.[6] Those cases remain relevant to the extent that they address freedom of religion more broadly.[7] Foreign sources are likewise canvassed for their general utility to the issues at hand.

15.1 The Significance of Religious Freedom

Societies like Canada place great value on freedom of religion. It is "cherished and promoted,"[8] flowing from the country's multicultural heritage, and deeply rooted in the idea that Canada is a free and democratic society. Freedom of religion embodies within it "concepts of liberty, equality, autonomy, and the recognition of human dignity."[9] It reflects not a trivial choice or preference but a "a fulcrum of individual identity, a framework through which to perceive and understand the world and one's place in it."[10]

During the pandemic, numerous international and domestic bodies stressed the need to anticipate possible conflicts between public health measures and freedom of religion. Recommended steps to address those conflicts include indicating the measures taken to protect religious minorities from discrimination,[11] itemizing "special sensitivities" around religious beliefs,[12] applying caution in suspending civil liberties,[13] and ensuring that any resulting rights restrictions are narrowly defined and are in proportion to achieving the state's objective.[14]

15.2 What Is Protected? Questions of Scope

A recurring issue in freedom of religion is how far it extends. In the Canadian context, that means deciding what exactly is protected as part of the "fundamental freedom of religion" under section 2(a) of the *Charter of Rights*. Does it, for example, include acts that cause harm to others? Must a practice be recognized by specific religious denominations? Must it correspond to a mandatory dictate in a religious text?

Canadian courts have adopted a broad understanding of religious freedom. Under that framework, the protection for the fundamental freedom is not internally limited because of any normative assessment of the harmfulness of a particular practice for which such protection is being sought.[15] Establishing a *prima facie* breach of religious freedom requires proof that (1) the claimant sincerely believes in a belief or practice that has a nexus with religion and (2) the impugned measure interferes with the claimant's ability to act in accordance with their religious beliefs in a manner that is more than trivial or insubstantial.[16] The cases discussed later largely focused on the question of the presence or absence of a religious nexus. They provided little discussion of the second element: whether the alleged infringement was trivial.

A refusal to be vaccinated must qualify as religious in nature. Notwithstanding the broad approach to religious freedom in Canadian law, at least some authorities have evinced a reluctance to accept such claims. The Ontario Human Rights Commission says that while receiving a vaccine is a voluntary decision, "a person who chooses not to be vaccinated based on personal preference does not have the right to accommodation under the *Code*." The Commission also notes that it is not "aware of any tribunal or court decision that found a singular belief against vaccinations or masks amounted to a creed within the meaning of the *Code*." Further, it stresses, "personal preferences or singular beliefs do not amount to a creed for the purposes of the *Code*."[17] Human rights commissions in New Brunswick, Alberta, Nova Scotia, Newfoundland and Labrador, and Yukon Territory have issued similar statements.[18]

The general tenor of such statements is that merely invoking religion is insufficient to challenge a vaccine mandate. There must be a demonstrable link to the claimant's religious beliefs. Additionally, the belief cannot be a political position operating in disguise.[19]

While in Canada, conformity with organized religious dogma is not a formal part of the test for freedom of religion,[20] the degree to which particular beliefs are supported by a broader religious community has cropped up in foreign legal analyses. Some decisions emphasize the fact that none of the world's major religions are theologically opposed to vaccines (and indeed, a number have endorsed them).[21] For example, in *R (Hussain) v Secretary of State for Health and Social Care* (2021), the English High Court of Justice considered public health measures suspending religious gatherings of two or more persons and, of particular concern to the applicants, preventing Muslim males from completing the "Jumu'ah prayer" obligation on Fridays. The Court considered a statement from the British Board of Scholars and Imams, which advised the following:

> (1) If the government issues a directive banning public gatherings this needs to be adhered to, and (2) high risk individuals (as previously identified) SHOULD NOT attend: not only is the obligation of Jumu'ah is [sic] lifted from them but their attendance, if any congregation does occur, should be severely and proactively precluded.[22]

The Court acknowledged that the claimant's and board's views diverged but found the "legitimate difference of opinion" relevant. In its view, achieving a "fair balance" would recognize "the indisputable point that the Claimant's beliefs as to communal Friday prayer in current circumstances are not beliefs shared by all Muslims."[23] (The issue of justification is developed further in this chapter.)

Some decisions show a degree of scepticism about the link between beliefs against COVID measures and religion itself. In one complaint against a store's mask policy, a man claimed that he could not wear a mask for even "a second or a minute" because "God created me in his own image and if he cannot see that image because it is covered with a face mask then I have committed sacrilege."[24] The Alberta Human Rights Tribunal found that the man failed to identify "what religion or faith tradition he follows," resorting instead to citing Bible passages with no evident link to "a tenet or practice of not covering one's face."[25] While Canadian jurisprudence did not require adherence to a "mainstream" religious faith, the claimant still had to explain "how that belief is tied to any particular religion, how it is religious in nature, or that the requirement to cover his face restricts his ability to practice his religious faith."[26] Ultimately, the tribunal found, he did not do so. In a separate case that did not ultimately turn on the issue, the Ontario Divisional Court dismissed one religiously-motivated attack against COVID vaccines: that they are derived from fetal cell tissue taken from selective abortions.[27]

Some of the cases strongly suggest that anti-vaccine beliefs in the main are only tenuously related to religion. To be clear, that position is inconsistent with Canadian precedent, which adopts a predominantly subjective approach to religious belief.[28] It would be possible for a claimant to articulate a cogent link between such views and their religious worldview—including how that view subjectively furthers their relationship with the divine. But in the absence of clear and convincing links between anti-vaccine views and one's personal religious beliefs, Canadian courts and tribunals may not readily accept such assertions.

15.3 Justification and Proportionality

Assuming that a claimant succeeds in establishing that a vaccine mandate has *prima facie* breached their freedom of religion, then under section 1 of the *Canadian Charter of Rights and Freedoms,* the state has an opportunity to justify that breach as a reasonable limit that is prescribed by law and demonstrably justified in a free and democratic society. The state must prove that the challenged law (a) has a pressing and substantial objective, (b) is rationally designed, (c) is minimally impairing of the specific *Charter* rights, and (d) achieves overall proportionality between its salutary and deleterious effects.[29]

In surveying decisions that have dealt with the general issue of religious freedom and public health measures, the Canadian approach to justification finds ready comparators in foreign jurisdictions. The discussion here draws on cases originating in Trinidad and Tobago, New Zealand, England, Wales, Scotland, and the United States, as well as a number of Canadian provinces.

While some of the terminology differs, adjudicators weigh facts and evidence against a similar backdrop of overarching questions. Those questions include: What threat was posed by COVID-19? What evidence and processes were relied upon to make decisions? How agile was a government in responding to new information? What consideration was given to the specific religious beliefs?[30]

Virtually every case recognizes that combatting COVID was or is a "pressing and substantial objective," that COVID "presents truly exceptional circumstances" and that it is "a genuine and present danger to" overall health and well-being.[31] Even more skeptical jurists, including some sitting on the United States Supreme Court, have acknowledged the state's "compelling interest" in managing COVID-19.[32]

Courts similarly have accepted as valid state arguments that restrictive measures can be rationally connected to attempts to minimize the effect of COVID. They tend to reject broadside attacks, of dubious scientific validity, on such measures. For example, in *Gateway Bible Baptist Church v. Manitoba*, a church contended that Manitoba's rights infringements were "based on unconvincing science, [that did] more harm than good."[33] The Court of King's Bench rejected this argument, finding "no new or convincing basis" to conclude that Manitoba lacked a basis for its actions. More specifically, no evidence supported the applicant's claims that:

> deaths from COVID-19 are not real, that positive PCR cases of COVID-19 are not real, that Manitoba's modelling projections were proven incorrect and/or that in making the difficult decisions required of them, these public health officials failed to properly balance collateral effects.[34]

Some claimants do not engage in outright science denialism but nonetheless argue that restrictions cannot be defended where the supporting science is uncertain. (This argument could be seen as a challenge either to the rationality or minimally impairing nature of the measure.) Generally, courts have been wary of second-guessing the information available to the state at the relevant time. To do so, one judge noted, would "set an impossible burden, particularly where, as here, the social problem defies scientific consensus."[35] In such cases, the precautionary principle, a key factor in public health, is engaged. As interpreted by some courts, under that principle, "certainty is not a reason to postpone harm reduction strategies. To wait for certainty is to wait too long."[36]

A couple of additional factors, which, again, could be relevant to either rational connection or to minimal impairment, warrant mention. The first is the degree to which the state response has accounted for changes in COVID itself. Given the various COVID waves and variants, this could well be a significant feature in a proportionality analysis. At least one court, however, rejected that argument in the context of the emergence of Omicron—finding that there remained a sufficient public health benefit to public health measures to justify the state's chosen policy.[37]

The second factor relates to instances where the state appears to subject religious activity to more stringent controls than other behavior. For example, in New York state, a public health rule limited religious gatherings to ten persons but did not impose similar limits on designated "essential" businesses in the same general locale. In the United States Supreme Court, that distinction proved fatal to the government. A majority of justices concluded that such differential treatment constituted "targeting" of the religious group in question and, on that basis, issued injunctive relief.[38] Similar reasoning appears in *Philip*, a case from the Scottish Court of Session. There, the Court found that once authorities allowed some (secular) exceptions to a "stay-at-home" rule, it fell on them "to justify why other [religious-activity based] exceptions [were] not allowed."[39] Other courts have found that such distinctions did not destroy the government's case, reasoning that some deference is required when considering the very complicated decisions that the virus forced authorities to make.[40]

Another issue that might bear on the question of minimal impairment is the degree to which COVID vaccines prevent infection and, therefore, the spread of the disease.[41] Where vaccines demonstrably prevent transmission of a dangerous virus, the balance between individual choice and overall societal benefit almost certainly tilts in favour of the latter. Where so-called "sterilizing immunity" is not as clear-cut, the state will have to point to additional justification to establish minimal impairment. One such factor is the need to prevent overburdening the healthcare system. That has indeed become a keen concern in Canada.[42] As stated by one court:

> A health system in which every available bed is occupied by someone infected with COVID-19 has no way to respond to people with heart attacks, hip fractures or strokes, potentially adding to the elevated mortality attributable to COVID-19. Put simply, the harms caused by COVID-19 would be compounded with additional preventable deaths due to heart attacks, hip fractures and other health conditions if there are no beds and no staff available to care for patients with these conditions.[43]

To the extent that vaccines reduce the severity of a COVID infection leading to reduced pressure on the overall health system, they can reasonably be assumed to contribute to this goal.

The final step of the section 1 analysis looks at the overall salutary effects of the impugned measure and weighs it against the deleterious effects on the *Charter* rights holder.[44] Although it is only occasionally decisive in a *Charter* claim,[45] this final stage in the section 1 analysis is where Canada's identity as a "free and democratic society" is put to the test. A measure, targeted at an important state objective, rationally designed to meet that objective, and imposing the least interference with a *Charter* right, might nonetheless be incompatible with the kind of society Canada has committed itself to be. Conflicts between otherwise valid state measures and religious beliefs can be especially tricky to navigate to the extent that they raise incommensurate values. Therefore, while it is rarely determinative in most *Charter* arguments, this final stage could be relevant in a conflict between vaccine refusal and public health measures.

While it is risky to make to broad predictions, the tenor of the case law to date suggests that courts will be reluctant to endorse the idea that the *Canadian Charter* requires governments to avoid valid health measures based on individual religious beliefs—no matter how sincerely they are held. It is almost certainly relevant here that, to date, any such regimes do not actually compel vaccination. Instead, they have conditioned the enjoyment of certain aspects of social citizenship upon a willingness to participate in a rational scheme to avoid the worst outcomes of a highly contagious disease. To be sure, the deleterious social effects upon an individual who refuses to get vaccinated are far from trivial. But the *Charter* is best understood as a document that both protects individuals from state overreach *and* ensures the continued conditions under which Canadian society can flourish and thrive. Viewed against that broader backdrop, it is very likely that future proof of vaccination regimes can withstand challenges from individuals who assert an honest religiously motivated belief against taking them.[46]

Notes

1 I benefited from Caroline Mercer's research assistance and thank the University of Ottawa Centre for Health Law, Policy and Ethics for facilitating it.
2 "Prime Minister announces mandatory vaccination for the federal workforce and federally regulated transportation sectors" (6 October 2021), online: *Government of Canada*. https://pm.gc.ca/en/news/news-releases/2021/10/06/prime-minister-announces-mandatory-vaccination-federal-workforce-and.
3 For a sample, see the proceedings of the Public Order Emergency Commission in the Fall of 2022: "Webcast of the commissioner's public statement" (2022), online (video): *Public Order Emergency Commission*. https://publicorderemergencycommission.ca/.
4 In Canada, there have been a number of labour board decisions, but these largely relate to conflicts over the scope of existing collective agreements. There are a smattering of reported decisions in other contexts, e.g., *Lewis v Alberta Health Services*, 2022 ABQB 479 (vaccination requirement for organ donation not subject to *Charter* scrutiny).
5 See the chapter by Dr. Kumanan Wilson on the differences between "sterilizing" and "protective" immunity in this volume. That sort of analysis would be relevant to the question of whether slightly more indirect harm (such as an overburdened healthcare system) might be a factor in any justification analysis.
6 The Supreme Court of Canada has described human rights codes as "quasi-constitutional": *Quebec (Commission des droits de la personne et des droits de la*

jeunesse) v. Montreal (city); Quebec (Commission des droits de la personne et des droits de la jeunesse) v. Boisbriand (City), [2000] 1 S.C.R. 665.

7 In Canada, "freedom of religion" has a common meaning in human rights and in constitutional law: *Syndicat Northcrest v. Amselem*, 2004 SCC 47 [*Amselem*]. The process for determining whether an infringement of the freedom might be justified is not identical between the two doctrinal areas but that distinction is not relevant to this discussion.

8 *Ontario v. Trinity Bible Chapel et al*, 2022 ONSC 1344, para 85 [*Trinity Bible Chapel*].

9 *Ibid*, para 86. See also Carissima Mathen, "What religious freedom jurisprudence reveals about equality" (2009) 6:2 *Journal of Law & Equality* 163.

10 *Trinity Bible Chapel*, *supra* note 8, para 87. See also Benjamin L. Berger, "Religious diversity, education, and the 'crisis' in state neutrality" (2014) 29 *The Centre for Justice, Law and Society* 103; Bruce Ryder, "State neutrality and freedom of conscience and religion" (2005) 29 S.C.L.R. (2d).

11 UNHRC, AL LKA 2/2020, Mandates of the Special Rapporteur on freedom of religion of belief (2020).

12 Council of Europe, *The impact of the Covid-19 pandemic on human rights and the rule of law*, Committee on Legal Affairs and Human Rights, AS/JUR (2020) 13.

13 Inter-American Commission on Human Rights, "Pandemic and human rights in the americas" (2020), online (pdf): www.oas.org/en/iachr/decisions/pdf/Resolution-1-20-en.pdf.

14 African Commission on Human and Peoples' Rights, "Press statement on human rights based effective response to the novel COVID-19 virus in Africa", online: https://achpr.au.int/pressrelease/detail?id=483.

15 *B. (R.) v. Children's Aid Society of Metropolitan Toronto*, [1995] 1 S.C.R. 315. In this case, a majority of judges found that section 2(a) *prima facie* protected parents' right to refuse a lifesaving transfusion for their infant daughter, although state intervention was justified under section 1.

16 *Amselem*, *supra* note 7.

17 Ontario Human Rights Commission, "OHRC policy statement on COVID-19 vaccine mandates and proof of vaccine certificates" (22 September 2021), online: www.ohrc.on.ca/en/news_centre/ohrc-policy-statement-covid-19-vaccine-mandates-and-proof-vaccine-certificates.

18 "COVID-19 and Human Rights: Best Practices", online: *Human Rights Commission of Newfoundland*. https://thinkhumanrights.ca/human-rights-and-covid-19-best-practices/; "COVID-19 FAQS", online: *Yukon Human Rights Commission*. https://yukonhumanrights.ca/covid-faqs/#1635981376432-000a41da-4cd7.

19 "Factsheet: COVID-19 and the human rights code", online: *Manitoba Human Rights Commission*. http://www.manitobahumanrights.ca/education/pdf/factsheets/factsheet_covid19.pdf.

20 *Amselem*, *supra* note 7, para 46.

21 *Ibid*, para 46.

22 *R (Hussain) v Secretary of State for Health and Social Care*, [2020] EWHC 1392 (Admin), para 16 (emphasis in original).

23 *Ibid*, para 17.

24 *Pelletier v 1226309 Alberta Ltd. o/a Community Natural Foods*, 2021 AHRC 192, paras 6–7 [*Pelletier*].

25 *Ibid*, para 35.

26 *Ibid*, para 35.

27 *Michalski v. McMaster University*, 2022 ONSC 2625, para 35.

28 A number of jurists have expressed disagreement with the breadth of that definition. See the dissenting arguments of Bastarache et al in *Amselem*, *supra* note 7

(a nexus between the believer's personal beliefs and the precepts of his or her religion must be established for *prima facie* breach); the majority judgment in *Ktunaxa Nation v. British Columbia (Forests, Lands and Natural Resource Operations)*, 2017 SCC 54 (excluding from the scope of 2(a) protection "sacred places" or other objects of a religious belief); and the concurring reasons of Rowe J. in *Law Society of British Columbia v. Trinity Western University*, 2018 SCC 32 (freedom of religion does not extend to beliefs that seek to constrain behaviour of nonbelievers).

29 *R. v. Oakes*, [1986] 1 S.C.R. 103.

30 Many of the cases dealt with measures that eliminated the possibility of religious gatherings, limited choices around funeral rites (such as cremation), or imposed other restrictions such as mask mandates.

31 *R (Hussain) v Secretary of State for Health and Social Care*, [2020] EWHC 1392 (Admin), para 19.

32 *Roman Catholic Diocese of Brooklyn, New York v. Andrew M. Cuomo, Governor of New York*, 592 U. S. ____ (2020) [*Roman Catholic Diocese of Brooklyn*].

33 2021 MBQB 219, para 322.

34 *Gateway Bible Baptist Church v. Manitoba*, 2021 MBQB 219, para 164. See also the court's dismissal of the underpinnings of the Great Barrington Declaration, an approach that urged states to avoid population-level measures entirely and focus instead on focused protection of the vulnerable: paras 306–315.

35 *Trinity Bible Chapel*, *supra* note 8, paras 143–145.

36 *Ibid*, paras 143–145.

37 *Orewa Community Church & Ors v Minister for COVID-19 Response; Free To Be Church v Minister for Covid-19 Response*, CIV-2022-485-123, para 252.

38 *Roman Catholic Diocese of Brooklyn*, *supra* note 32.

39 *Judicial Review of the closure of places of worship in Scotland*, [2021] CSOH 32, para 114.

40 Trinity Bible Chapel, *supra* note 8, para 144.

41 See the chapter by Dr. Kumanan Wilson in this volume.

42 Alan Drummond, "State of emergency: Inside Canada's ER Crisis" (10 November 2022), online: *Maclean's*. www.macleans.ca/longforms/er-doctor-healthcare-crisis-canada/; "CHEO opens 2nd pediatric ICU amid 'unprecedented' demand" (9 November 2022), online: *CBC News*. www.cbc.ca/news/canada/ottawa/cheo-second-pediatric-icu-surge-cases-1.6646324.

43 *Trinity Bible Chapel*, *supra* note 8, para 52.

44 *Alberta v. Hutterian Brethren of Wilson Colony*, 2009 SCC 37 [*Hutterian Brethren*]; *Dagenais v. Canadian Broadcasting Corp.*, [1994] 3 S.C.R. 835.

45 In other words, it is a rare for a court to find that the state has established all of the other arguments under section 1 but failed to show overall proportionality. Nonetheless, the Supreme Court has insisted this question remains an important one: *Hutterian Brethren*, *supra* note 44.

46 *Suraj & Ors v Attorney General of Trinidad and Tobago (Trinidad and Tobago)*, [2022] UKPC 26.

16

A BRIEF HISTORY OF THE SCIENCE OF VACCINE PASSPORTS AND WHAT THE FUTURE HOLDS

Kumanan Wilson

We are now in year three of a global pandemic that has claimed over six and a half million lives and caused mass disruptions in the economy and social fabric of society.

When it became clear that the world was being confronted by a unique viral challenge, it was recognized that a safe and effective vaccine would be critical to our ability to combat the pathogen. An unprecedented global effort was undertaken to develop vaccines against the novel coronavirus.[1] However, this endeavor faced substantial obstacles: effective vaccines had not previously been developed against coronaviruses; the timeline for developing the vaccine was remarkably short from a historical perspective; there were risks ensuant with the development of the vaccine; and the vaccines would not only have to be developed, they would have to undergo Phase 3 trials to ascertain safety and effectiveness.

And then one of the greatest medical accomplishments of our lifetime happened.[2] Highly safe and effective vaccines were developed and tested in unprecedented times. Two of these used a novel mRNA platform that had never created a widely used vaccine before, as reported in landmark studies that were published in the New England Journal of Medicine in December of 2020, less than one year from the emergence of the virus.[3] Hope was on the horizon.

Unfortunately, the story did not end there. New challenges emerged. How were we going to track the vaccine and know whether people were vaccinated? How were we going to communicate the importance of vaccination to the public? And how would public health pivot as the pandemic inevitably changed course? Our failure to adequately address these, as well as prepare for the eventual torrent of misinformation, ultimately created enormous

DOI: 10.4324/9781003394006-22

challenges that have threatened not only our response to COVID-19 but also future such threats, routine vaccination programs, and the foundations of our civil society. In particular, the simple idea of tracking vaccinations has created a deep schism in our country.

How did it go so wrong?

16.1 A Brief History of Vaccine Tracking

Knowing and tracking who has received vaccines is not new. During the smallpox pandemic, the vaccine scar was a passport to access. For example, to board a train, passengers would have to show evidence either of a scar suggesting previous smallpox infection or of vaccination.[4] Prior to the pandemic, Article 79 and Annex VI of the International Health Regulations described an International Certificate of Vaccination and Prophylaxis. This certificate was—and still is—used to confirm vaccination against yellow fever for travel to countries where the disease is endemic.[5] It has previously been used during the smallpox pandemic. More locally, in some provinces in Canada, proof of vaccination, or a valid exemption, is required for entry into school.[6] Proof of childhood immunization, either vaccination or antibodies, a negative TB test, and proof of influenza vaccination are routine requirements in many healthcare institutions for healthcare workers. Thus, the idea of tracking vaccination and requiring proof of vaccination is not novel.

16.2 Science of Vaccine Tracking

Given the implications on individual mobility, what are the scientific and medical arguments that have justified requiring proof of vaccination? At its root, this requirement is based on the concept of reducing risk not only to the individual vaccinated but also to reduce risk to others. As vaccination is not 100% effective, the unvaccinated, if infected, can still potentially transmit the pathogen, and consequent illness, to some vaccinated. And some individuals, the immunocompromised and older adults, for example, cannot be vaccinated or do not respond optimally to vaccination. To protect these vulnerable individuals, others who they may come in contact with need to be vaccinated.

However, there are also societal benefits to requiring vaccination. At a certain level of population vaccination coverage, the chain of transmission of the pathogen can be effectively disrupted to prevent disease spread. This concept is referred to as "herd immunity". The proportion of the population who needs to be vaccinated to achieve the "herd immunity" threshold can be determined by the following equation:

Critical Vaccine ("Herd Immunity") Threshold = (1–1/Ro)/Ve

In this equation, *Ro* refers to the basic reproduction number of the virus—the number of individuals infected for every infected individual in the absence of any intervention. *Ve* is the effectiveness of the vaccine's ability to protect individuals from being infected. Even if herd immunity level is not achievable, the more individuals vaccinated the more transmission is reduced. The following formula demonstrates how vaccination can reduce the effective reproduction number of the virus:

$$R_t = R_0 \, x \, (1 - P_{vax} \, x \, VE)$$

The goal of vaccination programs is to reduce R_t, the effective reproduction number of the virus, i.e., reduce the number of subsequent individuals infected by each infected individual. In this equation, P_{vax} is the proportion of the population effectively vaccinated. The more effective the vaccine and the more individuals vaccinated, the more the reproduction number of the virus is reduced. If it is reduced below 1, herd immunity is theoretically achieved and the chain of transmission is effectively disrupted, resulting in a decline in the number of cases. Table 16.1 demonstrates how differing vaccine effectiveness, differing R_t and differing coverage rates impact the effectiveness of vaccine campaigns. We will return to this formula later as it explains the implications of a changing virus on vaccination programs.

There is, however, one further benefit of vaccination that, unfortunately, was not well recognized or communicated during the early stages of the vaccination program. Vaccines can produce two types of immunity: sterilizing immunity, where they protect against infection, and protective immunity, where they reduce the health impacts of infection.

When we have traditionally thought of the justifications for vaccine programs, we have referred to the sterilizing benefits of many vaccines. However, reducing serious illness is also valuable not only for the individual being vaccinated but also to reduce the burden of illness in an already stressed healthcare system. The tetanus vaccine and pertussis vaccine work through this

TABLE 16.1 Median deaths averted by vaccinations per 10,000 people by country in the first year of COVID-19 vaccination

Vaccine	*Strain*	*Reproductive number* (R_0)[7]	*Vaccine effectiveness against symptomatic infection*	R_t *with 70% vaccine coverage* $R_0 \, x \, (1\text{-}P_{vax} \, x \, VE)$	*Critical vaccination threshold (1–1/Ro)/Ve*
mRNA vaccines	Wuhan	2.8	95%[8]	0.94	68%
mRNA vaccines	Delta	5	80%[9]	2.2	100%

mechanism.[10] With pertussis, the vaccine effectively prevents serious disease or "whooping cough". However, it does not as effectively prevent infection, and asymptomatic transmission to susceptibles can still occur. As we saw, overwhelming this system with seriously ill patients with COVID-19 results in the cancellation of other medical procedures and, ultimately, lockdowns—both of which have impacts beyond the individual who was not vaccinated. *Thus, the consequences of not being vaccinated, even in the absence of sterilizing immunity, are not borne by the individual alone in a Canadian-style healthcare system if the vaccine protects against serious illness.*

16.3 So What Happened during COVID-19?

At the outset of the pandemic, governments were examining different approaches to exiting lockdowns that would enable economies to reopen, protect the public's health, and be respectful of individual rights and freedoms. Even in advance of vaccinations being available, the idea of proof of the previous infection was being considered as one option to provide access.[11] There were several concerns about this approach, including whether prior infection actually provides immunity and the extent thereof, the creation of a perverse incentive to be infected, and equity issues related to impacts on marginalized populations, particularly racialized groups.[12] Nevertheless, the belief existed amongst some (including this author) that the creation of some form of digital record of immunity would eventually be needed for a vaccine, and there was a call for discussions about vaccine passports given the many ethical, political, and technological challenges that lay ahead.[13] This was strongly opposed by others, including many medical ethicists, who were worried about the impact on marginalized and racialized populations, raising the spectre of carding as one potential consequence.[14]

Then a vaccine became available with a remarkable 95% sterilizing immunity effectiveness. Based on the previous formula, approximately 60% of the population would need to be vaccinated to achieve herd immunity. The belief was that this could occur through voluntary means. There would be no need for mandates.

But just as vaccines began to be available at the beginning of 2021, at least for those in high-income countries, the virus changed. In June of that year, the Delta variant became the dominant strain globally and was more infectious with a basic reproduction almost double the ancestral strain.[15] There was also a decrease in vaccine effectiveness against the Delta variant to around 70–80%.[16] And the Delta variant was more harmful, overwhelming health systems and ICUs in particular.[17] Herd immunity now required close to 100% of the population to be vaccinated. Marginalized and racialized populations were being disproportionately impacted by the virus. Even libertarian premiers were forced to bring in proof of vaccination requirements.[18] These served to not only ensure individuals were vaccinated but incentivize individuals to be vaccinated. And they were successful in the latter respect.[19]

16.4 What Went Wrong?

But because of the absence of prior discussion, these were rushed. Some technological challenges were overcome. For example, the use of a smart health record standard allowed for a common standard across Canada. But there were ongoing issues related to technology for ascertaining vaccine status at international borders. More significantly, communication challenges about the need for vaccination undermined the vaccination programs.

Then the virus changed again with the emergence of the Omicron variant at the end of 2021 and beginning of 2022. The reproduction number further increased.[20] The variant was likely less harmful than Delta, but this was partly due to protective immunity that had developed in the population.[21] Sterilizing immunity all but disappeared, but the vaccine still provided protective immunity.[22] The latter was important to reduce the impact on the healthcare system, but its benefit was challenging to communicate. Transient sterilizing immunity was provided by boosters, but the argument about being vaccinated to protect others from being infected was no longer as relevant.

With the change in the virus and vaccine effectiveness came a change in public sentiment. While during the earlier stages of the pandemic there was strong support for public health measures, including vaccine mandates,[23] now there was an increasing belief we needed to learn to "live with the virus".[24] Out of the extreme opposition to vaccines passports emerged the trucker protests. But it was not the demographic that those who had concerns about passports thought would be disproportionately affected—marginalized visible minority communities. It was largely blue-collar and white populations. The movement garnered global attention. Partly, as a consequence of the protests and the changing science, mandates were lifted in many parts of the country.

16.5 Evidence for the Societal Impact of Vaccine Passports and Vaccination Programs

So did the mandates work? The short answer is yes. Vaccine hesitancy occurs on a spectrum, with many strongly supporting vaccination and a vocal minority who oppose vaccination. An important proportion of the population exists somewhere in between. An incentive to vaccinate provided by a passport could motivate these individuals to receive the vaccine if they were otherwise inclined not to. Complacency amongst young men, in particular, could be addressed by linking vaccines to access to entertainment

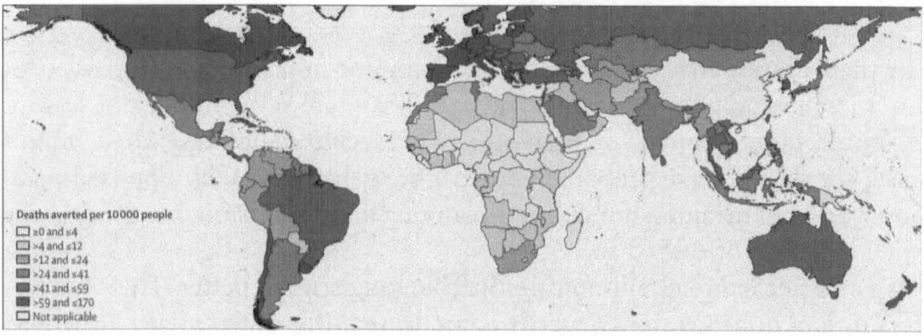

FIGURE 16.1 Median deaths averted by vaccinations per 10,000 people by country in the first year of COVID-19 vaccination.

Source: Oliver J Watson, "Global impact of the first year of COVID-19 vaccination: a mathematical modelling study" (2022) 22 Lancet Infectious Diseases P1293. Available under a CC BY 4.0 license: https://creativecommons.org/licenses/by/4.0/.

venues. Evidence supported this concept with passports increasing vaccination amongst younger populations.

It has been established that vaccination programs themselves were successful in reducing avoidable mortality. A mathematical model published in the Lancet Infectious Diseases estimated that COVID-19 vaccines saved 20 million lives globally in the first year of the program with a 2/3 reduction in deaths.[25]

Because of global inequities, higher income countries benefited disproportionately from vaccine access and the consequent reduction in vaccine-preventable deaths. As can be seen by the figure later, Canada was one of the countries that benefited the most from COVID-19 vaccination programs.

As for the impact of vaccine passports, an excellent review of the impact of vaccine passports can be found in Drew, 2022.[26] The findings are summarized as follows. A review of vaccine passports/mandates in Canada identified that on average, the mandates increase the pace of vaccination by 66% with significant interprovincial variability.[27] Benefits were greater when pre-vaccination rates were lower. According to this analysis, vaccine mandates accounted for approximately 1 million Canadians, or 2.9% of the eligible population, receiving vaccines.

Similar effects were identified internationally. In France, mandates reportedly resulted in an extra 8.6 million doses being administered.[28] According to one analysis, COVID certificates "accounted for 13% of the French population and 9.7% of the Italian population getting vaccinated in 2021."[29] This same analysis identified that the health passes saved 4,000 lives in France and boosted GDP by approximately half a percent. It was also believed that the mandates prevented the third lockdown in France. The benefits of vaccine passports were also noted in the US, UK, and Germany.[30]

16.6 What's Next?

Why then, despite the benefits of both vaccination and vaccination passports, were these interventions so controversial? There are some important lessons we should take from this experience with vaccine mandates. Most importantly, we should have prepared earlier. Efforts by those who opposed passports were well meaning but delayed planning and discussion, resulting in the implementation of rushed solutions.

We also needed to communicate the changing science better. This was easier said than done, as the science is complicated. But differentiating the way vaccines protect the public was important. And the lack of basic understanding of immunity in the population speaks to gaps in our education systems. It left the public susceptible to anti-vaccination misinformation disseminated through social media channels, something that should have been anticipated given that the WHO identified vaccine hesitancy as a major threat to global health in 2019.[31] The scientific ambiguity was exploited not only by those who had concerns about mandates but also by those who sought to disrupt civil society through the use of bots amongst other strategies.

The next phase in the use of vaccination to protect against COVID-19 is the introduction of multi-valent vaccines. These vaccines are "updated" to include better protection against the later Omicron variants. The mRNA platform, in particular, can allow for a more rapid iteration of vaccines to confront the challenge of a changing virus.

The introduction of multi-valent vaccines should result in longer and better protection against serious illness and potential infection against the Omicron variants. However, they have not gone through traditional Phase 3 randomized clinical trials. There will be a reliance on real-world data to ascertain their true effectiveness. The potential development of mucosal vaccines creates the possibility for the return of some level of sterilizing immunity, reducing infection and potentially protecting against outbreaks. This will create pressure to reintroduce mandates at work and healthcare institutions. Workplaces will be an important "battleground", as higher vaccination rates could result in fewer days lost to work and reduce the likelihood of work closures. Ironically, workplaces for which vaccination is most beneficial to employees are often blue collar, and these are the demographics that are more hesitant to be vaccinated.

The consequences of the COVID-19 vaccine protests, unfortunately, have not been limited to the COVID-19 vaccine. The protests have become symbolic of an "anti-government/libertarian" movement. And an emboldened anti-vaccination movement is challenging routine pediatric vaccination requirements.[32] This is a serious concern, as logistical challenges created by the pandemic have already impacted childhood vaccination rates and resulted in re-emergence of vaccine preventable diseases like measles and polio.[33]

16.7 A Better Way

As we move forward, we need to consider different approaches to encouraging vaccination programs, as it is apparent that the status quo has changed. Apparently, rapid oscillations on the part of governments—without clear justification and public health messaging—between opposing, favouring, to opposing mandates have undermined public confidence. The rhetoric of chastising the unvaccinated resulted in further alienation of some demographics. While it may seem like a platitude, returning to an approach of respectful communication and engagement is needed. Vaccination programs are designed to *protect* the unvaccinated and suboptimally vaccinated, not penalize them. School vaccination programs permit exemptions but require the unvaccinated to stay home when cases arise in school for their own protection. A similar approach may be needed for COVID-19. Workers can choose to not be vaccinated, but if cases arise at work, they will be informed to not come to the workplace. The issue of whether these individuals would be paid or not paid will be contentious and dependent on the strength of evidence for the protection the vaccines provide against reducing an individual's risk to their coworkers. And blue-collar workplaces may not have the same luxury of a work-from-home option. We also need to substantially improve our education of the population on vaccination. School programs should make this part of the curriculum, as otherwise, most children's experience with vaccines is but a painful shot in the arm.

While there has been much negative associated with the rollout of the COVID-19 vaccine, it is important to keep in mind the successes. A safe and effective vaccine was rapidly developed, tested, and distributed (at least in high-income countries) and may have saved 20 million lives in the first year of the programs. The novel vaccine platforms utilized are currently being repurposed to develop a plethora of other vaccines for both infectious and non-infectious diseases. It is more important than ever that we support this technological breakthrough with better communication and better technology.

16.8 Vaccine Passports as Metaphor

As a final reflection, it is important to consider that the anti-mandate movement may not have been just about vaccination. It is hard to believe that the simple act of getting a shot in the arm could justify the fevered protests we saw in Canada's capital as part of the trucker convoy. In my opinion, the vaccination programs came to represent more to some aspects of our society. While, overtly, this was a general distrust of government, one can't help but think that the exclusion felt by not being vaccinated may represent a general exclusion from society felt by rural and blue-collar populations—who may perceive that they and their children don't have the same opportunities as other "elites". With this frame, addressing increasing challenges to social mobility and divisions in wealth may be an important step towards addressing anti-vaccine sentiment.

Notes

1 Philip Ball, "The lightning-fast quest for covid vaccines—And what it means for other diseases" (18 December 2020), online: *Nature News*. www.nature.com/articles/d41586-020-03626-1; COVAX, "No one is safe, until everyone is safe", online: *World Health Organization*. www.who.int/initiatives/act-accelerator/covax.
2 Gerald Chan, "For all the lawyers who object to the Stmt of Principles . . ." (21 February 2019), online: *Twitter*. https://twitter.com/Gerald_Chan_law/status/1098586638790393856.
3 Fernando P. Polack et al, "Safety and efficacy of the BNT162b2 mRNA Covid-19 vaccine" (2020) 383 *The New England Journal of Medicine* 2603; Lindsey R. Baden et al, "Efficacy and safety of the mRNA-1273 SARS-CoV-2 vaccine" (2021) 384 *The New England Journal of Medicine* 403.
4 Kumanan Wilson, "Why we need a digital vaccination scar for the 21st century" (25 May 2020), online: *The Hamilton Spectator*. www.thespec.com/opinion/contributors/2020/05/25/why-we-need-a-digital-vaccination-scar-for-the-21st-century.html.
5 Kumanan Wilson, Katherine M. Atkinson & Cameron P. Bell, "Travel vaccines enter the digital age: Creating a virtual immunization record" (2016) 94 *The American Journal of Tropical Medicine and Hygiene* 485.
6 Erin Walkinshaw, "Mandatory vaccinations: The Canadian picture" (2011) 183 *The Canadian Medical Association* E1165.
7 Ying Liu & Joacim Rocklöv, "The reproductive number of the Delta variant of SARS-CoV-2 is far higher compared to the ancestral SARS-CoV-2 virus" (2021) 28:7 *Journal of Travel Medicine* 1.
8 Polack et al, *supra* note 3; Baden et al, *supra* note 3.
9 Sarah A. Buchan et al, "Estimated effectiveness of COVID-19 vaccines against omicron or delta symptomatic infection and severe outcomes" (2022) 5 *JAMA Network Open* e2232760.
10 Stacey McKenna, "Vaccines need not completely stop COVID transmission to curb the pandemic" (18 January 2021), online: *Scientific American*. www.scientificamerican.com/article/vaccines-need-not-completely-stop-covid-transmission-to-curb-the-pandemic1/#.
11 "'Immunity passports' in the context of COVID-19" (24 April 2020), online: *WHO*. www.who.int/news-room/commentaries/detail/immunity-passports-in-the-context-of-covid-19.
12 Natalie Kofler & Françoise Baylis, "Ten reasons why immunity passports are a bad idea" (21 May 2020), online: *Nature*. www.nature.com/articles/d41586-020-01451-0.
13 Raisa Patel, "Immunity passes could be an 'interim measure' on the way to reopening society, physician says" (25 April 2020), online: *CBC*. www.cbc.ca/radio/thehouse/immunity-passes-could-be-an-interim-measure-on-the-way-to-reopening-society-physician-says-1.5544368.
14 Françoise Baylis & Natalie Kofler, "Why Canadians should fight tooth and nail against proof-of-immunity cards" (7 May 2020), online: *CBC*. www.cbc.ca/news/opinion/opinion-pandemic-coronavirus-immunity-passport-1.5551528.

15 Berkeley Lovelace Jr., "WHO says delta is becoming the dominant Covid variant globally" (18 June 2021), online: *CNBC*. www.cnbc.com/2021/06/18/who-says-delta-is-becoming-the-dominant-covid-variant-globally.html.

16 Sarah A. Buchan et al, "Estimated effectiveness of COVID-19 vaccines against omicron or delta symptomatic infection and severe outcomes" (2022) *JAMA Network*.

17 Elizabeth Bast et al, "Increased risk of hospitalisation and death with the delta variant in the USA" (2021) 21 *Lancet* 12.

18 Nia Williams, "Canada's Alberta province brings in vaccine passport as Premier apologises" (15 September 2021), online: *Reuters*. www.reuters.com/world/americas/canadas-alberta-province-brings-vaccine-passport-premier-apologises-2021–09–16/.

19 Alexander Karaivanov et al, "COVID-19 vaccination mandates and vaccine uptake" (2022) *Nature Human Behaviour*.

20 Ying Liu & Joacim Rocklöv, "The effective reproductive number of the Omicron variant of SARS-CoV-2 is several times relative to Delta" (2022) 29:3 *Journal of Travel Medicine* taac037.

21 Chao Wang et al, "Differences in incidence and fatality of COVID-19 by SARS-CoV-2 Omicron variant versus Delta variant in relation to vaccine coverage: A world-wide review" (2023) 95:1 *Journal of Medical Virology* e28118.

22 Buchan et al, *supra* note 9.

23 Nicole Thompson, "Most Canadians in favour of vaccine passports for non-essential activities: Poll" (21 August 2021), online: *CTV News Montreal*. https://montreal.ctvnews.ca/most-canadians-in-favour-of-vaccine-passports-for-non-essential-activities-poll-1.5556167.

24 Melissa Couto Zuber, "Nearly 30% of Canadians say it's time to 'learn to live' with COVID-19: poll" (10 February 2022), online: *Global News*. https://globalnews.ca/news/8611838/covid-19-canada-poll-leger/.

25 Oliver J Watson, "Global impact of the first year of COVID-19 vaccination: A mathematical modelling study" (2022) 22 *Lancet Infectious Diseases* P1293.

26 Liam Drew, "Did COVID vaccine mandates work? What the data say" (6 July 2022), online: *Nature*. www.nature.com/articles/d41586-022-01827-4.

27 Alexander Karaivanov et al, "COVID-19 vaccination mandates and vaccine uptake" (2022), online: *Nature Human Behaviour*. www.nature.com/articles/s41562-022-01363-1

28 Miquel Oliu-Barton et al, "The effect of COVID certificates on vaccine uptake, health outcomes, and the economy" (2022) 13 *Nature Human Behaviour* 3942.

29 Drew, *supra* note 26.

30 James T Lee et al, "Employer requirements and COVID-19 vaccination and attitudes among healthcare personnel in the U.S.: Findings from national immunization survey adult COVID module, August—September 2021" (2022) 40 *National Library of Medicine* 7476.

31 Rada Akbar, "Ten threats to global health in 2019", online: *WHO* www.who.int/news-room/spotlight/ten-threats-to-global-health-in-2019.

32 Moises Velasquez-Manoff, "The anti-vaccine movement's new frontier" (25 May 2022), online: *The New York Times*. www.nytimes.com/2022/05/25/magazine/anti-vaccine-movement.html.

33 "COVID-19 pandemic fuels largest continued backslide in vaccinations in three decades" (15 July 2022), online: *WHO*. www.who.int/news/item/15-07-2022-covid-19-pandemic-fuels-largest-continued-backslide-in-vaccinations-in-three-decades.

17

RIGHTS DISCOURSE AND CANADIAN DEBATE OVER VACCINE PASSPORTS

Bryan Thomas

In responding to the unique exigencies of the COVID-19 pandemic, governments have been driven to enact restrictions on individual freedoms that are largely unprecedented in the modern era, including stay-at-home orders, restrictions on private and public gatherings and the forced closure of non-essential businesses. The endgame of these policies, in most countries,[1] has been to "flatten the curve" of infection rates to avert health system overload—a challenging goal for Canada, with its above-average population age[2] and below-average number of hospital beds per capita.[3]

The rollout of effective COVID-19 vaccines, in December 2020, offered a way to tailor these restrictions. While fully vaccinated individuals could still be infected, they were highly unlikely to require hospitalization and likely posed a reduced risk of transmitting the virus.[4] If individuals could certify their vaccination status at the entry point of public venues, using vaccine passports, they could resume indoor gathering without risking a significant spike in hospitalizations. Vaccine passports would also have the salutary effect of encouraging people to be vaccinated.[5] A critical assumption, in making the moral and legal case for vaccine passports, is that the alternative would be a resumption of restrictions for *everyone*—vaccinated and unvaccinated alike.

While polling at the time showed that a strong majority of Canadians supported the idea of vaccine passports,[6] the concept was critiqued as legally and ethically fraught by many academics and pundits.[7] Among the objections raised, it was alleged that vaccine passports effectively *coerce* people into getting vaccinated, in violation of their legal and moral right to bodily autonomy; violate the right to religious freedom and freedom of conscience of those who are ideologically opposed to vaccination; foster inequality and create a "two-tier society"; and enable mass surveillance, in violation of

DOI: 10.4324/9781003394006-23

privacy rights. In this chapter, I explore these allegations one-by-one, arguing that none are morally or legally compelling on close examination.[8]

By now, these conclusions are hardly revelatory; in the fall of 2021, as push came to shove with the fourth wave of the COVID-19 pandemic, vaccine passport regimes were implemented across most provinces, and there is scant evidence, if any at all, of the grave societal harms or myriad legal challenges predicted by doomsayers.[9] Nevertheless, these critiques had the effect, arguably, of shutting down debate and public consultation around the design of vaccine passport systems, as governments eschewed the idea until the fourth wave was underway. In the province of Ontario, for example, the government reacted with a "hard no" to the idea of vaccine passports well into the summer of 2021, citing concerns about rights violations; by mid-September, an *ad hoc* vaccine passport system was hurriedly enacted.[10] This made Ontario (and Canada) a relative latecomer, among OECD countries, in implementing vaccine passports.[11] This foot-dragging occurred as Ontario gained international notoriety for having one of the world's longest lockdowns.[12] In my conclusion, I offer some critical reflections on the regrettable role that "rights-talk" has played in polarizing debate and encouraging delay and inaction by governments.

17.1 Legal and Ethical Critiques of Vaccine Passports

17.1.1 Coercion and Bodily Autonomy

As indicated, one recurring objection has been that vaccine passports effectively coerce individuals to be vaccinated as a condition of resuming normal life, in violation of the right to bodily autonomy. Section 7 of the *Charter* provides that "Everyone has the right to life, liberty and security of the person and the right not to be deprived thereof except in accordance with the principles of fundamental justice."[13] It is well established in s.7 jurisprudence that patients have a right to autonomy and informed consent over medical treatments and a right to refuse even lifesaving medical treatment.[14] Of course, no proponents of vaccine passports have suggested that individuals should be forcibly vaccinated in violation of these longstanding and fundamental rights to patient autonomy and bodily integrity. It has been argued, nevertheless, that vaccine passport regimes—if sufficiently ubiquitous in their application—effectively coerce individuals to be vaccinated in a manner that violates patient autonomy.

A critical question here is whether the deprivations that might be incurred by a refusal to acquire a vaccine passport—e.g., exclusion from certain non-essential forms of travel, restaurant dining, indoor concerts, gyms and even one's workplace—rise to the level of engaging s.7 interests. The Supreme Court of Canada has emphasized that s.7 is meant to protect only "basic choices going to the core of what it means to enjoy individual dignity and independence."[15] It seems unlikely that pedestrian decisions over whether to dine in at a restaurant or exercise in a gym meet this test. The court's reasons for limiting the scope of s.7 in this way are explained in *R v. Malmo Levine* (2003), as the Court rejects a challenge to prohibitions on recreational marijuana use:

> the Constitution cannot be stretched to afford protection to whatever activity an individual chooses to define as central to his or her lifestyle. One individual chooses to smoke marihuana; another has an obsessive interest in golf; a third is addicted to gambling. The appellant . . . invokes a taste for fatty foods. A society that extended constitutional protection to any and all such lifestyles would be ungovernable.[16]

17.1.2 Religious Freedom and Freedom of Conscience

It has likewise been alleged that vaccine passports may violate the *Charter*'s section 2(a) right to freedom of conscience and religion.[17] The courts have given the *Charter*'s protection of religious freedom a very generous and expansive interpretation. In *Syndicat Northcrest v. Amselem* (2004), Justice Iaccobucci explained for the majority:

> at the first stage of a religious freedom analysis, an individual advancing an issue premised upon a freedom of religion claim must show the court that (1) he or she has a practice or belief, having a nexus with religion, which calls for a particular line of conduct, either by being objectively or subjectively obligatory or customary, or by, in general, subjectively engendering a personal connection with the divine or with the subject or object of an individual's spiritual faith, irrespective of whether a particular practice or belief is required by official religious dogma or is in conformity with the position of religious officials; and (2) he or she is sincere in his or her belief. Only then will freedom of religion be triggered.[18]

Claimants have a further burden of showing "that the impugned contractual or legislative provision (or conduct) interferes with his or her ability to act in accordance with his or her religious beliefs *in a manner that is more than trivial or insubstantial*."[19]

While no major religious denomination has come out against COVID-19 vaccination, no doubt some Canadians have declined vaccination on sincere religious grounds; sincerity is a highly subjective test, after all.[20] The next criterion is that the interference must be non-trivial, and it seems inarguable that the ubiquitous demand for proof of vaccination at restaurants, gyms, concerts and other facilities would constitute a non-trivial interference in the lives of people unvaccinated for religious reasons.[21]

Having established a *prima facie* infringement, the onus would then shift to government to justify its vaccine passport requirement, under s.1 of the *Charter*, as demonstrably justified in a free and democratic society.[22] Broadly speaking, the s.1 analysis would assess the rationality of vaccine passport policies, asking whether the government had a pressing objective that would be furthered by these policies (e.g., the effectiveness of passports in preventing transmission and/or bending the curve of hospitalizations), whether the government could have employed less intrusive policies to achieve that objective, and the proportionality of government objectives relative to the harm done to the rights of non-vaccinating religious groups.[23]

Had vaccine passports been challenged, it is conceivable that the courts might have ordered some accommodation for affected religious groups in some circumstances (e.g., the option of providing a recent test result before air travel). In *Multani v Commission scolaire Marguerite-Bourgeoys*,[24] for example, the Supreme Court granted an exemption to a general prohibition on weapons in schools, allowing a 13-year-old Sikh student to don a kirpan (ceremonial dagger) in the classroom.

It is also conceivable that the courts would have sided with governments on the importance and administrative efficiency of enforcing vaccine passports consistently. In *Alberta v. Hutterian Brethren of Wilson Colony*,[25] the claimants challenged a provincial law requiring that all licensed drivers be photographed. Then–Chief Justice McLachlin, writing for the majority, found the impugned law to be reasonably justified: the photo requirement is designed, in combination with a facial recognition database, to prevent identity theft, and allowing exemptions would undermine the integrity of this system.[26]

It is also possible that the courts would provide exemptions only in select contexts: in *Multani*, access to basic education was at stake, whereas in *Hutterian Brethren*, at issue was the claimants' ability to drive automobiles on highways; the latter is "not a right, but a privilege," the majority emphasized.[27]

What about those who oppose vaccination, not as a religious matter but as a matter of *conscience*? In most cases, the beliefs in question will fall under the heading of "vaccine hesitancy"—primarily rooted in philosophical scepticism, incorporating concerns about the safety of vaccines and the pharmaceutical industry's trustworthiness. There is scant Supreme Court jurisprudence on *Charter* protections for freedom of conscience, but it seems doubtful that vaccine hesitancy would qualify. In an early *Charter* ruling, *Edwards Books*, then–Chief Justice Dickson explained that "[t]he purpose of s. 2 (a) is to ensure that society does not interfere with profoundly personal beliefs that govern one's perception of oneself, humankind, nature, and, in some cases, a higher or different order of being."[28] The thinking here has echoes of the court's efforts, outlined earlier, to limit the scope of

Charter protections to beliefs and practices of a more profound nature. It seems unlikely that vaccine hesitancy—often rooted in misinformation about the science—would be construed by the courts as a "profoundly personal belief." Consider, by analogy, the 2004 Alberta Provincial Court ruling, *R. v. Locke*, where the plaintiff, skeptical of the science behind seatbelts, claimed that mandatory seatbelt laws infringed his freedom of conscience. The Court drew on *Edwards Books* to conclude that seatbelt hesitancy is not protected under the *Charter*'s protection of conscience because it does not reflect a "comprehensive value system," or "profoundly personal beliefs that govern one's perception of oneself, humankind, [and] nature."[29] It seems that such reasoning should lead to the rejection of s.2(a) protections for vaccine hesitancy; some provincial human rights boards have issued policy statements affirming this point.[30]

17.1.3 Inequality and the Fear of a Two-Tier Society

Another recurring concern has been that vaccine passports will exclude or discriminate against the unvaccinated, violating the moral and legal right to equality.[31] The *Charter*'s s.15 guarantee of equality rights prohibits "discrimination based on race, national or ethnic origin, colour, religion, sex, age or mental or physical disability,"[32] and the Supreme Court has ruled, in *Andrews v Law Society of BC*, that certain other "analogous grounds" are protected as well—notably, characteristics that are immutable or at least difficult for a person to change (e.g., sexual orientation, citizenship).[33] At its core, s.15 aims at the "promotion of a society in which all are secure in the knowledge that they are recognized at law as human beings equally deserving of concern, respect and consideration."[34] Section 15 protections are not satisfied by mere *formal* equality (e.g., offering a staircase to a public building that everyone is welcome to use), and courts will instead demand *substantive* equality (e.g., the installation of elevators for those unable to use stairs due to disability).

A critical question here is precisely *which* group suffers disadvantage under a vaccine passport regime and whether this group falls under some enumerated or analogous ground. Early in the vaccine rollout, there was an understandable concern that marginalized populations would face problems accessing vaccines and that vaccine passports would compound this inequality. But the solution to this problem is improved outreach and access for those marginalized populations, not the outright eschewal of vaccine passports.

Over time, allegations of discrimination were levelled on behalf of the unvaccinated generally—a group whose main common denominator is vaccine hesitancy. Yet it seems quite unlikely that the courts would accept vaccine hesitancy as an analogous ground under s.15. Crucially, vaccine hesitancy does not have the quality of being "unchangeable or changeable only at unacceptable personal costs"[35] required of analogous grounds. Indeed, governments have made a policy aim of educating the public, precisely to change minds on vaccine hesitancy. In *Malmo-Levine*, the Supreme Court pointed to this issue of mutability to find that a person's "substance orientation" towards marijuana is not an analogous ground.[36]

A more plausible case concerns those unable to be vaccinated due to health issues, which likely would count as a disability (an enumerated class under s.15). A vaccine passport regime threatens exclusion from restaurants, gyms, airline travel and even employment, and such deprivations could be construed as discriminatory. Yet there has always been an obvious work-around to this concern: issue vaccine passports to anyone who provides documentation attesting that they cannot be vaccinated for a legitimate medical reason. With few exceptions, provincial vaccine passport regimes have provided such exemptions.[37]

It is worth briefly interrogating the very idea that vaccine passports are discriminatory, in the wrongful sense of discrimination that s.15 aims to prevent—i.e., treating members of enumerated and analogous groups as *less deserving of respect and consideration.* The problem here is that vaccine passports were not proposed as a means of protecting the vaccinated population, who are assumed to face little risk of serious illness; they were proposed to control the risk of unvaccinated people interacting indoors, where they might contract the disease. There is no plausible sense in which vaccine passports can be described as excluding people on the basis of stereotypes or as discounting the interests of enumerated or analogous groups. On the contrary, this was a public health initiative aimed at protecting unvaccinated populations and preventing health system overload.

There is arguably a second conceptual confusion at play in the assumption that vulnerable or marginalized class will be unfairly disadvantaged by vaccine passports. The putative disadvantage, of course, is denial or limitations on entry to venues gated by vaccine passports. However, this is not a disadvantage conferred by vaccine passports *per se*; it is conferred by public health restrictions on indoor gatherings, which were bound to persist at least until the threat of health system overload abated. Eschewing vaccine passports in this context would only serve a perverse "levelling-down" conception of equality that has no basis in s.15 jurisprudence or, for that matter, sound ethical reasoning. Indeed, the suggestion that eschewing vaccine passports would level society down to some state of equality is unrealistic, empirically, as the burdens associated with maintaining the lockdown in full force would be borne disproportionately by the vulnerable and marginalized.

17.1.4 Privacy Rights

Finally, critics have alleged that vaccine passports pose a grave threat to privacy rights—with some critics even purporting to see in vaccine passports the beginnings of a totalitarian "show-me-your-paper" society. Canadian privacy law is a notoriously complex patchwork of federal and provincial statutes,[38] reinforced by principles rooted in common law, the exploration of which is beyond the scope of this chapter.[39] Moreover, there is a critical and complex technological dimension to compliance with privacy laws, inasmuch as a vaccine passport regime must be secure, and designed to minimize the sharing of personal information.

It is safe to say that the verification of information about a person's vaccination status *does* engage privacy rights; when this verification is carried out by private sector entities, as is generally the case under a vaccine passport regime that applies at restaurants, gyms, and so on, the default legal regime will be the federal *Personal Information Protection and Electronic Documents Act* (*PIPEDA*) or, in some provinces, provincial private sector privacy laws.[40] Broadly speaking, this legislation is built around a *reasonableness* standard, protecting consumers against the collection of personal information by private entities, except where this collection is necessary for a *legitimate business purpose*.[41]

Of course, once governments had mandated vaccine passport checks at non-essential businesses, it would be difficult to argue that compliance by businesses was unreasonable. But this raises the deeper question of whether government mandates themselves were reasonable from the standpoint of generally accepted principles of privacy law.

Beyond the requirements of individual consent for a transparent and legitimate purpose, privacy law principles specify that personal information collection, use, disclosure and retention be strictly limited to what is essential for the stated purpose. Again, the purpose of vaccine passport checks is to facilitate safe indoor gatherings, and provincial regimes hewed strictly to this aim; in many provinces, all that patrons were required to provide was a QR code bearing their name, along with photo ID. A green check, upon scanning the QR code, would provide only the barest information: the individual is either fully vaccinated or subject to a medical exemption. In Ontario, regulations stipulated that businesses could not retain this information or use it for any other purpose—under the threat of severe penalties.[42]

17.2 Conclusion: The Role of Rights Talk in Pandemic Response Discourse

At the level of academic theory, there is an emerging consensus that public health objectives are not in tension with civil, political and human rights.[43] If rights are understood to include a strong, positive right to health, then moves to restrict individual freedoms in the name of public health can be construed as respectful of rights overall. Whatever the philosophical merits of thinking about public health and individual rights in this way, it is not reflective of how rights-talk operates in ordinary public discourse. When decision-makers and the public at large turn their minds to legality of a policy like vaccine passports or mask mandates in schools, their concern is with the threat of legal challenges before courts—challenges invoking individual rights like those enumerated earlier that seek to overturn government policy. Real-world rights-talk seldom prompts questions like "Would government *inaction* in the face of this public health challenge constitute a rights violation?" This is understandable, of course, because Canadian courts have generally not embraced the concept of a positive right to health.[44]

This points to the need for caution and care when advancing rights-based arguments during a public health emergency. As an expert in law or ethics, fielding media requests in connection with pandemic response measures, the temptation is to begin by identifying every conceivable reason that a proposal *might* infringe some legal or moral right. There may even be a temptation to render these concerns vivid with dramatic historical analogies—repeated invocations of the "show-us-your-papers" trope in connection with vaccine passports is an especially common and egregious example here. When potential rights infringements are foregrounded in this way, equally important considerations tend to fall into the background. Bold exclamations about rights infringements make for good headlines, whereas nuanced discussions about proportionality testing do not. Expert commentary ought to militate against this dynamic.

On several topics related to COVID-19 response—health worker vaccination mandates, provincial borders closures and vaccine passports—government officials have invoked vague rights-talk as a reason for delay or inaction. The superficiality of legal analysis at work here should concern us; to my knowledge, at the crucial decision point of early-mid 2021, no critic had come forward with a detailed, well-referenced account of how vaccine passports infringe rights, in a manner that could not be addressed through their thoughtful design and implementation, or failing that, justified under a proportionality analysis. In drawing lessons for the next pandemic, this is one area in need of improvement. Promising public health measures should not be held hostage for months on end to vague and implausible rights-based concerns.

Notes

1 A handful of "zero Covid" countries pursued a more ambitious goal of eliminating the virus altogether. See DCG Skeggs, "Defining covid-19 elimination" (2021) 374 *BMG* 1794.
2 OECD, "Working age population", online: data.oecd.org/pop/working-age-population.htm.
3 OECD, "Hospital beds", online: data.oecd.org/healtheqt/hospital-beds.htm.
4 S Tan et al, "Infectiousness of SARS-CoV-2 breakthrough infections and reinfections during the Omicron wave" (2023) 29 *Nature Medicine* 358.

5 Melinda C. Mills & Tobias Rüttenauer, "The effect of mandatory COVID-19 certificates on vaccine uptake: synthetic-control modelling of six countries" (2021) 7 *Lancet Public Health* e15.
6 "Strong majority of Canadians support vaccination mandates; Open to measures including vaccine passports" (2021), online: *Ipsos*. www.ipsos.com/en-ca/news-polls/majority-of-canadians-support-vaccination-mandates.
7 Françoise Baylis, "COVID-19 vaccine certification: A contentious proposal" (8 January 2021), online: *Impact Ethics*. https://impactethics.ca/2021/01/08/covid-19-vaccine-certification-a-contentious-proposal/; "CCLA debates vaccine passports on TVO.org: Our letter that sparked the debate", online: *Canadian Civil Liberties Association*. ccla.org/privacy/surveillance-technology/ccla-debates-vaccine-passports-on-tvo-org-our-letter-that-sparked-the-debate.
8 While my discussion focuses on Canadian law, a similar analysis could be offered for many comparator countries. The leaders of *Lex Atlas*—a massive research project tracking the legalities around COVID-19 pandemic responses worldwide—have surveyed the evidence and conclude: "[a]s far as we know, no major constitutional or international court has found that a mandatory vaccination policy violates any general right to liberty." See Jeff King et al, "Mandatory COVID-19 vaccination and human rights" (2022) 399 *Lancet* 200.
9 One might argue that the "Freedom Convoy" protests which disrupted life in many Canadian cities in early 2022 are an example of serious harms resulting from vaccine passports. Given my conclusions about the first-order impact of vaccine passports on civil liberties, I think that to argue in this way is to engage in self-fulfilling prophecy: overstating the dangers of vaccine passports, inciting disruptive protests as a result, and then treating the latter harms as validation of one's initial alarmism.
10 Rob Ferguson, "Ontario scrambling on vaccination passports after Doug Ford rejects initial proposals" (31 August 2021), online: *The Toronto Star*. www.thestar.com/politics/provincial/2021/08/31/doug-ford-rejects-initial-proposals-for-covid-19-vaccination-passports.html.
11 Israel, Denmark, and Austria were early adopters, while 17 OECD countries adopted vaccine certificates by the summer of 2021—a move facilitated by launch of the EU Digital Certificate on 1 July 2021. By the end of 2021, some 28 OECD countries had implemented vaccine passports (Austria, Belgium, Bulgaria, Chile, Colombia, Croatia, Czech Republic, Denmark, Estonia, Finland, France, Germany, Greece, Israel, Ireland, Italy, Korea, Latvia, Lithuania, Luxembourg, Mexico, Netherlands, Portugal, Slovak Republic, Slovenia, Spain, Turkey, and the United States). See Nicolas Woloszko, "Do COVID certificates spur vaccination take-up? A snapshot of the recent evidence" (18 January 2022), online: *Ecoscope*: oecdecoscope.blog/2022/01/18/do-covid-certificates-spur-vaccination-take-up-a-snapshot-of-the-recent-evidence/.
12 "Toronto lockdown—One of the world's longest?" (24 May 2021), online: *BBC News*. www.bbc.com/news/world-us-canada-57079577.
13 *Canadian Charter of Rights and Freedoms*, s 7, Part I of the *Constitution Act, 1982*, being Schedule B to the *Canada Act 1982* (UK) 1982, c 11 [*Canadian Charter*].
14 *Rodriguez v British Columbia (AG)*, [1993] 3 S.C.R. 519.
15 *Godbout v Longueuil (City)*, [1997] 3 S.C.R. 844, para 66.
16 *R v Malmo-Levine; R v Caine* [2003] 3 S.C.R. 571, para 86 [*Malmo-Levine*].
17 *Canadian Charter*, *supra* note 13, s 2(a).
18 *Syndicat Northcrest v. Amselem*, 2004 SCC 47, para 56 [*Amselem*].
19 *Ibid* at para 59 (emphasis added).
20 There is no onus on believers to establish in any objective sense that the religious practice in question is mandated by their religious teachings; idiosyncratic beliefs

are protected. *Amselem*, *supra* note 18, para 47. There is perhaps a concern that the anti-vaccination movement might coach refusers to frame their vaccine resistance under the guise of a religious objection.

21 Note that the test for establishing an infringement under s.7—requiring an interference with *basic* life choices that engage one's core dignity—is more demanding than the requirement under s.2(a) of non-trivial interferences.

22 *Canadian Charter*, *supra* note 13, s 1.

23 *R v Oakes*, [1986] 1 S.C.R. 103,

24 [2006] 1 S.C.R. 256.

25 [2009] 2 S.C.R. 567.

26 Of course, the availability of medical exemptions somewhat undermines the integrity of vaccine passport regimes. However, allowing religious exemptions would presumably be far more undermining, as it would have to rely on self-reporting of religious beliefs—without the gatekeeping effect, in place with medical exemptions, of requiring documentation from a health professional.

27 *Alberta v Hutterian Brethren of Wilson Colony,* [2009] 2 S.C.R. 567, para 98.

28 *R. v. Edwards Books and Art Ltd*., [1986] 2 S.C.R. 713, para 97.

29 *R. v. Locke (J.),* 2004 ABPC 152.

30 "COVID-19 vaccines, vaccination mandates, and human rights" (2021), online: *Saskatchewan Human Rights Commission.* https://saskatchewanhumanrights.ca/education-resources/information-sheets/covid-19-vaccines-vaccination-mandates-and-human-rights/; "OHRC policy statement on COVID-19 vaccine mandates and proof of vaccine certificates" (2021), online: *Ontario Human Rights Commission.* www.ohrc.on.ca/en/news_centre/ohrc-policy-statement-covid-19-vaccine-mandates-and-proof-vaccine-certificates.

31 K. Bardosh et al, "The unintended consequences of COVID-19 vaccine policy: Why mandates, passports, and segregated lockdowns may cause more harm than good" (1 February 2022), online: *BMJ Global Health* (accepted for publication). https://ssrn.com/abstract=4022798.

32 *Canadian Charter*, *supra* note 14, s 15.

33 *Andrews v Law Society of British Columbia*, [1989] 1 S.C.R. 143 [*Andrews*]. See also *Corbiere v. Canada (Minister of Indian and Northern Affairs)*, [1999] 2 S.C.R. 203, para 60: "An analogous ground may be shown by the fundamental nature of the characteristic: whether from the perspective of a reasonable person in the position of the claimant, it is important to their identity, personhood, or belonging. The fact that a characteristic is immutable, difficult to change, or changeable only at unacceptable personal cost may also lead to its recognition as an analogous ground."

34 *Andrews*, *supra* note 33 at 171.

35 *Egan v Canada*, [1995] 2 S.C.R. 513 at 528.

36 *Malmo-Levine*, *supra* note 16, para 185.

37 See, e.g., "Proof of COVID-19 vaccination", online: *Government of Ontario.* covid-19.ontario.ca/proof-covid-19-vaccination#medical-exemptions.

38 *Personal Information Protection Act* (PIPA), SBC 2003, c 63; *Personal Health Information Protection Act* (PHIA), 2004, SO 2004, c 3, Sch A; Personal Health Information Act (PHIA), SNS 2010, c 41; *Personal Information Protection Act* (PIPA), SA 2003, c P-6.5; *Personal Information Protection and Electronic Documents Act* (PIPEDA), SC 2000, c 5.

39 See, generally, B. Thomas et al, "Vaccine ins and outs: An exploration of the legal issues raised by vaccine passports" (2021), online: *C.D. Howe Report.* https://covid-19.ontario.ca/proof-covid-19-vaccination#medical-exemptions; B. Thomas et al, "Privacy rights and private sector vaccination requirements" (2022), online (pdf): *C.D. Howe Intelligence Memo.* www.cdhowe.org/sites/default/files/2022-01/IM_Tho-Flo-Kri-Tan-Wil_2022_0128.pdf.

40 Many provinces have bespoke health information privacy laws. But these are only engaged—and only displace PIPEDA—when health information is collected or handled by "health information custodians" in the context of delivering care. When health information is collected by restaurants or other non-health-related commercial entities, this is regulated under the federal PIPEDA.
41 PIPEDA, *supra* note 38, ss 3, 4.3.3.
42 O Reg. 362/20: Rules for Areas at Step 3 and at the Roadmap Exit Step.
43 J. Mann et al, "Health and Human Rights" (1994) 1 Health and Human Rights 6.
44 Colleen M. Flood, "Litigating health rights in Canada: A white knight for equity?" in *The Right to Health at the Public/Private Divide: A Global Comparative Study*, edited by Colleen M. Flood & Aeyal Gross (New York: Cambridge University Press, 2014).

18

MOBILITY RESTRICTIONS, HUMAN RIGHTS, AND THE LEGAL TEST OF PROPORTIONALITY

Jeff King

Some commentators have considered COVID-19 lockdowns to be the advent of a 'totalitarian society' and a grave curtailment of civil liberties.[1] Anti-lockdown protests have in some cases turned violent, in the belief that the right to liberty is at stake. In the United States, some protests involved the open carrying of firearms and the occupation of public buildings.[2] Some human rights and constitutional lawyers have at times fed narratives that motivate such sentiments by characterizing mobility restrictions as draconian, disproportionate, or as having been made under dubious authority,[3] even where they have sympathized with the need for mobility restrictions. Equally interestingly, surveys of lay citizens' rights-consciousness during lockdowns in the UK revealed that 83% of participants believed that the lockdown "violated" at least one of nine "rights-ideas," with 57% further believing that the majority of the nine rights were "violated." Of this 57%, nevertheless, only 32% expressed the view that the lockdown was an unacceptable violation in the context of the pandemic, and of that fraction, 40% expressed that view only in relation to one rights-idea.[4] In other words, they believed that mobility restrictions "violated" their rights but were nevertheless justified.

The views expounded earlier reflect what I have elsewhere referred to as the "hazards" of the language of liberal constitutionalism: its tendency to promote "state scepticism" and "oversimplification" in the realm of law and policy.[5] An aim of this short essay is to demonstrate that there is no prima facie tension between mobility restrictions and human rights law. This point holds in relation to both the theory of human rights and the practice of human rights law in a number of important liberal democratic jurisdictions around the world. For the purposes of this essay, mobility restrictions include stay at home orders, restrictions on gatherings, shop closures, border closures, and

DOI: 10.4324/9781003394006-24

vaccine mandates restricting access to public and private venues. First, I aim to explain their general (not blanket) compatibility with the idea of rights and liberty. I will then show why the legal systems of a representative selection of liberal democratic constitutional systems have rejected the view that they are incompatible in practice. In essence, and as I show in Part I later, some of the views stated in the introductory paragraph earlier do not give adequate weight to the crucial distinction between an *infringement of rights that is justified*—which is everyday policy in a modern democracy—and a *violation of rights which is nearly never justified.* Contemporary global practice concerning human rights tends to converge around whether infringements of rights meet the legal test of proportionality. There is broad convergence in practice that they do in principle but can of course fail in points of detail.

The practical claims draw on the results from a comparative study of national legal responses to COVID-19 covering nearly 50 countries.[6] While a comprehensive survey and account will be reserved for other sources,[7] a selective survey of important jurisdictions will illustrate the points.

18.1 The Theory of Human Rights

When we consider the theory of human rights (sometimes called civil or constitutional rights), it is important to distinguish between non-paternalistic restrictions controlling disease transmission and paternalistic ones controlling infection of themselves. Paternalistic measures are those aimed at preventing one from harming oneself; non-paternalistic ones are those that are aimed at preventing one from harming others. In a pandemic, the distinction breaks down in practice—but we are here concerned with the theory. It breaks down in practice because in a viral context, mass infection can overwhelm public health services that are critical in delivering the intensive care that can, and did, prevent many of those who contracted the disease from dying from it. Yet for the sake of argument, I will separate paternalistic from non-paternalistic interventions.

Where mobility restrictions aim *at controlling transmission of disease to others*, there is no theory of liberty that would regard that as a violation of any right to liberty. We can put to the side consequentialist theories of rights (such as that of John Stuart Mill), which have no trouble accommodating public health restrictions. Instead, let us focus on deontological theories—those which recognize a conception of rights according to which are always absolute or can admit of being outweighed only in the most extreme circumstances.[8] In defending a conception of rights as trumps, Ronald Dworkin was careful to distinguish between abstract and concrete rights: "an abstract right is a general political aim the statement of which does not indicate how that general aim is to be weighed or compromised in particular circumstances against other political aims."[9] He continues to explain that "concrete rights are more precisely defined so as to express more definitely the weight they have against other political claims on particular occasions."[10] Adapting Dworkin's account to our context, we can say that an abstract right to liberty does not entail any concrete right to be free from mobility restrictions that protect the health of others.

Even libertarian theories of rights do not stop a state from restricting one person harming another. John Stuart Mill's harm principle is among the most libertarian versions of the liberty principle but nevertheless recognizes that harm to others is a valid reason for limiting liberty.[11] Transmission of a harmful disease constitutes harm to others. Therefore, if mobility restrictions are targeted reasonably and proportionately at curbing transmission, there is no violation of the right to liberty. Indeed, to the extent a state stands by and does nothing to protect someone from transmission, they are failing in a state's duty to protect the liberties of its citizens. In the liberal theories of the state ranging from John Locke,[12] to Immanuel Kant,[13] through Friedrich Hayek[14]—to take from among the most libertarian (or non-paternalistic) theories of state and liberty available—the function of the state is precisely *to protect spheres of individual liberty from both public and private interferences*.

As for paternalistic public health interventions, it should be noted that all the leading theories of autonomy and liberty in recent years recognize the role of hard paternalism in the area of seatbelts and helmet laws, mandatory pension saving, and some other areas.[15] Determining whether mobility restrictions motivated by paternalistic reasons would violate these conceptions of autonomy would require us to consider the matter policy by policy and theory by theory. For instance, a paternalistic mask mandate (should one exist) would probably be regarded as analogous to seatbelt laws, defended by nearly all the modern theories. A purely paternalistic compulsory vaccination mandate might or might not be a different story, depending on how plausible and developed a theory is for bodily autonomy in the vaccine context.[16] Time-bound stay-at-home orders are arguably liberty-promoting in the long run, even where paternalistic in the sense of blocking individuals from recklessly exposing themselves to quite harmful disease that carries much greater risk than does the seatbelt mandate. It's all a little complex.

Yet there is little reason to explore these complexities in depth here. This is because *in practice,* mobility restrictions are almost invariably framed in terms of protecting *others*, and because uncontrolled infection will, given the mortality levels typically present when mobility restrictions were enforced, unavoidably compromise public health services that are required to protect others. Put simply, then, the idea that one could claim immunity from mobility restrictions on anti-paternalistic grounds would probably be untenable in the COVID-19 context.

Such libertarian interpretations of liberty and human rights are anyway unduly narrow—quite out of line with the very widely ratified international human rights law framework. Public health interventions are positively required under international human rights law, especially article 11(2)(c) of the International Covenant on Economic, Social and Cultural Rights which identifies "the prevention, treatment and control of epidemic . . . diseases" as a "step" that "shall be taken" by States Parties to fulfil the right to health.[17] The rights to work and education, similarly recognized, would also call for positive state action to counter the epidemics and protect each of these social rights. Conventions on the rights of children, disabled persons, and on the elimination of discrimination against women and on the basis of race all create a dense network of obligations requiring robust state action to control epidemics or to pre-empt or mitigate their consequences for other rights.

The distinction between abstract and concrete rights was chosen to illustrate how a robustly deontological conception of rights-adjudication needs to address how general rights-claims are set off against competing rights and policy claims. It is, of course, only one helpful mode of conceiving of these relationships. The dominant language used by courts around the world—what one theorist simply refers to as the "global model"[18]—is to distinguish between public measures that *infringe* rights versus those that actually *violate* them. That distinction is crucial to correct the kind of public misunderstanding evidenced in the introduction to this essay. The framework used in public law systems around the world for determining whether policies *violate* constitutional or human rights is the test of proportionality. This distinction must be borne in mind because the idea that mobility restrictions violate rights, but justifiably, is a misguided understanding of the theory and practice of human rights. The violation of rights is never justified. The point is that mobility restrictions that are proportionate in the legal and moral sense will almost never violate rights.

18.2 The Legal Test(s) of Proportionality

Challenges by people aggrieved by mobility restrictions arose in dozens of countries. Most of them frame such restrictions as violations of some constitutional right to mobility, privacy, assembly, or religion. The first legal question is whether the restriction infringes a right. Arcane issues sometimes arise here. For example, it was relevant in German litigation whether the policy is a "deprivation of liberty" or merely an infringement of a right.[19] In Spain, an important constitutional case turned on whether the legal measures "restricted" or "suspended" rights.[20] In a 6:5 judgment with five dissenting opinions, the Constitutional Court found that the government had declared a "state of alarm" rather than "state of exception" or "state of siege" and that the only the latter two could be invoked to suspend rights. Yet in the vast majority of cases, courts will, and did, rightly find that mobility restrictions prima facie *infringe* rights, and the case will proceed to the proportionality or justification question to determine whether the right was actually violated. Such is the pattern in those examined next. This is true of many important public policies.

The legal test of proportionality is composed of four distinct questions, or branches. These are broadly similar in many jurisdictions, though emphasis can vary between them:[21]

1. Is the protection of public health a legitimate aim or compelling public purpose?
2. Are the means chosen rationally connected to that aim?
3. Are the means chosen necessary to protect that public interest?
4. Do the measures strike a "fair balance between the rights of the individual and the interests of the community?"[22]

There is also an overarching question that relates to each of these questions, namely:

> To what extent should judges show judicial restraint when evaluating (i) complex administrative schemes with many interconnecting variables (i.e. polycentric schemes); (ii) complex or conflicting social science evidence or (iii) acute problems whose appropriate resolution depends on quick reaction to evolving circumstances (i.e. flexibility)?

This last question, not any formal part of a legal proportionality test, concerns the institutional capacity of the judiciary for adjudicating complex policy questions. As such, it is related to the application of the precautionary principle in the face of epistemic uncertainty, and it arises in connection with the application of all four branches of the proportionality test by the judiciary.

18.3 Applying the Proportionality Test during the Pandemic

In the extensive *Oxford Compendium of National Legal responses to Covid-19*, country report authors were asked to report not only on mobility restrictions but also on important legal challenges thereto. Extremely few countries suspended or derogated from their bills of rights and virtually none derogated from any relevant international human rights conventions.[23] At the height of the pandemic, they reported very few successful direct legal challenges to particular mobility restrictions. Some hypothesize that as the pandemic progressed, and the challenges were ex post facto rather than to active measures, the courts would be more bold in hindsight. There is evidence of "a certain shift" in this direction, particularly in Israel.[24] Yet the overarching pattern was to find mobility restrictions in general lawful and proportionate—that is to say, not *violations* of rights. New statutes conferring powers to impose non-pharmaceutical interventions, or older ones used for that purpose, were invariably upheld.

I will briefly examine the different branches of the proportionality test, using representative examples from legal proceedings from jurisdictions whose public law courts remained open for business during the pandemic. The countries will naturally vary in their emphasis or perhaps intensity of judicial scrutiny of the measures when applying these legal categories. Yet the harmony is striking. For example, there are presently 46 States Parties to the European Convention on Human Rights who tend to apply the proportionality standard domestically in a quite similar manner, one that aligns with the approach of the European Court of Human Rights.

The first issue (legitimate aim) is fairly straightforward. The European Convention on Human Rights recognizes a series of grounds on which several of the rights can be limited, and "the protection of health or morals" is among them in each case.[25] In Germany, the protection of public health is an established category of "legitimate aim" that has been applied in COVID-19 litigation.[26] Legitimate aim was also recognized prominently in Canadian jurisprudence in older tobacco advertising litigation[27] and was well established for over 100 years in American constitutional law.[28] The legitimacy of the protection of public health (or the health of others) was applied in all major COVID-19 constitutional cases reviewed in a study for Lex-Atlas: COVID-19.[29]

The second issue (rational connection) requires that the means are "suitable"[30] to achieve the legitimate aim. It will require that there is some evidence base for the mobility restrictions. In the COVID-19 context, this burden is relatively easily discharged, as public health advice from epidemiologists tended to play a leading role nearly everywhere.[31] Of course, there were occasions where public health advice was not followed. This was more likely to occur, however, where lockdown scepticism (either about the efficacy of the lockdown measures or the consequences of widespread infection) prevailed among political leadership—for example, in Brazil and the United States.[32] In some countries, of course, the pandemic was used as a pretext to restrict liberties. For example, in Russia, lockdown laws were enforced against political protests but not against pro-government rallies of much greater size.[33] In Israel, the High Court of Justice struck down a law that prohibited attending demonstrations more than 1 kilometre from the protester's home, also limiting such demonstrations to 20 people.[34] The distance restriction was found to violate the rational connection standard in a situation where the law seemed designed to restrict ongoing protests taking place in front of the Prime Minister's house. This kind of pandemic opportunism was a phenomenon in some countries but an episodic, rather than chronic, issue in liberal democracies.

An interesting issue relevant to the test of rational connection is the strictness of the legal requirement for evidence. Its intensity of will likely vary with the urgency of the situation and the extent of possible risk (i.e., whether "precaution" is advised). This is held by the German Federal Constitutional Court:

> Where scientific knowledge is tentative and the legislator's possibilities to draw sufficiently reliable conclusions are therefore limited, it is enough for the legislator to proceed on the basis of a context-appropriate and tenable assessment of the available information and evidence.[35]

That conclusion applies with equal force to public health regulation-making. Policymakers have to act on the best available evidence and not wait until it is too late to contain the threat. This is noted in the UK *Dolan* case in the Court of Appeal:

> We bear in mind that the Secretary of State had access to expert advice which was particularly important in the context of a new virus *and where scientific knowledge was inevitably developing at a fast pace*. The fact that others may disagree with some of those expert views is neither here nor there. The Government was entitled to proceed on the basis of the advice which it was receiving and balance the public health advice with other matters.[36]

In brief, these courts found, rightly, that the requirement of rational connection does not necessarily mean that the government cannot act where the evidence base is developing rapidly and the consequences of inaction are severe.

The third legal question (necessity) relates to whether there is another, less rights-restricting alternative available that can achieve the same aim. In an early contribution on the question of COVID-19, Gostin, Hodge, and Wiley wrote that the "extensive use of federal quarantine powers has no modern precedent," that "coercive measures should be proportionate to the threat faced," and that "there should be no less restrictive alternatives to accomplish public health objectives."[37] This advice is solid so far as it goes, but in application, there were relatively few cases where a policy was challenged successfully on account of the Court thought another policy was less rights-restricting and, therefore, better. Of course, there were some such cases (which I itemize in the conclusion further later), but they did tend to turn on very specific facts, as one would expect under this branch of the proportionality test. There is a risk that broad polices, admitting of no exceptions, could be attacked. This view is underscored by the extent to which the relevant jurisprudence underscored the exceptions that were carved out from the general restriction. For instance, the European Court of Human Rights refers sometimes disparagingly to "blanket policies" that do not admit for exceptions.[38] In other court cases, judges have sometimes taken pains to show that the legislative scheme being challenged provides for exceptions to its blanket rules.[39] And in fact, some of the few cases where governments have lost in public law challenges have tended to succeed on these kinds of narrow grounds. For example, in a complex judgment in New Zealand, a High Court judge held that a booking system for allocating quarantine vouchers/places to returning residents and citizens violated their protected right to enter New Zealand.[40] The booking method was randomized, based on a lottery principle. The judge found this to be more restrictive than a method which took account either of the basis of waiting period or emergency need. Commentators pointed out that the government had, in fact, run an extensive process for vetting six other methods and that the judge had no evidence for finding that the alternative policies she mentioned were feasible.[41] At any rate, the relief was declaratory only, limited to a quite brief period in which the booking system was active, and it concerned a policy that had already been wound up. The *Grounded Kiwis* case was a highly fact-specific decision of limited general appeal.

The fourth branch of the test (fair balance) concerns whether the mobility restrictions strike a fair balance between the rights of the individual and the interests of the community. This part of the test has not to my knowledge, based on reviewing national legal responses as editor of the *Oxford Compendium*, arisen as a particularly significant issue in comparative case law yet.[42] The answer will be juridically straightforward when the impact on public health of unconstrained transmission can be potentially catastrophic, the scenario in contemplation for much of the high-mortality and extremely contagious COVID-19 pandemic. A knottier legal question arises, however, when both transmission and mortality tail off but do not disappear—i.e., that governments do not lift public health restrictions when the evidence no longer supports them as justified and proportionate. This scenario presented in Europe with the onset of the Omicron variant in December 2021. For example, Austria had laid draft laws for a general vaccination mandate in December 2021. However, as the extremely transmissible but comparatively benign Omicron variant took hold in January 2022, Austrian ministers observed that "[w]e see no need to actually implement this compulsory vaccination due to the variant that we are predominantly experiencing here."[43] This was a political decision, but there inevitably would have been legal challenges. It can be compared with the situation in Germany, where the government pressed on with its vaccine mandate for healthcare workers. Here, the Federal Constitutional Court rejected a constitutional complaint arguing that the Omicron variant had changed the equation:

> The legislator was not constitutionally required, in the context of its suitability prognosis, to refrain from enacting [the mandate] because of factual uncertainties regarding the effectiveness of vaccines against the Omicron variant, which was still novel at the start of December 2021. The legislator

> was entitled to take into consideration that the Delta variant continued to be the dominant variant at the time, accounting for more than 99% of new cases, while very few persons had yet been infected with the Omicron variant. It was therefore at least tenable for the legislator to assume that the Delta variant would continue to dominate pandemic activity, at least for a certain period of time.[44]

The Court was right to find as it did. A different approach would have invited litigants to submit complaints to Germany's Federal and *Länder* (state-level) constitutional courts asking them to micromanage, on the same legal theory, a task fit for public health experts and civil service–supported government acting on that advice. That task is namely to choose the right cocktail of mobility restrictions and vaccination policies to establish a projected level of risk mitigation—which is itself determined by speculating on what level of mortality and disease is tolerable, having regard to the capacity of the health system to bear it, extensive limits on personal freedom, and the cost of economic restrictions on trading.[45] Public law judges are well out of their epistemic comfort zone at multiple points of this equation, let alone in deciding on how they should all fit together. Serious judges recognize that instantaneously. It needs to be borne further in mind that democratically responsive political systems are already under severe political and economic pressure to avoid imposing costly restrictions for any longer than absolutely necessary.[46] None of this, it can be added, denies that there are many other more focused legal and human rights issues arising which are eminently suitable for adjudication. Nor does it deny that in theory there will be a point at which the mortality or welfare impact of uncontrolled transmission does tail off to the point that highly restrictive measures impose costs that exceed their benefits in a way that does not strike a fair balance. The point worthy of emphasis here is that it would only be for judges to make such a finding, unless in narrow circumstances, either in cases where it is so obvious that it is hard to see a democratically responsible government maintaining the highly unpopular and economically restrictive restrictions in the first place.

18.4 Judicial Restraint

I have drawn attention to some cases in which mobility restrictions were upheld and some others, exceptional as they were, in which they were found unlawful. What is clear and consistent throughout the jurisprudence has been a recognition of the necessity of judicial restraint in situations where judges are asked to second-guess rapidly evolving and scientifically complex assessments.

A few judgments of the German Federal Constitutional Court were quoted earlier. Across the first year of the pandemic, of the thousands of public law cases taken in Germany's administrative and constitutional courts, the vast majority of challenges were unsuccessful.[47] It bears recognizing that this is widely regarded as one of the most active judiciaries in the world. In Canada, clerics and activists challenged a provincial mass gathering order as an infringement of the section 2 freedom of assembly under the *Canadian Charter*. In a judgment of the British Columbia Supreme Court, the judge found that the transmission risk assessment had been reasonable and that the context warranted deference:

> [The] decision was made in the face of significant uncertainty and required highly specialized medical and scientific expertise. The respondents submit, and I agree, that this is the type of situation that calls for a considerable level of deference in applying the *Doré* test.[48]

The approach taken in *Beaudoin* largely chimes with the UK's *Dolan* case, a general challenge to the "lockdown" suite of mobility restrictions that included a stay-at-home order and school and shop closures. The Court of Appeal found that "[i]n this context . . . we consider that a wide margin of judgment must be afforded to the Government and to Parliament . . . on the well-established grounds of both democratic accountability and institutional competence."[49] The appeal to the Supreme Court was refused by the latter for having no reasonable prospect of success.[50] Similarly, in the *Vavricka v Czech Republic* case, the Grand Chamber of the European Court of Human Rights held that a mandatory requirement for the routine (non–COVID-19) vaccination of children did not violate the article 8 freedom of physical integrity. In the course of a lengthy judgment, the Court recalled that "[t]he Court has held that matters of healthcare policy are in principle within the margin of appreciation of the domestic authorities, who are best placed to assess priorities, use of resources and social needs."[51]

In the Netherlands, the District Court in the Hague rejected a challenge from the *Viruswaarheid* (Virus Truth) anti-Covid restriction campaign group that would have required the state to repeal all public health measures. The Court found that the measures are subject to the state's large degree of discretion where competing interests are balanced, a constant evaluation amidst shifting needs, and therefore, proportionate.[52]

In a study of COVID-19 case law before the European Court of Human Rights, the writers found only one case, which concerned restriction of political protest (which is definitely a grey area), where a challenge to a restrictive public health measure was upheld (and which is under appeal as this chapter goes to press).[53]

While the success rate of litigation was more variable in the United States, a review by Lindsey Wiley of the early period of the pandemic in the United States (up to October 2021) found that though hundreds of lawsuits against public health measures were filed, very few were successful.[54] She concluded that most "[US] courts rejected challenges to stay-at-home orders on the grounds that they infringed on personal liberty."[55] Most judges relied on the leading authority of *Jacobson v Massachussets* (1905),[56] in which the US Supreme Court upheld a statute that conferred power on local health boards to make smallpox vaccination compulsory if it was considered necessary for protecting public health. The Court held the regulations should be set aside only if they were a "plain, palpable violation" of fundamental rights. In the COVID-19 context, the narrow *Jacobson* standard was applied consistently by lower courts refusing constitutional challenges.[57] On religious freedom, the response of US state and federal courts was more divided. *Jacobson* was doubted in a Supreme Court case which struck down restrictions applying to religious gathering,[58] though a subsequent challenge to a measure for failing to provide a religious exemption from an occupational vaccine mandate was rejected and the mandate upheld by the US Supreme Court.[59] Yet there were a wave of successful challenges in state and federal courts on limits on places of worship.[60] State courts were also more divided on the constitutionality of internal travel restrictions and other limits on gatherings, though challenges to face covering mandates were "uniformly rejected by the courts"; however, school closures were not broadly challenged.[61] It is possible that US courts were more likely to uphold challenges because the system does not officially recognize the doctrine of proportionality, despite some judicial encouragement towards that end.[62] The point is ultimately speculative, however, as balancing has long been a feature of US public law.[63] So on the whole, although the US courts were significantly more open to legal challenges to mobility restrictions by comparison with all other states surveyed on this question in the *Oxford Compendium*, the tendency towards challenges being rejected is still more discernible than any appetite for judicial activism.

Some commentators take this general comparative posture of judicial non-interference to be an abdication of the judicial role. It was a posture which US Supreme Court Justice Gorsuch derided in his dissenting judgment in the *Does v Mills* case, claiming it was judges deciding to "shelter in place when the Constitution is under attack."[64] The view, which evokes imagery of cowardice, is both misguided and hubristic. It is so first because that type of view often offers no theory of why courts should have interfered more often and especially why widely accepted institutional competence grounds for judicial restraint suddenly evaporate when the measures constrain (e.g.) religious belief. Indeed, a developed theory of judicial restraint is required as a concomitant to the appropriately robust protection of social and other human rights in matters concerning complex social policy. For my part, and as an advocate of judicially enforced constitutional social rights who took pains to set out a theory of judicial restraint, it appears to me that the judges are broadly doing exactly what I argued they should do in 2012.[65] I argued there that considerations of democratic accountability, expertise, polycentricity/complexity, and flexibility *could* rightly justify judicial restraint. And in this pandemic, we see democratically adopted public health measures mostly challenged by non-marginalized groups, challenges to government judgments based on collective professional scientific expertise, public health measures that are nested within suites of interlocking restrictive measures and social policy benefits, and challenges brought in a context in which administration necessarily needs to experiment and adapt rapidly.

18.5 Conclusion

It is important to be clear about what I am not arguing in this short contribution: neither (a) that there were no notable cases where public health measures were found disproportionate nor (b) that law courts should not stand prepared to consider closely the proportionality of public health measures. On the first point, there are many instances of successful constitutional challenges. In addition to the US, Spanish, and New Zealand cases mentioned earlier, there are others and which may be of more merit. One area in which courts can and have played a more assertive role is in relation to political protest. In Germany, for instance, this was among the rare areas in which the courts consistently questioned and qualified, right from the beginning of the pandemic, the unrestricted power to maintain a general total ban on political protest.[66] This is consistent with similar case law in Israel, the United States, the European Court of Human Rights,[67] and the de facto tolerance of protest in many countries.

There were also challenges to entry and exit requirements. In a matter before the Israeli Supreme Court, a challenge to a measure which imposed limits on entry and exit of citizens into and from Israel was upheld, and the regulations were held to be unconstitutional violations of the basic law.[68] The Court found that the policy aims could be achieved in a less invasive manner, were of dubious effectiveness, and that they impacted the right to vote in impending Knesset elections. On the other hand, though the challenge was successful, the regulations expired three days after judgment, and there was no process for renewing them, so the matter was close to moot. The Administrative Court of Appeals in Lüneburg, Germany, issued a preliminary injunction against a prohibition of sport in outside sports facilities for people who had not been vaccinated.[69] The Court found that the measure was not proportionate because it failed to differentiate between different types of sport (and the degree of risk of transmission they posed), and it also did not ban sports outside of these facilities for non-vaccinated people. Often, the facts and holdings are complex and peculiar. In Spain, for example, the Constitutional Court found that a raft of health limitations in Royal Decree 926/2020 were compatible with human rights. But it also found that the extension of a state of emergency for six months was too long and unjustified and further that the conferral of powers on the autonomous communities (regional governments) in Spain, without restrictive criteria set out by the national government for the exercise of those powers, were unconstitutional.[70] The merits of both arguments depend on the particularities of the Spanish constitutional order.

Beyond these, there are of course dozens of successful public law claims and often rightly so because patently bad policymaking is a sad feature of administrative life even outside of emergencies. But that fact should not be converted into the mistaken view that most measures are of dubious legal authority or are inconsistent with rights. The basic point here is that well-designed public health measures including stay-at-home orders are not presumptively incompatible with basic human rights. A general understanding of the proportionality test and the role for a theory of judicial restraint is a crucial aspect of any proper approach to human rights law.

Notes

1 The author thanks Rebecca Freund and Justin Cai for very helpful research assistance. Cambridge Law Faculty, "Lord Sumption—Cambridge Freshfields Lecture: Government by Decree—Covid-19 and the Constitution" (27 October 2020), online (video): *YouTube*. www.youtube.com/watch?v=amDv2gk8aa0.

2 "Coronavirus: Armed Protesters Enter Michigan Statehouse" (1 May 2020), online: *BBC News*. www.bbc.co.uk/news/world-us-canada-52496514.

3 Adam Wagner, *Emergency State: Constitutional Catastrophe in a Time of Pandemic* (Penguin, 2022); Tom Hickman, "The Use and Misuse of Guidance during the UK's Coronavirus Lockdown" (2020), online: https://papers.ssrn.com/sol3/papers.cfm?abstract_id=3686857.

4 Simon Halliday et al, "Law, Lockdown and Liberty: Rights Consciousness in an Age of Proportionality" (forthcoming) *The Oxford Journal of Legal Studies*.

5 Jeff King, "The Future of Social Rights: Social Rights as Capstone" in *The Future of Social Rights,* edited by Katharine Young (Cambridge University Press, 2019) at 308–315.

6 Jeff King et al, eds, *The Oxford Compendium of National Legal Responses to Covid-19* (Oxford University Press, 2021, with updates); "Lex-Atlas: Covid-19: A Comparative Study of National Legal Responses to COVID-19" (2022), online: *Lex-Atlas*. https://oxcon.ouplaw.com/home/OCC19/.

7 See Jeff King & Octavio Ferraz, eds, *Comparing Covid Laws: A Critical Global Survey* (Oxford University Press, forthcoming).

8 Ronald Dworkin, *Taking Rights Seriously* (Harvard University Press, 1978).

9 *Ibid* at 119.

10 *Ibid.*

11 John Stuart Mill, *On Liberty*, 4th ed (Longman, Roberts & Green, 1869) at chapter 1.

12 John Locke, *Second Treatise of Government* (Hackett Publishing, 1988), at §137: "absolute arbitrary power, or governing without *settled standing laws*, can neither of them consist with the ends of society and government, which men would not quit the freedom of the state of nature for, and tie themselves up under, were it not to preserve their lives, liberties and fortunes by *stated rules* of right and property to secure their peace and quiet."

13 Immanuel Kant, "The Doctrine of Right," within *The Metaphysics of Morals*, in The Cambridge Edition of the Works of Immanuel Kant: Practical Philosophy (Cambridge University Press, 1996 [1797]). See further: Arthur Ripstein, Force and Freedom: Kant's Legal and Political Philosophy (Harvard University Press, 2009).
14 Friedrich A. Hayek, *The Constitution of Liberty* (Routledge, 1960) at Chapter 13.
15 See the discussion of the views of Gerald Dworkin, Joseph Raz, Ronald Dworkin, and John Rawls in Christopher McCrudden & Jeff King, "The Dark Side of Nudging: The Ethics, Political Economy, and Law of Libertarian Paternalism" in *Choice Architecture in Democracies, Exploring the Legitimacy of Nudging*, edited by Alexandra Kemmerer et al (Hart and Nomos, 2015) at 96–99.
16 See Jeff King, Octavio Ferraz & A. Jones, "Mandatory COVID-19 Vaccination and Human Rights" (2022) 399:10321 *Lancet* 220.
17 In the COVID-19 context, in addition to King, Ferraz & Jones, *ibid*, see also the decision of the European Court of Human Rights in *Le Maillouz v France* (Application No 18108/20) (3 December 2020): "La Cour rappelle que si le droit à la santé ne fait pas partie en tant que tel des droits garantis par la Convention, *les États ont l'obligation positive de prendre les mesures nécessaires à la protection de la vie des personnes relevant de leur juridiction et de protéger leur intégrité physique, y compris dans le domaine de la santé publique* (Lopes de Sousa Fernandes c. Portugal [GC], no 56080/13, § 165, 19 décembre 2017, Vasileva c. Bulgarie, no 23796/10, §§ 63–69, 17 mars 2016)" (emphasis added). The claim was rejected on admissibility grounds.
18 Kai Möller, *The Global Model of Constitutional Rights* (Oxford University Press, 2015).
19 BVerfG, Order of the First Senate of 19 November 2021–1 BvR 781/21 (5 October 2022), para 250.
20 Sección del Tribunal Constitucional, Judgment 148/2021 (2021). For a full analysis, see Dolores Utrilla, Manuel Antonio García-Muñoz & Teresa Pareja Sánchez, "Spain: Legal Response to Covid-19" in King et al, *supra* note 6 (forthcoming update), Part IV.A.1.
21 Möller, *supra* note 18.
22 Legal systems vary as to how much emphasis is put on this final category. It is marginal in Canadian jurisprudence and crucial in Germany: see Dieter Grimm, "Proportionality in Canadian and German Constitutional Jurisprudence" (2007) 57 UTLJ 383. And differently from both, the standard applied by the European Court of Human Rights allows a community interest to prevail over the right at this stage even if it is proportionate in all other respects.
23 Questions on these two topics are found in Part II.A of the Oxford Compendium's Author Guidance Code, and reports each contain the answers in Part II.A. See "Author Guidance Code" (online): *Oxford Constitutional Law*. https://oxcon.ouplaw.com/page/925.
24 Einat Albin et al, "Israel: Legal Response to Covid-19", in King et al, *supra* note 6, para 53.
25 "Convention for the Protection of Human Rights and Fundamental Freedoms." Council of Europe Treaty Series 005, Council of Europe, 1950, arts. 8(2), 9(2), 10(2), 11(2).
26 BVerfG, *supra* note 19, para 188.
27 *RJR-MacDonald Inc v Canada (AG)*, [1995] 3 SCR 199. RJR sought a declaration that the *Tobacco Products Control Act* of 1988 was invalid, as it entailed an unjustified infringement on the freedom of expression guaranteed by the *Canadian Charter of Rights and Freedoms*.
28 *Jacobson v Massachusetts* 197 US 11 (1905); *Zucht v King*, 260 US 174, 176–77 (1922). *Jacobson* revolved around a 14th Amendment challenge on the constitutionality of Massachusetts' smallpox vaccine mandate and is the authority for

the proposition that State legislatures have police powers to restrict constitutional rights for public health reasons—provided it is not excessive, arbitrary, or unreasonable.

29 Lex-Atlas, *supra* note 6.
30 The terminology used for this criterion in German constitutional law, EU law, and by the ECtHR.
31 See King et al, *supra* note 6. Every country report addresses the role of scientific advice in Part III.E.
32 See Lindsay F. Wiley, Ruqaiijah Yearby & Andrew Hammond, "United States: Legal Response to Covid-19", in King et al, *supra* note 6, Part III.E.
33 Tatiana Khramova, "Russia: Legal Response to Covid-19", in King et al, *supra* note 6, Parts VI.A, IV.A.3
34 *National Responsibility—Israel My Home Ltd. (PBC) v Government of Israel* [2020] 5469/20 HCJ; Albin et al, *supra* note 24, Part II.A & B, Part IV.A.3.
35 BVerfG, *supra* note 19, para 171.
36 *Dolan v Health Secretary* [2020] EWCA Civ 1605, at 97 (emphasis added) [*Dolan*]. Leave to appeal was refused by the Supreme Court for having no reasonable prospect of success.
37 Lawrence O. Gostin, James G. Hodge Jr. & Lindsay F. Wiley, "Presidential Powers and Response to COVID-19" (2020) 323:16 *Journal of the American Medical Association* 1547 at 1547.
38 Peter Cumper & Tom Lewis, "Blanket Bans, Subsidiarity, and the Procedural Turn of the European Court of Human Rights" (2019) 68 *Intl & Comp L Quarterly* 611.
39 *Dolan*, *supra* note 36, para 93 (lockdown exceptions): "[t]he obligation to stay at home in the original version of regulation 6(1) was subject to numerous, express exceptions, which were non-exhaustive, and the overriding exception of having a reasonable excuse." See also BVerfG, Order of the First Senate of 27 April 2022–1 BvR 2649/21 (mandatory vaccination, health exemptions) ["BVerfG 2"].
40 *Grounded Kiwis Group Inc v Minister of Health*, [2022] NZHC 832; *Grounded Kiwis Group Inc v Minister of Health (No 2)*, [2022] NZHC 1407.
41 Dean R. Knight & Jane C. Norton, "New Zealand's Pandemic Border Fortress: The Community's Health and Wellbeing Versus Citizens' Right To Return" (2022) 33 *Public Law Review*186.
42 It was, however, analysed in detail in BVerfG, *supra* note 19, paras 215–236. See also the English Court of Appeal in *Dolan*, *supra* note 36, paras 215–236 (restrictions on gatherings) and 289–303 (curfew).
43 "Austria Suspends Mandatory Covid Vaccination Law" (9 March 2022), online: *The Guardian*. www.theguardian.com/world/2022/mar/09/austria-suspends-mandatory-covid-vaccination-law.
44 BVerfG 2, *supra* note 39, para 174.
45 The question of whether efficiency gains are relevant to adjudication on rights is complex and frequently ignored by constitutional courts—though none would dare hold it an irrelevant and unlawful consideration. The legal complexities of recognizing it are explored in J. L. Mashaw, "The Management Side of Due Process" (1974) 59 *The Cornell Law Review* 772.
46 Were mobility restrictions not generally applicable—i.e., targeted at particular communities or were highly localised—this consideration would be diminished.
47 See generally Anna-Bettina Kaiser & R. Hensel, "Federal Republic of Germany: Legal Response to Covid-19", in King et al, *supra* note 6.
48 *Beaudoin v BC*, 2021 BCSC 512, para 244.
49 *Dolan*, *supra* note 36.
50 "Permission to Appeal Results: December 2020" (2020), online (pdf): *UK Supreme Court*. www.supremecourt.uk/docs/permission-to-appeal-2020-12.pdf.

51 *Vavřička and Others v. the Czech Republic* [2021] ECtHR no. 47621/13, para 274. See also *ibid*, para 273.
52 District Court The Hague, ECLI:NL:RBDHA:2020:6856 (24 July 2020). Subsequent challenges by the same organization alleging an absence of appropriate legal basis for the nationwide evening curfew imposed between 23 January to 28 April 2021 succeeded in the same court at first instance (ECLI:NL:RBDHA:2021:1100 [16 February 2021]) but was then overturned by the Court of Appeal in the Hague (ECLI:NL:GHDHA:2021:252 [26 February 2021]).
53 Lewis Graham, "Challenging State Responses to the Covid-19 Pandemic before the ECtHR" (18 October 2022), online: *Strasbourg Observers Blog*. https://strasbourgobservers.com/2022/10/18/challenging-state-responses-to-the-covid-19-pandemic-before-the-ecthr/.
54 See Wiley, Yearby & Hammond, *supra* note 32, Part IV.A.1.
55 *Ibid*, para 81.
56 Jacobson, *supra* note 28.
57 See Wiley, Yearby & Hammond, *supra* note 32, paras 12–13 and 80–81.
58 *Roman Catholic Diocese of Brooklyn v Cuomo*, 141 S.Ct. 63 (2020) [*Diocese of Brooklyn*].
59 *Does v Mills* 595 US (2021). The case was decided on narrow grounds, however, due to it coming on an emergency application.
60 See Wiley, Yearby & Hammond, *supra* note 32, Part IV.A.2–4.
61 *Ibid*, para 115.
62 Stephen Breyer, *Making Our Democracy Work: A Judge's View* (Vintage Books, 2010). For a scholarly—if, in my view, overcooked—statement that proportionality is a hugely significant difference, see Jamal Greene, *How Rights Went Wrong* (Harcourt, 2021) xxii-xxiii, referring to the "widespread refusal of many US judges and lawyers to accept proportionality."
63 T. Alexander Aleinikoff, "Constitutional Law in the Age of Balancing" (1987) 96 Yale L J 943. See also Steven Gardbaum, "The Myth and Reality of American Constitutional Exceptionalism" (2008) 107 *The Michigan Law Review* 391, especially 416ff.
64 *Diocese of Brooklyn*, *supra* note 58.
65 Jeff King, *Judging Social Rights* (Cambridge University Press, 2012); see also Jeff A. King, "Institutional Approaches to Judicial Restraint" (2008) 28 *The Oxford Journal of Legal Studies* 409.
66 Kaiser & Hensel, *supra* note 47, para 72. See, e.g., Federal Constitutional Court, Order of the First Chamber of the First Senate of 17 April 2020–1 BvQ 37/20.
67 See cases and discussion, *supra* notes 34, 53 and accompanying text. See also Wiley, Yearby & Hammond, *supra* note 32, paras 88–95 (Part IV.A.3) (indicating at least one successful claim arguing an unlawful restraint on freedom of assembly but also that legal exemptions were frequently made for political protest).
68 *Shemesh v The Prime Minister* [2021] 1107/21 HCJ.
69 Judgment No. 14 121/22 (Administrative Court of Appeals of Lüneburg, Germany) 25 January 2022.
70 Judgment 60/2022 (Supreme Court of Spain—Administrative) 25 January 2022.

PART VII

Vaccine Passports

Privacy Claims and Technology Fixes and Failures

19

PANDEMIC-FIGHTING TECHNOLOGIES? LESSONS FROM COVID-19 FOR THE PANDEMICS OF THE FUTURE

Vivek Krishnamurthy and Myka Kollmann

19.1 Introduction

COVID-19 is the first pandemic disease of the digital age, but it is unlikely to be the last—given the distressing regularity with which pandemic diseases have struck humanity since the dawn of the agricultural revolution.[1] Correspondingly, COVID-19 is likely to be the first of many pandemic diseases where digital technologies that are in wide use—such as cellphones and QR codes—will be leveraged for public health purposes.

Much has been written about the legal and ethical considerations surrounding the use of such technologies in the fight against COVID-19.[2] All of this work takes place against the backdrop of one particular (albeit rapidly evolving) disease, but the purpose of this paper is to begin a conversation on how we should assess the repurposing of technologies in widespread use to combat the pandemic diseases of the future. Specifically, we suggest that in conducting such evaluations, policymakers should consider three characteristics of the infectious disease they are attempting to combat with a technological intervention. These are (1) the severity of the illness the disease causes; (2) its level of infectiousness; and (3) its mode of transmission, which bears on the social stigma associated with contracting the disease.

The first part of this paper will provide a brief overview of technologies used to combat COVID-19, and of the broader technological context in which COVID-19 arose, while the second will consider how disease characteristics should be considered in evaluating the appropriateness of enlisting a particular technology in the fight against it.

DOI: 10.4324/9781003394006-26

19.2 Combatting COVID-19 with Digital Technology

Two main digital technologies have been used to combat the spread of COVID-19, namely, (1) digital contact tracing and (2) digital vaccine passports. Contact tracing and proof of vaccination requirements are well-established strategies for combatting infectious diseases, but their effectiveness was increased considerably at the height of the COVID-19 pandemic by leveraging existing technologies that were in widespread use to digitize and automate both—at least to some extent. Each of these digital interventions had two main variants during the COVID-19 pandemic, and as the discussion later will show, each had very different impacts on privacy and a range of other human rights.

19.2.1 Digital Contact Tracing

Contact tracing is the "process of identifying, assessing, and managing people who have been exposed to someone who has been infected" with a contagious disease to prevent them from spreading it further.[3] The World Health Organization has described contact tracing and the quarantining of contacts as "essential public health tools for controlling" the spread of COVID-19.[4]

Since its development in the early 20th century,[5] contact tracing has involved interviewing individuals infected with a disease and asking them to recall the people they have seen and the places they have been so that their contacts can be asked to take appropriate preventative actions. Contact tracing has been used successfully to fight outbreaks of diseases ranging from syphilis to measles to Ebola.[6] Since COVID-19 is spread by aerosols, technologists have been able to repurpose two features of smartphones to create two different digital contact tracing systems that are effective in dealing with this means of transmission.

19.2.1.1 Cellular Location-Based Contact Tracing

The first approach leverages a property of cellphone networks that requires their operators to know the location of their customers to provide seamless service as they talk, text, and surf the web while on the go. Cellphone network operators collect and store such cell site location information (CSLI) for various purposes, ranging from billing (i.e., to assess roaming charges) to compliance with government data retention mandates.[7]

Early in the pandemic, several governments—notably those of South Korea[8] and Israel[9]—used the CSLI records of patients infected with COVID-19 to alert others who may have been in close contact with them to isolate and/or test themselves. South Korea, for example, asked its cellphone network operators to send automated text messages to individuals whose phones had been near someone known to have COVID-19 to ask those individuals to isolate themselves.[10]

This method of digital contact tracing has the benefit of being quick and easy to deploy, as it merely requires the authorities to examine the CLSI of known COVID-19 carriers to notify those who have been close to them to take appropriate precautionary measures. The problem, however, is that this method carries significant privacy risks to all concerned, as CLSI is extraordinarily sensitive data that paints an intimate portrait of a person's life through the lens of their movements.[11] This, in turn, raises serious questions about whether the public health benefits of this technological approach to contact tracing are justified in view of the privacy risks it poses.[12]

19.2.1.2 Bluetooth Contact Tracing

The other main approach to digital contact tracing during the COVID-19 pandemic leverages Bluetooth wireless technology, which allows electronic devices such as laptops, keyboards, headphones, mobile phones, and a variety of "smart" devices to communicate with each other. When a device's Bluetooth radio is switched on, the device scans the environment for other devices with which it has previously been "paired," as well as other devices that are in range and offer pairing possibilities.[13]

A Bluetooth signal's strength can be used to determine how close two devices are to each other.[14] This property can be used to develop contact tracing applications to combat a respiratory disease, as physical proximity is a reasonable (albeit imperfect) proxy for sharing the same air.

Developers at Apple and Google did just that in building an ingenious, privacy-protective contact tracing system based on Bluetooth.[15] The Apple-Google system, which underpinned numerous governmental contact tracing apps, including Canada's COVID-19 Alert, begins with each enrolled device generating a new random digital token every 15 minutes.[16] When two smartphones with the contact tracing app installed come into Bluetooth signal range of each other, they exchange these tokens. Should an individual later test positive for COVID-19, they are asked to upload all of their tokens from the period they were infectious to a central server. The software on the other user's phone checks the tokens they have exchanged against the list of tokens associated with known COVID cases that are stored on the central server. In the event of a match, the app notifies the user of a potential COVID-19 exposure.[17]

This approach to digital contact tracing has been widely credited as being highly privacy protective, as it does not require the use of any location data and incorporates strong protections against individuals being reidentified based on the exchange of the randomly generated tokens.[18] That said, there is a great deal of debate about the effectiveness of both CSLI- and Bluetooth-based digital contact tracing technologies.[19] What is most interesting for the purposes of this paper, however, is how two features (CSLI and Bluetooth) of an underlying technology in widespread use (smartphones) were leveraged in record time to develop two different contact tracing systems, each of which had significantly different impacts on privacy and other human rights as well.

19.2.2 Digital Health Certificates

Proof of health status requirements have long existed in a variety of contexts, from education[20] to travel[21] to migration,[22] but the leveraging of smartphone capabilities allowed proof of health status requirements to be deployed much more widely in the fight against COVID-19 in comparison to any previous infectious disease outbreak. As with digital contact tracing, two very different kinds of digital health certificates developed during the COVID-19 pandemic, each of which has very different impacts on the right to privacy.

All digital health certificates—from China's Health Code system to Canada's digital vaccine certificates—store certain health information about an individual in a centralized database. The Chinese system stores an individual's vaccination status and recent COVID-19 test status and links them with a great deal of other data, including national ID card information and facial recognition information.[23] By contrast, the Canadian system of vaccine certificates requires provincial health ministries to record an individual's name, date of birth, health card number, and information about the date and type of vaccines they have received. Each government, in turn, issues its citizens a digital health certificate in the form of a QR code that encodes certain information about the individual. In the Chinese system, the QR code identifies an individual as having a green, yellow, or red health status, while QR codes issued by most Canadian jurisdictions encode the bearer's name, their date of birth, and details regarding the type and date of the vaccinations the bearer received.[24]

Beyond what information is encoded into the digital health certificates, the most salient difference involves how the certificates are verified and authenticated. When a Chinese Health Code is scanned, a central database is queried and a record is created therein that the individual to whom the code belongs attempted to gain entry to a given establishment at a particular date and time.[25] By contrast, the verification applications built by several Canadian provinces for their digital vaccine certificate systems do not record, store, or share any data about the bearer or the time, date, and place where they presented their vaccine certificates.[26] Rather, the verification applications are decentralized by design, and they use complex cryptographic techniques to extract the bearer's name from the QR code and assess whether the certificate is genuine.[27]

Correspondingly, the privacy implications associated with a vaccine certificate system like Canada's are an order of magnitude less severe than under a system such as China's, where the verification system creates a detailed record of a person's movements through society. This is true even leaving aside the vast differences in the level of respect for human rights and the quality of rule of law that prevails in both countries.

19.3 Interactions between Public Health Technologies and Disease Characteristics

What can we glean from our experience with leveraging existing technologies to combat COVID-19 that helps us assess the privacy implications of doing something similar to fight the pandemic diseases of the future? Everything that has been written about the privacy and human rights impacts of digital contact tracing and digital health certificates in the context of the COVID-19 pandemic takes this awful disease, and its various characteristics, as a constant. If, however, we treat COVID-19 as a variable that can be replaced with other diseases that possess other characteristics, we can develop a more generalizable framework for evaluating whether a particular technology constitutes a proportionate response to a given disease.

There are three disease characteristics that are salient to such an analysis: (1) the severity of the illness it causes; (2) its level of infectiousness; and (3) its mode of transmission, which bears on the social stigma associated with contracting the disease. Let us consider these characteristics of COVID-19 in turn, before considering how the characteristics of other diseases might bear on the use of particular technologies to fight them.

19.3.1 Severity of Illness

First, we must consider the severity of the disease we are combatting through technological means. COVID-19 may share symptoms in common with other respiratory illnesses, but it has been described as being a "serious vascular disease with primary symptoms of a respiratory ailment."[28] The reported death toll of the disease is staggering, but research suggests that excess mortality caused by the pandemic is far higher than the official death toll.[29] The effectiveness of therapies that have been developed to combat COVID-19, such as monoclonal antibodies, are declining as the virus continues to mutate rapidly,[30] and the long-term health consequences on the billions of COVID-19 survivors around the world are still unknown. Correspondingly, serious measures are justified to combat what is a very serious disease, whereas similar measures to fight a less serious disease might be disproportionate.

19.3.2 Level of Infectiousness

We must then consider the infectiousness of a transmissible disease against the backdrop of the severity of the illness it causes. A disease that is severe but not very transmissible might not support the use of the same range of measures to combat it as one that is severe and highly contagious. Of course, we all know that COVID-19 is a highly contagious disease, with a basic reproduction number estimated at 2.87 (95% CI, 2.39–3.44).[31]

19.3.3 Mode of Transmission

We now know that COVID-19 is airborne and that the disease is primarily spread by the inhalation of aerosols, rather than by the inhalation of respiratory droplets or through contact with contaminated surfaces.[32] The fact that COVID-19 is airborne has two significant implications for the leveraging of existing technologies to combat the disease.

First, airborne spread means that physical proximity between individuals is a reasonable proxy for breathing the same air. This has allowed technologists to leverage CSLI and Bluetooth to develop digital contact tracing systems that have had some impact in reducing the spread of the disease.[33]

Second, contracting an airborne disease such as COVID-19 is far less stigmatizing than contracting a disease that has a mode of transmission that is more revealing of an individual's behaviors and personal characteristics. Consider a sexually transmitted disease, such as syphilis. The stigma associated with revealing that one is infected with syphilis is far greater than what is associated with revealing that one has COVID-19, as the former is contracted through sexual activity, which is among the most intimate aspects of an individual's life.[34] By contrast, COVID-19 is associated with the activity of breathing, which is something that all people must do at all times.

To be sure, the technologies that were leveraged to construct proxies for sharing the same air for digital contact tracing purposes (namely, CSLI and Bluetooth signal strength) would be ill-suited to detecting the spread of diseases spread by other vectors, such as sexual contact or insect-based transmission. Yet the data generated by wearable health devices can be used to detect sexual activity in certain circumstances,[35] and future advances may yield technologies that provide us with useful proxies for other common modes of disease transmission.

19.3.4 Putting the Factors to Work

Future policymakers will need to take the characteristics of infectious diseases into account in making decisions about whether and how features of existing technologies in widespread use are enlisted to combat them.

Even though 2022 is on track to be the deadliest year of the COVID-19 pandemic in some countries,[36] many of the technological measures that were developed to combat the COVID-19 pandemic have already been withdrawn.[37] It therefore seems unlikely that governments will mandate technological tools to fight anything other than the most serious diseases in the future, but history teaches us that these will arise in due course.

Furthermore, the market may well develop technological solutions to combat the spread of infectious diseases—particularly among populations that are vulnerable to their spread. In such cases, the background law that governs privacy in society and the deployment of particular forms of technology will shape the possibilities for such technologies to be developed and sold.[38] At this stage of the COVID-19 pandemic, we have not seen the market step in to fill the vacuum left by the abandonment of digital contact tracing and digital health certificates in much of the world, but such a possibility cannot be dismissed. Correspondingly, policymakers today and in the future will have to consider not just whether to legislate particular technological measures to combat serious infectious diseases but also whether legal defaults should permit such technologies from being developed and deployed absent state action.

19.4 Conclusion

Necessity is the mother of invention, and the necessity of fighting COVID-19 to minimize the ravages of the disease while simultaneously minimizing the social cost of doing so fostered a wave of technological innovation. Just as Apple didn't foresee that third-party developers would want to create apps for the iPhone,[39] few observers before the COVID-19 pandemic would have predicted how existing technologies such as CSLI, Bluetooth, and QR codes would be leveraged in the fight against this disease. Now that we know that such innovations are possible, now is the time to begin reflecting how the installed base of technology in society can be leveraged to fight the pandemic diseases of the future. Doing so will allow us to be clear-eyed as to whether the public health benefits of such measures justify their costs in terms of privacy when the next pandemic does strike.

Notes

1 Jocelyne Piret & Guy Boivin, "Pandemics Throughout History" (2021) *Frontiers in Microbiology*.
2 Ignacio Cofone, "Immunity Passports and Contract Tracing Surveillance" (2021) 24:176 *The Stanford Technology Law Review*; Oskar Josef Gstrein, Dimitry Valdimirovich Kochenov & Andrej Zwitter, "A Terrible Great Idea? COVID-19 'Vaccination Passports' in the Spotlight" (2021) *The Centre on Migration, Policy, and Society*, *Working Paper No* 153, University of Oxford; Bryan Thomas et al, "Are Vaccine Passports Discriminatory?" (29 July 2021), online: *C.D. Howe Institute*. https://www.cdhowe.org/intelligence-memos/thomas-flood-krishnamurthy-tanner-wilson---are-vaccine-passports-discriminatory.
3 World Health Organization, "Coronavirus Disease (COVID-19): Contact Tracing" (31 May 2021), online: *World Health Organization*. www.who.int/news-room/questions-and-answers/item/coronavirus- disease-covid-19-contact-tracing.
4 *Ibid*.
5 Wafaa M. El-Sadr et al, "Contract Tracing: Barriers and Facilitators" (2022) 112:7 *The American Journal of Public Health* 1025.

6 Tamar Sharon, "Blind-sided by Privacy? Digital Contract Tracing, the Apple/Google API and Big Tech's Newfound Role as Global Health Policy Makers" (2021) 23(Supp 1) *Ethics and Information Technology* 45.
7 Bob Pegoraro, "Here's How Long You Wireless Carrier Holds on to Your Location Data" (29 August 2022), online: *PCMag*. www.pcmag.com/news/heres-how-long-your-wireless-carrier-holds-on-to-your-location-data.
8 Chamee Yang, "Digital Contract Tracing in the Pandemic Cities: Problematizing the Regime of Traceability in South Korea" (2022) 9:1 *Big Data and Society*. https://doi.org/10.1177/20539517221089294.
9 Amir Cahane, "The Israeli Emergency Regulations for Location Tracking of Coronavirus Carriers" (21 March 2020), online: *Lawfare*. www.lawfareblog.com/israeli-emergency-regulations-location-tracking-coronavirus-carriers.
10 Yang, *supra* note 8.
11 Trevor Moore, "Cell-Site Location Information and the Privacies of Life: The Impact of Carpenter v. United States" (2020) 53:3 *The Loyola of Los Angeles Law Review* 713.
12 Gyuwon Jung et al, "Too Much Information: Assessing Privacy Risks of Contact Trace Data Disclosure on People with COVID-19 in South Korea" (2020) 8:305 *Frontiers in Public Health*.
13 Curt Franklin & Chris Pollette, "How Bluetooth Works" (10 February 2021), online: *howstuffworks*. https://electronics.howstuffworks.com/bluetooth.htm.
14 Paul-Olivier Dehaye, "Inferring Distance from Bluetooth Signal Strength: A Deep Dive" (19 May 2020), online: *Medium*. https://medium.com/personaldata-io/inferring-distance-from-bluetooth-signal-strength-a-deep-dive-fe7badc2bb6d.
15 "Exposure Notifications: Frequently Asked Questions" (September 2020), online: *Apple Inc.* https://covid19-static.cdn-apple.com/applications/covid19/current/static/contact-tracing/pdf/ExposureNotification-FAQv1.2.pdf.
16 *Ibid.*
17 Government of Canada, "COVID Alert: COVID-19 Exposure Notification Application Privacy Assessment" (February 2021), online: www.canada.ca/en/public-health/services/diseases/coronavirus-disease-covid-19/covid-alert/privacy-policy/assessment.html.
18 Koustubh Bagachi et al, "Digital Tools for COVID-19 Contract Tracing: Identifying and Mitigating the Equity, Privacy and Civil Liberties Concerns" (2020), online: *Edmond J. Safra Center for Ethics, Open Tech Institute*. https://ethics.harvard.edu/files/center-for-ethics/files/22civilliberties.pdf.
19 "COVID Fueled Debate Over Centralized vs Decentralized Health Systems" (14 March 2022), online: *Exemplars News*. www.exemplars.health/stories/covid-fueled-debate-over-centralized; see also Michael Veale, in this volume.
20 Erin Walkinshaw, "Mandatory Vaccinations: The Canadian Picture" (2011) 183:16 *The Canadian Medical Association Journal*.
21 See Kumanan Wilson, in this volume.
22 Centre for Disease Control and Prevention, "New Vaccination Criteria for U.S. Immigration" (2012), online: *Centre for Disease Control and Prevention*. www.cdc.gov/immigrantrefugeehealth/laws-regs/vaccination-immigration/revised-vaccination-immigration-faq.html.
23 Ann Scott Tyson, "Why China's COVID-tracking QR Code Raises Surveillance Concerns" (6 December 2022), online: *The Christian Science Monitor*. www.csmonitor.com/World/Asia-Pacific/2022/1206/Why-China-s-COVID-tracking-QR-codes-raise-surveillance-concerns.
24 Quebec encoded the bearer's gender into their QR code, however. Peter Jackson, "More Than Just Your Name on Vaccine QR Codes" (14 October 2021), online: *The Star*. www.thestar.com/news/canada/2021/10/14/more-than-just-your-name-on-vaccine-qr-codes.html.

25 Tyson, *supra* note 23.
26 Gouvernement du Québec, "Help for VaxiCode" (14 March 2022), online: *Governement du Québec*. www.quebec.ca/en/health/health-issues/a-z/2019-coronavirus/progress-of-the-covid-19-vaccination/covid-19-vaccination-passport/help-for-vaxicode.
27 Marc-Étienne M. Léveillé, "Flaw in the Quebec Vaccine Passport: Analysis" (31 August 2021), online: *welivesecurity*. www.welivesecurity.com/2021/08/31/flaw-quebec-vaccine-passport-vaxicode-verif-analysis/.
28 Michael Kalafatis, "COVID-19: A Serious Vascular Disease with Primary Symptoms of a Respiratory Ailment" (2021) 6:5 *Journal of Applied Laboratory Medicine* 1099.
29 Haidong Wang et al, "Estimating Excess Mortality due to the COVID-19 Pandemic: A Systematic Analysis of COVID-19-related Mortality, 2020–21" (2022) 399:10334 *Lancet*.
30 Columbia University Irving Medical Center, "Vaccine and Antibody Treatment Effectiveness Blunted by all Three Omicron Subvariants" (3 March 2022), online: *ScienceDaily*. www.sciencedaily.com/releases/2022/03/220303125021.htm.
31 Arif Billah, Mamum Miah & Nuruzzaman Khan, "Reproductive Number of Coronavirus: A Systematic Review and Meta-analysis Based on Global Level Evidence" (2020) 15:11 *PLoS One* e0242128.
32 Raymond Tellier, "COVID-19 the Case for Aerosol Transmission" (2022) 12:2 *Interface Focus* 20210072.
33 Shuo Sun et al, "The Epidemiological Impact of the Canadian COVID Alert App" (2022) 113:4 *Canadian Journal of Public Health* 519.
34 Fahimeh Saeed et al, "A Narrative Review of Stigma Related to Infectious Disease Outbreaks: What Can Be Learned in the Face of the COVID-19 Pandemic?" (2020) 11 *Frontiers in Psychiatry* 565919.
35 Becca Gaddy, "From Cheating to Pregnancy Reveals, Wearables Know What You're Doing Intimately" (21 March 2020), online: *Inverse*. www.inverse.com/mind-body/from-cheating-to-pregnancy-reveals-wearables-know-what-you-are-doing-intimately.
36 Kwame McKenzie, "Canada is Set for Its Deadliest Pandemic Year Yet. Yes We're Tired, But We Cannot Give Up the Fight" (26 May 2022), online: *The Star*. www.thestar.com/opinion/contributors/2022/05/26/canada-is-set-for-its-deadliest-pandemic-year-yet-yes-were-tired-but-we-cannot-give-up-the-fight.html.
37 Elizabeth Payne, "Ontario to End Vaccine Passports, Lift Restrictions 'in Spite' of Protests" (14 February 2022), online: *Ottawa Citizen*. https://ottawacitizen.com/news/local-news/ontario-to-end-vaccine-passports-lift-restrictions-in-spite-of-protests.
38 Bryan Thomas et al, "Vaccine Ins and Outs: An Exploration of the Legal Issues Raised by Vaccine Passports" (2021), online: *C.D. How Institute Working Paper*. https://www.cdhowe.org/sites/default/files/attachments/research_papers/mixed/Working%20Paper%202021-07-13.pdf.
39 Stephen Silver, "The Revolution Steve Jobs Resisted: Apple's App Store Marks 10 Years of Third-party Innovation" (10 July 2018), online: *Apple Insider*. https://appleinsider.com/articles/18/07/10/the-revolution-steve-jobs-resisted-apples-app-store-marks-10-years-of-third-party-innovation.

20

VERIFICATION THEATRE AT BORDERS AND IN POCKETS

Michael Veale

20.1 Introduction

The COVID-19 pandemic saw individuals asked to prove health-related characteristics in a wide and varying array of situations. These differed across jurisdictions. Some countries imposed requirements in occupational and leisure situations. Others made little use of proof mechanisms, or left their use up to private actors. Internationally, however, the idea of 'vaccination passports' co-evolved with legal requirements to prove health-related characteristics *at the border*. This in turn placed domestic pressure on countries to either publicly provide or facilitate private provision of technical infrastructures that could meet emerging international standards of proof.

Before the COVID-19 pandemic, the most similar provision at borders was in relation to yellow fever. Requirements for travelers to have yellow fever vaccinations are typically imposed by countries without the virus but vulnerable to its establishment due to mosquito vectors and non-human primate hosts.[1] The International Certificate of Vaccination or Revaccination against Yellow Fever was replaced from 2007 by the more general International Certificate of Vaccination or Prophylaxis (ICVP).[2] Although the WHO describes ICVP paper certificates—often known as a yellow card, or *carte jaune*—as 'easily lost and prone to fraud',[3] use of these rarely if ever required 'proofs of the veracity of the document'.[4] This is despite significant evidence of forgery. In a recent study, two-thirds of the ICVPs from travelers interviewed at a Sudanese airport appeared to be counterfeit.[5] In these contexts, this could be considered a minimum, as features of the ICVP make it impossible to truly validate. These issues are compounded by challenges further up the supply chain such as vaccine falsification.[6]

DOI: 10.4324/9781003394006-27

Contrary to the ICVP, discussions of COVID-19 documentation had functionalities related to proof built into them from the start. European guidelines focused on verifiability as a key design criterion.[7] Several jurisdictions where the ICVP are used as the official record and 'source of truth' of COVID-19 vaccinations later removed their admissibility as proof in day-to-day circumstances.[8] This makes it important to consider what verifiability could and in practice does mean in these contexts.

20.2 Verifiability Theatre

We often verify our identities or verify we possess certain attributes. Verification of a characteristic of an individual is conceptually a two-step process. The first step is authentication of identity—linking the person in front of you to an identifier. The second step is the linkage of that identifier to a characteristic, such as vaccination, testing or recovery. This process further requires integrity of the data involved in this process.

It is worth considering what 'digital' means in this context. Digital is often thought of as an app or a website versus a paper document. This is an important distinction when considering a 'digital divide'; even in a country with high technology saturation such as the UK, 7% of individuals still lack a device which can connect to the Internet.[9] However, even a paper certificate with a QR code is 'digital' insofar as it relies on a 'stack' of infrastructure to generate, maintain, authenticate and interact with it. It is simply the case that the role of the individual in the digital infrastructure is only to obtain and display information—the 'intelligence' happens elsewhere in the network.[10]

20.2.1 Only as Strong as the Weakest Link

In practice, the deployed digital verifiability strategies provided little defence against moderately determined fraud.

Some countries recorded initial vaccinations on paper vaccination cards, such as the United States from the CDC or in the *carte jaune* in Germany. In the United States, these were accepted as proof directly. In Germany, these were both broadly directly accepted as proof, as well as used a source of truth, without reference to other databases, to convert them into digitally signed certificates by most pharmacies.[11]

Hand-signed paper vaccination cards are typically trivially forged. In a poll commissioned by *The Economist*, 12% of American adults under 30 admit knowing somebody with a fake US vaccination card.[12] Thousands of cases of forged *cartes jaunes* are subject to investigation and prosecution procedures in Germany.[13] Those prosecuted included high-profile celebrities, including football coaches.[14] Forgeries of such cards are commonplace concerning yellow fever vaccination in sub-Saharan Africa.[15]

Paper cards with no in-built mechanism of digital linkage of an identifier to a vaccination status were widely accepted around the world despite no practical method of verifying them. The Washington State Department of Health verification guidance illustrates this, with guidance to 'be suspicious of cards printed on thin paper or edges that appear cut by scissors'; to check all fields are completed and the template is the expected one; and to look up vaccine lot numbers to check if such a lot was ever distributed. CDC passes were not printed on secure paper (as ballot papers sometimes are), and so such paper is easily emulated. The latter check is easily passed by copying a valid vaccination batch-time combination from any other card.

Despite this, and seemingly for political reasons, US vaccination cards were accepted around the world as proof at borders and often within domestic regimes and in line with restrictions placed there.

In Germany, the situation was in some ways worse. As with many countries lacking health informatics, the *carte jaune* was used as the source of truth to populate the cryptographically assured digital vaccination pass database. Individuals would walk into pharmacies, who would examine evidence and enter it into a database. At this point, fraudulent *cartes jaunes* could effectively be laundered into a real vaccination pass. This author, holder of a valid UK vaccination record, presented the UK documents to a pharmacist in Berlin in 2021, who looked at the printout without seeking to validate the UK QR code (which at the time was not able to be validated with a German validator, a situation which later changed), and entered the record into the German database, issuing a German vaccination certificate.[16] Indeed, pharmacies in Germany stated they would transform CDC cards and other unverifiable and easily forged foreign vaccination records into German digital certificates.[17]

Fooling pharmacists was not even necessary for those forging at scale, who set up fake pharmacies in order to create irrevocable certificates in Germany. An investigation from the newspaper *Handelsblatt* in July 2022 revealed that it was trivial to register a fake pharmacy and issue digital certificates, even when a residential apartment address was used. The cryptographic set-up used in Germany meant that once issued, these certificates could not be revoked without invalidating the millions issued in that manner.[18] Nor could other European countries, who were part of the shared EU validation system for such certificates, selectively revoke German certificates that were part of proven forgeries.

Other issues in the chain concern the validity of vaccines and the identity of recipients. We know from yellow fever vaccination that falsified vaccines also exist on the market as part of chains that lead to documents for verification.[19] The market for falsified COVID-19 vaccines is large but has been difficult to estimate.[20] Furthermore, many countries did not require a robust process of identity assurance in order to receive a vaccination. There was no guarantee that the person inside a valid vaccination chain, being vaccinated with a valid vaccine, was the person whose name is on the certificate. This makes sense due to a need for rapid rollout, including amongst undocumented individuals who may be persecuted and marginalized by state authorities in other contexts. However, it creates a hole in a chain of trust which cannot be mended by a more solid certification verification process downstream.

In sum, many jurisdictions lacked a reliable and secure chain of trust from the actual act of vaccination through to the digital certificate. This created easy opportunities for forgery within these jurisdictions. The requirement to recognize certificates across borders, a necessity given their main use as international travel documents, meant that even a handful of weak jurisdictions undermined any technical security measures placed on the generation and use of vaccination certificates domestically. While not covered here, the same issues apply for records of testing and records of recovery.

20.2.2 Why Bother?

Just because forgery is possible does not mean that everyone *will* forge documents. The law can always impose serious penalties were fraud to be discovered and that will be enough to dissuade some. There have been penalties and prosecutions for withholding health information at airports since at least 1924, but significant compliance issues have persisted in spite of this.[21] Furthermore, vaccination, testing and recovery are typically all imperfect methods to prevent transmission, and insofar as borders are open to those meeting certain characteristics, pathogens may still enter the country in question. Documentation fraud adds to these errors, but the sum of the intervention of requiring certification may be beneficial if reduction, rather than total security, is an acceptable aim.

An approach of reduction rather than security casts the entire enterprise of verification in a different light. Such an approach would likely be unacceptable for many aims where we try to verify to secure. A nuclear power plant's security systems should not 'reduce' unauthorized entry but prevent the possibility. Yet other environments, such as supermarket self-checkouts or contactless cards, come with an expectation of abuse built into the policy, typically outweighed against a benefit, such as reduced staff cost or greater card usage, and, therefore, more transactions subject to intermediation fees.[22]

Considering vaccine verification in this light raises the question of whether the behavioral consequences of a digital proof infrastructure in a world where dodging it is relatively trivial is enough to justify it being built in the first place. Infrastructures to prove things to people come with serious social consequences. Is this just to give a veneer of fraud protection compared to analogue methods? That a system that many will not understand the workings of might seem more secure than it actually is? Other than the fact that there are many ways to build an opaque computer system, this ignores that systems designed to prove things to people are not just a performance, but they are also performative, in the sense that they have social effects that lead to change.[23]

20.3 Verification's Impacts beyond Biosecurity

A digital verification system is not just icing sugar added to an ICVP to increase its behavioral impact. Digital verification systems do real things in the real world and come with consequences far outside the realm of public health.

20.3.1 Repurposed Infrastructure

The digital systems created to enable verification are often used for purposes beyond that. More broadly, the introduction of technologies at borders typically goes beyond stated purposes to separate out 'legitimate' from 'illegitimate' forms of mobility and to allow surveillance to be practiced both at and away from the border by private actors, such as security firms, as well as state agents.[24] The affordances of digital systems, such as verification, invite extensions and further systems to be built upon them. These are not just systems built upon the vaccination record themselves but systems built on the connection to health databases, the connection to individual identities, the connections to individuals' mobile devices and so on.

One pandemic example is the 'ArriveCAN' app. Originally created as a method to capture data under Canada's Quarantine Act, the app became a mandatory way of submitting such information, first for air travelers in late 2020, then for all travelers in early 2021.[25] However, the Government of Canada stated that the app was 'not only keeping travellers safe, but [was] part of [their] ongoing efforts to modernize the border'. This became apparent, as the mandatory app was extended to contain components of previous border modernization attempts which had failed to get traction, such as the Advance Canada Border Services Agency (CBSA) 'declaration' feature, relating to customs and immigrations, with no link to public health and no debate or discussion.[26] Academic commentators have criticized ArriveCAN's transformation 'from a voluntary app intended to offer an alternative for paperwork to permit contact tracing into a mandatory app that had little connection to public health'.[27]

Another example comes in the form of the German 'Luca' app. This app was launched by a private firm to initially attempt to create a presence-tracing system, where individuals could 'check in' to locations to provide a list of who was there to the venue. This feature was criticized by scholars, who noted its poor design with significant security flaws,[28] and by journalists, who had highlighted the 21 million EUR regional governments had spent on this technology for just a single year of usage, largely in attempt to look active in relation to the federal government in advance of a regional election.[29] A regional court in Rostock later found the purchase of the Luca app by the government there to be illegal.[30] By this time, the app had also expanded beyond its initial features, allowing individuals to integrate their vaccination certificates for the purpose of proof at the border and in shops and restaurants and even to buy tickets to gigs and events through its portal. The firm was effectively attempting to create a public health–related platform to become a technology intermediary across a variety of sectors.

In general, a system that has at its core the ability to prove something to other people forms a strong platform to build on. Once built, such technologies rarely stay still. When a pandemic ends or is at a lull, these technologies enter into confusing situations. They may still have some users and uses. They certainly have maintenance and security issues that need care over time, as operating systems change and new security threats emerge. But maintenance and updating costs money, particularly to maintain infrastructures which may not have a purpose between public health crises. In these situations, maintaining such systems for a crisis with a certain set of functionality can be difficult to justify compared to finding a use for this technology in-between crises. Similarly, when such systems are developed by private actors, they need to locate revenue streams between crises which can keep the organization and the technologies afloat and ready. Preparedness in technologies appears difficult to reconcile with tendencies for 'function creep'.

20.3.2 Exclusionary Standards and Domestic IT Capture

The process around creating the underlying technical set-up for verification of vaccination had significant industry involvement in ways that risked capture of various types.

While an ICVP really only requires common document templates, and relies on stamps and signatures from vaccinating authorities (which may or may not be standardized), a digital verification process typically needs a *public key infrastructure*, or PKI. PKIs provide means to record, distribute and revoke bindings between users and cryptographic keys that relate to them. Public and private keys are core building blocks of cryptography. Entities like a public health authority generate one or more pairs of public and private keys. If they wish to *sign* an event (such as 'Jane Doe received vaccine X on 21.02.21'), they can do so using their private key, which they keep secret and secure. Individuals who want to verify that this was indeed signed by this authority can then check if the signature is valid by comparing it to the alleged signing authority's public key, which by definition should be 'public' and attributable to the authority in question. This makes it important that verifiers have somewhere where they know all the public keys will reliably be placed, alongside notices of revocation, for example, if a private key is hacked so people know not to trust corresponding signatures anymore.

PKIs are a crucial aspect of applied cryptography and one of the hardest to establish and maintain in practice. They are constant targets for surveillance authorities around the world, and the PKIs underpinning encryption on the web are sites of geopolitical tension in Internet governance.[31]

The WHO Smart Vaccination Certificate Working Group indicate in their report that in order to participate in their proposed standard, public health authorities will need to 'have access to a national public key infrastructure', and although they do 'not describe the PKI in detail', they require it to have a wide variety of features.[32] The European COVID certificate, which significantly influenced global standards, could build upon EU countries long having been urged, particularly through successive laws on electronic signatures, to have experience and state capacity in national PKIs.[33] However, countries in the Global South rarely have public sector PKIs established, although they are often part of future digital plans.[34]

The result of this state of affairs is a demand on all countries wishing to participate in international travel to rapidly develop and adopt a complex infrastructure in one of their most sensitive sectors—health. Health informatics is a sector with a lot of promise but also an extraordinary possibility for capture. Building a complex infrastructure during a crisis will only be achievable for poor countries by effectively handing over significant control to private entities. Regardless of the merits or drawbacks of privatization in the health and care sectors, this privatization can really only occur in a rush. The WHO Smart Vaccination Certificate Working Group appeared set up as a sales pitch, with many consultants as members, and the only eligible individuals to apply to this group were those who could at short notice provide a slide deck 'outlining a proposed global interoperability standard for issuing, certifying, and verifying a vaccination event'—a finished, or at least significantly developed, *product*.[35]

In sum, the rushed desire to create *digitally verifiable* vaccination certificates may contribute to rushed procurement of informatics capacity in many countries' public sectors in a way which would seem likely to lead to a loss of control over the problems, capacities, framings and even data flows within those organizations. Such procurement, however, provides little benefits, for the reasons outlined earlier. The extent of this impact requires further country-specific research and follow-up.

20.4 Privacy (Or Rather, Confidentiality) Theatre

As 2020 progressed, questions moved from whether vaccination was possible to how vaccination would affect society. When discussions moved to consider logistical challenges of demonstrating vaccination status, the predominant frame for discussing these questions was one of privacy.

From the perspective of this author, privacy had been a very important frame for pandemic technologies up until this point. We had been involved in the furore around Bluetooth contact tracing technologies, as states had proposed solutions with unnecessary publicity risk, whereas more decentralized solutions that have the same or similar functionality with greatly reduced risks were possible.[36] In the end, decentralized technologies were widely rolled out under the banner of 'Exposure Notification'. These technologies prevented detailed network data of who saw who in society from being accumulated by state actors around the world, including those with lacklustre human rights regimes or those with limited ability to keep this data secure.

Vaccination certificates were not exactly like this. For contact tracing technologies, the functionality itself—notifying individuals subject to a 'risky' encounter—was not particularly controversial. With design precautions, it could be repurposed only in limited ways.[37] For vaccination certificates, the controversial data is not a database of vaccination recipients (which typically exists) nor typically specific vaccination information that a checker may see in the process of checking. The controversial data is the 'tick' or the 'cross': Do you meet the policy of the verifier?[38] Privacy technologies exist which allow individuals to reveal nothing to a verifier except the fact they meet a certain policy that has been set.[39] The issue here becomes less about the data that is used during the process of verification—which is nice to minimize but not the focus—but the functionality that the system enables.

Drawing attention to the verifier's policy should also draw our attention to attributions we may not wish to be possible to be required to attest to. Lifestyle, travel history, occupation, age, socioeconomic grouping—all these have potential causative or correlative links to transmission and vulnerability to emerging pathogens. Individuals have information about most of these characteristics on their mobile devices, whether they inputted it manually or not. If they are not revealed to a querier, should they be able to form part of a policy? We could imagine law and rules governing this, but more than anything, this is governed by the technical possibilities of attesting to these characteristics. A path where individuals can technically attest, even privately and confidentially, to a variety of attributes, may leave us in quite a dark place indeed.

It should, however, be noted that functionality *can* be part of discussions about privacy, particularly when it is conceived of in terms that are relational, about autonomy and self-definition.[40] But in the health domain, privacy is often thought of as *confidentiality*, following the importance of medical confidentiality. Privacy is a concept that captures a bundle of interests. Verification and attestation do the same. Choosing a framing for analysis of the role of verification technologies and infrastructures in society will be key to establishing a wider debate on these practices.

20.5 Concluding Remarks

Perhaps some of these arguments seem moot now. Few countries at the time of writing retain entry requirements around COVID-19. The practical impacts of verification theatre were likely dampened by the United States lacking any national vaccination registry and geopolitically forcing countries to accept trivially forgeable paper cards, regardless of the standards they had invested in or the technologies they had built.

Nevertheless, the saga of verification and its limits in this pandemic should draw our attention more towards the interaction of law and technologies in crises. Both interventions and infrastructures matter, and they cannot be seen apart from each other. We cannot set aside infrastructural considerations simply because urgency calls or ignore the long-term legacies of the systems and schemes that societies dream up simply because we are in a rush. Preparedness should allow us to have deep consideration, and simultaneous discussions, of all issues that matter and which surround a proposed intervention such as vaccine certification. In an age of conspiracy, it can be difficult to speculate about the longer-term development and governance of technological systems without appearing to resort to a 'slippery slope' argument. But the design of infrastructures requires considering use and misuse in the future—how they reconfigure power and facilitate certain policy choices and possibilities over others. The COVID-19 pandemic should sharpen our understanding and sensitivity to the importance of these areas. We need this for both operational preparedness when another crisis arises and to support longer transdisciplinary debates about how to use technologies in societies in crises.

Notes

1 Max Hardiman & Annelies Wilder-Smith, "The Revised International Health Regulations and Their Relevance to Travel Medicine" (2007) 14:3 *Journal of Travel Medicine* 141.
2 International Health Regulations 2005, art 36; annex 6–7.
3 World Health Organization, "Digital Documentation of COVID-19 Certificates: Vaccination Status: Technical Specifications and Implementation Guidance" (27 August 2021) at 1, online: *WHO*. www.who.int/publications-detail-redirect/WHO-2019-nCoV-Digital_certificates-vaccination-2021.1.
4 e-Health Network, "Guidelines on Verifiable Vaccination Certificates—Basic Interoperability Elements" (12 March 2021), online: *European Commission*. https://health.ec.europa.eu/publications/guidelines-verifiable-vaccination-certificates-basic-interoperability-elements_en.
5 Razan Osman Abdalla et al, "The Global Health Challenge of Counterfeit Vaccination Certificates: The Case of Yellow Fever Vaccination among Travelers Departing from Khartoum International Airport in Sudan" (2022) 1:4 *Public Health Challenges* e45.
6 Pierre Saliou et al, "The Scourge of Vaccine Falsification" (2022) 40:14 *Vaccine* 2126.
7 e-Health Network, *supra* note 4.

8 As a convenient shorthand, this paper will talk primarily in terms of vaccination and vaccination documentation, which should be seen as inclusive of certificates intending to prove testing or recovery.
9 Ofcom, "Online Nation 2021 Report" (9 June 2021) at 18, online: *Ofcom*. https://perma.cc/8367-N6WW.
10 Compare to an analogue phone—which really just consists of a microphone and some buttons that make sounds, with all the processing happening in the telephone network.
11 Some *Länder* restricted the direct use of *cartes jaunes* from the beginning of 2022; see Charlotte Kurz, "In diesen Bundesländern reicht der gelbe Impfpass nicht mehr" (2 December 2021), online: *Pharmazeutische Zeitung*. www.pharmazeutische-zeitung.de/in-diesen-bundeslaendern-reicht-der-gelbe-impfpass-nicht-mehr-130002/.
12 Kathy Frankovic, "Are Americans OK with Lying to Get or Avoid Getting a COVID-19 Shot?" (22 October 2021), online: *YouGov*. https://today.yougov.com/topics/politics/articles-reports/2021/10/22/are-americans-ok-lying-get-avoid-covid-vaccine.
13 Buten un Binnen, "Mehr als 100 Fälle gefälschter Impfpässe bei Bremer Staatsanwaltschaft" (4 January 2022), online: *Radio Bremen*. www.butenunbinnen.de/nachrichten/gefaelschte-impfpaesse-impfung-bremen-polizei-100.html; "Bundesweite Ermittlungen: 12.000 Verfahren zu falschen Impfpässen" (19 January 2022), online: *Tagesschau*. www.tagesschau.de/inland/corona-impfpass-faelschung-verfahren-101.html.
14 Buten un Binnen, "Ex-Werder-Trainer Markus Anfang legt Geständnis ab" (5 January 2022), online: *Radio Bremen*. www.butenunbinnen.de/sport/werder-bremen-markus-anfang-impfausweis-faelschung-gestaendnis-100.html.
15 Abdalla et al, *supra* note 5.
16 This was done transparently, in good faith, and in line with the legal discretion pharmacists had at the time to recognize foreign vaccination certificates, in anticipation that the UK's departure from the EU would cause further recognition challenges for vaccinations.
17 "Local Pharmacies offer Transcription of CDC Vaccine Cards into EU Digital Standard" (30 March 2022), online: *Stuttgart Citizen*. www.stuttgartcitizen.com/news/local-pharmacies-offer-transcription-of-cdc-vaccine-cards-into-eu-digital-standard/.
18 Julian Olk, "IT-Experten finden Sicherheitslücke bei Digitalen Impfnachweisen—Ausstellung durch Apotheken gestoppt", online: www.handelsblatt.com/politik/deutschland/corona-pandemie-it-experten-finden-sicherheitsluecke-bei-digitalen-impfnachweisen-ausstellung-durch-apotheken-gestoppt/27443716.html.
19 Saliou et al, *supra* note 6.
20 Joseph Amankwah-Amoah, "COVID-19 and Counterfeit Vaccines: Global Implications, New Challenges and Opportunities" (2022) 11:2 *Health Policy and Technology* (The COVID-19 Pandemic: Vaccination Strategies and Global Health Policies) 100630.
21 Lucy Budd, Morag Bell & Tim Brown, "Of plagues, Planes and Politics: Controlling the Global Spread of Infectious Diseases by Air" (2009) 28:7 *Political Geography* 426.
22 Emmeline Taylor, "Supermarket Self-checkouts and Retail Theft: The Curious Case of the SWIPERS" (2016) 16:5 *Criminology & Criminal Justice* 552.
23 Stefania Milan et al, "Promises Made to Be Broken: Performance and Performativity in Digital Vaccine and Immunity Certification" (2021) 12:2 *The European Journal of Risk Regulation* 382.
24 Louise Amoore, "Biometric Borders: Governing MOBILITIES in the War on Terror" (2006) 25:3 *Political Geography* 336.

25 Public Health Agency of Canada, "Government of Canada announces new mandatory requirements for travellers to Canada", (2 November 2020), online: *Government of Canada*. www.canada.ca/en/public-health/news/2020/11/government-of-canada-announces-new-mandatory-requirements-for-travellers-to-canada.html; Public Health Agency of Canada, "Government of Canada expands restrictions to international travel by land and air" (12 February 2021), online: *Government of Canada*. www.canada.ca/en/public-health/news/2021/02/government-of-canada-expands-restrictions-to-international-travel-by-land-and-air.html.
26 Bianca Wylie & Matt Malone, "Canada's ArriveCAN App Is Fostering Inequity at the Border" (9 September 2022), online: *Centre for International Governance Innovation*. www.cigionline.org/articles/canadas-arrivecan-app-is-fostering-inequity-at-the-border/.
27 Matt Malone, "Lessons from ArriveCAN: Access to Information and Justice during a Glitch" (2023) 35:2 *Intellectual Property Journal* 99 at 115.
28 Theresa Stadler et al, "Preliminary Analysis of Potential Harms in the Luca Tracing System" (22 March 2021), online: *arXiv*. https://arxiv.org/abs/2103.11958.
29 Chris Köver & Markus Reuter, "Luca-App: Bund übernimmt Millionenkosten der Länder nicht" (12 January 2022), online: *netzpolitik.org*. https://netzpolitik.org/2022/luca-app-bund-uebernimmt-millionenkosten-der-laender-nicht/.
30 *Oberlandesgericht (OLG) Rostock* (Urt. v. 11.11.2021, Az. 17 Verg 4/21).
31 Ross Anderson, *Security Engineering: A Guide to Building Dependable Distributed Systems* (Newark: John Wiley & Sons, Incorporated, 2020) at 730; Laura DeNardis, *The Global War for Internet Governance* (New Haven: Yale University Press, 2014) at 95.
32 World Health Organization, *supra* note 3 at 4.
33 Stephen Blythe, "Digital Signature Law of the United Nations, European Union, United Kingdom and United States: Promotion of Growth in E-Commerce With Enhanced Security" (2005) 11:2 *The Richmond Journal of Law & Technology* 6 at 9.
34 See, e.g., United Nations Conference on Trade and Development, "Member States of the Economic Community of West African States eTrade Readiness Assessment" (2022) at 41–42, online (pdf): *UNCTAD/DTL/ECDE/2022/1*. https://unctad.org/system/files/official-document/dtlecdc2022d1_en.pdf.
35 World Health Organization, "World Health Organization Open Call for Nomination of Experts to Contribute to the Smart Vaccination Certificate Technical Specifications and Standards" (2 December 2020), online: *WHO*. www.who.int/news-room/articles-detail/world-health-organization-open-call-for-nomination-of-experts-to-contribute-to-the-smart-vaccination-certificate-technical-specifications-and-standards-application-deadline-14-december-2020.
36 Carmela Troncoso et al, "Decentralized privacy-preserving proximity tracing" (2020) 43:2 IEEE Data Eng Bull 36; Carmela Troncoso et al, "Deploying Decentralized, Privacy-preserving Proximity Tracing" (2022) 65:9 *Communications of the ACM* 48.
37 cf Jaap-Henk Hoepman, "Stop the Apple and Google Contact Tracing Platform. (Or be Ready to Ditch Your Smartphone.)" (11 April 2020), online: https://blog.xot.nl/2020/04/11/stop-the-apple-and-google-contact-tracing-platform-or-be-ready-to-ditch-your-smartphone/index.html (presenting examples of repurposing).
38 Seda Gürses & Michael Veale, "Societal Unknowns of Digital Rule Enforcement?" (10 June 2021), online (video): *YouTube*. www.youtube.com/watch?v=BG3QG7Yza00.

39 For example, attribute-based credentials. See Merel Koning et al, "The ABC of ABC: An Analysis of Attribute-based Credentials in the Light of Data Protection, Privacy and Identity" in *Internet, Law & Politics: A Decade of Transformations*, edited by J Balcells (Barcelona: Huygens Editorial, 2014) 357.

40 Julie E. Cohen, "What Privacy is For" (2012) 126 Harv L Rev 1904; Salome Viljoen, "A Relational Theory of Data Governance" (2021) 131 *The Yale Law Journal* 573; Mireille Hildebrandt, "Privacy as Protection of the Incomputable Self: From Agnostic to Agonistic Machine Learning" (2019) 20:1 *Theoretical Inquiries in Law* 83.

PART VIII

Bounded Vulnerabilities

Long-Term Care, Prisons, Psychiatric Care Institutions, and Homelessness

21

THE PARADOX OF PROTECTING THE VULNERABLE

An Analysis of the Canadian Public Discourse on Older Adults during the COVID-19 Pandemic

Martine Lagacé, Caroline D. Bergeron, Tracey O'Sullivan, Samantha Oostlander, Pascale Dangoisse, Amélie Doucet, and Philippe Rodrigue-Rouleau

21.1 Introduction

The COVID-19 pandemic affected all Canadians. During the first 15 months of the pandemic, adults aged 65 and over were particularly impacted, accounting for 64% of excess deaths and for 93% of deaths attributed to COVID-19.[1] The ongoing impact on older adults' mental health is also solidly documented, with increasing levels of depressive symptoms stemming from feelings of loneliness amongst others.[2] In many long-term care facilities, strict infection control protocols were implemented to try to control for the multiple COVID-19 outbreaks (due in part, as sustained by many studies, to a lack of planning[3]). For residents, such protocols translated into acute physical and social isolation with restricted or no human contacts at all for long periods of time. In short, studies suggest that these very restrictive public health measures, although put in place with the aim of "protecting" seniors, have had deleterious effects on the well-being of older adults, particularly those residing in long-term care, effects which are still felt to this day.

However, as will be demonstrated in this chapter, in addition to restrictive physical limitations, older adults faced attitudinal barriers manifested through ageist public discourse. Ageism, initially conceptualized by Butler (1969), as the negative age-based stereotypes and discriminatory attitudes targeting particularly older adults.[4] Since this seminal work, a plethora of studies have been conducted on ageism that not only refined the concept but also examined its possible sources and demonstrated its profoundly negative

DOI: 10.4324/9781003394006-29

impact at both a societal and individual level.[5] Ageism can take the form of "hostile" attitudes as we have seen during the first weeks of the pandemic with the social media infamous hashtag "Boomer Remover". However, ageism can also be expressed in less overt (and even well-intentioned) attitudes as is the case for "compassionate" (also referred to as "benevolent") ageism. Although compassionate ageism may appear less harmful, this is not the case because it relies on patronizing and even pitiful views of older adults that pave the way for social exclusion.[6]

Public discourse is a powerful means that shapes our understanding of a phenomenon.[7] By discourse, we refer to Burr's definition of a collection of "meanings, metaphors, representations, images, stories, statements and so on that in some way together produce a particular version of events".[8] The language used in public discourse, as expressed by Michel Foucault, is not neutral and does not merely reflect reality; on the contrary, it shapes reality by generating norms and ideologies, stemming from power relationships.[9] In the case of aging and older adults, findings from previous studies suggest that public discourse does convey ageist stereotypes through the creation of certain norms (contained in public policies) such as "aging well", "aging actively", or "aging productively" that *de facto* exclude those older adults that cannot achieve such norms.[10] Public discourse also expresses ageist stereotypes in the way that it often (if not solely) focuses on the deficits and losses stemming from the aging process. Either generated consciously or unconsciously, stereotypes are particularly useful in that they preserve cognitive resources when individuals are in a state of acute mental exhaustion[11] as was plausibly the case during the pandemic. Nonetheless, consciously, or unconsciously, expressed in the public discourse, stereotypes remain harmful to those who are the target of it. As Cotrina et al (2020)[12] have shown, stereotypes can be internalized and impact one's self-esteem. Hence, it is important to examine how and the extent to which stereotypes are conveyed in the public discourse, especially in a time of global health crisis. To this effect, let us recall that the World Health Organization (WHO) had warned of an *infodemic* phenomenon where an overabundance of information and the spread of misinformation and disinformation could erode public trust and undermine the public health response. Calls for action plans to combat the spread of misinformation and disinformation were made to stakeholders, such as media platforms.[13]

In light of the previous section, the aim of the current empirical study was twofold: 1) examine how older adults and the aging process were portrayed during the first year of the COVID-19 pandemic, and 2) assess if and the extent to which such portrayals expressed ageism and, as such, exacerbated barriers that older adults had to face.

21.2 Methods

We conducted a thematic content analysis of four types of public documents that related to a combination of two main key words "COVID-19 or coronavirus or pandemic" and "older adults or elder or aging or seniors". Selected documents were published during three turning points of COVID-19 in Canada: at the beginning of the lockdown period in April 2020, in mid-September to mid-October with the rise of the second wave, and in early December 2020 when there were important discussions about the vaccines and the winter holidays.

Within these three periods, a total of 20 opinion-editorial pieces written by journalists (representing the media discourse), 20 opinion-editorials authored by older adults or associations of older adults (representing the older adult discourse), 10 academic articles (representing the academic discourse), and 32 press briefings and 28 communications generated by the federal government and all 13 provincial and territorial governments of Canada (representing the government discourse) were randomly selected, for a total sample of 110 documents.[14]

The content of each document was organized in the QSR NVivo software according to the following categories: 1) main theme, 2) presence of ageism, 3) framing of the aging process, as well as 4) role of older adults during the pandemic. Pilot sessions were conducted to ensure inter-reliability coding between the three researchers who were responsible for this task.

21.3 Results

21.3.1 Themes

Across the four types of discourse, main themes focused on neglect of vulnerable older adults in long-term care, care and health, the negative impact of the pandemic on older adults as well as the need for government investments to support programming for older adults. However, above and beyond, the most prevalent and cross-cutting theme related to the "*vulnerability of all older adults*" (also framed in the discourse as "our" vulnerable older adults). The word "vulnerable" itself was the one mostly used (in terms of frequency) in the government documents and well as the media. The following representative quote illustrates this last theme:

> No one intentionally wants to take COVID into these facilities but staff [and] visitors can unintentionally bring it in [. . .] So we really need to protect our most vulnerable, especially in long-term care facilities, personal care homes but also people living independently who are our parents and grandparents. Be extra cautious if you do need to visit to assist them with something.
>
> *(government press briefings)*

21.3.2 Presence of Ageism

The media, government press briefings, and older adults themselves contributed to the ageist discourse. For example, a media article from the National Post published in April 2020 perpetuated ageism by focusing solely on the deficits of all older adults in care homes:

> By their very nature, people in care homes aren't able to create the sort of noise required to attract the attention of governments. They are old people, confined to their beds, or dependent on walkers or wheelchairs to get around. They aren't great at social networking, crowdsourcing or virtual campaigning. They are largely dependent on others, either relatives, medical professionals or care staff, for basic needs. Many of them, given the chance, would selflessly insist they don't want to be a bother or a burden.[15]

Some articles written by older adults themselves and associations of older adults also revealed the presence of self-ageism, where they endorsed existing negative stereotypes about their age, as illustrated in an editorial from December 2020: "Dear editor. When the vaccine for COVID-19 rolls out, it should not start with us old folk. [. . .] We old folk are not productive members of society and can shelter at home if concerned."[16]

On the other hand, few discourses from academics, ministry, or department communications and older adults criticized ageism and recognized the negative impact it can have on mental health and access to care. For example, a December 2020 scientific article discussed the following: "The current situation has highlighted the need to rethink the status and role of older adults in our society and to specifically address the impact and influence of ageism in decision-making and the delivery of care."[17]

Interestingly, articles from older adults denouncing ageism were mostly focused on healthy older adults who live independently within their own homes or communities and not older adults residing in long-term care, which may suggest some type of distancing within the same generation. As proposed by an older adult in the journal *La Presse*, "I would prefer us to be perceived as active citizens who are still full participants in the development of society and able to bear their share of the collective burden."[18]

21.3.3 Framing of Aging

More than half of all documents referred to aging as a process of loss, as opposed to a process of gain or a more neutral or balanced process. This framing of loss varied based on the type of discourse but were present in the majority of all documents. Press briefings were the most likely to associate aging with loss, as indicated in the following quote:

> We're facing an aging population—a population that has more needs and more requirements and we're really just at the very very beginning of an aging population, Ih will go on for a number of decades so we are looking at how we can reform long term care.

Formal ministry or department communications as well as communications produced by older adults or associations of older adults were the least likely to associate aging with this negative framing.

21.3.4 Older Adults' Contributions

Similar to the framing of aging, older adults' contributions to society were not often recognized throughout the various discourses. Their diverse strengths and contributions were acknowledged in about one-third of all documents with federal, provincial, and territorial ministries and departments highlighting this important fact the most. However, older adults' contributions were primarily attributed to "healthy" older adults—those who are "business owners and entrepreneurs, volunteers, mentors, caregivers and have a wealth of knowledge and expertise to share with other generations" (government press briefings)—again creating a divide with less independent older adults.

21.3.5 Role during the Pandemic

Across all discourses, older adults were mainly considered as "victims" of the pandemic, rather than being seen as combatting the pandemic alongside every other citizen. Rarely were they portrayed as fighters taking part in a resilient community. This assigned role of a victim suggested the need to receive care from others: "The elderly, particularly those with underlying health conditions, are at grave risk from the COVID-19 virus. We will maintain our vigilance on their behalf" (government press briefings). Academics were the least likely to attribute this role to older adults, although this role still emerged, as illustrated in this quote from a September 2020 scientific publication: "The differential mortality risks suggest that this is largely a 'gero-pandemic, which has brought the field of aging into center-stage, in both pathogenic and salutogenic contexts."[19]

In summary, results of the content analysis of the 110 documents suggest that older adults are portrayed in a homogeneous way as "vulnerable" individuals that need to be protected and as victims of the pandemic that cannot take part in the fight against the global health crisis. While ageism was criticized (although minimally) by scholars as well as older adults, the latter did so through a narrative that emphasized the negative impact of ageism on "healthy" and "active" older adults, living independently and not in long-term care.

21.4 Discussion

The goal of the current study was to examine how older adults and the aging process were portrayed during the first year of the COVID-19 pandemic and assess the degree to which such portrayals expressed ageism. Let us recall that previous research have documented the presence of ageism within multiple arenas of Western societies, such as work, education, and healthcare, long before the COVID-19 global pandemic.[20] Such is also the case as for the solidly documented negative effects of ageism at an individual, organizational, and societal level.[21] However, how and by whom is ageism expressed and conveyed—either consciously or unconsciously is yet to be fully understood, especially in the context of a global crisis whereby social tensions are exacerbated and as such pave the way for stereotyping processes against already marginalized groups. As stated previously, the public discourse (as well as public policies) play a central role in the framing and reframing of older adults, which in turn impact insights and perceptions of one's own aging process as well as relationship dynamics with older adults. The findings of our study suggest that the discourse on aging during the pandemic was framed in such a way that it restrained the psychological and social space of older adults (in addition to the physical space).

Let us recall that the media and government discourse strongly focused on both the vulnerability of "all" older adults (either consciously or unconsciously) as well as the losses related to the aging process. As such, these are not only portrayed in a homogenous and negative way but are subtly placed on the margins of society. Indeed, when all older adults are depicted as vulnerable, it implies that they need to be constantly "protected" which in turn paves the way for controlling behaviors and withdrawal of agency. While one could argue that such behaviors are acceptable as they underlie compassion (i.e., well intentioned), they nonetheless express ageism in that they lead to decision-making *on behalf* of older adults as well as patronizing attitudes. The roles attributed to older adults during the pandemic also suggest the presence of compassionate ageism in the public discourse: older adults are mostly framed as "victims" as opposed to individuals who are resilient and can take part in the collective effort to end the crisis or at least reduce its burden. All in all, these findings fall in continuity with the postulates of the stereotype content model[22] suggesting the prevalence of paternalistic prejudice as relates to older adults that, plausibly, were exacerbated during the pandemic.

On the other hand, some older adults did not keep silent when faced with compassionate ageism. Although a minority, these expressed concerns and criticized the lumping of all older adults into a vulnerability cluster; more so, they reminded the media and the government of the importance of differentiating healthy and autonomous older adults from those living in long-term care facilities. Their discourse implicitly agreed on the need for protecting the "vulnerable" older adults which they explicitly distanced themselves from. The fact that some older adults voiced their concerns against ageism during the pandemic is undoubtedly encouraging. However, their discourse points to some kind of a symbolic divide between those older adults who perfectly fit the social norm of "productive and successful" aging and those who have fallen off such norm, i.e., the "vulnerable" older adults living in long-term care facilities. This finding is particularly interesting, as it suggests the subtle presence of what Higgs and Gilleard (2021)[23] conceptualize as fourth ageism. Hence, in this conceptual framework, it is not so much the chronological age that is the driving force behind ageist stereotypes and discrimination but the (perceived) lack of agency and autonomy. Paradoxically, fourth ageism seems to stem from older adults themselves towards their own peers of the fourth age, generating intragenerational divides.

The first year of the COVID-19 pandemic was especially difficult for older adults due to forced quarantine and isolation measures, loneliness, illness, and high mortality. Moreover, as findings of the current research suggest, the public discourse, which amplified negative stereotypes against older adults, made it even more challenging. It is recommended that the media, academics, governments, and older adults themselves pay close attention to their discourses in the future to avoid ageist speech and better highlight older adults' resilience in these health crises.

Notes

1 Statistics Canada, *Impact of the COVID-19 pandemic on Canadian Seniors*, 2021, Catalogue No 75–006-X (Ottawa: Statistics Canada, October 18, 2021), online: https://www150.statcan.gc.ca/n1/pub/75-006-x/2021001/article/00008-eng.htm.

2 Parminder Raina et al, "A longitudinal analysis of the impact of the COVID-19 pandemic on the mental health of middle-aged and older adults from the Canadian Longitudinal Study on Aging" (2021) 1 *Nature Aging* 1137, online: https://doi.org/10.1038/s43587-021-00128-1.

3 Michael Liu et al, "COVID-19 in long-term care homes in Ontario and British Columbia" (2020) 192:47 *The Canadian Medical Association Journal* E1540, online: https://doi.org/10.1503/cmaj.201860.

4 Robert N. Butler, "Age-Ism: Another form of bigotry" (1969) 9:4.1 *Gerontologist* 243, online: https://doi.org/10.1093/geront/9.4_part_1.243.

5 Liat Ayalon & Clemens Tesch-Römer, eds, *Contemporary Perspectives on Ageism*, part of book series "International Perspectives on aging" vol 19 (Cham: Springer, 2018); E-Shien Chang et al, "Global reach of ageism on older persons'

health: A systematic review" (2020) 15:1 *PLoS One* e0220857; Becca R. Levy et al, "Longevity increased by positive self-perceptions of aging" (2002) 83:2 *Journal of Personality and Social Psychology* 261, online: https://doi.org/10.1037/0022-3514.83.2.261.

6 Lindssay A. Cary, Alison L. Chasteen & Jessica Remedios, "The ambivalent ageism scale: Developing and validating a scale to measure benevolent and hostile ageism" (2017) 57:2 *Gerontologist* 27, online: https://doi.org/10.1093/geront/gnw118.

7 Jan Blommaert, *Discourse: A Critical Introduction*, Series: Key Topics in Sociolinguistics (Cambridge: Cambridge University Press, 2005), online: https://doi.org/10.1017/CBO9780511610295; Marianne Jørgensen & Louise J. Phillips, *Discourse Analysis as Theory and Method* (London: SAGE Publications, 2002).

8 Vivien Burr, *Social Constructionism*, 3rd ed (London: Routledge, 2015) at 74–75.

9 Michel Foucault, *L'archéologie du savoir* (Paris: Éditions Gallimard, 1969).

10 Amanda Phelan, "Researching ageism through discourse" in Liat Ayalan & Clemens Tesch-Römer, eds, *Contemporary Perspectives on Ageism*, vol 19 (Cham: Springer, 2018) 549; Julia Rozanova, "Discourse of successful aging in *The Globe & Mail*: Insights from critical gerontology" (2010) 24:4 *Journal of Aging Studies* 213, online: https://doi.org/10.1016/j.jaging.2010.05.001.

11 Tom Gilovich et al, *Social Psychology*, 5th ed. (New York: WW Norton, 2018).

12 Anita del Rosario Zevallos Cotrina, Sofia Sabina Lavado Huarcaya & Márcia de Assunção Ferreira, "The middle-aged adult and their own old age: a structural approach to social representation" (2020) 23:6 *Revista Brasileira de Geriatria e Gerontologia*, online: https://doi.org/10.1590/1981-22562020023.200162.

13 WHO, "Global report on Ageism" (18 March 2021), online: *WHO*. www.who.int/publications/i/item/9789240016866.

14 To protect the confidentiality of each federal, provincial, and territorial government, information on the author or jurisdiction for each press briefing quote has been omitted.

15 National Post, "The COVID-19 crisis has exposed Canada's shameful treatment of its elderly" (17 April 2020), online: *National Post*. https://nationalpost.com/opinion/np-view-the-covid-19-crisis-has-exposed-canadas-shameful-treatment-of-the-elderly.

16 Ian Kimm, "Seniors should not be first for vaccination" (3 December 2020), online: *Cowichan Valley Citizen*. https://www.cowichanvalleycitizen.com/opinion/seniors-should-not-be-first-for-vaccination-815280.

17 Jane R. Rylett et al, "La COVID-19 et les priorités de recherche sur le vieillissement" (2020) 39:4 *Canadian Journal on Aging/La Revue Canadienne Du Vieillissement* 506 at 511.

18 Pierre Cliche, "J'ai 72 ans et je suis en bonne santé. Est-ce un tort?" (30 May 2020), online: *La Presse*. https://www.lapresse.ca/debats/courrier-des-lecteurs/2020-06-02/j-ai-72-ans-et-je-suis-en-bonne-sante-est-ce-un-tort.

19 Andrew Wister & Mark Speechley, "COVID-19: Pandemic Risk, Resilience and Possibilities for Aging Research" (2020) *The Canadian Journal on Aging* 1, online: www.ncbi.nlm.nih.gov/pmc/articles/PMC7322148/.

20 Ayalon & Tesch-Römer, *supra* note 5; Todd D. Nelson, ed, *Ageism: Stereotyping and Prejudice Against Older Persons* (Cambridge: MIT Press, 2002); Michael S. North & Susan T. Fiske, "An inconvenienced youth? Ageism and its potential intergenerational roots" (2012) 138:5 *The Psychological Bulletin* 982, online: https://doi.org/10.1037/a0027843.

21 Dominic Abrams, Anja Eller & Jacqueline Bryant, "An age apart: The effects of intergenerational contact and stereotype threat on performance and intergroup bias" (2006) 21:4 *Psychology and Aging* 691, online: https://doi.org/10.1037/0882-7974.21.4.691; Angelina R Sutin et al, "Perceived

discrimination and physical, cognitive, and emotional health in older adulthood" (2014) 23:2 *The American Journal of Geriatric Psychiatry* 171, online: https://doi.org/10.1016/j.jagp.2014.03.007.

22 Susan T. Fiske et al, "A model of (often mixed) stereotype content: Competence and warmth respectively follow from perceived status and competition" (2002) 82:6 *Journal of Personality and Social Psychology* 878, online: https://doi.org/10.1037/0022-3514.82.6.878.

23 Paul Higgs & Chris Gilleard, "Fourth Ageism: Real and imaginary old age" (2021) 11:1 *Societies* 12, online: https://doi.org/10.3390/soc11010012.

22

OF GOVERNMENTAL PRIORITIES, HUMAN RIGHTS, AND SOCIAL CONTROL

Prison Responses to the COVID-19 Pandemic

Adelina Iftene

22.1 Introduction

Loss of liberty is often one of the first legal consequences of committing a criminal offence. From arrest to pretrial detention, to prison sentences, to community sentences under various conditions, all of these include, to various degrees and under various legally accepted justifications, restrictions of liberty. However, even the most serious consequence of a criminal act (i.e., a custodial sentence) does not fully abolish any of the rights, liberties, and freedoms an individual has.

Incarcerated individuals maintain mobility rights within the institution and, under certain conditions, outside. They have the right to be detained in the least restrictive form of confinement for their security level, to access various spaces within an institution (e.g., the yard, the gym, the library, the visitation area, common spaces, canteen, showers, phones, etc.), and to not be confined to their cell for more time or for other reasons than those strictly regulated by national and international norms.[1] They have the right to apply for temporary leaves for work or family matters, and they have the right to be in regular contact with the outside world, especially their legal representatives.[2] Incarcerated people retain these residual liberties together with many other rights that should not be at all affected by incarceration, such as the right to healthcare.

The recognition of prisoner rights and liberties has a complicated history in Canada, and their protection, as imperfect as it is, is the result of decades of hard-fought battles by lawyers and social justice activists.[3] Upholding these rights is crucial. On an individual level, they allow for the preservation of some individual autonomy and dignity, promote well-being, and allow

DOI: 10.4324/9781003394006-30

individuals to work towards rehabilitation and reintegration. On a societal scale, they are essential in limiting and fighting against state control over individual bodies and groups that are overrepresented in prisons (e.g., Indigenous people, Black people, people with mental disabilities), not infrequently as a by-product of discriminatory laws and social policies.

Early in the COVID-19 pandemic, international human rights organizations and international health organizations warned that prisons would be some of the most impacted spaces, both because of the congregated living settings and because of the high vulnerability of those in custody. They urged governments to decarcerate to the fullest extent possible and to ensure prisoner rights were upheld during the pandemic.[4] Some of the Canadian provincial prison systems (responsible for the custody of those awaiting trial or those serving custodial sentences of less than two years) undertook measures to depopulate. However, many others, as well as the federal correctional system (responsible for those serving custodial sentences of two years or more), did not. In addition, after the first two waves of the pandemic, the incarceration rates have creeped back up, even in the provinces that were faring better.[5] Many prisons have had difficulties respecting even basic health prevention protocols, such as providing masks and soaps to those incarcerated. It is, thus, not surprising that the number of infections among incarcerated populations, federally and in some provinces, has been much higher than the rate of infection in the community.[6]

The harm inflicted on those in custody, and by extension, on the communities they belong to, went beyond endangering physical health. Not only did governments not take adequate measures to protect those in custody from infection but also, under the justification of the pandemic, prison systems and facilities were granted unfettered discretion to restrict, on a large scale, prisoner rights and residual liberties. It is these restrictions that will be the focus of this essay. In the next section, I will describe the measures taken in correctional institutions across Canada and their impact on individual rights and well-being. I will then turn to discussing the implications of these pandemic responses on society at large, on the rule of law, and on Canada's commitment to social justice.

The chapter reflects on the responses adopted earlier on, at the peak of the pandemic. Some of the pandemic measures continue to the present day, and the regular prison activities have not resumed in full, across the country, at the time of writing. That said, the restrictions that remain in place are milder now and are often not reported as "pandemic emergency measures" but rather as measures imposed due to staff shortage or budgetary issues (but which, of course, either derive from or were worsened by the pandemic). It is why this chapter often uses the past tense in describing the measures taken while acknowledging that the consequences of these measures are still unfolding.

22.2 Carceral Responses to COVID-19 and Their Impact on Prisoner Mobility and Well-Being

During the pandemic, many statutory correctional obligations were suspended, interrupted, or indefinitely withdrawn.[7] In Canada and elsewhere, these interruptions often occurred without a legislative basis. Framed as "emergency measures" taken in the name of public health, they were often the product of discretionary decisions made by commissioners, deputies, or institutional heads.[8]

22.2.1 Isolation Measures

The International Minimum Standards for the Treatment of Prisoners (The Mandela Rules) define solitary confinement as the situation where an individual is locked up for 22 hours, without meaningful human contact.[9] Because of the proven effects of isolation on mental and physical health, prolonged (over 15 days) or indefinite solitary confinement are considered torture, and thus, their use is prohibited under any circumstances, including during a pandemic.[10] In Canada, the use of certain forms of solitary confinement has been found unconstitutional under ss. 7 and 12 of the *Charter*.[11]

Yet extensive isolation was the first and main measure taken throughout the pandemic in many jurisdictions. It was reported that, in federal institutions, upon arrival, every individual was isolated for 14 days in conditions no different than solitary confinement. Also, full 24-hour isolation was used for both incubation and recovery periods, in conditions and for durations well beyond what was necessary and clinically justified.[12] In some institutions where there was an outbreak, the institution went into full lockdown, meaning nobody was allowed out of their cell for weeks, including for showers, phone calls, contact with their lawyers, or mental health services.[13]

In addition, the Office of the Correctional Investigator (OCI), the federal prison ombudsperson, reported that even in some of the institutions where there were no outbreaks, lockdowns or time in cells were also increased significantly, for weeks on end. Individuals were kept "incommunicado," in near total "cellular isolation," without access to a phone to call anyone, including family, lawyers, or the OCI.[14] There is less official information about the extent of isolation used in provincial settings, but the media and some researchers have reported similar or worse measures being taken.[15]

These measures did not prevent serious outbreaks and high rates of infections, but they did normalize lockdowns and isolation as a way of controlling prison populations.[16] They led to a significant deterioration in the mental health of the prison population, an increase in suicide attempts, unrest and violence in prisons, and a curtailing of essential prison services, including healthcare.[17] Essentially, these measures degraded the minimum standards for residual liberties and significantly jeopardized individual health.

22.2.2 Suspension of Programs and Access to Services

In most federal institutions (and likely provincial ones as well but this is less documented), programs and activities were suspended indefinitely during the pandemic. People were not able to access programs mandatory for their release or any kind of recreational activities.[18] The inability to access these programs translated into people remaining at higher levels of security since they were not able to demonstrate a decrease in their risk level, often measured by frequency and quality of engagement in educational, work, and recreational activities. Individuals were also not able to complete their correctional plans (which include a set of prison programs mandatory in order to be considered for early release), which resulted in many not being considered for early release on their early release eligibility date for no fault of their own.[19]

Being left idle has negatively impacted people's mental well-being but also their opportunities to reintegrate into society. Temporary work leaves outside prisons, institutional work programs, and preparation for release programs, all curtailed during the pandemic,[20] are essential for transitioning individuals back to the community and maximizing their chances of not being returned to prison.

22.2.3 Delayed Releases, Lack of Access to Justice, and Returns to Prison

Not only were the residual liberties of individuals hindered but also, many ended up spending time in prison beyond when they were entitled to be released to the community. As mentioned, the lack of program availability meant that they were not considered eligible for early release.[21] In addition, sometimes, even for those eligible, parole hearings were delayed due to staff shortage. Finally, there were reports of delays in releasing people who had already been granted parole.[22]

Of consequence is also the fact that during the pandemic, in most institutions, lawyer visits were suspended, and during extended periods of lockdown, incarcerated people were not able to reach their lawyer by phone either. This, of course, was particularly problematic for those in provincial prisons who were awaiting trial.[23] Moreover, lack of movement in the institutions meant people did not have access to libraries, which many depended on for preparing for their trials. The interruptions in communications with families and NGOs also meant they were not able to ask for assistance in filing or receiving documents. This undoubtedly led to delays in trial and sentencing hearings (beyond the delays already encountered because courts shut down during the first part of the pandemic) and perhaps also affected the quality of the defence individuals were able to put forward. Procedural access to justice is essential, and in the criminal justice context, it has a long-term impact on individual liberty. It is why access to lawyers and legal materials is a protected right in both national and international instruments.[24]

Finally, the fact that individuals were disconnected from their support systems (no visitations, sometimes no phone calls)[25] negatively impacted family relationships. Just like work and preparation for release programs, these are crucial for ensuring that individuals can reintegrate into society and are able to meet their conditions for release. Lack of support systems make it both less likely for people to be released on parole and more likely for those released to breach their conditions (which can be as simple as not having anywhere to stay or having a different residence from the one they initially declared) and thus be returned to prison.

22.3 Beyond Prison Walls: The Carceral Responses to COVID-19 in the Broader Context

The carceral responses to the pandemic constitute, at best, a missed opportunity to engage in decarceration measures for low-risk populations (including those serving intermittent sentences, short sentences, those close to release) and to promote the increased use of community sanctions.[26]

On a less generous take, these measures constituted a regressive move in the fight for social justice. As illustrated earlier, the pandemic was used to justify large-scale human rights abuses and to bolster security. In addition, recent steps towards reform were swiftly curtailed, and the pandemic was used as a justification to continue and, indeed, to increase the use of problematic pre-pandemic practices. As but one example, in 2019, as a result of litigation,[27] a Bill was passed that allegedly abolished solitary confinement in federal prisons.[28] Instead, supportive units were to be created, called Structured Intervention Units (SIU), where individuals would have access to programs and to adequate mental health services. Since the conditions were not meant to emulate solitary confinement, there was no limit on how long an individual could be kept in those places. Dr. Anthony Doob, who chaired an external oversight SIU implementation panel, together with his colleague Dr. Jane Sprott, reported extensively on the first year of the SIUs existence. The data CSC provided them with showed that SIU conditions were no different than solitary confinement, except that people could be legally held in these units for much longer.[29] Black individuals were the most likely to experience the highest rates of detention in these places and the longest stays.[30] The CSC responded to these reports explaining that the reason as to why the implementation was problematic was only because it coincided with the pandemic. Doob and Sprott provided a follow-up report, showing, with CSC's own data, that the two events were unrelated, that the implementation of SIUs and their misuse started over six months prior to the pandemic, and that its use during the pandemic was not necessarily related to institutional lockdowns.[31] Regardless, CSC maintained their justification, and to this day, the SIUs are still versions of solitary confinement.

At their worst, the measures taken constituted a new justification for yet again using criminal law tools to enhance control over certain populations through a narrative of where danger comes from, how risk is defined, and what counts as public safety. It is inescapable that the human rights abuses that took place in prison during the pandemic primarily impacted Indigenous and Black people, people living with mental health and other disabilities, and people living in poverty. These populations are notoriously overrepresented in prisons, and they are also disproportionately impacted by conditions of confinement.[32] It is hardly a surprise that the federal prisons most affected by outbreaks were those with the highest number of Indigenous people in custody,[33] while Black prisoners were, as discussed, some of the most impacted by isolation measures, such as the abusive use of the new SIUs.

It is difficult to see these impacts as unfortunate side effects of necessary emergency measures. Governments had received timely notice and guidance on prison policies and best practices during the pandemic.[34] There were multiple waves of the pandemic that also allowed for the further development of evidence-based practices. Governments were well informed that people in custody are at higher risk of getting the infection and developing complications from it. In addition, prison outbreaks will prolong the life of the pandemic in the community, as there is a continuous stream of people coming and going from prisons, such as officers and other prison workers, who return to the community at the end of their shifts.

Knowing full well who the measures will impact most, ineffective security responses were used. The message sent to the community was clear: incarcerated people, most from Indigenous, Black, and poor communities, regardless of what they have done, are more dangerous than a deadly virus. Risking their well-being by exposing them, and by extension, the community at large, to increased risk of infection and other harms due to confinement is considered better than having these people on the streets, despite the demonstrated low public safety risk many of them present.[35]

In this context, perhaps, the prison responses to the pandemic were not a missed opportunity at all from the state's perspective. Instead, in an era where efforts for reconciliation and social justice are more pronounced than ever, and where there is an understanding that achieving such goals will require a move away from using criminal justice as a tool of oppression, the pandemic provided the opportunity to increase, once again through criminal justice administration, the suppression of rights and the control of groups seeking social liberation.

22.4 Concluding Thoughts

The Canadian and provincial governments chose to ignore the evidence-based pandemic guidelines for correctional settings provided by health and human rights organizations and, instead, largely responded to a public health crisis by strengthening security measures. These security measures indefinitely suspended individual rights, including mobility rights and residual liberties within and outside institutions.

Essentially, the pandemic provided a widely accepted justification for violations of even the most basic human rights in the name of an undefined notion of public safety. Various court challenges to conditions of confinement and carceral treatment during the pandemic are currently underway, including *Charter* challenges and class actions. It will be up to the courts to reinstate the rights lost during the pandemic and to hold the governments accountable for the significant abuses. How these cases go will be a test on the ability and desire to uphold the rule of law and, given the overrepresentation of marginalized groups in prison, the commitment to reconciliation and social justice more broadly.

Notes

1 See, e.g., *Corrections and Conditional Release Act*, SC 1992, c 20 at ss. 68–71 [CCRA]; UNODC, *The Mandela Standard Minimum Rules for the Protection of Prisoners* (Vienna: UNODC, 2015) at Rules 3–5, 43–45, 64, online (pdf): www.unodc.org/documents/justice-and-prison-reform/Nelson_Mandela_Rules-E-ebook.pdf [https://perma.cc/BAZ5-P8MB] [Mandela Rules]; in Canada, various aspects of these residual liberties are also constitutionally protected under the writ of habeas corpus and under s. 7 of the *Canadian Charter of Rights and Freedoms*, Part 1 of the *Constitution Act, 1982*, being Schedule B to the *Canada Act 1982* (UK), 1982, c11 [*Charter*], the right not to be deprived of life, liberty, and security of the person in accordance with the principles of fundamental justice (see *BCCLA and JHSC v Attorney General of Canada*, 2018 BCSC 62 [*BCCLA*]; *Canadian Civil Liberties Association v Canada (Attorney General)*, 2019 ONCA 243 [*CCLA*]).

2 See, e.g., *CCRA*, *supra* note 1 at ss. 17–18, 115; Mandela Rules, *supra* note 1 at Rules 58–61.

3 See, e.g., Michael Jackson, *Justice Behind Walls: Human Rights in Canadian Prisons* (Vancouver: Douglas & McIntyre, 2002); Adelina Iftene, *Punished for Aging: Vulnerability, Rights and Access to Justice in Canadian Penitentiaries* (Toronto: University of Toronto Press, 2019).

4 See, e.g., World Health Organization, "Infection prevention and control during health care when novel coronavirus (nCoV) infection is suspected" (World Health Organization Publications, 19 March 2020), online (pdf): www.who.int/publications/i/item/10665-331495 [https://perma.cc/5WNC-7URB] ["WHO"]; International Committee of the Red Cross, News Release, "COVID-19: Authorities must protect health of detainees, staff and ultimately surrounding communities" (7 April 2020), online: www.icrc.org/en/document/covid-19-places-detention-must-protect-health-detainees-staff-and-ultimately-surrounding [https://perma.cc/MZ25-PCYX] ["Red Cross"]; UN, Subcommittee on Prevention of Torture and Other Cruel, Inhuman or Degrading Treatment or Punishment, *Advice of the*

Subcommittee to States parties and national preventive mechanisms relating to the coronavirus disease (COVID-19) pandemic, UN Doc CAT/OP/10, 2020 at 3 ["UN Subcommittee"].

5 For a description of the rates of decarceration, both provincially and federally, see Adelina Iftene, "COVID-19, human rights and public health in Prisons: A case study of nova scotia's experience during the first wave of the pandemic" (2021) 44:2 *The Dalhousie Law Journal.*

6 Canada, Office of the Correctional Investigator, *OCI Annual Report 2020–21* (Ottawa: OCI, 2021) at iii, online (pdf): www.oci-bec.gc.ca/cnt/rpt/pdf/annrpt/annrpt20202021-eng.pdf [https://perma.cc/RZR9-SR2B] [OCI 2020–21]; Anthony Doob, "Understanding imprisonment in the time of COVID-19, report" (2020) [Unpublished, archived at University of Toronto] at 1–2; for infection rates in provincial and federal systems, see "Tracking the politics of criminalization and punishment in Canada" (8 March 2022), online (blog): http://tpcp-canada.blogspot.com/ [https://perma.cc/2YZV-ZB67].

7 Canada, Office of the Correctional Investigator, *Third COVID 19 Status Update* (Ottawa: OCI, 23 February 2021) at 13, online (pdf): www.oci-bec.gc.ca/cnt/rpt/pdf/oth-aut/oth-aut20210223-eng.pdf> [https://perma.cc/C7CN-2RNC] [OCI, Update 3].

8 Frieder Dunkel, Stefan Harrendorf & Dirk van Zyl Smit, "Summary analysis of the state of prisons and penal policies before, during and after the COVID-19 pandemic" in Frieder Dunkel, Stefan Harrendorf & Dirk van Zyl Smit, eds, *The Impact of COVID-19 on Prison Conditions and Penal Policy* (London: Routledge, 2022) at 657 [Dunkel et al, "Impact of COVID-19"].

9 Mandela Rules, *supra* note 1.

10 Roisin Mulgrew & Dirk Van Zyl Smit, "International Rights and Covid-19 in prisons: medical isolation and independent oversight" in Dunkel et al, "Impact of COVID-19", *supra* note 8 at 598–599; Mandela Rules, *supra* note 1.

11 *BCCLA*, *supra* note 1; *CCLA*, *supra* note 1.

12 OCI 2020–21, *supra* note 6 at 79. For similar observations in the context of coercive psychiatric care, see Bernheim in this volume.

13 "Solitary by Any Other Name: The ongoing use of isolation in Canada's federal prisons" (2020) at 34, online (pdf): *West Coast Prison Justice Society.* https://prisonjustice.org/wp-content/uploads/2020/11/Solitary-by-another-name-report.pdf [https://perma.cc/D86P-U3K8] [WCPJS].

14 Canada, Office of the Correctional Investigator, *COVID-19 Status Update* (Ottawa: OCI, 2020) at 6, online (pdf): www.oci-bec.gc.ca/cnt/rpt/pdf/oth-aut/oth-aut20200423-eng.pdf [https://perma.cc/453C-ZMH7] [OCI].

15 See, e.g., Iftene, *supra* note 5 at 14–16; Sarah Smellie, "Calls grow for inmate releases as COVID-19 cases climb in Canada's jails and prisons" (4 January 2022), online: *CityNews.* halifax.citynews.ca [perma.cc/8Q6U-TXGC]; Ainslie MacLellan, "Inmates, advocates denounce 'inhuman' 24/7 COVID-19 lockdowns at Quebec's Leclerc jail" (11 February 2022), online: *CBC News.* cbc.ca [https://perma.cc/93VX-B9B5].

16 WCPJS, *supra* note 13 at 35.

17 OCI, *supra* note 14 at 5–6.

18 OCI, Update 3, *supra* note 7 at 20; OCI 2020–21, *supra* note 6 at v.

19 OCI, Update 3, *supra* note 7 at 20; OCI 2020–21, *supra* note 6 at v.

20 OCI, Update 3, *supra* note 7 at 20; OCI 2020–21, *supra* note 6 at v; Sandra Bucerius, Rosemary Ricciardelli & Luca Berardi "Canada," in Dunkel et al, "Impact of COVID-19", *supra* note 8 at 71.

21 Canada, Office of the Correctional Investigator, *Second COVID-19 Update* (Ottawa: OCI, 2020), online (pdf): www.oci-bec.gc.ca/cnt/rpt/pdf/oth-aut/oth-aut20200619-eng.pdf [https://perma.cc/775Z-HL9Q].

22 Doob, *supra* note 6 at 11–17.
23 Iftene, *supra* note 5 at 16; Sheila Wildeman, "East Coast Prison Justice Visiting Committee June Reporting Letter" (30 June 2022) [unpublished].
24 See, e.g., *Charter*, *supra* note 1, s. 11; Mandela Rules, *supra* note 1 at Rule 61.
25 OCI, *supra* note 14 at 5–6.
26 On the importance of criminal justice reform in light of the pandemic, see Iftene, *supra* note 5 at 16.
27 *BCCLA*, *supra* note 1; *CCLA*, *supra* note 1.
28 Bill C-83, an act to amend the Corrections and Conditional Release Act and another Act, 1st Sess, 42nd Parl, 2018, c 27 (assented to 21 June 2019).
29 Anthony N Doob & Jane B Sprott, "Understanding the Operation of Correctional Service Canada's Structured Intervention Units: Some Preliminary Findings" (2020), online (pdf): https://drive.google.com/file/d/1FiN_l3hbBUU-KNIHFQ3g4auN59KyRoOn/view [https://perma.cc/9A2K-BLC4]; Jane B Sprott & Anthony N Doob, "Solitary Confinement, Torture, and Canada's Structured Intervention Units" (2021), online (pdf): www.crimsl.utoronto.ca/sites/www.crimsl.utoronto.ca/files/Torture%20Solitary%20SIUs%20%28Sprott%20Doob%2023%20Feb%202021%29.pdf [https://perma.cc/X67L-Y3PH].
30 Jane B Sprott, Anthony N Dob & Adelina Iftene, "Do independent external decision makers ensure that 'An inmate's confinement in a structured intervention unit is to end as soon as possible'? [*Corrections and Conditional Release Act*, Section 33]" (2021) at 9, online (pdf): www.crimsl.utoronto.ca/sites/www.crimsl.utoronto.ca/files/SIU_Report4-IEDM%28SprottDoobIftene%2910May21.pdf [https://perma.cc/H2SJ-EHDN].
31 Jane B Sprott & Anthony N Doob, "Is there clear evidence that the problems that have been identified with the operation of correctional service Canada's 'structured intervention units' were caused by the COVID-19 outbreak? An examination of data from correctional service Canada" (2020), online (pdf): https://drive.google.com/file/d/1RMye7xxEZONGA0mS8Arb0G_yheo2k2ui/view [https://perma.cc/HE6U-9BK3].
32 There are numerous official reports on the increased number of Indigenous and Black people in the criminal justice system and calls for action. See *Honouring the Truth, Reconciling for the Future: Summary of the Final Report of the Truth and Reconciliation Commission of Canada* (Ottawa: Truth and Reconciliation Commission of Canada, 2015) at 170–172; Canada, National Inquiry into Murdered and Missing Indigenous Women and Girls, *Reclaiming Power and Place: The Final Report of the National Inquiry into Missing and Murdered* (Vancouver: Privy Council Office, 2019) at 635–645; Scot Wortley, *Halifax, Nova Scotia: Street Checks Report* (Halifax: Nova Scotia Human Rights Commission, 2019); UNHRC, *Report of the Working Group of Experts on People of African Descent on its mission to Canada*, UNGAOR, 36th Sess, UN Doc A/HRC/36/60/Add1 (2017).
33 OCI, *supra* note 14.
34 See WHO, *supra* note 4; Red Cross, *supra* note 4; UN Subcommittee, *supra* note 4.
35 Doob, *supra* note 6. For a similar argument in the context of coercive psychiatric care, see Bernheim in this volume.

23

EXTENDING THE BOUNDARIES OF THE PSYCHIATRIC HOSPITAL

The Use and Misuse of Psychiatric Coercion during the COVID-19 Pandemic in Quebec and Ontario

Emmanuelle Bernheim

23.1 Introduction: The Rise of Psychiatric Coercion

Over the past few decades, the boundaries around involuntary admission and treatment in psychiatry ("psychiatric coercion" or "coercive psychiatry") have become blurred. On the one hand, between the 1970s and 2000, the use of involuntary admissions decreased, along with the number of available hospital beds. On the other hand, in order to rationalize expenses, alternatives to involuntary admission were developed.[1] The use of involuntary hospitalization and treatment in the community ("community treatment order," "compulsory community care," "authorization for care") became increasingly important in several jurisdictions.

This coercive care blurs the boundaries between hospital, clinic, and community and between what is coerced and what is voluntary. In many jurisdictions, such as Ontario, community treatment orders ("CTOs") are agreed upon by psychiatrists and their patients, who consent to undergo treatment in exchange for their release from hospital. This freedom is conditional on their compliance with treatment, with involuntary admission remaining a possibility, like a sword of Damocles hanging over their heads. As freedom is exchanged for submission to treatment, the meaning and value of consent in psychiatry is diminished, enabling practices that are not permissible in other areas of the healthcare field. In practice, as freedom is exchanged for submission to treatment, hospitals move into communities. In the days of the asylum, coercion was explicit. The coercion of current practices, in contrast, is implicit, masked as negotiation and consent, taking place in the private sphere of homes—what some authors have called the "invisible asylum."[2]

DOI: 10.4324/9781003394006-31

Although the clinical effectiveness of these community-based measures has been controversial,[3] their coercive dimension is significant. In addition to threatening the rights to freedom and integrity, psychiatric coercion allows for exceptional surveillance and control. Apart from criminal law and child welfare, coercive psychiatry is the only way to impose a place to live, to prohibit the use of drugs or alcohol, and to deploy a panoply of professionals to document a person's daily activities, in addition to imposing medication. These exceptional powers—implemented on the basis of indeterminate and controversial concepts such as risk and capacity—make psychiatry a very powerful tool for monitoring and controlling poor, racialized, and marginalized people.[4] Moreover, the use of psychiatric coercion has been steadily increasing for over a decade in most of the northern global countries,[5] despite significant differences in implementation criteria and procedures, suggesting that legal frameworks are not a central determinant of psychiatric practices and, in particular, of coercive practices.

The COVID-19 pandemic appears to have been a pivotal moment in the use of coercive psychiatry. During the pandemic, while social inequalities worsened, health and social services were less and less accessible. Not surprisingly, international research shows that the use of psychiatric coercion has increased during this period.[6]

Using the Quebec and Ontario cases as examples, I will (1) show how the use of coercive psychiatry during the COVID-19 pandemic reveals systemic adverse treatment against most marginalized people. In light of the inconsistency of court decisions, I will (2) demonstrate that coercive psychiatry was used during this period for control and surveillance purposes, not for mental or even public health reasons. I will then conclude with a reflection on the slippery slope the judicial practices represent when it comes to psychiatric coercion.

23.1.1 Psychiatric Coercion and Systemic Adverse Treatment in Quebec and Ontario during the COVID-19 Pandemic

The comparative study of the use of involuntary admission and treatment in the provinces of Ontario and Quebec during the COVID-19 pandemic is significant in several respects. First, consistent with international trends, the use of coercive psychiatric practices has been increasing in these two provinces over more than a decade, including during the COVID-19 pandemic.[7] Second, the criteria and procedures for implementing involuntary admission and treatment are substantially different in the two provinces. Third, the role of the Quebec and Ontario courts in the context of coercive psychiatry differs significantly. In Ontario, the Consent and Capacity Board, an administrative tribunal, conducts a review at the request of a person involuntarily admitted or treated based on the decision of a psychiatrist. In Quebec, hospitals must apply to the civil court to obtain a court order before admitting or treating a person against their will. Finally, from the beginning of the COVID-19 pandemic, both provinces issued decrees or orders allowing the involuntary quarantine of people who resisted public health restrictions or who were at risk of contracting or transmitting COVID-19.

To document the justifications for the use of psychiatric coercion during the pandemic, I collected court decisions regarding involuntary admission and treatment from the Consent and Capacity Board, the Court of Quebec, and the Superior Court of Quebec, available in the CanLII database between March 2020, when governments in Canada declared a state of emergency due to the COVID-19 pandemic and September 2022. I obtained 523 Ontario decisions and 144 Quebec decisions, a difference that can be explained by, among other factors, the fact that many Quebec decisions are rendered orally and are not published. Since no reliable public statistics on the use of psychiatric coercion are available in either province,[8] it is impossible to know the extent to which the figures obtained from the database reflect a broader reality.

Many of the decisions are short and mention the pandemic only briefly (e.g., "considering the COVID-19 pandemic" in the Quebec decisions). I randomly selected decisions that allowed a discourse analysis (Ontario = 42, Quebec = 38). This body of decisions is supplemented by higher-court decisions—two decisions of the Ontario Superior Court of Justice, sitting in judicial review of the Consent and Capacity Board, and one decision of the Ontario Court of Appeal. No decisions of the Court of Appeal of Quebec rendered during this period were relevant. Since the Ontario decisions are written in English and the Quebec decisions in French, I will quote only from the Ontario decisions to avoid the risk of altering the meaning through my translation.

Despite the significant legal and contextual differences, similarities are evident between the decisions of the Ontario and Quebec courts, with the risk of contracting and/or transmitting COVID-19 used to partly justify psychiatric coercion.[9] Decisions are peppered with references to precarious living conditions—living in homelessness or in unsanitary housing, lack of hygiene, promiscuity, etc.—that do not allow for the implementation of public health restrictions, such as lockdowns or social distancing. For example, in one of its decisions, the Consent and Capacity Board did the following:

> concluded that if AT [the defendant] left the closely monitored and structured hospital environment, he was likely to suffer serious physical impairment whether from becoming malnourished to the point of starvation or being unable to keep himself safe from Covid-19, or quite possibly both together.[10]

In some cases, psychiatrists and relatives reported being unsure whether defendants were following the public health restrictions or understood their importance. In the vast majority of cases, Quebec and Ontario courts recognized the need for involuntary admission or treatment, accepting arguments about the risks of COVID-19.

These court decisions and the practices they reflect, in addition to being a dangerous expansion of the legal concepts used to admit and treat involuntarily in psychiatry, adversely impact members of marginalized groups. First, they create a double standard between wealthy people and poor people, between those who were able to choose whether or not to follow the public health restrictions and those who had no choice because of their living conditions. Indeed, decrees and orders to force quarantine were used very infrequently in the general population, even though surveys conducted during the period of the study show that a growing proportion of Canadians were not following public health restrictions. Second, while governments tried to minimize the length and number of hospital stays to reduce the spread of disease and to unburden the healthcare system, involuntary psychiatric admissions took place under poor conditions. Psychiatric facilities are not set up for infection control and were inadequately prepared to deal with infection management; inpatients remained isolated in their rooms, sometimes for months on end, including at times when the general population came out of lockdown. Although little information was made available, some hospitals reported an increase in the use of seclusion rooms and restraints to manage crises and incidents. Community groups and relatives of people in psychiatric wards and hospitals reported not being able to communicate with them and being concerned about their mental health.[11] Third, despite these particularly severe restrictions, several outbreaks occurred in psychiatric facilities, exposing hospitalized individuals to a risk that involuntary admissions and treatments were intended to minimize. People subjected to coercive psychiatry during the COVID-19 pandemic experienced much harsher restrictions than the general population while being exposed to high COVID-19 risk.

23.1.2 Coercive Psychiatry, Control, and Surveillance during the COVID-19 Pandemic

The use and misuse of coercive psychiatry during the COVID-19 pandemic demonstrates that the concerns underlying these practices are not related to mental or public health but to the control and surveillance of the most marginalized social groups. I will discuss this issue in light of the inconsistency of court decisions.

In addition to the adverse nature of the coercive psychiatry that was used, in practice, to enforce quarantine, and the extraordinarily strict conditions of hospitalization, several court decisions have effectively placed people at risk of contracting COVID-19. One example is the authorization for care issued by the Superior Court of Quebec in the spring of 2020 to force a 63-year-old man to enter a long-term care facility. At the time of this decision, Quebec was the province most affected by the pandemic in Canada, especially in long-term care facilities. The repeated COVID-19 outbreaks, as well as the lack of staff and the deplorable sanitary conditions in these facilities—which, at that time, made daily headlines—were not even mentioned in the judicial decision.[12] Another example is a decision of the Ontario Superior Court of Justice. In this case, the appellant argued that the community treatment order issued by the Consent and Capacity Board required him "to travel across Toronto and Peel Region to periodic appointments [. . .] in ways which did not accommodate for applicable public health precautions."[13] According to the Court, it was unreasonable for the Board "to require the Appellant to risk being infected by COVID-19 in order to comply with the Community treatment order."[14]

The review of the Ontario and Quebec court decisions thus demonstrates that coercive psychiatry, though purportedly intended in some cases to protect some people from COVID-19–related risks, in practice exposed other people in other instances to increased risks. However, the quality of evidence of risk of contracting and/or transmitting COVID-19 in support of or against coercive psychiatry was fundamentally different. On the one hand, when hospitals claimed, to argue in favour of coercion, that a person could contract and/or transmit COVID-19, the arguments were based on impressions and hearsay about their living conditions and behavior. Apart from the few cases where people themselves said they did not follow the public health restrictions, psychiatrists or relatives reported believing that individuals did not understand or follow those measures. Courts, applying the precautionary principle, accepted these arguments without noting the weakness of the evidence. In an Ontario Consent and Capacity Board decision, for example, the psychiatrist testified that "LG [the defendant] would not engage in the measures which have been put in place to reduce the risk of contracting and spreading COVID -19."[15] The Board concluded:

> on a balance of probabilities based on clear, cogent, and compelling evidence that as a result of mental disorder, if not in hospital, LG would likely suffer serious physical impairment in the form of medical complications associated with epilepsy, titration of anti-psychotic medication, and potentially COVID -19.[16]

On the other hand, the courts did not consider the risk of contracting COVID-19 in healthcare facilities, and the severity of the restrictions in those facilities, in an overall risk assessment or a cost-benefit calculation. Before the Ontario Superior Court of Justice, where the appellant claimed that the community treatment order issued by the Consent and Capacity Board did put him at risk of contracting COVID-19, the respondent, his psychiatrist, replied that there was no evidence to support this argument. For the Court, the pandemic and the public health restrictions are common knowledge and do not require the submission of evidence, a principle largely ignored in the decisions studied. For example, the Consent and Capacity Board, relying on the psychiatrist's argument that no staff or patients in their facility had COVID-19, considered that "[w]hile the Board could take judicial notice of the COVID-19 pandemic, a blanket statement about its effect in detention units would likely not be sufficient to exercise a discretion that is to be used cautiously and in 'egregious' situations."[17]

Clearly, courts were more seriously concerned about a marginalized person potentially transmitting COVID-19 to the public than about the same person potentially contracting COVID-19 in an outbreak-prone psychiatric facility or being subjected to severe restrictions, with potentially harmful consequences.

Court decisions are inconsistent in several respects and reflect a wide variation in the use of psychiatric coercion. The expansive interpretation of the legal concept of risk to include a variety of considerations, such as those related to COVID-19, demonstrates how easy it is to instrumentalize both law and coercive psychiatry for various purposes. While some might suggest that trying to control the spread of COVID-19 through psychiatry is a lesser evil under the circumstances, the analysis of the decisions shows that the courts have acceded to these arguments at face value, without sufficiently discussing them. More worryingly, the rights of those targeted by coercive psychiatry were not at the core of the judicial arguments.

This finding is consistent with research on judicial practices in matters of psychiatric coercion in Canadian courts[18] and around the world.[19] On the one hand, this research shows that hospitalization and treatment are generally seen as positive and necessary for people with psychiatric diagnoses.[20] On the other hand, coercion and infringement of rights are seen as lesser evils when it comes to protecting the defendants or other persons from risk, even hypothetical ones.[21] Through these practices, courts have not only been failing to protect and enforce rights; analysis of the decisions made during the COVID-19 pandemic shows that they have also been failing to protect health and mental health, as well as to enforce public health measures.

23.2 Conclusion: The Slippery Slope of Judicial Practices in Matter of Psychiatric Coercion

The role of the courts in coercive psychiatry is ambiguous—between the protection of the rights of defendants, including the right to consent to treatment, and the protection of health and safety of the same people, sometimes against their own will. The purpose of the judicialization and proceduralization of involuntary admission and treatment is twofold: first, taking decisions out of the hands of psychiatrists and involving a neutral third party, and second, making coercive psychiatry a matter of rights, not only a clinical matter.

By failing to protect and enforce laws and rights, courts have played a major role in expanding, in practice, the boundaries of the psychiatric hospital. The results of the analysis of court decisions during the COVID-19 pandemic demonstrate that arguments outside the legal framework were readily used by hospitals and psychiatrists to justify new uses of coercive psychiatry. It is evident that such arguments might be used in the future, especially since the current increase in the use of coercive psychiatry can hardly be justified other than by an extensible interpretation of the legal criteria and by the development of new uses and practices.

Considering the current legal frameworks, the expansion of the psychiatric hospital's boundaries is possible only through the law and the courts. In addition to the questions that these findings raise in terms of the role of judges and lawyers, it may be concluded that the judicial system has become an essential component of the "invisible asylum," exercising and facilitating coercive psychiatry inside and outside the psychiatric institution—and thus undermining already precarious rights.

Notes

1 Stephan Sjöström, Liv Zetterberg & Urban Markström, "Why Community Compulsion Became the Solution: Reforming Mental Health Law in Sweden" (2011) 34:6 *International Journal of Law and Psychiatry* 419.
2 Lucy Series, *Deprivation of Liberty in the Shadows of the Institution* (Bristol: Bristol University Press, 2022).
3 Jorun Rugkåsa, "Effectiveness of Community Treatment Orders: The International Evidence" (2016) 61:1 *The Canadian Journal of Psychiatry* 15.
4 China Mills, "The Psychiatrization of Poverty: Rethinking the Mental Health—Poverty Nexus" (2015) 9:5 *Social and Personality Psychology Compass* 213; Phoebe Barnett & al, "Ethnic Variations in Compulsory Detention under the Mental Health Act: A Systematic Review and Meta-analysis of International Data" (2019) 6 *Lancet Psychiatry* 305 (for a similar observation in the context of prisons, see Iftene in this volume).
5 Luke Sheridan Rains et al, "Variations in Patterns of Involuntary hospitalization and in Legal Frameworks: An International Comparative Study" (2019) 6:5 *The Lancet* 403; Jorun Rugkasa & Tom Burns, "Community Treatment Orders: Are they Useful?" (2017) 23:4 *BJPsych Advances* 222.
6 See, e.g., Julia Ambrosetti et al, "Impact of the COVID-19 Pandemic on Psychiatric Admissions to a Large Swiss Emergency Department: An Observational Study" (2021) 18 *International Journal of Environmental Research and Public Health* 1174; Bernardo Carpiniello et al, "Psychiatry during the Covid-19 Pandemic: A Survey on Mental Health Departments in Italy" (2020) 20 *BMC Psychiatry* 593; Erich Flammer & al, "Increase in Coercive Measures in Psychiatric Hospitals in Germany during the COVID-19 Pandemic" (2022) 17:8 *PLoS One* e0264046; Mohammed J. Abbas, "The Early Impact of the COVID-19 Pandemic on Acute Care Mental Health Services" (2021) 72:3 *Psychiatric Services* 242.
7 In Ontario, involuntary admission has increased by nearly 75% between 2009 and 2013. In Quebec, involuntary admission increased by 29% and forced treatment by 45% between 2015 and 2020. See Michael Lebenbaum et al, "Prevalence and Predictors of Involuntary Psychiatric Hospital Admissions in Ontario,

Canada: A Population-based Linked Administrative Database Study" (2018) 4:2 *The British Journal of Psychiatry Open* 31; Emmanuelle Bernheim, "The triumph of the 'Therapeutic' in Quebec Courts: Mental Health, Behavioral Reform and the Decline of Rights" (2022) 38 *Windsor Yearbook of Access to Justice* 125.

8 As part of access-to-information requests, the Quebec Ministry of Justice has provided statistics on the number of judicial trials for involuntary hospitalization and authorization for care that differ significantly from one document to another, suggesting that public data collection is unreliable.

9 An international trend. See Azgad Gold, Rael D. Strous & Paul S. Appelbaum, "COVID-19 and Involuntary Hospitalization: Navigating the Challenge" (2020) 7:7 *Lancet Psychiatry* 572.

10 *AT(Re)*, 2020 CanLII 33214 (ON CCB).

11 Suze G Berkhout, Lindsey MacGillivray & Kathleen Sheehan, "Carceral Politics, Inpatient Psychiatry, and the Pandemic: Risk, Madness, and Containment in COVID-19" (2021) 4:1 *International Journal of Computing and Digital Systems* 74; Emmanuelle Bernheim, "Pandemic Injustice in Mental Health: Quebec Punitive Risk-based Approach in the Coronavirus Era" (2021) 10 *The Annual Review of Interdisciplinary Justice Research* 270. For similar observations in the context of prisons, see Iftene in this volume.

12 Mauricie-et-du-Centre-du-Québec Integrated University Health and Social Services Center (CIUSSS MCQ) c RM, 2020 QCCS 1666 (CanLII).

13 *Edem v Kantor*, 2020 ONSC 4729 (CanLII) at para 28.

14 *Ibid* at para 31.

15 *LG (Re)*, 2020 CanLII 33296 (ON CCB) at 7.

16 *Ibid* at 10.

17 *BD (Re)*, 2020 CanLII 32317 (ON CCB) at 19 (between quotation marks in the decision). See also *KM v Banik*, 2020 ONSC 4829 (CanLII); *KM v Banik*, 2021 ONCA 481 (CanLII).

18 Anne Nordberg, "Therapeutic Governmentality and Biopower in a Canadian Mental Health Court" (2016) 11:2 BioSocieties 240; Tess Sheldon, Karen Spector & Mercedes Perez, "Re-Centering Equality from the Inside: The Interplay Between Sections 7 and 15 of the Charter in Challenges to Psychiatric Detention" (2016) 35:2 *National Junior Classical League* 193; Laura Johnston, *Operating in Darkness: BC's Mental Health Act Detention System*, Community Law Program, Community Legal Assistance Society, 2017; Bernheim, *supra* note 7.

19 Katey Thom & Ivana Nakarada-Kordic, "Mental Health Review Tribunals in Action: A Systematic Review of the Empirical Literature" (2014) 21 *Psychiatry, Psychology and Law* 126; Agnieszka Doll, "Lawyering for the 'Mad': Social Organization and Legal Aid Representation in Involuntary Admissions Cases in Poland" in Bonnie Burstow, ed, *Psychiatry Interrogated* (New York: Palgrave Macmillan, 2016) 183; William Brooks, "The Tail Still Wags the Dog: The Pervasive and Inappropriate Influence by the Psychiatric Profession on the Civil Commitment Process" (2010) 86 *NDL Rev* 260; Series, *supra* note 2.

20 James Davies, ed, *The Sedated Society: The Causes and Harms of our Psychiatric Drug Epidemic* (New York: Palgrave Macmillan, 2017); Bonnie Burstow, *Psychiatry and the Business of Madness: An Ethical and Epistemological Accounting* (New York: Palgrave Macmillan, 2015).

21 Nicholas Rose, "Governing Risky Individuals: The Role of Psychiatry in New Regimes of Control" (1998) 5:2 *Phonographic Performance Limited* 177; Paul S. Applebaum, "Dangerous Persons, Moral Panic, and the Uses of Psychiatry" (2003) 54:4 *Psychiatric Services* 441.

24

PUNISHING MOBILITY

Curfews and Homelessness in Quebec during the COVID-19 Pandemic

Véronique Fortin and Céline Bellot

24.1 Introduction

On January 6, 2021, at 5 P.M., the Prime Minister of the province of Quebec, François Legault, gave a highly anticipated press conference on the new measures his government would be implementing to curb the spread of COVID-19. Cases of COVID-19 were fast increasing, with an average of around 2,500 new cases a day;[1] hospitals were overcrowded, the population was still largely unvaccinated, and the province's COVID-19 death toll kept rising, with more than 350 COVID-19 deaths in the first week of January.[2] So on that early January evening, Legault declared, with a shaking voice, and visibly more nervous than usual, that we needed a shock treatment to limit contacts, especially in private homes:

> Starting next Saturday, for four weeks, we are going to have a curfew in Quebec, from 8pm until 5am, which means that except to go to work, people will not be allowed to be outside their residence, between 8pm and 5am, from January 9th until February 8th.[3]

Quebecers will brutally remember that in most regions of the province, this curfew did not last four weeks but five months. Moreover, another curfew was imposed again from December 31, 2021, until January 17, 2022.

In this chapter, we will first explain the legal underpinnings of the Quebec curfew; we will then present some results of a research project on the punitive strategy of the Quebec government during the first year and a half of the COVID-19 pandemic; and we will finally argue that the curfew amounts to a legal technology of bordering, tragically pushing people in spaces of

DOI: 10.4324/9781003394006-32

nonexistence. We will conclude with a plea to decision-makers to avoid adopting punitive public health policies, such as curfews, that disproportionately impact the most vulnerable.

24.2 The Legal Mechanics of the Quebec Curfew

Quebec was the only Canadian province to impose a curfew during the COVID-19 pandemic.[4] The legal technology implementing the curfew is a government Order in Council issued under the *Public Health Act* (*PHA*).[5] Section 123 of the *PHA* allows the government, while a public health emergency is in effect, to order any "measure necessary to protect the health of the population." In Quebec, the public health emergency was in effect from March 13, 2020, until June 1, 2022. The Order in Council no 2–2021 made on January 8, 2021, said the following: "between 8:00 p.m. and 5:00 a.m., no person may be outside the person's residence or its equivalent, or its grounds."[6] Several exceptions applied, and people were allowed to be outside for a variety of reasons, such as to perform employment work or provide professional services, to obtain care or services required by a person's state of health, or even for the needs of their dog. Any person violating a measure imposed in an Order in Council or a Ministerial Order during a public health emergency could be found guilty of a regulatory offence and be liable to a fine of $1,000 to $6,000.[7] In other words, police officers had the power to ticket people for being outside their residence after 8 P.M. As we will see in the next section, this power was heavily relied on.

At the beginning of January, no specific exception existed for homeless people, with the very unfortunate result that they were not exempted from a rule requiring them to be in a residence they did not have. The Prime Minister mentioned they should be in shelters after 8 P.M. and even declared in a press conference that there was room for everyone in the shelters,[8] thus demonstrating his ignorance of the reality on the ground.[9]

On January 17, 2021, Raphaël André, an Innu man originally from Matimekush-Lac John and who was then homeless, was found dead in a Montreal portable toilet. Apparently hiding from the police during the curfew, he died on a cold Montreal night. The Open Door, the shelter he used to go to, was closed that night because of a COVID-19 outbreak.[10] That tragedy provoked outrage across the province. After being pressed by community organizations[11] and the Montreal mayor[12] for a curfew exemption, on January 19, the Prime Minister reiterated he had the greatest confidence in the police who, according to him, exercised common sense when deciding whether to ticket homeless people for violating the curfew.[13] Moreover, he justified his refusal to include a curfew exemption for homeless people by the fear that people would claim to be homeless to avoid tickets.[14]

On January 25, even the President of the Quebec Human Rights Commission published a letter to the Prime Minister asking again for an exemption and warning:

> Requiring people experiencing homelessness not to be in public space between 8:00 p.m. and 5:00 a.m. when the occupation of this space is often at the heart of their life and survival strategies is not adapted to their realities and could have a discriminatory impact on several of their rights and freedoms, notably their right to security and integrity of the person.[15]

It finally took a court decision,[16] rendered by Justice Chantal Masse of the Superior Court of Quebec on January 26, 2021, ordering the suspension of the curfew for homeless people for a first period of ten days for the government to give in and specify in a Ministerial Order that the curfew did not apply to homeless persons.[17]

24.3 The Curfew: The Most Frequent Reason for Judicialization

In a recent collaborative research project on the punitive practices during the pandemic, along with a team of researchers from the Observatoire des Profilages, we analyzed police and judicial data from the Quebec Ministry of Public Safety and Ministry of Justice.[18] In the following pages, we present data pertaining to statements of offence issued under the *Public Health Act* and served to people in a manner to initiate penal court proceedings. All in all, over a period of about 15 months, i.e., between March 22, 2020, and June 27, 2021, 31,845 statements of offence were issued in Quebec. To give an idea of the scale of this punitive treatment, although we should be wary of comparisons given the scarcity of comparable data, the Canadian Civil Liberties Association and the Policing the Pandemic Mapping Project estimated that between October 2020 and February 2021, Quebec had a ratio of 0,51 statement of offence issued per capita, whereas Ontario had a ratio of 0,22 and British Columbia 0,28.[19] These near 32,000 statements of offence amounted to about 50 million dollars in fines and fees at the moment of the data extraction (January 2022).

Seventy-eight percent (78%) of the statements of offence (i.e., 24,812) were issued during the five months when the curfew was in place, from January to May 2021. As shown in graph 1 later, curfew violation was the most frequent reason for judicialization: 56.8% of the statements of offence in our database were issued for this reason. The next two most common reasons for offences were "gathering in private residences" (17.5%) and "gathering in public places" (15.2%). The curfew appears to have been an important tool of repression.

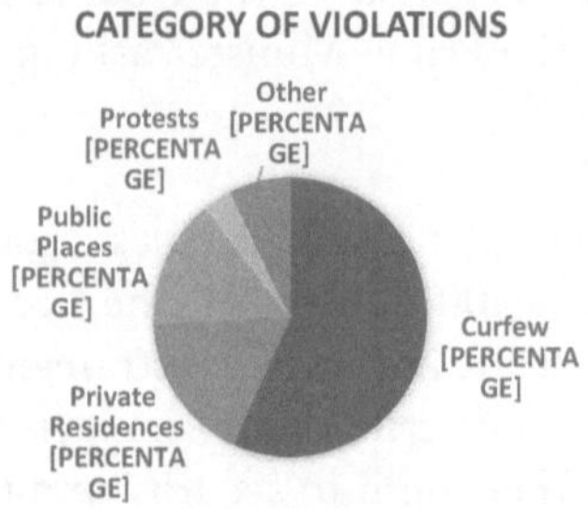

FIGURE 24.1 Category of violations, in percent.

TABLE 24.1 Statements of offence served to homeless people, per category of offence and across time

Category of offence	*Apr. 20*	*May 20*	*Oct. 20*	*Nov. 20*	*Dec. 20*	*Jan. 2021*	*Feb. 21*	*Mar. 21*	*Apr. 21*	*May 21*	*Jun. 21*
Curfew	0	0	0	0	0	52	30	19	29	21	0
Public places	66	12	0	0	0	3	0	0	0	0	0
Private residences	0	0	2	3	3	5	3	0	1	0	0
Other	1	0	0	1	1	2	6	3	4	7	1

The data obtained from the Ministry of Justice does not allow for a picture of the socioeconomic conditions of the individuals who received statements of offence. It is, therefore, impossible to directly identify the statements of offence served to homeless people. To know if homeless people received statements of offence, we used the same indirect methodological strategy as the one we used in our previous studies on the judicialization of homelessness.[20] We identified the individuals in the ministry database that reported the address of one of the many shelters or organizations that work with people experiencing homelessness in Quebec.[21] This strategy allows us to identify only the tip of the iceberg of their judicialization for offences related to the COVID-19. Other people may have declared the address of a friend, a family member, or any other address when receiving a statement of offence and thus escape our accounting.

All in all, using that methodology, we could identify that 275 COVID-19–related statements of offence were served to people giving the address of a shelter or a community organization as their residence.[22] As shown in Table 1, 99 of these were served for curfew violations from February until May 2021, which is during the period where homeless people were specifically exempted from respecting the curfew. In other words, 99 homeless persons were ticketed despite the legal exemption, either because they could not advocate for their situation to the police or because police officers did not care about the legal exemption covering them. As a result, 99 people were, if found guilty, potentially liable to fines of more than $1,500. Those fines could result in imprisonment for nonpayment of fines if people are unable to pay them.[23] To put it bluntly, 99 people could ultimately be imprisoned for having nowhere to go during the curfew hours of a winter pandemic night.

24.4 The Curfew: A Legal Technology of Bordering

Curfews are spatiotemporal legal technologies that draw borders around one's private residence, a border between legality and illegality. Between 8 P.M. and 5 A.M., a person found outside their residence or its equivalent or its ground, is within a space of illegality. At night, curfews had the consequence of confining unhoused people in spaces of illegality, or what we could call, with the legal anthropologist Susan Bibler Coutin, spaces of nonexistence.[24] Bibler Coutin argues that undocumented migrants in the United States are forced to occupy spaces of nonexistence. They are physically present in their country of adoption, yet they are legally absent. Once they cross the borders without legal authorization, "a disjuncture between physical and legal presence arises."[25] But this space of nonexistence, like the migrants themselves, is both there and not there. It *is* inasmuch as it has real consequences (constant fear, police harassment, etc.), but of course, it also only exists as an imagined locus. Moreover, the undocumented migrants, as a matter of fact, are not always confined to this space of nonexistence; though they are legally absent, they are nevertheless physically real and present. On a day-to-day basis, they are getting jobs, going to school, renting apartments, etc. And their illegal presence becomes relevant in certain circumstances only, for example, when driving:

> The undocumented thus move in and out of existence. Much of the time they are undifferentiated from those around them, but suddenly, when legal reality is superimposed on daily life, they are once more in a space of nonexistence. The borders between existence and nonexistence remain blurred and permeable.[26]

Like the presence of undocumented migrants in a country, the homeless presence under curfew is unauthorized. The homeless then exist only "in a non-domain, a space of illegality."[27] In other words, the curfew territorializes in a way to operate a disconnection between legal and physical presence. The homeless physically exist in public spaces, but their legal existence is denied by the curfew and the ticketing practices. Curfews, like immigration policies in the United States, became porous borders between existence and nonexistence. In a study on red zones and other conditions of release imposed on marginalized people, which often include curfews, Sylvestre, Blomley, and Bellot write, "Red zones are not simply discrete spacetimes, but rework extant social relations of care, need, politics and affect, lived in and through different but entangled spatiotemporalities."[28] In other words, curfews "sever and rearrange spatiotemporal "geographies of being."[29] The tragic story of Raphaël André is a painful demonstration of how the curfew in Quebec rearranged geographies of being, from the shelter to the hiding spot of the portable toilet, in and out of spaces of nonexistence.

As part of a research project funded by the Canadian Institutes of Health Research on the reorganization of homelessness services during the COVID-19 pandemic, 25 people experiencing homelessness in Montreal were interviewed over two periods, in November 2020 (before the imposition of the curfew) and from August to November 2021 (this time after the curfew ended).[30] They reported that because of the various health measures that were implemented, like the lockdown and the curfew, they were unable to meet their basic needs, such as finding shelter, food, water, and a place to shower. They lost their bearings because of these measures highly disrupting of their survival strategies. They also condemned the complete lack of recognition by the government of their particular situation, which includes life in public space. This nonrecognition or contempt, as Axel Honneth might refer to it,[31] bears witness to the invisible borders that separate those who are domiciled from those who cannot or are not. As we have seen, the impossibility of respecting the curfew for homeless people has never been considered by the government. Again, unrecognized homeless people experienced the curfew as another illustration of the social, penal, and even lethal consequences of the repression of their occupation of public space.[32]

24.5 Conclusion

The curfew, as a legal technology of bordering, operated a discretionary spatiotemporal distinction between legality and illegality. As such, it had dramatic consequences on homeless people, and some of them are still dealing with the burden of unpaid fines almost two years after having been ticketed. While the stated goal of the curfew was to reduce contacts and curb the raging spread of COVID-19, it was revealed to have been implemented without definitive scientific evidence of its efficiency.[33] Among other things, it is very difficult to "separate any impact a curfew might have on coronavirus infections from the impact of other public health measures, like lockdowns and bar and restaurant closings."[34] If some scientists found that the curfew did reduce mobility[35] (and mobility appears to be a predictor of the growth rate of COVID-19 cases),[36] others considered the measure to be nothing more than a spectacle[37]—a spectacle that impacted disproportionately vulnerable people, such as homeless people. But the curfew did not only have consequences on homeless people. For example, drug users might have been using in very dangerous settings during the curfew, rather than at the safe injection sites they used to visit at night. Deaths due to a drug overdose in Quebec skyrocketed in 2021 and amounted to 450, compared to 312 in 2020 and 203 in 2019.[38] Of course, we cannot attribute all those fatalities to the curfew, but community organizations did ring the alarm bell on the curfew and the threat it posed for thousands of people.[39]

In the future, we urge the government to assess the needs and respect the rights of everyone in the population. Decision-makers need to have marginalized populations fair and square in their rearview mirror and not only in their blind spot as it was the case when implementing the curfew. As we wrote elsewhere, "the management of a health crisis should be based on justified, recognized, fair, and equitable health measures, and not on coercive and punitive measures that reinforce social inequalities and discrimination."[40] Unfortunately, the curfew turned out to be a discriminatory and even deadly spatiotemporal legal technology.

Notes

1 Institut national de santé publique du Québec, "Données COVID-19 au Québec", online: *INSPQ*. www.inspq.qc.ca/covid-19/donnees.
2 *Ibid.*
3 CPAC, "COVID-19 au Québec: Confinement prolongé et couvre-feu—6 janvier 2021" (6 January 2021), online (video): *YouTube*. www.youtube.com/watch?v=bQA6djSN5WY. [CPAC, "COVID-19 au Quebec"].
4 Emily Cameron-Blake et al, "Variation in the Canadian provincial and territorial responses to COVID19" (2021), online: *Blavatnik School of Government Working Paper*. www.bsg.ox.ac.uk/sites/default/files/2021-03/BSG-WP-2021-039.pdf.
5 *Public Health Act*, CQLR c S-2.2.
6 Ordering of measures to protect the health of the population amid the COVID-19 pandemic situation, OIC No 2–2021, (2021) GOQ II, 2102B-E.
7 *Public Health Act*, *supra* note 5, s 139.
8 CPAC, "COVID-19 au Quebec", *supra* note 3.
9 Caroline Leblanc, Opinion, *La Presse* (8 January 2021), online: https://plus.lapresse.ca/screens/136e26a1-ca09-4619-b682-4500618e07c6%7C_0.html; Jeanne Corriveau, "Legault will not exempt homeless people from curfew, despite requests" (20 January 2021), online: *Le Devoir*. www.ledevoir.com/societe/593572/couvre-feu-valerie-plante-demande-une-exemption-pour-les-itinerants (shelter occupation rate was around 95% in Montreal in January 2021).
10 Jeanne Corriveau & Annabelle Pebble, "The death of a homeless sows consternation" (19 January 2021), online: *Le Devoir*. www.ledevoir.com/societe/593511/un-itinerant-trouve-mort-dans-une-toilette-portable-a-montreal.
11 Support Network for Alone and Homeless People of Montreal (RAPSIM), News Release, "The curfew, a counter-productive and dangerous measure for the homeless community" (16 January 2021), online: *Presse-Toia Gauche*. www.pressegauche.org/Le-couvre-feu-une-mesure-contre-productive-et-dangereuse-pour-le-milieu-de-l.
12 Corriveau, *supra* note 9.
13 CPAC, "COVID: Le PM Legault demande l'interdiction des vols internationaux non essentiels—19 jan. 2021" (19 January 2021), online (video): *YouTube*. www.youtube.com/watch?v=R2_B2oEEEIA&t=1384s.

14 *Ibid.*
15 Letter from Philippe-Andre Tessier to Mr François Legault (22 January 2021) as President of the Commission des droits de la personne et des droits de la jeunesse, "Commission recommends amendment to curfew decree to prevent discrimination against homeless people", online: www.cdpdj.qc.ca/fr/actualites/lettre-couvre-feu-discrimination-itinerance.
16 *Clinique juridique itinérante c Procureur général du Québec*, 2021 QCCS 182 (CanLII).
17 Ministerial Order 2021–004 of the Minister of Health and Social Services, (2021) GOQ II, 2105A-E.
18 Véronique Fortin et al, "Une approche punitive alarmante face à la pandémie de COVID-19: analyse des données policières" (2022), online (pdf): *Observatoire Des Profilages*. www.observatoiredesprofilages.ca/une-approche-punitive-alarmante-face-a-la-pandemie-de-covid-19-analyse-des-donnees-policieres/; Céline Bellot et al, "Surengagement policier et judiciaire dans la gestion de la pandémie: Conséquences pour les personnes judiciarisées et le système penal" (2022), online (pdf): *Observatoire Des Profilages*. www.observatoiredesprofilages.ca/surengagement-policier-et-judiciaire-dans-la-gestion-de-la-pandemie-consequences-pour-les-personnes-judiciarisees-et-le-systeme-penal/.
19 "COVID-10 and law enforcement in Canada: The second wave" (2021) at 11, online (pdf): *Association canadienne des libertés civiles et Policing the Pandemic Mapping Project*. https://ccla.org/wp-content/uploads/2021/06/2021-05-13-COVID-19-and-Law-Enforcement-The-second-wave.pdf.
20 Céline Bellot et al, "Judiciarisation de l'itinérance à Montréal: Des données alarmantes témoignent d'un profilage social accru (2012–2019)" (2021), online (pdf): *Observatoire Des Profilages*. www.observatoiredesprofilages.ca/judiciarisation-de-litinerance-a-montreal/.
21 A list of addresses of organizations working with homeless people was compiled from the lists of member organizations of the Réseau solidarité itinérance du Québec, the Réseau d'aide aux personnes seules (RAPSIM), and organizations that are members of regional or municipal homelessness networks. See Bellot et al, *supra* note 18 at 37.
22 Despite a list of more than 100 organizations, our analysis reveals that only a few specific addresses of organizations were given by people, usually the best-known emergency shelters or organizations whose mandate is to provide a postal box to people experiencing homelessness.
23 *Code of Penal Procedure*, CQLR c C-25.1, s 347.
24 Susan Bibler Coutin, *Legalizing Moves: Salvadoran Immigrants' Struggle for US Residency* (Ann Arbor: University of Michigan Press, 2000).
25 *Ibid* at 29.
26 *Ibid* at 40.
27 *Ibid* at 29.
28 Marie-Ève Sylvestre, Nicholas Blomley & Céline Bellot, *Red Zones. Criminal Law and the Territorial Governance of Marginalized People* (Cambridge: Cambridge University Press, 2020) at 165.
29 *Ibid.*
30 Céline Bellot et al, "Covid et itinérance: de la réorganisation des services au point de vue des personnes en situation d'itinérance", forthcoming research report.
31 Axel Honneth, *La société du mépris: Vers une nouvelle Théorie critique* (Paris: Éditions La Découverte, 2006).
32 Véronique Fortin, Taking the Law to the Streets: Legal and Spatial Tactics Deployed in Public Spaces to Control Protesters and the Homeless in Montreal (PhD Dissertation, University of California, Irvine, 2015) [unpublished].

33 Emma Jean & Julien Simard, "L'illusion du couvre-feu" in J Cossette & J Simard, eds, *Traitements-chocs et tartelettes: Bilan critique de la gestion de la Covid-19 au Québec*, (Montreal: Éditions Somme Toute, 2022) at 205–226; Julien Simard, "Le couvre-feu: Mesure épidémiologique ou outil de communication politique?" (2022) 24:1 *Éthique Publique*. https://journals.openedition.org/ethiquepublique/6979.

34 Jonathan Jarry, "Do Curfews Work", McGill Office for Science and Society, online: *McGill*. www.mcgill.ca/oss/article/covid-19-general-science/do-curfews-work.

35 Amir Ghasemi et al, "Impact of a nighttime curfew on overnight mobility" (April 7, 2021), online: *MedRxiv*. www.medrxiv.org/content/10.1101/2021.04.04.21254906v1.

36 Kevin A. Brown et al, "The mobility gap: Estimating mobility thresholds required to control SARS-CoV-2 in Canada" (2021) 193:17 *Canadian Medical Association Journal* E592.

37 Vincent Duclos, "Le couvre-feu comme mesure-spectacle" (3 Avril 2021), online: *Le Devoir*. www.ledevoir.com/opinion/idees/598163/coronavirus-le-couvre-feu-comme-mesure-spectacle; see also Simard, *supra* note 33.

38 Special Advisory Committee on the Epidemic of Opioid Overdoses, *Harms Associated with Opioids and Stimulants in Canada* (Ottawa: Public Health Agency of Canada, September 2022), online: https://sante-infobase.canada.ca/mefaits-associes-aux-substances/opioides-stimulants/graphiques?index=565.

39 Émilie Roberge, "How the curfew is putting the lives of thousands at risk" (13 May 2021), online (blog): *Ligue des droits et libertés*. https://liguedesdroits.ca/carnet-le-couvre-feu-met-la-vie-de-milliers-de-personnes-en-danger/; CACTUS Montreal et al, News Release, "Curfews and overdoses: A marked drop in visits to supervised consumption sites worries harm reduction organizations" (28 January 2021), online: www.newswire.ca/fr/news-releases/couvre-feu-et-surdoses-une-baisse-marquee-de-la-frequentation-des-sites-de-consommation-supervisee-inquiete-les-organismes-en-reduction-des-mefaits-889888572.html.

40 Bellot et al, *supra* note 18.

PART IX

Access to Services, Care, and Medical Necessities

25

BODIES ACROSS BORDERS

A History of Cross-Border Travel for Abortion Services in Poland and Canada

Christabelle Sethna and Krystyna Dzwonkowska-Godula[1]

As international and domestic borders began closing in March 2020 in response to the COVID-19 pandemic, reproductive justice activists raised concerns about potential barriers to abortion access. These included medical staff shortages, reduced operating hours at medical facilities, stay-at-home orders, and the delisting of abortion as an essential medical service. High up on the list was cross-border travel to an abortion provider, which could be hampered by enforced quarantines, travel bans, flight and rail interruptions, and border shutdowns.[2] The pandemic thus drew attention to a commonplace but relatively understudied phenomenon: travel across international and domestic borders to access abortion services. It occurs when abortion access is illegal, or legal but restricted, unavailable, or otherwise inaccessible and often involves traveling long distances from one's place of residence. After several Western countries liberalized their abortion laws in the late 1960s and 1970s, abortion travel became a popular work-around option for women who could afford the costs of travel, accommodation, and surgical termination.[3] Paradoxically, abortion upon request in many communist and socialist Eastern European governments was legalized years earlier to facilitate gender equality and women's workforce participation. However, soon after the collapse of the Soviet Union in 1989, several new democratic governments in former Eastern bloc countries began restricting access to legal abortion.[4] What follows is a comparative overview between the chronological trajectory of abortion provision in Canada and Poland. It illustrates how legislative changes can drive cross-border abortion travel and tracks how grassroots groups, feminist networks, and non-governmental organizations (NGOs) respond by facilitating access to abortion services, thereby providing a vital alternative to healthcare systems that fail women's reproductive health needs.[5]

DOI: 10.4324/9781003394006-34

Before a 2018 national referendum in Ireland overturned the ban on abortion known as the 8th Amendment, thousands of Irish women traveled to Great Britain annually to access abortion services.[6] With Ireland now offering, under the *Health (Regulation of Termination of Pregnancy) Act*, free and legal abortions on request up to 12 weeks of pregnancy, as well as for indications such as a risk to the pregnant woman's life or health or evidence of fatal fetal anomaly,[7] it is Poland (and Malta) that now boasts some of the strictest anti-abortion laws in Europe. Ironically, Polish abortion laws were once among the most progressive in the world. Abortion was legalized as early as 1932 for medical and criminal indications; however, written permission from two doctors was required in the former case and permission from the prosecutor in the latter. Between 1956 and 1959 postwar socialist Poland, then an Eastern bloc member country aligned with the Soviet Union, broadened these indications to include socioeconomic difficulties, effectively permitting abortion on request.[8] Liberal Polish abortion laws compelled some Western European women to travel to Poland for abortions in the 1960s and 1970s.[9]

However, in the 1980s, anti-abortion sentiment rose alongside a tide of anti-Soviet resistance allied with the Catholic Church. Following the collapse of the Soviet Union in 1989, the process of democratizing the Polish government was intimately bound to the implementation of restrictions on reproductive rights, including abortion and contraception, with the Church, physicians, and conservative politicians playing an active role in mobilizing a powerful anti-abortion movement in the country.[10] A conscience clause permitting doctors to refuse provision of some medical services, such as abortion, according to the dictates of their own conscience, and regulations requiring additional consultations with physicians performing abortion under the socioeconomic indication in public hospitals were introduced. Unsurprisingly, the numbers of officially recorded abortions dropped rapidly, from 82,137 terminations in 1989 to just 1,240 in 1993.[11]

In that year, the Polish government passed the Family Planning, Protection of the Human Fetus, and Conditions for Termination of Pregnancy Act. The legislation reflected the sway of the Church and was touted as an "abortion compromise." It limited access to legal abortion by permitting only three indications: the pregnancy constituted a risk to the life or health of the pregnant woman, there was a high probability of severe and irreversible fetal impairment or illness, or the pregnancy resulted from a sexual assault. The socioeconomic indication was removed.[12]

The Foundation (earlier, the Federation) for Women and Family Planning, also known as FEDERA, has been working for access to abortion and contraception in Poland since 1991. It estimates that approximately 80,000 to 100,000 Polish women access abortion services annually.[13] The 1993 legislation spurred the growth of an "abortion underground" of medical personnel providing illegal abortions for unregulated high prices, even though physicians could be penalized.[14] It also encouraged travel to neighbouring countries like Slovakia, the Czech Republic, Lithuania, and Ukraine for abortion services or to more expensive abortion clinics in Austria, Germany, Great Britain, and the Netherlands.[15] The legal changes entrenched social, economic inequality. Poor women, young women, migrants, and rural women faced financial hurdles, especially if traveling abroad, in addition to limited access to computer and Internet services and a lack of knowledge of foreign languages, although some abortion clinics display web pages in Polish and/or have Polish-speaking personnel.[16]

In Canada, abortion was illegal until 1969 when the federal government, led by Prime Minister Pierre Elliot Trudeau, introduced an Omnibus Bill that legalized abortion, decriminalized contraception, and legalized homosexual acts between consenting adults. These significant legislative changes were supposed to signal the emergence of a modern, secular, and pluralistic Canada.[17] Before the passage of the new abortion law, women seeking abortions had little choice but to bring the pregnancy to term, seek out illegal abortion providers, some of whom were medical personnel providing clandestine abortion services, or travel to countries like Great Britain, a popular destination hub for legal abortion services that were available for purchase in the private healthcare sector.[18] The 1969 abortion law was intended to alleviate the problem of illegal abortion. However, it proved obstructive by medicalizing the practice; hospital-based therapeutic abortion committees (TACs) composed of three physicians were now empowered to decide, on a case-by-case basis, whether the pregnancy posed a threat to the life or health of the pregnant woman. These indications were never defined and were interpreted broadly or narrowly, at each TAC's discretion.[19] Assisted by grassroots groups, feminist organizations, and NGOs, Canadian women continued to travel to Great Britain for abortions and, after some American states like New York legalized abortion, many more Canadian women headed south of the border. These journeys spoke to class and race privilege in accessing abortion services outside the country, an issue that pro-choice activists highlighted as central to the law's unworkability.[20]

Once the Supreme Court of the United States ruled in the 1973 landmark decision, *Roe v. Wade*, that abortion was a constitutionally protected right, even more Canadian women crossed into the USA. The unworkability of the 1969 abortion law galvanized the Vancouver Women's Caucus and the Canadian Association for the Repeal of the Abortion Laws (later, the Canadian Abortion Rights Action League), as well as physicians, clergy, and laypersons to campaign for its repeal. Their energies eventually coalesced around a socialist-leaning pro-choice movement supporting Dr. Henry Morgentaler, a Polish-born Canadian family physician and Holocaust survivor who first performed abortions in his Montreal clinic in contravention of the law.[21] The 1977 *Report of the Committee on the Operation of the Abortion*, an investigation into the functioning of the 1969 law that the Canadian federal government commissioned, confirmed that by 1976, only 20% of all civilian hospitals had established TACs, leading to regional variation in abortion provision, arbitrary decision-making on the part of TACs, and delays accessing abortion despite the time-sensitive nature of the procedure.[22] Referrals to American abortion services boomed and, in some cases, became a profitable business. Between 1970 and 1975, an estimated 16% to 24% of Canadian women had abortions in the USA.[23]

In 1988, after years of bruising legal battles that also involved Morgentaler clinics in Toronto and Winnipeg, the Supreme Court of Canada struck down the 1969 abortion law in *R. v. Morgentaler*, ruling that it violated women's right to security of the person protected by the *Canadian Charter of Rights and Freedoms*. In the early 1990s, Prime Minister Brian Mulroney attempted to introduce another abortion law but failed, making Canada one of the few countries in the world that does not have a national abortion law.[24] The anti-abortion movement flourished in this decade, as American anti-abortion violence influenced by the politics of the New Christian Right, spilled northward. Morgentaler's Toronto abortion clinic was firebombed in 1992. Between 1995 and 1998, three Canadian physicians were shot and seriously wounded.[25] Politicians from various parties introduced into parliament dozens of private members bills and motions beginning in 1987, and extending well into the 1990s and 2000s, to restrict or ban abortion, but these measures have been unsuccessful thus far.[26]

Without a national law governing abortion, the administration of abortion services came under the jurisdiction of individual provinces and territories, resulting in a "patchwork quilt with many holes."[27] Notwithstanding the argument that abortion should be considered a medically necessary procedure protected throughout the country by the *Canada Health Act*'s guarantee of universal public healthcare,[28] regional disparities in abortion provision became apparent. An important study of hospital abortion access conducted for Canadians for Choice in 2006 showed that only 15% of hospitals were providing abortion services, down from the 1977 figure of 20%. This drop may have had to do with the growth of clinic abortions in some urban centres, but it was likely due primarily to the many barriers to abortion access that the study identified. These barriers included a lack of abortion providers, judgmental healthcare professionals, the complications of reciprocal billing for abortions, and the costs of travel and expenses related to accessing abortion services outside pregnant women's residential area.[29]

A 2013 study, this time specifically on travel to abortion clinics, confirmed that abortion services for women living in or close to urban centres were easy to access, but those in the Atlantic provinces, rural areas, and northern Canada were underserviced, sometimes necessitating long journeys to an abortion clinic and bypassing hospital abortion services. Younger women and poorer women traveled the greatest distances.[30] Medication (or medical) abortion in pill form known as mifepristone, combining the drugs mifepristone and misoprostol, was approved for prescription use by Health Canada only in 2015, decades later than many other European countries. After restrictions on medication abortion were lifted in 2017, and as more provincial and territorial healthcare plans covered the costs of the medication, uptake increased but is uneven regionally.[31]

Meanwhile in Poland, Church-backed conservative politicians dissatisfied with the so-called abortion compromise represented by the 1993 Family Planning, Protection of the Human Fetus, and Conditions for Termination of Pregnancy Act moved to ban abortion altogether. As of 1997, the Polish Criminal Code criminalized abortion providers and individuals assisting women seeking abortions but does not penalize pregnant women who have abortions.[32] The criminalization of abortion had a "chilling effect" on physicians, some of whom refused to perform any abortions and denied referrals for prenatal testing under the conscience clause, treating women's requests for prenatal testing as a prelude to a legal abortion.[33] In response, an international coalition working to loosen legal restrictions on abortion, counteract the abortion stigma, and support the termination of unwanted pregnancies emerged to aid Polish women. Women on Waves, founded by Dutch physician Rebecca Gomperts, chartered a ship equipped with a mobile abortion clinic and sailed to international waters off the coast of Poland in 2003.[34] Since 2006, Kobiety w Sieci (Polish Women on Web) has created a virtual space for sharing abortion experiences and for disseminating information in Polish about medication abortion. Notably, abortion pills have not been approved for use, although misoprostol is used off label in Polish hospitals to induce labour and expel the contents of the uterus after miscarriage.[35] Kobiety w Sieci is based on Women on Web, a telemedicine service pioneered by Gomperts, "to help women access mifepristone and misoprostol in countries with no safe care for termination of pregnancy."[36] It launched a telephone information hotline in 2013.[37] Women on Waves later collaborated with Polish women to deliver packages of abortion pills by drone from Germany to Poland.[38]

Anti-abortion measures intensified once the right-wing Law and Justice Party was elected as Poland's majority government in 2015.[39] The party's populism, nationalism, and pro-natalism is manifested in its opposition to immigration, sex education, contraception, and abortion and in its vilification of feminist and LGBTQ activists for the spread of a putative "gender ideology" that threatens Catholic heteronormative family values.[40] From 2016 onward, proposed anti-abortion bills that penalize women having abortions animated mass demonstrations and strikes known as "Black Protests."[41] The Abortion Dream Team was established to destigmatize abortion, starting with a 2016 meeting about aborting pregnancies at home.[42] Three years later, Polish Women on Web and the Abortion Dream Team joined with Women Help

Women (international), Aunt Basia (Germany), Abortion Network Amsterdam (Netherlands), and the Abortion Support Network (United Kingdom) to found Abortion Without Borders.[43] Notably, the Abortion Support Network arose initially to help support Irish women both financially and logistically in traveling to Great Britain for abortion services.[44] Abortion Without Borders provides Polish women with information about surgical and medication abortion options, assists them financially and logistically with travel to another country for an abortion, and supports a telephone information hotline.

Managing abortion services during the COVID-19 pandemic in Canada posed challenges that the National Abortion Federation Canada, the Abortion Rights Coalition of Canada, and Action Canada for Sexual Health and Rights foresaw and tried to address.[45] There have been some likely positive outcomes. A recent study indicates that the majority of medical personnel practicing abortion healthcare during the pandemic considered surgical and medication abortion essential, transitioned quickly to online consultations with patients, and increased access to medication abortion (except in Quebec due to the province's regulations). This kind of healthcare delivery could potentially reduce regional variation in abortion provision.[46] Various provincial bubble zone laws intended to protect abortion clinics, hospitals providing abortions, and pharmacies dispensing the abortion pill from anti-abortion harassment could be boosted by new federal Criminal Code amendments that intend to shield healthcare workers and facilities from abuse by anti-vaccine protesters but are applicable to a range of threats.[47] In addition, the federal government's 2021 budget under openly pro-choice Prime Minister Justin Trudeau earmarked $45 million over three years for community-based organizations providing sexual and reproductive healthcare information and services to "vulnerable populations," including "travel and logistical support to individuals who have to go long distances to access abortion care."[48]

In Poland, the lack of access to abortion services was exacerbated during the pandemic by the suspension of international passenger air and rail services for nearly a month and a mandatory 14-day quarantine requirement upon returning home from abroad in 2020. Border closures also prevented Polish women from traveling to abortion clinics in other countries for a time.[49] Whereas some European Union (EU) member states liberalized or updated their abortion policies during the pandemic others, like Poland, "pushed for restrictions."[50] On 22 October 2020, Poland's highest court, the Constitutional Tribunal (with judges selected by the right-wing Law and Justice Party), determined that abortion based on the indication of "severe and irreversible fetal defect or incurable illness that threatens the fetus's life" was unconstitutional. This ruling went into effect in early 2021. It permits abortions only if there is a risk to the pregnant woman's life or health or the pregnancy occurs as the result of a criminal act but outlaws abortions due to fetal anomalies (which make up over 90% of the approximately 1,000 legal abortions conducted in Polish hospitals annually).[51]

On behalf of abortion providers and activists, Natalia Broniarczyk, a member of the Abortion Dream Team, underlined:

> We build abortion solidarity in a time of crisis. We are cheated by the government, we are cheated by the Tribunal, and we are constantly stigmatized by the Church for making decisions about our families. But this gives us a chance to build support networks, and until things are normal, we will provide abortions in feminist support networks with our sisters. We'll look for help on the Internet, we'll help each other travel for abortion, and we'll survive it.[52]

In widespread revolt against the Constitutional Tribunal ruling, Polish men and women publicized the telephone information hotline of Abortion Without Borders by sharing it on their social media profiles, placing it on their profile photos and displaying it on buildings, sidewalks, and bus stops for maximum visibility. Grassroots "Abortion Guerrilla" activists also turned to public spaces to post stickers, homemade banners, or leaflets containing information about access to abortion and relevant contact data.[53]

After the death of a Polish woman who was refused an abortion, the European Parliament condemned Poland for forcing women to carry a pregnancy to term, undergo an unsafe abortion, or travel abroad to an abortion provider. It requested EU member states "to cooperate more effectively to facilitate cross-border access to abortion, for example by granting Polish women access to a free and safe abortion in other national healthcare systems."[54] Nevertheless, EU health laws and policies have been criticized for not protecting women from the punitive impact of anti-abortion laws in member states that restrict access to surgical and/or medication abortion.[55] Abortion Without Borders noted on its webpage: "Coronavirus is simply YET ANOTHER obstacle faced by people living in countries with inadequate provision of abortion services."[56] The scale of the need for abortion access support is shown by the following data: between 2020 and 2021, FEDERA fielded approximately 8,000 telephone calls and 5,000 emails.[57] In that same period, Abortion Without Borders received more than 8,000 telephone calls and almost 3,000 emails seeking information or access to abortion services. It also helped 34,000 Polish women access abortion, and 1,080 of them were able to terminate a pregnancy in a foreign clinic in the second trimester of pregnancy.[58] According to the Abortion Dream Team, every day, four women from Poland travel abroad for abortions, and at least 90 access abortion pills, whereas in Polish hospitals, only 107 abortions were performed under the anti-abortion law in 2021.[59]

After Russia attacked Ukraine in early 2022, the massive influx of Ukrainian women into Poland posed an additional challenge. Some of the refugees needed a range of reproductive healthcare services, including those women who had been raped and impregnated by Russian soldiers.[60] Several Polish and international organizations immediately prepared information in Polish, Russian, English, and Ukrainian about the possibilities and limitations of reproductive healthcare in Poland.[61] The Abortion Dream Team announced online:

> Abortion in Poland is not available as a formal health care service, but a person terminating their own pregnancy is not punished. Pharmacological [medication] abortion and help from the organization Abortion Without Borders are possible [+48 22 29 22 597]. Proven and trusted sources of abortion pills in Poland are: Abortion Poland—Women Help Womenhelp.org and Women on Web. Do you need emergency contraception—the "morning after" pill? Write to *dzienpo@riseup.net*[62]

In 2021 and 2022, the Belgium government donated a total of 30,000 euros to help Polish women to travel out of the country for abortion services,[63] and in 2022, the French government provided 60,000 euros to Abortion Without Borders in support of Ukrainian refugees seeking abortions.[64]

Shortly before the American Supreme Court overturned *Roe v. Wade* in the *Dobbs v Jackson Women's Health* decision in the summer of 2022,[65] Venny Ala-Siurua, Executive Director of Women on Web, remarked, with no small irony, "Many American women will have to do what Polish women are already doing to get safe abortions,"[66] and Karina Gould, Canadian Minister of Families, Children and Social Development, declared that Americans would be able to obtain abortion services north of the border.[67] These comments recognize the significance of cross-border abortion travel to women seeking pregnancy termination.

In the case of Poland, the government has perversely been able to tighten its anti-abortion laws over the years because international cross-border abortion travel, in addition to the abortion underground, has served as a convenient pressure release valve. In Canada, functioning without a national abortion law on the books since 1988, domestic abortion travel serves as a stop-gap measure that allows the federal, provincial, and territorial governments to ignore shortcomings in providing equitable reproductive healthcare delivery across the country.[68] In the similar and dissimilar experiences of both Poland and Canada, it is obvious that grassroots groups, feminist networks, and NGOs facilitating access to abortion services internationally and domestically are the unsung heroes of this history. Running on a combination of dedication, moxie, and innovation, they have picked up the slack for national healthcare systems that continue to fail women in fundamental ways. The COVID-19 pandemic and the bleak post–*Roe v. Wade* abortion landscape in the USA[69] have cast a spotlight on the necessity of integrating fair and workable access to surgical and medication abortion into the DNA of national healthcare systems. These strategies should include vetted arrangements for abortion access across international and domestic borders whenever and wherever necessary and consequent protections at the highest levels of supranational bodies.

Notes

1 The authors are grateful to the Social Sciences and Humanities Research Council of Canada and the Bekker Scholarship Programme of the Polish National Agency for Academic Exchange.
2 Laura Hurley, "How will the corona virus affect access to safe abortion?" (20 March 2020), online (blog): *IPPF Blog*. www.ippf.org/blogs/how-will-coronavirus-affect-access-safe-abortion.
3 Christabelle Sethna, "All Aboard? Canadian Women's Abortion Tourism, 1960–1980" in Cheryl Krasnick Warsh, ed, *Gender, Health, and Popular Culture* (Waterloo: Wilfred Laurier University Press, 2011) 89.
4 Susan Gal & Gail Kligman, *The Politics of Gender after Socialism: A Comparative-Historical Essay* (Princeton: Princeton University Press, 2000) 16–17. See also Silvia De Zordo, Joanna Mishal & Lorena Anton, "Introduction" in Silvia De Zordo, Joanna Mishtal and Lorena Anton, eds, *A Fragmented Landscape: Abortion Governance and Protest* (New York and Oxford: Berghahn Books, 2017) 1–8.
5 For a similar argument, see Leslie J. Reagan, "Crossing the border for abortions: California activists, Mexican clinics, and the creation of a feminist health agency in the 1960s" (2000) 26 *Feminist Studies* 323; Agata Ignaciuk & Christabelle Sethna, "Charters for choice: Abortion travel, abortion referral networks and Spanish women's transnational reproductive agency, 1975–1985" (2020) 32:2 *Gender & History* 286.
6 Ann Rossiter, *Ireland's Hidden Diaspora: The "Abortion Trail" and the Making of a London-Irish Underground, 1980–2000* (London: IASC Publishing, 2009).
7 "Ireland's abortion provisions: Health (Regulation of Termination of Pregnancy) Act 2018", online: *Center for Reproductive Rights*. https://reproductiverights.org/maps/provision/irelands-abortion-provisions/.
8 Atina Krajewska, "Revisiting Polish abortion law: Doctors and institutions in a restrictive regime" (2022) 31:3 *Social & Legal Studies* 416. See also Ewelina Ciaputa, "Abortion and the Catholic Church in Poland" in Christabelle Sethna & Gayle Davis, eds, *Abortion Across Borders: Transnational Travel and Access to Abortion Services* (Baltimore: Johns Hopkins University Press, 2019) 278.
9 Lena Lennerhed, "Sherri Finkbine Flew to Sweden: Abortion and Disability in the Early 1960s" in Sethna & Davis, *supra* note 8 at 41–42.
10 Ann Snitow, "Poland's abortion law: The Church wins, women lose", 256:16 *The Nation* (26 April 1993) 556; Wanda Nowicka, "Roman Catholic fundamentalism against women's reproductive rights in Poland" (1996) 4:8 *Reproductive Health Matters* 21; Jacqueline Heinen & Stéphane Portet, "Reproductive rights in Poland: When politicians fear the wrath of the Church" (2010) 31:6 *Third World Quarterly* 1007; Joanna Mishtal, *The Politics of Morality: The Church, the State, and Reproductive Rights in Postsocialist Poland* (Ohio: Ohio University Press, 2015).
11 Krajewska, *supra* note 8; Joanna Misthal, "Matters of 'conscience': The politics of reproductive healthcare in Poland" (2009) 23:2 *Medical Anthropology Quarterly* 161 at 163. See also Joanna Mishtal, "Mobilisation, protest, and resistance against reproductive rights restrictions in Poland" (2018) 5:2 *Anthropologica* 33.
12 Atina Krajewska, *supra* note 8 at 417. See also Agata Ignaciuk, "In sickness and in health: Expert discussions on abortion indications, risks, and patient-doctor

relationships in Postwar Poland" (2021) 95:1 *Bulletin of the History of Medicine* 83; Wanda Nowicka, "The struggle for abortion rights in Poland" in Richard Parker, Rosalind Petchesky and Robert Sember, eds, *Sex Politics: Reports from the Front Line* (Rio de Janeiro: Sexuality Policy Watch, 2004) 167.

13 Federation for Women and Family Planning, *Twenty Years of Anti-Abortion Law in Poland: Report* (Warsaw: Federation for Women and Family Planning, 2013) 1 at 22.

14 Françoise Girard & Wanda Nowicka, "Clear and compelling evidence: The Polish tribunal on abortion rights" (2022) 10:19 *Reproductive Health Matters* 1 at 22–30; Joanna Mishtal, "Neoliberal reforms and privatisation of reproductive health services in post-socialist Poland" (2010) 18:36 *Reproductive Health Matters* 56; Agata Chełstowska, "Stigmatisation and commercialisation of abortion services in Poland: Turning sin into gold" (2011) 19:37 *Reproductive Health Matters* 98.

15 Lula Mecinska, Carolyne James & Kate Mukungu "Criminalization of women accessing abortion and enforced mobility within the European Union and the United Kingdom" (2020) 30:5 *Women & Criminal Justice* 398; Caitlin Gerdts et al, "Experiences of women who travel to England for abortions: An exploratory pilot study" (2016) 21:5 *The European Journal of Contraception & Reproductive Health* Care 401.

16 Chełstowska, *supra* note 14; Ewelina Ciaputa, "Abortion and the Catholic Church in Poland" in Sethna & Davis, *supra* note 8, 278 at 279; Mishtal, *supra* note 11 at 43.

17 Criminal Law Amendment Act, SC 1968–69, c 38. See also: Angus McLaren & Arlene Tigar McLaren, *The Bedroom and the State: The Changing Practices and Politics of Contraception and Abortion in Canada, 1880–1980* (Toronto: McClelland and Stewart, 1986); Christopher Dummitt & Christabelle Sethna, eds, *No Place for the State: The Omnibus Bill: The Origins and Legacies of the 1969 Omnibus Bill* (Vancouver: UBC Press, 2020). For more on abortion history, see Shannon Stettner, "A brief history of abortion in Canada" in Shannon Stettner, ed, *Without Apology: Writings on Abortion in Canada* (Edmonton: AU Press, 2016) 31.

18 Christabelle Sethna, "From Heathrow Airport to Harley Street: The ALRA and the travel of non-resident women for abortion services in Britain" in Sethna & Davis, *supra* note 8, 46.

19 Janine Brodie, Shelley A. M. Gavigan & Jane Jenson, *The Politics of Abortion* (Toronto: Oxford University Press, 1992) 36.

20 Sethna, *supra* note 3. See also Beth Palmer, "Lonely, tragic, but legally necessary pilgrimages: Transnational abortion travel in the 1970s" (2011) 92:4 *The Canadian Historical Review* 637.

21 See Judy Rebick, *Ten Thousand Roses: The Making of a Feminist Revolution* (Toronto: Penguin Canada, 2005); Ann Thomson, *Winning Choice on Abortion: How British Columbian and Canadian Feminists Won the Battles of the 1970s and 1980s* (Victoria, British Columbia: Trafford Publishing, 2004); Catherine Dunphy, *Morgentaler: A Difficult Hero* (Toronto: Random House, 1996); Bruce Douville, Katrina Ackerman & Shannon Stettner, "'Is abortion ever right?', The United Church of Canada and the debate over abortion law reform, 1960–1980" in Dummitt & Sethna, *supra* note 17.

22 Canada, *The Report of the Committee on the Operation of the Abortion Law* (Ottawa: Ministry of Supplies and Services, 1977) at 27–39.

23 *Ibid* at 381–384.

24 Joanna Erdman, "Constitutionalizing abortion rights in Canada" (2017) 49 *Ottawa Law Review* 221.

25 Jack Fainman with Roland Penner, *They Shoot Doctors, Don't They? A Memoir* (Winnipeg: Great Plains Publications, 2011).
26 "Anti-choice private member bills and motions introduced in Canada since 1987" (last modified 6 June 2021), online: *Abortion Rights Coalition of Canada*. www.arcc-cdac.ca/presentations-anti-bills/.
27 Laura Eggertson, "Abortion services in Canada: A patchwork quilt with many holes" (2001) 164 *The Canadian Medical Association Journal* 847.
28 Howard Palley, "Canadian abortion policy: National policy and the impact of federalism and political implementation on access to services" (2006) 36:4 *Publius: The Journal of Federalism* 565. See also Rachael Johnstone, *After Morgentaler: The Politics of Abortion in Canada* (Vancouver and Toronto: UBC Press, 2018) at 110–115.
29 Jessica Shaw, *Reality Check: A Close Look at Accessing Abortion Services in Canadian Hospitals* (Ottawa: Canadians for Choice, 2006).
30 Christabelle Sethna & Marion Doull, "Spatial disparities and travel to freestanding abortion clinics in Canada" (2013) 38 *Women's Studies International Forum* 52.
31 Sarah Munro et al, "Perspectives among Canadian physicians on factors influencing implementation of mifepristone medical abortion: A national qualitative study" (2020) 18 *Annals of Family Medicine* 413; Enav Z. Zusman et al, "Pharmacist direct dispensing of mifepristone for medication abortion in Canada: a survey of community pharmacists" (2022) 12 *British Medical Journal Open* 1; "Abortion coverage by region" (4 December 2022), online: *National Abortion Federation Canada*. https://nafcanada.org/abortion-coverage-region/.
32 Atina Krajewska, *supra* note 8 at 418.
33 *Ibid* at 419; Federation for Women and Family Planning, *Twenty Years of Anti-Abortion Law in Poland: Report* (Warsaw: Federation for Women and Family Planning, 2013) 1 at 12 and 19; Ludovica Anedda et al, *Sexual and Reproductive Health Rights and the Implication of Conscientious Objection* (Luxembourg: Publications Office of the European Union, 2018) 1 at 66.
34 Wanda Nowicka & Joanna Regulska, "Repressive policies and women's reproductive choices in Poland. The case of state violence against women" in Kristen Zaleski, Annalisa Enrile, Eugenia L. Weiss & Xiying Wang, eds, *Women's Journey to Empowerment in the 21st Century: A Transnational Feminist Analysis of Women's Lives in Modern Times* (Oxford University Press, 2019) 238; Wanda Nowicka, *Solidarność kobiet ponad granicami: Kronika wydarzeń (Women's Solidarity across Borders: A Chronicle of Events)* (Warsaw: Federation for Women and Family Planning, 2003).
35 Jakub Mlodawski & Marta Mlodawska, "Prostaglandins in the induction of labour—do we have the optimal substance, dose, and route of administration? Literature review" (2021) 37:2 *Medical Studies/Studia Medyczne* 165.
36 Rebecca Gomperts et al, "Using telemedicine for termination of pregnancy with mifepristone and misoprostol in settings where there is no access to safe services" (2008) 115 *BJOG: an International Journal of Obstetrics and Gynaecology* 1171. See also Rebecca Gomperts et al, "Regional differences in surgical intervention following medical termination of pregnancy provided by telemedicine" (2012) 91 *Acta Obstetricia et Gynecologica Scandinavica* 227.
37 Justyna Wydrzyńska & Natalia Broniarczyk, "Bezpieczna aborcja w naszych rękach (Safe abortion in our hands)" (7 March 2019), online: *Codziennik Feministyczny*. http://codziennikfeministyczny.pl/bezpieczna-aborcja-naszych-rekach/.
38 Joanna Mishtal, "Quietly 'beating the system' " in De Zordo, Misthal & Anton, *supra* note 4, 226.
39 Nowicka, *supra* note 12.

40 Krzysztof Jasiecki, "'Conservative modernization' and the rise of Law and Justice in Poland" in Katharina Bluhm & Mihai Varga, eds, *New Conservatives in Russia and East Central Europe* (London and New York: Routledge, 2019) 130; Elżbieta Korolczuk & Agnieszka Graff, "Gender as 'Ebola from Brussels': The anticolonial frame and the rise of illiberal populism" (2018) 43:4 *Signs* 797. See also Agnieszka Graff & Elżbieta Korolczuk, *Anti-gender Politics in the Populist Moment* (London and New York: Routledge, 2022).

41 Agnieszka Wierzcholska, "Gender in the resurgent Polish conservatism" in Katharina Bluhm & Mihai Varga, eds, *New Conservatives in Russia and East Central Europe* (London and New York: Routledge, 2019) 198; Elżbieta Korolczuk, "Explaining mass protests against abortion ban in Poland: The power of connective action" (2016) 7 *Zoon Politikon* 91; Agnieszka Król & Paula Pustułka, "Women on strike: mobilizing against reproductive injustice in Poland" (2018) 20:3 *International Feminist Journal of Politics* 366; Bogumila Hall, "Gendering resistance to right-wing populism: Black protest and a new wave of feminist activism in Poland?" (2019) 63:10 *American Behavioral Scientist* 1497.

42 Anna Louie Sussman, "How to make abortion great again" (4 November 2019), online: *The Harper's Bazaar*. www.harpersbazaar.com/culture/features/a28690537/abortion-dream-team-poland/#sidepanel.

43 See the Abortion Without Borders webpage, https://abortion.eu/.

44 Fiona Bloomer, Claire Pierson & Sylvia Estrada Claudio, *Reimagining Global Abortion Politics. A Social Justice Perspective* (Bristol: Bristol University Press 2019) 95.

45 "Joint statement on essential abortion care during COVID-19" (20 March 2020), online: *Action Canada for Sexual Health and Rights*. www.actioncanadashr.org/news/2020-03-20-joint-statement-essential-abortion-care-during-covid-19; "Abortion rights and healthcare during COVID-19" (6 January 2022), online: *Abortion Rights Coalition of Canada*. www.arcc-cdac.ca/covid-19/.

46 Madeline Ennis et al, "The perspective of Canadian health care professionals on abortion service during the COVID-19 pandemic" (2021) *Family Practice* 30.

47 "Safe zones laws and court injunctions in Canada (to protect abortion access)" (22 August 2022), online: *Abortion Rights Coalition of Canada*. www.arcc-cdac.ca/media/2020/06/Bubble-Zones-Court-Injunctions-in-Canada. See also Diana Duong with files from Lauren Vogel, "What do new intimidation laws mean for health workers and patients?" (17 February 2022), online: *CMAJ News*. https://cmajnews.com/2022/02/17/intimidation-1095988/.

48 Department of Finance Canada, "A resilient and inclusive recovery: Supporting the health of Canadians" (last modified 19 April 2021), online: *Government of Canada*. www.budget.gc.ca/2021/report-rapport/p3-en.html#188.

49 Paulina Januszewska, "Nie jesteś sama. Aborcja w czasach pandemii (You are not alone. Abortion in a time of pandemic)" (2020) 28 *Krytyka Polityczna*. https://krytykapolityczna.pl/kraj/nie-jestes-sama-aborcja-w-czasach-pandemii/.

50 Neva Bojovic, Jovana Stanisljevic & Guido Giunti, "The impact of COVID-19 on abortion access: Insights from the European Union and the United Kingdom" 125 *Health Policy* 841 at 853.

51 Wiktor Ferfecki, "Raport Ministerstwa Zdrowia: 1076 aborcji w Polsce w 2020 r. W tym legalne byłyby 23 (Health Ministry Report: 1076 abortions in Poland in 2020. Of which 23 would be legal this year.)" (19 July 2022), online: *Rzeczpospolita*. www.rp.pl/kraj/art10701-raport-ministerstwa-zdrowia-1076-aborcji-w-polsce-w-2020-r-w-tym-legalne-bylyby-23.

52 Dorota Roman & Weronika Fabjańska, "Aborcyjny Dream Team Nie zostawimy kobiet bez pomocy. Jest aborcja za granicą (Abortion dream team: We will not leave women without help. There's abortion abroad)" (30 January 2021), online: *Gazeta Wyborcza*. https://wyborcza.pl/7,82983,26736169,aborcyjny-dream-team-nie-zostawimy-kobiet-bez-pomocy-jest.html.

53 Maciej Rutkowski, "'Najczęściej z nami robią aborcje osoby, które już mają dzieci'. Natalia Broniarczyk o realiach po wyroku TK" ("'Most often abortions are done with us by people who already have children.' Natalia Broniarczyk on the reality after the CT verdict)" (17 May 2021), online: *impuls.press*. https://impuls.press/najczesciej-z-nami-robia-aborcje-osoby-ktore-juz-maja-dzieci-natalia-broniarczyk-o-realiach-po-wyroku-tk/.

54 Zof the restrictive law on abortion" (11 November 2021), online: www.europarl.europa.eu/news/en/press-room/20211108IPR16844/poland-no-more-women-should-die-because-of-the-restrictive-law-on-abortion.

55 Tamara Hervey & Sally Sheldon, "Abortion by telemedicine in Northern Ireland: Patient and professional rights across borders" (2017) 68:1 *The Northern Ireland Legal Quarterly* 1.

56 "Coronavirus update" (last accessed 20 October 2022), online: *Abortion Without Borders*. https://abortion.eu/.

57 "Rok cierpienia i emancypacji: Nasze działania po pseudowyroku TK (A year of suffering and emancipation: Our actions after the CT pseudo-judgment)" (22 October 2021), online: *Foundation for Women and Family Planning*. https://federa.org.pl/rocznica-wyroku-tk/.

58 "Sprawozdanie: Aborcja Bez Granic pomogła 34 tysiącom osób w dostępie do aborcji od wyroku TK (Report: Abortion Without Borders has helped 34,000 people access abortion since the CT ruling)" (21 October 2021), online: *Abortion Dream Team*. https://aborcyjnydreamteam.pl/aborcja-bez-granic-pomogla-34-tysiacom-osob-w-dostepie-do-aborcji-od-wyroku-tk-raport-z-dzialalnosci/.

59 Abortion Dream Team, "Codziennie na zabieg aborcji za granicą wyjeżdżają 4 osoby z . . ." (2 August 2022), posted on *Abortion Dream Team*, online: *Facebook*. www.facebook.com/aborcyjnydreamteam/photos/pb.100064786806923.-2207520000./403332106891139/?type=3.

60 Weronika Strzyżyńska, "'Declare it to a doctor, and it's over': Ukrainian women face harsh reality of Poland's abortion laws" (16 May 2022), online: *The Guardian*. www.theguardian.com/global-development/2022/may/10/ukrainian-women-face-harsh-reality-poland-abortion-laws.

61 Abortion Dream Team, "Medication abortion—Instruction in Ukrainian" (3 March 2022), posted on *Abortion Dream Team*, online: *Facebook*. www.facebook.com/photo/?fbid=389795121376256&set=pb.100064786806923.-2207520000; "Brochure on gynecological care for women refugees and asylum-seekers in Poland" (9 May 2022), online: *Foundation for Women and Family Planning*. https://en.federa.org.pl/healthcare-refugees-poland/; "Access to sexual and reproductive health services for Ukrainians in Poland" (10 May 2022), online: *Foundation for Women and Family Planning*. https://federa.org.pl/ukrainki-w-polsce/.

62 Abortion Dream Team, "Nigdy nie płać za aborcje bitcoinami. To oszustwo!" (4 March 2022), posted on *Abortion Dream Team*, online *Facebook*. www.facebook.com/photo/?fbid=389877378034697&set=pb.100064786806923.-2207520000; Abortion Dream Team, "Potrzebujesz antykoncepcji awaryjnej—tabletki 'dzień po'?" posted on *Abortion Dream Team*, online: *Facebook*. www.facebook.com/photo/?fbid=390092136013221&set=pb.100064786806923.-2207520000.

63 Agata Czarnacka, "PiS wyeksportował aborcję. Polkom chętnie pomagają inne kraje (PiS has exported abortion. Polish women are willingly helped by other countries)" (26 November 2021), online: *Polityka*. www.polityka.pl/tygodnikpolityka/spoleczenstwo/2101351,1,pis-wyeksportowal-aborcje-polkom-chetnie-pomagaja-inne-kraje.read.

64 "Wsparcie finansowe na aborcje dla Polek i Ukrainek od francuskiego rządu (Financial support for abortions for Polish and Ukrainian women from French government)" (4 July 2022), online: *Abortion Dream Team*. https://aborcyjnydreamteam.pl/rzad-francuski-przeznacza-60-000-euro-na-aborcje-bez-granic/.

65 Benjamin Rader et al., "Estimated travel time and spatial access to abortion facilities in the US before and after the *Dobbs v Jackson Women's Health* Decision" (2022) 328:20 *Journal of the American Medical Association* 2041.
66 Lauren Egan & Corky Siemaszko, "What U.S. women can learn from Poland's recent abortion restrictions" (16 May 2022), online: *NBC News*. www.nbcnews.com/news/world/us-women-can-learn-polands-recent-abortion-restrictions-rcna28750.
67 Peter Zimonjic, "American women can obtain abortions in Canada if Roe v. Wade falls, minister says" (3 May 2022), online: *NBC News*. www.cbc.ca/news/politics/canada-provide-abortion-access-american-women-1.6440238>.
68 Jillian Schneidman & Camille Zeitouni, "Opinion: Canadian physicians need better abortion training" (21 September 2022), online: *Montreal Gazette*. https://montrealgazette.com/opinion/opinion-canadian-physicians-need-better-abortion-training.
69 Marielle Kirstein et al, "100 days post-Roe: At least 66 clinics across 15 US States have stopped offering abortion care" (6 October 2022), online: *The Guttmacher Institute*. www.guttmacher.org/2022/10/100-days-post-roe-least-66-clinics-across-15-us-states-have-stopped-offering-abortion-care.

26

BORDERS DRAWN ACROSS BODIES

Advocating for Maternal Health in Times of Crisis

Sarah J. Lazin

While the COVID-19 virus did not discriminate in who it infected, the effects of the pandemic were far-reaching and deeply gendered, uniquely impacting women and girls. It is well-known that infectious diseases pose substantial risks to pregnant women, their fetuses, and neonates, yet impacts of outbreaks specific to maternal health have been consistently overlooked and underreported. Even less attention is paid to how pandemics impact fertility care, as well as the social and economic barriers preventing women from accessing reproductive healthcare.

This chapter examines how women of child-bearing age have been uniquely impacted by the COVID-19 pandemic. It takes up persisting tensions between autonomy and paternalism and the power imbalances that shape a woman's ability to freely exercise autonomy over her own healthcare decisions. Further, it discusses borders drawn between social groups that isolate women from both community and care. These borders include timely access to vaccinations (or lack thereof), as well as barriers preventing women from accessing healthcare.

This chapter will argue that women's reproductive health is uniquely and disproportionately affected by healthcare crises and, as such, must be reflected in local and international approaches to future and ongoing public health disasters. In doing so, this chapter will proceed on the assumption that the reproductive autonomy of a woman is paramount.[1]

26.1 Maternal Health in Times of Crisis

As with countless past healthcare crises, COVID-19 continues to disproportionately affect pregnant women, both medically and socially. During the 2014 Ebola outbreak, for example, pregnancy was associated with extremely

DOI: 10.4324/9781003394006-35

high maternal fatality rates, as well as nearly guaranteed miscarriage, stillbirth, or neonatal death.[2] Thousands of pregnant women were denied emergency obstetrical care, regardless of whether or not they actually had Ebola, due to the risk posed by potentially contagious bodily fluids expelled during childbirth.[3] Many of these pregnant women ultimately died from otherwise preventable causes,[4] overshadowed by fear and emergency.

In the context of the COVID-19 pandemic, pregnant women who contract the virus are nearly five times more likely to be admitted to a hospital and at least ten times more likely to be admitted to an ICU than their non-pregnant counterparts.[5] More worryingly, a study by the University of Washington reported COVID-19 mortality to be 13 times higher in pregnant women than their non-pregnant counterparts.[6] There are also much higher rates of pre-term birth among pregnant women who have COVID-19, which subsequently poses additional risks to both mother and child.[7] Of those infants carried to term by a COVID-positive mother, nearly 10% are subsequently admitted to the neonatal ICU (NICU).[8] There has also been a small, but noted, rate of pregnancy loss (approximately 2%), and the high fevers caused by serious COVID-19 infection can raise the risk of birth defects, especially during the first trimester.[9] In fact, COVID-19 was the leading cause of maternal deaths in Mexico and Colombia in 2021.[10]

Importantly, it is likely that pandemic-related maternal deaths continue to be systematically undercounted and underreported, if counted at all.[11] This contributes to dangerous gaps in health data which influence how much attention individual countries and international organizations pay to maternal health when addressing healthcare crises.[12]

26.2 Barriers to Vaccines

The first "border" discussed in this chapter is that drawn between pregnant women and the general population in terms of vaccine development and testing. This exclusion is not novel, new, or unique to COVID-19,[13] and barriers to vaccine equity are imposed both by governments and/or pharmaceutical companies, as well as by social influences.[14]

26.2.1 Exclusion from Vaccine Testing

Maternal vaccinations are fundamental to public health outcomes, yet pregnant women were specifically excluded from most COVID-19 vaccine trials. Women have been—and continue to be—"inappropriately excluded from participating in some research."[15] As expressed in the Tri Council Policy Statement on Research Ethics:

> This exclusion of women, where unwarranted, has **delayed the advancement of knowledge, denied potential benefits to women, and exposed**

> **women to harm** when research findings from male-only research projects were generalized inappropriately to women, as has often been the case in clinical drug trials. The inclusion of women in research advances the commitment to Justice, improves the generalizability of research findings to women where that is a goal of the research, and is essential to ensure that women and men benefit equally from research.[16]

In their 2013 study, Shields and Lyerly estimated that only 1% of industry-sponsored studies were designed specifically for pregnant women and approximately 95% of Phase 4 clinical trials excluded pregnant women.[17] The hesitancy to include women of child-bearing age (whether pregnant or not) from clinical research stems largely from the ethical (and liability) consideration that both mother and fetus are involved and could potentially be impacted. And while this concern is understandable, the near-total exclusion of young women from clinical trials risks harming more people than it protects. The significant lack of data surrounding pregnancy and pharmaceuticals ultimately requires pregnant women and their healthcare providers to make decisions without being fully aware of the risks and/or benefits[18]—a dilemma not faced by most other adult patients who see themselves reflected in trials. For example, Shields and Lyerly estimate that over 50% of pregnant women use at least one prescription drug during their pregnancy—the safety of which is unknown due to a lack of clinical testing and human data.[19] Until women are adequately represented in pharmaceutical trials, pregnant patients will continue to be caught between a rock and a hard place, making partially informed decisions.

Perhaps unsurprisingly, all early COVID-19 vaccine trials and testing excluded pregnant and lactating women, despite a lack of safety concerns arising from decades of post-market data on other maternal vaccinations.[20] COVID-19 vaccine research involving pregnant women is finally underway now—mirroring the 2009 H1N1 influenza vaccine testing carried out on pregnant women only after years of post-market data demonstrated the safety of seasonal influenza vaccines in pregnant women.[21]

26.2.2 The Impact of Mixed Messaging

The lack of maternal-focused clinical data regarding COVID-19 vaccines has led to extremely mixed messaging by governments and public health bodies. And while the vaccine is now widely recommended for pregnant women in Canada, there remains ongoing vaccine hesitancy and proliferation of dangerous misinformation.

In January 2021, the safety and efficacy of maternal vaccines was decidedly unsettled. On January 7, the Center for Disease Control in the United States recommended that vaccination "is a personal choice for people who are pregnant."[22] The next day, the World Health Organization "recommended withholding [the Pfizer] vaccine from pregnant women unless the benefit of vaccination outweighs the potential risk, as in the case of healthcare workers or those who have comorbidities linked with severe COVID-19"; the organization gave the same advice for the Moderna vaccine two weeks later.[23] With no consensus in sight, the beginning of 2021 also saw a number of vaccination centres across Canada turning away pregnant or breastfeeding women.[24] At that time, Ontario explicitly recommended against vaccinating pregnant and breastfeeding people: because pregnant women were not involved in the vaccine trials, there was no sufficient data available on the safety and efficacy of either the Pfizer or Moderna vaccine for that group. The government of Quebec similarly held that the vaccination of "pregnant women will be determined based on future studies on vaccine safety and efficacy in these people."[25]

This stance was problematic for two key reasons: rather than advising pregnant women of the risks relating to vaccination and leaving them to make their own informed choice, the governments of Ontario and Quebec barred them from having the option. While other vulnerable populations were prioritized to receive protection against the pandemic, pregnant women were denied the same opportunity to exercise their healthcare decision-making autonomy. Second, a significant portion of the pregnant women urgently seeking vaccines were frontline healthcare workers.[26] While this data does not appear to have been collected in Canada, at any given point in the United States, approximately 300,000 healthcare workers are pregnant.[27] This is an enormous number of women who were constantly exposed to infection while caring for their communities yet were not permitted to make fundamental healthcare decisions for themselves. As a result, over 1,000 healthcare workers signed an online petition calling for Ontario to change its official position.[28] The petition cited the increased risk of pregnant women for contracting COVID-19 and the importance of a woman making her own healthcare decisions.[29]

In contrast, British Columbia's official recommendation was that while more research on vaccine safety in pregnancy was needed, those interested should talk to their healthcare provider and make their own decisions.[30] As a result, women in one province were able to exercise their autonomy while women in other parts of the country were not. And even if some pregnant women were able to cross provincial borders in search of a vaccine, they would then have to spend more time and money than their non-pregnant counterparts in order to be vaccinated. Furthermore, such travel would only be an option for some pregnant women, as many would already have familial and/or work obligations preventing them from leaving the province at the drop of a hat—deepening the vaccine inequity experienced across the country.

26.2.3 Misinformation and Vaccine Hesitancy

Nearly two years into the pandemic and one year into vaccine rollout, at the time of writing, the real-world data collected after pregnant women received the COVID-19 vaccine around the world has not raised any safety flags. In

Canada, vaccines are now widely recommended during pregnancy by numerous organizations including the Provincial Council for Maternal and Child Health, the Ontario Society of Obstetricians and Gynaecologists, the Society of Obstetricians and Gynecologists of Canada, and the National Advisory Committee on Immunization.[31] However, pregnant women are now making up an alarming number of hospital and ICU admissions, virtually all of whom are unvaccinated.[32] While the majority of the general antivax population cites "personal freedoms" as their reason for avoiding vaccines, pregnant women primarily cite a lack of clinical data and rampant misinformation.[33]

Whether described as "misinformation," "disinformation," or even an "infodemic," false or misleading information about healthcare poses significant risks to public health. Per the World Health Organization:

> [Misinformation] causes confusion and risk-taking behaviours that can harm health. It also leads to mistrust in health authorities and undermines the public health response. An infodemic can intensify or lengthen outbreaks when people are unsure about what they need to do to protect their health and the health of people around them.[34]

Rumours circulating social media linking the COVID-19 vaccine with infertility and miscarriages are among the most common.[35] While quickly disproven, in many cases, that seed of doubt has been enough to dissuade hundreds of people from getting vaccinated. Countless doctors around the world have dispelled the (in)fertility rumour. According to Jennifer Blake, the CEO of the Society of Obstetricians and Gynaecologists of Canada, not only is there no scientific evidence of any of the vaccines causing fertility issues, but such a connection would not be plausible, given that the vaccines have nothing to do with ovaries, eggs, or sperm.[36] This particular point of misinformation is thought to stem from reports of menstrual cycles changing after receiving the vaccine. By September 2021, over 30,000 reports of menstrual changes—including unexpected vaginal bleeding and changes in periods—were received in the United Kingdom alone.[37] While underreported and rarely studied, other vaccinations have also been associated with menstrual changes, likely due to a link between immunological responses and hormones.[38]

This point of misinformation thus becomes somewhat understandable. Thousands of women experienced similar side effects after receiving the vaccine, yet at the time of writing, no studies have been published that can explain precisely *why*. There are a handful of academic articles, such as the one written by Male, that clarify this potential link does not equate to infertility; however, there are hundreds of clickbait articles popping up online to suggest otherwise.[39] It is unclear whether this dearth in knowledge is due to a lack of academic interest or whether the speed of academic research and reporting is simply too slow to quell public fears (whereas misinformation can be readily shared online in seconds). If women's unique health experiences are not adequately researched and understood in a timely manner, or if the resulting publications are hidden behind paywalls (or are written only in medical or legal jargon), the public is left to unravel the science themselves and to make potentially unsupported conclusions. Importantly, mere "[p]erceptions of safety risk, even mild ones, may exert a disproportionate effect on the willingness of pregnant women to accept vaccinations."[40] In the case of COVID-19, this has resulted in mass vaccine hesitancy in young women.[41]

26.3 Barriers to Community and Care

The second "border" taken up in this chapter concerns barriers to reproductive care throughout the pandemic. Access to reproductive care was deeply impacted by COVID-19. An estimated 14 million women and girls lost access to contraception, while millions more had limited (if not outright non-existent) access to maternal and newborn healthcare.[42,43]

26.3.1 The Closure of Clinics

In the spring of 2021, fertility clinics across Ontario stood divided as to whether they should remain open following a provincial directive to pause "non-urgent and non-emergent" procedures.[44] The directive allowed each specialty to classify procedures as lifesaving (or not), leaving substantial room for interpretation, especially amongst providers offering out-of-hospital procedures.[45] As a result, fertility societies in Canada, the United States, and Europe classified fertility care as "essential."[46] However, while "essential," the classification of fertility care as "emergent" or "urgent" remains unsettled. While its impact on "life or limb" is perhaps not as obvious as other types of healthcare, the inability to access fertility care—especially in the face of months-long disruptions—has caused tremendous emotional and psychological harm for some patients. The situation mirrors other healthcare procedures impacted by the COVID-19 pandemic. Dr. Alana Cattapan observed:

> [W]e've asked people to suspend cancer screening, and hip and knee replacements and a wide variety of other treatments that, I hesitate to use the word elective, because they so dramatically affect the quality of people's lives, and in many cases address the pain that they live with every day.[47]

Given that many patients pursuing fertility care are already at an advanced reproductive age, even a short delay could snowball down the road.[48] In some cases, such as preserving eggs or sperm before a patient undergoes imminent chemotherapy, time really is of the essence.[49] However, ongoing disruptions to fertility care have caused immense harm to patients, even without extenuating circumstances. Nearly 25% of patients surveyed by the American Society for Reproductive Medicine described the loss of a cycle as akin to "the loss of a child."[50] Patients at advanced reproductive age or with lower financial resources available to them were the least likely to accept "fertility treatment as an elective procedure that could be indefinitely postponed."[51] This is especially true for rural patients who have to travel to receive care (and now may have to start over and pay for more visits).

Importantly, many patients surveyed did understand the necessity of closing clinics.[52] Their concerns centred largely on (1) the lack of clear information, timelines, and next steps and (2) the lack of consideration paid to fertility patients by policymakers. Could it not have been possible, for example, to allow women to finish an egg retrieval or IVF cycle, without allowing other patients to begin new cycles?[53]

26.3.2 Alone in Labour

For those patients who gave birth during the COVID-19 pandemic, public health measures intended to reduce the spread of the virus often had unintended consequences on birth and maternal health outcomes. In attempting to limit the transmission of COVID-19, hospitals around the world imposed restrictions on how many visitors pregnant women could have prior to, during, and following labour.[54] This is particularly true of COVID-19–positive women, who were often denied any visitors whatsoever.[55] In fact, COVID-19–positive women were 11 times more likely to be denied a support person during labour than those uninfected.[56]

Social isolation surrounding childbirth can be frightening, lonely, and stressful.[57] Further, it is known to increase the risk for maternal morbidity; in fact, the WHO recommends continuous companionship during labour "for all pregnant women to potentially improve labor outcomes."[58] COVID-19–positive women who were denied visitors were six times more likely to report acute stress symptoms during or following labour.[59] Denying women a support person during labour is also linked to greater pain in delivery, elevated NICU admission rates, and increased maternal mental illness during the postpartum period.[60]

Social isolation policies also caused notable harm to patient partners.[61] Partners and support persons "experienced a sense of 'missing out' from the pregnancy and maternity care experience . . . They reported feelings of isolation, psychological distress, and reduced bonding time with babies."[62]

Public health measures pertaining to labour also extended beyond the hospital walls. In the UK, for example, home births were suspended during COVID-19, necessitating pregnant women give birth in-hospital.[63] Such drastic changes to a patient's birth plan were described as "traumatic," while the constant changes to public health guidance and measures created significant fear and stress among pregnant patients and their families.[64] While it does appear that homebirths were permitted in Canada throughout the pandemic,[65] requiring all births occur in-hospital is reminiscent of Canada's birth evacuation policy, where women from remote communities are required to give birth in urban hospitals.[66] This ongoing policy burdens Indigenous women—and particularly Inuit women—with social, emotional, and financial harms, including the loss of emotional ties and familial support during labour, as well as the loss of intergenerational knowledge exchanges and traditional practices.[67]

Similarly, COVID-19–positive women were far more likely to be separated from their newborns, contributing to immense stress.[68] While little has been written on this topic to date (within the COVID-19 context, that is), it is likely that such separation would be particularly traumatizing for Indigenous mothers, who have good reason to be fearful of hospitals separating them from their children.[69]

Many have argued that the correct balance was not always struck when imposing visitor restrictions; as such, many complete visitor bans were amended to exclude maternity wards, allowing one support person for at least part of the labour and delivery process.[70] In moving forward through this pandemic and those to come, more research is needed into the stress and trauma experienced by women without support available to them during labour and delivery. Specifically, future research should focus on women with low health literacy (who may not feel comfortable or safe in clinical settings) and on women from rural or Indigenous communities who were required (whether by policy or simply due to reduced community resources during the pandemic) to come into urban centres to give birth.

26.4 In Conclusion: Moving Forward

The past three years have been universally challenging, to say the least. However, it has been widely recognized that certain populations have been disproportionately harmed by the COVID-19 pandemic. In Canada, and elsewhere, this pandemic has highlighted—and indeed, worsened—reproductive health inequities. And when the healthcare system was stretched too thin during the COVID-19 pandemic, equitable access to reproductive healthcare quickly fell through the cracks.

We have seen the following time and time again:

> [T]he consequences of living in a world built around male data can be deadly. [Yet] one of the most important things to say about the gender data gap is that it is not generally malicious, or even deliberate. Quite the opposite. It is simply the product of a way of thinking that has been around for millennia and is therefore a kind of *not* thinking.[71]

Thus, whether focused on female inclusion in clinical trials, contradictory or confusing public health messaging, rampant misinformation, or on specific public health measures that disproportionately impact women, significantly more research is needed on the unique positionality of women—and particularly of pregnant women—during this and future pandemics.

It is unclear when the next pandemic will emerge and how long we have to make meaningful progress in including women's voices and data in public health policy and emergency preparedness. What is certain, however, "is that pregnancy and childbirth, even during global health disasters and humanitarian emergencies, will always happen."[72]

Notes

1 See, e.g., Erin Nelson, "Autonomy, equality, and access to sexual and reproductive health care" (2017) 54:3 *The Alberta Law Review* 707. See also: "Women's autonomy, equality and reproductive health" (2017), online: *UN Human Rights Office of the High Commissioner*. www.ohchr.org/en/special-procedures/wg-women-and-girls/womens-autonomy-equality-and-reproductive-health.

2 Lisa B. Haddad, Denise J. Jamieson & Sonia A. Rasmussen, "Pregnant women and the ebola crisis," (2018) 379:26 *The New England Journal of Medicine* 2492 at 2492. See also Sam F. Halabi, "Zika, pregnancy, and the law" (2017) 70:3 *Arkansas Law Review* 707 at 718.

3 Severine Caluwaerts & Patricia Kahn, "Ebola and pregnant women" in David A. Schwartz et al, eds, *Pregnant in the Time of Ebola* (Switzerland: Springer Nature, 2019) 87 at 89.

4 John E. Deaver & Wayne R. Cohen, "Ebola virus screening during pregnancy in West Africa: unintended consequences" (2015) 43:6 *Journal of Perinatal Medicine* 649.

5 Nicole Ireland, "Why doctors are so worried about pregnant people getting COVID-19" (4 November 2021), online: *CBC News*. cbc.ca/news/health/fertility-and-pregnancy-covid-19-vaccine-1.6233434; Lauren Pelley, "COVID-19 during pregnancy means 10 times higher risk of ICU admission, Canadian data suggests," *CBC News* (16 September 2021), online: cbc.ca/news/health/covid-pregnancy-risk-icu-hospitalization-1.6176742.

6 Erica M. Lokken et al, "Disease severity, pregnancy outcomes, and maternal deaths among pregnant patients with severe acute respiratory syndrome coronavirus 2 infection in Washington State" (2021) 225 *The American Journal of Obstetrics and Gynecology* 77.e1.

7 Muriel Draaisma & Paula Duhatschek, "Ontario doctors to urge pregnant women to get vaccinated against COVID-19" (30 October 2021), online: *CBC News*. cbc.ca/news/canada/toronto/oma-pregnancy-vaccination-covid-19–1.6231642.

8 "Canadian surveillance of COVID-19 in pregnancy: Epidemiology, maternal and infant outcomes" Report 1 (2020) at 2, online (pdf): med-fom-ridprogram.sites.olt.ubc.ca/files/2021/10/CANCOVID-Preg-report-1–19Oct2021.pdf.

9 Jeanne Sheffield, "Coronavirus and pregnancy: What you should know" (last modified 4 February 2021), online: *Johns Hopkins Medicine*. hopkinsmedicine.org/health/conditions-and-diseases/coronavirus/coronavirus-and-covid-19-what-pregnant-women-need-to-know.

10 "PAHO Director urges countries to prioritize pregnant and lactating women for COVID-19 vaccinations" (8 September 2021), online: *Pan American Health Organization*. paho.org/en/news/8–9–2021-paho-director-urges-countries-prioritize-pregnant-and-lactating-women-covid-19.

11 Sedigheh Hantoushzadeh et al, "Maternal death due to COVID-19" (2020) 223 *The American Journal of Obstetrics and Gynecology* 109.e1 at 109.e10. See also Erica M. Lokken et al, "Disease severity, pregnancy outcomes, and maternal deaths among pregnant patients with severe acute respiratory syndrome coronavirus 2 infection in Washington State" (2021) 225 *The American Journal of Obstetrics and Gynecology* 77.e1 at 77.e8.
12 Caroline Criado Perez, *Invisible Women: Data Bias in a World Designed for Men* (New York: Abrams Press, 2019). See, in particular, Chapter 16: "It's Not the Disaster That Kills You," *ibid* at 296.
13 See, e.g., Sam F. Halabi, "Zika, pregnancy, and the law" (2017) 70:3 *Arkansas Law Review* 707.
14 For further discussion on (in)equities in vaccine access, see Adam R. Houston's chapter in this volume.
15 Panel on Research Ethics, "Tri-council policy statement" (2018), online: *Government of Canada.* ethics.gc.ca/eng/tcps2-eptc2_2018_chapter4-chapitre4.html#b. See also Halabi, *supra* note 13.
16 Panel on Research Ethics, "Tri-Council Policy Statement" (2018), online: *Government of Canada.* ethics.gc.ca/eng/tcps2-eptc2_2018_chapter4-chapitre4.html#b [emphasis added].
17 Kristine E. Shields & Anne Drapkin Lyerly, "Exclusion of pregnant women from industry-sponsored clinical trials" (2013) 122:5 *The American College of Obstetricians and Gynecologists* 1077 at 1077.
18 *Ibid* at 1077.
19 *Ibid* at 1081.
20 Rita Rubin, "Pregnant people's paradox—Excluded from vaccine trials despite having a higher risk of COVID-19 complications" (2021) 325:11 *Journal of the American Medical Association* 1027 at 1027.
21 See, e.g., "NIH begins study of COVID-19 vaccination during pregnancy and postpartum" (2021), online: *National Institutes of Health.* www.nih.gov/news-events/news-releases/nih-begins-study-covid-19-vaccination-during-pregnancy-postpartum; Tom T. Shimabukuro et al, "Preliminary findings of mRNA COVID-19 vaccine safety in pregnant persons" (2021) 384 *The New England Journal of Medicine* 2273; "New study further demonstrates COVID-19 mRNA vaccines are safe during pregnancy" (2022), online: *UBC Faculty of Medicine.* www.med.ubc.ca/news/new-study-further-demonstrates-covid-19-mrna-vaccines-are-safe-during-pregnancy/.
22 Rubin, *supra* note 20 at 1027.
23 *Ibid* at 1027.
24 Lauren Pelley, "Ontario ob-gyns push back on policies advising against COVID-19 vaccine for pregnant or breastfeeding women" (5 January 2021), online: *CBC News.* cbc.ca/news/canada/toronto/pregnant-women-covid-vaccine-1.5861631.
25 *Ibid.*
26 *Ibid.*
27 Rubin, *supra* note 20 at 1028.
28 Pelley, *supra* note 24.
29 *Ibid.*
30 *Ibid.*
31 Muriel Draaisma & Paula Duhatschek, "Ontario doctors to urge pregnant women to get vaccinated against COVID-19" (30 October 2021), online: *CBC News.* cbc.ca/news/canada/toronto/oma-pregnancy-vaccination-covid-19–1.6231642.
32 *Ibid.* See also: Kathryn Ivey, "If you are pregnant, I am begging you to get the covid vaccine. The only young, healthy women in our ICU have all been pregnant. Every single one. They crash harder and faster and with worse outcomes than any

other patient group I've seen. Please get the vaccine" (27 April 2021 at 23:31), online: *Twitter*. https://twitter.com/kathryniveyy/status/1387247990977478656.

33 See, e.g., Leigh Ann Simmons et al, "Understanding COVID-19 vaccine uptake during pregnancy: 'Hesitance', knowledge, and evidence-based decision-making" (2022) 40 *Vaccine* 2755.

34 "Infodemic", online: *World Health Organization*. who.int/health-topics/infodemic#tab=tab_1.

35 Colleen Underwood, "Spike of unvaccinated pregnant women in COVID-19 ICUs concerning, says Calgary doctor" (10 September 2021), online: *CBC News*. cbc.ca/news/canada/calgary/pregnant-covid-eliana-castillo-icu-1.6170575.

36 Nicole Ireland, "Why doctors are so worried about pregnant people getting COVID-19" (4 November 2021), online: *CBC News*. cbc.ca/news/health/fertility-and-pregnancy-covid-19-vaccine-1.6233434.

37 Victoria Male, "Menstrual changes after COVID-19 vaccination" (2021) 15 *BMJ Open* 1 at 1.

38 *Ibid*.

39 *Ibid*.

40 Halabi, *supra* note 13 at 720.

41 Male, *supra* note 37 at 1.

42 "Restore sexual, reproductive health rights lost during COVID, rights expert urges" (20 October 2021), online: *UN News*. https://news.un.org/en/story/2021/10/1103562.

43 While abortion is a fundamental pillar of reproductive health, the impact of the COVID-19 pandemic on abortion access will not be discussed in this chapter. For further reading on the subject, see the chapter by Christabelle Sethna and Krystyna Dzwonkowska-Godula in this volume.

44 Brooke Taylor, "Ontario fertility clinics left in limbo after directive to cease non-emergency procedures" (24 April 2021), online: *CTV News*. www.ctvnews.ca/health/coronavirus/ontario-fertility-clinics-left-in-limbo-after-directive-to-cease-non-emergency-procedures-1.5400833.

45 *Ibid*.

46 *Ibid*; See also "CFAS COVID-19 update # 17: April 22, 2021" (22 April 2021), online: *Canadian Fertility & Andrology Society*. https://cfas.ca/CFAS_Communication_on_COVID-19.html.

47 Taylor, *supra* note 44.

48 *Ibid*. Importantly, maternal age of 35 is also associated with worsened morbidity and mortality when infected with COVID during pregnancy, thus furthering the risks and challenges facing many fertility care patients. See Ashley Raeside, Manavi Handa & Rachel Spitzer, "The disproportionate impact of COVID-19 on already marginalized communities: Considerations for sexual and reproductive health care" (2021) 43:11 *Journal of Obstetrics and Gynaecology Canada* 1229.

49 Taylor, *supra* note 44; Raeside, Handa & Spitzer, "*supra* note 48.

50 "Most patients resumed IVF treatment during the COVID-19 pandemic shutdown immediately when able" (19 October 2020), online: *American Society for Reproductive Medicine*. www.asrm.org/news-and-publications/covid-19/covid-19-press-releases-and-announcements/most-patients-resumed-ivf-treatment-during-the-covid-19-pandemic-shut-down-immediately-when-able/.

51 Karen N. DSouza et al, "Impact of the COVID-19 Pandemic on Patient Fertility Care" (2022) 9 *Journal of Patient Experience* 1 at 5.

52 Lindsay Kalter, "Infertility amid COVID-19: 'Our hopes were taken away'" (24 January 2022), online: *WebMD*. www.webmd.com/infertility-and-reproduction/news/20220124/infertility-amid-covid.

53 DSouza et al, *supra* note 51 at 5.

54 Kavita Shah Arora, Jaclyn T. Mauch & Kelly Smith Gibson, "Labor and delivery visitor policies during the COVID-19 pandemic: Balancing risks and benefits" (2020) 323:24 *Journal of the American Medical Association* 2468.
55 Gus Mayopoulos et al, "Giving birth under hospital visitor restrictions: Heightened acute stress in childbirth in COVID-19 positive women" (2020) *Research Square* (Preprint) 1.
56 *Ibid* at 2.
57 Ezra Aydin et al, "Giving birth in a pandemic: Women's birth experiences in England during COVID-19" (2022) 22 *BMC Pregnancy & Childbirth* 1 at 8.
58 Arora, Mauch & Gibson, *supra* note 54, citing "Companion of choice during labour and childbirth for improved quality of care" (2016), online (pdf): *World Health Organization*. https://apps.who.int/iris/bitstream/handle/10665/250274/WHO-RHR-16.10-eng.pdf;jsessionid=C416229E2871679B16D791787E1CF326.
59 Mayopoulos et al, *supra* note 55 at 11.
60 *Ibid.*
61 Vidanka Vasilevski et al, "Receiving maternity care during the COVID-19 pandemic: Experiences of women's partners and support persons" (2022) 35 *Women & Birth* 298.
62 *Ibid.*
63 Aydin et al, *supra* note 57 at 6.
64 *Ibid* at 6–7.
65 "Home birth during the COVID-19 pandemic: A viable option for all clients at low risk of complications" (2020), online (pdf): *Midwives of Mississauga*. www.midwivesofmississauga.ca/wp-content/uploads/AOM-Choice-of-Birthplace-during-the-COVID-19-Pandemic-April-2020.pdf.
66 Jaime Cidro, Rachel Bach & Susan Frohlick, "Canada's Forced Birth Travel: Towards Feminist Indigenous Reproductive Mobilities" (2020) 15:2 *Mobilities* 173 at 173.
67 *Ibid* at 176; Erika Finestone & Cynthia Stirbys, "Indigenous birth in Canada: Reconciliation and reproductive justice in the Settler State" in Hannah Tait Neufeld & Jaime Cidro, eds, *Indigenous Experiences of Pregnancy and Birth* (Brantford: Demeter Press, 2017) 176 at 4–5.
68 Mayopoulos et al, *supra* note 55 at 11.
69 Finestone & Stirbys, *supra* note 67 at 5.
70 Arora, Mauch & Gibson, *supra* note 54; Aydin et al, *supra* note 57.
71 Caroline Criado Perez, *Invisible Women: Data Bias in a World Designed for Men* (New York: Abrams Press, 2019) at XII [emphasis in original].
72 Sharon A. Abramowitz, "Ebola's assault on women, children, and family reproduction" in David A. Schwartz et al, eds, *Pregnant in the Time of Ebola* (Switzerland: Springer Nature, 2019) 3 at 3.

27

KEEPING BORDER RESTRICTIONS LIGHT ENOUGH TO TRAVEL

A Humanitarian Perspective on Canada's Border Control Measures during COVID-19

Jason W. Nickerson and Joseph Belliveau

27.1 Introduction

As the world has quickly learned, public health is highly influenced and impacted by global events. Simplistically, viruses do not respect borders and can represent transnational threats warranting global responses that mutualize and optimize the use of global resources, such as health workers with expertise in emerging infectious diseases, medical supply chains capable of meeting global demand, and research and development for new vaccines, therapeutics, diagnostic tests, and medical devices. Amidst this competition for human and other health resources during the COVID-19 pandemic, countries made controversial and at times unpopular policy choices to enact restrictive measures that significantly limited the movement of people and goods domestically and internationally by, for example, closing borders, imposing curfews, and limiting access to public spaces. In this chapter, we argue that a more careful balance is needed between restrictive measures to mitigate the impact and spread of infectious diseases and the need to ensure the continuity of global ongoing health and humanitarian programming both related and unrelated to pandemics to ensure that people continue to be able to access lifesaving medical care and that throughout the pandemic, this balance was not adequately struck. We draw on the specific example of Canada's border restrictions to illustrate this.

As countries rushed to close their borders to attempt to slow or stop the transmission of COVID-19, they created blockages—either inadvertent or deliberate—to the flow of essential medical personnel and cargo. Governments sought, for example, to limit the export of medical equipment, such as personal protective equipment (PPE) that was in high demand and low

DOI: 10.4324/9781003394006-36

availability.[1] States quickly realized that most, if not all, countries lacked the domestic manufacturing capabilities needed to produce the full complement of medical supplies to protect populations and provide often complex clinical care requiring protective equipment to keep their health workforce healthy and deliver medical care to the sick.

Taken together, attempts to hermetically seal countries from one another and to hoard supplies amidst uncertain but escalating domestic needs quickly resulted in limiting the flow of essential medical goods from countries where they were manufactured or stockpiled to countries where the pandemic was raging.[2] They also impeded the ability of health workers to move to where they were needed most if that entailed crossing an international border. The movement of health and humanitarian personnel became particularly important, as many countries realized they lacked suitable quantities of qualified health personnel and emergency managers capable of and experienced in responding to this public health emergency, as most health systems in the world had never faced such strain. While governments did enact some exemptions to these rules, they were often clumsily designed and self-serving, designed with domestic needs in mind but neglecting the global response that was truly needed to fully respond to the pandemic as a matter of shared global public health responsibility, as well as global health ethics. The most egregious recent example of this was COVID-19 vaccine inequity, whereby wealthy countries reserved and hoarded billions of doses of vaccines, placing them out of reach of billions of people living in low- and middle-income countries for months.[3] This rich-country-first approach severely hamstrung humanitarian and other actors' ability to fight COVID-19 globally and almost certainly lengthened and worsened the impact of the pandemic overall.

Border closures also played a role in humanitarian organizations' abilities to respond to the pandemic as well as to other humanitarian crises by limiting these organizations' staff from traveling to and from emergencies and, in some cases, unjustifiably placing restrictions on humanitarian medical cargo that was needed to save lives and alleviate suffering during armed conflicts, forced displacement, natural disasters, and disease epidemics.

Such restrictions had very real consequences for Doctors Without Borders/ Médecins Sans Frontières' (MSF's) humanitarian response. MSF is a medical and humanitarian organization responding to crises in more than 70 countries affected by armed conflict, disease epidemics, forced displacement, and other emergencies. Our programs provide both emergency and essential life-saving medical care to people who are often systematically excluded from accessing it for a variety of reasons, including the absence of other formal or high-quality health services. Moreover, our teams bring expertise in the response to acute medical emergencies, including disease outbreaks such as COVID-19 and others, which meant that as the world began to close its borders to limit international and domestic travel and mobility, our organization needed to continue, even scale up, its operations and keep moving across borders. During the COVID-19 pandemic, our operational footprint increased to include multiple high-income countries whose health systems were collapsing or were neglecting people experiencing vulnerability. This meant that overly restrictive measures placed enormous stress on MSF's ability to respond both to COVID-19 and non-COVID-19 humanitarian needs globally.

As a medical organization, we are acutely aware of the value of public health measures designed to curb the spread and impact of an infectious disease outbreak. However, we are equally aware of the need to build trust in health systems, services, and professionals[4] as essential for ensuring the success of any public health measures and of the need to strike a balance between restrictive measures and the freedom of movement required to provide essential health services both in response to such an outbreak as well as for other urgent health needs.

27.2 Scope and Scale of Humanitarian Travel Restrictions: People and Planes

Border restrictions introduced in response to the global spread of COVID-19 were extensive and varied, with different countries forbidding and allowing different people and things, resulting in a complex and often unclear picture of who and what could go where and which permissions were required to do so. Here, we focus on two aspects of humanitarian responses that were particularly impacted by COVID-19 restrictions, both because of direct and specific restrictions on them as well as their omission from national guidelines and restrictions: humanitarian personnel and humanitarian flights.

More than 80% of MSF staff are locally hired program staff.[5] However, the success of our operations also depends on having regular and reliable international air transportation and access to projects in crisis settings for our international program staff who bring expertise in medical specialties, humanitarian logistics, and emergency operations management. In March 2020, international borders closed, most countries imposed significant and strict quarantine measures for anyone entering their territories, and international flights quickly disappeared as the global commercial aviation industry ground to a halt. In almost all cases, at least initially, medical and humanitarian personnel were not exempted from these quarantine restrictions, creating significant logistical barriers and delays for our operations.

The COVID-19 pandemic created substantial disruptions to health systems around the world, reducing access to lifesaving health services and disrupting basic disease control and response activities, such as routine immunizations.[6] As a medical and humanitarian organization that is often the provider of last resort for millions of people affected by crises, it was not an option for our staff to stop traveling to provide lifesaving assistance.

With few options available to us to access commercial flights, MSF booked more than 150 flights on the United Nations Humanitarian Air Service, with our staff accounting for more than half of the air services' passenger volume by May 2020.[7] MSF also made use of humanitarian flight hubs established in Addis Ababa, Ethiopia, Accra, and Ghana, allowing a limited number of our staff to travel to and from our medical projects in East, Central, and West Africa to allow the continuity of lifesaving medical programs. In other locations, MSF staff benefited from being able to put staff and cargo onto repatriation flights that were often organized by governments, including the Canadian government.

Prior to the COVID-19 pandemic, approximately 650 MSF staff were departing from various countries, including Canada, for international assignments each month. However, by April 2020, this number had dropped to 114 and rose only slightly to 202 in May. MSF also saw a significant decrease in our international departures of Canadian field staff, in part due to travel restrictions and the collapse of international flight routes that challenged our organization's ability to guarantee staff could predictably be given the opportunity to leave a field assignment if they needed to, for example, to return home in the event of a family emergency or even for medical care—at least in part because of overly restrictive border measures. While border restrictions and quarantine requirements presented significant barriers, they were not the only relevant challenges we faced in recruiting and deploying staff to the field. They were, however, the one thing that was clearly in the hands of Canadian policymakers.

On March 20, 2020, Canada enacted its first border control measures restricting who could enter or transit through the country but made no mention of who could leave the country which still allowed us to deploy staff from Canada, provided they could enter or transit through other countries—including their final destination. Canada's border control measures were enacted through an Order in Council, pursuant to section 58 of the *Quarantine Act*, which established broad prohibitions on people entering Canada for any purpose and initially contained few exemptions.[8] The restrictive prohibitions on entering the country were immediately decried by our organization along with other legal and human rights actors for closing Canada's borders to asylum seekers.[9] Although there were a small number of criteria establishing nonapplication of the Order in Council, none of them were applicable to international humanitarian workers.

The first Order in Council expired one month after coming into effect. Over the coming months, guided by pragmatic realizations that some travel into Canada was essential for maintaining basic societal functions, subsequent Orders in Council expanded the list of classes of individuals for whom the border entry restrictions did not apply. As the orders were regularly updated, over time, they came to include exemptions for airplane crew members, members of the armed forces, health professionals working in Canada, students attending post-secondary institutions in Canada, medical couriers delivering blood products, human organs, and other tissues, and several others. On November 29, 2020, Canada introduced a framework for approving travel by a "high-performance athlete" attending an international single-sport event, requiring a letter of permission to be issued by the Deputy Minister of Canadian Heritage upon application from individuals satisfying these criteria.[10] Other travelers were able to return to Canada provided they completed a mandatory isolation period of 14 days.[11] For several months, Canada also required that returning travelers complete an isolation period in a government-approved hotel until they obtained a negative polymer chain reaction (PCR) test and could complete the remainder of the 14-day isolation at another location, such as their home. In short, Canada gradually loosened its border restrictions to ensure that individuals whose presence in Canada was deemed to be "in the national interest" could enter—including professional hockey players—and to allow Canadians returning to the country to do so if they completed a prolonged period of quarantine.

The imposition of these restrictions by Canada created multiple problems for humanitarian organizations like ours, who at no point were exempted from any Canadian border control or immigration measures. While these measures created logistical hurdles for our Canadian staff returning home (discussed later in this chapter), these were not impossible barriers to overcome. Reaching field locations in the Americas was, however, more complicated and not served by the humanitarian air hubs that were established in Ethiopia and Ghana. Access to MSF's medical projects in Haiti became particularly challenging, as our teams operate a trauma and burns hospital, a trauma stabilization point in a neighborhood affected by gang violence, one of the only 24/7 sexual and gender-based violence clinics, plus emergency responses to peaks of violence, disease outbreaks, natural disasters, and other emergencies. Prior to the COVID-19 pandemic, there were multiple flights to and from the Caribbean nation from Canada and the United States, along with regular flights from some European cities. However, at various moments in the pandemic, transiting through Canada became the sole option for a variety of operational reasons.

Humanitarian workers who needed to transit through Canadian airports to reach humanitarian programs in places such as Haiti were also not exempted from any of Canada's border restrictions. Under the orders, individuals who transited through Canada and remained in the "sterile" area of an airport were able to travel and could reach connecting flights in Canada. However, because of the disruptions to commercial flights and the few flights departing from Canada to Haiti, such an arrangement would have required humanitarian staff to sleep in airport terminals sometimes for more than a day, which is neither practical nor consistent with public health guidance to limit exposure to public spaces during a respiratory disease pandemic. Under Canada's border restrictions, some ministers were given the ability to issue exemptions to entry prohibitions on a case-by-case basis and granted several thousand of them throughout the pandemic for various, largely commercial, reasons.[12] A limited number of National Interest Exemption Letters were issued for humanitarians by the Minister of Foreign Affairs, though this was an incomplete solution dependent on an unclear process for applying for such an exemption. The impact of these restrictions led to several gaps of essential medical and other profiles in our projects amidst a worsening humanitarian emergency. This remaining travel route to Haiti from Canada became even further disrupted and inaccessible when Canada announced on January 1, 2021, that airlines had agreed to suspend all flights to and from Mexico and Caribbean countries, including Haiti, until April 30, 2021—a measure clearly designed to limit vacation travel but with humanitarian staff becoming collateral damage in these restrictions.

Canada's quarantine hotel regime posed additional challenges for humanitarian organizations, as hotel reservations could be made only 48 hours prior to arriving and had to cover the first 72 hours that an individual would be in Canada. This posed two challenges: first, travel from humanitarian projects, particularly in armed conflicts, is complex. Staff traveling from remote locations may conceivably have to travel by car, boat, motorbike, and a domestic flight before reaching a capital city and an international flight, creating the possibility of substantial delays which made the 48-hour booking window impractical at times. Moreover, the cost of these hotels—which were nonrefundable—imposed a substantial burden on charities who had to cover this expense to comply with these Canadian government regulations.

27.3 Discussion

Canada's border restrictions were removed on October 1, 2022, for all travelers, including individuals who had not completed a primary series of vaccinations against COVID-19. At no point were humanitarians specifically exempted from them.

Canada's imposition of border control measures restricting the transit of humanitarian personnel through Canadian territory to reach humanitarian crises or when returning from them failed to take into consideration the reality that humanitarians played—and continue to play—an essential role in responding to the direct and indirect effects of the COVID-19 pandemic. Ensuring the continuity of medical programs in crisis-affected areas necessitates that medical, logistic, administrative, and other humanitarian personnel can reach people affected by crises, and their travel should not be impeded intentionally or unintentionally by government regulations. Entry requirements for Canadian staff returning to Canada were logistically complex;

however, the inability of staff to transit through Canadian airports without formally entering Canada during prolonged, multiday layovers while transiting to reach humanitarian emergencies—and subsequently being required to complete a 14-day quarantine before being allowed to exit—made travel by essential humanitarian personnel at times impossible.

It was, of course, possible for Canada to have created an exemption for humanitarian workers as it did for essential health workers and even professional athletes. If entire teams of hockey players can be exempted from border restrictions, surely, humanitarian medical personnel traveling to provide lifesaving assistance can be as well.

In the future, Canadian legislators should include, by default, exemptions for humanitarian workers in any restrictive measures and should consider the unintended consequences of legislation or regulations designed to limit the flow of people, materials, and finances across borders to ensure that a balance exists between restrictions and the necessary movement of essential personnel and goods. Beyond a moral responsibility to ensure the continued availability of humanitarian assistance, Canada also has a legal obligation to not impede humanitarian assistance, either directly or indirectly, pursuant to article 70(2) of Additional Protocol I to the *Geneva Conventions*, which specifically requires a state that is not party to a conflict to allow and facilitate the rapid and unimpeded passage of humanitarian personnel and equipment to reach an armed conflict where the *Geneva Conventions* apply.[13] While Haiti was not, and as of this writing, is not, declared to be in an armed conflict, many of the places where MSF and other humanitarian organizations work are, and the basic principle that Canada should allow and facilitate the rapid passage of humanitarian medical relief to a country affected by crisis is clearly consistent with Canada's global responsibilities.

A lack of a humanitarian exemption in Canada's COVID-19 travel restrictions ought to be closely scrutinized, particularly in light of recent criticism that a lack of humanitarian exemption in Canada's anti-terror provisions in the *Criminal Code* has impeded humanitarian organizations' abilities to deliver assistance to the people of Afghanistan.[14] This suggests that Canada may not be systematically considering the impacts of Canadian legislation on the activities of impartial humanitarian organizations and is negligently creating domestic legislative barriers in contradiction to its international obligations and stated commitments.

The removal of restrictive measures that impede humanitarian assistance is not simply a matter for Canadian domestic law but should be viewed as part of a broader initiative underway to ensure that international legal instruments do not inadvertently or deliberately restrict access to humanitarian assistance. Recently, for example, the United Nations Security Council reached an agreement to create a standing humanitarian exemption to asset freeze measures in United Nations sanctions regimes, through the adoption of resolution 2664 (2022), removing a longstanding restrictive measure in these regimes.[15] Canadian legislators and policymakers ought to establish a clear process for scrutinizing future legislation to assess its potential impact on the operations of impartial humanitarian organizations. The present approach of enacting broad restrictions, blind to their consequences on some of the world's most vulnerable people living in crisis and in conflict-affected areas, is simply inadequate. It makes no accommodation for efforts aiming at saving lives and alleviating suffering. Humanitarian organizations are not asking to be exempted of responsibilities to take reasonable precautions to protect domestic public health. Rather, what we are asking is for Canada to be mindful of its responsibilities to ensure and facilitate access to humanitarian assistance and to take reasonable steps to make this a reality in current and future legislation and practice.

Notes

1 Chuan De Foo et al, "COVID-19 public health and social measures: a comprehensive picture of six Asian countries" (2022) 7 *BMJ Glob Health* e009863.
2 Sharmila Devi, "Travel restrictions hampering COVID-19 response" (2020) 395 *The Lancet* 10233, 1331–1332.
3 See Adam R. Houston's chapter in this volume.
4 Andrew S. Boozar, Paul E. Farmer & Ashish K. Jha, "The ebola outbreak, fragile health systems, and quality as a cure" (2014) 312 *Journal of the American Medical Association* 1859.
5 "International activity report 2021: 2021 in figures", online: *Médecins Sans Frontieres*. www.msf.org/international-activity-report-2021/2021-figures.
6 "Immunization" (last modified July 2022), online (statistics): *UNICEF Data*. https://data.unicef.org/topic/child-health/immunization/.
7 Médecins Sans Frontières, "Responding to COVID-19 global accountability report—March to May 2020" (19 August 2020), online: *MSF*. www.doctorswithoutborders.ca/responding-covid-19-global-accountability-report-march-may-2020.
8 PC 2020–161, (2020) C Gaz I. Minimizing the Risk of Exposure to COVID-19 in Canada Order (Prohibition of Entry into Canada from any Country Other than the United States).
9 "Closing Canada's border to refugee claimants is dangerous and illegal, and must be reversed" (30 March 2020), online: *Doctors Without Borders*. www.doctorswithoutborders.ca/article/closing-canada%E2%80%99s-border-refugee-claimants-dangerous-and-illegal-and-must-be-reversed. See also Audrey Macklin's chapter in this volume.
10 PC 2020–0967, (2020) C Gaz I. Minimizing the Risk of Exposure to COVID-19 in Canada Order (Prohibition of Entry into Canada from any Country Other than the United States).
11 Public Health Agency of Canada, News Release, "Government of Canada to remove COVID-19 border and travel measures effective October 1" (26 September 2022), online: *Government of Canada*. www.canada.ca/en/public-health/news/2022/09/government-of-canada-to-remove-covid-19-border-and-travel-measures-effective-october-1.html (2022).
12 Refugees and Citizenship Canada Immigration, "CIMM—Travel restrictions and exemptions—June 2, 2021" (22 September 2021), online: *Government of Canada*. www.canada.ca/en/immigration-refugees-citizenship/corporate/transparency/committees/cimm-jun-02-2021/travel-restrictions-exemptions.html.

13 "Treaties, states parties, and commentaries—Protocol additional to the Geneva Conventions, of 12 August 1949, and relating to the Protection Of Victims Of International Armed Conflicts (Protocol I), 8 June 1977.—Relief actions", online: *International Committee of the Red Cross*. https://ihl-databases.icrc.org/applic/ihl/ihl.nsf/Article.xsp?action=openDocument&documentId=609876DAFD3EEEACC12563CD0051DF9A.
14 Report of the Special Committee on Afghanistan: Honouring Canada's Legacy in Afghanistan: Responding to the Humanitarian Crisis and Helping People Reach Safety (Ottawa: 44–1, 2022), online: www.ourcommons.ca/DocumentViewer/en/44-1/AFGH/report-1. In June 2023, the Canadian Government passed legislation via Bill C-41 exempting humanitarian assistance from counter-terror finance laws.
15 UNSC, *Res 2664 (2022)*, S/RES/2664 (2022).

28

"WHERE YOU LIVE SHOULDN'T DETERMINE WHETHER YOU LIVE"

Canada and the Line between Rhetoric and Reality in Global COVID-19 Vaccine Equity

Adam R. Houston

Borders have impacted not only the movement of people and pathogens but also the tools to combat the COVID-19 pandemic. The successful development of multiple effective vaccines within a year of identifying a novel disease is an unprecedented scientific triumph. However, for billions of people in low- and middle-income countries (LMICs) who have yet to receive even a single dose, the benefits of this triumph have failed to accrue. As UN Secretary-General Guterres described the global vaccine rollout: "We passed the science test. But we are getting an F in ethics".[1]

Canada offers a striking case study in global vaccine equity. It has long tried to project the image of a leading proponent of global health. In July 2020, Prime Minister Trudeau's name sat atop an op-ed from eight world leaders in the *Washington Post*, which concluded by stating, "We call on global leaders to commit to contributing to an equitable distribution of the COVID-19 vaccine, based on the spirit of a greater freedom for all".[2] Canada's actions have not reflected its self-image or its equitable distribution rhetoric. By August 2020, Canada had embarked on a purchasing spree that within just a few months would lead to it securing the most doses per capita of any country in the world.[3] It would also do so without producing any vaccines domestically; every dose distributed in Canada as of the end of 2022—nearly 120 million doses—was manufactured elsewhere.[4]

Canada's procurements were trumpeted in the House of Commons; the 2020 Fall Economic Statement emphasized, "Canada has secured the most diverse and extensive vaccine portfolio of any country in the world", with up to 429 million doses—11 for every Canadian—from seven companies.[5] The government had considerably less to say about another important facet of procurement: if Canada was acquiring so much of what was, as the global

DOI: 10.4324/9781003394006-37

rollout began, a scarce commodity, what was left for other countries? And in turn, would Canada be willing to share?

Canadian officials dodged these questions throughout the fall of 2020. Not until December 17—during a televised media interview rather than in an official statement—would Trudeau finally publicly state that if there were any surplus, Canada would share.[6] This "if" would underpin Canadian vaccine policy for months to come. The resulting paradox might be termed Schrödinger's Vaccine: Canada would regularly offer forecasts for domestic supplies, with particular numbers of doses meant for Canadian arms arriving on specific timelines; however, the possibility of any of those very same doses from the very same contracts ever being shared remained a hypothetical.[7]

28.1 COVAX

There was, of course, a mechanism intended to ensure global vaccine equity. That mechanism was COVAX, a public-private partnership led by Gavi, the Vaccine Alliance. COVAX was meant to provide vaccines to cover a certain percentage of the population of all participating countries: the poorest countries would receive doses financed by the contributions of others, while wealthier countries, like Canada, would help support the mechanism while also receiving vaccines for themselves.

Crucially, COVAX, as initially conceived, was based entirely on procurement; it included no means of redistributing surplus doses from one country to another. The subsequent shift towards reliance on surplus doses underscores how wrong things went. A dissection of these failures is beyond the scope of this paper.[8] However, its designers drastically underestimated how badly COVAX would be undermined by national self-interest, particularly in the face of limited supply. By the time COVAX was procuring vaccines, most doses were already spoken for, placing COVAX well back in the queue. This affected not only the lowest-income countries, reliant on doses financed by other participants, but also wealthier countries, who were paying their own way but had relied primarily or entirely on COVAX to do so rather than procuring doses bilaterally from pharmaceutical companies. By mid-January 2021, while over 39 million doses had been received in 49 higher-income countries, just 25 doses had been administered in any lowest-income country.[9]

Critics of this disparity soon characterized the gap in access as "vaccine apartheid".[10] The World Health Organization (WHO) called for an end to further bilateral deals, with WHO Director-General Dr. Tedros criticizing countries that had scooped up more than their share: "Even as they speak the language of equitable access, some countries and companies continue to prioritize bilateral deals, going around COVAX, driving up prices and attempting to jump to the front of the queue".[11] Ignoring both pleas and criticisms, Canada entered into its eighth bilateral agreement, this time with the Serum Institute of India (SII) for COVISHIELD (SII's licensed version of the AstraZeneca vaccine).[12] Canada's SII deal was especially egregious from the perspective of vaccine equity, for reasons highlighting another serious COVAX flaw: COVAX was almost wholly dependent on SII to supply LMICs. Notably, however, Canada was not competing against its own allotment of COVAX doses; while SII's COVISHIELD was destined for LMICs, Canada's own doses received from COVAX were brand name AstraZeneca doses, manufactured in South Korea.[13] Thus, Canada was accepting doses from COVAX while simultaneously undercutting it.

To be clear, Canada had every *legal* right to take doses from COVAX. Indeed, COVAX was in part premised on just such a "skin-in-the-game" model. Canada's *moral* right to double-dip into the limited global supply is a different matter. Notably, Canada was the only G7 country, and one of just three high-income countries (HICs), to accept doses in the first round of COVAX allocations, suggesting Canada's actions were out of step with global norms.[14]

The consequences of COVAX reliance on SII would shortly, and tragically, become clear. While much of this volume focuses on borders closing to keep people out, it must be remembered they also closed to keep medical supplies in. Canada received its first shipment from SII on March 3, 2021.[15] Later that month, amidst a massive wave of COVID-19, India closed its borders to vaccine exports, keeping domestically-manufactured vaccines for its own population; COVAX was promptly cut off from much of its supply.[16] This should not have been a surprise to the COVAX designers. Earlier in the pandemic, multiple countries, including India, had restricted or banned exports of other pharmaceuticals thought useful in the pandemic, most notoriously hydroxychloroquine.[17] This illustrates an advantage of Canada's diverse vaccine portfolio. Even so, the spectre of restrictions on European vaccine exports did raise concerns for Canada's own supply, which it attempted to resolve diplomatically even as it remained silent on even prospective timelines for sharing with others.[18]

By March of 2021, Procurement Minister Anand stated Canada would continue to take doses from COVAX and would not share until every Canadian had been vaccinated.[19] Nevertheless, Canada had no compunctions about accepting doses from elsewhere. For instance, on June 17, Canada would accept a donation of one million doses of Moderna from the United States.[20] It did so at a time Canada's first doses outpaced those of its donor and when many countries around the world had yet to receive even a single dose.[21] Ultimately, it was the lack of stock available for COVAX to acquire that led to a major shift in COVAX: the addition of a mechanism to share domestic surplus. Ironically, Canada was the sole country to publicly announce that it was contributing funding specifically to set up this donation mechanism; it did so before it had committed even in principle to share any of its own surplus doses.[22]

28.2 Paying Indulgences

It must be recognized that Canada has been a major financial contributor to COVAX; indeed, it has been one of the biggest financial donors per capita.[23] At the same time, paying indulgences does not grant absolution for hoarding vaccines. First, given that the primary barrier faced by COVAX in 2021 was that rich countries had left few doses on the shelves for it to buy, the value of providing money to purchase non-existent doses is unclear. To analogize, consider the person in front of you at the pizzeria ordering 20 pizzas (considerably more than they could conceivably consume). Even if they offer to pay for your pizza as well, you still won't get yours until after they've received their order.

Second, Canada's attempts to frame financial support in terms of actual doses have been unsatisfactory. Despite claiming that by the end of 2022, it had donated the financial "equivalent of" 150 million doses, Canada has never shown receipts to verify this equivalence.[24] This is important, given different vaccines come with different price tags. COVAX itself has been unable to confirm Canada's figures.[25] A more precise figure—if that is indeed even possible—would be a better indicator of impact; Canada's in-kind donations of physical vaccines have on multiple occasions been in the range of 20,000 or 30,000 doses, or a fraction of a tenth of a percent of claimed "equivalent doses".[26] Similarly, given difficulties COVAX faced in procuring doses, the delivery status of these "equivalent" doses—where and when, if at all—remains unknown. This raises questions about the tangible impact of Canada's financial contribution, even if the financial contribution itself is accepted.

28.3 Pledging Surplus

Canada would enter the high-profile G7 vaccine summit in June 2021 without having made any concrete pledges of timelines or amounts around sharing physical doses. It would also leave said summit without pledging any of its world-beating portfolio of bilateral doses; Canada's G7 pledge of 100 million doses to COVAX consisted of 87 million financial "equivalent of" doses plus foregoing the remaining 13 million from Canada's COVAX allotment.[27] This allotment notably included doses of Novavax, still months from approval anywhere, demonstrating that pledging doses of as-yet unapproved vaccine was entirely possible. Meanwhile, the only physical doses Canada exported abroad were to vaccinate personnel in 134 of Canada's diplomatic missions in countries where vaccines were scarce.[28]

Finally, on July 12, Canada committed 17.7 million doses of AstraZeneca from its own bilateral orders.[29] By this time, Canada was already phasing out use of AstraZeneca domestically.[30] Just over two weeks later, on July 27, 2021, Canada would announce it had physically received enough vaccine to double dose everyone in Canada then eligible for vaccination.[31] By contrast, pledges for sharing abroad did not immediately translate into physical access, demonstrating that a shot in the arm is worth more than one in a press release. Canada would deliver its first vaccines—82,030 doses of AstraZeneca—in a bilateral shipment to Trinidad & Tobago on August 4, 2021.[32] No Canadian surplus would be delivered via COVAX until September 2.[33]

Canada in turn received criticism from recipient countries for sending doses close to their expiry date.[34] Thus, even doses Canada shared were transferred in a way that greatly increased the chance they would go to waste. Stunningly, 13.6 million doses of AstraZeneca promised by Canada—equivalent to over 75% of the 17.7-million-dose pledge—would expire before delivery.[35] Canada would nevertheless choose to continue to count these undelivered, expired vaccines towards achieving its pledge to COVAX, a remarkably cynical move.[36]

Meanwhile, lack of clarity continued to plague Canada's approach to sharing. In August 2021, Minister Anand stated that Canada would maintain a buffer of 4 million doses and begin donating beyond that; following this announcement, however, Canada's Central Vaccine Inventory often held over 10 million, never dipping below 6 million.[37] In other words, millions of doses sat unused in freezers for months, benefitting nobody. Ultimately, in May 2022, Canada stopped including the Central Vaccine Inventory on its main vaccine information page. Since then, there has been no transparent public indicator of how many doses are held by the federal government.

At the G20 summit in October 2021, Canada increased its COVAX pledge to 200 million doses by the end of 2022; however, even as doses sat idle in Canadian freezers, Canadian officials, including Deputy Prime Minister Freeland, blamed manufacturers for the slow pace of delivery on pledges.[38] When Canada wanted to speed up delivery for domestic use early in the pandemic, it pressured manufacturers to pick up the pace; there is no public evidence it did the same to hasten delivery elsewhere.[39] By the end of 2022, the country that secured the world's most doses per capita had shared less than 26 million surplus doses with COVAX.[40] In the interim, Canada had entered into further contracts for well over 200 million additional booster doses for its 38 million people.[41]

28.4 Baking a Bigger Pie?

Even as Canada secured far more than its share, it was also stymying efforts to increase the global vaccine supply. This was most evident at the World Trade Organization (WTO). Canada never officially expressed a stance on the "TRIPS Waiver" proposal to temporarily waive intellectual property (IP) rights on vaccines and other tools for the COVID-19 response under the WTO Agreement on Trade-Related Aspects of Intellectual Property Rights (TRIPS).[42] Its public silence was noticeable, particularly in contrast to the United States, a usually fervent proponent of IP rights, who openly supported a waiver for vaccines.[43] Behind the scenes, Canada also questioned the need for the TRIPS Waiver on the grounds that existing TRIPS flexibilities, particularly those in Article 31bis of TRIPS (on compulsory licensing of patented pharmaceuticals for export to other countries without production capacity), were sufficient.[44] To this end, Canada argued that its own experience was ample proof—and indeed, Canada's history of serving as an exporting country on one sole occasion also has the dubious honour of making it the only exporting country ever to use this flexibility at all.[45] In stark contrast to Canada's rhetoric at the WTO, however, an attempt by Bolivia to use Article 31bis to contract vaccines from a Canadian manufacturer was completely stonewalled by the Government of Canada, who took zero action to even permit the process to be initiated.[46] The need to address problems with Canada's Access to Medicines Regime (CAMR), Canada's domestic mechanism for operationalizing Article 31bis, has been highlighted in a report on COVID-19 vaccines released by the Standing Committee on Foreign Affairs and International Development but no action taken as yet.[47]

Attracting less attention, but similarly unhelpful, is Canada's approach to tech transfer, an issue perhaps even more important than intellectual property rights like patents. In particular, the mRNA vaccines from both Pfizer and Moderna rely upon Canadian-invented lipid nanoparticle technology, developed at the University of British Columbia.[48] Despite writing cheques to support WHO tech transfer iniatives, Canada has applied neither stick nor carrot to ensure that Canadian technology, originating from research at a publicly funded Canadian university, is shared with the world.

28.5 Consequences of Vaccine Inequity

Why is vaccine equity important? Putting aside moral arguments around humans caring for each other across geographical divides or the self-interest of staving off the emergence of new viral variants abroad, vaccine access is also a prerequisite for many of the legal interventions discussed elsewhere in this volume. Most obviously, imposing vaccine requirements for international travel places countries without vaccine access at a serious disadvantage. Moreover, such lack of access tends to overlap with other pre-existing barriers to international mobility, like disproportionately facing visa requirements.[49] Such impacts have had further ramifications for international law beyond the health sphere; for instance, a lack of access to COVID-19 vaccines threatened to prevent some countries from participating in climate talks.[50] The *kind* of vaccine can also have impacts, as not every vaccine is accepted for entry by other countries. An ironic footnote to Canada taking vaccines from SII is that COVISHIELD wasn't initially accepted under the vaccination requirements of the European Union, meaning Canadians who received it received health benefits but not the mobility benefit of EU entry.[51] There are domestic repercussions too. Consider vaccine mandates. Requiring a vaccine to work or to access public spaces may be a defensible infringement upon individual liberties.[52] If there are no vaccines available, however, these requirements become indefensibly difficult to meet. Within societies where the wealthy and well connected are more likely to have access to a limited supply, they also perpetuate existing societal inequalities.

There are implications for the future as well, which Canada again aptly illustrates. For one, the COVID-19 vaccine saga raises questions about whether Canada will be accepted as a good-faith negotiator on issues such as equitable access to vaccines and other medical tools in the context of the WHO Pandemic Treaty currently under negotiation. Certainly, it has not bolstered Canada's reputation as a promoter of global health.[53] Nor is it likely to aid Canada's broader soft-power aspirations.[54] Is Canada likely to learn any lessons? Well, it has announced funding opportunities to research international vaccine equity.[55] It must be hoped that such research looks inward as well, as Canada's hoarding is not a new or isolated phenomenon. Over a decade ago, despite obtaining an oversupply of H1N1 vaccine, Canada's reticence to share left it "in the unusual position of being odd-man-out of an international agreement brokered by U.S. President Barack Obama's White House to donate vaccine to the World Health Organization" involving ten donor countries.[56] More recently, even against the backdrop of COVID-19, Canada has behaved similarly around mpox vaccine. Despite being one of the only countries with a longstanding stockpile, and statements by Canada's Chief Medical Officer of Health that Canada has a sufficient supply, Canada has remained conspicuously silent in the face of WHO requests to share.[57]

Today, the global vaccine supply is no longer the primary barrier to access in the way it was in 2021. Other barriers, from ensuring the infrastructure necessary to turn vaccines into vaccinations is available to combatting vaccine hesitancy, also need to be addressed. At the same time, as HICs start to phase out earlier vaccines in favour of bivalent boosters, the same questions of equitable global access are arising again. And as those HICs find themselves sitting on massive stockpiles of first-generation vaccines that are likely to expire unused, it must be recalled that had those doses been shared—or equitably allocated in the first place—months earlier, lives could have been saved.[58] Canada trumpeted its domestic first-doses-fast campaign as world-leading; it is all too telling that it didn't show global leadership by taking the practical steps necessary to extend that policy beyond its borders.[59]

Notes

1 António Guterres, "Secretary-general's address to the 76th session of the UN general assembly" (21 September 2021), online: *United Nations Secretary General*. www.un.org/sg/en/content/sg/speeches/2021-09-21/address-the-76th-session-of-general-assembly.
2 Justin Trudeau et al, "The international community must guarantee equal global access to a covid-19 vaccine" (15 July 2020), online: *Washington Post*. www.washingtonpost.com/opinions/2020/07/15/international-community-must-guarantee-equal-global-access-covid-19-vaccine/.
3 Asher Mullard, "How COVID vaccines are being divvied up around the world" (30 November 2020), online: *Nature*. www.nature.com/articles/d41586-020-03370-6.
4 "COVID-19 vaccination in Canada" (2 January 2023), online: *Government of Canada*. https://health-infobase.canada.ca/covid-19/vaccine-distribution/.
5 Canada, Department of Finance, *Supporting Canadians and Fighting COVID-19 - Fall Economic Statement 2020* (Quebec: Department of Finance, 2020), online: www.budget.gc.ca/fes-eea/2020/report-rapport/FES-EEA-eng.pdf.
6 Rachel Aiello, "If Canada has excess COVID-19 vaccines they 'absolutely' will be shared: PM" (17 December 2020), online: *CTV News*. www.ctvnews.ca/politics/if-canada-has-excess-covid-19-vaccines-they-absolutely-will-be-shared-pm-1.5236745.
7 John D. Trimmer, "The present situation in quantum mechanics: A translation of Schrödinger's 'cat paradox' paper" (1980) 124:5 *Proceedings of the American Philosophical Society* 323; see, e.g., Zi-Ann Lum, "Too early for talk about Canada's 'hypothetical surplus' of vaccines: Minister" (20 December 2020), online: *Huffington Post*. www.huffpost.com/archive/ca/entry/canada-coronavirus-vaccine-surplus_ca_5fdfe4f0c5b60f8288576132.
8 But see, e.g., Médecins Sans Frontières Access Campaign, *COVAX: A Broken Promise to the World*, online: https://msfaccess.org/covax-broken-promise-world.
9 Michael Safi, "WHO: just 25 Covid vaccine doses administered in low-income countries" (18 January 2021), online: *The Guardian*. www.theguardian.com/society/2021/jan/18/who-just-25-covid-vaccine-doses-administered-in-low-income-countries.
10 See, e.g., "World has entered stage of 'vaccine apartheid'—WHO head" (17 May 2021), online: *Reuters*. www.reuters.com/business/healthcare-pharmaceuticals/world-has-entered-stage-vaccine-apartheid-who-head-2021-05–17/.
11 Tedros Adhanom Ghebreyesus, "WHO director-general's opening remarks at 148th session of the executive board" (18 January 2021), online: *World Health Organization*. www.who.int/director-general/speeches/detail/who-director-general-s-opening-remarks-at-148th-session-of-the-executive-board.
12 Public Services and Procurement Canada, "Canada to receive 2 million doses of AstraZeneca's COVID-19 vaccine manufactured by the Serum Institute of India" (26 February 2021), online: *Government of Canada*. www.canada.ca/en/public-services-procurement/news/2021/02/canada-to-receive-2-million-doses-of-astra-zenecas-covid-19-vaccine-manufactured-by-the-serum-institute-of-india.html.
13 Mia Rabson, "Canada's deliveries from COVAX join growing list of COVID-19 vaccine confusion" (3 February 2021), online: *CBC News*. www.cbc.ca/news/politics/covax-million-doses-anand-1.5898821.
14 Marieke Walsh & Geoffrey York, "Canada the only G7 country to take vaccines from fund that helps developing countries" (3 February 2021), online: *Globe and Mail*. www.theglobeandmail.com/politics/article-canada-the-only-g7-country-to-take-vaccines-from-fund-for-developing/.

15 Hannah Jackson, "Canada sees 2,812 new COVID-19 cases as country receives first AstraZeneca vaccine shipment" (3 March 2021), online: *Global News*. https://globalnews.ca/news/7675748/coronavirus-canada-march-3-2021/.
16 Rajesh Roy & Vibhuti Agarwal, "India suspends COVID-19 vaccine exports to focus on domestic immunization" (25 March 2021), online: *Wall Street Journal*. www.wsj.com/articles/india-suspends-covid-19-vaccine-exports-to-focus-on-domestic-immunization-11616690859.
17 Ed Silverman, "India bans exports of drug touted by Trump as potential Covid-19 treatment" (25 March 2020), online: *STAT News*. www.statnews.com/pharmalot/2020/03/25/india-trump-hydroxychloroquine-coronavirus-covid19/.
18 Peter Zimonjic, "Trudeau 'concerned' by latest threat to vaccine supply from EU" (24 March 2021), online: *CBC News*. www.cbc.ca/news/politics/vaccine-shipments-canada-eu-india-1.5961888.
19 Peter Zimonjic & Catherine Cullen, "Canada to take COVAX vaccines, won't share doses until every Canadian is inoculated: Anand" (5 March 2021), online: *CBC News*. www.cbc.ca/news/politics/covax-anand-vaccine-timetable-1.5939270.
20 "The United States donates one million COVID-19 vaccine doses to Canada" (17 June 2021), online: *United States Embassy & Consulates in Canada*. https://ca.usembassy.gov/the-united-states-donates-one-million-covid-19-vaccine-doses-to-canada/#:~:text=OTTAWA%20%E2%80%93%20The%20United%20States%20Embassy,Administration's%20global%20vaccine%20sharing%20framework.
21 Phil Hahn, "Canada's first-dose vaccinations surpass U.S., as American daily rate declines" (21 May 2021), online: *CTV News*. www.ctvnews.ca/health/coronavirus/canada-s-first-dose-vaccinations-surpass-u-s-as-american-daily-rate-declines-1.5438413.
22 Global Affairs Canada, "Canada announces additional support for equitable access to COVID-19 tests, treatments and vaccines" (14 December 2020), online: *Government of Canada*. www.canada.ca/en/global-affairs/news/2020/12/canada-announces-additional-support-for-equitable-access-to-covid-19-tests-treatments-and-vaccines.html.
23 See, e.g., Prime Minister of Canada, "Prime Minister announces additional funding for COVID-19 vaccination in lower-income countries" (8 April 2022) online: *Canada*. https://pm.gc.ca/en/news/news-releases/2022/04/08/prime-minister-announces-additional-funding-covid-19-vaccination.
24 Government of Canada, "Canada's COVID-19 vaccine supply and donation strategy" (last modified 30 December 2022), online: *Government of Canada*. www.canada.ca/en/public-health/services/diseases/coronavirus-disease-covid-19/vaccines/supply-donation.html.
25 Mia Rabson, "Canada offers more money to COVAX to aid in the delivery of vaccine donations" (8 April 2022), online: *CTV News*. www.ctvnews.ca/health/coronavirus/canada-offers-more-money-to-covax-to-aid-in-the-delivery-of-vaccine-donations-1.5854455.
26 Government of Canada, *supra* note 24.
27 Mia Rabson, "Canada's vaccine donations to COVAX to come only from its COVAX supply: Gould" (14 June 2021), online: *CTV News*. www.ctvnews.ca/health/coronavirus/canada-s-vaccine-donations-to-covax-to-come-only-from-its-covax-supply-gould-1.5470027.
28 Geoffrey York, "Canada ships COVID-19 vaccines to 134 of its diplomatic missions in countries where vaccines are scarce" (6 July 2021), online: *Globe and Mail*. www.theglobeandmail.com/world/article-canada-ships-covid-19-vaccines-to-134-of-its-diplomatic-missions-in/.
29 Global Affairs Canada, "Canada announces new contribution to global vaccination efforts and launch of matching fund with UNICEF Canada" (12 July 2021),

online: *Government of Canada*. www.canada.ca/en/global-affairs/news/2021/07/canada-announces-new-contribution-to-global-vaccination-efforts-and-launch-of-matching-fund-with-unicef-canada.html.

30 Jeff Gray & Marieke Walsh, "More provinces turn away from AstraZeneca COVID-19 vaccine" (12 May 2021), online: *Globe and Mail*. www.theglobeandmail.com/canada/article-more-provinces-turn-away-from-astrazeneca-covid-19-vaccine/; Sarah Turnbull, "mRNA vaccine now preferred as second dose following AstraZeneca shot: NACI" (17 June 2021), online: *CTV News*. www.ctvnews.ca/health/coronavirus/mrna-vaccine-now-preferred-as-second-dose-following-astrazeneca-shot-naci-1.5475020.

31 Prime Minister of Canada, "Canada reaches major vaccine campaign milestone" (27 July 2021), online: *Canada*. https://pm.gc.ca/en/news/news-releases/2021/07/27/canada-reaches-major-vaccine-campaign-milestone.

32 Government of Canada, *supra* note 24.

33 *Ibid*.

34 Geoffrey York, "Canada donates soon-to-expire COVID-19 vaccines to Africa as global shortage worsens" (9 September 2021), online: *The Globe and Mail*. www.theglobeandmail.com/world/article-canada-donates-soon-to-expire-vaccines-to-africa-as-global-shortage/.

35 The Canadian Press, "More than half of Canada's AstraZeneca COVID-19 vaccine doses expired in spring, will be thrown out" (5 July 2022), online: *The Globe and Mail*. www.theglobeandmail.com/canada/article-more-than-half-of-canadas-astrazeneca-covid-19-vaccine-doses-expired/.

36 Government of Canada, *supra* note 24.

37 Stephanie Dubois, "Canada's vaccine reserve exceeds 4 million doses, prompting calls for better tracking of donations" (17 December 2021), online: *CBC News*. www.cbc.ca/news/health/extra-vaccines-donation-pledge-1.6288998.

38 Eric Reguly, "Canada will ramp up vaccine donations, overcome past shortfalls" (30 October 2021), online: *Globe and Mail*. www.theglobeandmail.com/politics/article-canada-will-donate-10-million-doses-of-modernas-covid-19-vaccine-to/.

39 See, e.g., Leyland Cecco, " 'I knew supply was coming': How Canada's push for Covid vaccines paid off" (13 August 2021), online: *The Guardian*. www.theguardian.com/world/2021/aug/13/canada-anita-anand-covid-vaccine.

40 Government of Canada, *supra* note 24.

41 Government of Canada, "Procuring vaccines for COVID-19" (last modified 14 September 2022), online: *Government of Canada*. www.canada.ca/en/public-services-procurement/services/procuring-vaccines-covid19.html.

42 See, e.g., World Trade Organization, Waiver from Certain Provisions of the TRIPS Agreement for the Prevention, Containment and Treatment of COVID-19, Document IP/C/W/669 (2020).

43 Thomas Kaplan, Sheryl Gay Stolberg & Rebecca Robbins, "Taking 'extraordinary measures,' biden backs suspending patents on vaccines" (5 May 2021), online: *New York Times*. www.nytimes.com/2021/05/05/us/politics/biden-covid-vaccine-patents.html.

44 Government of Canada, "Item 15—Waiver from certain provisions of the TRIPS agreement for the prevention, containment and treatment of COVID-19" (10 December 2020), online: *Government of Canada*. www.international.gc.ca/world-monde/international_relations-relations_internationales/wto-omc/2020-12-10-TRIPS-ADPIC.aspx?lang=eng.

45 *Ibid* See also Médecins Sans Frontières Canada, *WTO COVID-19 TRIPS Waiver—Doctors Without Borders Canada Briefing Note* (2021), online: www.doctorswithoutborders.ca/sites/default/files/msf_canada_briefer_on_trips_waiver.pdf.

46 Muhammad Zaheer Abbas, Canada's political choices restrain vaccine equity: The bolivia-biolyse case, *Research Paper* 136 (South Centre, 2021), online:

www.southcentre.int/wp-content/uploads/2021/09/RP136_Canadas-Political-Choices-Restrain-Vaccine-Equity-The-Bolivia-Biolyse-Case_EN-1.pdf; Ahmar Khan, "Canada lacks 'political will' to waive COVID-19 vaccine patents, Bolivian minister says" (6 October 2021), online: *Global News*. https://globalnews.ca/news/8243635/bolivian-minister-canada-covid-vaccine-waiver/.

47 House of Commons, Standing Committee on Foreign Affairs and International Development, *Overcoming the Barriers to Global Vaccine Equity and Ending the Pandemic*, 44–1 (October 2022), online: www.ourcommons.ca/Content/Committee/441/FAAE/Reports/RP11968481/faaerp05/faaerp05-e.pdf.

48 University of British Columbia, "UBC-grown biotech leads global pandemic efforts" (26 April 2021), online: https://science.ubc.ca/news/ubc-grown-biotech-leads-global-pandemic-efforts.

49 See Will Tao's chapter in this volume.

50 Susanna Twidale, "Poor countries say lack of vaccines may exclude them from climate talks" (10 September 2021), online: *Reuters*. www.reuters.com/business/healthcare-pharmaceuticals/poor-countries-say-lack-vaccines-may-exclude-them-climate-talks-2021–09–10/.

51 Rachel Gilmore & Redmond Shannon, "Over 270K Canadians got the Covishield vaccine. They may not be eligible for EU travel" (30 June 2021), online: *Global News*. https://globalnews.ca/news/7992959/covid-coronavirus-vaccine-passport-europe-eu-travel-covishield/.

52 See Jeff King's chapter in this volume.

53 Adam R. Houston & Srinivas Murthy, "Canada is no global health leader on COVID-19 vaccine equity" (2021) 397:10287 *The Lancet* 1803; Alex Boyd, "Canada has failed to deliver on its COVID-19 promises to the world—and some say they won't forget it" (17 February 2022), online: *The Toronto Star*. www.thestar.com/news/world/2022/02/17/canada-has-failed-to-deliver-on-its-covid-19-promises-to-the-world-and-some-say-they-wont-forget-it.html.

54 Stephen Brown, "Canada's COVID-19 vaccine fix" (2022) 28:1 Canadian Foreign Policy Journal 98; Jillian Kohler, "Developing countries won't forget Canada's 'me-first' approach to vaccines" (8 February 2021), online: *Globe and Mail*. www.theglobeandmail.com/opinion/article-developing-countries-wont-forget-canadas-me-first-approach-to-vaccines/.

55 See, e.g., Canadian Institutes of Health Research, "Pre-announcement: Notice of upcoming COVID-19 research funding opportunity" (27 July 2021), online: *Government of Canada* https://cihr-irsc.gc.ca/e/52568.html.

56 The Canadian Press, "Canada mulls options for H1N1 vaccine leftovers" (27 November 2009), online: *CTV News*. www.ctvnews.ca/canada-mulls-options-for-h1n1-vaccine-leftovers-1.458861.

57 "PHAC urges gay, bisexual men to practise safe sex as monkeypox spreads" (27 July 2022), online: *CBC News*. www.cbc.ca/news/politics/phac-monkey-pox-spreadf-canada-1.6533909; Tedros Adhanom Ghebreyesus, "WHO director-General's opening remarks at the COVID-19 media briefing—27 July 2022" (27 July 2022), online: *World Health Organization*. www.who.int/director-general/speeches/detail/who-director-general-s-opening-remarks-at-the-covid-19-media-briefing—27-july-2022.

58 See, e.g., Sam Moore et al, "Retrospectively modeling the effects of increased global vaccine sharing on the COVID-19 pandemic" (2022) *Nature Medicine* 2416.

59 Department of Finance, Canada, *Economic and Fiscal Update 2021* (2021), online: https://budget.gc.ca/efu-meb/2021/report-rapport/EFU-MEB-2021-EN.pdf.

PART X

Borders, Boundaries, and the Future of Global Health Law

29

CROSS-BORDER MOBILITY OF PERSONS AND GOODS DURING PANDEMICS

Exposing Normative Duality in International Law

Pedro A. Villarreal

The regulation of movement across territorial borders was a core feature of public health responses to the COVID-19 pandemic, considering the unprecedented degree of restrictions on international travel and trade implemented during the crisis.[1] During the pandemic, travel restrictions were at their peak on the week of 15–21 June 2020. At that point, of the 174 Member States of the United Nations International Organization of Migration (IOM), 130 (i.e., 75%) reported total entry restrictions to travelers from either one or several countries, another 21 (12%) held conditions for entry of travelers, and only 23 (13%) reported no restrictions to travel whatsoever.[2] In the case of trade, by the second and third quarters of 2020, 124 restrictions of trade in services and 58 export restrictions directly related to COVID-19 had been identified.[3]

The World Health Organization (WHO)'s International Health Regulations (IHR) of 2005 enshrine broad legal criteria for restrictions on the entry of persons and goods in the territory of countries during disease outbreaks. Each subject falls under the purview of a different legal regime. What results is a normative duality, wherein international rules on the cross-border movement of goods—with the General Agreement on Tariffs and Trade (GATT) of 1947 and the World Trade Organization (WTO) at the core—are more sophisticated than rules on the international mobility of persons, which centre mostly on soft law documents. Furthermore, neither the legally binding Constitution of the IOM nor the Refugee Convention of 1951 regulate international movement as such. Rather, the former gives said organization the mandate to generally support persons in need of migration to countries willingly accepting them;[4] whereas the latter determines instances in which states must accept persons seeking refuge in a foreign country, which must be

DOI: 10.4324/9781003394006-39

granted on the basis of threats to life and freedom they may be subjected to in a different country.[5] There is a greater onus of justification for restrictions on trade as opposed to restrictions on cross-border travel of persons; with the latter, there is much less clarity on the evidentiary thresholds to be met. This chapter critically assesses this normative duality with a focus on vaccine passports and their legal consequences for the international mobility of persons, contrasting it with the more robust criteria for sanitary certificates for goods.

29.1 Regulating International Travel and Trade during Pandemics

Communicable disease control has been among the historical reasons for denying travelers entry into a country. Even before the debacle with international mobility during the COVID-19 pandemic, the increase of sea and air travel and trade brought with it an uptick in the likelihood of the cross-border spread of disease.[6] A major point of contention is whether and to what extent restricting transit across borders is effective at mitigating the spread of communicable diseases. Absent effective vaccines and other medical treatments, mobility restrictions are one of the tools available alongside other public health measures. Data has shown how mobility restrictions were effective during the COVID-19 pandemic when adopted in conjunction with other non-pharmaceutical interventions.[7] But when adopted bluntly, such restrictions may unnecessarily disrupt key aspects of pandemic response. Although it did not reach the status of a pandemic, the West African Ebola crisis of 2014 highlighted how measures restricting travel can hamper the international delivery of humanitarian assistance to countries experiencing health emergencies, while eliciting a broader economic impact and increasing the stigma of local populations.[8]

Assessing the legality of the restriction of mobility across borders is contingent upon whether it involves a person, i.e., a traveler, or a tangible good. Here, the normative duality is blatant. International trade law has been shaped through the obligations of the GATT since 1947. All States Parties must conform with the GATT's provisions on how to impose restrictions on imports and exports of goods. Importantly, the preamble of the GATT enshrined the goal of gradually lifting the restrictions on international trade, including tariffs and border controls, as one of its key tenets. Thus, decisions restricting trade under the argument of protecting against the spread of communicable diseases must fulfil common minimum criteria. These criteria are addressed later. The core goal is to grant stability to the course of international trade.

In contrast, the regulation of international travel does not have a functional equivalent to the GATT. The multilateral agreement fostering regulatory coordination, the Convention on International Civil Aviation ("Chicago

Convention") of 1944, is focused on air travel and does not impose any substantive limitations on how states limit movement across borders. In turn, the conventions within the purview of the International Maritime Organization regulate traffic by sea undertaken for commercial purposes, mostly the transport of goods. The only rules governing restrictions imposed on international travel due to the cross-border spread of disease are found in the WHO's International Health Regulations (IHR) of 2005. Particularly, the IHR (2005) is the outcome of the 2002–2003 SARS crisis. Back then, in light of the reluctance by the Chinese government to openly share information on the nature of the disease, and facing the cross-border spread of a novel communicable disease, the WHO Director-General recommended against traveling to affected areas—including China and Canada.[9] This practice was lauded afterwards as an assertion of authority by the WHO in times of need, despite its not having the explicit mandate to do so. Drawing lessons from this experience, Article 43 IHR (2005) now obliges states to refrain from imposing restrictions on travel and trade that are more restrictive than necessary. The key legal analysis is how to properly gauge "necessity". Conditioning entry into a country to showing proof of vaccination or other prophylaxis is allowed for under the IHR (2005). It is within the leeway of a state's authorities to decide whether to request them or not.

29.1.1 International Law on Vaccine Passports and Import/Export Health Certificates: Overview

The normative duality in the treatment of persons and goods is visible in how a similar scenario is split in two different, albeit not opposing, legal directions. When persons and goods arrive at a territorial border, a number of domestic migration and trade laws are triggered, with each legal regime following different paths. Both proof of vaccination or prophylaxis and health certificates for agricultural goods[10] may be legally requested from travelers and goods, respectively, as means to protect a population from the potential cross-border spread of diseases.

In the case of agricultural goods, including products derived from animals, import or export licenses can be a requirement for moving them across borders. Should the interested party, either a physical person or a company, fail to show such a license, the good in question may not be legally imported or exported. Complying with minimum sanitary standards is among the conditions for issuing those licenses, the purpose of which is to ensure that animal-derived goods are disease-free. These standards fall under the purview of the WTO's Sanitary and Phytosanitary Agreement, and there is an overlap with a number of criteria for animal health developed by other organizations, such as the World Animal Health Organization (WOAH).[11] Under these criteria, the onus is on national authorities to demonstrate that, first, these permits and their features fulfil a public policy goal like the protection of health or the environment and, second, that these permits are the least restrictive alternative. Trade in services is still, notwithstanding electronic commerce, primarily an in-person activity.[12] The in-person supply of services contingent upon international mobility is not regulated under the GATT but rather under the General Agreement of Trade in Services (GATS). Under its Article XIV, states may adopt restrictions necessary to protect, among other things, "animal or plant life or health". "Services trade costs" are a side effect of mobility restrictions ranging from blanket travel bans or border closures to specific visa and quarantine requirements.[13]

In the case of the international mobility of persons, migration and customs officials at the border have considerable leeway in deciding who may enter the country. Authorities may require a proof of immunization—a "vaccine" or "immunity" passport—meeting certain features when attempting to enter a country. Similar to how they may be legally required at the national, provincial, and local or municipal level as a condition for conducting specific activities,[14] proofs of vaccination as a condition of entry into a country have been imposed during the COVID-19 pandemic either to travelers from all countries—with exceptions allowed for countries due to economic or political considerations—or, alternatively, on the basis of persons' presence in particular countries or regions with high rates of transmission. Moreover, demanding proof of vaccination as a condition of entry is certainly possible during non-pandemic times, for example, against yellow fever, and even for travelers from countries with no reports of an active spread of the disease.[15] A key challenge when adopting restrictions on international travel is how to assess evidence on their effectiveness in mitigating the cross-border spread of a disease, when such evidence is absent or inconclusive. This raises the question on whether the precautionary principle is warranted and, if so, to what extent. Said principle, originally devised in the environmental field, affirms that when there is a threat against, for instance, public health, insufficient scientific evidence does not impede states from taking measures offering the highest level of protection against the possible source of the threat.[16] The precautionary principle might lead to restricting international travel or trade[17] for protecting the population against the risk posed by a disease with the potential for cross-border spread, even when available evidence either on is inconclusive. Nevertheless, in order to apply the precautionary principle, a particular risk must be identified at least prima facie through scientific evidence.[18] Deciding what the acceptable level of risk, however, involves not only technical/scientific considerations but rather also economic and political factors. There is, therefore, no universally accepted threshold for determining from which point onwards in a threat the precautionary principle should apply. Different societies may decide upon different levels of threat that they are willing to accept. From a legal point of view, when restrictive measures are adopted under a precautionary principle, there must be an explanation provided on why they are necessary given the absence of alternatives, and proportionate in light of their benefits outweighing their costs.[19]

As for different degrees of restrictiveness, during the COVID-19 pandemic states adopted measures affecting the movement of persons and of goods across borders seldom seen during "ordinary" periods. The two most atypical measures were arguably export restrictions[20] and restrictions on the right of persons to return to their countries of origin or residence due to blanket travel bans that prevent people from either leaving or from entering a particular country.[21] Both fulfilled nationalist goals: export restrictions were imposed under the justification of the need to maintain scarce resources in the country, whereas refusal of the right to return to one's country was based on the justification of keeping persons present in areas with high transmission of COVID-19 from importing the disease into their countries. The legality of both these instances of restrictions of international travel and trade was highly contested.

There are visible disparities in terms of the legal requirements when conditioning the entry of goods or persons in a country on grounds of public health. Over time, the regulation of trade has become ever more sophisticated—and, arguably, convoluted—than that of international travel. For instance, if and when an import/export certificate places an unreasonable burden on goods from a particular state, the latter can resort to dispute settlement at the WTO. Existing case law in the field has addressed the intricacies of how exactly these import/export certificates must achieve the proper balance between protecting public health and not being more restrictive of trade than necessary. Specific criteria are found in the dispute *India—Agricultural Products*.[22] The dispute emerged after the government of the United States of America challenged a measure by the Indian government banning imports of US poultry products—which, under WTO law, are classified as "agricultural goods"—on the basis of a zoonotic risk. This happened following the notification of highly pathogenic avian influenza in parts of the US. While the Indian government argued that the measure was adopted for preventing the further spread of avian influenza across poultry and, potentially, humans, the US government disagreed with the blanket import ban. In its report, the Appellate Body affirmed that the onus for offering proper scientific evidence justifying the restriction lay with the Indian government. As it did not uphold the criteria in the matter, namely, those within the WOAH's Terrestrial Code, India failed to meet the relevant provisions of the Sanitary and Phytosanitary Agreement. In fact, the Appellate Body went as far as scrutinizing the scientific arguments put forward by the Indian government, deeming them insufficiently sound for justifying a ban of poultry products from across all of the United States of America. Consequently, India's import ban was deemed to be in breach of the WTO's Sanitary and Phytosanitary Agreement. At the moment of writing, however, the Indian government has yet to fully conform its policies to as required by the decision of the WTO's Dispute Settlement Body.[23]

By contrast, there is no case law at the international level dealing with restrictions on international travel on grounds of the protection against the cross-border spread of disease. This may be explained by several factors. First, until before COVID-19, there was a relative infrequency of epidemics and pandemics and an overall decreasing burden of disease posed by communicable diseases.[24] The theory of epidemiological transition first developed by Abdel Omran in 1971 posited a steady downward trend in the incidence and prevalence of communicable diseases.[25] Although by 2019, these diseases were still a considerable threat, the downward trend had been generally steady throughout the second half of the 20th century and the beginning of the 21st.[26] As highlighted by COVID-19, however, the trend was and continues to be subject to the continuous risk of new and re-emerging diseases.[27] Second, only states and not individuals have standing under Article 56 IHR (2005).[28] There are a few instances of national court cases dealing with travel restrictions due to the COVID-19 pandemic, but none have been settled citing international standards. Instead, what is available internationally is soft law, by way of legally non-binding recommendations issued by the WHO Director-General. In public health emergencies of international concern declared so far under the IHR (2005), recommendations have been issued against imposing travel restrictions. Several scholars criticize how states constantly disregard the WHO's recommendations on international travel when responding to disease outbreaks occurring in other countries, be they H1N1 Influenza, Ebola, or COVID-19.[29] Thus, when the spread of the SARS-CoV-2 virus was first declared to be a public health emergency of international concern on 30 January 2020, the WHO—on the basis of advice given by an Emergency Committee composed of external experts—recommended against adopting travel restrictions to respond to the threat.[30] A group of legal scholars opined that travel restrictions imposed in the wake of this event were a violation of the IHR (2005) because, among other reasons, "evidence belies the claim that illegal (sic) travel restrictions make countries safer".[31] The evidentiary basis cited for such an argument referred to past events, particularly the spread of influenza and of the Ebola virus.

The conflation of evidence related to different pathogens when assessing the effectiveness of travel restrictions leads to misleading legal reasoning. An open question is whether and how restrictive measures can be justified under the precautionary principle, when evidence of effectiveness is unavailable or inconclusive. Beyond this debate, on 1 May 2020, the WHO revised its preceding stance on international travel and recognized that states may impose those restrictions, albeit through risk assessments balancing public health needs with their socioeconomic impact.[32]

29.2 Critically Assessing Legal Duality between International Travel and Trade

While there are parallelisms in the regulation of both international travel and trade, closer scrutiny displays a duality in the legal requirements within each regime for conditioning the entry of persons. Two nuances can be highlighted: 1) the question of how exactly international travel and trade in goods are restricted and 2) what the burden of justification, or lack thereof, might be. International travel and trade may be legally restricted to different degrees, falling within a wide spectrum. Thus, for example, "blanket" travel and trade bans both stand at the highest end of the restrictiveness spectrum. On the other side, there is the absence of barriers either through free trade agreements reducing tariffs to zero[33] or the elimination of all routine border controls for persons as in the Schengen Area.[34] Standing in the middle of these two options is the requirement to demonstrate the disease-free status of either a good or a person. These types of measures are available for states under both the GATT and the IHR (2005)[35] and can be considered functional equivalents in their respective fields.

In terms of the expected justification for these mid-level travel and trade restrictions, while there is no mathematical formula, the degree of restrictiveness is correlated with how high the burden of proof for demonstrating its necessity will be. Through its case law, the Appellate Body of the WTO has shaped legal criteria on how to properly frame the requirements of health certificates for agricultural goods.

Similarly, migration authorities may require travelers to show a proof of immunization or prophylaxis when they wish to transit through or visit a country. This is allowed under the IHR (2005),[36] though they quite explicitly limit their scope to international travelers, understood as persons not having the intent to establish temporary or permanent residence in a country. In the latter case, states have considerable leeway in how they will regulate the residence status of persons. The IOM Constitution has a limited reach, as it confirms states' leeway in terms of defining "standards of admission and the number of immigrants to be admitted".[37] Meanwhile, the 1951 Refugee Convention and its protocol apply to cases where persons face threats in another country, leading to the principle of *non-refoulement* proscribing national authorities from returning them to said country. Health considerations, including vaccine passports, can fall within the purview of such standards of admission, and yet this scenario remains beyond the reach of the IHR (2005), as it is not an instrument tackling migration as such. Instead, migration is subject to a high degree of legal variation in how states regulate it, often leading to easing the requirements for some groups of persons but not for others and particularly during a pandemic.[38]

29.2.1 The Normative Duality of Travel and Trade as a Bulwark of Lopsided Globalization

The visible contrast between the international regulation of travel and trade during pandemics is telling of how the ongoing process of globalization has prioritized regulating the mobility of goods over that of persons. Thus, the normative duality portrayed in this contribution plays out in how disruptions of trade in goods, including multinational supply chains, during the COVID-19 pandemic have led to a stronger international law- and policymaking momentum[39] than the disruptions of international travel. Not even the most dramatic standstill of international travel on record[40] triggered a consensus on formulating clear international law norms on the subject. To the contrary, in the ongoing negotiations for a pandemic convention, or other legal instrument, states have so far reaffirmed their sovereignty interests when deciding which public health measures to implement as part of their pandemic response.[41] This includes the possibility of adopting travel restrictions when facing future pandemics. It is not surprising, considering how the main mode of cross-border spread of COVID-19 was from person to person and not through goods. Nevertheless, the persistent risk of zoonotic spillover, i.e., the transmission of a disease from a non-human animal to a person, leaves open a possibility of future trade-related disease outbreaks in humans.[42]

The duality described earlier is visible in how, despite the increasing interdependence between states due to globalization, the mobility of goods across borders has been prioritized over the mobility of persons. States generally have fewer political incentives to foster consensus on harmonized requirements for allowing the entry of non-resident foreigners into a country. Other authors have posited a more stringent legal interpretation of the issue, by raising the argument that blanket travel bans to all countries when facing a pandemic can be legally justified, whereas travel bans targeting particular countries cannot.[43] First, this understanding goes beyond the wording of Article 43 IHR (2005), which rests on the basis that states may adopt restrictions as long as they are deemed "necessary" from a public health perspective. Second, even such a stringent interpretation of "necessity" rests upon the basis that states, indeed, withhold the legal prerogative to impose travel restrictions to protect their population against the cross-border spread of diseases.

Current developments regarding potential amendments to the IHR (2005) might lead to a change in the status quo regarding the health certificates of international travelers. The European Union's Member States have proposed granting the World Health Assembly—which is itself a meeting of WHO Member State representatives—the legal power to establish common requirements for the interoperability of digital travel forms.[44] These forms include digital certificates demonstrating vaccination or other prophylaxis.[45] There is, moreover, a concern for ensuring the protection of private data shared across multiple jurisdictions. National and regional requirements on this matter vary considerably.[46] If, eventually, such amendments to the IHR (2005) are approved and the World Health Assembly enshrines common standards on the interoperability of digital health certificates, then national authorities would no longer be able to legally reject certificates meeting those standards. Nevertheless, national authorities would retain the prerogative to refuse the entry of persons holding digital health certificates that do not meet international standards. In terms of what that interoperability may look like, an opportunity emerges for cross-fertilization from import/export licenses in the field of international trade law. The evolution of international trade law on this subject in the last decades[47] could be a point of comparison for devising coherent legal criteria regarding certificates of immunization or prophylaxis for the purpose of international travel. Ultimately, considering the wild divergence in how countries regulate them domestically, it is unclear whether there will be any consensus on how legal criteria on travelers' health certificates can be harmonized at the multilateral level.

Notes

1 For an overview, see Mathieu Poirier et al, "Quasi-experimental evaluation of national border closures on COVID-19 transmission" (2023) 3 *PLoS Global Public Health* e0000980.
2 See the travel restriction matrix developed by United Nations International Organization on Migration, *Human Mobility Impacts*: "Displacement Tracking Matrix", online: *IOM* https://migration.iom.int.
3 WTO World Trade Report: Economic Resilience and Trade (2021), at 66.
4 *Constitution*, 1953, IOM, art. 1.
5 Convention Relating to the Status of Refugees (1951) and its Protocol (1967). See also on both the IOM Constitution and the 1951 Convention; Ian Hurd, *International Organizations*, 4th edition (Cambridge: Cambridge University Press 2021) 195–218.
6 Kelley Lee & Richard Dodgson, "Globalization and cholera" in *Health Impacts of Globalization*, edited by Kelley Lee (London: Palgrave Macmillan, 2003) 138.
7 Elsewhere, research has shown how international mobility restrictions are effective mostly in conjunction with other public health measures. Timothy Russell et al, "Effect of internationally imported cases on internal spread of COVID-19: A mathematical modelling study" (2021) 6 *Lancet Public Health* e13; see also Lisa Forman's chapter in this volume.
8 WHO, Report of the Review Committee on the Role of the International Health Regulations (2005) in the Ebola Outbreak and Response, A69/21, 13 May 2016, para. 74.
9 Annelies Wilder-Smith, "The severe acute respiratory syndrome: Impact on travel and tourism" (2006) 4 *Travel Medicine & Infectious Disease* 53 at 56.
10 Michael Ryan, Ellie Avery & Sarah Kahn, "Electronic Sanitary Certificates for Trade in Animal Products: Opportunities and Challenges" (2023) OECD Food, Agriculture and Fisheries Paper No. 190. https://doi.org/10.1787/5417ff4f-en.
11 Colin Carlson & Alexandra Phelan, "International law reform for one health notifications" (2022) 400 *Lancet* 462 at 464.

12 It is not coincidental, then, that trade in in-person services during the COVID-19 pandemic declined twice as much as trade in goods. Organization for Economic Cooperation and Development, *International Trade during the COVID-19 Pandemic: Big Shifts and Uncertainty* (10 March 2022), online (pdf): www.oecd.org/coronavirus/policy-responses/international-trade-during-the-covid-19-pandemic-big-shifts-and-uncertainty-d1131663/. See also Lukasz Gruszczynski, "The COVID-19 pandemic and international trade: Temporary turbulence or paradigm shift?" (2020) 11 *The European Journal of Risk Regulation* 337.

13 Sebastian Benz, Frédéric Gonzales & Annabelle Mourougane, "The impact of COVID-19 international travel restrictions on services-trade costs" (2020) *OECD Trade Policy Papers No.* 237 1 at 5.

14 Bryan Thomas et al, "Vaccine ins and outs: An exploration of the legal issues raised by vaccine passports" (2021) *C.D. Howe Institute Working Paper*. http://www.cdhowe.org/public-policy-research/vaccine-ins-and-outs-exploration-legal-issues-raised-vaccine-passports.

15 "International travel and health" (1 July 2020), online (pdf): *WHO*. www.who.int/docs/default-source/documents/emergencies/travel-advice/yellow-fever-vaccination-requirements-country-list-2020-en.pdf.

16 Jacqueline Peel, *Science and Risk Regulation in International Law* (Cambridge: Cambridge University Press, 2010) 129–132.

17 On the corresponding risks posed by international trade, see WTO, *supra* note 3 at 66.

18 Vera Lúcia Raposo, "Quarantines: Between precaution and necessity. A look at COVID-19" (2021) 14 *Public Health Ethics* 42.

19 James Childress et al, "Public health ethics: Mapping the terrain" (2002) 30 *Journal of Law, Medicine & Ethics* 173.

20 WTO, *supra* note 3, at 90.

21 Australia was a particular case in point. See Olivera Simic, "Australia, COVID-19, and the India travel ban" (2022) 9 *The Griffith Journal of Law & Human Dignity* 2; see also Steven Hoffman, Isaac Weldon & Roojin Habibi, "A virus unites the world while national border closures divide it: Epidemiologic, legal, and political analysis on border closures during COVID-19" (2022) 77:2 *International Journal* 188.

22 WTO, *India—Measures Concerning the Importation of Certain Agricultural Products,* DS430. See also Pedro Villarreal, "India—Agricultural products" in *Max Planck Encyclopedia of Public International Law*, edited by Rüdiger Wolfrum & Anne Peters (Oxford: Oxford University Press, 2019).

23 As of March 2023. See the current status of the dispute at "India—Measures concerning the importation of certain agricultural products", online: *WTO*. www.wto.org/english/tratop_e/dispu_e/cases_e/ds430_e.htm.

24 As a matter of practice, prior to the COVID-19 pandemic, yellow fever vaccination certificates were the only ones requested as condition to enter a country. See "The scientific and technical advisory group on geographical yellow fever risk mapping (GRYF)", online: *WHO*. www.who.int/groups/gryf.

25 Abdel Omran, "The epidemiologic transition: A theory of the epidemiology of population change" (1971) 49 *Milbank Memorial Fund Quarterly* 509.

26 "Global burden of 369 diseases and injuries in 204 countries and territories, 1990–2019: A systematic analysis for the Global Burden of Disease Study 2019" (2020) 396 *Lancet* 1204.

27 Rachel E. Baker et al, "Infectious disease in an era of global change" (2022) *Nature Reviews Microbiology* 193 at 202–203.

28 Article 56 of the International Health Regulations gives legal standing only to states for challenging travel restrictions by other states and initiating dispute settlement.

29 Benjamin Mason Meier et al, "Travel restrictions and variants of concern: global health laws need to reflect evidence" (2022) 100 *Bulletin of the WHO* 178.
30 See the temporary recommendations issued in WHO, "Statement on the second meeting of the International Health Regulations" (2005) Emergency Committee regarding the outbreak of novel coronavirus (2019-nCoV) (30 January 2020).
31 Roojin Habibi et al, "Do not violate the international health regulations during the COVID-19 outbreak" (2020) 395 *Lancet* 664 at 665.
32 WHO, "Statement on the third meeting of the international health regulations (2005) emergency committee regarding the outbreak of coronavirus disease (COVID-19)" (1 May 2020), online: www.who.int/news/item/01-05-2020-statement-on-the-third-meeting-of-the-international-health-regulations-(2005)-emergency-committee-regarding-the-outbreak-of-coronavirus-disease-(covid-19).
33 A full removal of other barriers to trade at the international level is mostly inoperative. While tariff restrictions may be reduced, other requirements such as technical standards may be present.
34 Pedro A. Villarreal, "The role of interstate adjudication in public health emergencies: incompatible at the core" (2021) 85 *QIL Zoom-out* 29.
35 I say "mostly," as there are limits in how states can exercise such sovereign prerogatives. Thus, restrictions that are disproportionate or lack a sufficient scientific basis. In the case of trade in goods, see Villarreal, *supra* note 22. For international travel, see Lisa Forman & Roojin Habibi, "Revisiting the Legality of Travel Restrictions under International Law during COVID-19" (2022) 71 *The International & Comparative Law Quarterly* 743.
36 International Health Regulations (2005), 2509 UNTS 79, arts 31, 36 [IHR].
37 IOM Constitution, *supra* note 4, art 1(3).
38 See Audrey Macklin's chapter in this volume.
39 On 21 March, 2022, a "Global Supply Chains Forum" took place at the WTO. The report is scheduled to be published in the yearly report of 2022, likely in 2023.
40 International Organization on Migration, *supra* note 2.
41 WHO, "Second meeting of the intergovernmental negotiating body to draft and negotiate a WHO convention, agreement or other international instrument on pandemic prevention, preparedness and response" (13 July 2022), online (pdf): https://apps.who.int/gb/inb/pdf_files/inb2/A_INB2_3-en.pdf.
42 Wildlife trade has been pinpointed as a trigger of pandemic risk. Tanya Wyatt, *Is CITES Protecting Wildlife? Assessing Implementation and Compliance* (London and New York: Routledge, 2021) 4–6; Independent Panel for Pandemic Preparedness and Response, *COVID-19: Make it the Last Pandemic* (2021) 20.
43 Hoffman, Weldon & Habibi, *supra* note 21.
44 The proposal was made by the Czech Republic on behalf of all EU Member States and, in the case of digital health certificates, touches upon Articles 23, 35, 36, and Annex 6 IHR (2005). See Working Group on Amendments to the International Health Regulations, "Proposed Amendments to the International Health Regulations (2005) submitted in accordance with decision WHA75(9)(2022)", online (pdf): https://apps.who.int/gb/wgihr/pdf_files/wgihr1/WGIHR_Submissions-en.pdf.
45 As established in Annex 6 of the IHR, *supra* note 36.
46 There is, moreover, some variation even between EU countries. See Bart Custers et al, "A comparison of data protection legislation and policies across the EU" (2018) 34 *The Computer Law and Security Review* 234.
47 Ryan, Avery & Kahn, *supra* note 10.

30

MODELLING APPROACHES TO BORDERS, GEOGRAPHY, AND INFECTIOUS DISEASES

David Fisman[1]

30.1 Mathematical Models of Movement of Disease in Space

Mathematical models of infectious diseases have been in use since Bernoulli's attempts to model the utility of smallpox inoculation in the 18th century,[2] and many current mathematical modelling applications are fundamentally based on the work of Kermack and McKendrick,[3] and Ross,[4] which are now about a century old. However, modelling of changes in infectious disease risk in space, or space and time, are relatively new endeavors. Noble[5] conceptualized the movement of a disease in space as analogous to diffusion; we could imagine the diffusion of disease in one-dimensional space (e.g., movement of cholera along the rivers and canals of 19th century New York)[6] or two dimensions (e.g., movement of the Black Plague through 14th century Europe) (**Figure 30.1**).[7]

Contacts between, and behaviors of, individuals may be better captured using more computationally intensive agent- or individual-based models, which can incorporate network structure. In such models, space isn't necessarily physical space but rather connectedness between individuals (or individuals and places). The edges that connect nodes in these models can either be fixed or dynamic, and agents themselves can be mobile. An important insight yielded by an early agent-based model was the degree to which the combined dynamics of contagion and fear (e.g., hiding and fleeing) can change the trajectory of an epidemic.[8]

Spatial models need to be modified when confronted with natural, or constructed, barriers that divide space. One such type of barrier would be a jurisdictional border. Borders disrupt the free movement of people (and diseases) in space and may also define spatial "patches" that have different levels of immunization, different degrees of investment in disease-preventing

DOI: 10.4324/9781003394006-40

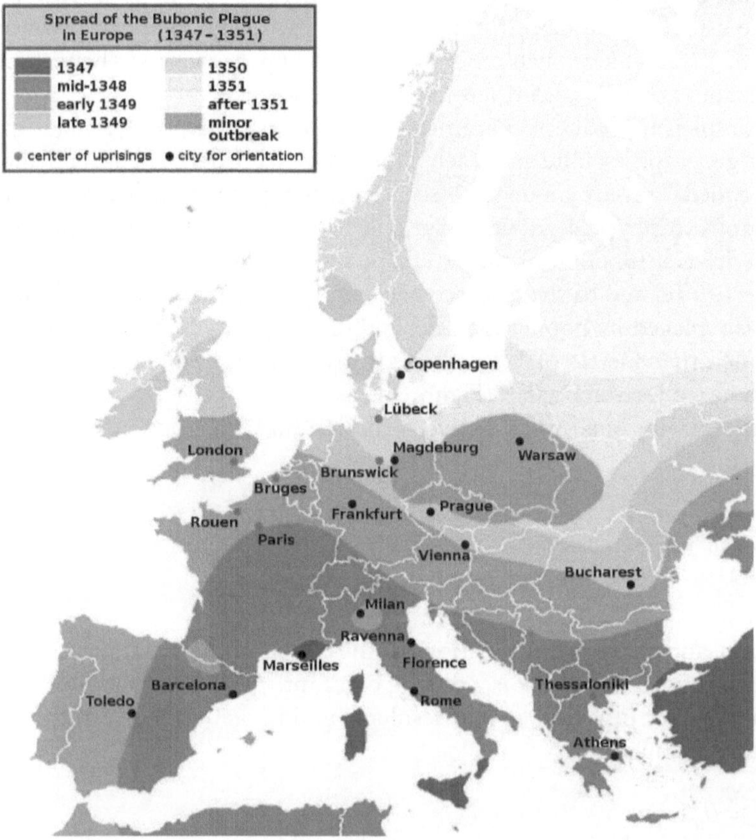

FIGURE 30.1 Movement of bubonic plague across Europe in the 14th century. This process can be modeled as a diffusion process in two-dimensional space.

Source: Figure available via Wikimedia Commons at https://commons.wikimedia.org/w/index.php?curid=4142024#/media/File:Bub.

infrastructure (e.g., sewage and water treatment infrastructure), or different disease control policies.[9]

Such "metapopulation" models are analogous to multilevel statistical models in that they consider dynamics within patches and also consider interaction between patches. Movement of populations and disease between patches can be parameterized explicitly. For example, we can capture the impact of immigration, emigration, trade, and tourism on disease in a very simple way by using a "patch model", such that for each of *i* regions, there is a possibility of traveling to region *j*; travel between regions can be described using an *i x j* matrix that describes reciprocal movement of susceptible, infectious, and immune individuals between patches. There has been recent enthusiasm for the use of digital data (for example, the use of mobile phone movement data) to parameterize such models, but such approaches may be technically challenging and may also result in privacy concerns.[10]

A simpler approach to parameterizing the way disease dynamics in different geographies influence each other across borders is through the use of so-called "gravity models".[11] Such models represent such interactions as analogous to physical gravitational pull between bodies (e.g., planets); that is, gravity is a function of the product of the masses of the two bodies and is inversely related to the distance between them. In metapopulation model, mass is replaced by population size, and distance may be physical distance[12] or some other metric of "closeness" (for example, number of daily flights between two jurisdictions)[13] (**Figure 30.2**).

The "gravitational pull" between the ith and j[th] regions (θ) is defined as follows:

$$\theta_{ij} = \kappa \frac{p_i p_j}{d_{ij}}$$

Where p_i and p_j are the populations of the communities *i* and *j*, and d_{ij} is the distance between *i* and *j*. κ is a scaling constant.

The force of infection (l) that results from interaction between the ith and j[th] patches is thus:

$$\lambda_{ij} = \theta_{ij} I_j S_i$$

Where I_j represents the number of infectives and S_i the number of susceptibles in the jth and i[th] patches respectively. We implicitly assume symmetry (non-directionality, $\theta_{ij} = \theta_{ji}$) which effectively makes gravity a property of the

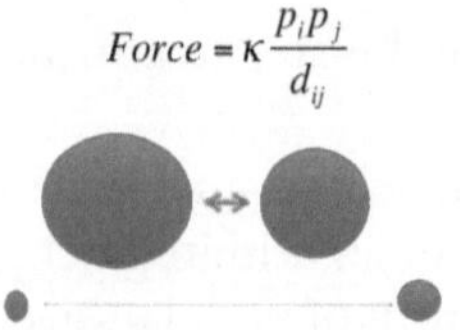

FIGURE 30.2 Schematic model of a "gravity model" for movement of infectious diseases between jurisdictions. Gravity is determined by the product of jurisdiction sizes and is inversely proportional to the distance between them. The two large close jurisdictions depicted earlier would have large gravitational pull on one another; the small far jurisdictions depicted earlier would have little gravitational pull on one another.

individual borders between patches, and for *n* patches, we have (n)(n–1)/2 unique borders.

30.2 A Simple Metapopulation Model

We used this approach to accurately predict the sequential spread of cholera through Haitian *departments* during the 2010 cholera epidemic in that country.[14] Indeed, when compared to models parameterized using cell phone movement data from the telecommunications company Digicel, simple gravity models performed well.[15] We can use this simple approach to gain qualitative insights into the impacts that interventions at borders can, and cannot, have on epidemic spread upon emergence of a novel disease. We use a simple compartmental differential equation model with four patches as follows:

$$dSi / dt = \beta_i S_i I_i + \rho R_i - \Sigma\theta_{ij} S_i I_j$$

$$dI_i / dt = \beta_i S_i I_i - \gamma I_i + \Sigma\theta_{ij} S_i I_j$$

$$dR_i / dt = \gamma I_i - \rho R_i$$

The model is represented schematically in **Figure 30.3.** β represents the transmission coefficient, ρ represents the rate of loss of immunity, and γ represents rate of recovery from infection. The basic reproduction number (R_0) is β/γ, and > 1, such that once introduction occurs, an epidemic will result. Other parameters are defined earlier. We initially assume that all four patches are equidistant from one another and have identical populations. I arbitrarily label patch 1 as the "home country", which in this model will be the decision-maker for policies regarding borders between itself and the three other patches.

1 We can use such a model to gain the following three insights: *Border measures can delay but not eliminate introduction.*

We assume that disease emerges in country 2. There is progressively greater delay in introduction of disease into the home country as θ_{12} is progressively decreased. However, even reducing traffic by 99% does not prevent introduction but simply delays it. We can completely seal the border between the home country and country 2, where the disease of interest originated, and emergence still occurs in the home country, as countries 3 and 4 are still connected both country 2 and the home country. It might be imagined that if governments in countries 3 and 4 are aware of the possibility of border closure if they announce that disease has emerged in their countries, there might be significant moral hazard related to the decision to do so. As the dynamics of the disease are identical in all countries, equilibrium prevalence of infection is identical in country 2 and in the home country (**Figure 30.4**). Note

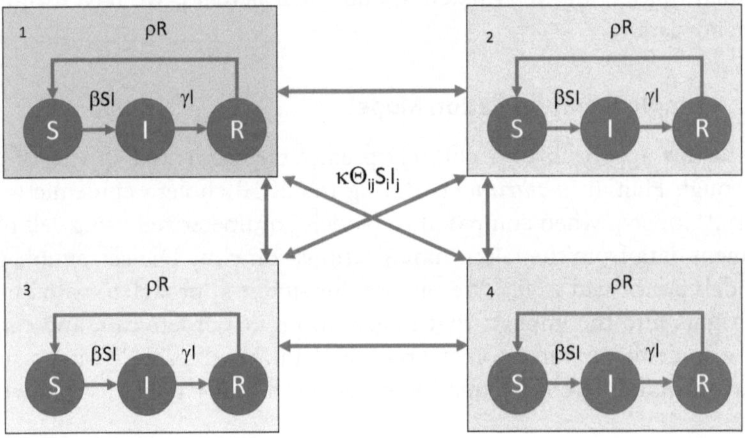

FIGURE 30.3 Schematic diagram of a metapopulation model of an infectious disease with between country transmission defined by "gravity". Arrows within patches represent flows between compartments as defined by model equations. Flow of disease between patches is defined by the term $\kappa\Theta_{ij}S_iI_j$ as described in the text. A novel disease emerges in patch 2; policy is made in the "home country" (patch 1).

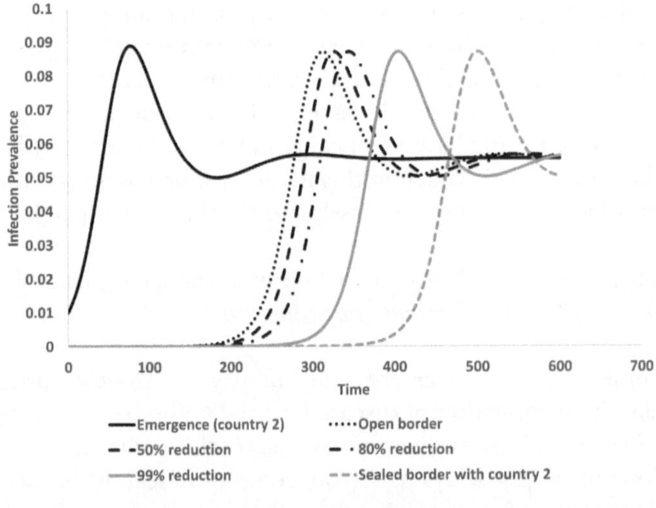

FIGURE 30.4 Figure shows outputs from a gravity model with four countries (patches). Disease emerges in country 2. No degree of border control, including complete closing of the border, prevents disease emergence in country 1. Progressive increases in stringency of border control results in increasing delay in emergence. As factors determining disease dynamics are identical in country 1 and country 2, epidemic trajectories and equilibrium prevalence are identical following emergence.

that this does not mean that the delay of emergence is without value; as noted later, delaying importation of a novel disease may be favoured as creating a window of opportunity for preparedness that might reduce the impact of the disease following importation, as described later.

2 *Big and close is more important than far and small.*

We initially assumed that all countries were identical in size and equally distant from one another. The gravity of the country of emergence strongly influences time to emergence. If we increase the size of country 2, the time to emergence in the home country decreases; decreasing the size of country 2 has the opposite effect (**Figure 30.5**).

In fact, the gravity of individual countries other than the country in which the disease emerges is highly influential in the timing of emergence in the home country. Indeed, when country 2 is identical in size to the home country, and country 3 has a 10-fold larger population than the home country, disease emerges earlier in country 3 than in the home country, and disease

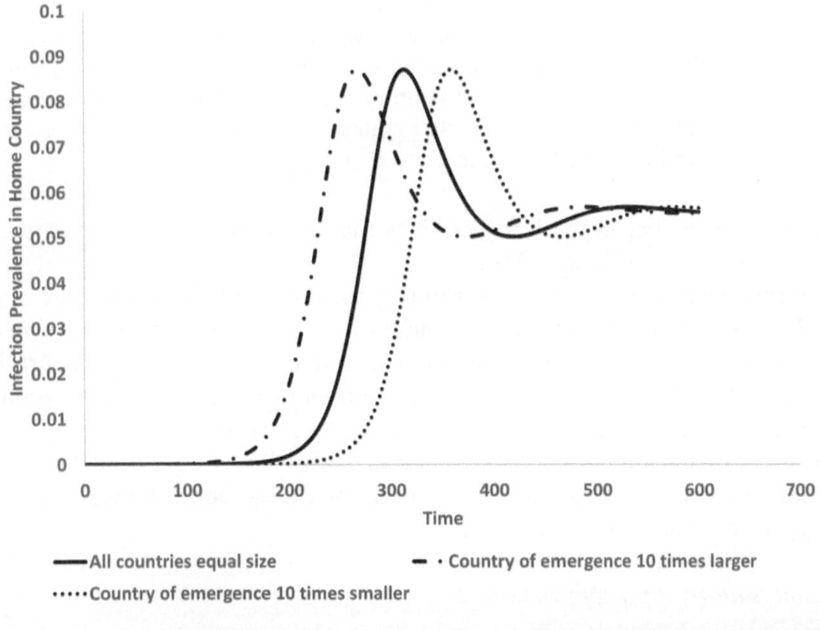

FIGURE 30.5 Impact of changing the size of country 2 (country of emergence) on timing of emergence in the home country. The timing of emergence in the home country when all countries are identical in size is represented by the orange curve. When country 2 increases in size 10-fold, emergence in the home country occurs more rapidly; emergence is slower when the size of country 2 is decreased 10-fold.

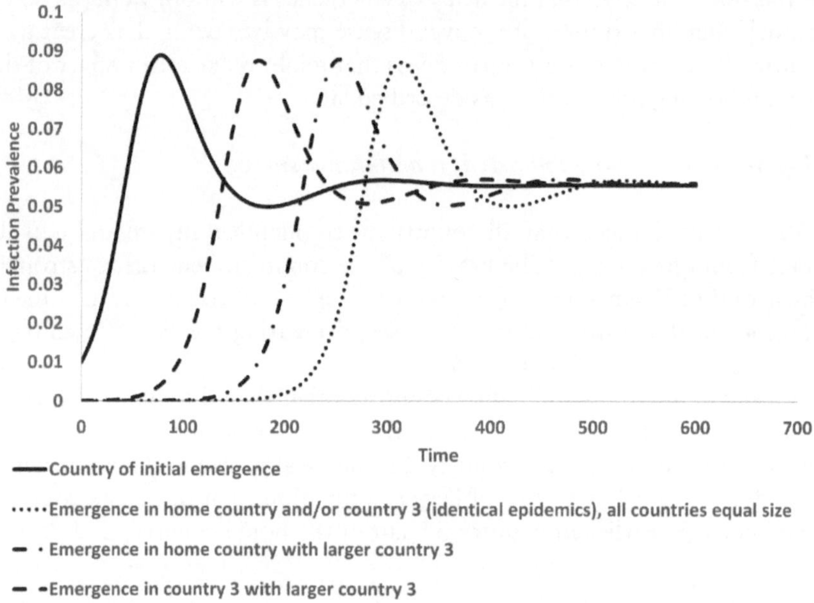

FIGURE 30.6 The effect of adding a far larger country to the network. Disease emerges initially in country 2. When all countries are identical in size, disease emerges simultaneously in the home country and country 3. When the size of country 3 is substantially increased, emergence occurs earlier in that country than in others in the network but is also earlier in the home country.

also emerges earlier in the home country than it would have if all countries were the same size (**Figure 30.6**).

In this latter scenario, notwithstanding emergence of the disease in country 2, imposing border controls on country 3 results in greater delay in emergence of the disease in the home country than does imposing border controls on country 2 (**Figure 30.7**). This creates an important dilemma: large highly connected countries are likely to be more economically influential than smaller more distant countries, meaning that while border controls targeting the larger country will have a greater impact on disease control, they will also be more economically disruptive.

3 Soil is more important than seed.

Emergence of a novel infectious disease in any jurisdiction can be likened to growing a garden; a "seed" (the pathogen) needs to be introduced, but the "soil" (environmental and population conditions necessary for $R_0 > 1$) must be sufficiently fertile to support growth of an epidemic.

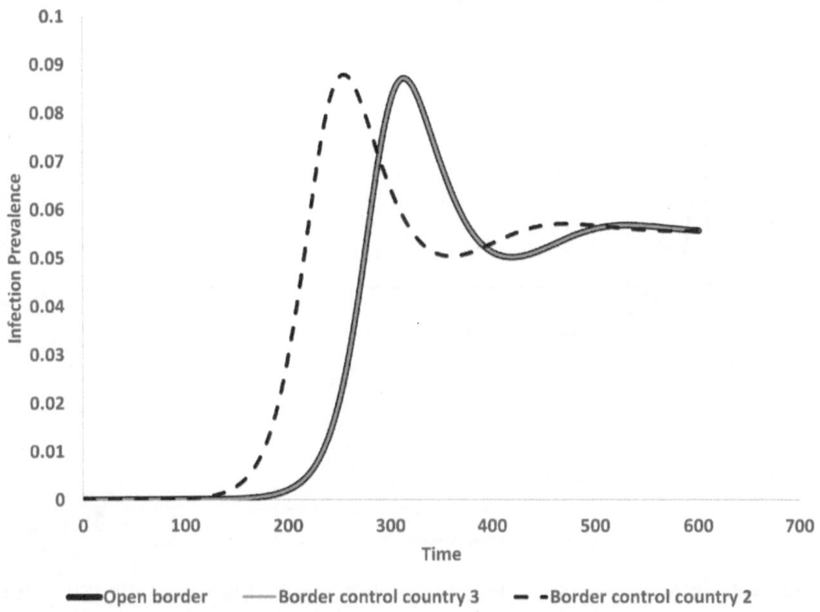

FIGURE 30.7 The impact of border controls to reduce disease transmission in the presence of a very large third country in the network. Disease initially emerges in country 2; the home country makes policy. When a large third country (country 3) is present in the network, no meaningful difference is seen in the timing of emergence of disease in the home country with or without border controls focused on country 2 (overlaid curves). However, because of the large gravity of country 3, imposition of border controls with country 3 delays emergence in the home country.

We can vary the R_0 across countries and see that having high R_0 in the country of emergence (country 2) may slightly reduce time to emergence in the home country but has no influence on the contour of the resultant epidemic in the home country, which is determined entirely by within-country R_0 (**Figure 30.8**). Because of the presence of borders, the disease dynamics resulting in higher equilibrium prevalence in the country of emergence do not impact equilibrium prevalence in the home country.

Conversely, when local conditions result in a reproduction number < 1 in the country of initial emergence, with resultant local fade-out of the disease, that emergence can nonetheless spark epidemics and high level endemicity in the home country, if the home country has R0 > 1. (**Figure 30.9**).

Lastly, and perhaps intuitively, when conditions in the home country to not permit emergence of the infectious disease, even with importation, as

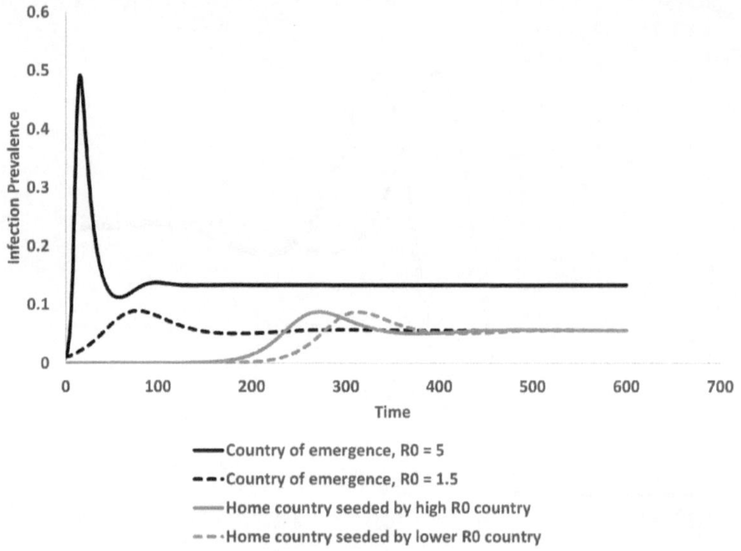

FIGURE 30.8 When disease emerges in a country with high R_0, time until emergence in the home country is slightly shortened, but dynamics are otherwise identical to disease emergence in a low R_0 country.

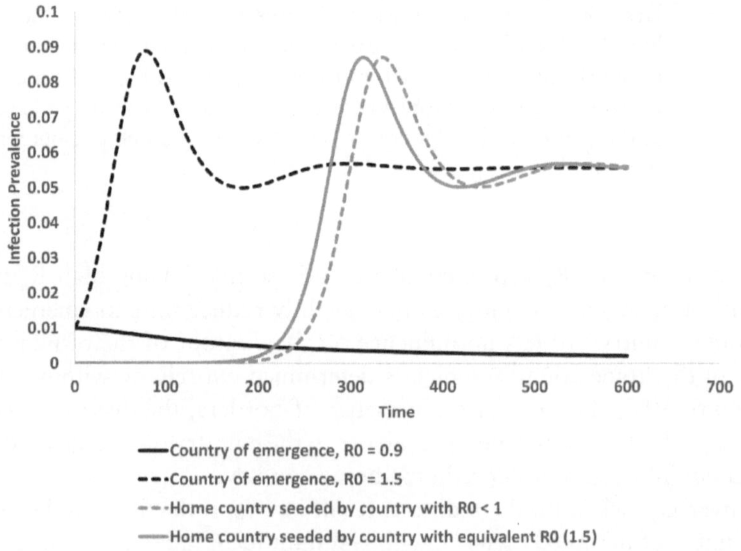

FIGURE 30.9 When disease emerges in a country with low R_0, even below 1 (preventing epidemic spread in the country of emergence with $R_0 < 1$), it nonetheless generates a slightly delayed but otherwise identical epidemic in the home country as if the disease emerged in a country with higher R_0 country.

R_0 in the home country is < 1, disease importation becomes unimportant at a population level. This may occur, for example, due to water and sewage infrastructure (for waterborne diseases like cholera) or due to the presence of herd immunity for vaccine preventable diseases. Maintaining a low R_0, even an R_0 that is above the threshold for emergence, has far more impact on prevention or delay of emergence than can be achieved through border controls (**Figure 30.10**). As noted earlier, border restrictions delay but do not eliminate introduction and might be justified as buying time for preparedness activities that reduce transmissibility of a newly introduced pathogen.

This key insight (that both seed and soil are important but the focus in pandemic preparedness tends to be on seed) is helpful in understanding recent policy pitfalls related to communicable disease emergence.

- The initial SARS-CoV-2 emergence in China may have been controlled; however, close connections to other countries with less ability to contain SARS-CoV-2 epidemics (such as Iran[16]) ensured that a global pandemic would result.

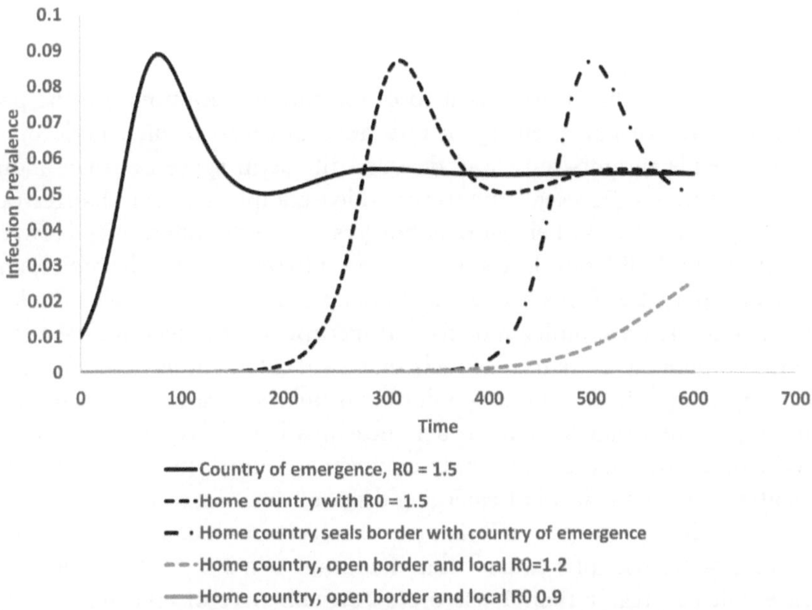

FIGURE 30.10 Disease emergence in country 2 is followed by emergence in the home country when the two countries have equivalent R_0. Sealing the border between country 2 and the home country delays emergence but not by as much as reducing the within-country R_0 from 1.5 to 1.2. Having R_0 < 1 (0.9) prevents emergence in the home country entirely, notwithstanding ongoing importation of cases.

- The emergence of cholera in Haiti in 2010 reflected introduction into a cholera-free country in which weak infrastructure for sewage management ensured a high local R_0. By contrast, notwithstanding close travel ties between Haiti and Canada (particularly Montreal), sewage management infrastructure in Canada prevented cholera emergence, notwithstanding the introduction of imported cholera cases.
- The emergence of Zika virus in the Western hemisphere led to investigations of possible linkages between specific international gatherings in Brazil (e.g., the 2014 football World Cup) and importation.[17] Concerns regarding exportation of Zika to other countries led to calls for the cancellation of the 2016 Olympic Games.[18] However, given the vast volume of human trafficking between Zika-endemic areas of Africa and Brazil over the course of a centuries-long transatlantic slave trade, and the fact that other arboviruses from the same parts of Africa (with identical mosquito vectors),[19] as well as African malaria species,[20] were imported into South America as a result of the slave trade, it is highly improbable that Zika's emergence was the result of a novel importation of the pathogen. Rather, it is likely that climate change-driven alterations in vector biting rates pushed this pathogen's R_0 above 1,[21] allowing invasion to occur.

30.3 Conclusions

Spatial models represent important tools for gaining intuition into the predicted behavior of newly emerging infectious diseases. While simple models can provide insights into how diseases diffuse in space or travel along networks, borders represent important added complexity that changes our expectations for disease behavior, as borders create discontinuities between populations with different levels of risk, and different disease dynamics, and represent a potential focus for jurisdictional disease control policy. While it is possible to create complex models that incorporate borders, we have seen here that even simple "patch" models that treat interactions between countries in a manner analogous to gravitational pull between planets can yield some important insights: that border measures can delay but not prevent introductions; that large and highly connected countries may be far more influential in dissemination of emerging diseases than the countries in which the disease initially emerged; and that the social, environmental, and immunological characteristics of a country that determine whether the R_0 of the novel disease will be greater than 1 are more determinative of epidemic growth than importation. These models also show us that border-focused prevention interventions are not meaningful in the absence of gradients in risk between countries. More realistic models, incorporating non-random, within-patch mixing patterns,[22] and other factors that may be country-specific (economic, cultural, values-based, political, etc.) are possible but are beyond the scope of this chapter. In the simple models presented here, R decreases with time simply as a result of acquired immunity in the population, but of course, dynamic imposition and relaxation of public health policies, and risk perception and behavior change by individuals, would also be expected to result in changes in effective reproduction number over time.[23]

Lastly, it is worth noting that borders can serve not only as barriers that may slow spread of disease but can also serve as important checkpoints for gathering information about disease prevalence and epidemic size in other countries,[24] as well as to characterize emerging pathogen strains that might be of concern if imported.[25] Discussion of borders as tools that create opportunities for gathering such intelligence is beyond the scope of this paper but is an important area for future research.

Notes

1 Supported by a grant to DNF from the Canadians Institutes for Health Research (2019 COVID-19 rapid researching funding OV4–170360).

2 Sally Blower & Daniel Bernoulli, "An attempt at a new analysis of the mortality caused by smallpox and of the advantages of inoculation to prevent it 1766" (2004) 14:5 *Review in Medical Virology* 275, doi: 10.1002/rmv.443.

3 W. O. Kermack & A. G. McKendrick, "Contributions to the mathematical theory of epidemics–I. 1927" (1991) 53:1–2 *Bulletin of Mathematical Biology* 33, doi: 10.1007/BF02464423.

4 R. Ross, "Some a priori pathometric equations" (1915) 1:2830 *British Medical Journal* 546, doi: 10.1136/bmj.1.2830.546.

5 J. V. Noble, "Geographic and temporal development of plagues" (1974) 250:5469 *Nature* 726, doi: 10.1038/250726a0.

6 Ashleigh R. Tuite, Christina H. Chan & David N. Fisman, "Cholera, canals, and contagion: Rediscovering Dr. Beck's report" (2011) 32:3 *Journal of Public Health Policy* 320, doi: 10.1057/jphp.2011.20.

7 Noble, *supra* note 5.

8 Joshua M. Epstein et al, "Coupled contagion dynamics of fear and disease: mathematical and computational explorations" (2008) 3:12 *PLoS One* e3955, doi: 10.1371/journal.pone.0003955.

9 Richard S. Ostfeld, Gregory E. Glass & Felicia Keesing, "Spatial epidemiology: An emerging (or re-emerging) discipline" (2005) 20:6 *Trends in Ecology & Evolution* 328, doi: 10.1016/j.tree.2005.03.009; G. R. Fulford, M. G. Roberts & J. A.P. Heesterbeek, "The metapopulation dynamics of an infectious disease: tuberculosis in possums" (2002) 61:1 *Theoretical Population Biology* 15, doi: 10.1006/tpbi.2001.1553.

10 Michele Tizzoni et al, "On the use of human mobility proxies for modeling epidemics" (2014) 10:7 *PLoS Computational Biology* e1003716, doi: 10.1371/journal.pcbi.1003716.

11 Yingcun Xia, Ottar N. Bjørnstad & Bryan T Grenfell, "Measles metapopulation dynamics: a gravity model for epidemiological coupling and dynamics" (2004) 164:2 *The American Naturalist* 267, doi: 10.1086/422341; Tuite et al, "Cholera epidemic in Haiti, 2010: Using a transmission model to explain spatial spread of disease and identify optimal control interventions" (2011) 154:9 *Annals of Internal Medicine* 593, doi: 10.7326/0003-4819-154-9-201105030-00334 [Tuite et al, "Cholera in Haiti"]; Cécile Viboud et al, "Synchrony, waves, and

spatial hierarchies in the spread of influenza" (2006) 312:5772 *Science* 447, doi: 10.1126/science.1125237.
12 Tuite et al, "Cholera in Haiti", *supra* note 11.
13 Viboud et al, *supra* note 11.
14 Tuite et al, "Cholera in Haiti", *supra* note 11.
15 Linus Bengtsson et al, "Using mobile phone data to predict the spatial spread of cholera" (2015) 5:8923 *Scientific Reports*, doi: 10.1038/srep08923.
16 Ashleigh R Tuite et al, "Estimation of Coronavirus Disease 2019 (COVID-19) Burden and Potential for International Dissemination of Infection From Iran" (2020) 172:10 *Annals of Internal Medicine* 699–701, doi: 10.7326/M20-0696 [Tuite et al, "Estimation of COVID-19 Burden"].
17 Nuno Rodrigues Fariaet al, "Zika virus in the Americas: Early epidemiological and genetic findings" (2016) 352:6283 *Science* 345, doi: 10.1126/science.aaf5036.
18 Rebecca Coombes, "Call to cancel 2016 Olympics because of Zika risk is not backed by WHO guidance" (2016) *BMJ* 353:i2899, doi: 10.1136/bmj.i2899.
19 Juliet E. Bryant, Edward C. Holmes & Allan D. T. Barrett, "Out of Africa: a molecular perspective on the introduction of yellow fever virus into the Americas" (2007) 3:5 *PLoS Pathogens* e75, doi: 10.1371/journal.ppat.0030075.
20 Erhan Yalcindag et al, "Multiple independent introductions of Plasmodium falciparum in South America" (2012) 109:2 *Proceedings of the National Academy of Sciences of the United States of America* 511, doi: 10.1073/pnas.1119058109.
21 Blanka Tesla et al, "Temperature drives Zika virus transmission: evidence from empirical and mathematical models" (2018) 285:1884 *Proceedings: Biological Sciences*, doi: 10.1098/rspb.2018.0795; Lillian L. M. Shapiro, Shelley A. Whitehead & Matthew B. Thomas, "Quantifying the effects of temperature on mosquito and parasite traits that determine the transmission potential of human malaria" (2017) 15:10 *PLoS Biology* e2003489, doi: 10.1371/journal.pbio.2003489.
22 G.P. Garnett & R. M. Anderson, "Sexually transmitted diseases and sexual behavior: Insights from mathematical models" (1996) 174 (Suppl 2) *Journal of Infectious Diseases* S150–S161, doi: 10.1093/infdis/174.supplement_2.s150.
23 Epstein et al, *supra* note 8; Jean-Paul R Soucy et al, "Characterizing responsiveness to the COVID-19 pandemic in the United States and Canada using mobility data" (2022) medRxiv 2022.11.08.22282050, doi: 10.1101/2022.11.08.22282050.
24 Tuite et al, "Estimation of COVID-19 Burden", *supra* note 16; Christophe Fraser et al, "Pandemic potential of a strain of influenza A (H1N1): Early findings" (2009) 324:5934 *Science* 1557–1561, doi: 10.1126/science.1176062.
25 Natsuko Imai et al, "COVID-19 in Japan, January-March 2020: insights from the first three months of the epidemic" (2022) 22:1 *BMC Infectious Diseases* 493, doi: 10.1186/s12879-022-07469-1; Li-Qun Fang et al, "Travel-related infections in mainland China, 2014–16: an active surveillance study" (2018) 3:8 *Lancet Public Health* e385–e394, doi: 10.1016/S2468-2667(18)30127-0.

31

ADVANCING A RISK-BASED APPROACH TO BORDER MANAGEMENT DURING PUBLIC HEALTH EMERGENCIES OF INTERNATIONAL CONCERN

Lessons from the COVID-19 Pandemic

Kelley Lee, Julianne Piper and Jennifer Fang

31.1 Background

The universal use of travel measures has proven among the most controversial policy issues during the COVID-19 pandemic. Previous infectious disease outbreaks, notably the Ebola virus in 2014–2015 and Middle Eastern Respiratory Syndrome (MERS) since 2012, suggest restricting travel is generally of limited value, and can even be counterproductive, to public health goals.[1,2] For this reason, upon declaring COVID-19 a public health emergency of international concern (PHEIC) on 30 January 2020, the World Health Organization (WHO) recommended against the adoption of travel restrictions for controlling the international spread of SARS-CoV-2.[3] Despite this recommendation, and the commitment by States Parties to comply with WHO guidance under the International Health Regulations (IHR), all IHR States Parties adopted a variety of travel measures including restrictions for border management by the end of March 2020.[4] Some international legal experts deemed restrictions in violation of IHR commitments.[5,6] However, due to the novel nature of the virus, and clear role of human mobility in the initial and ongoing spread of the virus and its (sub)variants worldwide, evolving evidence suggests the precautionary and stringent use of travel restrictions[7] may be warranted during certain types of events.[8] Moreover, there is new recognition that appropriately applied travel measures can facilitate, rather than simply restrict, mobility by enhancing public health safety.

In this context, there is need for an improved and agreed upon approach for deciding when and how a broad range of possible travel measures should be used in response to major public health events, including PHEICs. The clear lack of consensus among States Parties and the WHO on an agreed approach is

DOI: 10.4324/9781003394006-41

evidenced by the highly varied, uncoordinated, and frequently changing policies adopted by different jurisdictions. Private actors, such as airlines and cruise ship companies, have also applied their own diverse and changing measures. Alongside questions about the effectiveness of these different measures for advancing public health goals, notably limiting pathogen introduction and onward transmission, the "travel chaos"[9] created during the COVID-19 pandemic has inflicted large-scale and inequitable economic, social, and political costs on populations worldwide. Public trust and compliance have, in turn, been undermined. For these reasons, a risk-based approach to decision-making on the use of travel measures has been supported by the WHO, governments, and the business sector. Attention has turned to understanding what an agreed risk-based approach would need to entail and how such an approach could align with efforts to revise the IHR and strengthen global pandemic governance.

31.2 Travel-Related Risk Analysis

The concept of risk is the possibility of a negative event occurring which has adverse impacts on something valued (e.g., good health, natural environment, wealth accumulation). The negative event is referred to as the *threat* or *hazard*, while the likelihood for the event to occur during a specified time and the likely magnitude of the consequences of any adverse impacts is known as the *risk*.[10] Emergency or disaster risk is defined, specifically, as "the potential loss of life, injury, or destroyed or damaged assets which could occur to a system, society or a community in a specific period of time, determined probabilistically as a function of hazard, exposure, vulnerability and capacity".[11] A pandemic such as COVID-19 causing large-scale morbidity and mortality, along with wider negative societal impacts, can thus be approached as an emergency or disaster risk.

For this purpose, *risk analysis* comprises three main components—risk assessment, risk management, and risk communication (Figure 1). *Risk assessment* concerns the "systematic process for gathering, assessing and documenting information to assign a level of risk" to a potential threat, incorporating hazard, exposure, and context assessments.[10] *Risk management* is defined as follows:

> the process of weighing policy options in the light of a risk assessment and, if required, selecting and implementing appropriate intervention options, including regulatory measures . . . to manage and reduce the negative consequences of acute public health risks.[10]

Risk communication is defined as follows:

> the range of communication principles, activities and exchange of information required through the preparedness, response and recovery phases

of a serious public health event between responsible authorities, partner organizations and communities at risk to encourage informed decision-making, positive behaviour change and the maintenance of trust.[10]

Applying these three components, *travel risk analysis* is routinely conducted by governments, employers (public and private), and others to identify potential hazards associated with travel. The hazard may be to traveler health and well-being or broader threats to the ability to travel to individuals, business sectors, or broader societies due to, for example, political unrest, terrorism, or natural disasters. A travel risk assessment provides the basis for identifying and ranking such threats by likelihood and consequence.[12] Governments, for example, regularly issue and update advisories based on ongoing assessment of the risk of potential threats to travel.

Our review of the existing travel medicine literature shows that the application of risk assessment routinely focuses on individual travelers. For outbound travel, risk assessment is used to identify potential health-related hazards at a designated destination for the arriving traveler. To mitigate such risks, advice may be issued regarding safer behaviors, prophylactic measures such as immunization, or preparations for if an event were to occur, such as insurance or carrying medical supplies.[13,14] Risk assessment is also used to manage health-related hazards posed by inbound travelers arriving from designated jurisdictions. This practice has been normalized for the immigration processes of many countries, with assessment of the potential hazard based, for example, on disease prevalence in the source country (e.g., tuberculosis). Inbound travelers may be required to provide a personal health history (e.g., immunization records) or documented proof of health insurance or undergo screening pre-, upon-, or post-arrival.[15,16]

While risk assessment in travel medicine is well-established, with tools and resources focused on individual travelers (either outbound or inbound), methodologies for assessing travel-related health risks at the population level remain underdeveloped. Advancing such methodologies is challenged by the increased scale and interconnectedness of population mobility in a globalized world. As Leder et al write, while "travel medicine has definitely progressed scientifically . . . there are distinct issues about the travelling population that add unique complexities to the risk discussion."[17] Over the past two decades, major public health events including PHEICs have led to greater attention to assessing travel-related risks. This includes expanded approaches to assess, for example, risk of pathogen introduction,[18] international spread through air travel,[19] and cost-benefit analysis[20] of efforts to prevent travel-related importations. However, in several of the public health events preceding the COVID-19 pandemic—such as SARS-CoV-1 (2003), H1N1 (2009), and the Ebola virus outbreak in West Africa (2014–2016)—travel-related risks for most countries proved less significant than initial government and public perceptions. The COVID-19 pandemic, however, has proven different, with travel playing a key role in the initial and ongoing introduction and onward transmission of the virus worldwide. This includes the rapid and large-scale spread of SARS-CoV-2 variants of concern globally, with significant morbidity and mortality alongside societal harms resulting from the prolonged pandemic. The continued struggle by States Parties to appropriately apply travel measures to mitigate these hazards has catalysed calls for risk-based approaches during major public health events.

31.3 Key Decision Points for Advancing a Risk-Based Approach to Travel Measures

To advance travel-related risk analysis, elsewhere, we reviewed 11 publicly available risk-based approaches to the use of travel measures during the COVID-19 pandemic.[21] These methodologies were put forth by Hong Kong, New Zealand, South Korea, Taiwan, the United Kingdom, the United States, the International Civil Aviation Organization (ICAO), the International Air Transport Association (IATA), the WHO, the Organisation for Economic Co-operation and Development (OECD), and the European Union. It should be noted that this review does not evaluate the extent to which each methodology informed real-world decision-making or their effectiveness in achieving stated goals. This will require detailed case studies of how each were operationalized during the pandemic and the extent to which decisions regarding the use of travel measures applied the methodology put forth. It is also noted that the methodologies reviewed may not represent all available methodologies. Other countries may have applied methodologies that are not presently publicly available online and in English. Moreover, some of the methodologies reviewed changed over time. A fuller discussion of this review can be found elsewhere.

Briefly, in comparing risk assessment and risk management (see Figure 31.1) by these methodologies, we found substantial variation in approach, including what is the primary source of the hazard (e.g., inbound versus outbound travelers), who is at risk (e.g., domestic versus other populations), how risk is characterized (e.g., epidemiological trends versus impact on healthcare system), and what level of risk is deemed tolerable (e.g., no infected inbound travelers permitted entry versus reduced number of inbound travelers permitted entry without vaccination). This significant variation in methodologies explains the wide diversity and frequent changes of practice by governments during this pandemic.

Towards greater international consensus on an agreed methodology, it is useful to recognize two decision instruments that currently inform risk analysis during international disease outbreaks. The first is a decision instrument of the IHR (Appendix 2) for the assessment of events to determine if

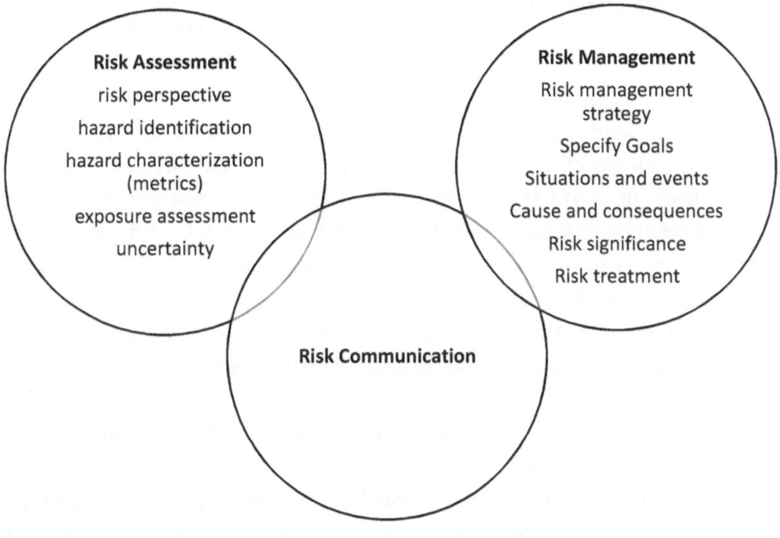

FIGURE 31.1 Basic structure of risk analysis.

Source: Spencer Henson & Julie Caswell, "Food safety regulation: An overview of contemporary issues" (1999) 24:6 *Food Policy* 592.

the WHO should be notified. The decision points include whether an event is "unusual or unexpected", is of "unknown causes or sources", poses a potentially serious public health impact, and can "spread rapidly internationally".[22] For assessing a potential travel-related risk, this instrument provides useful questions for the initial characterizing of a pathogen. Second, the ICAO sets out a basic decision aid that "can support the development of operationally viable inter-agency risk management processes" for cross-border commercial airline travel.[23] This four-stage framework sets out an approach that informs the implementation of risk management measures to achieve a state of "residual risk". The framework provides guidance on *what* analysis should be conducted at each stage (e.g., draft scenarios, assess likelihood of scenarios, select mitigation measures) but not *how* such analyses should be conducted (i.e., methodology).[24]

Building on our review and the two decision instruments described earlier, we argue that an agreed approach to travel-related risk analysis during major public health events requires a broader framework. This framework should encompass a) agreed scientific and technical evidence and b) agreed normative frameworks for navigating diverse values, perspectives, and interests. To date, risk-based approaches to the use of travel measures have focused on the former, with an assumption that decisions can be driven by certain types of evidence alone. In light of the unprecedented challenges of the COVID-19 pandemic, there is undoubtedly a need for the science of border management to continue to evolve. This includes the development of agreed scientific and technical methods and shared datasets to assess the characteristics of a pathogen, as well as the role of human mobility in its introduction and transmission. The assessment criteria might include the capacity for human-to-human transmission, mode of transmission, transmissibility, and virulence of the pathogen (severity of the illness caused). A review of pathogens causing previous major public health events, and their association with travel, can provide the basis of an agreed set of scientific and technical criteria for this first decision point.

A second decision point is based on an assessment of a jurisdiction's characteristics. Risk analysis is concerned with assessing the likelihood and potential impacts of a hazard. Pathogens will vary in their impact depending on contextual factors, such as population demographics (e.g., age, sex, occupation, income), human (e.g., urban and rural settlements, population density) and physical (e.g., landforms, climate) geography, population mobility patterns, economic systems (e.g., trade dependence, role of migrant workers), and public infrastructure (e.g., healthcare system, points of entry). The degree to which the pathogen in question is already present within the jurisdiction is also an important consideration. Methods for assessing jurisdictional characteristics can draw, for example, on the study of human mobility dynamics to identify spaces and populations of vulnerability.[25]

A third decision point concerns the prioritization of policy goals (i.e., trade-offs among public health, social, and economic impacts) and overall response strategy. During the COVID-19 pandemic, Wu et al describe governments adopting three main response strategies—aggressive containment, suppression, and mitigation.[26] Our review of the 11 methodologies found that how risk analysis was applied was closely linked with the chosen response strategy. For example, what level of risk is deemed tolerable (risk evaluation) depends on which strategy is being maintained. Countries pursuing an aggressive containment strategy, a so-called COVID zero strategy, tolerate a much lower level of risk (i.e., no importation of test positive cases in inbound travelers) than countries maintaining a mitigation strategy (i.e., importation of test positive cases permitted as long as healthcare capacity not exceeded). Importantly, this decision point is informed by a jurisdiction's normative frameworks informed by shared values, moral principles, and ethical standards. There may be contestation within a jurisdiction on what normative frameworks take precedence and what trade-offs are chosen. Jurisdictions will also differ with each other on what normative frameworks will guide decision-making. Supports for the prioritization of policy goals may come from improved governance processes that enhance engagement with key stakeholders, equity deserving populations and applied ethics frameworks. This decision point would also benefit from policy mapping, stakeholder analysis, impact assessment (e.g., environmental, equity, economic), and public opinion polls to inform political choices.

Once pathogen characteristics, jurisdictional characteristics, and prioritization of policy goals are considered, they can be combined with what is currently analyzed by the reviewed methodologies, using largely technical indicators, as risk assessment and risk management into a more encompassing decision instrument. We argue that this would form a more complete framework for decision-making on travel measures which, as noted earlier, should bring together scientific and technical evidence with normative frameworks. Both inputs will evolve over time. Monitoring and review of outcomes in real time should provide ongoing feedback to be taken account alongside changes in the pathogen (e.g., variants of concern, immune escape), jurisdictional characteristics (e.g., increased vaccination), priority policy objectives (e.g., increased priority to economic recovery, unforeseen social consequences), and even response strategy (e.g., shift from elimination to mitigation).

31.4 Towards an Expanded Approach to Travel-Related Risk Analysis during PHEICs

We identify four lessons for advancing analyses of travel-related risks during major public health events. First, there is need for greater consensus on the approach and methodology applied by IHR States Parties. Patterns of human mobility in a globalized world mean that travel is highly interconnected and how one government manages inbound and outbound travel can have profound implications for other jurisdictions. Lack of consistency in screening, quarantine, vaccination, and other travel measures across jurisdictions has diminished the public health effectiveness of the global pandemic response on a population level. Importantly, this does not mean that consensus will necessarily lead to the same practices when using travel measures. Decisions will invariably be shaped by different capacities and varied normative frameworks that, in turn, lead to particular priorities, choices, and trade-offs. States Parties and other relevant actors can thus move towards an agreed process for applying a risk-based approach rather than an agreed set of decision outcomes.

Second, any agreed methodology must be more transparent in its approach, assumptions, and limitations. While most jurisdictions claimed to undertake evidence-informed decision-making on the use of travel measures during COVID-19, our review found only a limited number of publicly available methodologies. Methodologies used by the private sector have also not been publicly available.[27,28] Datasets used to design and apply these methodologies have been largely unavailable. Improved transparency enables the ongoing evaluation and refinement of decision-making processes. This, in turn, enables fuller understanding of how risk-based approaches can support policymakers, as well as recognizing the limitations of such approaches. Transparency also improves the ability of governments to communicate risk and uncertainty more effectively to the public as rationales for decisions. Given the significant impacts travel measures can have, it is important to prevent or mitigate disproportionate effects and unintended consequences. Transparency also enables equity deserving groups to be identified and consulted if needed.[29]

Third, future use of travel-related risk analysis requires better quality and timely data. Ideally, rather than data availability constraining how risk analysis is approached, an agreed-upon methodology should guide how and what data is collected. Given the unprecedented nature of the COVID-19 pandemic, evidence available to support decision-making on travel measures has been largely limited to modelling studies. These studies rely on the evolving science on SARS-CoV-2, estimates or projections of travel and outbreak dynamics, and assumptions about pathogen evolution. There has been limited real-world and real-time data from observational studies to inform risk analysis (e.g., travel volumes, test positivity rates among travelers, test positivity by immunity status). Available data is largely nationally aggregated which prevents exposure assessment and risk mitigation for subpopulations or subregions.[30] The COVID-19 pandemic has disproportionately impacted vulnerable populations, with the risks and outcomes of both illness and deaths inequitably distributed in ways that are often not captured in epidemiological data.[31] These data are also produced by health systems with diverse capacities and priorities on data collection and dissemination, with differing and often unknown data reliability, accuracy, and comprehensiveness. Finally, the lack of standardized datasets prevents cross-national comparisons using risk analysis.

Finally, a risk-based approach that combines scientific and normative considerations into a decision instrument to inform policy processes on travel measures during major public health events should be integrated into a revised IHR. In May 2022, the World Health Assembly formed a dedicated Member States *Working Group on Revision on the IHR* (WG IHR), to be informed by technical recommendations of an IHR Review Committee.[32] The Committee, which conducted its work between October 2022 and January 2023, is tasked with reviewing hundreds of proposed IHR revisions. The Committee's report will be submitted to the Director-General and discussed at the WHA in May 2023. At the time of writing, the proposed amendments are not publicly available. Given no currently agreed methodology, it is unlikely that proposed revisions will include a new decision instrument to support a risk-based approach to travel measures to strengthen Article 43.[33] One alternative to this formal intergovernmental process, for revising the core text of the IHR, is to build upon the technical guidelines issued by WHO in July 2021.[34] New guidelines would need to acknowledge the dual importance of scientific and normative considerations. Another option is to adopt a decision instrument as an additional appendix to the IHR, similar to the decision instrument to determine WHO notification. A further option, given the importance of more coherent use of travel measures to stakeholders far beyond the health sector, is to include a decision instrument in the legal instrument for pandemic preparedness and response currently under negotiation. This is perhaps the more challenging route, given the diversity of perspectives already at play, but also where political traction might be most forthcoming. There is widespread recognition across state, market, and civil society actors that the absence of an agreed travel-related, risk-based approach during future PHEICs will inflict large-scale public health, economic, and social harms in a globalized world.

Notes

1 Timothy C. Germann et al, "Mitigation strategies for pandemic influenza in the United States" (2006) 103:15 *Proceedings of the National Academy of Sciences* 5935.
2 Lawrence Gostin & Rebecca Katz, "The international health regulations: The governing framework for global health security" (2016) 94:2 *Milbank Quarterly* 264.
3 World Health Organization, "Statement on the second meeting of the International health regulations (2005) emergency Committee regarding the outbreak of novel coronavirus (2019-nCoV)" (30 January 2020), online: www.who.int/news/item/30-01-2020-statement-on-the-second-meeting-of-the-international-health-regulations-(2005)-emergency-committee-regarding-the-outbreak-of-novel-coronavirus-(2019-ncov).
4 Catherine Worsnop et al, "The unintended consequences of information provision: The world health organization and border restrictions during COVID-19" (2022) *International Studies Perspectives* 1.
5 Benjamin Mason Meier, Roojin Habibi & Y. Tony Yang, "Letter: Travel measures violate international law" (27 March 2020) 367: 6485 *Science* 1436.
6 Roojin Habibi et al, "Do not violate the international health regulations during the COVID-19 outbreak" (2020) 395:10225 *Lancet* 664.
7 Nina Haug et al, "Ranking the effectiveness of worldwide COVID-19 government interventions" (2020) 4 *Nature Human Behaviour* 1303.
8 Jacob Burns et al, "International travel-related control measures to contain the COVID-19 pandemic: A rapid review" (2021) 3:3 *Cochrane Database of Systematic Reviews* CD013717.
9 "Travel chaos will last well beyond summer" (14 August 2021), online: *The Economist*. www.economist.com/international/2021/08/14/travel-chaos-will-last-well-beyond-summer.
10 World Health Organization, "Rapid risk assessment of acute public health events" (1 January 2012), online: www.who.int/publications/i/item/rapid-risk-assessment-of-acute-public-health-events.
11 World Health Organization, "Health Emergency and Risk Management Framework" (2019), online (pdf): apps.who.int/iris/bitstream/handle/10665/326106/9789241516181-eng.pdf?sequence=1&isAllowed=y.
12 WorldAware, "Best practices for implementing a travel risk management program" (2019), online (pdf): drj.com/wp-content/uploads/2019/08/Travel-Risk-Management-Best-Practices-WorldAware-043019.pdf.
13 Peter A. Leggat, "Risk assessment in travel medicine" (2006) 4:3–4 *Travel Medicine and Infectious Disease* 127.

14 Stephen Toovey, "Travelling to Africa: Health risks reviewed" (2006) 4:3–4 *Travel Medicine and Infectious Disease* 147.
15 US Centers for Disease Control and Prevention, "Immigrant, refugee and migrant health" (2022), online: www.cdc.gov/immigrantrefugeehealth/index.html.
16 Government of Canada, "Medical inadmissibility" (online): www.canada.ca/en/immigration-refugees-citizenship/services/immigrate-canada/inadmissibility/reasons/medical-inadmissibility.html#public-health.
17 Karin Leder et al, "Risk assessment in travel medicine: How to obtain, interpret, and use risk data for informing pre-travel advice" (2015) 22:1 *Journal of Travel Medicine* 13.
18 See, for example, Annelies Wilder-Smith, Nicholas I. Paton & Kee Tai Goh, "Experience of severe acute respiratory Syndrome in Singapore: Importation of cases, and defense strategies at the Airport" (2003) 10:5 *Journal of Travel Medicine* 259; US Centers for Disease Control and Prevention, "Lessons learned supplement E: Managing international travel-related transmission risk", online: www.cdc.gov/sars/guidance/e-travel/lessons.html; Tianmu Chen et al, "Risk of imported Ebola virus disease in China" (2014) 12:6 *Travel Medicine and Infectious Disease* 650; Shiori Otsuki & Hiroshi Nishiura, "Reduced risk of importing Ebola virus disease because of travel restrictions in 2014: A retrospective epidemiological modeling study" (2016) 11:9 *PLoS One* e0163418.
19 See, for example, Sonia J. Olsen et al, "Transmission of the severe acute respiratory syndrome on aircraft" (2003) 349:25 *New England Journal of Medicine* 2416; Annelies Wilder-Smith, Nicholas I. Paton & Kee Tai Goh, "Low risk of transmission of severe acute respiratory syndrome on airplanes: The Singapore experience" (2003) 8:11 *Tropical Medicine and International Health* 1035; Michael G. Baker et al, "Transmission of pandemic A/H1N1 2009 influenza on passenger aircraft: retrospective cohort" (2010) 340 *BMJ* c2424; Isaac Bogoch et al, "Assessment of the potential for international dissemination of Ebola virus via commercial air travel during the 2014 west African outbreak" (2015) 385:9962 *Lancet* 29.
20 See, for example, Annelies Wilder-Smith, "The severe acute respiratory syndrome: impact on travel and tourism" (2006) 4:2 *Travel Medicine and Infectious Disease* 53; Ronald K. St. John et al, "Border screening for SARS" (2005) 11:1 *Emerging Infectious Diseases* 6.
21 Kelley Lee, Julianne Piper & Jennifer Fang, *Using Risk Analysis to Shape Border Management: A Review of Approaches during the COVID-19 Pandemic* (Washington, DC: Migration Policy Institute, 2023).
22 WHO, "Annex 2 of the international health regulations (2005)" (30 November 2017), online: www.who.int/publications/m/item/annex-2-of-the-international-health-regulations-(2005).
23 International Civil Aviation Organization, "Manual on COVID-19 cross-border risk management" (2021), online (pdf): www.icao.int/covid/cart/Documents/10152_manual_3rd_edition.en.pdf.
24 *Ibid.*
25 International Organization for Migration, *Assessing Population Mobility Dynamics and Patterns for Public Health Emergency Preparedness and Response* (Geneva: The International Organization for Migration, 2017).
26 Shishi Wu et al, "Aggressive containment, suppression, and mitigation of COVID-19: Lessons learnt from eight countries" (2021) 376 *BMJ* e067508.
27 "What the COVID-19 outbreak reveals about airlines' approach to risk", (online): *Kearney*. www.kearney.com/covid-19/article/-/insights/what-the-covid-19-outbreak-reveals-about-airlines-approach-to-risk.
28 Michael Bielecki et al, "Air travel and COVID-19 prevention in the pandemic and peri-pandemic period: A narrative review" (2021) 39 *Travel Medicine and Infectious Disease* 101915.

29 Nirosha Elsem Varghese et al, "Risk communication during COVID-19: A descriptive study on familiarity with, adherence to and trust in the WHO preventive measures" (2021) 16:4 *PLoS One* e0250872.
30 Michele Tizzoni et al, "Addressing the socioeconomic divide in computational modeling for infectious diseases" (2022) 13 *Nature Communications* 2897.
31 Efrat Shadmi et al, "Health equity and COVID-19: global perspectives" (2020) 19:104 *International Journal of Equity and Health*. https://doi.org/10.1186/s12939-020-01218-z.
32 World Health Organization, "Strengthening WHO preparedness for and response to health emergencies" (2022) 75:9 *The World Health Assembly*, online (pdf): apps.who.int/gb/ebwha/pdf_files/WHA75/A75(9)-en.pdf.
33 World Health Organization, "Review committee regarding amendments to the international health regulations (2005)" (2022), online: www.who.int/teams/ihr/ihr-review-committees/review-committee-regarding-amendments-to-the-international-health-regulations-(2005).
34 World Health Organization, "Technical considerations for implementing a risk-based approach to international travel in the context of COVID-19: Interim guidance" (2 July 2021), online (pdf): www.who.int/publications/i/item/WHO-2019-nCoV-Risk-based-international-travel-2021.1.

32

GLOBAL HEALTH LAW

Overcoming the Shortfall in Human Resources

Tim G. Evans and Priyanka Saksena

32.1 Introduction

In May 2019, a Lancet-O'Neill Institute Commission on Global Health and Law released its findings and recommendations.[1] With an explicit view that laws and policies at every level—local, national, and global—are necessary to achieve a world that is healthier and safer, the Commission elaborated an ambitious agenda to realize the potential of law as a major determinant of health. From realizing the right to health to addressing inequities and pressing health challenges of the 21st century, such as tobacco control, road traffic safety, health emergencies, and universal health coverage, the Commission pointed to myriad areas where law is an important instrument for advancing global health with justice. Critical to harnessing the power of law for this broad and rapidly growing agenda, the Commission noted the importance of building legal capacity, defined as the intersection of an effective legal environment, a strong evidence base, and an empowered health law workforce.[2]

With the advent of the SARS-CoV-2 pandemic shortly after the release of the Lancet Commission report, the demands related to health law capacity have continued to grow. Dimensions of this demand include pandemic countermeasures—ranging from behavioral mandates to lockdowns to accelerated production of and access to diagnostics, vaccines, and therapeutics and related liability arrangements, as well as the closing of international borders. The scope and speed with which health-related laws have had to be developed and implemented in countries across the world has been staggering during the SARS-CoV-2 pandemic.[3] There is a plethora of examples of the challenges faced by public health authorities and the limited governmental capacities to analyze, develop, and implement laws, especially in areas where

DOI: 10.4324/9781003394006-42

there was a strong imbalance of capacity in health law—for example, in negotiations with pharmaceutical companies on liability around access to new products.

This growth in demand for health law competencies is accompanied by a wider health workforce crisis that the pandemic and its aftermath have exposed.[4] Longstanding shortfalls in health workforce capacity have limited the ability of health systems to from keep up with increasing needs for timely, accessible and quality care and public health. This has been exacerbated by the SARS-COV-2 pandemic, be it directly related to the health needs associated with infection or its sequelae (i.e., long-COVID) or public health surveillance as well as the indirect effects related to widespread mental stress, forgone care for other health conditions, and the erosion of public trust in the health system and government. In short, the rapid growth in demands and needs for a health workforce is far outpacing the ability of workforce supply to keep up. Exacerbating this supply shortfall is accelerated attrition arising from macro-labour market trends related to the "great resignation"—widespread burnout and the demographic greying of the workforce.[5] Further, there is relative inelasticity among supply-side institutions (i.e., the academy) to accelerate the production of appropriately trained cadres to address these growing needs and demands.

32.2 The Global Workforce for Health Crisis and Its Extension to Global Health Law

This acute crisis facing the workforce for health is by no means new. In the race to achieve the Millennium Development Goals targets by 2015, evidence emerged of a global health workforce crisis. The Report of the Joint Learning Initiative on Human Resources for Health pointed to a global workforce crisis as a primary impediment to the achievement of the MDGs by 2015, characterized by a massive shortage of around 4 million health workers globally.[6] Currently, the global health workforce shortage is estimated to be in the order of between 15–17 million health workers required to meet the SDG 3 in health.[7] The scope of this chronic workforce shortfall extends well beyond clinically trained workers who provide patient care to public health and other workers whose efforts also constitute vital contributions to improving health.

This includes the workforce with competencies related to global health law, where demands and needs have been far outrunning supply for many years. The MDG workforce crisis raised contentious issues related to the trans-border flows of health workers, especially from low- to high-income countries. Additionally, in a connected world, the chances of global pandemics grow, even as critical health workers are taken away from under-resourced settings to high-income countries. In 2004, South Africa proposed a resolution for the World Health Assembly (WHA), calling for compensation from high-income countries that were actively recruiting health workers they had trained. Deliberations in the WHA led to the adoption of a resolution on ethical recruitment of health workers.[8] Current strategies in Canada and other high-income countries to address their health workforce shortages rely heavily on recruitment from low-income countries, which have further intensified since the SARS-CoV-2 pandemic, raising the continued importance of competencies related to design, implementation, and evaluation of ethical recruitment policies.[9]

Similarly, issues of equitable access to lifesaving medicines—which figured prominently in the Doha round of the Trade Related and Intellectuals Property Rights (TRIPs) agreement—were a central focus of a WHO Commission on Intellectual Property Rights, Innovation and Public Health, and remain active in current debates about a TRIPS wavier related to COVID-19–related products.[10] The Framework Convention on Tobacco Control (FCTC) required a massive law capacity in agreeing on its components, ratifying, and subsequently monitoring its implementation.[11] To come to grips with the 2003 outbreak of SARS, there was a revision of the International Health Regulations in 2005. Less than 20 years later, following SARS-CoV-2, a further revision is now underway, alongside a new Pandemic Treaty.[12] Through all of these internationally negotiated efforts, the voices of lower- and middle-income countries (LMIC) have been constrained by the imbalance in negotiation capacity between poorer and richer countries. This reflects a dearth of expertise in global health law and effective negotiating representation amongst LMICs, as well as the much larger numbers of experts that represent the interests of HICs.[13] This disparity in legal expertise likely contributes to the very limited use of compulsory licensing provisions, and lack of use of export oriented compulsory licensing, by developing countries.[14]

It is safe to say, therefore, that the needs and demands for health law competencies are large, diverse, and growing. It is also safe to say that the requisite supply-side response, in terms of increasing the numbers of persons with health law competencies, is lagging far behind and, without greater attention to its distribution, may well perpetuate and accentuate inequities.

The implementation of the International Health Regulations (IHRs) is a good illustration of the challenges with respect to the lack of recognition of the importance of a health law workforce. To help monitor the IHRs' implementation following their second revision in 2005, a Joint External Evaluation (JEE) methodology was established with specific targets in 13 core capacity areas.[15] For the core capacity on human resources, the target is that State Parties should have "skilled and competent health personnel for sustainable and functional public health surveillance and response at all levels of the health system and the effective implementation of the IHR".[16] Of note, this target on human resources is embedded in the "detect" function of the JEE framework and not in either of the other two functions, "prevent" and "respond".[17] Moreover, for other JEE targets such as that for national legislation, policy, and financing, capacities for health law are not explicitly mentioned. The absence of explicit articulation of specific health law competencies required to implement the IHRs is likely significant, given the breadth and complexity of issues. For example, managing risk related to antimicrobial resistance or infectious diseases spillover raises enormous challenges for laws related to healthcare prescription behavior, agro-industrial use of antibiotics, and regulation of wet markets. Similarly, a government's ability to negotiate agreements with pharmaceutical companies, such as advance purchase agreements, rests to a large extent on bench strength of its lawyers with appropriate training.

The implications of this limited characterization of the health workforce needs and its relative blindness to health law can be demonstrated in Canada's reporting on the human resources target as part of its JEE.[18] Canada's 2018 JEE report identifies "significant progress" in developing its public health workforce, as expected under the International Health Regulations. It goes on to describe the diversified workforce that includes epidemiologists, public health advisors, physicians, nurses, surveillance analysts, veterinarians, laboratory specialist, environmental health officers, information system and technology specialists, and public health communications specialists. Across this diverse workforce, there is no mention of cadres with health law competencies, be they lawyers, law enforcement officers, legislators, or human rights specialists. Paradoxically, this JEE assessment that is relatively blind to health law contrasts with broader plan for the development of the public health workforce in Canada in 2005, in which public health lawyers are identified as one of the critical regulated professions to mobilize.[19]

32.3 The State of the Global Health Law Workforce: Who Constitutes the Health Law Workforce, and How Are They Trained?

In 1842, in his report on the Sanitary Conditions of the Labouring Population in Great Britain, Sir Edwin Chadwick recommended the development of a new public health cadre, the District Medical Officer:

> for the general means necessary to prevent disease, it would be good economy to appoint a district medical officer, independent of private practice, with the securities of special qualifications, and responsibilities to initiate sanitary measures and reclaim the execution of the law.[20]

Despite this promising reference to the execution of the law in Chadwick's report, there has been little formal development of global health law workforce over the last 180 years.

This contrasts with the major advances in development of the health workforce in the areas of medicine, nursing, and public health through the early 20th century—as demonstrated in the landmark reports of Flexner, Goldmark, and Welch-Rose respectively.[21] On the centenary of the Flexner Report, the Lancet Commission on Health Professionals for a New Century provided a refreshed vision for health professional education through instructional and institutional reforms fostering greater health equity.[22] In all of these efforts, however, health law either as a profession or health law competencies have been conspicuously absent!

While the area of global health law may not require dedicated schools, its backwater or orphaned status in the context of health professional education has led to the absence of a clear route to professionalization—and, therefore, constitutes one of the primary constraints to the realization of a competent and appropriately scaled workforce. This relative neglect may reflect its interdisciplinary nature, drawing on the evolving span of law from medical to health to public health to global health and to global health security, as well as the overlapping disciplines of (bio-)ethics, rights, equity, and policy.

An appropriate health law workforce is also impeded by an opaque career structure. Full-time jobs in health law practice are few, often specialized (e.g., medical malpractice), but likely growing given the size and complexity of the health sector. Moreover, persons with training in law are being called upon to engage in health sector issues but often lack sufficient competencies to understand health and public health issues in order to appropriately design, implement, and evaluate health laws. In practice, health law competencies are often critical adjuncts that enhance the work of health professionals to engage in policy, legislation, employment conditions, partnerships, and conventions or other agreements that address health issues.

32.4 Pathways to Acquiring Global Health Law Competencies

For the purposes of understanding the acquisition of competencies, there appear to be two primary pathways. The first is through law schools, with lawyers pursing a master's (LLM) or diploma-level training in "health law". A different pathway is available through dedicated courses or concentrations on law within masters in public health, global health, or public policy programs.

By searching combinations of the terms "health", "medical", and "law" with "diploma", "degree", and "certificate" in English, French, and Spanish on the Google search engine, we have conducted a very cursory review of specialized programs in "health law" globally by WHO region (see Table 32.1). Of the 106 masters in health law programs identified globally, 93 are found in the European and Pan-American regions, revealing a massive skew towards high-income countries. While data for diploma in health law

TABLE 32.1 Specialized trainings in health law

WHO region	*Master's in health law*	*Diploma in health law*
AFRO	7 (RSA 4)	0
EMRO	0	0
EURO	55 (UK 14, France 16)	Note 1
PAHO	38 (US 27, CA 6)	18
SEARO	1	3
WPRO	5 (3 ANZ)	3

Note 1: Some universities in the Europe offer certificates and/or diplomas in addition to master's degrees in health law. However, this type of training in general does not seem to exist in most European countries.

programs are even more sparse, a similar concentration in high-income countries is seen. This paucity of health law programs in LMICs reflects a broader pattern of global inequality with respect to distribution of health professional workforce training institutions—a structural imbalance that condemns these countries to a trickle of the workforce they require. Additionally, it is notable that there are no readily available international accreditation standards that individual training programs can compare themselves against or adhere to.

A second pathway focuses on the acquisition of health law competencies amongst health professionals. This pathway takes the form of courses most often offered within the context of health professional training, such as public health. Following on the Welch-Rose report and the adoption of an accreditation standard for schools of public health based on five core disciplines (epidemiology, biostatistics, socio-behavioral sciences, environmental science, and health services administration), there was little or no room in the formal curricula for health law competencies. On the 100th anniversary of the Welch-Rose report, the US-based Association of Schools and Programs of Public Health (ASPPH) identified "legal, ethical, economic and regulatory dimensions of health care and public health"[23] as critical content for the MPH in the 21st century.

More recently, the Association of Schools of Public Health in the European Region (ASPHER) have adopted a new competencies framework in which health law is explicitly identified.[24] This recent recognition of health law competencies within public health training programs appears to be in the early stages of adoption. For this paper, we explored the supply of this sort of training through a review of eight well-established master of public health programs in different countries and found courses on law were offered in three programs, two of which were mandatory.

The third pathway for acquisition of competencies arises through practice and experience. Perhaps the most important example of this is the CDC's Public Health Law Academy and its efforts to establish competencies and career pathways in "legal epidemiology".[25] This is further elaborated in Box 1. This is an interesting complement to other health law training opportunities since it targets health professionals who are already working in public health, thus adopting a continuing education approach.

BOX 1 LEGAL EPIDEMIOLOGY AND CDC'S LEGAL COMPETENCY MODEL

According to the CDC's definition, legal epidemiology is the scientific study and deployment of law as a factor in the cause, distribution, and prevention of disease and injury in a population. The emergence of legal epidemiology intends to understand the need for, and appropriate application of, legal approaches to address public health challenges.

To encourage this, the CDC has developed a legal epidemiology competency model, which provides guidelines on minimum competencies for public health practitioners. These competencies including research, assessment and evaluation, design of strategies, as well as knowledge transfer. Competencies are grouped into three areas, including general legal epidemiology, legal mapping, and legal evaluation, along with three tiers corresponding to different professional levels, ranging from early career to senior manager and principal investigator levels.

General Legal Epidemiology

- Articulate the importance of legal epidemiology concepts to inform health, fiscal, administrative, legal, social, and political research and discourse
- Apply legal epidemiology principles to research studies, funding opportunities, and policy agendas
- Communicate legal epidemiology findings, methodologies, and recommendations to lay and professional audiences
- Analyze the use of legal epidemiology findings to inform health, fiscal, administrative, legal, social, and political activities

Legal Mapping

- Identify opportunities for legal mapping to inform the process, nature, and impact of policies and laws on public health
- Develop policy surveillance or legal assessment studies to address specific research questions
- Analyze laws, policies, and political and programmatic priorities using evidence-based or empirical guidelines (including health-related principles

or trends, stakeholder or special interests, and other key developments or concerns)
- Validate and synthesize results that compare and contrast meaningful variations in law and policy related to health

Legal Evaluation

- Identify opportunities for a legal evaluation study to address existing legal, health, or other issues
- Design a legal evaluation to study potential associations between law and health
- Collect and analyze qualitative and quantitative study data using generally accepted research methodologies
- Interpret results, draw conclusions, and formulate key findings towards the improvement of public health

This list of comprehensive and systematic competencies provides a useful framework for developing curricula and pedagogical materials to train public health practitioners. Indeed, an online course has been developed as partnership between the CDC, the Public Health Law Academy, and Temple University's Beasley School of Law. There is significant scope for developing trainings in other languages and for other country and global contexts, using the work of the CDC as a base.

32.5 From Bare Threads to a Robust Supply Side Fabric for Mobilizing the Health Law Workforce

As noted earlier, there are some foundations and recent reforms to build upon that can help improve the supply of workers with global health law competencies. From a broader systems perspective, however, without a major push, the supply of workers with health law competencies is unlikely to be sufficient to address the burgeoning needs and demands of today and tomorrow. This prospect should be a clarion for thinking more ambitiously about how to mobilize the supply side to narrow, or even fully close, this gap.

Fortunately, there are convergent forces around which a major mobilization of the supply side for global health law can be configured. From a global advocacy perspective, a road map for the development of adequate global health law competencies needs to be created, building on the recommendations of the Lancet Commissions on Global Health Law and Health Professionals for a New Century. Critical inputs to this road map could be requested from, or piggybacked on, a range of health-related legal instruments, including—but not limited to—the international treaty to strengthen pandemic prevention, preparedness, and response and the revision of the International Health Regulations. The road map could be given profile and prominence as a key plank of the broader agenda to address global health workforce challenges in pursuit of goal 3 of the Sustainable Development Goals, which focuses on health.[26]

The road map for the development of competencies can be implemented through national policies to revitalize the workforce for health and public health. In 2005, for example, Canada explicitly advocated for significantly increasing the number of public health lawyers, in an effort to revitalize the public health workforce. Moreover, the experience of enhancing legal frameworks and competencies nationally may build on the experience of other social issues where law has been instrumental. For example, documentation of the history and impact of the Indian residential school system on Indigenous peoples led Canada's Truth and Reconciliation Commission to recommend a set of new programs, regulations, and laws related to various aspects of health and social services for Indigenous populations. This creates a significant opportunity to further training in area of health law to ensure there are sufficient numbers of practitioners to develop and implement new policies and radically move away from the discriminatory and abusive practices of the past.

In addition to taking advantage of these global and national contextual opportunities, it is important to target specific health law constituencies. As noted in Table 1 earlier, there are more than 100 masters in health law programs globally. This important nidus of experience and expertise could be encouraged to make recommendations on improving the scope, the standards, and the coverage of masters in health law training. For example, in view of the paucity and inequitable distribution of existing programs, there might be a consensus to establish at least one accredited masters in health law in every country by 2030. In advancing this agenda, it would be important to draw on existing legal networks such as the European Association of Health Law, committees covering health in the International Bar Association or the International Law Association, as well as associations focused on legal education.

In addition to health lawyers, it is important to build on efforts to provide training on the principles and practice of health law for health professionals. The adoption of health law or legal competencies as part of expected standards for public health training needs to be implemented widely by different stakeholders including governments and academic institutions and extended to other health professional training reform, such as physicians, nurses, and pharmacists. Integrating health law education through courses or modules may find greater success as part of broader reforms in interprofessional education and revitalization of academic health centres.[27] Beyond curricular reforms, establishing a greater research and scholarship presence of health law in academies is also likely to yield further opportunities for improved student education.

Creating opportunities for health law training through continuing education initiatives are also important. The CDC's legal epidemiology competency model provides a good starting point in this area, which can be built upon by academies in different countries and adapted according to their legal, social, and health contexts. For civil servants working in the health sector—be it in Ministries of Health or the range of public health agencies—it is worthwhile to explore whether governments can partner with academies to enable health law oriented continuing education, at least for selected employees.

Overall, these types of initiatives can facilitate exchange and collaboration between various stakeholders and build capacity in the critical area of health law. In establishing these initiatives, governments and other stakeholders, such as law schools and law associations, should be encouraged to define explicit targets for health law training, alongside plans for financing. Concerted and explicit efforts to increase health law training are critical for ensuring sufficient momentum in this instrumental area.

Finally, it is important to ensure that efforts to improve health law capacity through further and improved training are also adequately monitored. The numbers of people getting preservice and continuing education on health law should be monitored alongside the broader monitoring of the health workforce. This is imperative to confront the numerous challenges in today's health landscape, including global health security and international treaties related to NCDs. It also important to recognize that implementation of global health laws not only depends on a more robust global health law workforce but also on a broad range of professionals—some of whom are mainstream health workers, while others, such as border officials, are not. As such, the state of the workforce in general is critical to effective implementation and emphasizes the importance of vital health workforce policies both nationally and globally.

Notes

1 Lawrence O. Gostin et al, "The legal determinants of health: Harnessing the power of law for global health and sustainable development" (2019) 393:10183 *Lancet* 1857.

2 *Ibid* at 1893–99.

3 OECD, "No policy maker is an island: The international regulatory co-operation response to the COVID-19 crisis" (2020), online (pdf): *OECD Library*. https://read.oecd-ilibrary.org/view/?ref=134_134311-cbjgrk3pwj&title=No-policy-maker-is-an-island-the-international-regulatory-co-operation-response-to-the-COVID-19-crisis.

4 Yuan-Sheng Ryan Poon et al, "A global overview of healthcare workers' turnover intention amid COVID-19 pandemic: a systematic review with future directions" (2022) 20:1 *Human Resources for Health* 70.

5 Ian Cook, "Who is driving the great resignation?" (15 September 2021), online: *Harvard Business Review*. https://hbr.org/2021/09/who-is-driving-the-great-resignation.
6 Lincoln Chen et al, "Human resources for health: overcoming the crisis" (2004) 364:9449 *Lancet* 1984.
7 Richard M. Scheffler et al, "Forecasting imbalances in the global health labor market and devising policy responses" (2018) 16:1 *Human Resources for Health* 5; Jenny X Liu et al, "Global health workforce labor market projections for 2030" (2017) 15:1 *Human Resources for Health* 11.
8 World Health Assembly, Fifty-Seventh World Health Assembly, International migration of health personnel: a challenge for health systems in developing countries, A57/11 (2004).
9 Stephanie Nolen, "Rich countries lure health workers from low-income nations to fight shortages" (24 January 2022), online: *New York Times*. www.nytimes.com/2022/01/24/health/covid-health-worker-immigration.html>.
10 "TRIPS Council welcomes MC12 TRIPS waiver decision, discusses possible extension" (6 July 2022), online: www.wto.org/english/news_e/news22_e/trip_08jul22_e.htm.
11 World Health Organization, "Framework convention on tobacco control" (25 May 2003), online: https://fctc.who.int/publications/i/item/9241591013.
12 World Health Organization, News Release, "World Health Assembly agrees to launch process to develop historic global accord on pandemic prevention, preparedness and response" (1 December 2021), online: www.who.int/news/item/01-12-2021-world-health-assembly-agrees-to-launch-process-to-develop-historic-global-accord-on-pandemic-prevention-preparedness-and-response.
13 Nicholas Chan, "Beyond delegation size: Developing country negotiating capacity and NGO 'support' in international climate negotiations" (2021) 21:2 *International Environmental Agreements: Politics, Law and Economics* 201; "Strengthening developing countries' capacity for trade negotiations: Matching technical assistance to negotiating capacity constraints", (2004), online (pdf): www.g77.org/doha/Doha-BP04%20-Strengthening_Southern_trade-related_negotiating_capacity.pdf.
14 Susan Vastano Vaughan, "Compulsory licensing of pharmaceuticals under TRIPS: What standard of compensation" (2001) 25:1 *Hastings International and Comparative Law Review* 87.
15 World Health Organization, "Joint external evaluation tool: International Health Regulations (2005)—third edition (23 June 2022), online (pdf): *WHO*. www.who.int/publications/i/item/9789240051980.
16 *Ibid* at 67.
17 *Ibid* at iii.
18 Public Health Agency of Canada, "International health regulations—Joint external evaluation of Canada self-assessment report" (17 June 2021), online: www.canada.ca/en/public-health/services/emergency-preparedness-response/international-health-regulations-joint-external-evaluation-canada-self-assessment-report.html (last modified 12 August 2022).
19 Joint Task Group on Public Health Human Resources, "Building the public health workforce for the 21st century: A pan-Canadian framework for public health human resources planning" (October 2005), online (pdf): https://publications.gc.ca/collections/collection_2008/phac-aspc/HP5-12-2005E.pdf.
20 Edwin Chadwick, *Report on the Sanitary Condition of the Labouring Population of Great Britain (1842)* (emphasis added).
21 Abraham Flexner, *Medical Education in the United States and Canada* (California: Carnegie Foundation, 1910); Josephine Goldmark, "Nursing and nursing

education in the United States. Report of the Committee for the Study of Nursing Education, and report of a survey" (1923) 80:21 *Journal of the American Medical Association* 1538; William Henry Welch & Wickliffe Rose, *Institute of Hygiene: Being a Report Submitted by Dr. William H Welch and Wickliffe Rose to the General Education Board* (New York: Rockefeller Foundation, 1915).

22 Julio Frenk et al, "Health professionals for a new century: Transforming education to strengthen health systems in an interdependent world" (2010) 376:9756 *Lancet* 1923.

23 *A Master of Public Health Degree for the 21st Century*, by Association of Schools and Programs of Public Health (2014).

24 World Health Organization, "WHO-ASPHER competency framework for the public health workforce in the European region" (2022), online (pdf): www.euro.who.int/__data/assets/pdf_file/0003/444576/WHO-ASPHER-Public-Health-Workforce-Europe-eng.pdf.

25 CDC, "Legal epidemiology" (12 May 2021), online: *Centers for Disease Control and Prevention*. www.cdc.gov/dhdsp/policy_resources/legal_epi.htm; ChangeLab Solutions, "Public health law academy", online: www.changelabsolutions.org/good-governance/phla.

26 World Health Organization, "Fifth global forum on human resources for health", online: www.who.int/news-room/events/detail/2023/04/03/default-calendar/fifth-global-forum-on-human-resources-for-health.

27 Victor J. Dzau, Melissa H. Laitner & Celynne A. Balatbat, "Has traditional medicine had its day? The need to redefine academic medicine" (2022) 400:10361 *Lancet* 1481.

33

CONCEPTUAL AND TANGIBLE BORDERS UNDER A REVISED INTERNATIONAL HEALTH REGULATIONS OR NEW INTERNATIONAL PANDEMIC AGREEMENT

Sam Halabi

33.1 Introduction

The COVID-19 pandemic resulted from fundamental defects in the world's only international public health emergency agreement: the International Health Regulations (IHR) (2005). The IHR (2005) failed to ensure countries prepared for an infectious disease outbreak or promptly alerted the World Health Organization (WHO) of the initial outbreak of COVID-19. It failed to drive global collaboration and cooperation in the face of an emergency or stop high-income countries (HICs) from hoarding vaccines and other medical treatments. In late 2021, roughly a year after the first approved vaccines were manufactured, only 3.07% of people in low- or middle-income countries (LICs/MICs) had been vaccinated, compared to 60.18% of people in HICs.[1]

The IHR (2005), the latest iteration of regulations last agreed in 1969, resulted from the world's experience with SARS-CoV-1, where internal and global failures of cooperation and preparation greatly exacerbated the outbreak. In late 2002, informal reports arose about an epidemic of atypical pneumonia in China's Guangdong Province.[2] In January 2003, a regional health office in China reported that there were over 100 cases of a novel pneumonia emerging. Bureaucratic obstacles and stringent rules around public information sharing meant that there was a news blackout among the general public, and even many health professionals, until well into February.[3] During this time, the Chinese Ministry of Health took few steps to limit spread, convinced that the outbreak was contained.[4] This information blackout created widespread panic among the public and meant that health professionals were unaware of the necessary procedures to treat and contain the virus. The Chinese Ministry of Health was also slow to alert the WHO

DOI: 10.4324/9781003394006-43

and share diagnostic information with neighbouring countries, leading to delays in the identification of the virus in Mongolia and Hong Kong. The pathogen then spread across the globe. Other nations were unprepared to respond to and contain an infectious disease. For example, in Toronto, the most impacted city outside of Asia, no hospital prioritized infectious disease, and there was no regional framework to for outbreak management to coordinate responses across institutions or health service sectors.[5] Within four months, there were around 8,500 cases and 800 deaths globally.[6]

The absence of international legal authority—at the World Health Organization or elsewhere—to investigate and respond was one of the key factors which facilitated the International Health Regulations (2005). That agreement required that countries adequately prepare to detect events with epidemic or pandemic potential[7] rapidly communicate information to the World Health Organization and then follow the measures it recommended in response.[8]

The COVID-19 pandemic has shown that even these changes were not enough, as many of the same problems observed during SARS reoccurred.[9] Two-thirds of countries never fulfilled their commitments under the IHR (2005) to adequately prepare, most because they could not afford to do so. Even when events were detected early, countries were incentivized to hide rather than disclose information because other countries imposed punitive and counterproductive measures like travel bans, import embargoes, and visa restrictions, almost always in contravention of those measures the World Health Organization recommended.[10] A desire to avoid these consequences contributed to state-level denial of COVID-19 in nations as diverse as Belarus,[11] China,[12] Tanzania,[13] and Turkmenistan,[14] even when evidence strongly indicated that caseloads far exceeded official statements. This rendered the surveillance and early response mechanisms outlined in the IHR (2005) far less effective. The IHR (2005) never required any commitment by wealthy countries to ensure that lifesaving medicines, vaccines, and medical equipment flowed efficiently, equitably, and rationally to the people and places that needed them most. Indeed, rich-world hoarding of medicines and vaccines has been predictable and persistent.[15] Not only wilful neglect of resource inequality but also few or no mechanisms for accountability, dispute resolution, or incorporation of rapidly advancing technologies and transfer of those technologies doomed the IHR (2005) in its current iteration. If early surveillance and notification had occurred, WHO recommendations had been complied with, and vaccines and other medical products equitably shared between nations, the impacts of the COVID-19 pandemic could have been significantly reduced.

In November 2020, Charles Michel, President of the European Council, began circulating the idea of an "international pandemic treaty" at the Paris Peace Forum to address these deficiencies.[16] In December 2020, Michel met with Tedros Adhanom Ghebreyesus, the Director-General of the World Health Organization, to discuss the treaty idea.[17] In January 2021, Tedros endorsed the EU's international pandemic treaty proposal as a way to guarantee countries' political commitment to fighting future disease outbreaks. He expressed WHO's support of such a treaty, saying, "[i]t will give the IHR [International Health Regulations] the political dimension" it needs.[18] On May 21, 2021, the World Health Assembly, the governing body of the World Health Organization, agreed to call a Special Session to take place November 29, 2021, through December 1, 2021, to decide how governments could better prevent, prepare for, coordinate during, and respond to the next pandemic. This was only the second such "special" meeting in its 75-year history.

The result of the Special Session was the decision to establish an Intergovernmental Negotiating Body (INB) with the goal of adopting a framework convention on pandemic preparedness and response, targeted revisions of the International Health Regulations (2005), and/or other international agreement.

This chapter evaluates the outcome of the Special Session and the ensuing negotiations conducted by the INB. It remains too early to say whether a new agreement will be formed, but if it is, it will be binding in nature like the IHR (2005), with advisory components that may draw in currently reluctant major powers. A binding treaty becomes part of international law, meaning that states are obligated to follow it, with the possibility of sanctions for non-compliance if specified in the treaty. States are not obligated to adhere to advisory components. Separately, the IHR (2005) will almost certainly be revised, with intense negotiations likely over the amount of sovereignty governments must cede when potential emergencies arise.

These revisions will almost certainly include efforts to increase accountability and clarity around the WHO's decision-making. From its first pandemic declaration in 2009 to the present, there has been little transparency into how WHO decisions were made nor why. This lack of accountability and explanation has led to confusion and ambiguity around key terms and measures used to respond to public health emergencies. For example, the WHO has failed to clarify the legal basis, effect, or even definition of a "pandemic"—unsanctioned in the IHR (2005)—despite the term's widespread use by multilateral development banks, governments, and the organization itself. It also decreases trust in WHO decision-making. Nearly every decision to declare or not declare a Public Health Emergency of International Concern (PHEIC), a formal designation by the WHO of an extraordinary health risk that triggers provisions of the IHR (2005), has been challenged by governments or global health experts in some material respect, as a lack of transparency has led to speculations about the WHO's motives. For example, the WHO's failure to declare a PHEIC during the 2018–2019 Ebola outbreak in

Uganda was criticized by influential publications as a political, rather than technical, decision.[19] Similarly, while the IHR (2005) requires the WHO to review its own actions, the dispute resolution mechanism between nations is strictly voluntary. This again has led to criticisms that the resolutions the WHO mediates are driven by political influence, rather than legal norms.[20]

The IHR (2005) failed to effectively respond to COVID-19 because true global preparedness requires a commitment to distribute resources to the people and places that need them most, including surveillance technologies and personnel, rapid communication and response capabilities, and research and manufacturing technologies and know-how. It requires reliable and efficient availability of funding should rapid response to an infectious disease emergency be necessary. After the Ebola PHEIC in West Africa in 2014, the World Bank established a Pandemic Emergency Financing Facility, in light of precisely such resource needs. Little was known about the algorithm that would be used to trigger availability or allocation of the funds or how much investors and insurance companies had made available through the arcane instruments used to finance it.[21] As it turns out, the money available has been extraordinarily limited and was fully committed by September 2020.[22] While an emerging financial intermediary fund (FIF) will replace it, critical questions remain unanswered.

Four key measures would have made COVID-19 response more effective. The first was effective surveillance in the first place, for both interfaces between animals and humans and with respect to the regulation of biosafety practices at research facilities. The second was increased transparency between parties at the very beginning of the outbreak, from provincial level officials in China up to the communications between Beijing and WHO. Thirdly, a well-informed and transparent process through which the WHO Emergency Committee could have deliberated with good evidence as to necessary travel and trade measures would have facilitated more accountable and clear decision-making. Finally, a commitment from the global community to financially and medically support those countries who suffered most, including through the sharing of intellectual property and technology as well as finished medicines and vaccines, to combat the spread of the pandemic would have benefitted of the rest of the world.

Ideally, these measures would be incorporated into the new framework agreement proposed by the INB. However, the World Health Assembly, the supreme decision-making body of the World Health Organization, has adopted only one framework convention in its history—a Framework Convention on Tobacco Control with evidence-based norms for tobacco prevention and control. Treaties like framework conventions are arduous and time-consuming to negotiate; they require governments to give up some of their ability to decide for themselves what they will do, with whom they will work, and how much money they will spend. The political difficulties of treaty negotiation are even more acute when the subject matter is politically sensitive or relevant to national security—like registering biological research laboratories; sharing vaccines, medicines, and especially the technology to produce them; and committing domestic resources to support patients and people who are not citizens of the supporting government. These obstacles are especially acute in the context of future emergencies and crises, when a government cannot fully predict circumstances.

33.2 Pandemic Treaty, Revised IHR (2005), Both or Neither?

Over the course of summer 2022, the WHA-appointed working group (WGPR) identified important benefits that would accrue through the adoption of a new instrument which could not otherwise be addressed through the IHR (2005) or a revision thereof. These included attracting high-level political commitment to the common goal of preparedness; strengthening the role of WHO as the leading authority on global health; sharing of data, samples, technology, and benefits; ensuring more equitable access to medical countermeasures, including diagnostics, therapeutics, and vaccines; and adopting a One Health approach,[23] which attempts to integrate, balance, and optimize the health of people, animals, and ecosystems.[24]

Over the course of the autumn, the INB convened so-called informal, focused consultations around the themes of equity, intellectual property, law and governance, and One Health as an effort to shape the content of a new agreement. The WGPR recommended developing a new instrument under the auspices of WHO in tandem with strengthening the IHR. The WGPR submitted its second report discussing all recommendations to WHO's Executive Board at its 150th session in January 2022. These recommendations included strengthening the IHR (2005); implementing the One Health approach; strengthening WHO governance and oversight; and adopting measures to enhance equity.[25] A draft agreement is due to the World Health Assembly in May 2024. So far, there is little agreement on text and coverage.

Separately, a review committee of the performance of the IHR (2005) over the course of the COVID-19 has been convened and governments including the US, Russia, and 47 African governments have submitted proposed revisions to the IHR (2005). Other governments, or collections of governments, are expected to follow.

The United States' proposed revisions for the IHR (2005) focused on enhancing the surveillance and response mechanisms centred on the World Health Organization and removing some of the discretionary authority currently granted to governments. For example, the US advocates that the WHO periodically review states' disease surveillance capacity and facilitate technical support and financial resources to develop and enhance the abilities of outreach governments that lack capacity or are assessed as having a high risk of failing to detect a threat. The US further argues that States Parties must either accept or reject an offer of assistance from WHO when a potential public health threat of international concern arises and, if rejecting, must provide a rationale for such rejection. It also details legal mechanisms for the assumption of rejection based on State Party inaction. Relatedly, the US calls for the removal of WHO's current obligation to consult with a State Party before notifying others when it receives "other reports" of any significant public health event potentially covered by the IHR (2005). The US proposal also calls for more coordination with international organizations including the Food and Agriculture Organization (FAO), the World Organisation for Animal Health (OIE), and the UN Environment Program (UNEP), among others.

The US also calls for an intermediate level of emergency, where an event has not yet been determined to meet the criteria for a PHEIC but requires heightened international awareness and potentially an international response, akin to so-called "traffic light" approaches to readiness and alerts. Under this proposed system, the Director-General would be specifically empowered to declare this intermediate form of alert. Relatedly, a regional director in one of the six WHO regions may declare a regional public health event of regional concern.

The US proposals also call for the Director-General to be able to deploy expert teams as part of temporary measures, a response to perceived hesitation to allow international investigations, as well as closer coordination with other international organizations and exemptions for healthcare workers from travel and trade restrictions.

The US asks that the Emergency Committee created under the IHR (2005) be diversified and include regional directors and calls for the establishment of a Compliance Committee with broad powers to seek expert advice, request action from the Director-General, and coordinate with other international organizations. The US also recommends shortening the time that amendments to the IHR (2005) take effect from two years to six months.[26]

The Russian Federation, submitting on behalf of the Eurasian Economic Union (EAEU), calls for ensuring that National Focal Points (NFPs)—the IHR-mandated national office that is accessible at all times for IHR-related communications with WHO and acts as the communication backbone of the IHR (2005)—are able to perform their functions. Over the course of nearly two decades, many NFPs have shown themselves to be under-resourced and lacking legal authority to gather relevant information. As with the US proposal, the EAEU proposal calls for the Director-General to have the ability to declare an intermediate alert, in addition to a PHEIC.

The EAEU proposal puts data sharing at the centre of its proposals, including genetic sequence data in the list of relevant information to be shared (like the US) but also focusing on building detection capacity, using digital platforms to share, and cooperating with other States Parties. The EAEU proposal also gives more authority to the WHO to recommend that States demand evidence of vaccination.

Meanwhile, the Africa Region has focused on equity in both IHR (2005) revisions and in the new pandemic agreement context. It has submitted a broader set of desired outcomes including the following:

1 Equity in obligations on prevention, detection, and control of pandemic threats (e.g., a requirement for States to adhere to a WHO-run allocation mechanism for health products required to control the pandemic);
2 Provision of financial assistance and technology transfer to developing countries;
3 Subjecting all WHO actions in a pandemic to the provisions of the IHR and any complementary future international instruments;
4 Obligation on the part of all states to provide support to WHO to coordinate the response;
5 Obligations on the part of all states to facilitate production, availability and access to medical countermeasures; and
6 Ensuring equal footing of pathogen and genomic sequence sharing and benefit sharing; WHO Executive Board Decision EB150(3) has urged Member States to consider potential targeted IHR amendments including for improving equity.[27]

Operative Paragraph 2 of EB150(3) specifically requires Member States to consider amendments to IHR:

> address specific and clearly identified issues, challenges, including equity, technological or other developments, or gaps that could not effectively be addressed otherwise but are critical to supporting effective implementation and compliance of the International Health Regulations (2005), and their universal application for the protection of all people of the world from the international spread of disease in an equitable manner.[28]

It is not clear whether either the new framework, the IHR amendments, or both will achieve meaningful outcomes. The European Union and some 70 countries now support the legally binding treaty approach.[29] Russia, Brazil, and China—three critical players—have either rejected the idea of a new agreement or issued public statements suggesting support is unlikely.[30] Russia and Brazil also expressed broader concerns shared by other governments, arguing that a binding treaty would curtail their national sovereignty and impede private sector innovation. Many states are concerned about duplication and inconsistency between the revised IHR (2005) and a new agreement.

The United States has generally focused its efforts on revising the IHR (2005) and, while not explicitly rejecting the idea of a new agreement, has largely evaded evincing specific support. The World Health Assembly's Framework Convention on Tobacco Control, its only treaty formed under Article 19 of its Constitution, adopted a governance structure whereby a Conference of the Parties served as the decision-making body and could both issue guidelines and subsequent treaties or protocols. One option that appears to be increasingly possible is to allow a framework convention, which Brazil, China, the US, and others would probably not join, and then allow governments to join subsequent agreements so that each state might pick and choose. Guidelines regularly issued by a treaty governing body (often called a Conference of the Parties) might similarly direct national policies. This is how the FCTC operates.

33.2.1 The Road to May 2024

In diplomatic and international law terms, the world is moving at lightning speed. The World Health Assembly directed the INB to update its progress to the Assembly in May 2023 and submit a draft instrument to the Assembly in May 2024.[31] By contrast, it took almost ten years from authorization of negotiations to entry into force of the Framework Convention on Tobacco Control (FCTC), although guidelines and a subsequent protocol of course took additional time.[32]

In August 2022, the INB agreed that the agreement would include binding elements under WHO's Article 19 treaty making authority, which allows the World Health Assembly to adopt binding agreements and treaties on any matter within the WHO's competence. However, it left flexibility for some parts, and perhaps even most parts, to be concluded under WHO's Article 21 regulation-issuing authority (the current form of the IHR [2005]), which allows the WHA to make binding rules for a significantly more limited set of topics and its Article 23 power to issue recommendations only. Recommendations made under Article 23 are not binding.

The topics for informal, focused consultations revolve around equity, One Health, and access-and-benefit sharing and IP, but it remains unknown what will be included in a new pandemic preparedness and response agreement or what is politically possible given the disparate views. Given there are hundreds of possibilities to evaluate—including some sensitive topics closely related to economic competitiveness and national security—there are nearly infinite directions the process and negotiations may go.

Broadly, WHO and the INB have committed to inclusiveness, transparency, consensus, member state leadership, including respect for sovereignty, and efficiency. To do this, the INB is consulting international organizations, non-state actors, and "other relevant stakeholders and experts". So far, the process has allowed civil society participation and has made information abundantly available on the INB webpage.

Given the positions of several influential governments in the lead-up to the WHA's final decision on a future framework or amendments to the

IHR (2005), the text of the agreed-upon document itself, and the normative changes accompanying its development, the world can anticipate at least four possible outcomes:

1 The revision of the IHR (2005) to fill gaps and enhance compliance, especially a more robust process for dispute resolution.
2 A new pandemic agreement or other instrument. This will take the form of a binding agreement but could also be supplemented by versions of "soft" law instruments with language taken from the IHR (2005).
3 Reformed decision-making at the WHO around pandemic declarations and ensuing measures. This is included in both suggested revisions to the IHR (2005) and in statements made by major powers about a new pandemic agreement.[33]

33.2.2 Conclusion

COVID-19 became an international public health emergency because the world was ill-prepared, communication and coordination deteriorated in the early months of the pandemic, and the response unfolded in deeply inequitable ways. A binding, new pandemic agreement may not ultimately be concluded, but the INB has moved quickly, decisively, and inclusively to give it a chance. What is almost certain is that the IHR (2005) will be revised, although those changes may be incremental, and there is significant disagreement between countries around necessary edits. The IHR was substantially revised in 2005 in response to the SARS epidemic. With 196 States Parties, the IHR is one of the most broadly accepted treaties in the world. In order to properly prepare and address the next pandemic, nations will need to meaningful recommit to enhanced surveillance, reporting, data sharing, and adherence with international guidelines. To build trust in those guidelines, decision-making bodies like the WHO will need to be more accountable to their members. Finally, wealthy countries will need to commit to equitable distribution of medical products. However, given that the world's experience with SARS-CoV-1 was a near miss—and so few lessons were internalized during COVID-19—expectations should be measured.

Notes

1 UN News, "COVID vaccines: Widening inequality and millions vulnerable" (19 September 2021), online: *United Nations*. https://news.un.org/en/story/2021/09/1100192.
2 Rui-Heng Xu et al, "Epidemiologic clues to SARS origin in China" (2004) 10 *Emerging Infectious Diseases* 1030 ("On March 12, 2003, the World Health Organization (WHO) issued a global alert about cases of atypical pneumonia in Guangdong Province and Hong Kong Special Administrative Region, China, and in Vietnam (footnote omitted)); Zixue Tai & Tao Sun, "The rumouring of SARS during the 2003 epidemic in China" (2011) 33 *Socio Health & Illness* 677 at 680

("The outbreak of the lethal virus in Guangdong in early 2003 prompted a site investigation by an expert team comprising officials from the provincial government and the national Ministry of Health, which concluded on 21 January that the infection was atypical pneumonia and recommended measures of prevention and treatment.")

3 Yanzhong Huang, "The SARS epidemic and its aftermath in China: A political perspective" in *Institute of Medicine (US) Forum on Microbial Threats. Learning from SARS: Preparing for the Next Disease Outbreak: Workshop Summary* (Washington, DC: National Academic Press, 2004).

4 David L. Heymann, "The international response to the outbreak of SARS in 2003" (2004) 359 *Philosophical Transactions of the Royal Society B: Biological Sciences* 1127.

5 National Advisory Committee on SARS and Public Health, "Learning from SARS: Renewal of public health in Canada" (2003), online: *Health Canada*. www.canada.ca/content/dam/phac-aspc/migration/phac-aspc/publicat/sars-sras/pdf/sars-e.pdf.

6 Fiona Fleck, "How SARS changed the world in less than six months" (2003) 81 *Bulletin World Health Organization* 625.

7 Lawrence O. Gostin & Rebecca Katz, "The international health regulations: The governing framework for global health security" (2016) 94:2 *The Milbank Quarterly* 264.

8 Christian Kreuder-Sonnen, "China vs the WHO: A behavioural Norm conflict in the SARS crisis" (2019) 95 *International Affairs* 535 at 544.

9 David P. Fidler, "Revision of the World Health Organization's international health regulations" (16 April 2004), online: *ASIL Insights*. www.asil.org/insights/volume/8/issue/8/revision-world-health-organizations-international-health-regulations; Rebecca Katz & Julie Fischer, "The Revised International Health Regulations: A Framework for Global Pandemic Response" (2010) 3 *Global Health Governance* 1 at 2.

10 Barbara von Tigerstorm & Kumanan Wilson, "COVID-19 travel restrictions and the International Health Regulations (2005)" (2020) 5 *BMJ Global Health* e002629.

11 Tom Parfitt, "Coronavirus: Belarus dictator 'hiding death toll' in lone stand against lockdown" (11 April 2020), online: *Times of London*. www.thetimes.co.uk/article/coronavirus-belarus-dictator-hiding-death-toll-in-lone-stand-against-lockdown-9bmccgt5f.

12 Yanzhong Huang, "China's hidden COVID catastrophe: How Xi obscured a lethal virus wave -and what it means for the future of his regime" (16 February 2023), online: *Foreign Policy*. www.foreignaffairs.com/china/chinas-hidden-covid-catastrophe.

13 "Coronavirus in Tanzania: The country that's rejecting the vaccine" (6 February 2021), online: *BBC*. www.bbc.com/news/world-africa-55900680.

14 Hashim Talib Hashim, "COVID-19 denial in Turkmenistan veiling the real situation" (2002) 80 *Archives in Pub Health* 8.

15 David P. Fidler, "Negotiating equitable access to influenza vaccines: Global health diplomacy and the controversies surrounding avian influenza H5N1 and pandemic influenza H1N1" (2010) 7:5 *PLoS Medicine* e1000247.

16 David M. Herszenhorn, "Charles Michel proposes 'international pandemic treaty'" (12 November 2020), online: *Politico*. www.politico.eu/article/charles-michel-proposes-international-pandemic-treaty/.

17 Svět Lustig Vijay, "WHO proposes new "pandemic treaty" to tighten global monitoring and enforcement of disease outbreak response" (20 January 2021), online: *Health Policy Watch*. https://healthpolicy-watch.news/who-proposes-new-pandemic-treaty-to-tighten-global-monitoring-and-enforcement-of-disease-outbreak-response/.

18 *Ibid.*

19 "The politics of PHEIC" (18 June 2019), online: *LANCET*. www.thelancet.com/journals/lancet/article/PIIS0140-6736(19)31406-0/fulltext.
20 Steven J. Hoffman, "Mending dispute resolution under the International Health Regulations" (2022) 19 *The International Organizations Law Review* 1.
21 "Fact sheet: Pandemic emergency financing facility" (27 April 2021), online: *World Bank*. www.worldbank.org/en/topic/pandemics/brief/fact-sheet-pandemic-emergency-financing-facility.
22 *Ibid.*
23 *Draft Report to Member States Working Group on Strengthening WHO Preparedness and Response to Health Emergencies to the Special Session of the World Health Assembly* (12 November 2021), online (pdf): *WHO*. https://apps.who.int/gb/wgpr/pdf_files/wgpr5/A_WGPR5_2-en.pdf.
24 "One health" (2023), online: *WHO*. www.who.int/health-topics/one-health#tab=tab_1.
25 "Strengthening WHO preparedness for and response to health emergencies" (19 January 2020), online (pdf): *WHO*. https://apps.who.int/gb/ebwha/pdf_files/EB150/B150_16-en.pdf.
26 *Proposal for Amendments to the International Health Regulations (2005)* (12 April 2022), online (pdf): *WHO*. https://apps.who.int/gb/ebwha/pdf_files/WHA75/A75_18-en.pdf.
27 *Proposed Amendments to the International Health Regulations (2005) submitted in accordance with decision WHA75(9) (2022)*, online (pdf): *WHO*. https://apps.who.int/gb/wgihr/pdf_files/wgihr1/WGIHR_Submissions-en.pdf.
28 "Africa Region calls for amendment of IHR to address equity" (2 March 2022), online: *Third World Network Berhad*. www.twn.my/title2/health.info/2022/hi220301.htm (emphasis added).
29 Stephanie Nebehay, "WHO nears consensus on future international pact to prevent pandemics -diplomats" (26 November 2021), online: *Reuters*. www.reuters.com/business/healthcare-pharmaceuticals/who-nears-consensus-future-international-pact-prevent-pandemics-diplomats-2021–11–26/.
30 Lawrence O. Gostin et al, "O'Neill Briefing: World Health Assembly special session launches historic intergovernmental negotiating body to develop a who convention or other international instrument on pandemic preparedness and response" (4 December 2021), online: *O'Neill Institute for National and Global Health Law*. https://oneill.law.georgetown.edu/oneill-briefing-world-health-assembly-special-session-launches-historic-intergovernmental-negotiating-body-to-develop-a-who-convention-or-other-international-instrument-on-pandemic-preparedn.
31 "The world together: Establishment of an intergovernmental negotiating body to strengthen pandemic prevention, preparedness, and response" (1 December 2021), online (pdf): *WHO*. https://apps.who.int/gb/ebwha/pdf_files/WHASSA2/SSA2(5)-en.pdf.
32 Report of the Secretary General, "Coordination questions: Multisectoral collaboration on tobacco or health -Progress made in the implementation of multisectoral collaboration on tobacco or health" (15 May 1997), online: *UN Economic and Social Council*. www.un.org/esa/documents/ecosoc/docs/1997/e1997-62.htm.
33 Gostin et al, *supra* note 30.

INDEX

Note: Page numbers in *italics* indicate a figure and page numbers in **bold** indicate a table on the corresponding page.